Handbook of Research on Soft Computing and Nature-Inspired Algorithms

Shishir K. Shandilya
Bansal Institute of Research and Technology, India

Smita Shandilya
Sagar Institute of Research Technology and Science, India

Kusum Deep
Indian Institute of Technology Roorkee, India

Atulya K. Nagar
Liverpool Hope University, UK

DISSEMINATOR OF KNOWLEDGE

www.igi-global.com

A volume in the Advances in Computational
Intelligence and Robotics (ACIR) Book Series

Published in the United States of America by
IGI Global
Information Science Reference (an imprint of IGI Global)
701 E. Chocolate Avenue
Hershey PA, USA 17033
Tel: 717-533-8845
Fax: 717-533-8661
E-mail: cust@igi-global.com
Web site: http://www.igi-global.com

Library of Congress Cataloging-in-Publication Data

Names: Shandilya, Shishir K., 1981- editor. | Shandilya, Smita, 1982- editor.
  | Deep, Kusum, editor. | Nagar, Atulya K., editor.
Title: Handbook of research on soft computing and nature-inspired algorithms
  / Shishir K. Shandilya, Smita Shandilya, Kusum Deep, and Atulya K. Nagar,
  editors.
Description: Hershey, PA : Information Science Reference, [2017] | Includes
  bibliographical references and index.
Identifiers: LCCN 2016054993| ISBN 9781522521280 (hardcover) | ISBN
  9781522521297 (ebook)
Subjects: LCSH: Soft computing--Handbooks, manuals, etc. | Natural
  computation--Handbooks, manuals, etc. | Algorithms--Handbooks, manuals,
  etc.
Classification: LCC QA76.9.S63 H354 2017 | DDC 006.3--dc23 LC record available at https://lccn.loc.gov/2016054993

This book is published in the IGI Global book series Advances in Computational Intelligence and Robotics (ACIR) (ISSN: 2327-0411; eISSN: 2327-042X)

British Cataloguing in Publication Data
A Cataloguing in Publication record for this book is available from the British Library.

All work contributed to this book is new, previously-unpublished material. The views expressed in this book are those of the authors, but not necessarily of the publisher.

For electronic access to this publication, please contact: eresources@igi-global.com.

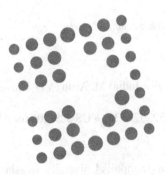

Advances in Computational Intelligence and Robotics (ACIR) Book Series

Ivan Giannoccaro
University of Salento, Italy

ISSN:2327-0411
EISSN:2327-042X

MISSION

While intelligence is traditionally a term applied to humans and human cognition, technology has progressed in such a way to allow for the development of intelligent systems able to simulate many human traits. With this new era of simulated and artificial intelligence, much research is needed in order to continue to advance the field and also to evaluate the ethical and societal concerns of the existence of artificial life and machine learning.

The **Advances in Computational Intelligence and Robotics (ACIR) Book Series** encourages scholarly discourse on all topics pertaining to evolutionary computing, artificial life, computational intelligence, machine learning, and robotics. ACIR presents the latest research being conducted on diverse topics in intelligence technologies with the goal of advancing knowledge and applications in this rapidly evolving field.

COVERAGE

- Artificial Intelligence
- Adaptive and Complex Systems
- Natural language processing
- Agent technologies
- Computer Vision
- Neural Networks
- Synthetic Emotions
- Evolutionary Computing
- Automated Reasoning
- Fuzzy Systems

IGI Global is currently accepting manuscripts for publication within this series. To submit a proposal for a volume in this series, please contact our Acquisition Editors at Acquisitions@igi-global.com or visit: http://www.igi-global.com/publish/.

Titles in this Series

For a list of additional titles in this series, please visit: www.igi-global.com/book-series

www.igi-global.com

701 East Chocolate Avenue, Hershey, PA 17033, USA
Tel: 717-533-8845 x100 • Fax: 717-533-8661
E-Mail: cust@igi-global.com • www.igi-global.com

To our little Champ 'Samarth Koshagra Shandilya'

— S. K. S., S. S.

To my son Aakash and daughter Paluck

— K. D.

To my beloved daughters – Kopal and Priyel

— A. K. N.

List of Contributors

Table of Contents

Detailed Table of Contents

In the last decade nature-inspired Optimizers such as genetic algorithms (GAs), particle swarm (PSO), ant colony (ACO), honey bees (HB), bacteria feeding (BFO), firefly (FF), bat algorithm (BTO), invasive weed (IWO) and others algorithms, has been successfully adopted as a powerful optimization tools in several areas of applied engineering, and in particular for the solution of complex electromagnetic problems. This chapter is aimed at presenting an overview of nature inspired optimization algorithms (NIOs) as applied to the solution of complex electromagnetic problems starting from the well-known genetic algorithms (GAs) up to recent collaborative algorithms based on smart swarms and inspired by swarm of insects, birds or flock of fishes. The focus of this chapter is on the use of different kind of natured inspired optimization algorithms for the solution of complex problems, in particular typical microwave design problems, in particular the design and microstrip antenna structures, the calibration of microwave systems and other interesting practical applications. Starting from a detailed classification and analysis of the most used natured inspired optimizers (NIOs) this chapter describes the not only the structures of each NIO but also the stochastic operators and the philosophy responsible for the correct evolution of the optimization process. Theoretical discussions concerned convergence issues, parameters sensitivity analysis and computational burden estimation are reported as well. Successively a brief review on how different research groups have applied or customized different NIOs approaches for the solution of complex practical electromagnetic problem ranging from industrial up to biomedical applications. It is worth noticed that the development of CAD tools based on NIOs could provide the engineers and designers with powerful tools that can be the solution to reduce the time to market of specific devices, (such as modern mobile phones, tablets and other portable devices) and keep the commercial predominance: since they do not require expert engineers and they can strongly reduce the computational time typical of the standard trial errors methodologies. Such useful automatic design tools based on NIOs have been the object of research since some decades and the importance of this subject is widely recognized. In order to apply a natured inspired algorithm, the problem is usually recast as a global optimization problem. Formulated in such a way, the problem can be efficiently handled by natured inspired optimizer by defining a suitable cost function (single or multi-objective) that represent the distance between the requirements and the obtained trial solution. The device under development can be analyzed with classical numerical methodologies such as FEM, FDTD, and MoM. As a common feature, these environments usually integrate an optimizer and a commercial numerical simulator. The chapter ends with open problems and discussion on future applications.

Chapter 2

Bilal Ervural, Istanbul Technical University, Turkey
Beyzanur Cayir Ervural, Istanbul Technical University, Turkey
Cengiz Kahraman, Istanbul Technical University, Turkey

Soft Computing techniques are capable of identifying uncertainty in data, determining imprecision of knowledge, and analyzing ill-defined complex problems. The nature of real world problems is generally complex and their common characteristic is uncertainty owing to the multidimensional structure. Analytical models are insufficient in managing all complexity to satisfy the decision makers' expectations. Under this viewpoint, soft computing provides significant flexibility and solution advantages. In this chapter, firstly, the major soft computing methods are classified and summarized. Then a comprehensive review of eight nature inspired – soft computing algorithms which are genetic algorithm, particle swarm algorithm, ant colony algorithms, artificial bee colony, firefly optimization, bat algorithm, cuckoo algorithm, and grey wolf optimizer algorithm are presented and analyzed under some determined subject headings (classification topics) in a detailed way. The survey findings are supported with charts, bar graphs and tables to be more understandable.

Chapter 3

Luciano Mescia, Politecnico di Bari, Italy
Pietro Bia, EmTeSys Srl, Italy
Diego Caratelli, The Antenna Company, The Netherlands & Tomsk Polytechnic University, Russia
Johan Gielis, University of Antwerp, Belgium

The chapter will describe the potential of the swarm intelligence and in particular quantum PSO-based algorithm, to solve complicated electromagnetic problems. This task is accomplished through addressing the design and analysis challenges of some key real-world problems. A detailed definition of the conventional PSO and its quantum-inspired version are presented and compared in terms of accuracy and computational burden. Some theoretical discussions concerning the convergence issues and a sensitivity analysis on the parameters influencing the stochastic process are reported.

Chapter 4

Snehal Mohan Kamalapur, K. K. Wagh Institute of Engineering Education and Research, India
Varsha Patil, Matoshree College of Engineering and Research Center, India

The issue of parameter setting of an algorithm is one of the most promising areas of research. Particle Swarm Optimization (PSO) is population based method. The performance of PSO is sensitive to the parameter settings. In the literature of evolutionary computation there are two types of parameter settings

- parameter tuning and parameter control. Static parameter tuning may lead to poor performance as optimal values of parameters may be different at different stages of run. This leads to parameter control. This chapter has two-fold objectives to provide a comprehensive discussion on parameter settings and on parameter settings of PSO. The objectives are to study parameter tuning and control, to get the insight of PSO and impact of parameters settings for particles of PSO.

Chapter 5

This chapter subscribes in the framework of an analytical study about the computational intelligence algorithms. These algorithms are numerous and can be classified in two great families: evolutionary algorithms (genetic algorithms, genetic programming, evolutionary strategy, differential evolutionary, paddy field algorithm) and swarm optimization algorithms (particle swarm optimisation PSO, ant colony optimization (ACO), bacteria foraging optimisation, wolf colony algorithm, fireworks algorithm, bat algorithm, cockroaches colony algorithm, social spiders algorithm, cuckoo search algorithm, wasp swarm optimisation, mosquito optimisation algorithm). We have detailed each algorithm following a structured organization (the origin of the algorithm, the inspiration source, the summary, and the general process). This paper is the fruit of many years of research in the form of synthesis which groups the contributions proposed by various researchers in this field. It can be the starting point for the designing and modelling new algorithms or improving existing algorithms.

Chapter 6

Machining of hard metals and alloys using Conventional machining involves increased demand of time, energy and cost. It causes tool wear resulting in loss of quality of the product. Non-conventional machining, on the other hand produces product with minimum time and at desired level of accuracy. In the present study, EN19 steel was machined using CNC Wire Electrical discharge machining with predefined process parameters. Material Removal Rate and Surface roughness were considered as responses for this study. The present optimization problem is single and as well as multi-response. Considering the complexities of this present problem, experimental data were generated and the results were analyzed by using Taguchi, Grey Relational Analysis and Weighted Principal Component Analysis under soft computing approach. Responses variances with the variation of process parameters were thoroughly studied and analyzed; also 'best optimal values' were identified. The result shows an improvement in responses from mean to optimal values of process parameters.

Chapter 7

Vo Ngoc Dieu, Ho Chi Minh City University of Technology, Vietnam
Tran The Tung, Ho Chi Minh City University of Technology, Vietnam

This chapter proposes an augmented Lagrange Hopfield network (ALHN) for solving combined economic and emission dispatch (CEED) problem with fuel constraint. In the proposed ALHN method, the augmented Lagrange function is directly used as the energy function of continuous Hopfield neural network (HNN), thus this method can properly handle constraints by both augmented Lagrange function and sigmoid function of continuous neurons in the HNN. For dealing with the bi-objective economic dispatch problem, the slope of sigmoid function in HNN is adjusted to find the Pareto-optimal front and then the best compromise solution for the problem will be determined by fuzzy-based mechanism. The proposed method has been tested on many cases and the obtained results are compared to those from other methods available the literature. The test results have shown that the proposed method can find good solutions compared to the others for the tested cases. Therefore, the proposed ALHN could be a favourable implementation for solving the CEED problem with fuel constraint.

Chapter 8

Mridusmita Sharma, Gauhati University, India
Rituraj Kaushik, Tezpur University, India
Kandarpa Kumar Sarma, Gauhati University, India

Speaker recognition is the task of identifying a person by his/her unique identification features or behavioural characteristics that are included in the speech uttered by the person. Speaker recognition deals with the identity of the speaker. It is a biometric modality which uses the features of the speaker that is influenced by one's individual behaviour as well as the characteristics of the vocal cord. The issue becomes more complex when regional languages are considered. Here, the authors report the design of a speaker recognition system using normal and telephonic Assamese speech for their case study. In their work, the authors have implemented i-vectors as features to generate an optimal feature set and have used the Feed Forward Neural Network for the recognition purpose which gives a fairly high recognition rate.

Chapter 9

Sanjiban Sekhar Roy, VIT University, India
Marenglen Biba, University of New York – Tirana, Albania
Rohan Kumar, VIT University, India
Rahul Kumar, VIT University, India
Pijush Samui, NIT Patna, India

Online social networking platforms, such as Weblogs, micro blogs, and social networks are intensively being utilized daily to express individual's thinking. This permits scientists to collect huge amounts of data and extract significant knowledge regarding the sentiments of a large number of people at a scale that was essentially impractical a couple of years back. Therefore, these days, sentiment analysis has the potential to learn sentiments towards persons, object and occasions. Twitter has increasingly become a significant social networking platform where people post messages of up to 140 characters known as 'Tweets'. Tweets have become the preferred medium for the marketing sector as users can instantly indicate customer success or indicate public relations disaster far more quickly than a web page or traditional media does. In this paper, we have analyzed twitter data and have predicted positive and negative tweets with high accuracy rate using support vector machine (SVM).

Chapter 10

Omveer Singh, Maharishi Markandeshwar University, India

A new technique of evaluating optimal gain settings for full state feedback controllers for automatic generation control (AGC) problem based on a hybrid evolutionary algorithms (EA) i.e. genetic algorithm (GA)-simulated annealing (SA) is proposed in this chapter. The hybrid EA algorithm can take dynamic curve performance as hard constraints which are precisely followed in the solutions. This is in contrast to the modern and single hybrid evolutionary technique where these constraints are treated as soft/hard constraints. This technique has been investigated on a number of case studies and gives satisfactory solutions. This technique is also compared with linear quadratic regulator (LQR) and GA based proportional integral (PI) controllers. This proves to be a good alternative for optimal controller's design. This technique can be easily enhanced to include more specifications viz. settling time, rise time, stability constraints, etc.

Chapter 11

Shailendra Aote, Ramdeobaba College of Engineering and Management, India
Mukesh M. Raghuwanshi, Yeshwantrao Chavan College of Engineering, India

To solve the problems of optimization, various methods are provided in different domain. Evolutionary computing (EC) is one of the methods to solve these problems. Mostly used EC techniques are available like Particle Swarm Optimization (PSO), Genetic Algorithm (GA) and Differential Evolution (DE). These techniques have different working structure but the inner working structure is same. Different names and formulae are given for different task but ultimately all do the same. Here we tried to find out the similarities among these techniques and give the working structure in each step. All the steps are provided with proper example and code written in MATLAB, for better understanding. Here we started our discussion with introduction about optimization and solution to optimization problems by PSO, GA and DE. Finally, we have given brief comparison of these.

Chapter 12

Dilip Kumar Choubey, Birla Institute of Technology Mesra, India
Sanchita Paul, Birla Institute of Technology Mesra, India

The modern society is prone to many life-threatening diseases which if diagnosis early can be easily controlled. The implementation of a disease diagnostic system has gained popularity over the years. The main aim of this research is to provide a better diagnosis of diabetes. There are already several existing methods, which have been implemented for the diagnosis of diabetes. In this manuscript, firstly, Polynomial Kernel, RBF Kernel, Sigmoid Function Kernel, Linear Kernel SVM used for the classification of PIDD.

Secondly GA used as an Attribute selection method and then used Polynomial Kernel, RBF Kernel, Sigmoid Function Kernel, Linear Kernel SVM on that selected attributes of PIDD for classification. So, here compared the results with and without GA in PIDD, and Linear Kernel proved better among all of the noted above classification methods. It directly seems in the paper that GA is removing insignificant features, reducing the cost and computation time and improving the accuracy, ROC of classification. The proposed method can be also used for other kinds of medical diseases.

The desirable merits of the intelligent computational algorithms and the initial success in many domains have encouraged researchers to work towards the advancement of these techniques. A major plunge in algorithmic development to solve the increasingly complex problems turned out as breakthrough towards the development of computational intelligence (CI) techniques. Nature proved to be one of the greatest sources of inspiration for these intelligent algorithms. In this chapter, computational intelligence techniques inspired by insects are discussed. These techniques make use of the skills of intelligent agent by mimicking insect behavior suitable for the required problem. The diversities in the behavior of the insect families and similarities among them that are used by researchers for generating intelligent techniques are also discussed in this chapter.

Chapter 14

Bio inspired algorithms are computational procedure inspired by the evolutionary process of nature and swarm intelligence to solve complex engineering problems. In the recent times it has gained much popularity in terms of applications to diverse engineering disciplines. Now a days bio inspired algorithms are also applied to optimize the software testing process. In this chapter authors will discuss some of the popular bio inspired algorithms and also gives the framework of application of these algorithms for software testing problems such as test case generation, test case selection, test case prioritization, test case minimization. Bio inspired computational algorithms includes genetic algorithm (GA), genetic programming (GP), evolutionary strategies (ES), evolutionary programming (EP) and differential evolution(DE) in the evolutionary algorithms category and Ant colony optimization(ACO), Particle swarm optimization(PSO), Artificial Bee Colony(ABC), Firefly algorithm(FA), Cuckoo search(CS), Bat algorithm(BA) etc. in the Swarm Intelligence category(SI).

Fahad Parvez Mahdi, Universiti Teknologi Petronas, Malaysia
Pandian Vasant, Universiti Teknologi Petronas, Malaysia
Vish Kallimani, Universiti Teknologi Petronas, Malaysia
M. Abdullah-Al-Wadud, King Saud University, Saudi Arabia
Junzo Watada, Universiti Teknologi Petronas, Malaysia

Economic emission dispatch (EED) problems are one of the most crucial problems in power systems. Growing energy demand, limited reserves of fossil fuel and global warming make this topic into the center of discussion and research. In this chapter, we will discuss the use and scope of different quantum inspired computational intelligence (QCI) methods for solving EED problems. We will evaluate each previously used QCI methods for EED problem and discuss their superiority and credibility against other methods. We will also discuss the potentiality of using other quantum inspired CI methods like quantum bat algorithm (QBA), quantum cuckoo search (QCS), and quantum teaching and learning based optimization (QTLBO) technique for further development in this area.

Jose Luis Calvo-Rolle, University of A Coruña, Spain
José Luis Casteleiro-Roca, University of A Coruña, Spain
María del Carmen Meizoso-López, University of A Coruña, Spain
Andrés José Piñón-Pazos, University of A Coruña, Spain
Juan Albino Mendez-Perez, Universidad de La Laguna, Spain

This chapter describes an approach to reduce significantly the time in the frequency sweep test of a Quartz Crystal Microbalance (QCM) characterization method based on the resonance principle of passive components. On this test, the spent time was large, because it was necessary carry out a big frequency sweep due to the fact that the resonance frequency was unknown. Moreover, this frequency sweep has great steps and consequently low accuracy. Then, it was necessary to reduce the sweeps and its steps gradually with the aim to increase the accuracy and thereby being able to find the exact frequency. An intelligent expert system was created as a solution to the disadvantage described of the method. This model provides a much smaller frequency range than the initially employed with the original proposal. This frequency range depends of the circuit components of the method. Then, thanks to the new approach of the QCM characterization is achieved better accuracy and the test time is reduced significantly.

Goutam Kumar Bose, Haldia Institute of Technology, India
Pritam Pain, Haldia Institute of Technology, India

In the present research work selection of significant machining parameters depending on nature-inspired algorithm is prepared, during machining alumina-aluminum interpenetrating phase composites through electrochemical grinding process. Here during experimentation control parameters like electrolyte concentration (C), voltage (V), depth of cut (D) and electrolyte flow rate (F) are considered. The response data are initially trained and tested applying Artificial Neural Network. The paradoxical responses like higher material removal rate (MRR), lower surface roughness (Ra), lower overcut (OC) and lower cutting force (Fc) are accomplished individually by employing Cuckoo Search Algorithm. A multi response optimization for all the response parameters is compiled primarily by using Genetic algorithm. Finally, in order to achieve a single set of parametric combination for all the outputs simultaneously fuzzy based Grey Relational Analysis technique is adopted. These nature-driven soft computing techniques corroborates well during the parametric optimization of ECG process.

Chapter 18

Swarm Intelligence is defined as collective behavior of decentralized and self-organized systems of a natural or artificial nature. In the last years and today, Swarm Intelligence has proven to be a branch of Artificial Intelligence that is able to solving efficiently complex optimization problems. Some of well-known examples of Swarm Intelligence in natural systems reported in the literature are colony of social insects such as bees and ants, bird flocks, fish schools, etc. In this respect, Artificial Bee Colony Algorithm is a nature inspired metaheuristic, which imitates the honey bee foraging behaviour that produces an intelligent social behaviour. ABC has been used successfully to solve a wide variety of discrete and continuous optimization problems. In order to further enhance the structure of Artificial Bee Colony, there are a variety of works that have modified and hybridized to other techniques the standard version of ABC. This work presents a review paper with a survey of the modifications, variants and applications of the Artificial Bee Colony Algorithm.

Chapter 19

The chapter at hand seeks to provide a general survey of the Cuckoo Search Algorithm and its most highlighted variants. The Cuckoo Search Algorithm is a relatively recent nature-inspired population-based meta-heuristic algorithm that is based upon the lifestyle, egg laying, and breeding strategy of some species of cuckoos. In this case, the Lévy flight is used to move the cuckoos within the search space of the optimization problem to solve and obtain a suitable balance between diversification and intensification. As discussed in this chapter, the Cuckoo Search Algorithm has been successfully applied to a wide range of heterogeneous optimization problems found in practical applications over the last few years. Some of the reasons of its relevance are the reduced number of parameters to configure and its ease of implementation.

Foreword

I would like to first congratulate the editors on the publication of this book and thank them for the invitation to write a foreword. I am a keen student of both soft computing and nature-inspired computing. Both of these paradigms help us push the boundaries of traditional mathematics in real-world applications. The domain of each of the two paradigms is not well-defined and the boundary between the two is fuzzy (pun intended).

Some researchers use the term soft computing when the solutions are imprecise, uncertain, imperfect, and – in many cases – unpredictable. Imprecision is almost inevitable in most practical applications. For real-world applications, we are only looking for an acceptable level of precision. For example, we only need to be precise to the closest half-inch when specifying the size of a shirt. Students of fuzzy logic tell us that when we use words such as "hot", "warm", "cool" and "cold", it is impossible to be precise. Instead, in most cases, we assign a degree of membership to describe our imprecision. Uncertainty needs to be taken into account in our knowledge of the existing state of the system or our prediction of the future. The theory of probability provides one of the earliest formalization of uncertainty. A number of alternative methodologies have been used to represent uncertainty when the probability axioms make the computing cumbersome. Lack of sufficient information is another joy of working in the real world. Rough set theory is a popular methodology for dealing with insufficient or uncertain information.

This book brings together soft computing and nature-inspired computing. Imperfection is an issue generally shared by soft computing and nature-inspired computing. While it is theoretically possible to come up with the perfect solution in a number of problems, it is not realistic to reach the optimal solution in practice. Therefore, we have to settle for an imperfect but a reasonably good solution. We see this principle used in a number of nature-inspired techniques, such as genetic algorithms, particle swarm, ant colony, and bee colony optimizations.

Unpredictability is another aspect seen in both soft computing and nature-inspired computing. In many nature-inspired and soft computing attempts, the optimization is the initial solution that is used as a starting point in the search for the optimal solution. Depending on where we begin in the search space, we may end up with a different quasi-optimal solution. Therefore, unlike traditional computing algorithms, the soft and nature-inspired computing solutions are unpredictable, i.e. they may change from one execution to the next. Most nature-inspired algorithms safeguard against spiraling into some local minima. One example is the use of the mutation operation in genetic algorithms. Despite such safeguards, our experience suggests that these optimizations tend to produce variable solutions. We typically run the optimization a number of times and cluster the resulting solutions. The medoids of these clusters are then analyzed in greater detail for practical implementation.

In addition to the bio-inspired techniques such as genetic algorithms, particle swarm, ant colony, and bee colony optimizations, simulated annealing is another nature-inspired optimization technique discussed in this book. I have often wondered whether simulated annealing can be called a nature-inspired computing technique. In addition to being nature-inspired, the former four techniques correspond to biological processes. While simulated annealing is analogous to an industrial/engineering process that is initiated by humans, annealing is still a natural process, albeit not bio-inspired. I believe that simulated annealing may be especially appropriate for some engineering applications. In fact, this book uses simulated annealing in an engineering application. Overall, I notice a strong emphasis on engineering applications in this book. It is interesting to consider the strengths and weaknesses of these intriguing nature-inspired techniques in different real-world situations.

Other nature-inspired techniques that have been investigated in this book are various extensions of neural networks. Neurocomputing has come a long way over the previous half-century since the rise and fall of the perceptron algorithm. Despite initial criticism of the perceptron's inability to accommodate a non-linear real-world system, researchers have been coming up with variations that are pushing the boundaries of computational intelligence. While the modeling of artificial neural networks is an over-simplification of extremely complex biological neural networks, the models have shown a remarkable ability to solve complex problems. Deep learning that is being explored by giants in both academia and industry may help enhance human intelligence and spare us from more mundane mental activities. The two neurocomputing techniques that appear in this book represent two different directions in which the perceptron was refined. The Hopfield networks represent more complex interconnections of neurons, including recurrent feedback. Support vector machines (SVM), on the other hand, derive their ability to address non-linearity through non-linear transformations using kernel functions, which are further supported by operations research.

In summary, I would like to say that this book presents a diversity of nature-inspired techniques with soft-computing refinements for real-world applications. I believe engineering practitioners will especially enjoy reading this work.

Pawan Lingras
Saint Mary's University, Canada

Pawan Lingras is a graduate of IIT Bombay with graduate studies from the University of Regina. He is currently a Professor and the Director of Computing and Data Analytics at Saint Mary's University, Halifax. He is also involved with a number of international activities, having served as a visiting professor at Munich University of Applied Sciences and IIT Gandhinagar, as a research supervisor at Institut Superieur de Gestion de Tunis, as a University Grants Commission (India) Scholar-in-Residence, and as a Shastri Indo-Canadian scholar. He has delivered more than 35 invited talks at various institutions around the world. He has authored more than 200 research papers in various international journals and conferences. He has also co-authored three textbooks, and co-edited two books and eight volumes of research papers. His academic collaborations/ co-authors include academics from Canada, Chile, China, Germany, India, Poland, Tunisia, the U.K. and USA. His areas of interests include artificial intelligence, information retrieval, data mining, web intelligence and intelligent transportation systems. He has served as a general co-chair, program co-chair, review committee chair, program committee member and reviewer for various international conferences on artificial intelligence and data mining. He is also on the editorial boards of a number of international journals. His fundamental research has been supported by the Natural Science and Engineering Research Council (NSERC) of Canada for twenty-five years, and the applications of his research to the industry are supported by a number of funding agencies, including NSERC, the Government of Nova Scotia, NRC-IRAP and MITACS.

Preface

Soft computing refers to a collection of imprecision-tolerant techniques which can fairly deal with uncertainty, partial truth, and approximation. The basic constituents of Soft Computing are Fuzzy Logic, Neural Computing, Evolutionary Computation, and Machine Learning. Soft Computing may be viewed as a foundation component for the emerging field of conceptual intelligence to generate human-type intelligence in computers. Whereas Nature-inspired Computing techniques have successfully been experimented and applied to machine-learning and advanced artificial intelligence. Nature-inspired Computing underlines the concept of learning and behaving as per the biological species to achieve the adaptability for survival by fulfilling certain objectives. It is still less-explored area but has potential to change the meaning of learning process of machines. Most of the current researches are focused on one or the other method encouraged by these concepts and therefore attracting students. Soft computing is having especially important role in science and engineering in many ways and becoming a back-bone of almost all the upcoming technologies. This handbook contains research contributions from leading scholars from all over the world with comprehensive coverage of each specific topic, highlighting recent and future trends and describing the latest advances.

Handbook of Research on Soft Computing and Nature-Inspired Algorithms is focused on current researches while highlighting the empirical results along with theoretical concept to provide a good comprehensive reference for students, researchers, scholars, professionals and practitioners in the field of advanced artificial intelligence, nature-inspired algorithms and soft computing. This book is a collection of 19 chapters written by various authors from all over the sphere, covering the applications of nature-inspired algorithms and various soft-computational systems

We express our heartfelt gratitude to all the authors, reviewers and IGI-Global personnel, especially Ms. Lindsay Johnston, Mr. Josh Witman, and Ms. Jan Travers for their kind support. Special thanks to Dr. Pawan Lingras, Ms. Kayla Wolfe, Ms. Emily Markovic, Mr. Joshua Herring, Ms. Melissa Wagner and Ms. Rachel Ginder, for their endless motivation and patience. We hope that this handbook will be beneficial to all the concerned readers.

Shishir K. Shandilya
Bansal Institute of Research and Technology, India

Smita Shandilya
Sagar Institute of Research, Technology, and Science, India

Kusum Deep
Indian Institute of Technology Roorkee, India

Atulya K. Nagar
Liverpool Hope University, UK

Chapter 1

Application of Natured-Inspired Algorithms for the Solution of Complex Electromagnetic Problems

Massimo Donelli
University of Trento, Italy

ABSTRACT

In the last decade nature-inspired Optimizers such as genetic algorithms (GAs), particle swarm (PSO), ant colony (ACO), honey bees (HB), bacteria feeding (BFO), firefly (FF), bat algorithm (BTO), invasive weed (IWO) and others algorithms, has been successfully adopted as a powerful optimization tools in several areas of applied engineering, and in particular for the solution of complex electromagnetic problems. This chapter is aimed at presenting an overview of nature inspired optimization algorithms (NIOs) as applied to the solution of complex electromagnetic problems starting from the well-known genetic algorithms (GAs) up to recent collaborative algorithms based on smart swarms and inspired by swarm of insects, birds or flock of fishes. The focus of this chapter is on the use of different kind of natured inspired optimization algorithms for the solution of complex problems, in particular typical microwave design problems, in particular the design and microstrip antenna structures, the calibration of microwave systems and other interesting practical applications. Starting from a detailed classification and analysis of the most used natured inspired optimizers (NIOs) this chapter describes the not only the structures of each NIO but also the stochastic operators and the philosophy responsible for the correct evolution of the optimization process. Theoretical discussions concerned convergence issues, parameters sensitivity analysis and computational burden estimation are reported as well. Successively a brief review on how different research groups have applied or customized different NIOs approaches for the solution of complex practical electromagnetic problem ranging from industrial up to biomedical applications. It is worth noticed that the development of CAD tools based on NIOs could provide the engineers and designers with powerful tools that can be the solution to reduce the time to market

DOI: 10.4018/978-1-5225-2128-0.ch001

of specific devices, (such as modern mobile phones, tablets and other portable devices) and keep the commercial predominance: since they do not require expert engineers and they can strongly reduce the computational time typical of the standard trial errors methodologies. Such useful automatic design tools based on NIOs have been the object of research since some decades and the importance of this subject is widely recognized. In order to apply a natured inspired algorithm, the problem is usually recast as a global optimization problem. Formulated in such a way, the problem can be efficiently handled by natured inspired optimizer by defining a suitable cost function (single or multi-objective) that represent the distance between the requirements and the obtained trial solution. The device under development can be analyzed with classical numerical methodologies such as FEM, FDTD, and MoM. As a common feature, these environments usually integrate an optimizer and a commercial numerical simulator. The chapter ends with open problems and discussion on future applications.

INTRODUCTION

Nature inspired optimization (NIO) algorithms has been successfully adopted for many years as powerful optimization tools in several areas of applied engineering (P. H. King, 2006; James M. Whitacre et al. 2008; S. He, Q. H. Wu, & J. R. Saunders, 2009; M. D. Gregory, J. S. Petko, et al. 2010; Fang Liu, Leping Lin, et al. 2015). They are very effective to solve various complex problems because of their effectiveness, simplicity and flexibility. The goal of this chapter is to report the evolution of the most common NIOs, trying to provide their keys strength and weakness. Before the development of NIOs, all the available optimization algorithms were based on the estimation of the gradient or conjugate gradient (CG) (R. Ringlee, 1965; S. Mitter, L. S. Lasdon, & A. D. Waren, 1966; L. Lasdon, S. Mitter, & A. Waren, 1967; B. N. Pshenichny, & Y. M. Danilin, 1978; Z. Wu, 2001; Zhengwei Xu, Michael, & S. Zhdanov, 2015), of the cost function. The CGs are commonly known as deterministic algorithms because if they are launched several times with the same initialization they always lead to the same solution. This is due because the CG update equation estimate the new position at iteration k+1, considering the previous position at iteration k, plus the gradient of the cost function, which indicates the direction of movement in the nth dimensional search space multiplied for a constant called step size t. The main advantage of CG based is their convergence rate since they are able to reach a very good solution in few iterations. The application of a CG based algorithm requires the analytical knowledge of the cost function (for the estimation of the gradient), a good initialization point. The main drawback of CG based algorithms is that they can be easily trapped in local minima because in presence of a local minima the gradient is zero and this correspond keep the new position equal to the old one. The CG based algorithm are the best solution for quadratic cost function, unfortunately almost all scientific and engineering problems show non-quadratic cost function characterized by different local minima. The problem of local minima led to the development of a new class of algorithms able to avoid the problem of the local minima. The new family of algorithms inspired to natural behaviour belong the family of evolutionary algorithms and they family of stochastic algorithms. They are also called non-deterministic algorithm because if we run several time a stochastic algorithm considering always the same initialization point, the obtained results will be always different because these kind of algorithms use stochastic operators. The first developed NIO algorithm was the genetic algorithm (GA) an optimizer that mimic the process of natural selection (discovered by Charles Darwin). A direct evolution of the GAs aimed at improve the convergence rate is the differential evolution DE algorithm developed in the 1997. The nineties have seen the emergence of a new class of algorithms inspired by animal with a social behavior such as swarm of bee, birds, insects and flock of fishes. Also this new class of algorithms belong the family of EA but they are based on the collaboration between individuals and not on the competition as in natural evolution. In a collaborative algorithm the individuals of a population or a swarm work together and share information with the goal to find the best solution in a fast way. Thanks to this change of philosophy, the problem of the stationary population typical of GAs and DEs is theoretically solved. This chapter presents a survey of the most common natured inspired optimizer namely as applied to the solution of electromagnetic problems. The outline of the chapter is as follows. A detailed description of different natured inspired optimizers is described in Section 2. Section 3, presents some applications of NIOs for the optimization and synthesis of microwave circuits and devices. In particular a set of selected and representative synthesis results concerned microwave passive devices such as rectangular patch antenna, filters and broadband matching transformer are presented and commented. Finally some conclusions are drawn (Section 4).

2. DESCRIPTION OF NIO ALGORITHMS

This section describes the behavior and the characteristics of the most known natured inspired algorithms starting from the GAs up to the IWO. All the algorithms described in this section belong the family of meta-heuristic algorithms which generally perform better with respect to simple heuristic algorithms. Heuristic algorithms try to find a solution considering a trial and error procedure. In such kind of algorithm the solution can be found in a reasonable amount of time, but there is no guarantee that optimal solution will be found. Meta-heuristic algorithms use stochastic operators that permit to combine global search an local search, in particular stochastic operator provide a way to move away from local search and avoid the problem of being trapped in false solution characterized by local minima. It can be demonstrated that if the iteration number of algorithm cycle can be extended to infinity the optimal solution will be reached. The only hypothesis that guarantee to reach the optimal solution is the use of a good random number generator, and this is a challenging problem for modern computer since they can provide only pseudo random numerical generator. To solve a electromagnetic or any kind of practical problem, the optimization algorithm must be inserted into an optimization loop. A typical optimization loop is reported in Figure 1. In particular any practical problem can be solved by defining a suitable cost function, that represent the distance between the requirements and the performances of a trial solution. The goodness of a trial solution can be determined by considering a suitable analytical, numerical or semi analytical model of the system under investigation.

2.1. Genetic Algorithm (GA)

GAs are the first developed NIO methods. They are based on Darwinian theory of evolution (H. Holland, 1975; D. E. Goldberg, 1989; R. Haupt, 1995; R. Haupt, 1995b; D. S. Weile & E. Michielssen, 1997; J. Johnson & Y. Rahmat-Samii, 1997; A. Massa, M. Donelli, et. al. 2004; M. Donelli, S. Caorsi, et al. 2004; C. Sacchi, F. De Natale, et al. 2004; cM. Donelli, S. Caorsi, ET AL., 2004b; M. Donelli, 2013). They simulate the evolution of a population of individuals (i.e., a set of trial solutions for the addressed problem dealt with) over time favoring the improvement of individual characteristics (i.e., the fitting with some constraints evaluated by means of a fitness function). In a genetic algorithm three

Figure 1. Schema of a classical optimization loop

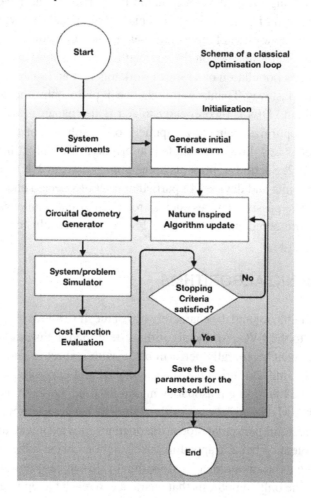

operators are iteratively applied namely the Selection, Crossover and Mutation operators (H. Holland, 1975; D. E. Goldberg, 1989). In the following a brief description of such operators will be reported. To generate new individuals two parents must be selected to generate two children. There are different selection techniques. The principal selection techniques are: the completely random selection, the Roulette Wheel Selection, and the tournament selection. The last two techniques take into account the chromosome fitness, a chromosome with a good fitness presents an high probability to be selected for reproduction. The crossover is aimed at exchanging gene information between chromosomes. The use of the crossover to improve the offspring production is undoubtedly problem-oriented. The most diffuse crossover technique widely considered for binary encoding is the single point crossover. A point in the chromosome is randomly chosen and two parts of the chromosomes are exchanged to generate two new individuals. The crossover operator is performed with probability p_c on the chromosomes of the population. A crossover occurs, with a very high probability $p_c = 0.95$. The mutation operator is performed with probability p_m on a chromosome of the population. A mutation occurs, with a very low probability $p_m = 0.05$. The mutation operator changes the value of a string position in order to introduce some variations into the chromosome. The mutation is performed following different strategies according to the type of the gene to mutate. The gene can be randomly selected considering a single double or block of point is the chromosome is binary-encoded. A random mutation has been designed for real-valued genes as well being a random value such that the obtained solution be physically admissible. To avoid losing the fittest individual from one generation to another, the elitism is applied. At each generation the best chromosome obtained so far is reproduced in the new population, and considered as the best solution found at iteration k. GAs demonstrated their effectiveness in many practical applications as reported before the main drawback of GAs is the problem of the stationary condition of the population, a condition that occurs when the genetic code of the chromosomes is quite similar, with similar genetic code the population cannot further evolve to a better solution. Figure 2 shown the flowchart of a standard genetic algorithm.

2.2. Differential Evolution (DE)

The Differential Evolution Algorithm has been originally proposed by Storn and Price (R. Storn, & K. Price,1997) and it is an evolution of genetic algorithm specifically designed for the global optimization over continuous spaces. Like GAs the DE is a competitive algorithm since it is based on the same evolution rules(G. Stumberger, D. Dolinar, et al. 2000; S. Yang, Y. B. Gan, & A. Qing, 2002; S. Caorsi, M.

Figure 2. Flowchart of a simplex genetic algorithm

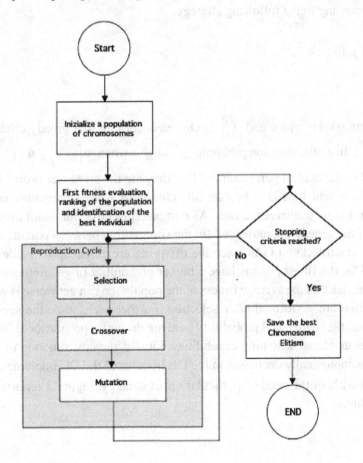

Donelli, A. et al., 2004; X. Chen, K. O'Neill, et al., 2004; A. Massa, M. Pastorino, & A. Randazzo, 2006, A. Qing, 2007; A. Breard, G. Perrusson, & D. Lesselier, 2008; A. Semnani, M. Kamyab, & I. T. Rekanos, 2009; F. Zhang, F.-S. Zhang, et al. 2009; E. Aksoy & E. Afacan, 2009; M. Donelli, A. Massa, et al. 2010; P. Rocca, G. Oliveri, & A. Massa, 2011). They were mainly aimed at simplifying the evolution process of GAs as well to enhance the convergence rate. The iterative evolution of the DE is similar to that of the GAs and it suffers of the main limitation of GAs the stationary condition of the population. Each current population is replaced by better individuals obtained by applying the DE operators, *LDE*, still based on genetic but now executed in a different sequence: the mutation,*M*, the crossover, *C*, and selection, *S*. The DE iteratively evolves as shown in Figure 3. During the mutation process, an intermediate solution is generated in correspondence with each individual $\underline{f}_k^p$ as follows:

$$\underline{t}_{k+1}^{(p)} = \underline{f}_k^{(p1)} + \epsilon(\underline{f}_k^{(p2)} - \underline{f}_k^{(p3)}), \ p = 1,\ldots,P \tag{1}$$

where $p, \ p_1, p_2, p_3 \in [1,P](p_1 \neq p_2 \neq p_3 \neq p)$ are the indices of different individuals randomly chosen in the population. The agents $\underline{f}_k^{(p_1)}$, $\underline{f}_k^{(p_2)}$ and $\underline{f}_k^{(p_3)}$ are called *donor* vectors or *secondary* parents, and $0 < \epsilon \leq 2$ is a real and constant value that controls the amplitude of the differential variation $\left(\underline{f}_k^{(p_2)} - \underline{f}_k^{(p_3)}\right)$. The crossover is then applied between the intermediate solution, $\underline{t}_{k+1}^{(p)}$, called *mutant* vector and the *primary* parent, $\underline{f}_k^{(p)}$ according to the following strategy.

$$\underline{u}_{k+1}^{(p)} = \begin{cases} \underline{t}_{k+1}^{(p)} \ if \ (r < p_c) \\ \underline{f}_k^{(p)} \ otherwise. \end{cases} \tag{2}$$

Finally, the selection takes place and $\underline{f}_{k+1}^{(p)}$ is chosen according to a greedy criterion by comparing $\Phi\left(\underline{f}_k^{(p)}\right)$ with $\Phi\left(\underline{u}_{k+1}^{(p)}\right)$. In a minimization problem, $\underline{f}_{k+1}^{(p)} = \underline{k}_{k+1}^{(p)}$ when $\Phi\left(\underline{u}_{k+1}^{(p)}\right) \leq \Phi\left(\underline{f}_k^{(p)}\right)$, while $\underline{f}_{k+1}^{(p)} = \underline{f}_k^{(p)}$ otherwise. In regard to the control parameters of DE, they are the crossover probability p_c and the amplification coefficient ε, which need to be carefully chosen to avoid a premature convergence to suboptimal solutions or a slow convergence rate. As compared to GAs, the main differences are (*a*) the order of execution of the genetic operators and (*b*) the competition between parents and children during the selection phase which lacks in GAs since the offspring are all accepted while the parents are all discarded. Unlike GAs, the fittest parents have a higher probability of generating children with better fitness. Moreover, the risk that the average fitness of the population can get worse is greater in GAs since crossover and mutation are performed after selection. Furthermore, since the secondary parents are chosen from the population with equal probability (and not through a proportional fitness selection), the DE usually increases its global searching capabilities. Finally, the cost function of the best individual Φ_k^{opt}, $k = 1, \ldots, K$, monotonically decreases in the DE because of the DE implementation of the selection mechanism and without the need of particular elitist strategy. Figure 3 reports the flowchart of a standard DE algorithm.

Figure 3. Flowchart of a standard differential evolution algorithm

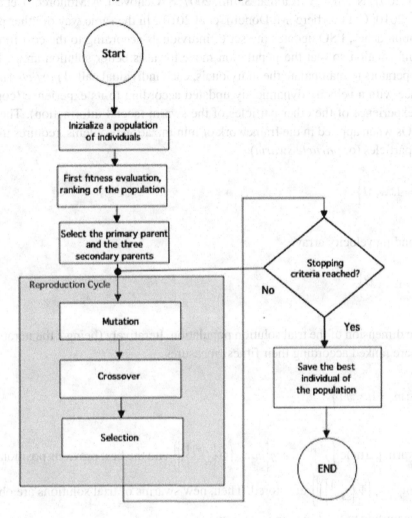

2.3. Particle Swarm Optimizer (PSO)

As reported in the introduction the PSO is a stochastic multiple-agent algorithm for finding optimal regions of complex search spaces through the interaction/collaboration of individuals in a population of individuals called particles. The algorithm is inspired on a metaphor of social interactions and it simulates the collective behavior of simple individuals interacting with their environment and each other (J. Kennedy, R. C. Eberhart, & Y. Shi, 2001; J. Robinson, S. Sinton, & Y. Rahmat-Samii, 2001; Clerc, M., & Kennedy, J., 2002; J. Robinson & Y. Rahmat-Samii, 2004; S. Caorsi, M. Donelli, et al. 2004; J. Robinson & Y. Rahmat-Samii, 2004; Donelli, M., & Massa, 2005; N. Jin & Y. Rahmat-Samii, 2005; D. Boeringer & D. Werner, 2005; M. Donelli, R. Azaro, et al. 2006; S. Mikki & A. Kishk, 2006; A. Adly & S. Abd-El-Hafiz, 2006; S. Ho, S. Yang, et al. 2006; S. Cui & D. Weile, 2006; R. Azaro, F. De Natale, et al. 2006; M. Donelli, R. Azaro, et al. 2006; F. Grimaccia, M. Mussetta, & R. E. Zich, 2007; T. Huang

& A. S.Mohan, 2007; N. Jin & Y. Rahmat-Samii, 2007; S. Genovesi, A.Monorchio, et al. 2007; L. Poli, P. Rocca, et al. 2010; C. Forestiere, M. Donelli, et al 2010). In the same way of other population based optimization approaches, PSO updates the set of individuals according to the cost function (or *fitness function*, Φ) information so that the population move towards better solution areas. Instead of using evolutionary operators to manipulate the individuals, each individual called *particle* flies as a "bird" in the search space with a velocity dynamically updated according to its experience (cognitive information) and the experience of the other particles of the swarm (social information). The PSO, as all the considered NIOs when applied in the framework of minimization problems, requires the definition of a population of particles (or *particle swarm*)

$$P_0 = \left\{ \underline{f}_0^{(m)}; m = 1,...,M \right\}$$
(3)

and a corresponding velocity array

$$V_0 = \left\{ v_0^{(m)}; m = 1,...,M \right\}$$
(4)

M being the dimension of the trial solution population. Iteratively (being *k* the iteration number), the trial solutions are ranked according their fitness measures

$$F_k = \left\{ \Phi \left\{ \underline{f}_k^{(m)} \right\}; m = 1,...,M \right\}$$
(5)

The best swarm particle $\left[\underline{f}_k^{(opt)} = arg \left[min_m \left(\Phi \left\{ \underline{f}_k^{(m)} \right\} \right) \right] \right]$ and the best previous position of each particle $\left[\underline{f}_k^{(m)} = arg \left[min_{k=1,...,k} \left(\Phi \left\{ \underline{f}_h^{(m)} \right\} \right) \right] \right]$ are stored. Then, new swarms of trial solutions are obtained updating each particle according to the following equation

$$f_{i,k+1}^{(m)} = f_{i,k}^{(m)} + v_{i,k+1}^{(m)}$$
(6)

Being

$$f_{i,k+1}^{(m)} = \omega v_{i,k}^{(m)} + \alpha C_1 (f_{i,k}^{(m-pbest)} - f_{i,k}^{(m)}) + \beta C_2 (f_{i,k}^{(gbest)} - f_{i,k}^{(m)})$$
(7)

where β and γ are two random values included in the range [0, 1] with a uniform distribution generated by a pseudo-random number generator, C_1 and C_2 are the two constants called acceleration terms, for almost all problem a good choice for the acceleration terms is $C_1 = C_2 = 2$, ω is the *inertia* weight. The iterative process stops when the termination criterion, based on a maximum number of iterations, *K* (i.e., $k = K$) or on a threshold on the fitness measure, is verified and *the global best* is assumed as the problem solution. As reported in the previous section the collaboration between individuals of the swarm is the key force of the algorithm. It prevents the stationary condition typical of genetic algorithm. The flowchart of the PSO is reported in Figure 4.

2.4. Ant Colony Optimizer (ACO)

The ACO is another population-based global optimization algorithm inspired by the foraging behavior of ant colonies looking for food sources(M. Dorigo, V. Maniezzo, & A. Colorni, 1996; Jun Zhang, Henry Shu-Hung Chung, & Alan Wai-Lun Lo, 2009; P. Rocca, L. Manica, & A. Massa, 2010; Carlos M. Fernandes, Antonio M. Mora, & C. Rosa, 2014; Hai Jin, & Longbo Ran, 2015). The ants move in the space surrounding the nest looking for the best (shortest) path between the food sources and the nest. Like PSO, the ACO is based on the concepts of swarm intelligence and sharing information, but it also exploits the paradigm of self-organization. In this sense, the activity of each agent $\underline{f}_k^{(p)}$ called *ant* in the

Figure 4. Schema of a standard particle swarm optimizer

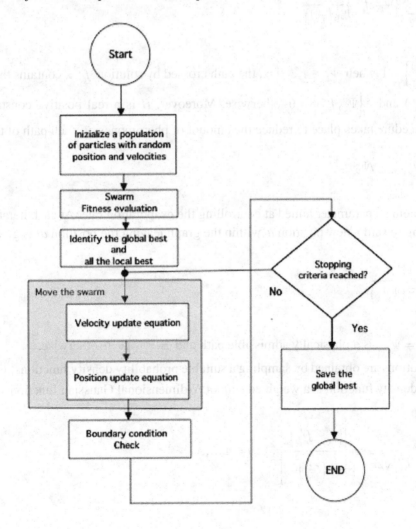

colony F_k is guided not only by the work in progress (the goal of optimization), but also from the information available in the local environment. To modify the local environment, each ant leaves a chemical substance called *pheromone* while moving within the solution space along a path, so in ACO the sharing of information is performed by means of chemical substances. The amount of pheromones on a path quantifies its degree of optimality, but it decays with time (*evaporation* mechanism). These mechanisms allow one to avoid poor food sources on one hand and on the other hand to efficiently sample the whole solution space. The basic version of ACO concern with the search of a path within a discrete space (a typical problem is the traveling salesman problem), each ant codes a vector $\underline{f}_k^{(p)}$ which represents of a set of discrete symbols or locations, $\underline{f}_k^{(p)} = \{a_1, \dots, a_N\}$. Let us suppose that Ψ_k^{ij} be the amount of pheromones on the edge between the location a_i and a_j, a_{ij} $i,j \in [1,N]$, with $i \neq j$. Every vector, $\underline{f}^{(p)}, p = 1, \dots, P$, is randomly initialized at the first iteration ($k = 0$) and a uniform level of pheromone is assigned to each path within the search space, $\Psi^{ij} = cost$. Successively, the pheromone level of each edge of the path covered by the pth ant is updated as

$$\Psi_{k+1}^{i,j} = \Psi_k^{i,j} + \sum_{i=1}^{P} \delta\left\{\Psi_k^{i,j}, \underline{f}_k^{(p)}\right\} \frac{H}{\Phi\left(\underline{f}_k^{(p)}\right)} \qquad (8)$$

where $\delta\left\{\Psi_k^{ij}, \underline{f}_k^{(p)}\right\} = 1$ when $\Psi_k^{ij} \in \underline{f}^{(p)}$ (i.e., the path crossed by solution $\underline{f}_k^{(p)} k$ contains the branch individuated by Ψ_k^{ij}) and $\delta\left\{\Psi_k^{ij}, \underline{f}_k^{(p)}\right\} = 0$ otherwise. Moreover, H is a real positive constant term. The evaporation procedure takes place to reduce the amount of pheromones on each path of the graph

$$\Psi_{k+1}^{i,j} = (1 - \rho)\Psi_{k+1}^{i,j}, \qquad \forall \Psi_{k+1}^{i,j} \qquad (9)$$

with $\rho \in (0, 1]$ being a parameter aimed at controlling the evaporation rate. At each iteration, the probability of moving toward a new position a_j within the graph leaving the position ai is given by

$$p_\Psi\left(\Psi_{k+1}^{i,j}\right) = \frac{\Psi_{k+1}^{i,j}}{\sum_j \Xi\left(\Psi_{k+1}^{i,j}\right)} \qquad (10)$$

where $\Xi\left(\Psi_{k+1}^{i,j}\right) = \Psi_{k+1}^{i,j}$ is a physically admissible path and $\Xi\left(\tau_{k+1}^{i,j}\right) = 0$ otherwise.

The new solutions are obtained by sampling a suitable probability density functions, Θ_k_k. Usually, the probability density function is a weighted sum of N-dimensional Gaussian functions

$$\Theta_k\left(f_n\right) = \sum_{p=1}^{Y} w_k^{(p)} \frac{1}{\zeta_{n,k}^{(p)}\sqrt{2\pi}} exp\left[\frac{\left(f_n - \underline{f}_n^{(p)}\right)^2}{2\left(\zeta_{n,k}^{(p)}\right)^2}\right], \qquad n = 1, \dots, N \qquad (11)$$

where the mean value $\underline{f}_p^{(p)}$ and the standard deviation $\zeta_{n,k}^{(p)}$ are given by $\underline{f}_p^{(p)} = f_{n,k}^{(p)}$, $n = 1,...,N$, and $\zeta_{n,k}^{(p)} = \rho \sum_{i=1}^{Y} \dfrac{\left| a_{n,k}^i - a_{n,k}^p \right|}{Y-1}$. Moreover, the weights of the Gaussian functions are defined as

$$w_k^{(p)} = \frac{1}{\varpi Y \sqrt{2\pi}} exp\left[\frac{(p-1)^2}{2(\varpi Y)^2} \right], \quad p = 1,...,P \tag{12}$$

with ε being a parameter modeling a sort of convergence mechanism. When ω is small, the best-ranked solutions are preferred, while when it is large, the probability becomes more uniform. The following Figure 5 shown the ACO flowchart.

2.5. Honey Bee Optimizer

In the following a brief description of the artificial bee colony optimizer behavior and control parameters will be described, a more detailed description of the algorithm can be found in the cited references (Y. Yonezawa & T. Kikuchi, 1996; M. Donelli, I. Craddock, et al. 2011; Xin Zhang, Xiu Zhang, et al. 2013;

Figure 5. A standard Ant Colony Optimizer ACO flowchart

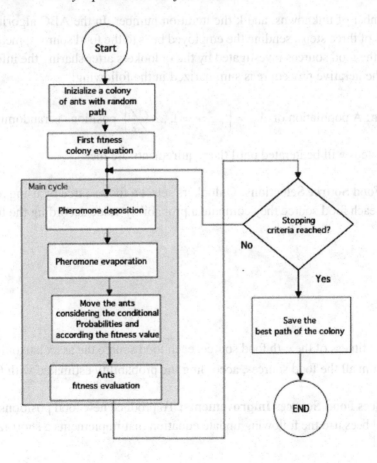

Shyh-Jier Huang, Xian-Zong Liu, et al. 2013; Nikola Todorovic & Sanja Petrovic, 2013; Sotirios K. Goudos, Katherine Siakavara & John N. Sahalos, 2014; Lina Yang, Xu Sun, et al., 2015; Assem M. Abdelhakim, Hassan I. Saleh, et al. 2016). In the ABC algorithm, the colony of artificial bees is composed of three groups of bees: employed bees, onlookers and scouts. A bee waiting on the dance area to make a decision about choosing a food source, is called an onlooker, the bee going to the food source it visited previously is called an employed bee, and a bee carrying out a new random search is called a scout. In the following these three main processes, which govern the ABC algorithm, will be discussed. In order to describe the ABC algorithm, let us consider a colony Π of C bees

$$\Pi = \left\{ \underline{B}_o; o = 1, \dots O = \frac{C}{2} \right\} \cup \left\{ \underline{B}_e; e = 1, \dots E = \frac{C}{2} \right\} \qquad (13)$$

where O and E are the number of onlooker and employed bees respectively. In this implementation we consider the first half of the colony as employed artificial bees and the second half as onlookers. For each employed bee a food source position, which represents a trial solution of the optimization problem, is defined as follows:

$$\underline{x}_k^e = \left\{ x_k^{e,j}; j = 1, \dots, J \right\} \qquad (14)$$

where J is the number of unknowns, and k the iteration number. In the ABC algorithm, each cycle of the search consists of three steps: sending the employed bees to the food sources; measuring the amount of food; selecting the food sources investigated by the onlookers after sharing the information found by employed bees. The iterative procedure is summarized in the following:

- **Initialization:** A population of $X_k = \left\{ \underline{x}_k^e; e = 1, \dots, \frac{C}{2} \right\}$ positions is randomly generated.

  The following steps will be iterated until the requirements are met:

- **Onlookers Food Source Selections:** Onlookers select a food source by using a probability based process. For each food source they compute a probability value according the following relation:

$$p_e = \frac{\varphi^e \left\{ \underline{x}_k^e \right\}}{\sum_{e=1}^{C/2} \varphi^e \left\{ \underline{x}_k^e \right\}} \qquad (15)$$

Where φ_k^e is the fitness of the e-th food source. each food source the associate onlooker bee chooses a source food h, from all the food sources, according the probability estimated with (4).

- **Employed Bees Food Sources Improvements:** To produce new food positions from the old one, the employed bees use the following update equation that implements a short range exploration:

$$x^{e,j}_{(k+1)} = x^{e,j}_k + R^{e,j}(x^{e,j}_k - x^{h,j}_k) \quad j=1,...,J \ e=1,...,\%_2 \tag{16}$$

where e is the food source index, h is the source position chosen by the onlooker bee, and $R^{e,j}$ is a random number generator, between 0 and 1.

- **Scouts Explorations:** If a solution representing a food source is not improved after a predetermined maximum number of iterations (L_{max}), then that food source is abandoned by its employed bees. A bee is converted into a scout which, and it is placed at a randomly generated new food source in order to implement a long range exploration. L_{max} is known as the food source limit it is an important control parameter of the Bee algorithm. A schema which summarizes the algorithm behavior is reported in Figure 6.

Figure 6. Flowchart of the honey bee algorithm

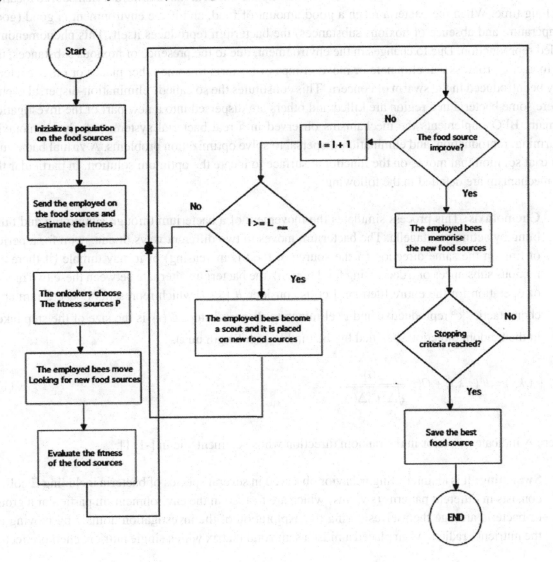

2.6. BFO

The bacteria feeding optimizer is inspired to the foraging behavior of the real bacteria, in particular the E. Coli bacterium (Y. Liu, & K. M. Passino, 2002). The locomotion of the E. Coli is achieved by a set of moving flagella (S. Gholami-Boroujeny, & M. Eshghi, 2012; Tao Zhang, Xiaoqin, et al. 2014; Mounir Amir, Sami Bedra, et al. 2014; Arvind Kumar Jain, Suresh Chandra Srivastava, et al. 2015; Jun Yi, Di Huang, et al. 2016) .The flagella help an E. Coli bacterium to tumble or swim, which are two basic operations performed by a bacterium when he is looking for food. In particular when the bacterium rotate the flagella in the clockwise direction, each flagellum produce a movement. When the bacterium move the flagella independently the bacterium tumbles with lesser number of tumbling whereas in a harmful place it tumbles frequently to find a nutrient gradient. If the bacterium move the flagella in the counterclockwise direction, the bacterium swim very fast rate in a given direction. In the BFO the combination of tumble and swim is called chemotaxis step. Bacteria like to move towards a rich nutrient sources and avoid noxious environment. Generally the bacteria move toward a rich source location for long time. When the bacteria reach a good amount of food, and if the environment is good (good temperature and absence of noxious substances) the bacterium reproduces itself. This phenomenon if called reproduction. Due to changes in the environment, due to the presence of noxious substances, the chemotactic progress can eliminate or move groups of bacteria to some other places or other bacteria may be introduced in the swarm of concern. This constitutes the so called "elimination-dispersal event" where some bacteria in a region are killed and others are dispersed into a new part of the investigation domain. BFO implements the mechanisms observed in a real bacterial system, namely chemotaxis, swarming, reproduction, and elimination-dispersal to solve optimization problems. A virtual bacterium is a trial solution that moves on the functional surface to locate the optimum solution. In particular the for mechanism are detailed in the following:

- **Chemotaxis:** This process simulates the movement of a bacterium through swimming and tumbling by acting via flagella. The bacterium moves in two different ways. It can swim for a period of time in the same direction (if the source of food is increasing) or it may tumble (if there are noxious substances or a decreasing food region), the bacterium alternate between these two modes of operation for the entire lifetime. Let us consider $\theta^i\left(j,k,l\right)$ which represents i^{th} bacterium at j^{th} chemotactic, k^{th} reproductive and l^{th} elimination-dispersal step. $C\left(i\right)$ is the size of the step taken in the random direction specified by the tumble (run length unit).

$$\theta^i(j+1,k,l) = \theta^i(j,k,l) + C(i)\frac{\Delta(i)}{\sqrt{\Delta^T(i)\Delta(i)}} \tag{17}$$

where Δ indicates a vector in the random direction whose elements lie in [-1, 1].

- **Swarming:** It is an interesting behavior observed in several species of bacteria including E.coli. It consists in different patterns (swarms) which are formed in the environment. In particular a group of bacteria arrange themselves during the exploration of the investigation domain by moving up the nutrient gradient when placed amidst a semisolid matrix with a single nutrient chemo-effecter.

The cells when stimulated by a high level of food, release an attractant substance, which helps them to aggregate into groups and thus move as concentric patterns of sub-swarms with high bacterial density. This is the way to share information and it can be expressed by the following function:

$$\Phi_{cc}(\theta, P(j,k,l)) = \sum_{i=1}^{S}\left[-D_{attrac\,tan\,t}\,\exp^{\left(-W_{attrac\,tan\,t}\sum_{m=1}^{P}(\theta_m-\theta_m^i)^2\right)}\right] + \sum_{i=1}^{S}\left[H_{repellant}\,\exp^{\left(-W_{attrac\,tan\,t}\sum_{m=1}^{P}(\theta_m-\theta_m^i)^2\right)}\right]$$ (18)

where $\Phi_{cc}\left(\theta, P\left(j,k,l\right)\right)$ is the objective function value to be added to the actual objective function (to be minimized) to present a time varying objective function, S is the total number of bacteria, p is the number of variables to be optimized, which are present in each bacterium and $\theta = \left[\theta_1, \theta_2, ..,\theta_p\right]$ is a point in the p-dimensional search domain. $D_{attractant}$, $W_{repellant}$, $H_{repellant}$, $W_{attractant}$, are different coefficients that should be chosen properly.

- **Reproduction:** When the least healthy bacteria the others healthier bacteria reproduce and split them into two bacteria, which are then placed in the same location. This keeps the number of bacteria constant. Elimination and Dispersal: Gradual or sudden changes in the local environment where a bacterium population lives may occur due to various reasons e.g. a significant local rise of temperature may kill a group of bacteria that are currently in a region with a high concentration of nutrient gradients.

- **Elimination and Dispersal:** If changes in the local environment where a bacterium population lives happens, all the bacteria in a region are killed or the group is dispersed into a new locations. To simulate this phenomenon in BFO some bacteria are moved at random positions with a very small probability while the new replacements are randomly initialized over the whole search space. The flow-chart of the complete BFO is presented in Figure 7. It is worth noticing that the main drawback of the BFO is the high number of parameters that requires a complex calibration phase.

2.7. Bat Optimizer

The bat algorithm is a meta-heuristic algorithm inspired to the eco-localization behavior of the bats. Bats flying searching food (insect) by using acoustical pulses with different pulse rates of emission and loudness. In particular bats emits acoustic signals to localize and identify preys (food) (Teodoro C. Bora, Leandro dos S. Coelho & Luiz Lebensztajn, 2012; Taher Niknam, Rasoul Azizipanah-Abarghooee, et al. 2013; Taher Niknam, Farhad Bavafa & Rasoul Azizipanah-Abarghooee, 2014; Farzan Rashidi, Ebrahim Abiri, et al. 2014; Ahmed Al-Muraeb & Hoda Abdel-Aty-Zohdy, 2015; Nien-Che Yang & Minh-Duy Le, 2015; Abdollah Kavousi-Fard, Taher Niknam & Mahmud Fotuhi-Firuzabad, 2016). The acoustical signals are reflected when they hit a target and bats are able to interpret the reflected signals and to correctly identify if the target is big, small, moving toward or far away from the hunter. For the implementation of the bat algorithm the following simplified ruled have been considered

Figure 7. Bacteria Foraging algorithm flowchart

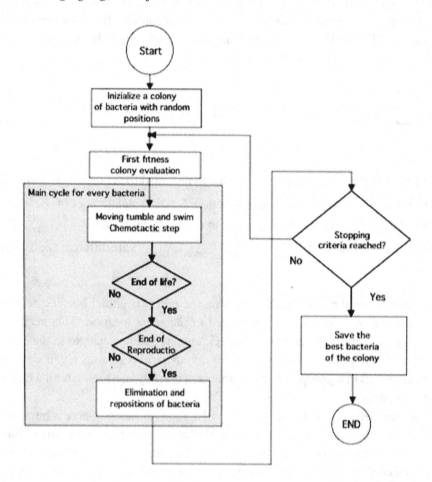

1. The bats of the colony are able to detect the distance and they know the difference between food location and the boundary of the investigation domain.
2. Bats fly randomly in the space of solution with a given velocity vector $\mathbf{v}_i$ starting from a $\mathbf{x}_i$ and considering acoustical signal with a fixed frequency f_{min}, the frequency and the loudness A_0 of the acoustical signals are varied to search prey.
3. Although the loudness can vary in different ways it is assumed that the loudness can vary from a large positive value A_{max} to a minimum constant value A_{min}.

The movement of virtual bats is regulated by the following update equations that estimate the new velocity and position vector:

$$\underline{v}_i^{k+1} = \underline{v}_i^{k} + (\underline{x}_i^{k} - \underline{x}_{best}^{k}) \cdot (f_{min} + (f_{max} - f_{min})\beta) \tag{19}$$

$$\underline{x}_i^{k+1} = \underline{x}_i^{k} + \underline{v}_i^{k+1} \tag{20}$$

where $\beta \in [0,1]$ is a random number, $\underline{x}_{best}^{k}$ is the global best solution known by all the bats of the colony (is the same of the G_{best} particle of the PSO). In order to permit the short range exploration, once a solution is selected among the current best solution a new solution for each bat is generated and move locally considering the following relation:

$$\underline{x}_{i}^{k+1} = \underline{x}_{i}^{k} + \varepsilon A^{k} \tag{21}$$

where $\varepsilon \in [-1,1]$ is a random number, and A^{t} is the average loudness of all the bats at k^{th} iteration. Moreover the loudness Ai and the repetition rate ri of pulse emission are updated with the iteration, in particular $A_{i}^{k+1} = \alpha A_{i}^{k}$ and $r_{i}^{k+1} = r_{i}^{0}\left[1 - e^{(-\gamma t)}\right]$ are the loudness and repetition pulse expression respectively. $\alpha = \gamma = 0.9$ are two real constant empirically chosen. The flowchart of the bat algorithm is reported in Figure 8.

Figure 8. Bat algorithm flowchart

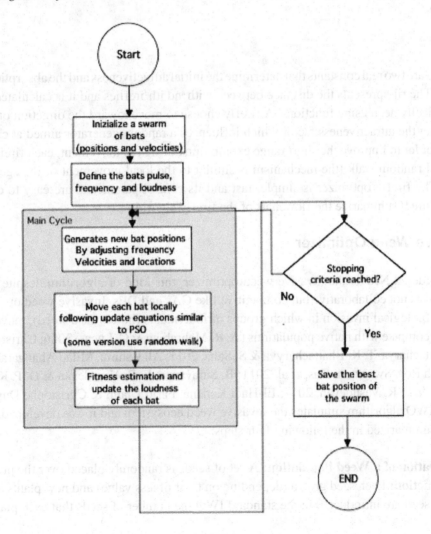

2.8. Firefly

In the previous sub-section aimed the bat optimizer has been described. In the bat optimizer the individuals share the social information considering the same mechanism of the PSO (a global best individual), and they search for the best solution considering a synthetic implementation of the bat's echo localization. In the firefly algorithm the agents are fireflies (Rock Z. Shi, Timothy & K. Horiuchi, 2006; Hongjun Su, Bin Yong, & Qian Du, 2016; Lindenberg Isac Silva, Edmarcio Antonio Belati, et al 2016; Husham J. Mohammed, Abdulkareem S. Abdullah, et al. 2016; Mariappan Kadarkarainadar Marichelvam, Thirumoorthy Prabaharan & Xin She Yang, 2014; Abdollah Kavousi Fard & Taher Niknam, 2014; Kinattingal Sundareswaran, Sankar Peddapati & Sankaran Palani, 2014; Urvinder Singh & Munish Rattan, 2014). Fireflies are nocturnal luminous insects which belong the beetle family. Fireflies are able to product light thanks to special photogenic organs. The fireflies use light to communicate each other or to attract prey, social orientation or as warning signals for predators. In the FFO a population of M agents (fireflies) is randomly initialized in the solution space with a given position $\mathbf{x}_i$ which represent a trial solution. Each fireflies has its distinctive attractiveness η which implies haw strong it can be attract the other fireflies of the colony. In particular the attractiveness of each firefly is given by the following relation:

$$\eta = \eta_0 e^{-\gamma r_{ij}} \tag{22}$$

where $\eta 0$ and γ are two real constants that determine the initial attractiveness and the absorption coefficient respectively. The r_{ij} epresents the distance between a ith ªnd jth ⁱireflies and it is calculated considering any monotonically decreasing functions. A firefly choose to move toward the direction of another firefly considering the attractiveness factor which influences a random generator aimed at choose a given direction. In order to improve the short range exploration during the movement, each firefly implement a sort of local random walk (the mechanism is similar to the local movement of the agents in the bat algorithm). The firefly optimizer is simple, fast and its control parameters are easy to calibrate. The following Figure 9 summarize the flowchart of the firefly algorithm.

2.9. Invasive Weed Optimizer

The last considered NIO is the invasive weed optimizer, this kind of algorithm despite it belongs to NIOs family it is not collaborative but competitive like GAs and DEs. Invasive weed optimizer (IWO) is inspired to biological invasion in which groups of individuals (in this case weed), move toward new locations and compete with native populations (A. R. Mehrabian & C. Lucas, 2006; Christian Veenhuis, 2010; R. Bhattacharya, T. K. Bhattacharyya & S. Saha, 2011; Ali Rahimi, Milad Ahangaran, et al. 2011; Gourab Ghosh Roy, Swagatam Das, et al. 2011; B. Saravanan, E. R. Vasudevan & D. P. Kothari, 2013; B. Saravanan & E. R. Vasudevan, 2014; El-Hadi Kenane, Farid Djahli & Christophe Dumond, 2015). In particular IWO algorithm simulates the invasive weed ecosystem and it was developed in 2006. The IWO can be summarized in the following four steps:

- **Initialization of a Weed Population:** A set of seeds is randomly placed over the problem space.
- **Reproduction:** Each seed grown (depending on their fitness value) and new plants able to generate new seed are introduced. In the standard IWO the number of seeds that each plant can gener-

Figure 9. The standard firefly algorithm flowchart

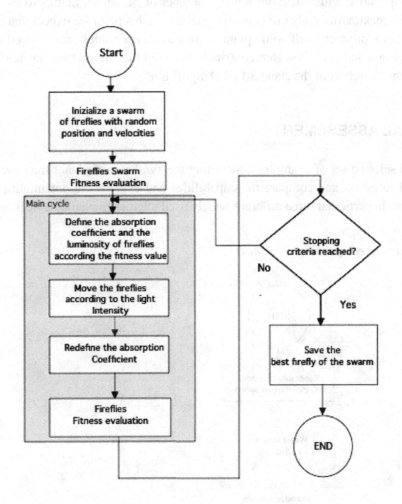

ates increase linearly from a minimum number of seeds corresponding to the worst fitness value up to the maximum number of seeds corresponding to the best fitness values.

- **Spatial Dispersal:** The seed are randomly distributed along the investigation domain considering a normal distribution with mean zero and a decreasing variance over the time. This permits to locate plants near the parent plant and to eliminate plants on the tail of the distribution. The standard deviation is calculated at every iteration k of the algorithm considering the following equation:

$$\sigma_k = \frac{(k_{max} - k)^n}{(k_{max})^n}(\sigma_{init} - \sigma_{fin}) + \sigma_{fin} \tag{23}$$

where σ_{init} and σ_{fin} are the initial an final value of the standard deviation for the normal distribution respectively. Where k_{max} is the maximum number of iterations, and n is an index usually set to 2 for almost all problems.

- • **Competition and Exclusion:** After a given number of iterations, thanks to the reproduction of the weed the maximum number of plants is reached. At this point we expect that plants with good fitness further reproduce itself while plants with bad fitness values are removed from the colony. The competition and exclusion step contributes to keep the colony to a constant number. Figure 10 shown the flowchart of the standard IWO algorithm.

3. NUMERICAL ASSESSMENT

In this section a selected set of examples concerning the synthesis of planar microwave devices have been considered to assess and compare the capabilities and explore the potentialities of natured in-spired algorithms. In particular three different widely used microstrip planar devices have been used as

Figure 10. Invasive weed optimizer flowchart

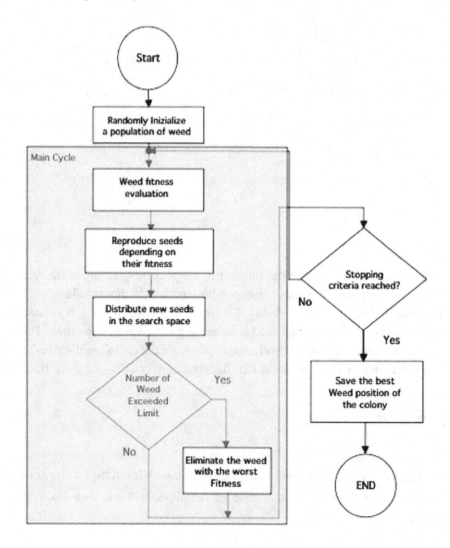

benchmarks. In the following the algorithms described in the previous section 2 will be considered for the design of a rectangular patch antenna equipped with a quarter wavelength matching transformer, a third order microstrip Chebichev filter, and a multi-sections Chebichev matching transformer. For all the considered experiments the NIOs will be initialized with the same population (of 100 different individuals) randomly chosen. Due to the stochastic nature of the considered algorithms each considered NIO has been run for 1000 times and the obtained results statistically analyzed. As far as the other NIOs parameters are concerned, a maximum number of iteration equal to K_{max}=100, and a threshold ε=10^{-3} have been considered. The NIOs have been implemented in matlab language and run under Windows 7 operative system, a standard four processors laptop equipped with 4Gb RAM has been considered. The specific algorithm parameters have been chosen considering the literature reported in the reference section. It is worth noticing that all the three following experiments are unconstraint optimization problems and the cost function is

3.1. Design of A Rectangular Antenna Patch with A Quarter Wavelength Matching Transformer

The geometry of the considered problem is reported in Figure 11. It consists of a rectangular patch antenna with a microstrip feeding network (I. Bahl & P. Bhartia, 1980). The feeding microstrip is connected on the center of the antenna side, which presents an high impedance value called R_{edge}, to match the antenna impedance with a standard 50Ω the use of a matching transformer is mandatory. In this experiment a quarter wavelength narrow band matching transformer has been considered as shown in Figure 11 (J. R. James & P. S. Hall, 1989). The matching transformer is a segment of microstrip line of length $L_L=\lambda/4$ characterized by an input impedance equal to $Z_{in} = Z_0^2 / Z_{edge}$ where Z_0 is the characteristic impedance of the microstrip antenna, and Z_{in} =50Ω is the required input impedance. The value of the characteristic impedance able to perfectly match the antenna with a 50Ω microstrip line is given by the following equation $Z_0 = \sqrt{Z_{edge} \bullet Z_{in}}$.

Figure 11. Geometry of the considered rectangular patch antenna

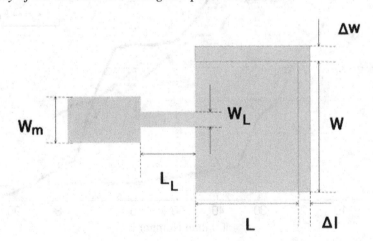

To properly design the antenna structure reported in Figure 11, a vector of seven real values unknowns must be optimized $\underline{X} = \{W_m, W_L, W, \triangle W, L_L, L, \triangle L\}$. In particular the goal is to obtain an antenna perfectly matched at a frequency of f=10GHz and characterized by a $S_{11} < $ -10 dB. In order to do this the following cost function $\varphi(\underline{X}) = min\{0, S_{11}(\underline{X})\}$ has been considered and minimized by using the NIOs described in Section 2. The antenna characteristics and in particular the cost function $S_{11}(\underline{X})$ has been estimated by mean of a commercial electromagnetic simulator, namely HFSS Designer. The mean of the fitness obtained after 1000 runs of the nine NIOs described in Section 2 are reported in Figure 12. As it can be noticed from the data reported in Figure 12, almost all optimizers were able to found a satisfactory solution, and they shown a good convergence rate. Almost all optimizer were able to found the optimal antenna parameters with an error of less than 0.1 mm, in particular W+$\triangle W$ =9.869 mm, L+$\triangle L$ =7.632 mm, L_L= 4.3 mm, W_m=1.7 mm, W_L=0.6 mm.

The behavior of the S_{11} versus the working frequency is reported in Figure 13 and clearly demonstrate the correct resonance frequency of the considered geometry, and the potentialities of the considered NIOs as effective microwave design tools. The data reported in Figure 13 clearly show that almost all considered NIOs are able to provide a good antenna design leading to the conclusions that all the considered NIOs provided similar results and they can be considered good tool for antenna design.

Figure 12. Rectangular antenna patch design. Comparisons between the fitness obtained with the nine NIOs described in section 2 (the data are mediated considering 1000 different runs)

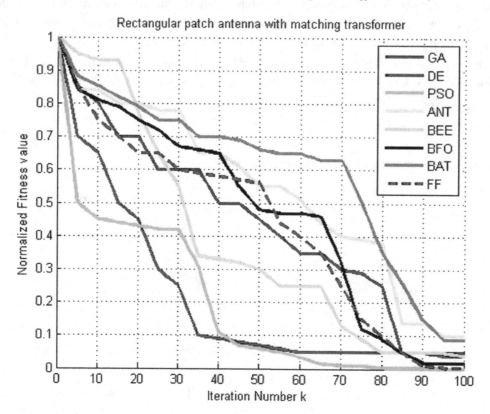

For a more accurate representation of this figure, please see the electronic version.

Figure 13. Rectangular antenna patch design. S11 vs. frequency. Optimized antenna parameters

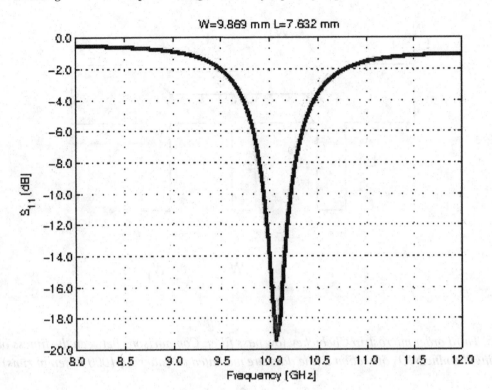

3.2. Design of a Low Pass Microstrip Chebichev Filter

The following experiment consider a low pass third order low pass Chebichev filter characterized with a ripple level R_L=0.5 dB, and a cut-off frequency of f_c=10GHz. Chebichev filters are very sensitive to the components tolerances and usually they require a tuning phase for their design (D. M. Pozar, 2012). The proposed microstrip filter geometry is reported in Figure 14, it consists of three open end stubs which act as reactive elements. The stubs are commensurate to a fixed length L. The goal of the design methodology is to obtain a low S_{11} parameters before the cut-off frequency f_c (for both input and output ports) and a $|S_{12}|$=1 in the pass band of the filter. The study of filter behavior is not the goal of this chapter so we remind to specific scientific literature. The goal is to solve the filter design problem by defining a suitable cost function as in the previous example and then minimize it by means of the nine NIOs described in Section 2.

The filter design requires the optimization of vector of five real values unknowns namely $\underline{X} = \{W_0, W_1, W_2, W_3, L\}$. In particular the goal is to obtain a filter perfectly matched in the pass band from zero up to f_c =10 GHz and characterized by a $|S_{11}|$< -15 dB. Moreover a $|S_{12}|$ = 1 in the filter passband must be reached. Also in this experiment the filter characteristics the cost function taking into account the $|S_{11}(\underline{X})|$ and $|S_{12}(\underline{X})|$ has been estimated by mean of the commercial electromagnetic simulator HFSS Designer particularly suitable for the analysis of planar microwave structures. The fitness obtained after 1000 runs of the nine NIOs described in Section 2 are reported in Figure 15 (as in the previous experiment the data are mediated). As it can be noticed from the data reported in Figure

Figure 14. Third order microstrip Chebichev low pass filter geometry

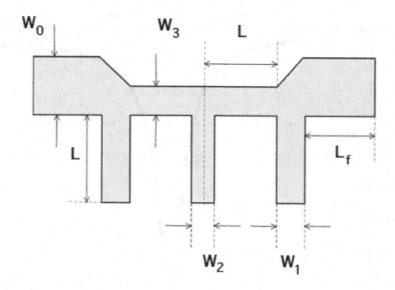

Figure 15. Third order microstrip Chebichev low pass filter. Comparisons between the fitness obtained considering the nine NIOs of section 2 (the data are mediated considering 1000 different runs)

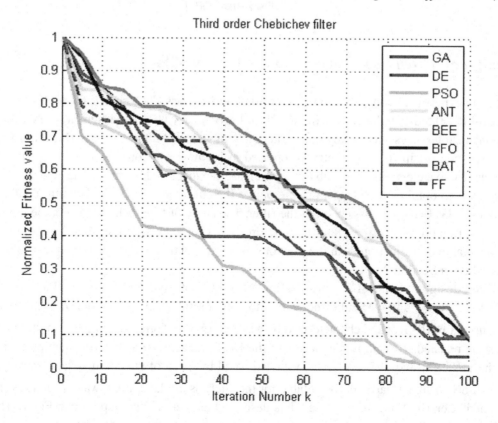

15, also in this case almost all optimizers shown a good convergence rate. All optimizers were able to found the filter parameters able to accomplish the requirements, in particular the following values have been obtained W_0=1.73 mm, W_1=0.82 mm, W_2=1.83 mm, W_3=0.26 mm, L=2.32 mm (negligible tolerances of about 0.02 mm has been obtained by the different algorithms).

3.3. Design of a Multisections Chebichev Matching Transformer

The last considered experiment deal with a four sections Chebichev matching transformers (D. M. Pozar, 2012), the requirements for such devices are the following $S_{11}(f) < $ -20 dB for a frequency f range between 8.0 GHz and 12.0 GHz. The design of the multi-sections transformer requires the optimization of six real values unknowns namely $\underline{X} = \{W_0, W_1, W_2, W_3, W_4, L\}$. The matching transformer geometry is reported in Figure 16. The considered cost function is represented by the value of the $S_{11}(f)$ parameter, also in this case the matching transformer characteristic have been simulated with the commercial electromagnetic simulator HFSS Designer and its geometrical parameter optimized with the algorithms reported in Section 2. The results obtained with the nine optimizers after 100 iterations are quite satisfactory all the optimizers reached the goal imposed by the requirements and the following geometrical parameters (with a negligible tolerance of 0.02 mm) have been obtained W_0=1.71 mm, W_1=1.22 mm, W_2=0.63 mm, W_3=0.25 mm, W_4=0.09 mm, L=4.21 mm. The behavior of the fitness obtained at the end of the optimization procedure are shown in Figure 17. As it can be observed also in this case the convergence rate of all the optimizers is quite satisfactory, they are able to reach similar fitness values at the end of the maximum number of iterations.

CONCLUSION

In this chapter, a review of nature inspired algorithms as applied to electromagnetic problems has been presented. In particular in this chapter three classical microwave design problems have been managed with different NIOs approaches. The obtained results demonstrated that a suitable information exchange

Figure 16. Multi sections Chebichev broadband matching transformer geometry

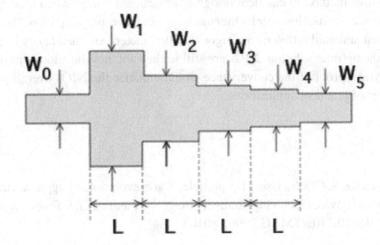

Figure 17. Multi sections Chebichev broadband matching transformer. Comparisons between the fitness of obtained with the nine NIOs (the data are mediated considering 1000 different runs)

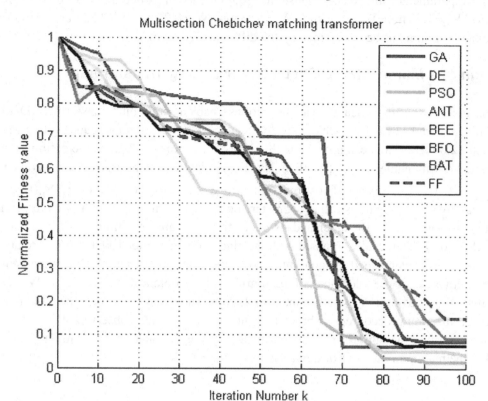

*For a more accurate representation of this figure, please see the electronic version.

between the individuals of the population is the key of force of recent NIOs, although it cannot be stated that a NIO algorithm is better then others algorithms (considering the "no free launch theorem"), NIOs based on collaboration generally outperform the performances of competitive algorithms such as GA and DE in terms of performances and convergence rate. NIOs therefore demonstrated to represent a reliable and effective alternative method to classical design approach, especially when dealing with problems characterized by real unknowns. However further mathematical investigations on NIOs convergence rate, computational burden and calibration of the algorithm parameters are mandatory to assure a fast and effective search of the optimal solution. NIOs are still in their infancy, development of fast calibration procedure and analytical proof of the convergence would enhance the NIOs overall performances and reveal additional area of practical applications.

REFERENCES

Adly, A., & Abd-El-Hafiz, S. (2006). Using the particle swarm evolutionary approach in shape optimization and field analysis of devices involving nonlinear magnetic media. *IEEE Transactions on Magnetics, 42*(10), 3150–3152. doi:10.1109/TMAG.2006.880103

Aksoy & Afacan. (2009). Planar Antenna Pattern Nulling Using Differential Evolution Algorithm. *International Journal on Electronics and Communications, 63*(2), 116-122.

Al-Muraeb, A., & Abdel-Aty-Zohdy, H. (2015). Optimal Design of Short Fiber Bragg Grating Using Bat Algorithm With Adaptive Position Update. *IEEE Photonics Journal, 8*(1).

Amir, M., Bedra, S., Benkouda, S., & Fortaki, T. (2014). Bacterial foraging optimisation and method of moments for modelling and optimisation of microstrip antennas. *IET Microwaves, Antennas & Propagation, 8*(4), 295–300.

Azaro, R., De Natale, F., Donelli, M., & Massa, A. (2006). PSO-based optimization of matching loads for lossy transmission lines. *Microwave and Optical Technology Letters, 48*(8), 1485–1487. doi:10.1002/mop.21738

Bahl, I., & Bhartia, P. (1980). *Microstrip Antennas.* Dedham, MA: Arthec House.

Bhattacharya, R., Bhattacharyya, T. K., & Saha, S. (2011). Sidelobe level reduction of aperiodic planar array using an improved invasive weed optimization algorithm. *Applied Electromagnetics Conference (AEMC).* IEEE. doi:10.1109/AEMC.2011.6256797

Boeringer, D., & Werner, D. (2005). *Effciency-constrained particle swarm optimization of a modified bernstein polynomial for conformal array excitation amplitude synthesis* (Vol. 53). IEEE Transactions on Antennas and Propagation.

Breard, Perrusson, & Lesselier. (2008). Hybrid Differential Evolution and Retrieval of Buried Spheres in Subsoil. *IEEE Geoscience and Remote Sensing Letters, 5*(4), 788-792.

Caorsi, S., Donelli, M., Lommi, A., & Massa, A. (2004). Location and imaging of two-dimensional scatterers by using a Particle Swarm algorithm. *Journal of Electromagnetic Waves and Applications, 18*(4), 481–494. doi:10.1163/156939304774113089

Caorsi, S., Donelli, M., Massa, A., Pastorino, M., & Randazzo, A. (2004). Detection of Buried Objects by an Electromagnetic Method Based on a Differential Evolution Approach. *Proceedings IEEE Instrumentation and Measurement Technology Conference, 2*, 1107-1111. doi:10.1109/IMTC.2004.1351257

Chen, X., ONeill, K., Barrowes, B. E., Grzegorczyk, T. M., & Kong, J. A. (2004). Application of a Spheroidal-Mode Approach and a Differential Evolution Algorithm for Inversion of Magneto-Quasistatic Data in UXO Discrimination. *Inverse Problems, 20*(6), 27–40. doi:10.1088/0266-5611/20/6/S03

Clerc, M., & Kennedy, J. (2002). The particle swarm—explosion, stability, and convergence in a multidimensional complex space. *IEEE Transactions on Evolutionary Computation, 6*(1), 58–73. doi:10.1109/4235.985692

Cui, S., & Weile, D. (2006). Application of a parallel particle swarm optimization scheme to the design of electromagnetic absorbers. *IEEE Transactions on Antennas and Propagation, 54*(3), 1107–1110.

Donelli, M. (2013, February). Design of broadband metal nanosphere antenna arrays with a hybrid evolutionary algorithm. *Optics Letters, 38*(4), 401–403. doi:10.1364/OL.38.000401 PMID:23455082

Donelli, M., Azaro, R., De Natale, F., & Massa, A. (2006, March). An innovative computational approach based on a particle swarm strategy for adaptive phased-arrays control. *IEEE Transactions on Antennas and Propagation*, *54*(3), 888–898. doi:10.1109/TAP.2006.869912

Donelli, M., Azaro, R., Massa, A., & Raffetto, M. (2006). Unsupervised synthesis of microwave components by means of an evolutionary-based tool exploiting distributed computing resources. *Progress in Electromagnetics Research*, *56*, 93–108. doi:10.2528/PIER05010901

Donelli, M., Caorsi, S., De Natale, F., Franceschini, D., & Massa, A. (2004). A versatile enhanced genetic algorithm for planar array design. *Journal of Electromagnetic Waves and Applications*, *18*(11), 1533–1548. doi:10.1163/1569393042954893

Donelli, M., Craddock, I., Gibbins, D., & Sarafianou, M. (2011). A three-dimensional time domain microwave imaging method for breast cancer detection based on an evolutionary algorithm. *Progress in Electromagnetic Research M*, *18*, 179–195. doi:10.2528/PIERM11040903

Donelli, M., & Massa, A. (2005). Computational approach based on a particle swarm optimizer for microwave imaging of two-dimensional dielectric scatterers. *IEEE Transactions on Microwave Theory and Techniques*, *53*(5), 1761–1776. doi:10.1109/TMTT.2005.847068

Donelli, M., Massa, A., Oliveri, G., Pastorino, M., & Randazzo, A. (2010). A differential evolution based multi-scaling algorithm for microwave imaging of dielectric structures. *Proceedings of IEEE International Conferences on Imaging Systems and Techniques, IST, 2010*, 90–95.

Dorigo, M., Maniezzo, V., & Colorni, A. (1996). Ant system: optimization by a colony of cooperating agents. IEEE Trans. Syst. Man Cybern. B, 26(1), 29-41.

Fard, A. K., & Niknam, T. (2014). Optimal stochastic capacitor placement problem from the reliability and cost views using firefly algorithm. *IET Science, Measurement & Technology*, *8*(5), 260–269. doi:10.1049/iet-smt.2013.0231

Fernandes, C. M., Mora, A. M., Merelo, J. J., & Rosa, A. C. (2014). KANTS: A Stigmergic Ant Algorithm for Cluster Analysis and Swarm Art. *IEEE Transactions on Cybernetics*, *44*(6), 843–856. doi:10.1109/TCYB.2013.2273495 PMID:23912505

Forestiere, C., Donelli, M., Walsh, G., Zeni, E., Miano, G., & Dal Negro, L. (2010). Particle-swarm optimization of broadband nanoplasmonic arrays. *Optics Letters*, *35*(2), 133–135. doi:10.1364/OL.35.000133 PMID:20081945

Genovesi, S., Monorchio, A., Mittra, R., & Manara, G. (2007). A subboundary approach for enhanced particle swarm optimization and its application to the design of artificial magnetic conductors. *IEEE Transactions on Antennas and Propagation*, *55*(3), 766–770. doi:10.1109/TAP.2007.891559

Goldberg, D. E. (1989). *Genetic Algorithms in Search, Optimization, and Machine Learning*. Boston, MA: Addison-Wesley.

Goudos, S. K., Siakavara, K., & Sahalos, J. N. (2014). Novel Spiral Antenna Design Using Artificial Bee Colony Optimization for UHF RFID Applications. *IEEE Antennas and Wireless Propagation Letters*, *13*, 528–531. doi:10.1109/LAWP.2014.2311653

Gregory, M. D., Petko, J. S., Spence, T. G., & Werner, D. H. (2010). Nature-Inspired Design Techniques for Ultra-Wideband Aperiodic Antenna Arrays. *IEEE Antennas and Propagation Magazine, 52*(3), 28–45. doi:10.1109/MAP.2010.5586571

Grimaccia, F., Mussetta, M., & Zich, R. E. (2007). Genetical swarm optimization: self-adaptive hybrid evolutionary algorithm for electromagnetics. IEEE Transactions on Antennas and Propagation, 55(3), 781–785.

Haupt, R. (1995). An introduction to genetic algorithms for electromagnetics. *IEEE Antennas Propag. Mag., 37*(2), 7–15. doi:10.1109/74.382334

Haupt, R. (1995). Comparison between genetic and gradient-based optimization algorithms for solving electromagnetics problems. *IEEE Transactions on Magnetics, 31*(3), 1932–1935. doi:10.1109/20.376418

He, S., Wu, Q. H., & Saunders, J. R. (2009). Group Search Optimizer: An Optimization Algorithm Inspired by Animal Searching Behavior. *IEEE Transactions on Evolutionary Computation, 13*(5), 973–990. doi:10.1109/TEVC.2009.2011992

Ho, S., Yang, S., Ni, G., & Wong, H. (2006). A particle swarm optimization method with enhanced global search ability for design optimizations of electromagnetic devices. *IEEE Transactions on Magnetics, 42*(4), 1107–1110. doi:10.1109/TMAG.2006.871426

Holland, H. (1975). *Adaptation in Natural and Artificial Systems*. Ann Arbor, MI: University of Michigan Press.

Huang, S.-J., Liu, X.-Z., Su, W.-F., & Ou, T.-C. (2013). Application of Enhanced Honey-Bee Mating Optimization Algorithm to Fault Section Estimation in Power Systems. *IEEE Transactions on Power Delivery, 28*(3), 1944–1951. doi:10.1109/TPWRD.2013.2264142

Huang, T., & Mohan, A. S. (2007). A microparticle swarm optimizer for the reconstruction of microwave images. IEEE Transactions on Antennas and Propagation, 55(3), 568–576.

Jain, A. K., Srivastava, S. C., Singh, S. N., & Srivastava, L. (2015). Bacteria Foraging Optimization Based Bidding Strategy Under Transmission Congestion. *IEEE Systems Journal, 9*(1), 141–151. doi:10.1109/JSYST.2013.2258229

James, J. R., & Hall, P. S. (1989). *Handbook of Microstrip Antennas* (Vols. 1-2). London, UK: Petergrinus.

James, M. (2008). The Self-Organization of Interaction Networks for Nature-Inspired Optimization. *IEEE Transactions on Evolutionary Computation, 12*(2), 220–230. doi:10.1109/TEVC.2007.900327

Jin & Ran. (2015). A Fair-Rank Ant Colony Algorithm in Distributed Mass Storage System. *IEEE Journals & Magazines Canadian Journal of Electrical and Computer Engineering, 38*(4).

Jin, N., & Rahmat-Samii, Y. (2005). Parallel particle swarm optimization and finite-difference time-domain (PSO/FDTD) algorithm for multiband and wide-band patch antenna designs. *IEEE Transactions on Antennas and Propagation, 53*(11), 3459–3468. doi:10.1109/TAP.2005.858842

Jin, N., & Rahmat-Samii, Y. (2007). Advances in particle swarm optimization for antenna designs: real-number, binary, single-objective and multi-objective implementations. IEEE Transactions on Antennas and Propagation, 55(3), 556–567.

Johnson, J., & Rahmat-Samii, Y. (1997). Genetic algorithms in engineering electromagnetics. *IEEE Transactions on Antennas and Propagation, 39*(4), 7–21. doi:10.1109/74.632992

Kavousi-Fard, A., Niknam, T., & Fotuhi-Firuzabad, M. (2016). A Novel Stochastic Framework Based on Cloud Theory and \theta -Modified Bat Algorithm to Solve the Distribution Feeder Reconfiguration. *IEEE Transactions on Smart Grid, 7*(2), 740–750.

Kenane, E.-H., Djahli, F., & Dumond, C. (2015). A novel Modified Invasive Weeds Optimization for linear array antennas nulls control. *2015 4th International Conference on Electrical Engineering (ICEE),* 1-4. doi:10.1109/INTEE.2015.7416784

Kennedy, J., Eberhart, R. C., & Shi, Y. (2001). *Swarm Intelligence.* San Francisco: Morgan Kaufmann.

King. (2006). Biomimetics: Biologically Inspired Technologies. Bar-Cohen.

Lasdon, L., Mitter, S., & Waren, A. (1967). The conjugate gradient method for optimal control problems. *IEEE Transactions on Automatic Control, 12*(2), 132–138. doi:10.1109/TAC.1967.1098538

Li, T.-H. S., Kao, M.-C., & Kuo, P.-H. (2015). Recognition System for Home-Service-Related Sign Language Using Entropy-Based K-Means Algorithm and ABC-Based HMM. *IEEE Transactions on Systems, Man, and Cybernetics Systems, 46*(1), 150–162. doi:10.1109/TSMC.2015.2435702

Liu, F., Lin, L., Jiao, L., Li, L., Yang, S., Hou, B., & Xu, J. et al. (2015). Nonconvex Compressed Sensing by Nature-Inspired Optimization Algorithms. *IEEE Transactions on Cybernetics, 45*(5), 1042–1053. doi:10.1109/TCYB.2014.2343618 PMID:25148677

Marichelvam, M. K., Prabaharan, T., & Yang, X. S. (2014). A Discrete Firefly Algorithm for the Multi-Objective Hybrid Flowshop Scheduling Problems. *IEEE Transactions on Evolutionary Computation, 18*(2), 301–305. doi:10.1109/TEVC.2013.2240304

Massa, A., Donelli, M., De Natale, F., Caorsi, S., & Lommi, A. (2004, November). Planar antenna array control with genetic algorithms and adaptive array theory. *IEEE Transactions on Antennas and Propagation, 52*(11), 2919–2924. doi:10.1109/TAP.2004.837523

Massa, A., Pastorino, M., & Randazzo, A. (2006). Optimization of the Directivity of a Monopulse Antenna With a Subarray Weighting by a Hybrid Differential Evolution Method. *IEEE Antennas and Wireless Propagation Letters, 5*(1), 155–158. doi:10.1109/LAWP.2006.872435

Mehrabian, A. R., & Lucas, C. (2006). A novel numerical optimization algorithm inspired from weed colonization. *Ecological Informatics, 1*(4), 355–366. doi:10.1016/j.ecoinf.2006.07.003

Mikki, S., & Kishk, A. (2006). Quantum particle swarm optimization for electromagnetics. *IEEE Transactions on Antennas and Propagation, 54*(10), 2764–2775. doi:10.1109/TAP.2006.882165

Mitter, S., Lasdon, L. S., & Waren, A. D. (1966). The method of conjugate gradients for optimal control problems. *Proceedings of the IEEE, 54*(6), 904–905. doi:10.1109/PROC.1966.4922

Mohammed, H. J., Abdullah, A. S., Ali, R. S., Abd-Alhameed, R. A., Abdulraheem, Y. I., & Noras, J. M. (2016). Design of a uniplanar printed triple band-rejected ultra-wideband antenna using particle swarm optimisation and the firefly algorithm. *IET Microwaves, Antennas & Propagation, 10*(1), 31–37. doi:10.1049/iet-map.2014.0736

Niknam, T., Azizipanah-Abarghooee, R., Zare, M., & Bahmani-Firouzi, B. (2013). Reserve Constrained Dynamic Environmental/Economic Dispatch: A New Multiobjective Self-Adaptive Learning Bat Algorithm. *IEEE Systems Journal, 7*(4), 763–776. doi:10.1109/JSYST.2012.2225732

Niknam, T., Bavafa, F., & Azizipanah-Abarghooee, R. (2014). New self-adaptive bat-inspired algorithm for unit commitment problem. *IET Science, Measurement & Technology, 8*(6), 505–517. doi:10.1049/iet-smt.2013.0252

Poli, L., Rocca, P., Manica, L., & Massa, A. (2010, April). Handling sideband radiations in time-modulated arrays through particle swarm optimization. *IEEE Transactions on Antennas and Propagation, 58*(4), 1408–1411. doi:10.1109/TAP.2010.2041165

Pozar, D. M. (2012). *Microwave Engineering*. Wiley & Sons.

Pshenichny, B. N., & Danilin, Y. M. (1978). *Numerical Methods in extrema problems*. Moscow: MIR Publisher.

Qing, A. (2007). A Parametric Study on Differential Evolution Based on Benchmark Electromagnetic Inverse Scattering Problem. *Proceedings 2007 IEEE Congress on Evolutionary Computation (CEC 2007)*, 1904-1909. doi:10.1109/CEC.2007.4424706

Rahimi, A., Ahangaran, M., Ramezani, P., & Kashkooli, T. (2011). An Improved Artificial Weed Colony for Continuous Optimization. *Computer Modeling and Simulation (EMS), 2011 Fifth UKSim European Symposium on*, 1-5. doi:10.1109/EMS.2011.30

Rashidi, F., Abiri, E., Niknam, T., & Salehi, M. R. (2014). On-line parameter identification of power plant characteristics based on phasor measurement unit recorded data using differential evolution and bat inspired algorithm IET Science. *Measurement Techniques, 9*(3), 376–392.

Ringlee, R. (1965). Bounds for convex variational programming problems arising in power system scheduling and control. *IEEE Transactions on Automatic Control, 10*(1), 28–35. doi:10.1109/TAC.1965.1098077

Robinson, J., & Rahmat-Samii, Y. (2004, February). Particle swarm optimization in electromagnetics. *IEEE Transactions on Antennas and Propagation, 52*(2), 397–407. doi:10.1109/TAP.2004.823969

Robinson, J., & Rahmat-Samii, Y. (2004). Particle swarm optimization in electromagnetics. *IEEE Transactions on Antennas and Propagation, 52*(2), 397–407. doi:10.1109/TAP.2004.823969

Robinson, J., Sinton, S., & Rahmat-Samii, Y. (2001). Particle swarm, genetic algorithm, and their hybrids: Optimization of a profiled corrugated horn antenna. *IEEE Antennas Propagat. Soc. Int. Symp. Dig., 1*, 314–317. doi:10.1109/APS.2002.1016311

Rocca, P., Manica, L., & Massa, A. (2010, January). Ant colony based hybrid approach for optimal compromise sum difference patterns synthesis. *Microwave and Optical Technology Letters, 52*(1), 128–132. doi:10.1002/mop.24882

Rocca, P., Oliveri, G., & Massa, A. (2011, February). Differential Evolution as applied to electromagnetics. *IEEE Antennas Propag. Mag.*, *53*(1), 38–49. doi:10.1109/MAP.2011.5773566

Roy, G. G., Das, S., Chakraborty, P., & Suganthan, P. N. (2011). Design of Non-Uniform Circular Antenna Arrays Using a Modified Invasive Weed Optimization Algorithm. *IEEE Transactions on Antennas and Propagation*, *59*(1), 110–118. doi:10.1109/TAP.2010.2090477

Sacchi, C., De Natale, F., Donelli, M., Lommi, A., & Massa, A. (2004, July). Adaptive antenna array control in presence of interfering signals with stochastic arrivals: Assessment of a GA-based procedure. *IEEE Transactions on Wireless Communications*, *3*(4), 1031–1036. doi:10.1109/TWC.2004.830845

Saravanan, B., & Vasudevan, E. R. (2014). Emission constrained unit commitment problem solution using invasive weed optimization Algorithm. *Advances in Electrical Engineering (ICAEE),2014International Conference on*, 1-6. doi:10.1109/ICAEE.2014.6838532

Saravanan, B., Vasudevan, E. R., & Kothari, D. P. (2013). A solution to unit commitment problem using Invasive Weed Optimization algorithm. *Power, Energy and Control (ICPEC),2013International Conference on*, 386-393. doi:10.1109/ICPEC.2013.6527687

Semnani, Kamyab, & Rekanos. (2009). Reconstruction of One-Dimensional Dielectric Scatterers Using Differential Evolution and Particle Swarm Optimization. *IEEE Geoscience and Remote Sensing Letters*, *6*(4), 671-675.

Silva, L. I., Belati, E. A., & Ivo, C. S. J. (2016). Heuristic Algorithm for Electrical Distribution Systems Reconfiguration Based on Firefly Movement Equation. *IEEE Latin America Transactions*, *14*(2), 752–758. doi:10.1109/TLA.2016.7437219

Singh, U., & Rattan, M. (2014). Design of thinned concentric circular antenna arrays using firefly algorithm. *IET Microwaves, Antennas & Propagation*, *8*(12), 894–900. doi:10.1049/iet-map.2013.0695

Storn, R., & Price, K. (1997). Differential Evolution – a simple and efficient heuristic for global optimization over continuous spaces. *Journal of Global Optimization*, *11*(4), 341–359. doi:10.1023/A:1008202821328

Stumberger, Dolinar, Palmer, & Hameyer. (2000). Optimization of Radial Active Magnetic Bearings Using the Finite Element Technique and Differential Evolution Algorithm. *IEEE Transactions on Magnetics, 36*(4), 1009-1013.

Su, H., Yong, B., & Du, Q. (2016). Perspectral Band Selection Using Improved Firefly Algorithm. *IEEE Geoscience and Remote Sensing Letters*, *13*(1), 68–72. doi:10.1109/LGRS.2015.2497085

Sundareswaran, K., Peddapati, S., & Palani, S. (2014). MPPT of PV Systems Under Partial Shaded Conditions Through a Colony of Flashing Fireflies. *IEEE Transactions on Energy Conversion*, *29*(2), 463–472. doi:10.1109/TEC.2014.2298237

Teodoro, C. (2012). Bat-Inspired Optimization Approach for the Brushless DC Wheel Motor Problem. *IEEE Transactions on Magnetics*, *48*(2), 947–950. doi:10.1109/TMAG.2011.2176108

Todorovic, N., & Petrovic, S. (2013). Bee Colony Optimization Algorithm for Nurse Rostering. *IEEE Transactions on Systems, Man, and Cybernetics Systems*, *43*(2), 467–473.

Veenhuis, C. (2010). Binary Invasive Weed Optimization. *Nature and Biologically Inspired Computing (NaBIC),2010Second World Congress on*, 449-454. doi:10.1109/NABIC.2010.5716311

Weile, D. S., & Michielssen, E. (1997, March). Genetic algorithm optimization applied to electromagnetics: A review. *IEEE Transactions on Antennas and Propagation, 45*(3), 343–353. doi:10.1109/8.558650

Wu, Z. (2001). Tomographic imaging of isolated ground surfaces using radio ground waves and conjugate gradient methods. *IEE Proceedings. Radar, Sonar and Navigation, 148*(1), 27–34. doi:10.1049/ip-rsn:20010111

Xu, Z. (2015). Three-Dimensional Cole-Cole Model Inversion of Induced Polarization Data Based on Regularized Conjugate Gradient Method. *IEEE Geoscience and Remote Sensing Letters, 12*(6), 1180–1184. doi:10.1109/LGRS.2014.2387197

Yang, L., Sun, X., Peng, L., Yao, X., & Chi, T. (2015). An Agent-Based Artificial Bee Colony (ABC) Algorithm for Hyperspectral Image Endmember Extraction in Parallel. *IEEE Journal of Selected Topics in Applied Earth Observations and Remote Sensing, 8*(10), 4657–4664. doi:10.1109/JSTARS.2015.2454518

Yang, N.-C., & Le, M.-D. (2015). Multi-objective bat algorithm with time-varying inertia weights for optimal design of passive power filters set. *IET Generation, Transmission & Distribution, 9*(7), 644–654. doi:10.1049/iet-gtd.2014.0965

Yang, S., Gan, Y. B., & Qing, A. (2002). Sideband Suppression in Time-Modulated Linear Arrays by Differential Evolution Algorithm. *IEEE Antennas and Wireless Propagation Letters, 1*(1), 173–175. doi:10.1109/LAWP.2002.807789

Yi, J., Di Huang, S. F., He, H., & Li, T. (2016). Multi-Objective Bacterial Foraging Optimization Algorithm Based on Parallel Cell Entropy for Aluminum Electrolysis Production Process. *IEEE Transactions on Industrial Electronics, 63*(4).

Yonezawa, Y., & Kikuchi, T. (1996). Micro Machine and Human Science. *Proceedings of the Seventh International Symposium Ecological algorithm for optimal ordering used by collective honey bee behaviour*, 249-256.

Zhang, F., Zhang, F.-S., Lin, C., Zhao, G., & Jiao, Y.-C. (2009). Pattern Synthesis for Planar Array Based on Element Rotation. *Progress In Electromagnetics Research Letters, 11*, 55–64. doi:10.2528/PIERL09070705

Zhang, J., Chung, H. S.-H., Lo, A. W.-L., & Huang, T. (2009). Extended Ant Colony Optimization Algorithm for Power Electronic Circuit Design. *IEEE Transactions on Power Electronics, 24*(1), 147–162. doi:10.1109/TPEL.2008.2006175

Zhang, X., Zhang, X., Yuen, S. Y., Ho, S. L., & Fu, W. N. (2013). An Improved Artificial Bee Colony Algorithm for Optimal Design of Electromagnetic Devices. *IEEE Transactions on Magnetics, 49*(8), 4811–4816. doi:10.1109/TMAG.2013.2241447

Chapter 2
A Comprehensive Literature Review on Nature-Inspired Soft Computing and Algorithms:
Tabular and Graphical Analyses

Bilal Ervural
Istanbul Technical University, Turkey

Beyzanur Cayir Ervural
Istanbul Technical University, Turkey

Cengiz Kahraman
Istanbul Technical University, Turkey

ABSTRACT

Soft Computing techniques are capable of identifying uncertainty in data, determining imprecision of knowledge, and analyzing ill-defined complex problems. The nature of real world problems is generally complex and their common characteristic is uncertainty owing to the multidimensional structure. Analytical models are insufficient in managing all complexity to satisfy the decision makers' expectations. Under this viewpoint, soft computing provides significant flexibility and solution advantages. In this chapter, firstly, the major soft computing methods are classified and summarized. Then a comprehensive review of eight nature inspired – soft computing algorithms which are genetic algorithm, particle swarm algorithm, ant colony algorithms, artificial bee colony, firefly optimization, bat algorithm, cuckoo algorithm, and grey wolf optimizer algorithm are presented and analyzed under some determined subject headings (classification topics) in a detailed way. The survey findings are supported with charts, bar graphs and tables to be more understandable.

DOI: 10.4018/978-1-5225-2128-0.ch002

INTRODUCTION

Nature is the main source of inspiration among scientists in order to develop several scientific methods and solution algorithms. To survive in natural life, speed, adaptability, flexibility and cooperation are the a few basic features. Actually, all these characteristics are expected from the development of a software in the computational environment. The nature-inspired soft computing techniques are emerged as a simulation of the real biological system or a modelization of human mind. Many nature-inspired soft computing techniques have been developed to solve combinatorial optimization problems. If these techniques are compared with the traditional methods, they can provide more successful performances since the nature-inspired soft computing techniques can easily be adapted to real life problems and they can deal with huge, inconsistent and incomplete model data thanks to their reasoning capabilities.

Soft Computing techniques are relatively efficient methods to describe real world complexity. Soft computing methods are widely used in various applications due to the capability of dealing with uncertain, incomplete and complicated data or model structures. Soft computing approaches are emerged as an alternative in case traditional approaches could not find appropriate solutions in multidimensional models which consist of multiple variables, complicated structures and ill-defined real cases. The core methodologies of soft computing are Fuzzy logic (FL), evolutionary computation (EC) and swarm intelligence (SI), neural networks (NN) and probabilistic models that all mainly concern with making rational decisions in imprecise and unstable conditions taking example of human thinking system in various applied area. Beside these techniques, the soft computing methods include machine learning (ML), belief networks, chaos theory, and support vector machines.

Soft computing techniques and computational intelligence methods are generally confused with each other because of the similar structures and working principles. According to Kacprzyk (2015), these methods are not the same but closely related to each other. Computational Intelligence (CI) is integrating the fields of Artificial Neural Networks, Evolutionary Computation, and Fuzzy Logic. Soft Computing is the collocation for the same fields as CI expanded with Probabilistic Reasoning, Swarm Intelligence, and partly Chaos Theory. These techniques provides a broader view of scope in complex mathematical modelling than traditional approaches.

Through the review of the existing literature, nature-inspired soft computing techniques have become one of the most promising tools that help to implement hard combinatorial problems. Particularly, in real world we have to design some strict mathematical models, but these models may not respond the decision makers' expectations due to the hardness of transferring all reality to the model. Most of the researchers have preferred to use nature-inspired soft computing techniques in various computational science areas and difficult engineering problems with a growing interest because of their easiness and flexibilities. The aim of this chapter is to provide a comprehensive review of nature inspired soft computing methods. This survey led to some observations and the identification of some deficiencies on nature-inspired soft computing literature. Based on the review, we will also present our suggestions on inspired soft computing and algorithms for future research.

In this chapter, a brief outline of soft computing techniques are discussed in Section 2. Section 3 provides a brief outline of the nature inspired soft computing techniques and tabular and graphical analyses of these techniques. Some directions for future research are provided in Section 4 and the conclusions are presented in Section 5.

SOFT COMPUTING

In the early 1990s, Zadeh introduced the concept of Soft Computing (SC). The definition of soft computing is 'a collection of methodologies that aim to exploit tolerance for imprecision and uncertainty to achieve tractability, robustness, and low solution cost' (Lotfi A. Zadeh, 1994). Soft computing methodologies have been advantageous in many areas. In contrast to hard methods, soft computing methodologies mimic consciousness and cognition in several important respects: they can learn from experience; they can universalize into domains where direct experience is absent; and lastly, they can perform mapping from inputs to the outputs faster than inherently serial analytical representations by means of parallel computer architectures that simulate biological processes (Chaturvedi, 2008).

Soft computing has four main branches: Fuzzy logic (FL), evolutionary computation (EC) and swarm intelligence, neural networks (NN) and probabilistic models. Beside these techniques, the soft computing methods include machine learning, belief networks, chaos theory, support vector machines, etc. as shown in Figure 1.

Soft computing provides the opportunity to represent ambiguity in human thinking with the uncertainty in real life (Roy, Furuhashi, & Chawdhry, 1999). The major soft computing techniques are briefed as follows.

Fuzzy Logic

Fuzzy logic is one of the techniques of soft-computing. In 1965, the concept of Fuzzy Logic (FL) was conceptualized by Lotfi Asker Zadeh, a professor at the University of California at Berkley. Zadeh published the first paper, called "fuzzy sets", on the theory of fuzzy logic. Fuzzy set is a class of objects whose memberships are not precisely defined (L.A. Zadeh, 1965). Fuzzy set theory was developed to characterize non-probabilistic uncertainties for representing and computing data and information that are uncertain and imprecise.

Figure 1. Classification of Soft Computing Techniques

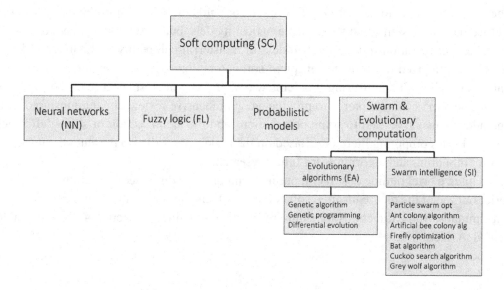

Many problems in real world deal with uncertain and imprecise data so conventional approaches cannot be effective to reach the best solution. To deal with this uncertainty, fuzzy set theory has been developed as an effective mathematical algebra under vague environment (Ruan, 2010). In the recent years, ordinary fuzzy sets and their extensions have been used in many areas such as energy, medicine, material, economics and pharmacology sciences (Kahraman, Öztayşi, & Çevik Onar, 2016).

Ordinary fuzzy sets have recently been extended to interval fuzzy sets, hesitant fuzzy sets, intuitionistic fuzzy sets, type-2 fuzzy sets, nonstationary fuzzy sets, and fuzzy multisets (Kahraman et al., 2016; Rodriguez, Martinez, & Herrera, 2012). An interval-valued fuzzy set is a special case of type 2 fuzzy set. Interval-valued fuzzy sets were introduced independently by Zadeh (1975), Grattan-Guiness (1976), Jahn (1975). Later, Zadeh (1978) introduced type-2 fuzzy sets. A type-2 fuzzy set lets us incorporate uncertainty about the membership function into the fuzzy set theory. Atanassov (1986) developed the intuitionistic fuzzy sets which include the membership value as well as the non-membership value. Another significant extension of the regular fuzzy sets is Hesitant fuzzy sets (HFSs), initially developed by Torra (2010). Hesitant fuzzy sets handle the situations where a set of values are possible for the membership of a single element.

Neural Networks

Scientists have long been inspired by the human brain. The artificial neural networks (ANN) were first introduced by W. McCulloch and W. Pitts in (1943). They suggested that the biological function of the human brain could be emulated by a simplified computational model. Artificial neural networks (ANNs) are systems that can obtain, store, and utilize knowledge gained from experience. An artificial neural network is capable of learning from an experimental data set to describe the nonlinear and interaction effects with great success (Chandrasekaran, Muralidhar, Krishna, & Dixit, 2010). The ANNs are structured with a set of inter connected layers, each of them composed of nodes; the typology of connections and nodes (called neurons) characterizes the different typologies of neural networks (Bertini et al., 2010). ANNs consist of an input layer used to current data to the network, output layer to generate ANN's response, and one or more hidden layers in between. The most important feature of ANN is that it does not need any mathematical model, since it learns from experimental data. Researchers from many scientific disciplines are designing ANNs to solve various problems such as pattern recognition, prediction, optimization, speech recognition, data mining, classification, control, and many others.

Probabilistic Reasoning

Probabilistic models are one of the techniques of soft-computing. The probabilistic reasoning (PR) is based on knowledge-driven reasoning. PR gives the mechanism to evaluate the outcome of systems affected by randomness or other types of uncertainty (Bonissone, 1997). PR with graphical models, known as Bayesian networks or Belief networks, is an active field of research and practice in soft computing. Bayesian probability theory and the Dempster-Shafer theory of belief functions are two theories for modeling and reasoning with knowledge in uncertain areas.

Swarm and Evolutionary Computation

Swarm intelligence (SI) is the collective behavior of decentralized, self-organized natural or artificial systems. Most of the basic ideas are derived from the real swarms in the nature, which includes particle swarm, ant colonies, bird flocking, fish schooling, honeybees, bacteria and microorganisms, etc. The concept of SI is introduced by Gerardo Beni and Jing Wang in (1993) in the context of cellular robotic systems. Swarm intelligence can be accepted as part of the evolutionary computation, but the interests in swarm intelligence are so dominant that SI has almost become a field of itself (Xin-She Yang & He, 2015). Some of the SI techniques can be listed as below:

- Particle swarm optimization algorithm
- Ant colony algorithm
- Artificial bee colony algorithm
- Firefly optimization algorithm
- Bat algorithm
- Cuckoo search algorithm
- Grey wolf optimizer algorithm

On the other hand, evolutionary computation (EC) refers to computer-based problem solving methods that use computational models of evolutionary processes, such as natural selection, survival of the fittest and reproduction, as the fundamental components of such computational systems. The evolutionary algorithms (EAs) which are inspired by the biological genetics found in living nature which is simple, powerful, and probabilistic approach to general problem solving approach (Chaturvedi, 2008). EAs are well known and successful algorithms among nature inspired algorithms. EAs can be subdivided as follows:

- Genetic algorithm
- Genetic programming
- Differential evolution

The following section gives an overview of some nature inspired soft computing techniques.

NATURE-INSPIRED SOFT COMPUTING

Genetic Algorithm

Genetic algorithms (GAs) are the most popular nature inspired soft computing algorithms in terms of the diversity of their applications. GAs were formally developed in the 1960s and 1970s by John Holland at University of Michigan and his collaborators.

GAs are a particular type of evolutionary computation. GAs can be categorized as population based global search algorithms. GA is a stochastic algorithm that mimics the evolutionary process of natural selection. GA uses operators such as selection, recombination (crossover) and mutation, which are inspired from the mechanics of natural selection. The initial population of GA is randomly selected and then a search is conducted by moving from the initial population to a new population using operators in order to obtain an optimum solution.

GA has three main applications, namely, optimization, intelligent search and machine learning. In recent years, for solving more complex problems, GAs have been used along with neural networks and fuzzy logic (Konar, 2000). In the literature, there are various review studies and book chapters related to GAs. Some of these studies are given in the following. Konak et al. (2006) present an overview of GAs developed specifically for problems with multiple objectives. Espejo et al. (2010) survey the existing literature about the application of genetic algorithms to classification. Sastry et al. (2005) give a brief introduction to simple genetic algorithms and associated terminology.

Some of the most cited and prominent articles on GA are given in the following. Deb et al. (2002) present a multi objective evolutionary algorithm, named nondominated sorting genetic algorithm (NSGA-II). Altiparmak et al. (2006) propose a new solution procedure based on GAs to find the set of pareto-optimal solutions for multi-objective supply chain network design problem. Stach et al. (2005) propose a novel learning method based on GA that is able to generate fuzzy cognitive map models from input historical data, and without human interference. Hidalgo et al. (2012) propose the use of a GA to optimize the type-2 fuzzy inference systems.

A literature review for GA using SCOPUS gives 69,996 published articles (in article title, abstract, and keywords). The frequencies of published articles using genetic algorithm listed on SCOPUS database as of end of 2015 are shown in Figure 2. The results clearly show the increasing trend in articles for genetic algorithm, with the frequencies of articles increasing dramatically over the last 15 years.

Figure 2. Genetic Algorithm articles based on years

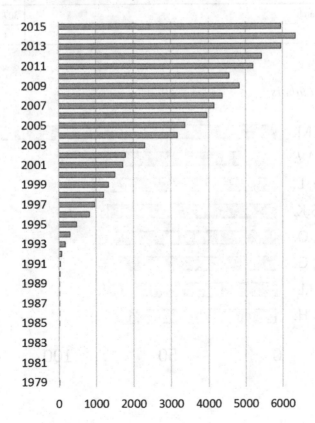

When the articles are classified according to the journals they are published in, Expert Systems with Applications is found to have the highest number of articles (900 articles). Table 1 shows the journals most-publishing genetic algorithm based articles.

Authors M. Gen (with 142 articles), W. Pedrycz (with 98 articles) and L. Jiao (with 84 articles) are the most productive researchers in this field. The frequencies of genetic algorithm articles by authors are shown in Figure 3. China has been studying on this subject (with 21,274 articles). Distribution of GA articles by countries is given in Figure 4.

Genetic algorithms have been used in different areas. These areas can be categorized as follows: Engineering, Computer Science, Mathematics, Biochemistry, Genetics and Molecular Biology, Physics and Astronomy, Materials Science, Energy, Decision Sciences, Medicine, Chemistry etc. As seen in Figure 5, especially in the engineering and computer science areas GAs have been widely used.

Table 1. Distribution of GA studies by journals

Journal	Frequency
Expert Systems with Applications	900
Bioinformatics	657
International Journal of Advanced Manufacturing Technology	648
International Journal of Production Research	460
Computers and Industrial Engineering	421
European Journal of Operational Research	381
Computers and Operations Research	307
Information Sciences	294

Figure 3. Documents by authors

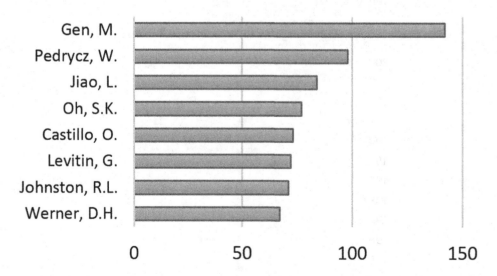

Figure 4. Documents by countries/territories

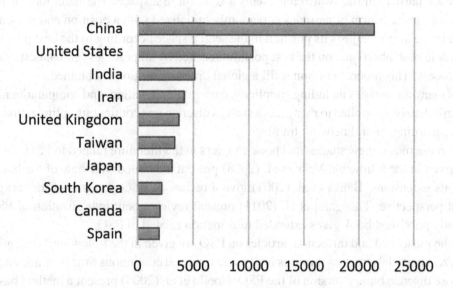

Figure 5. Documents by subject area

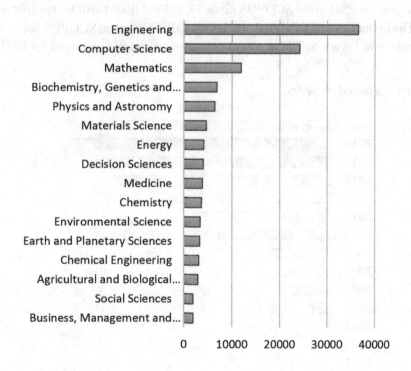

Particle Swarm Optimization

Particle Swarm Optimization (PSO) was developed by Kennedy and Eberhart (1995). PSO is a nature inspired soft computing oriented, stochastic and population-based global optimization technique. It is inspired by the social behavior of bird and fish flocking.

In PSO, each particle in the swarm represents a solution in a space. The main idea of PSO can be described as follows: a swarm of particles is randomly initialized with a position and velocity and then each particle in the swarm adjusts its position in the search space according to the best position reached by itself (particle best, pbest) and on the best position reached by all particles (global best, gbest) during the search process. This process continues till a global optimal solution is obtained.

Due to its many advantages including simplicity, easy implementation, and computational efficiency PSO has been extensively applied to many areas such as discrete and continuous optimization, classification, machine learning, neural network training.

There are numerous review studies and book chapters in the literature related to PSO. Some of these studies are given in the following. Valle et al. (2008) present a detailed overview of the basic concepts of PSO and its extensions. Banks et al. (2007) give a review of PSO in terms of its background and development perspective. Thangaraj et al. (2011) present review about hybridization of PSO. Clerc's (2010) recently published book gives extended information related to PSO.

Some of the most cited and influential articles on PSO are given in the following. Clerc and Kennedy (2002) analyze a particle's track as it moves in discrete time and continuous time. Kennedy and Eberhart (1997) propose discrete binary version of the PSO. Coello et al. (2004) present a method based on PSO to handle problems with several objective functions. Trelea (2003) analyse PSO algorithm in terms of convergence analysis and parameter selection.

A literature review for PSO using SCOPUS gives 18,423 published articles (in article title, abstract, and keywords). The frequencies of published articles using PSO listed on SCOPUS database with respect to the years are shown in Figure 6. The results clearly show the increasing trend for PSO.

Figure 6. PSO articles based on years

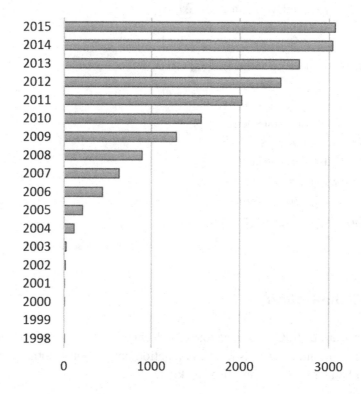

PSO based articles have been published in various journals. Table 2 shows the significant journals most-publishing PSO based articles. When the articles are classified according to the journals they are published in, Expert Systems with Applications is found to have the highest number of articles (365 articles). International Journal of Electrical Power and Energy Systems, International Journal of Advanced Manufacturing Technology, Neurocomputing and Information Sciences have published a considerable number of articles related to PSO.

Authors A. Abraham (with 69 articles), J. Zeng (with 55 articles) and J. Sun (with 48 articles) are the most productive researchers in this field. The frequencies of PSO articles by authors are shown in Figure 7. PSO has received the most attention from Chinese researchers (with 9,306 articles). Distribution of ACO articles by countries is given in Figure 8.

PSO has been used in different areas. These areas can be categorized as follows: Engineering, Computer Science, Mathematics, Energy, Physics and Astronomy, Materials Science, Decision Sciences, Chemical Engineering etc. As seen in Figure 9., especially in the engineering and computer science areas GA has been widely used.

Table 2. Distribution of PSO studies by journals

Journal	Frequency
Expert Systems with Applications	365
Int J of Electrical Power and Energy Systems	242
Int J of Advanced Manufacturing Technology	150
Neurocomputing	149
Information Sciences	130
Engineering Applications of Artificial Intell.	112
Soft Computing	83

Figure 7. Documents by authors

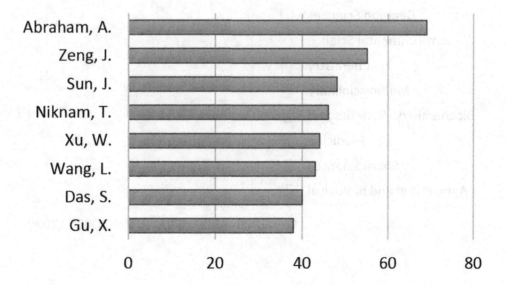

Figure 8. Distribution of PSO studies by countries

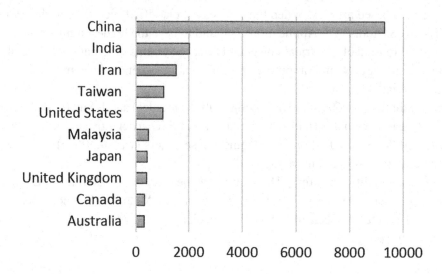

Figure 9. Distribution of PSO studies by subject areas

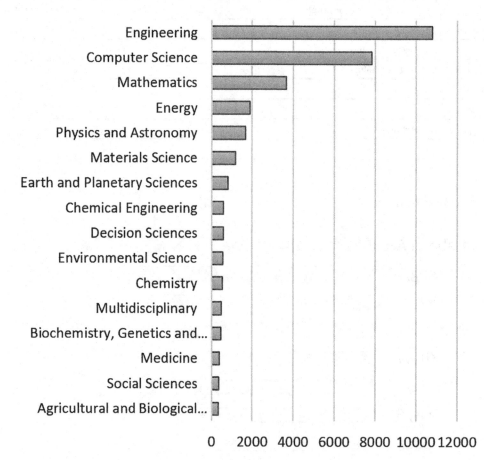

Ant Colony Optimization

Ant Colony Optimization (ACO) is among the most successful swarm intelligence based soft computing algorithms. Ant algorithms were first introduced by Dorigo (1992) and Dorigo et al. (1996) as a novel heuristic approach to different combinatorial optimization problems such as the traveling salesman problem and the quadratic assignment problem. The ACO framework was developed by Dorigo and Caro (1999).

ACO was inspired by the ability of real ant colonies to efficiently organize the foraging behavior of the colony using pheromone trails by means of communication between the ants. The pheromone trail allows the ants to find for the shortest path back to the food source or to the nest.

The ACO is a stochastic optimization technique for solving complex, combinatorial optimization problems. A number of successful ACO algorithms in such diverse application areas including exploratory data analysis, graph coloring, partitioning, scheduling problems, vehicle routing problems, design of communication networks and machine learning.

In the related literature, there are numerous review studies and books. Some of these studies are given in the following. Duan et al. (2012) give a comprehensive survey on the recent progresses of ant colony optimization. Blum (2005) presents an outline of ACO, gives some of the ACO variants, and demonstrates how ACO can be applied to continuous optimization problems. Angus and Woodward (2009) propose a taxonomy for multiple objective ACO algorithms. Pedemonte et al. (2011) present a systematic and comprehensive survey of the state-of-the-art on parallel ACO applications and introduce a taxonomy for classifying parallel ACO algorithms.

Some of the most cited and influential articles on ant systems are given in the following. Stützle and Hoos (2000) present MAX-MIN Ant System. Dorigo et al. (1999) propose ant algorithms for discrete optimization. Parpinelli et al. (2002) present an ant colony based algorithm for data mining. Socha and Dorigo (2008) propose an extension of ACO to continuous problems. Gambardella et al. (1999) present a hybrid ant colony system coupled with a local search, applied to the quadratic assignment problem.

A literature review for ACO using SCOPUS gives 5,667 published papers (article title, abstract, or keywords). Yearly distribution of articles using ACO listed on SCOPUS database is given in Figure 10. As shown in Figure 10, most of the articles were published in 2013. After 2013, the results clearly show the decreasing trend in the frequencies of articles related to ACO.

ACO based articles have been published in various journals. Table 3 shows the significant journals most-publishing ACO based articles. When the articles are classified according to the journals they are published in, Expert Systems with Applications is found to have the highest number of articles (110 articles). Computers and Operations Research, International Journal of Production Research, and European Journal of Operational Research have also published a considerable number of articles related to ACO.

Authors A. Kaveh (with 35 articles), L. Chen (with 27 articles) and M. Dorigo who also developed ACO algorithm (with 24 articles) are the most productive researchers in this field. The frequencies of ACO algorithm articles by authors are shown in Figure 11. ACO has received the most attention from Chinese researchers (with 2791 articles). Distribution of ACO articles by country is given in Figure 12.

ACO has been used in different areas. These areas can be categorized as follows: Engineering, Computer Science, Mathematics, Decision Sciences, Physics and Astronomy, Materials Science, Biochemistry, Genetics and Molecular Biology, Energy, Social Sciences. As seen in Figure 13., especially in the engineering and computer science areas ACO has been widely used.

Figure 10. ACO articles based on years

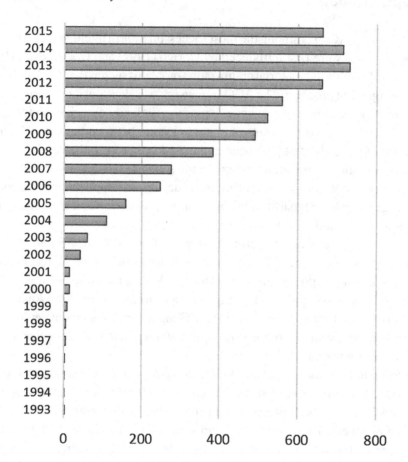

Table 3. Distribution of ACO studies by journals

Journal	Frequency
Expert Systems with Applications	110
Computers and Operations Research	52
International Journal of Production Research	46
European Journal of Operational Research	40
Engineering Applications of Artificial Intell.	34
Information Sciences	33
Computers and Industrial Engineering	27

Artificial Bee Colony (ABC) Optimization

In the literature, various bees-inspired algorithms based on swarm intelligence are available such as the Virtual Bee Algorithm, Bee Swarm Optimization, Bee Colony Optimization, and Bees Algorithm. The most popular algorithm based on bees-inspired algorithms is Artificial Bee Colony (ABC) algorithm was developed by Karaboga in 2005.

Figure 11. Documents by authors

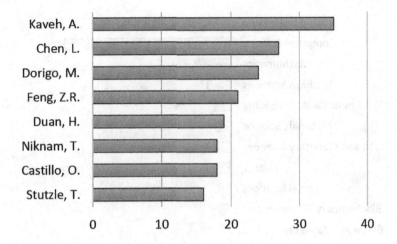

Figure 12. Distribution of ACO studies by countries

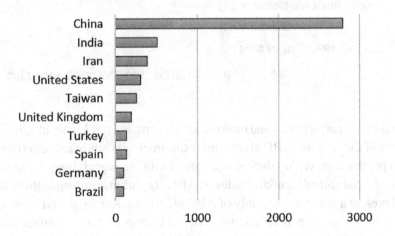

The basic idea of designing ACO algorithm is to imitate the foraging behaviour of honey bees. In ABC algorithm, the position of a food source represents a possible solution to the optimization problem and the nectar amount of a food source corresponds to the quality of the solution. Typically, the colony of artificial bees consists of two essential groups of bees: employed artificial bees that are employed at, and currently exploiting, a certain food source and unemployed artificial bees (onlookers and scouts) that are looking for a food source to exploit (Dervis Karaboga & Akay, 2009).

Similar to the ACO algorithm, bee algorithms are also very suitable in dealing with discrete optimization problems. Combinatorial optimization problems such as routing, determining optimal paths and scheduling have been successfully solved by ABC algorithm. Besides that, ABC optimization algorithm has been implemented on clustering problems due to the quality of solution when compared with other stochastic approaches.

In the literature, there are a few number of reviews and book chapters related to ABC algorithm. Some of these studies are given in the following. Bansal et al. (2013) present a review on ABC developments,

Figure 13. Distribution of ACO studies by subject areas

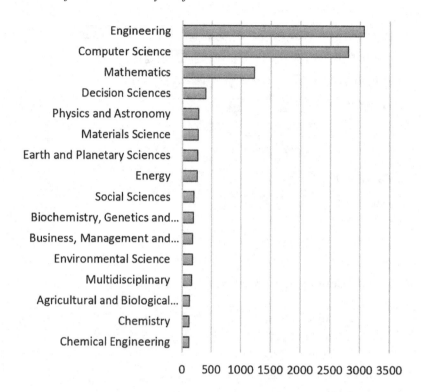

applications, comparative performance and future research perspectives. Liao et al. (2013) present a review of various variants of the original ABC algorithm, experimentally study and improvements. Akay and Karaboga (2015) present a survey on the applications of ABC in signal, image, and video processing.

Some of the most cited and influential articles on ABC algorithm are given in the following. Karaboga and Akay (2009) present a comparative study of ABC algorithm. Karaboga and Ozturk (2011) use ABC algorithm for data clustering on benchmark problems and compare with classification techniques from the literature. Pan et al. (2011) propose a discrete ABC algorithm to solve the lot-streaming flow shop scheduling problem. Gao and Liu (2012) present a modified ABC algorithm.

A literature review for ABC using SCOPUS gives 1,425 published papers (article title, abstract, or keywords). Yearly distribution of articles using ABC listed on SCOPUS database is given in Figure 14. The results clearly show the increasing trend for ABC.

ABC based articles have been published in various journals. Table 4 shows the significant journals most-publishing ABC based articles. When the articles are classified according to the journals they are published in, International Journal of Electrical Power and Energy Systems is found to have the highest number of articles (34 articles). Information Sciences, Engineering Applications of Artificial Intelligence and Expert Systems with Applications have published a considerable number of articles related to ABC.

Authors D. Karaboga who also developed ABC algorithm (with 24 articles), S.Y. Liu (with 18 articles) and H. Chen (with 15 articles) are the most productive researchers in this field. The frequencies of ABC algorithm articles by authors are shown in Figure 15. Particularly researchers from China have been studying on this subject (with 552 articles). Distribution of ABC articles by countries is given in Figure 16.

Figure 14. ABC articles based on years

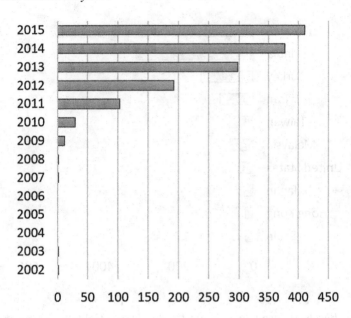

Table 4. Distribution of ABC studies by journals

Journal	Frequency
International Journal of Electrical Power and Energy Systems	34
Information Sciences	25
Engineering Applications of Artificial Intelligence	22
Expert Systems with Applications	21
Applied Mathematics and Computation	18
Swarm and Evolutionary Computation	16
Soft Computing	14

Figure 15. Documents by authors

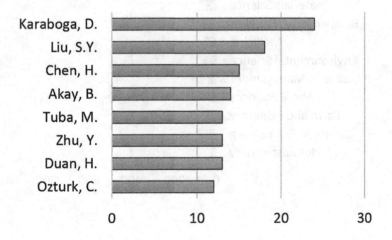

Figure 16. Distribution of ABC studies by countries

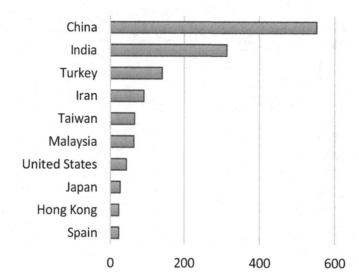

ABC methodology has been used in various fields. These fields can be categorized as follows: Engineering, Computer Science, Mathematics, Energy, Decision Sciences, Physics and Astronomy, Materials Science, Biochemistry, Medicine, Genetics and Molecular Biology, and Social Sciences. As seen in Figure 17, especially in the engineering and computer science fields ABC has been widely used.

Figure 17. Distribution of ABC studies by subject areas

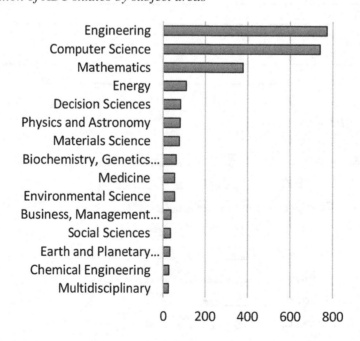

Firefly Algorithm

The Firefly Algorithm (FA) is one of the recent swarm intelligence techniques developed by Xin-She Yang in 2008 at Cambridge University. FA is a kind of nature-inspired soft computing, meta-heuristic and stochastic algorithm.

FA is inspired by the flashing lights of fireflies in nature. The main characteristic of fireflies is their flashing light. These lights have two principal functions: to attract mating partners and to warn potential predators. The algorithm has three rules: i) all fireflies are unisex so that one firefly will be attracted to other fireflies regardless of their gender, ii) attractiveness is represented by their brightness, which increases or decreases depending on distances between the flies, iii) the brightness of a firefly is affected or determined by the landscape of the objective function (X.S. Yang, 2008).

In recent years, Firefly Algorithm (FA) has attracted much attention among researchers and has been applied to solving a wide range of diverse real-world problems due to simple, flexible and easy to implement. FA can efficiently solve highly nonlinear, multimodal optimization problems, continuous optimization, combinatorial optimization, classification and engineering application such as image processing, robotics, chemistry.

In the literature, there are several reviews and book chapters related to FA algorithm. Some of these studies are given in the following. Yang (2014) presents an overview of firefly algorithm as well as their latest developments and applications. Fister et al. (2014) provide a brief review of the expanding and state-of-the-art literature. Fister et al. (2015) present a comprehensive overview of firefly algorithms that are enhanced with chaotic maps, to describe the advantages.

Some of the most cited and influential articles on FA algorithm are given in the following. Gandomi et al. (2011) present the FA for solving mixed continuous/discrete structural optimization problems. In Senthilnanth et al.'s study (2011), the FA is used for clustering on benchmark problems and the computational performance of the FA is compared with other nature inspired soft computing techniques. In another study, Gandomi et al. (2013) introduce chaotic FA-based methods to increase its global search mobility for robust global optimization. Yang (2013) extends the FA to solve multiobjective optimization problems.

A literature review for FA methodology using SCOPUS gives 495 published articles (in article title, abstract, and keywords). The frequencies of published articles using firefly algorithm listed on SCOPUS database as of end of 2015 are shown in Figure 18. The results clearly show the increasing trend for firefly algorithm.

Figure 18. FA articles based on years

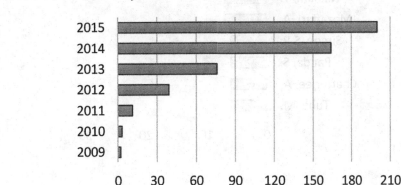

FA based articles have been published in different journals. Table 5 shows the significant journals most-publishing FA based articles. When the articles are classified according to the journals they are published in, International Journal of Electrical Power and Energy Systems is found to have the highest number of articles (18 articles). Expert Systems with Applications, Journal of Intelligent and Fuzzy Systems and Energy have published a considerable number of articles related to FA.

Authors X.S. Yang who also developed FA algorithm (with 24 articles), M.A. Vega-Rodriguez (with 9 articles), M.H. Horng, K. Chandrasekaran and T. Niknam (with 7 articles) are the most productive researchers in this subject. The frequencies of FA algorithm articles by authors are shown in Figure 19. Especially researchers from India have been studying on this field (with 150 articles). Distribution of FA articles by countries is given in Figure 20.

FA methodology has been used in diverse areas. These areas can be categorized as follows: Engineering, Computer Science, Mathematics, Energy, Physics and Astronomy, Materials Science, Environmental Science, Biochemistry, Genetics and Molecular Biology, Medicine, Decision Sciences. As seen in Figure 21, the FA has been widely used in the engineering and computer science areas.

Table 5. Distribution of FA studies by journals

Journal	Frequency
Int J of Electrical Power and Energy Systems	18
Expert Systems with Applications	11
Journal of Intelligent and Fuzzy Systems	9
Energy	7
Neurocomputing	5
Knowledge Based Systems	4

Figure 19 Documents by authors

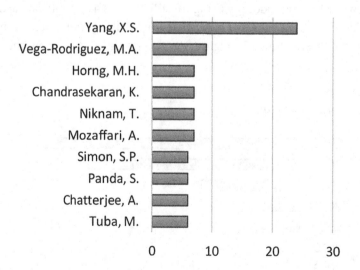

Figure 20. Distribution of FA studies by countries

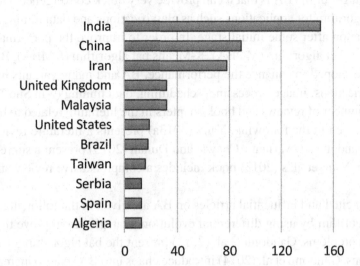

Figure 21. Distribution of FA studies by subject areas

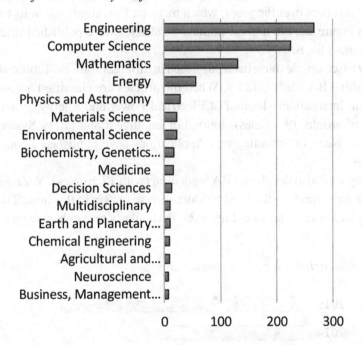

Bat Algorithm

Bat algorithm (BA) is a relatively novel bio-inspired algorithm. BA was first introduced by Xin-She Yang in (2010) and inspired by the echolocation behavior of microbats. Microbats use a form of radar called echolocation that is a process of detecting an object by reflected sound. It is used to detect its prey, avoid obstacles, and locate their roosting crevices in the dark. Microbats fly randomly with some velocity, frequency and sound in searching space. The objective of algorithm is to detect preys at minimum distance.

One of the advantages of the BA is that it can provide very quick convergence. Due to this advantage it is very efficient algorithm for applications such as classifications and data mining. But in some cases, it may lead to stagnation after some initial stage. In order to improve the performance, many variants such as Multiobjective bat algorithm (MOBA), K-Means bat algorithm (KMBA), Binary bat algorithm (BBA), have been developed to enhance the performance. BA and many variants have been applied in optimization, classifications, image processing, scheduling, data mining (Xin She Yang & He, 2013).

There are a few number of reviews and book chapters in the literature related to bat algorithm. Some of these studies are given in the following. Yang (2013a) presents a literature review and applications of the bat algorithm and its new variants. Chawla and Duhan (2015) present a survey of the state of the art on Bat algorithm. Yang et al.'s (2013) book includes a comprehensive review and tutorial of BA as a chapter.

Some of the most cited and influential articles on BA are given in the following. Fister et al. (2013) hybridize the bat algorithm by using differential evolution strategies to improve the bat-algorithm behaviour for complex problems. Gandomi et al. (2013) present the bat algorithm for solving constrained optimization problems. Gandomi et al. (2014) introduce chaos into BA so as to increase its global search mobility for robust global optimization.

A literature review for BA methodology using SCOPUS gives 206 published papers. Figure 22 shows the distribution of 206 papers over the years, which mention Bat Algorithm in its title, abstract, or keywords. As shown in Figure 22, the highest number of articles were published in 2015 and the results show the increasing trend for BA.

BA methodology based articles have been published in different sources. Table 6 shows the substantial journals most-publishing BA based articles. When the articles are classified according to the journals they are published in, International Journal of Electrical Power and Energy Systems is found to have the highest number of articles (9 articles). Journal of Intelligent and Fuzzy Systems, Expert Systems with Applications and Neural Computing and Applications have published a considerable number of articles related to BA.

Authors X.S. Yang who also developed BA algorithm (with 17 articles), Y. Zhou (with 8 articles), J. Xie and Q. Wu (with 6 articles) are the most productive researchers in this area. The frequencies of BA algorithm articles by authors are shown in Figure 23. Particularly researchers from China and India have

Figure 22. Bat Algorithm articles based on years

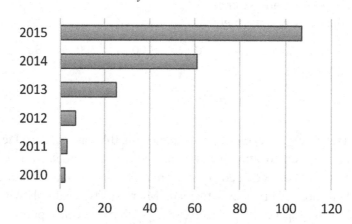

Table 6. Distribution of BA studies by journals

Journal	Frequency
Int J of Electrical Power and Energy Systems	9
Journal of Intelligent and Fuzzy Systems	7
Expert Systems with Applications	5
Neural Computing and Applications	3
Energies	2

Figure 23. Documents by authors

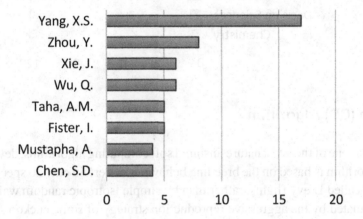

been studying on this field (with 64 articles and 54 articles, respectively). Distribution of BA articles by countries is given in Figure 24.

Bat algorithm has been used in diverse fields. These fields can be categorized as follows: Engineering, Computer Science, Mathematics, Energy, Materials Science, Physics and Astronomy, Biochemistry, Genetics and Molecular Biology, Environmental Science, Medicine, Decision Sciences, Chemistry etc. As seen in Figure 25, particularly in the engineering and computer science areas (with 105 article), the BA has been widely used.

Figure 24. Distribution of BA studies by countries

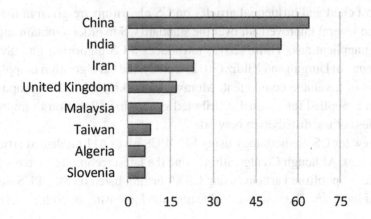

Figure 25. Distribution of BA studies by subject areas

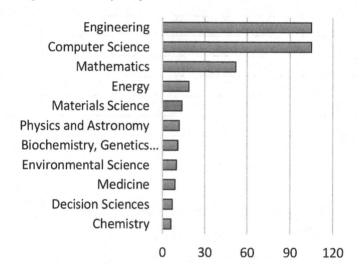

Cuckoo Search (CS) Algorithm

Cuckoo search (CS) is one of the latest nature-inspired soft computing algorithms, developed by Yang and Deb (2009). CS algorithm is based on the breeding behaviour of certain cuckoo species. CS algorithm is enhanced by the so-called L´evy flights, rather than by simple isotropic random walks. In addition, this algorithm was stimulated by the aggressive reproduction strategy of some cuckoo species.

CS algorithm was firstly proposed as a tool for numerical function optimization and continuous problems. Nowadays, there have been a lot of attention and recent studies using cuckoo search with diverse range of applications such as function optimization, engineering optimization, image processing, scheduling, planning, feature selection, forecasting, and real-world applications. Recent studies show that CS is potentially far more efficient than PSO and genetic algorithms (Fister et al., 2014). A brief literature review has been carried out by Yang and Deb (2014) and Fister et al. (2014).

In the literature, there are several reviews related to CS algorithm. Some of these studies are given in the following. Fister et al. (2013) present a review of all the state-of-the-art developments and research directions for future development. Mohamad et al. (2014) present an overview of CS algorithm as well as an overview of CS applications for solving optimization problems. Yang and Deb (2014) investigate the fundamental ideas of cuckoo search and the latest developments.

Some of the most cited and influential articles on CS algorithm are given in the following. Walton et al. (2011) propose several improvement over the standard CS in order to obtain superior performance on real engineering applications. Yildiz (2013) introduces a CS algorithm for solving manufacturing optimization problems. In Durgun and Yildiz (2012)'s study, the CS algorithm is applied to the structural design optimization of a vehicle component. Moravej and Akhlaghi (2013) propose a new approach based on CS which is applied for optimal distributed generation allocation to improve voltage profile and reduce power loss of the distribution network.

A literature review for CS methodology using SCOPUS gives 411 published articles (in article title, abstract, and keywords). Although CS algorithm is one the latest techniques, it has gained a lot of attention. The frequencies of published articles using CS algorithm listed on SCOPUS database as of end of 2015 are shown in Figure 26. The results clearly show the increasing trend for firefly algorithm.

Figure 26. CS Algorithm articles based on years

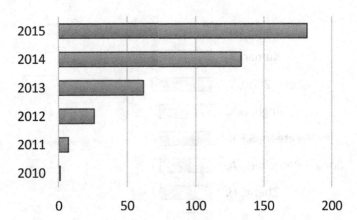

CS algorithm based articles have been published in various journals. Table 7 shows the significant journals most-publishing CS algorithm based articles. When the articles are classified according to the journals they are published in, International Journal of Bio Inspired Computation is found to have the highest number of articles (13 articles). Expert Systems with Applications, Journal of Intelligent and Fuzzy Systems International Journal of Electrical Power and Energy Systems and Neural Computing and Applications have published a considerable number of articles related to CS algorithm.

Authors X.S. Yang who also developed CS algorithm (with 22 articles), A. Kumar and Y. Zhou (with 8 articles) are the most productive researchers in this subject. The frequencies of CS algorithm articles by authors are shown in Figure 27. Especially researchers from India and China have been studying on this field. Distribution of CS algorithm articles by countries is given in Figure 28.

CS algorithm has been used in different areas. These areas can be categorized as follows: Computer Science, Engineering, Mathematics, Energy, Physics and Astronomy, Environmental Science, Medicine, Biochemistry, Genetics and Molecular Biology, Materials Science, Decision Sciences, Chemistry etc. As seen in Figure 29, especially in the computer science and engineering areas the CS algorithm has been widely used.

Table 7. Distribution of CS Algorithm studies by journals

Journal	Frequency
Int Journal of Bio Inspired Computation	13
Expert Systems with Applications	11
Int J of Electrical Power and Energy Systems	8
Neural Computing and Applications	6
Journal of Intelligent and Fuzzy Systems	5
Swarm and Evolutionary Computation	5
Energy	5
Energy Conversion and Management	5

Figure 27. Documents by authors

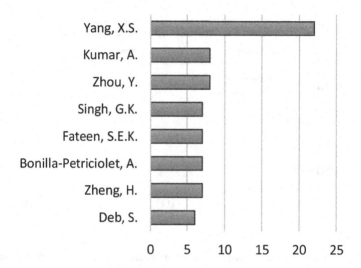

Figure 28. Distribution of CS algorithm studies by countries

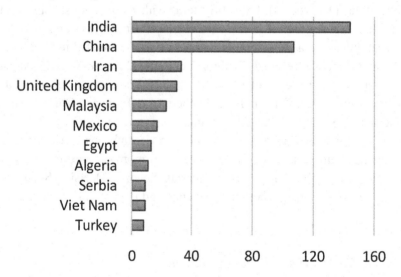

Grey Wolf Optimizer Algorithm

Grey Wolf Optimizer Algorithm (GWO) is a novel meta-heuristic algorithm. GWO was first proposed by Mirjalili et al. (2014) and inspired by grey wolves. The GWO algorithm mimics the leadership hierarchy and hunting mechanism of grey wolves in nature. Four types of grey wolves such as alpha, beta, delta, and omega are employed for simulating the leadership hierarchy. In addition, there are three major steps of hunting: searching, encircling, and attacking prey.

The GWO algorithm was able to provide highly competitive results compared to the most commonly used heuristics such as PSO, differential evolution, evolutionary programming. The results of the continuous problems on the unimodal functions showed the superior exploitation of the GWO algorithm and the exploration ability of GWO was supported by the results on multimodal functions. The results of

Figure 29. Distribution of CS algorithm studies by subject areas

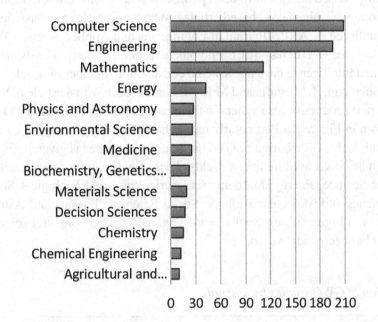

the analyses showed high local optima avoidance (Seyedali Mirjalili et al., 2014). The GWO algorithm can be applied to many areas such as classical engineering design problems and real application with unknown search spaces.

In the literature there has been no review and book chapter related to GWO algorithm since it is a recent developed algorithm. Some of the most cited and influential articles on GWO algorithm are given in the following. Sulaiman et al. (2015) present the use of GWO to solve optimal reactive power dispatch problem which is a well-known nonlinear optimization problem in power system. Mirjalili (2015) implements the recently proposed GWO for training multi-layer perceptron for the first time. Saremi et al. (2015) propose the use of evolutionary population dynamics in the GWO. Song et al. (2015) apply GWO algorithm for parameter estimation in surface waves. Komaki and Kayvanfar (2015) propose the use of GWO to solve two stage assembly flow shop scheduling problem with release time.

A literature review for GWO methodology using SCOPUS gives 30 published articles. Figure 30 shows the distribution of 30 papers over the years, which mention GWO in its title, abstract, or keywords. In Figure 30, most articles were published in 2015 and the results show that the usage of GWO algorithm will be increased drastically in a short term due to its success.

Figure 30. GWO algorithm articles based on years

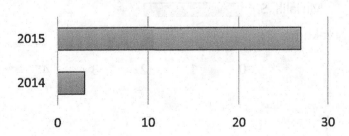

GWO methodology based articles have been published in different sources. Table 8 shows the substantial journals most-publishing GWO based articles. When the articles are classified according to the journals they are published in, ARPN Journal of Engineering and Applied Sciences is found to have the highest number of articles (3 articles). IEEE Photonics Technology Letters, Advances In Engineering Software and Applied Intelligence have published a considerable number of articles related to GWO.

Authors M.H. Sulaiman, Z. Mustaffa and M.R. Mohamed (each with 4 articles), S.M. Mirjalili (with 3 articles) are the most productive researchers in this area. The frequencies of GWO algorithm articles by authors are shown in Figure 31. Particularly researchers from Iran, Malaysia, China and India have been studying on this field. Distribution of GWO articles by countries is given in Figure 32.

GWO algorithm has been used in diverse fields. These fields can be categorized as follows: Engineering, Computer Science, Energy, Mathematics, Agricultural and Biological Sciences, Medicine, Biochemistry, Genetics and Molecular Biology, Social Sciences, Physics and Astronomy, Materials Science etc. As seen in Figure 33, especially in the engineering and computer science areas (with 27 articles), the GWO has been widely used.

Table 8. Distribution of GWO studies by journals

Journal	Frequency
ARPN Journal Of Eng. And Applied Sciences	3
IEEE Photonics Technology Letters	2
Advances In Engineering Software	1
Applied Intelligence	1
Applied Soft Computing	1

Figure 31. Documents by authors

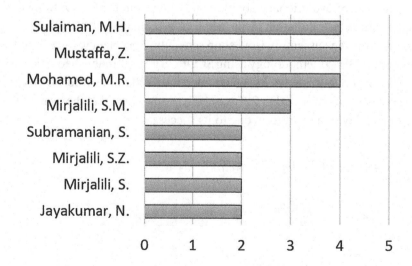

Figure 32. Distribution of GWO studies by countries

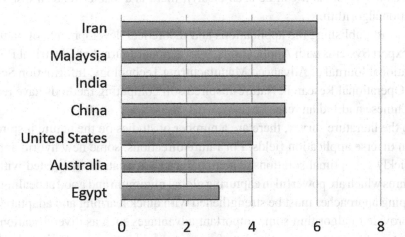

Figure 33. Distribution of GWO studies by subject areas

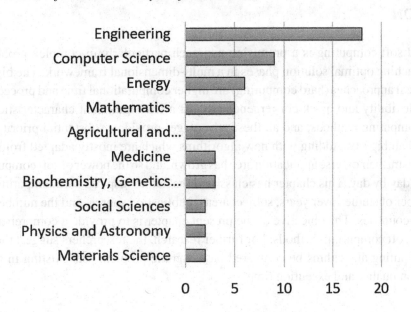

FUTURE OF NATURE-INSPIRED SOFT COMPUTING

Application areas of the nature inspired soft computing techniques are mainly focused on complex computer science and engineering problems. Their implementations can be extended with various study fields such as business, finance, economics, government and social sciences since the huge data challenges have become major issue actually in these areas.

This study has pointed that there is a clear upward movement in the usage of relatively novel bio-inspired algorithm namely firefly algorithm, bat algorithm, cuckoo search algorithm, grey wolf algorithm and their extensions. In the future years, this trend is predicted to continue. On the other hand, recently, scholars have shown a decreased interest in genetic algorithm and ant colony optimization algorithm compared to previous years. As it can be seen clearly, there is a stable trend in last years on particle swarm optimization algorithm.

The journals most publishing the applications and theoretical developments of nature-inspired soft computing are Expert Systems with Applications, International Journal of Electrical Power and Energy Systems, International Journal of Advanced Manufacturing Technology, Information Science and European Journal of Operational Research. Nature-inspired soft computing methods have received the most attention from Chinese and Indian researchers.

According to the literature survey, there are a number of studies on the nature inspired soft computing techniques in diverse application fields. For future directions, some new hybrid approaches can be developed to quickly get optimal solutions. Their characteristics can be integrated with well-designed effective algorithms which are powerful in capturing global minimum and good at dealing with uncertainties. The developing approaches must be strengthened with quick learning and adaptability capabilities. These features provide to algorithm some important advantages such as diversification of the solution space and guarantee of convergence optimal performance besides the time limit and solution quality.

CONCLUSION

Nature inspired soft computing is a promising approach particularly in complex problems' defining, solving, and reaching optimal solution phases in a multi-dimensional framework. The biggest disadvantages of analytical approaches (hard computing) are higher computational time and procedure/result cost. Adaptability, flexibility and quick convergence are just a few significant characteristics of the nature inspired soft computing methods, and all these advantages provide a substantial priority to tackle with complexity and ambiguity. Adding with new algorithms which are mostly adapted from biological and natural mechanism, their diverse application area has grown, and so the power of soft computing techniques have increased day by day. This chapter has classified the nature inspired soft computing methods with respect to number of studies over years, subject areas, publication source, and the number of documents by authors and countries. The objective of the present chapter is to provide a comprehensive review of nature inspired soft computing methods. For further research, the researchers suggest the performances of the soft computing algorithms be compared based on the problem sets existing in the literature in terms of solution quality and execution time.

REFERENCES

Akay, B., & Karaboga, D. (2015). A survey on the applications of artificial bee colony in signal, image, and video processing. *Signal. Image and Video Processing*, *9*(4), 967–990. doi:10.1007/s11760-015-0758-4

Altiparmak, F., Gen, M., Lin, L., & Paksoy, T. (2006). A genetic algorithm approach for multi-objective optimization of supply chain networks. *Computers & Industrial Engineering*, *51*(1), 196–215. doi:10.1016/j.cie.2006.07.011

Angus, D., & Woodward, C. (2009). Multiple objective ant colony optimisation. *Swarm Intelligence*, *3*(1), 69–85. doi:10.1007/s11721-008-0022-4

Atanassov, K. T. (1986). Intuitionistic fuzzy sets. *Fuzzy Sets and Systems*, *20*(1), 87–96. doi:10.1016/S0165-0114(86)80034-3

Banks, A., Vincent, J., & Anyakoha, C. (2007). A review of particle swarm optimization. Part I: Background and development. *Natural Computing*, *6*(4), 467–484. doi:10.1007/s11047-007-9049-5

Bansal, J. C., Sharma, H., & Jadon, S. S. (2013). Artificial bee colony algorithm: A survey. *International Journal of Advanced Intelligence Paradigms*, *5*(1-2), 123–159. doi:10.1504/IJAIP.2013.054681

Beni, G., & Wang, J. (1993). Swarm Intelligence in Cellular Robotic Systems. In P. Dario, G. Sandini, & P. Aebischer (Eds.), *Robots and Biological Systems: Towards a New Bionics?* (pp. 703–712). Berlin: Springer Berlin Heidelberg. doi:10.1007/978-3-642-58069-7_38

Bertini, I., Ceravolo, F., Citterio, M., De Felice, M., Di Pietra, B., Margiotta, F., & Puglisi, G. et al. (2010). Ambient temperature modelling with soft computing techniques. *Solar Energy*, *84*(7), 1264–1272. doi:10.1016/j.solener.2010.04.003

Blum, C. (2005). Ant colony optimization: Introduction and recent trends. *Physics of Life Reviews*, *2*(4), 353–373. doi:10.1016/j.plrev.2005.10.001

Bonissone, P. P. (1997). Soft computing: The convergence of emerging reasoning technologies. *Soft Computing*, *1*(1), 6–18. doi:10.1007/s005000050002

Chandrasekaran, M., Muralidhar, M., Krishna, C. M., & Dixit, U. S. (2010). Application of soft computing techniques in machining performance prediction and optimization: A literature review. *International Journal of Advanced Manufacturing Technology*, *46*(5-8), 445–464. doi:10.1007/s00170-009-2104-x

Chaturvedi, D. K. (2008). *Soft computing: techniques and its applications in electrical engineering*. Berlin: Springer. doi:10.1007/978-3-540-77481-5

Chawla, M., & Duhan, M. (2015). Bat algorithm: A survey of the state-of-the-art. *Applied Artificial Intelligence*, *29*(6), 617–634. doi:10.1080/08839514.2015.1038434

Clerc, M. (2010). *Particle Swarm Optimization*. Academic Press.

Clerc, M., & Kennedy, J. (2002). The particle swarm-explosion, stability, and convergence in a multidimensional complex space. *IEEE Transactions on Evolutionary Computation*, *6*(1), 58–73. doi:10.1109/4235.985692

Coello, C., Pulido, G. T., & Lechuga, M. S. (2004). Handling multiple objectives with particle swarm optimization. *IEEE Transactions on Evolutionary Computation*, *8*(3), 256–279. doi:10.1109/TEVC.2004.826067

Deb, K., Pratap, A., Agarwal, S., & Meyarivan, T. (2002). A fast and elitist multiobjective genetic algorithm: NSGA-II. *IEEE Transactions on Evolutionary Computation*, *6*(2), 182–197. doi:10.1109/4235.996017

del Valle, Y., Venayagamoorthy, G. K., Mohagheghi, S., Hernandez, J.-C., & Harley, R. G.del. (2008). Particle swarm optimization: Basic concepts, variants and applications in power systems. *IEEE Transactions on Evolutionary Computation*, *12*(2), 171–195. doi:10.1109/TEVC.2007.896686

Dorigo, M. (1992). *Optimization, Learning and Natural Algorithm*. Milan, Italy: Dipartimento di Elettronica, Politecnico di Milano.

Dorigo, M., & Caro, G. D. (1999). Ant colony optimization: a new meta-heuristic. In *Proceedings of the 1999 Congress on Evolutionary Computation, 1999. CEC 99* (Vol. 2, p. 1477). doi:10.1109/CEC.1999.782657

Dorigo, M., Di, C., & Gambardella, L. M. (1999). Ant algorithms for discrete optimization. *Artificial Life, 5*(2), 137–172. doi:10.1162/106454699568728 PMID:10633574

Dorigo, M., Maniezzo, V., & Colorni, A. (1996). Ant system: Optimization by a colony of cooperating agents. *IEEE Transactions on Systems, Man, and Cybernetics. Part B, Cybernetics, 26*(1), 29–41. doi:10.1109/3477.484436 PMID:18263004

Duan, H., Yu, Y., Zou, J., & Feng, X. (2012). Ant colony optimization-based bio-inspired hardware: Survey and prospect. *Transactions of the Institute of Measurement and Control, 34*(2-3), 318–333. doi:10.1177/0142331210366689

Durgun, I., & Yildiz, A. R. (2012). Structural design optimization of vehicle components using Cuckoo search Algorithm. *Materialpruefung/Materials Testing, 54*(3), 185–188.

Espejo, P. G., Ventura, S., & Herrera, F. (2010). A survey on the application of genetic programming to classification. *IEEE Transactions on Systems, Man and Cybernetics. Part C, Applications and Reviews, 40*(2), 121–144. doi:10.1109/TSMCC.2009.2033566

Fister, I. Jr, Perc, M., Kamal, S. M., & Fister, I. (2015). A review of chaos-based firefly algorithms: Perspectives and research challenges. *Applied Mathematics and Computation, 252*, 155–165. doi:10.1016/j.amc.2014.12.006

Fister, I., Yang, X.-S., & Fister, D. (2014). Firefly algorithm: A brief review of the expanding literature. *Studies in Computational Intelligence, 516*, 347–360. doi:10.1007/978-3-319-02141-6_17

Fister, I., Yang, X.-S., Fister, D., & Fister, I. (2014). Cuckoo Search: A Brief Literature Review. In X.-S. Yang (Ed.), *Cuckoo Search and Firefly Algorithm* (Vol. 516, pp. 49–62). Cham: Springer International Publishing. doi:10.1007/978-3-319-02141-6_3

Fister, J., Fister, D., & Fistar, I. (2013). A comprehensive review of Cuckoo search: Variants and hybrids. *International Journal of Mathematical Modelling and Numerical Optimisation, 4*(4), 387–409. doi:10.1504/IJMMNO.2013.059205

Fister, J., Fister, D., & Yang, X.-S. (2013). A hybrid bat algorithm. *Elektrotehniski Vestnik/Electrotechnical Review, 80*(1-2), 1–7.

Gambardella, L. M., Taillard, É. D., & Dorigo, M. (1999). Ant colonies for the quadratic assignment problem. *The Journal of the Operational Research Society, 50*(2), 167–176. doi:10.1057/palgrave.jors.2600676

Gandomi, A. H., & Yang, X.-S. (2014). Chaotic bat algorithm. *Journal of Computational Science, 5*(2), 224–232. doi:10.1016/j.jocs.2013.10.002

Gandomi, A. H., Yang, X.-S., & Alavi, A. H. (2011). Mixed variable structural optimization using Firefly Algorithm. *Computers & Structures*, 89(23-24), 2325–2336. doi:10.1016/j.compstruc.2011.08.002

Gandomi, A. H., Yang, X.-S., Alavi, A. H., & Talatahari, S. (2013). Bat algorithm for constrained optimization tasks. *Neural Computing & Applications*, 22(6), 1239–1255. doi:10.1007/s00521-012-1028-9

Gandomi, A. H., Yang, X.-S., Talatahari, S., & Alavi, A. H. (2013). Firefly algorithm with chaos. *Communications in Nonlinear Science and Numerical Simulation*, 18(1), 89–98. doi:10.1016/j.cnsns.2012.06.009

Gao, W.-F., & Liu, S.-Y. (2012). A modified artificial bee colony algorithm. *Computers & Operations Research*, 39(3), 687–697. doi:10.1016/j.cor.2011.06.007 PMID:23086528

Grattan-Guinness, I. (1976). Fuzzy Membership Mapped onto Intervals and Many-Valued Quantities. *Mathematical Logic Quarterly*, 22(1), 149–160. doi:10.1002/malq.19760220120

Hidalgo, D., Melin, P., & Castillo, O. (2012). An optimization method for designing type-2 fuzzy inference systems based on the footprint of uncertainty using genetic algorithms. *Expert Systems with Applications*, 39(4), 4590–4598. doi:10.1016/j.eswa.2011.10.003

Jahn, K.-U. (1975). Intervall-wertige Mengen. *Mathematische Nachrichten*, 68(1), 115–132. doi:10.1002/mana.19750680109

Kacprzyk, J. (2015). Computational Intelligence and Soft Computing: Closely Related but Not the Same. In L. Argüelles Méndez & R. Seising (Eds.), *Accuracy and Fuzziness. A Life in Science and Politics* (Vol. 323, pp. 267–280). Cham: Springer International Publishing. doi:10.1007/978-3-319-18606-1_26

Kahraman, C., Öztayşi, B., & Çevik Onar, S. (2016). A Comprehensive Literature Review of 50 Years of Fuzzy Set Theory. *International Journal of Computational Intelligence Systems, 9*(sup1), 3–24. http://doi.org/10.1080/18756891.2016.1180817

Karaboga, D. (2005). *An idea based on honey bee swarm for numerical optimization*. Technical report-tr06, Erciyes University, Engineering Faculty, Computer Engineering Department.

Karaboga, D., & Akay, B. (2009). A comparative study of Artificial Bee Colony algorithm. *Applied Mathematics and Computation*, 214(1), 108–132. doi:10.1016/j.amc.2009.03.090

Karaboga, D., & Ozturk, C. (2011). A novel clustering approach: Artificial Bee Colony (ABC) algorithm. *Applied Soft Computing*, 11(1), 652–657. doi:10.1016/j.asoc.2009.12.025

Kennedy, J., & Eberhart, R. (1995). Particle swarm optimization. *IEEE International Conference on Neural Networks, 1995. Proceedings* (Vol. 4, pp. 1942–1948). doi:10.1109/ICNN.1995.488968

Kennedy, J., & Eberhart, R. C. (1997). Discrete binary version of the particle swarm algorithm. *Proceedings of the IEEE International Conference on Systems, Man and Cybernetics, 5*, 4104-4108. doi:10.1109/ICSMC.1997.637339

Komaki, G. M., & Kayvanfar, V. (2015). Grey Wolf Optimizer algorithm for the two-stage assembly flow shop scheduling problem with release time. *Journal of Computational Science*, 8, 109–120. doi:10.1016/j.jocs.2015.03.011

Konak, A., Coit, D. W., & Smith, A. E. (2006). Multi-objective optimization using genetic algorithms: A tutorial. *Reliability Engineering & System Safety, 91*(9), 992–1007. doi:10.1016/j.ress.2005.11.018

Konar, A. (2000). *Artificial intelligence and soft computing: behavioral and cognitive modeling of the human brain.* Boca Raton, FL: CRC Press.

Liao, T., Aydin, D., & Stützle, T. (2013). Artificial bee colonies for continuous optimization: Experimental analysis and improvements. *Swarm Intelligence, 7*(4), 327–356. doi:10.1007/s11721-013-0088-5

McCulloch, W. S., & Pitts, W. (1943). A logical calculus of the ideas immanent in nervous activity. *The Bulletin of Mathematical Biophysics, 5*(4), 115–133. doi:10.1007/BF02478259

Mirjalili, S. (2015). How effective is the Grey Wolf optimizer in training multi-layer perceptrons. *Applied Intelligence, 43*(1), 150–161. doi:10.1007/s10489-014-0645-7

Mirjalili, S., Mirjalili, S. M., & Lewis, A. (2014). Grey Wolf Optimizer. *Advances in Engineering Software, 69*, 46–61. doi:10.1016/j.advengsoft.2013.12.007

Mohamad, A. B., Zain, A. M., & Bazin, N. E. N. (2014). Cuckoo search algorithm for optimization problems - A literature review and its applications. *Applied Artificial Intelligence, 28*(5), 419–448. doi:10.1080/08839514.2014.904599

Moravej, Z., & Akhlaghi, A. (2013). A novel approach based on cuckoo search for DG allocation in distribution network. *International Journal of Electrical Power & Energy Systems, 44*(1), 672–679. doi:10.1016/j.ijepes.2012.08.009

Pan, Q.-K., Fatih, T., Suganthan, P. N., & Chua, T. J. (2011). A discrete artificial bee colony algorithm for the lot-streaming flow shop scheduling problem. *Information Sciences, 181*(12), 2455–2468. doi:10.1016/j.ins.2009.12.025

Parpinelli, R. S., Lopes, H. S., & Freitas, A. A. (2002). Data mining with an ant colony optimization algorithm. *IEEE Transactions on Evolutionary Computation, 6*(4), 321–332. doi:10.1109/TEVC.2002.802452

Pedemonte, M., Nesmachnow, S., & Cancela, H. (2011). A survey on parallel ant colony optimization. *Applied Soft Computing, 11*(8), 5181–5197. doi:10.1016/j.asoc.2011.05.042

Rodriguez, R. M., Martinez, L., & Herrera, F. (2012). Hesitant Fuzzy Linguistic Term Sets for Decision Making. *IEEE Transactions on Fuzzy Systems, 20*(1), 109–119. doi:10.1109/TFUZZ.2011.2170076

Roy, R., Furuhashi, T., & Chawdhry, P. (Eds.). (1999). *Advances in soft computing: engineering design and manufacturing.* London: Springer. doi:10.1007/978-1-4471-0819-1

Ruan, D. (2010). *Computational Intelligence in Complex Decision Systems* (Vol. 2). Paris: Atlantis Press. doi:10.2991/978-94-91216-29-9

Saremi, S., Mirjalili, S. Z., & Mirjalili, S. M. (2015). Evolutionary population dynamics and grey wolf optimizer. *Neural Computing & Applications, 26*(5), 1257–1263. doi:10.1007/s00521-014-1806-7

Sastry, K., Goldberg, D., & Kendall, G. (2005). Genetic algorithms. In *Search Methodologies* (pp. 97–125). Introductory Tutorials in Optimization and Decision Support Techniques. doi:10.1007/0-387-28356-0_4

Senthilnath, J., Omkar, S. N., & Mani, V. (2011). Clustering using firefly algorithm: Performance study. *Swarm and Evolutionary Computation, 1*(3), 164–171. doi:10.1016/j.swevo.2011.06.003

Socha, K., & Dorigo, M. (2008). Ant colony optimization for continuous domains. *European Journal of Operational Research, 185*(3), 1155–1173. doi:10.1016/j.ejor.2006.06.046

Song, X., Tang, L., Zhao, S., Zhang, X., Li, L., Huang, J., & Cai, W. (2015). Grey Wolf Optimizer for parameter estimation in surface waves. *Soil Dynamics and Earthquake Engineering, 75*, 147–157. doi:10.1016/j.soildyn.2015.04.004

Stach, W., Kurgan, L., Pedrycz, W., & Reformat, M. (2005). Genetic learning of fuzzy cognitive maps. *Fuzzy Sets and Systems, 153*(3), 371–401. doi:10.1016/j.fss.2005.01.009

Stützle, T., & Hoos, H. H. (2000). MAX-MIN Ant System. *Future Generation Computer Systems, 16*(8), 889–914. doi:10.1016/S0167-739X(00)00043-1

Sulaiman, M. H., Mustaffa, Z., Mohamed, M. R., & Aliman, O. (2015). Using the gray wolf optimizer for solving optimal reactive power dispatch problem. *Applied Soft Computing, 32*, 286–292. doi:10.1016/j.asoc.2015.03.041

Thangaraj, R., Pant, M., Abraham, A., & Bouvry, P. (2011). Particle swarm optimization: Hybridization perspectives and experimental illustrations. *Applied Mathematics and Computation, 217*(12), 5208–5226. doi:10.1016/j.amc.2010.12.053

Torra, V. (2010). Hesitant fuzzy sets. *International Journal of Intelligent Systems*. http://doi.org/10.1002/int.20418

Trelea, I. C. (2003). The particle swarm optimization algorithm: Convergence analysis and parameter selection. *Information Processing Letters, 85*(6), 317–325. doi:10.1016/S0020-0190(02)00447-7

Walton, S., Hassan, O., Morgan, K., & Brown, M. R. (2011). Modified cuckoo search: A new gradient free optimisation algorithm. *Chaos, Solitons, and Fractals, 44*(9), 710–718. doi:10.1016/j.chaos.2011.06.004

Yang, X. S. (2008). Firefly algorithm. *Nature-Inspired Metaheuristic Algorithms*, 79–90.

Yang, X.-S. (2010). A new metaheuristic Bat-inspired Algorithm. *Studies in Computational Intelligence, 284*, 65–74. doi:10.1007/978-3-642-12538-6_6

Yang, X.-S. (2013b). Multiobjective firefly algorithm for continuous optimization. *Engineering with Computers, 29*(2), 175–184. doi:10.1007/s00366-012-0254-1

Yang, X.-S. (2014). Cuckoo search and firefly algorithm: Overview and analysis. *Studies in Computational Intelligence, 516*, 1–26. doi:10.1007/978-3-319-02141-6_1

Yang, X.-S., Cui, Z., Xiao, R., Gandomi, A. H., & Karamanoglu, M. (2013). *Swarm Intelligence and Bio-Inspired Computation*. Academic Press.

Yang, X.-S., & Deb, S. (2009). Cuckoo Search via Levy Flights. *World Congress on Nature & Biologically Inspired Computing (NaBIC 2009)*, (pp. 210-214). IEEE. doi:10.1109/NABIC.2009.5393690

Yang, X.-S., & Deb, S. (2014). Cuckoo search: Recent advances and applications. *Neural Computing & Applications*, *24*(1), 169–174. doi:10.1007/s00521-013-1367-1

Yang, X. S., & He, X. (2013). Bat algorithm: Literature review and applications. *International Journal of Bio-inspired Computation*, *5*(3), 141. doi:10.1504/IJBIC.2013.055093

Yang, X.-S., & He, X. (2013a). Bat algorithm: Literature review and applications. *International Journal of Bio-inspired Computation*, *5*(3), 141–149. doi:10.1504/IJBIC.2013.055093

Yang, X.-S., & He, X. (2015). Swarm Intelligence and Evolutionary Computation: Overview and Analysis. In X.-S. Yang (Ed.), *Recent Advances in Swarm Intelligence and Evolutionary Computation* (Vol. 585, pp. 1–23). Cham: Springer International Publishing. doi:10.1007/978-3-319-13826-8_1

Yildiz, A. R. (2013). Cuckoo search algorithm for the selection of optimal machining parameters in milling operations. *International Journal of Advanced Manufacturing Technology*, *64*(1-4), 55–61. doi:10.1007/s00170-012-4013-7

Zadeh, L. A. (1965). Fuzzy sets. *Information and Control*, *8*(3), 338–353. doi:10.1016/S0019-9958(65)90241-X

Zadeh, L. A. (1975). The concept of a linguistic variable and its application to approximate reasoning—I. *Information Sciences*, *8*(3), 199–249. doi:10.1016/0020-0255(75)90036-5

Zadeh, L. A. (1978). Fuzzy sets as a basis for a theory of possibility. *Fuzzy Sets and Systems*, *1*(1), 3–28. doi:10.1016/0165-0114(78)90029-5

Zadeh, L. A. (1994). Fuzzy logic, neural networks, and soft computing. *Communications of the ACM*, *37*(3), 77–84. doi:10.1145/175247.175255

Chapter 3
Swarm Intelligence for Electromagnetic Problem Solving

Luciano Mescia
Politecnico di Bari, Italy

Diego Caratelli
*The Antenna Company, The Netherlands &
Tomsk Polytechnic University, Russia*

Pietro Bia
EmTeSys Srl, Italy

Johan Gielis
University of Antwerp, Belgium

ABSTRACT

The chapter will describe the potential of the swarm intelligence and in particular quantum PSO-based algorithm, to solve complicated electromagnetic problems. This task is accomplished through addressing the design and analysis challenges of some key real-world problems. A detailed definition of the conventional PSO and its quantum-inspired version are presented and compared in terms of accuracy and computational burden. Some theoretical discussions concerning the convergence issues and a sensitivity analysis on the parameters influencing the stochastic process are reported.

INTRODUCTION

Optimization is an important paradigm widely used in various fields, including engineering, economics, management, physical sciences, social sciences, etc.. The goal of the optimization is the identification of the global maximum or minimum of a fitness function. Indeed, finding all optimal points of an objective function is helpful to select a robust design where different constraints and performance criteria are taken into account simultaneously.

The designers of microwave and antenna systems are constantly challenged in searching optimum solutions for a variety of electromagnetic problems of increasing complexity. This is typically an arduous subject to solve since it requires the evaluation of electromagnetic fields in three dimensions, involves a large number of parameters and complex constraints. Furthermore, the computational domain could contain non-differentiable and discontinuous regions (Mescia et al., 2016; Bia et al., 2015; Ciuprina et

DOI: 10.4018/978-1-5225-2128-0.ch003

al., 2002; Robinson & Rahmat-Samii, 2004). These optimization problems are in many cases non-linear and more difficult to solve than the linear ones, especially when the problem has many local optimal solutions in the feasible region.

As the availability of unprecedented computational resources has become common, numerically based electromagnetic methodologies useful to the design of antenna and microwave devices as well as to the understanding of the underlying physics have turned to be significantly advantageous. However, the increasing complexity of antenna and microwave systems makes the computation of three-dimensional electromagnetic field distributions still time consuming and cumbersome. This results in a continuously growing demand for better speed and efficiency of computational approaches. Moreover, contrary to the design of electrical circuits, the development of electromagnetic systems requires special attention in the modeling of coupling processes between design elements. As a consequence, a direct application of brute-force computational techniques is often replaced by the state-of-the-art optimization procedures.

The computer-based optimization techniques can be classified into deterministic and stochastic methods. Contrary to deterministic search techniques, stochastic ones are potentially able to find the global optima of the problem regardless the initial points of the search procedure. Therefore, the so-called metaheuristics algorithms have become increasingly popular because of their potential in solving large-scale problems efficiently in a way that is impossible by using deterministic algorithms.

Swarm intelligence offers insight into metaheuristics. This is quite a general concept based on the interaction and information exchange between multiple agents. In particular, a swarm intelligence system consists of a population with members having characteristic behaviors and interacting locally with each other within their environment following simple rules. Such simple systems can show complex and self-organized behavior. Moreover, even if a dictating centralized mechanism is not embedded, said interactions yield a collective intelligence resulting in a more organized and directive behavior than that of a stand-alone individual.

The resulting metaheuristic algorithms are gaining popularity within the electromagnetic research community and among electromagnetic engineers as design tools and problem solvers thanks to their capability to efficiently find global optima without being trapped in local extrema, and the possibility to address nonlinear and discontinuous problems possibly characterized by great numbers of variables (Fornarelli & Mescia, 2013; Jin & Rahmat-Samii, 2007). Metaheuristic algorithms tend to be flexible, efficient and highly adaptable, as well as easy to implement. They also allow dealing with very complex fitness functions since the computation of derivatives is not needed during the optimization procedure. Furthermore, contrary to more traditional searching methods, their convergence do not strongly depend on the starting point. Therefore, the high efficiency of these algorithms make them an invaluable tool to optimize non-differentiable cost functions in complex multimodal search spaces. However, due to the strong stochastic behavior, these algorithms need a lot of iterations to get a meaningful result (Aboul Ella Hassanien & Eid Emary, 2015).

Since descriptors and number of unknowns to be determined is different in each optimization problem, a variety of swarm intelligence-based optimization algorithms have been developed. They include particle swarm optimization, ant colony optimization, cuckoo search, firefly algorithm, bat algorithm, artificial fish swarm algorithm, flower pollination algorithm, artificial bee colony, wolf search algorithm, gray wolf optimization (Aboul Ella Hassanien & Eid Emary, 2015). As a result, the choice of a proper algorithm is a key issue especially considering that a general rule for this choice does not exist, yet. Typical features helping to a fair decision in this matter regard good convergence properties, ease of use, ability to manage complex fitness function, limited number of control parameters, good exploitation of the parallelism offered by the modern computational architecture.

Since its introduction, particle swarm optimization (PSO) has attracted the attention of many researchers in the electromagnetic community that has resulted in the development of many variants of the original algorithm relying on different parameter automation strategies. In particular, PSO has been used as a powerful and promising optimization method to solve several EM and antenna design problems including antenna pattern synthesis, reflector antenna shaping, patch antennas and EM absorber designs, microwave filter design. The parallel implementation of PSO also allows the simultaneous evaluation of the fitness of all the agents involved in the procedure, and substantially speeds up the optimization process. PSO has been often used as an optimization algorithm because of its effectiveness in addressing difficult problems. Moreover, compared to other evolutionary methods, the PSO scheme provides better results in a faster and cheaper way with fewer parameter adjustments.

MAIN FOCUS OF THE CHAPTER

The main objective of this chapter is to highlight the flexibility and reliability of a novel quantum-behaved PSO algorithm in treating a class of problems encountered in electromagnetic engineering. This task is accomplished by addressing design and analysis challenges associated with complex real-world problems.

In the first section, a detailed definition of classic PSO algorithms is provided. Attention is initially put on the analysis and formulation of the optimization problem, which quantify the information content of the solution itself. Subsequently, the challenges in determining problem unknowns, suitable cost functions and constraints are thoroughly discussed. The cost function is the only link between the optimization problem and the physical one and great attention needs to be paid in its definition in order to obtain representative and reliable solutions. To this end, the complexity of the cost function and relevant computational burden are discussed as well.

The trade-off between exploration and exploitation is a key aspect in the PSO algorithm. A strong exploitation may lead to a focused search, this reducing the diversity of the population that may in turn speed up the convergence of the search procedure. Otherwise, excessive exploitation may lead to the premature convergence. On the other hand, too much diversity and exploration may result in meandered search paths leading to a slow convergence. In order to balance exploration and exploitation, a right amount of randomness is needed. An algorithm having very low randomness loses the exploration ability. At the other extreme, an algorithm dominated by high randomness is characterized by reduced ability to exploit the landscape information. It is clear that the overall performance of a PSO algorithm strongly depends on its parameter settings, tuning and control. In this framework, details about velocity and position updating rules of each particle and the sampling of the solution space to find the global optimum are provided. The optimal selection of the swarm population size, as well as the definition of suitable stopping criteria and problem constraints or boundary conditions are properly addressed. As far as the convergence criteria are concerned, termination conditions based on user-defined threshold and maximum iterations number are discussed. Finally, a dedicated verification procedure on the solution is needed in order to determine whether the particle pitches on local or global extrema.

In classical PSO algorithm, the searching procedure is guided by the global and personal best positions. This neighborhood topology generates algorithms more prone to encounter premature convergence when solving harder optimization problems. In fact, this algorithm is based on semi-deterministic search procedure that may weaken the global search ability of the algorithm itself. In order to overcome this limitation, a PSO algorithm based on a quantum–inspired dynamics (QPSO) is illustrated. Numerical experiments and analysis show that the QPSO algorithm offers good performance in solving a wide range of continuous optimization problems.

Many efficient strategies have been proposed in the scientific literature in order to improve the basic PSO algorithm [Sun et al., 2011]. To this end, a quantum-based modifications to the conventional PSO algorithm is presented here. In order to justify the introduced modifications and verify the performance of the resulting algorithm in terms of accuracy and computational burden, several benchmarks are illustrated.

In the second section, based on our studies presented in (Bia et al., 2013; Mescia et al., 2016; Bia et al., 2015), we present a detailed overview on the application of quantum-behaved PSO algorithm in a more challenging and, of course, more intriguing scenario, such as lens antenna design. In particular, a systematic and detailed study of a new class of dielectric lens antennas (supershaped dielectric lens antenna) having a surface described by the so-called 3D Gielis' formula is illustrated. Dielectric lens antennas are widely used in various applications due to their attractive features as beam collimating/shaping capability, mechanical and thermal stability, integration easiness in densely populated electronic circuits. In comparison to known classes of shaped lenses, supershaped dielectric lens antenna technology provides an higher degree of versatility allowing antenna radiation characteristics to be optimized for a wide variety of applications. In fact, the unified geometrical description provided by Gielis' transformation allows tailoring the lens shape in such a way as to radiate electromagnetic energy in a more efficient way in comparison to conventional lens antennas. The adoption of Gielis' formula translates into the possibility of using any automated optimization procedure to identify the lens parameters yielding optimal antenna performance in accordance to specified requirements. In our study, an enhanced version of QPSO is introduced in order to study the problem of synthesis of lens antennas having special radiation characteristics. Details concerning the definition of the fitness function giving reliable numerical results, as well as criteria for fast convergence of the antenna directivity to the target one are provided. Furthermore, the dynamic selection of suitable antenna characterization techniques useful to enhance the effectiveness of the proposed lens synthesis procedure is discussed while addressing the impact of the antenna feeding structure on the radiation pattern characteristics.

In the third section, the application of PSO in an even more challenging and attractive context is discussed. Here, the algorithm will be used to estimate the thickness and the dielectric response of an unknown material inside a lossy and dispersive multilayer structures. In particular, the unknown parameters of the medium are recovered from the knowledge of the reflected electromagnetic field of an incident wave illuminating the multilayer structure. From a mathematical point of view, the problem is non-unique, ill-posed, and intrinsically non-linear. In fact, the amount of independent data achievable is essentially limited, hence only a finite number of parameters can be accurately recovered. Furthermore, increasing the number of unknowns leads to a more severe ill-posedness of the problem, this potentially resulting in the divergence of the problem. Unfortunately, conventional optimization-based methods are not suitable to solve this class of problems especially when the number of the parameters to recover is large. To overcome this drawback, an optimization method based on the extended quantum-behaved PSO algorithm and a novel finite difference time domain scheme (FDTD) is analyzed. This study has great importance especially for the detection of tumors in human body tissues. In this context, the main challenge to be addressed is the accurate evaluation of the interaction between the illumination electromagnetic pulse and the cancer tissue. The goal of the proposed analysis is to demonstrate that, by properly elaborating the time-domain properties of the reflected wave, and by adopting the fractional calculus-based FDTD algorithm developed by the authors in (Mescia et al., 2015; Bia[1] et al., 2015; Mescia et al., 2014; Mescia et al., 2015, Piro et al., 2016), the developed algorithm can successfully detect the permittivity values of various layers in human tissues and, in this way, the identification of potential tumors.

CLASSIC PSO ALGORITHM – GENERAL FRAMEWORK

PSO algorithm was presented by Kennedy and Eberhart in 1995 (Kennedy & Eberhart, 1995). It is a population-based optimizer that models the behavior of a swarm of bees, school of fish, or flock of birds emphasizing the interaction between independent agents and the social or swarm intelligence. Similar to other evolutionary computation, a number of particles are embedded in the swarm, each of them representing a candidate solution to the optimization problem. Each particle searches the global optimal point in a multi-dimensional solution space adjusting its position according to its own experience as well as the experiences of other particles. In particular, each particle changes its position by simply varying its associated velocity utilizing the best position it has visited so far, called personal best, and the best position reached by all the particles during their paths, called global best.

Let us consider a swarm of M particles in a N-dimensional search space. Each swarm can be characterized by two $N \times M$ matrices, the position matrix $\mathbf{X}$ and the velocity matrix $\mathbf{V}$:

$$X(t) = \begin{bmatrix} x_{11}(t) & x_{12}(t) & \cdots & x_{1M}(t) \\ x_{21}(t) & x_{22}(t) & \cdots & x_{2M}(t) \\ \vdots & \vdots & \vdots & \vdots \\ x_{N1}(t) & x_{N2}(t) & \cdots & x_{NM}(t) \end{bmatrix} \tag{1}$$

$$V(t) = \begin{bmatrix} v_{11}(t) & v_{12}(t) & \cdots & v_{1M}(t) \\ v_{21}(t) & v_{22}(t) & \cdots & v_{2M}(t) \\ \vdots & \vdots & \vdots & \vdots \\ v_{N1}(t) & v_{N2}(t) & \cdots & v_{NM}(t) \end{bmatrix} \tag{2}$$

where t is a unit pseudotime increment (iteration counter), $x_{nm}(t)$ is the nth position element of the mth particle at tth iteration, $v_{nm}(t)$ is the nth velocity element of the mth particle at tth iteration, every column $x_m(t)$ in matrix $\mathbf{X}$ is a possible solution for the problem. Moreover, the personal best position matrix $\mathbf{X}^b$ and the global best position vector $\mathbf{G}^b$ are introduced:

$$X^b(t) = \begin{bmatrix} x_{11}^b(t) & x_{12}^b(t) & \cdots & x_{1M}^b(t) \\ x_{21}^b(t) & x_{22}^b(t) & \cdots & x_{2M}^b(t) \\ \vdots & \vdots & \vdots & \vdots \\ x_{N1}^b(t) & x_{N2}^b(t) & \cdots & x_{NM}^b(t) \end{bmatrix} \tag{3}$$

$$G(t) = \begin{bmatrix} g_1(t) \\ g_2(t) \\ \vdots \\ g_N(t) \end{bmatrix} \tag{4}$$

where $x_{nm}^b(t)$ is the nth personal best position element of the mth particle at tth iteration, and $g_n(t)$ is the nth global best position of the swarm at tth iteration. The swarm is randomly initialized and, subsequently, the position matrix is updated by application of a suitable velocity matrix as follows:

$$X(t+1) = X(t) + V(t+1) \tag{5}$$

The update rule on the velocity field represents the main PSO operator since it defines the motion of the entire swarm towards the global optimum. In order to predict the best update for the position in the next iteration, the information on global and local best positions should be properly processed. In this respect, a right balance between cognitive and social perspectives is beneficial to improve the efficiency of the PSO algorithm. Said perspectives can be illustrated as follows:

- **Cognitive Perspectives:** At tth iteration the mth particle compares its fitness ($\mathcal{F}[x_m(t)]$) with the one ($\mathcal{F}[x_m^b(t-1)]$) corresponding to (t-1)th personal best position. If $\mathcal{F}[x_m(t)] > \mathcal{F}[x_m^b(t-1)]$ then the algorithm sets $x_m^b(t) = x_m(t)$. In this way, a record of the best positions achieved by an individual particle is kept for the velocity update.
- **Social Perspectives:** At tth iteration the mth particle compares its fitness ($\mathcal{F}[x_m(t)]$) with the one ($\mathcal{F}[G(t)]$) corresponding to tth global best position. If $\mathcal{F}[x_m(t)] > \mathcal{F}[G(t)]$ then the algorithm sets $G(t) = x_m(t)$. So, by updating the global best position, a particle shares its information with the rest of the swarm.

In the classical PSO algorithm, the velocity component is updated so that the contribution due to the cognitive/social perspectives are directly proportional to the difference between the current position of the particle and the previously recorded personal/global best, respectively. More precisely, the velocity vector of each particle is the sum of three vectors: one representing the current motion, one pointing towards the particle's best position, this being steered by the individual knowledge accumulated during the evolution of the swarm, and, finally, one pointing towards the global best position, and modeling the contribution of the social knowledge. In particular, the mth particle updates its velocity and position according to the following equations:

$$v_{nm}(t+1) = \underbrace{wv_{nm}(t)}_{current\ motion\ term} + \underbrace{c_1 r_1 [x_{nm}^b(t) - x_{nm}(t)]}_{individual\ knowledge\ term} + \underbrace{c_2 r_2 [g_n(t) - x_{nm}(t)]}_{social\ knowledge\ term} \tag{6}$$

$$x_{nm}(t+1) = x_{nm}(t) + v_{nm}(t+1) \tag{7}$$

where $w \in [0,1]$ is a constant *or variable* value, called inertia weight, c_1 and c_2 are two positive constants, called the cognitive and social parameters, respectively; r_1 and r_2 are two random numbers uniformly distributed in the range [0,1]. The objective function evaluated at the new positions is compared with a user defined error criterion. If this criterion is not satisfied, the random numbers r_1 and r_2 generate different numerical values in the next update and the process is iterated until the error criterion is met. The personal best position of each particle is updated using the following equation

$$x_{nm}^b(t+1) \begin{cases} x_{nm}^b(t) & if \quad \mathcal{F}[x_{nm}(t+1)] \geq \mathcal{F}[x_{nm}^b(t)] \\ x_{nm}(t+1) & if \quad \mathcal{F}[x_{nm}(t+1)] \leq \mathcal{F}[x_{nm}^b(t)] \end{cases} \tag{8}$$

where $\mathcal{F}$ denotes the fitness function.

Experience shows that the success or failure of the search algorithm as well as the algorithm performance strongly depend on the values of the parameters w, c_1, and c_2. The main causes for failure are: i) particles move out of the search space since their velocity increases rapidly, ii) particles become immobile since their velocity rapidly decreases, iii) particles cannot escape from locally optimal solutions. The random variables $\phi_1 = c_1 r_1$ and $\phi_2 = c_2 r_2$ model the stochastic exploration of the search space. The weighting constants c_1 and c_2 regulate the relative importance of the cognitive perspective versus the social perspective. In particular, different weighting constants are used in recent versions of PSO to control the search ability in a finer way, by biasing the new particle position toward its historically best position or globally best position. High values of c_1 and c_2 result in new positions in the search space that are relatively far away from the former ones, this leading to a finer global exploration but also, potentially, to a divergence of the particle motion. Small values of c_1 and c_2 are useful to achieve a more refined local search around the best positions due to the limited movement of the particles. The condition $c_1 > c_2$ endorses the search behaviour towards the particle best experience. The condition $c_1 < c_2$ endorses the search behaviour towards the global best experience. The inertial weight w is used to control the algorithm convergence. Large values of w improve exploration, while a small w results in a confinement within an area surrounding the global maximum. The convergence speed is an important aspect to assess in electromagnetic problems since the numerical evaluation of the fitness function generally takes a considerable amount of time. Convergence speed can be tuned by properly setting the swarm size, as well as the initial population and boundary conditions. In particular, the parameters of the algorithm can be varied so as to adapt to the specific type of problem and, in this way, achieve a better search efficiency. Special attention is to be put in the selection of the algorithm parameters in order to control divergence and convergence of the particles. Recent researches have been presented in the literature in order to illustrate these key aspects (Mahanfar et al., 2007; Iwasaki et al., 2006; Yasuda et al., 2008; Jaco et al., 2005; Huang T. & Mohan 2005).

When the global best position turns to be a local optimum, the PSO search performance could be degraded and a premature convergence can occur. In fact, the particles located close to the local optimum solution could became inactive since their velocities could get close to zero. As result, the PSO algorithm would be trapped in an undesired state of slow evolution. Such limitation becomes more restrictive when PSO is applied to more complex optimization problems characterized by large search spaces and multiple local optima. In this context, specific solutions are to be implemented in order to prevent the phenomenon of so-called swarm explosion and, at the same time, facilitate convergence (Valle et al., 2008; Jin & Rahmat-Samii, 2007; Yasuda et al., 2008; Shi & Eberhart, 1998). The goal is to develop a PSO algorithm characterized by an optimal balance between global and local searching abilities. Without any control or constraint on the velocity field, some particle could fly out of the physically meaningful solution space. Such process could lead to swarm divergence especially when the problem search space is very large. One approach for preventing this problem to occur is to enforce a clamping rule based on the definition of upper and lower limits on the velocity, as follows:

$$v_{nm}\left(t+1\right)\begin{cases}v_{max} & if \quad v_{nm}\left(t+1\right)>v_{max}\\ -v_{max} & if \quad v_{nm}\left(t+1\right)<-v_{max}\end{cases} \tag{9}$$

The value of the parameter v_{max} is selected empirically and can affect the behavior of the algorithm significantly. A too large value of v_{max} may cause good solutions to be overlooked, whereas small values would reduce the motion of the particles and, therefore, prevent portions of the search domain from being explored efficiently. Instead, proper settings of the algorithm can result in an enhanced global exploration ability of the algorithm, while avoiding trapping in local optima. Generally, the threshold velocity is problem-dependent and dimension-dependent (Parsopoulos & Vrahatis, 2010; van den Bergh & Engelbrecht, 2006). Modifications of the PSO learning have been proposed (Ratnaweera et. al, 2004; Shi[1] & Eberhart, 1999; Clerc & Kennedy, 2002). In particular, a variant of the learning equation has been introduced by Clerc M. in 2002. In this scheme, the velocity is updated by the following equation (Clerc & Kennedy, 2002):

$$v_{nm}\left(t+1\right)=\mathcal{X}\left\{v_{nm}\left(t\right)+\vartheta_1 r_1\left[v_{nm}^b\left(t\right)-v_{nm}\left(t\right)\right]+\vartheta_2 r_2\left[g_n\left(t\right)-v_{nm}\left(t\right)\right]\right\} \tag{10}$$

where

$$\mathcal{X}=\frac{2}{2-\vartheta-\sqrt{\vartheta^2-4\vartheta}},\vartheta=\vartheta_1+\vartheta_2 \ and \ \vartheta>4 \tag{11}$$

is the constriction factor. The use of the update equations (10)-(11) enhances the convergence properties of the algorithm (Eberhart & Shi, 2000). As a matter of fact, this approach proved to be effective in a large number of problems (van den Bergh[1] & Engelbrecht, 2004; Fornarelli[1] et al, 2013). Furthermore, it allows for a very simple identification of the optimal value of the algorithm parameter; in fact the inertial weight and the cognitive constants are defined when only one value is set. This aspect makes the method very attractive and usable by not expert users.

QUANTUM-BEHAVED PSO ALGORITHM – GENERAL FRAMEWORK

The PSO algorithm variants based on the velocity threshold and the constriction factor generally increase the convergence speed with improved accuracy. Such variants are essentially semi-deterministic since the particles follow a deterministic trajectory defined by the velocity update equation where two random acceleration coefficients are implemented. Such property may weaken the global search ability especially during the late stage of the search process. Moreover, the search pattern of PSO strongly depends on personal and global best positions and if these best particles get stuck, all the particle in the swarm will quickly converge to the trapped position. In order to overcome this drawback, the quantum-behaved particle swarm optimization algorithm has been developed (Sun et al, 2004; Sun et al, 2011). Such algorithm relies on a probabilistically driven procedure. As a matter of fact, it permits all particles to move under quantum-mechanical rules rather than the classical Newtonian dynamics. Moreover, compared to the original PSO, QPSO eliminates the velocity vectors, it has a reduced number of control parameters (strictly speaking only one parameter), this making it easier to implement, with a faster convergence rate, as well as a stronger search ability when applied to complex problems.

By using the δ potential well, QPSO generates new particles around the previous best point and receives feedback from the mean best position to enhance the global search ability.

Assuming that the PSO is a quantum system, the mth particle can be treated as a spin-less particle moving in a N-dimensional search space with a δ potential well centred at the point $p_m(t), 1 \leq n \leq N$. So, the quantum state of the nth component of particle m is characterized by the wave function Ψ, instead of position and velocity. In such framework, the exact values of X and V cannot be determined simultaneously since only the probability of the particles appearing in position X can be evaluated. It is defined by the probability density function $\left| \Psi\left(r_{nm}, t\right) \right|^2$ satisfying the general time-dependent Schrödinger equation

$$j\hbar \frac{\partial \Psi\left(r_{nm}, t\right)}{\partial t} = \hat{H}\left(r_{nm}\right) \Psi\left(r_{nm}, t\right) \tag{12}$$

where $\hbar$ is the reduced Plank's constant and $\hat{H}$ is a time-independent Hamiltonian operator given by

$$\hat{H}\left(r_{nm}\right) = -\frac{\hbar^2}{2m} \nabla^2 - \delta\left(r_{nm}\right) \tag{13}$$

where m is the mass of the particle, $\delta\left(r_{nm}\right)$ is the potential energy distribution, $r_{nm} = x_{nm} - p_{nm}$ is the nth component of the vector difference between the mth particle position and the corresponding δ potential well position. Applying the separation variables method, it is possible separate the time dependence of the wave function from the spatial dependence obtaining

$$\Psi\left(r_{nm\circ} t\right) = \varphi\left(r_{nm}\right) \exp\left(-jEt / \hbar\right) \tag{14}$$

where E is the energy of the particle and $\varphi\left(r_{nm}\right)$ satisfies the stationary Schrödinger equation

$$\frac{\partial^2 \varphi\left(r_{nm}\right)}{\partial^2_{nm}} + \frac{2m}{\hbar^2}\left[E + \delta\left(r_{nm}\right)\right]\varphi\left(r_{nm}\right) = 0 \tag{15}$$

and the normalization condition

$$\int_{\mathbb{R}^N} \left|\Psi\left(r_{nm}, t\right)\right|^2 d^N r = 1 \tag{16}$$

Solving eq. (15) and taking into account (16) the probability density function is found to be

$$\left|\Psi\left(r_{nm}, t\right)\right|^2 = \frac{1}{L_{nm}\left(t\right)} \exp\left[-2\left|x_{nm}\left(t\right) - p_{nm}\left(t\right)\right| / L_{nm}\left(t\right)\right] \tag{17}$$

where $L_{nm}\left(t\right)$ is standard deviation of the distribution. Employing the Monte Carlo inverse method (Woolfson & Pert, 1999) it is possible to show that the update equation relevant the nth position component of particle m is

$$x_{nm}\left(t+1\right) = \begin{cases} p_{nm}\left(t\right) + \dfrac{L_{nm}\left(t\right)}{2}\ln\left(\dfrac{1}{u_{nm}}\right) & if\ s_{nm} \geq 0.5 \\ p_{nm}\left(t\right) - \dfrac{L_{nm}\left(t\right)}{2}\ln\left(\dfrac{1}{u_{nm}}\right) & if\ s_{nm} \leq 0.5 \end{cases} \tag{18}$$

where

$$p_{nm}\left(t\right) = \xi_{nm}\left(t\right)x^b_{nm}\left(t\right) + \left[1 - \xi_{nm}\left(t\right)\right]g_n\left(t\right) \tag{18}$$

u_{nm}, ξ_{nm} and s_{nm} are independent random numbers generated according to a uniform probability distribution in range (0,1). In order to improve the QPSO algorithm efficiency, the mean best of the population, $\bar{x}^b_n\left(t\right)$, is defined as the mean of the personal best positions of all particles

$$\bar{x}^b_n\left(t\right) = \frac{1}{M}\sum_{m=1}^{M} x^b_{nm}\left(t\right) \tag{19}$$

In this way, the value of $L_{nm}\left(t\right)$ is given by

$$L_{nm}\left(t\right) = 2\beta\left|\bar{x}^b_n\left(t\right) - x_{nm}\left(t\right)\right| \tag{20}$$

β being the contraction-expansion coefficient. Considering that both the population size and the number of iteration are common requirements, β is the only parameter of the QPSO algorithm that can be tuned to control the its speed and convergence (Omkar et al, 2009) remarking the very easy implementation of the algorithm. In particular, to balance the local and global search of the algorithm, a dynamic adjustment of the contraction-expansion coefficient in the range [0,1] can be used

$$\beta(t) = 1 - \frac{t}{2t_{max}} \tag{21}$$

t_{max} being the maximum number of iterations.

The illustrated QPSO algorithm is proven to be more effective than traditional PSO algorithm in various standard optimization problems (Omkar et al, 2009; dos Santos Coelho, 2008; Sun[1] et al., 2011; Fu et al, 2013; Yumin & Li, 2014). However, from eq. (19) it can been seen that each particle affects in the same way the value of $\bar{x}_n^b(t)$ since the mean best position is just the average of the personal best position of all particles. This approach takes into account the search scope of each particle and in some cases it can be reasonable. It is to be noticed however that, based on general rules of real-life social culture, the equally weighted mean position could represent not the best choice. To this aim, a control method based on the promotion of the particle importance has been developed (Xi et al, 2008). In such approach, the elitism is associated with the particle's fitness value. In particular, the greater the fitness value, the more important the particle. In this way, the particle has a weighted coefficient α_m linearly decreasing with the corresponding fitness function. The closer is the fitness function to the optimal value, the larger is the weight of the particle. So the mean best position is calculated as:

$$\bar{x}_n^b(t) = \frac{1}{M} \sum_{m=1}^{M} \alpha_m x_{nm}^b(t) \tag{22}$$

where the weighting coefficient linearly ranges from 1.5, for the best particle, down to 0.5 for the worst one. The corresponding QPSO algorithm is called weighted QPSO (WQPSO). In order to further improve the convergence rate of the WQPSO algorithm we have developed an enhanced weighting methodology where the computation of the mean best position $\bar{x}_n^b(t)$ is carried out by directly embedding the information associated with the error function ε. The convergence speed is important in electromagnetic problems since every run of the objective function takes a considerable amount of time and any effort to reduce the relevant computational time and, in this way, shorten the design process is much relevant. The resulting enhanced weighted QPSO (EWQPSO) algorithm is based on the following adaptive update equation

$$\bar{x}_n^b(t) = \frac{\sum_{m=1}^{M} \Lambda_m(t) x_{nm}^b(t)}{\sum_{m=1}^{M} \Lambda_m(t)} \tag{23}$$

where

$$\Lambda_m(t) = \begin{cases} 1 - \dfrac{\varepsilon\left(\mathrm{x}_m^b(t)\right)}{\max\left\{\varepsilon\left(\mathrm{x}_1^b(t)\right), \varepsilon\left(\mathrm{x}_2^b(t)\right), \dots \varepsilon\left(\mathrm{x}_M^b(t)\right)\right\}} & \textit{Minimization problem} \\[4mm] 1 - \dfrac{\min\left\{\varepsilon\left(\mathrm{x}_1^b(t)\right), \varepsilon\left(\mathrm{x}_2^b(t)\right), \dots \varepsilon\left(\mathrm{x}_M^b(t)\right)\right\}}{\varepsilon\left(\mathrm{x}_m^b(t)\right)} & \textit{Maximization problem} \end{cases}$$

(24)

In this way, the positions close to the optimum value will stochastically guide the movements of the swarm. Moreover, the absorbing boundary condition has been implemented in the EWQPSO algorithm. In particular, every particle which flies outside the search range in one specific dimension is going to be moved back at the boundary of the search range along that dimension. The flowchart of the execution algorithm regarding the solution of the minimization problem is illustrated in Figure 1.

Figure 1. Flowchart of the EWQPSO algorithm regarding the minimization problem

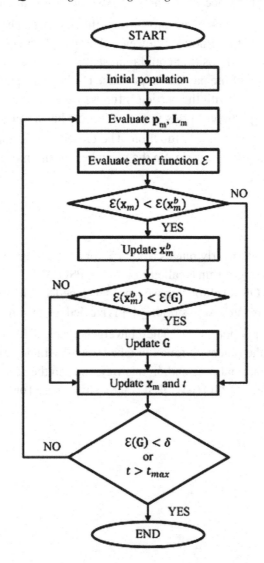

BENCHMARK TESTS FOR THE EWQPSO ALGORITHM

In order to verify the effectiveness and performance of the proposed EWQPSO, several tests have been carried out. In particular, the minimum searching problem regarding the test functions Ackley, Griewank, Iperspherical, Alpine and De Jong is considered, by changing both the domain dimension N and the number of particles M (Xi et al, 2008; Sun[1] et al, 2011). The maximum generation value is set to $t_{max} = 500 + 10N$. For each function, the results calculated by using EWQPSO, WQPSO and QPSO algorithms have been compared. The search algorithm is applied 100 times for each test function and the mean and standard deviation values relevant to the best particle have been calculated.

Ackley Test Function

The searching problem of the minimum value pertaining the Ackley function defined in the N-dimensional space is fulfilled considering a swarm composed of M particles. The Ackley function is defined as follows:

$$f(\mathrm{x}) - 20\exp\left(-0.2\sqrt{\frac{1}{N}\sum_{i=1}^{N}x_i^2}\right) - \exp\left[\frac{1}{N}\sum_{i=1}^{N}\cos\left(2\pi x_i\right)\right] + 20 + \exp\left(1\right) \tag{25}$$

where the global minimum $f(\mathrm{x}_{min}) = 0$ corresponds to $\mathrm{x}_{min} = (0,0,...,0)$ coordinates. For the test the following searching domain $x_i \in (-32,32), i = 1,2,...,N$, is set. Figure 2 shows the evolution of the mean value corresponding to the best particle position considering a population of M=30 particles and a) N=5 and b) N=10. Even if at the end of the computation all the QPSO algorithms provide almost the same optimum value, it is worthwhile to note the EWQPSO finds results faster than the other approaches.

Figure 2. Evolution of the mean value corresponding to the best particle position of the EWQPSO, WQPSO and QPSO applied to Ackley function for (a) N=5 and (b) N=10. A swarm composed of M = 30 particles is considered

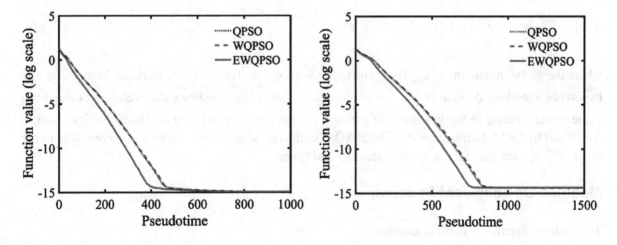

Griewank Test Function

The Griewank function is defined as follows:

$$f\left(\mathrm{x}\right) = \sum_{i=1}^{N} \frac{x_i^2}{4000} - \prod_{i=1}^{N} \cos\left(\frac{x_i}{\sqrt{i}}\right) + 1 \tag{26}$$

where the global minimum $f\left(\mathrm{x}_{\min}\right) = 0$ corresponds to $\mathrm{x}_{\min} = \left(0,0,...,0\right)$ coordinates. In this case, the searching domain $x_i \in \left(-600, 600\right), i = 1,2,...,N$, is considered. Figure 3 shows the evolution of the mean value corresponding to the best particle position considering a population of M=30 particles and a) N=5 and b) N=10. From the obtained results it is possible to underline that the tested QPSO algorithms have comparable performance. However, the EWQPSO finds more accurate optimal values.

Iperspherical Test Function

The Iperspherical function is defined as follows:

$$f\left(\mathrm{x}\right) = \sum_{i=1}^{N} x_i^2 \tag{27}$$

where the global minimum $f\left(\mathrm{x}_{\min}\right) = 0$ corresponds to $\mathrm{x}_{\min} = \left(0,0,...,0\right)$ coordinates. For the test the following searching domain $x_i \in \left(-100, 100\right), i = 1,2,...,N$, is set. Figure 3 shows the evolution of the mean value corresponding to the best particle position considering a population of M=30 particles and a) N=15 and b) N=20. As it can be noticed in Figure 4, the EWQPSO is faster and provides a minimum mean value smaller than those calculated using alternative methods.

Alpine Test Function

The Alpine function is defined as follows:

$$f\left(\mathrm{x}\right) = \sum_{i=1}^{N} \left| x_i \sin\left(x_i\right) + 0.1 x_i \right| \tag{28}$$

where the global minimum $f\left(\mathrm{x}_{\min}\right) = 0$ corresponds to $\mathrm{x}_{\min} = \left(0,0,...,0\right)$ coordinates. In this case, the hypercube searching domain is $x_i \in \left(-10, 10\right), i = 1,2,...,N$. Figure 5 shows the evolution of the mean value corresponding to the best particle position considering a population of M=30 particles and a) N=10 and b) N=15. In this case, the EWQPSO exhibits remarkable performance in comparison to the other PSO approaches since it is more accurate and faster.

Modified De Jong Test Function

The de Jong function is defined as follows:

Figure 3. Evolution of the mean value corresponding to the best particle position of the EWQPSO, WQPSO and QPSO applied to Griewank function for (a) N=5 and (b) N=10. A swarm composed of M = 30 particles is considered

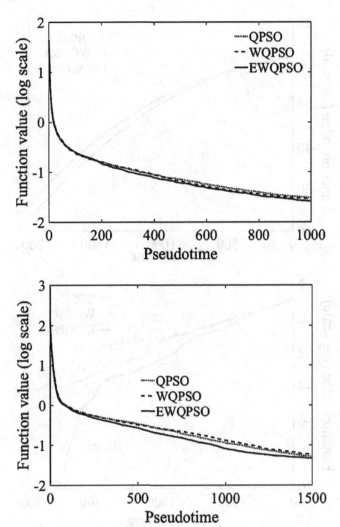

$$f\left(\mathbf{x}\right) = \sum_{i=1}^{N} i x_i^4 \tag{29}$$

where the global minimum $f\left(\mathbf{x}_{\min}\right) = 0$ corresponds to $\mathbf{x}_{\min} = \left(0,0,...,0\right)$ coordinates. For the test the following searching domain $x_i \in \left(-100,100\right), i = 1,2,...,N$, is set. Figure 6 shows the evolution of the mean value corresponding to the best particle position considering a population of M=30 particles and a) N=5 and b) N=10. Also in this case it can be noticed that the EWQPSO is faster and more accurate than the alternative QPSO algorithms.

In Table 1 are listed the mean and standard deviation (STD) values taking into account the minimum value associated to the best particle found in each of the 100 runs and by changing the particles number

Figure 4. Evolution of the mean value corresponding to the best particle position of the EWQPSO, WQPSO and QPSO applied to the iperspherical function for (a) N=15 and (b) N=20. A swarm composed of M = 30 particles is considered

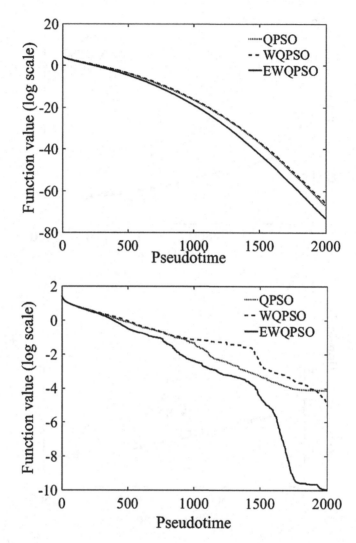

and the test function. By visual inspection of the results one can easily conclude that the developed EWQPSO algorithm is characterized by improved accuracy.

EWQPSO FOR SUPERSHAPED LENS ANTENNA SYNTHESIS

Dielectric lens antennas have attracted the attention of various researchers and companies because of their potential use in several application fields such as wireless communication systems [Raman et al, 1998], smart antennas (Ravishankar & Dharshak, 2014), radar systems (Raman et al., 1998). The attractive features of this class of antennas mainly consist in the ease of integration as well as in their

Figure 5. Evolution of the mean value corresponding to the best particle position of the EWQPSO, WQPSO and QPSO applied to the Alpine function for (a) N=10 and (b) N=15. A swarm composed of M = 30 particles is considered

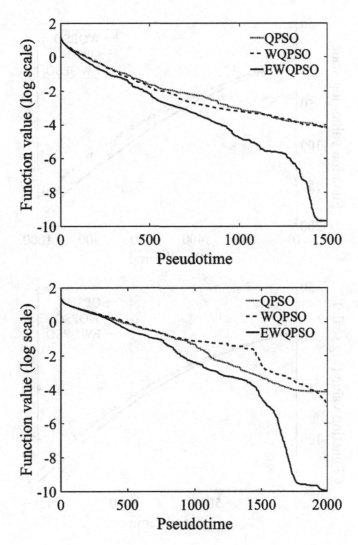

beam collimating/shaping capability. Many research activities have been devoted to the development of 3D dielectric lenses characterized by canonical or axial-symmetrical geometry (Filipovic & Rebeiz, 1993) and only a few scientific studies have been dedicated to the study of more complex shaped lens (Chantraine-Bars et al., 2005).

In recent years, a systematic and detailed study of a new class of shaped dielectric lens antennas whose geometry is described by Gielis' superformula has been presented (Mescia et al., 2016; Bia et al., 2015; Simeoni et al., 2011). Thanks to Gielis' formulation it is possible to generate a wide range of 3D shapes in a simple and analytical way by changing a reduced number of parameters. As result, an automated optimization procedure based on QPSO algorithm could be conveniently developed to identify the geometrical parameters yielding optimal antenna performance.

Figure 6. Evolution of the mean value corresponding to the best particle position of the EWQPSO, WQPSO and QPSO applied to de Jong function for (a) N=5 and (b) N=10. A swarm composed of M = 30 particles is considered

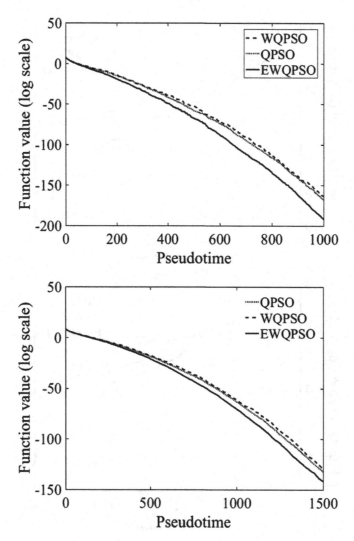

Assuming a Cartesian coordinate system, the lens surface is described by general Gielis' surface characterized by the following parametric equations

$$x\left(v,\mu\right) = R\left(v\right)\cos vR\left(\mu\right)\cos\mu \tag{30}$$

$$y\left(v,\mu\right) = R\left(v\right)\sin vR\left(\mu\right)\cos\mu \tag{31}$$

Table 1. Mean and STD values of the global best calculated applying the EWQPSO, WQPSO and QPSO algorithms and considering the different test functions

Test function	N	QPSO		WQPSO		EWQPSO	
		mean	STD	mean	STD	mean	STD
Akley	5	1.03e-15	7e-16	1.1e-15	8.48e-16	1.17e-15	9.67e-16
	10	4.41e-15	3.55e-16	4.41e-15	3.55e-16	4.44e-15	0
	15	4.83e-15	1.11e-15	4.87e-15	1.16e-15	4.69e-15	9.11*e-16
	20	6.75e-15	1.70e-15	7.21e-15	1.48e-15	6.79e-15	1.69e-15
Griewank	5	3.02e-2	1.99e-2	2.85e-2	1.74e-2	2.55e-2	1.56e-2
	10	5.16e-2	3.19e-2	5.89e-2	5.07e-2	4.70e-2	3.51e-2
	15	2.77e-2	2.10e-2	3.31e-2	3.58e-2	2.92e-2	2.03e-2
	20	5.76e-2	4.58e-2	6.33e-2	3.99e-2	4.38e-2	2.45e-2
Iperspherical	5	2.69e-93	2.02e-92	9.70e-92	7.64e-91	9.59e-107	9.37e-106
	10	1.49e-80	1.07e-79	9.28e-79	7.40e-78	2.23e-89	1.48e-88
	15	6.05e-68	4.27e-67	5.34e-67	3.95e-66	6.16e-74	2.97*e-73
	20	7.80e-57	4.88e-56	7.43e-57	2.74e-56	5.96e-61	5.36e-60
Alpine	5	3.63e-5	1.64e-4	7.99e-5	4.7e-4	1.42e-6	8.31e-6
	10	6.94e-5	3.1e-4	6.35e-5	3.61e-4	2.05e-10	1.74e-9
	15	7.46e-5	7.45e-4	9.23e-6	6.11e-5	1.08e-10	1.08e-9
	20	5.50e-4	5.50e-3	5.09e-4	3.63e-3	2.51e-4	1.77e-3
de Jong	5	1.27e-169	6.48e-169	9.32e-165	6.56e-164	6.37e-193	6.05e-192
	10	3.58e-133	2.73e-132	1.0*e-130	9.31e-130	1.04e-142	1.00e-141
	15	3.31e-104	1.44e-103	1.5*e-101	7.46e-101	2.35e-108	1.92e-107
	20	3.72e-81	2.59e-80	3.4*e-80	1.8e-79	2.29e-84	1.34e-83

$$z(\mu) = R(\mu)\sin\mu \tag{32}$$

$$R(v) = \left[\left|\frac{\cos(m_1 v / 4)}{a_1}\right|^{n_1} + \left|\frac{\sin(m_2 v / 4)}{a_2}\right|^{n_2}\right]^{-1/b_1} \tag{33}$$

$$R(\mu) = \left[\left|\frac{\cos(m_3\mu / 4)}{a_3}\right|^{n_3} + \left|\frac{\sin(m_4\mu / 4)}{a_4}\right|^{n_4}\right]^{-1/b_2} \tag{34}$$

where m_p, a_p, n_p, $p = 1,2,3,4$ are positive real number and b_q, $q = 1,2$ are strictly positive real number selected in such a way that the surface of the lens is closed and characterized, at any point, by curvature radius larger than the working wavelength. The parameters $v \in (-\pi, \pi)$ and $\mu \in (0, \pi/2)$ denote convenient angle values, whereas the spherical angles are obtained by the equations

$$\theta = \arccos\left(\frac{z}{r}\right) \tag{35}$$

$$\varphi = \arccos\left(\frac{y}{x}\right) \tag{36}$$

where $r = \sqrt{x^2 + y^2 + z^2}$.

As depicted in Figure 7, the antenna structure considered in the synthesis procedure consists of an electrically large dielectric lens placed at the centre of a perfectly electric conductor circular plate, with diameter d, acting as a ground plane and, at the same time, as a shield useful to reduce the back-scattered radiation. The lens is illuminated by the electromagnetic field emitted by open ended circular waveguide, with diameter d_n, filled up by the same dielectric material forming the lens. The tube tracing approach based on the combined geometrical optics/physical optics (GO/PO) approximation is used to model the electromagnetic propagation inside the homogeneous dielectric lens. This approximation, allows a significant simplification of the mathematical model making the simulation of electrically large structures possible with a lower computational effort in comparison to full-wave numerical methods. In fact, by virtue of the GO/PO approximation the travelling electromagnetic wave can be approximated by a set of tubes propagating over a rectilinear path inside the lens (Bia et al., 2015, Bia et al., 2013, Mescia et

Figure 7. Geometrical structure of the electromagnetic system based on dielectric lens antenna

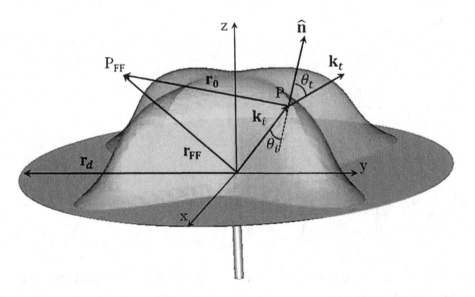

al., 2016). The accuracy of the method can be further improved by considering the effects of multiple internal reflections occurring within the lens.

The developed GO/PO tube-tracing algorithm has been validated by comparison with the full-wave finite integration technique (FIT) adopted in the commercially available electromagnetic solver CST Microwave Studio (Bia et al., 2015, Bia et al., 2013, Mescia et al., 2016). A dedicated novel synthesis procedure based EWQPSO is adopted to design a particular lens antenna showing a fixed 3D radiation pattern at frequency f=60 GHz. Such antenna could be used to improve the channel capacity in communication systems implementing a spatial-division multiplexing. The lens is made out of a dielectric material with relative electric permittivity equal to $\varepsilon_r = 2$, the cylindrical open ended waveguide and the metal plate have diameter $d_n = 2.3 mm$ and $d = 20 cm$, respectively. A swarm of M=48 particles has been launched over a maximum pseudotime $t_{max} = 40$. The position vector relevant to the mth particle is $\mathrm{x}_m = \begin{bmatrix} n_1 & n_2 & n_3 & n_4 & b_1 & b_2 \end{bmatrix}^T$. The multidimensional search space has been restricted by assuming that all the components of the vector position can range from 1 to 5, while the remaining Gielis' parameters are $a_1 = a_2 = a_3 = a_4 = 1$ and $m_1 = m_2 = m_3 = m_4 = 1$.

The developed modelling technique is adopted for synthesising a lens antenna featuring a radiation beam pattern having four main lobes at the frequency f=60 GHz. This type of antenna could be adopted in communication systems implementing a spatial-division multiplexing useful for increasing the channel capacity where the position of the receiver is known. The fitness function value is evaluated as

$$\mathcal{F}\left(\mathrm{x}_m\right) = \sum_{p=1}^{N_\theta} \sum_{q=1}^{N_\phi} \left| \frac{\hat{D}_{p,q}^T - \hat{D}_{p,q}^m}{1 + \hat{D}_{p,q}^T} \right| \tag{37}$$

where $\hat{D}^T$ is the target normalised directivity, expressed in dB, $\hat{D}^m$ is the normalised directivity, in dB, relevant to the mth particle, N_θ and N_ϕ denote the number of points in which the azimuthal and polar coordinates are discretised, respectively. The directivity of the considered radiating system can be obtained by the following expression

$$D\left(\theta_{FF}, \phi_{FF}\right) = \frac{4\pi r_{FF}^2 \left| \mathrm{E}_{FF} \right|^2}{\eta_0 P_{tot}} \tag{38}$$

where E_{FF} is the electric far-field radiated by the lens antenna at the observation point $\mathrm{P}_{FF}\left(r_{FF} q_{FF} f_{FF}\right)$, η_0 is is the characteristic impedance of the vacuum, r_{FF} is the distance between the observation point and the origin of the coordinate system, P_{tot} is the total power radiated by the lens. Under these assumptions, by using the EWQPSO procedure, the optimal lens parameters are found to be: $n_1 = 4.161$, $n_2 = 4.004$, $b_1 = 1.017$, $b_2 = 1.001$, $n_3 = 2.837$, and $n_4 = 1.010$.

The radiation solid illustrated in Figure 8(a) is generated by the current density distribution on the lens surface shown in Figure 8(b). From Figure 8(a) four main lobes can be observed pointing in four different directions $\phi = 45°$, $\phi = 135°$, $\phi = 225°$, and $\phi = 315°$ with a directivity of about 10 dBi.

Figure 9 shows both the target and EWQPSO recovered polar section of the radiation solids for $\phi = 0°$ and $\phi = 45°$. It is worth noting that the synthesised radiation patterns are in excellent agreement with

Figure 8.(a) radiation solid generated by (b) the densities current distribution on the lens surface

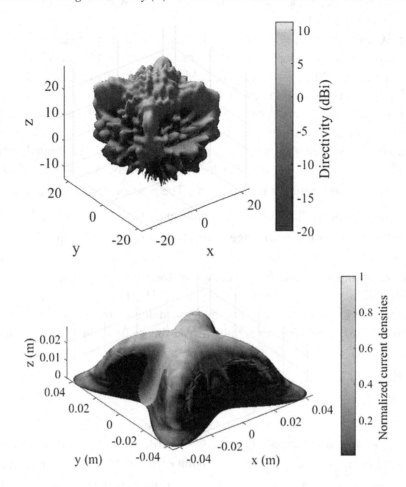

the target masks. Moreover, it is clear that accounting for the multiple wave reflections occurring within the lens is instrumental to the enhancement of the modelling accuracy of the procedure. Figure 10 shows the convergence rate of the new optimisation procedure (EWQPSO) when applied to the synthesis of the lens antenna illustrated in Figure 8. The convergence of the average value of the fitness function of the whole swarm to the one corresponding to the global best demonstrates the capability of the whole swarm to search the optimal solution in an effective way.

The illustrated lens antenna structures feature specific properties in terms of radiation pattern that can be beneficial for the newly introduced Wi-Fi 802.11ad communication protocol working at frequency $f = 60GHz$. However, in previously published articles by the authors (Mescia et al., 2016; Bia et al., 2015) more detailed studies have been illustrated in order to demonstrate the effectiveness of the proposed EWQPSO model in the design of the special class of dielectric lens antennas defined by Gielis' formula. It was also verified that the EWQPSO technique outperforms both the classical PSO and genetic algorithms (GAs), as well as the conventional WQPSO procedure in terms of convergence rate, accuracy, and population size. Such properties are highly attractive in the considered contest since the computational burden associated with the computation of the fitness function is not negligible.

Figure 9. Comparison between the target directivity and the directivity of the Gielis' lens antenna synthesized by means of the EWQPSO procedure: (a) $\phi = 0°$ and (b) $\phi = 45°$

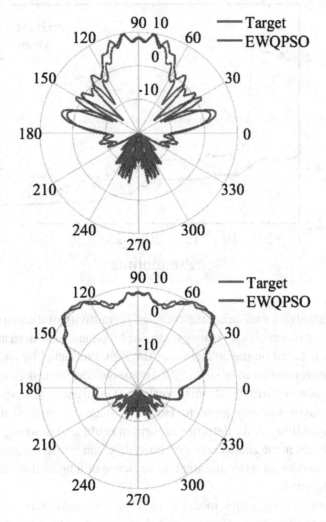

FDTD/EWQPSO METHOD FOR ELECTROMAGNETIC CHARACTERIZATION OF DISPERSIVE LAYERED SYSTEMS

The EWQPSO algorithm can be used to address more complex and challenging problems such as the identification of the inner structure of unknown multilayered materials. The solution of this type of electromagnetic problems has potential applications in the modern-day military and civil industries (Lee et al., 2015; Roy et al., 2015), security and non-destructive testing, microwave imaging, radio propagation, and non-ionizing radiation dosimetry (Fang et al., 2004; Fhager et al., 2012; Skaar & Haakestad, 2012). In fact, microwave absorbers are often used to suppress radar echoes, to reduce spurious radiation from electronic sources, and for more complex stealth applications, as well as to diminish electromagnetic interference between microwave components and electronic components. Furthermore, detailed knowledge of the permittivity of biological tissues is essential to understand the behavior of light propagating in biological tissues, and such knowledge is also important for diagnostics and treatments.

Figure 10. Convergence rate of the EWQPSO procedure

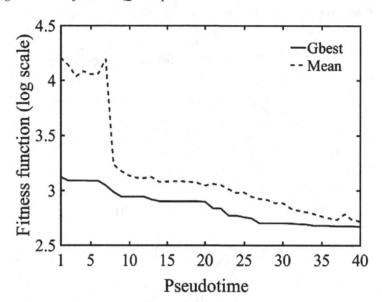

There are several methods for measuring the complex permittivity of dielectric materials: resonant, free space and transmission line methods. Among these, the broadband non-destructive and non-invasive measurement technique is based on the collection of the signal reflected by an unknown structure illuminated by a pulsed or continuous wave signal. As a consequence, the task is to recover the dielectric properties as well as the geometry structure from the reflected signal characteristics. From a mathematical point of view, this is a classical inverse problem. However, since the involved materials are lossy and dispersive, numerical instabilities of the detection algorithm could lead to wrong estimates. A basic approach to reduce instabilities in the characterization procedure consists in the adoption of measurement data. To this end, the time-domain reflection impulse response of a layered structure is regarded as the input of the detection algorithm.

In order to have a realistic propagation model of the electromagnetic waves inside lossy media, it is necessary to account for the frequency dispersion of the materials. This leads to complex-valued permittivity functions having frequency-dependent real and imaginary parts. Generally, there are several different mechanisms affecting the polarization of a medium exposed to an electric field. These processes typically result in a specific frequency-domain behavior of the permittivity function. In particular, the disordered nature and microstructure of dielectric matter produces non-symmetric experimental dielectric response in the frequency domain which cannot be described by a simple Debye expression having a single relaxation time. To this end, an empirical relation incorporating the Debye-type functions and the "universal" response, as its particular cases, is used (Raicu, 1999)

$$\varepsilon_r(\omega) = \varepsilon_{r,\infty} + \sum_{p=1}^{P} \frac{\Delta\varepsilon_p}{\left[\left(j\omega\tau_p\right)^{\gamma_p} + \left(j\omega\tau_p\right)^{\alpha_p}\right]^{\beta_p}} - j\frac{\sigma_s}{\omega\varepsilon_0} \tag{39}$$

where $0 \leq \alpha_p, \beta_p, \gamma_p \leq 1$ are heuristically derived fitting parameters, P is maximum number of relaxation processes, $\varepsilon_{r,\infty}$ is the relative permittivity at high frequency, σ_s is the static conductivity, $\Delta\varepsilon_p$ is a dimensional constant, ε_0 is the free space permittivity, τ_p is the relaxation time. Equation (39) reduces to the Debye dispersion function for $\alpha_p = \beta_p = 1$ and $\gamma_p = 0$, to the Cole-Cole function for $\gamma_p = 0$ and $\beta_p = 1$, to the Davidson-Cole function for $\alpha_p = 1$ and $\gamma_p = 0$. Moreover, for $\beta_p = 1$ and $\alpha_p = \gamma_p$ the constant-phase angle function or Jonscher's universal response can be modelled.

In recent years, a lot of interest has been devoted in the development of time domain numerical methods for solving electromagnetic problems. In particular, the continuous progress of the available computational resources has stimulated many advances in the finite-difference time-domain (FDTD) method. The FDTD technique is a powerful and efficient numerical procedure exhibiting good accuracy, robustness, and low computational footprint. However, the inclusion of the dielectric response function equation (39) into the FDTD scheme causes difficulties since fractional powers in frequency domain lead to fractional derivatives in time domain, this requiring advanced mathematics to be adopted for the embedding of such operators in the core of the algorithm. In order to tackle this problem, we have developed a novel FDTD scheme based on a general fractional polynomial series approximation and the fractional calculus theory. Dedicated uniaxial perfectly matched layer boundary conditions, ohmic losses and total field/scattered field approach have been also derived and implemented in combination with the basic time-marching scheme [Bia[1] et al, 2015; Mescia et al, 2015; Mescia[1] et al, 2015; Mescia et al, 2014; Caratelli et al, 2016]. Moreover, a dedicated EWQPSO based procedure has been coupled with the developed FDTD scheme in order to solve the inverse problem associated with the retrieval of the dielectric response of a dispersive material, as well as the identification of the geometrical parameters of a stratified medium consisting of dispersive materials.

Dispersive Dielectric Response Retrieving

As a numerical example of the FDTD/EWQPSO algorithm the two-layer slab structure illustrated in Figure 11 is considered. We assume that the half-space $x < 0$ is filled with vacuum, whereas a material having unknown permittivity $\varepsilon_r^*(\omega)$ is contained in the slab for $0 < z < d$ against a bulk material having known permittivity $\varepsilon_r^b(\omega)$ for $z > d$. The system is illuminated by a pulsed plane wave propagating along the positive x-direction, with electric field linearly polarized along the y-direction and generated at a given abscissa $x = x_s$. Both materials are assumed to be modelled by eq. (39) with only one relaxation process (P=1). In particular, the permittivity parameters of the bulk material are: $\Delta\varepsilon = 3$, $\varepsilon_{r,\infty} = 2.5$, $\alpha = 0.2$, $\beta = 0.08$, $\gamma = 0.93$, $\tau = 160\text{ns}$, and $\sigma = 0.01\text{S/m}$.

So, the task is to determine the parameters of the dielectric function $\varepsilon_r^*(\omega)$ and the thickness d by using the reflection coefficient evaluated at $x = x_s$ in a finite frequency band ranging from $\omega_{\min} = 500MHz$ to $\omega_{\max} = 10GHz$.

In order to tackle the considered problem, a swarm of M=48 particles is launched over a maximum pseudotime $t_{\max} = 40$ The position vector relevant to the mth particle is $x_m = \left[\alpha^* \beta^* \gamma^* \tau^* \Delta\varepsilon^* d\right]^T$. The multidimensional search space is restricted by assuming that $\alpha^*, \beta^*, \gamma^*$ can range from 0.001 to 1, τ^* from 1 to 20 ps, $\Delta\varepsilon^*$ from 2 to 1000, d from 0.3 to 3 mm. The optimization method is steered in order to minimize the following fitness function

Figure 11. Two layers slab structure used for dielectric response retrieving problem

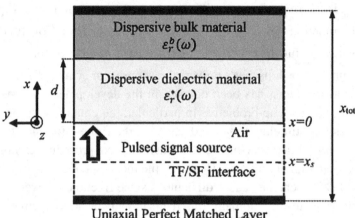

$$\mathcal{F}\left(\mathrm{x}_m\right) = \sqrt{\frac{\int_{\omega_{\min}}^{\omega_{\max}} \left|R^T\left(\omega\right) - R^m\left(\omega\right)\right|^2 d\omega}{\int_{\omega_{\min}}^{\omega_{\max}} \left|R^m\left(\omega\right)\right|^2 d\omega}} \tag{40}$$

where $R^T\left(\omega\right)$ is the target reflectance spectrum, $R^m\left(\omega\right)$ is the reflectance spectrum relevant to the mth particle. The frequency-domain behaviour of the reflection coefficient is calculated by the following expression:

$$R\left(\omega\right) = \frac{E_r\left(\omega, x = 0^-\right)}{E_{inc}} \tag{41}$$

where $E_r\left(\omega, x = 0^-\right)$ is the reflected electric field at the air-dielectric dispersive material interface (x=0), and E_{inc} is the incident electric field. The time-domain signal source is an electric current density placed at the specified position $x = x_s$ within the computational domain

$$\mathcal{J}_0\left(\omega\right) = \exp\left\{-\frac{\left(t - T_c\right)^2}{T_d^2}\right\} \sin\left[2\pi f_e\left(t - T_c\right)\right]\delta\left(x - x_s\right)\hat{y} \tag{42}$$

where $T_d = 1/\left(2.1 f_e\right)$, $T_c = 4T_d$, and $f_e = 6GHz$ are selected in such a way as to achieve a spectral bandwidth of about 10 GHz. Under these assumptions, by using the EWQPSO procedure, the optimal material parameters are found to be: $\alpha^* = 0.1$, $\beta^* = 0.38$, $\gamma^* = 0.52$, $\tau^* = 5.4ps$, $\Delta\varepsilon^* = 17.15$, and $d = 2mm$. Figure 12(a) shows the target and EWQPSO recovered reflectance spectra, while the corresponding target and EWQPSO recovered real and imaginary parts of the complex permittivity are illustrated in Figure 12(b). It can be observed that the proposed optimization algorithm is able to recover both reflectance and complex permittivity spectrum in excellent agreement with the target ones. Such result is further confirmed by Figure 13 showing the convergence rate of the new FDTD/EWQPSO optimization algorithm when applied to the retrieval of the dielectric response.

Figure 12. (a) Comparison between the target reflectance spectrum and the reflectance spectrum synthesized by means of the EWQPSO procedure, (b) target and EWQPSO recovered real and imaginary part of the complex permittivity spectrum

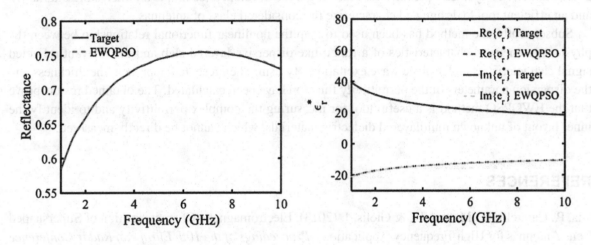

Figure 13. Convergence rate of the FDTD/EWQPSO optimization algorithm

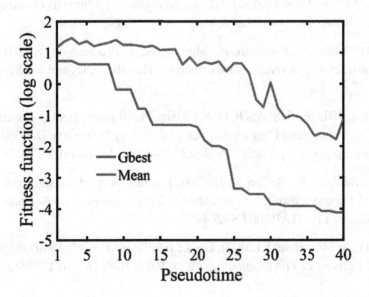

CONCLUSION

In this chapter, an optimization algorithm based on the quantum-behaved PSO approach, called EWQPSO, has been proposed to solve complex electromagnetic problems. The presented method has been usefully employed to identify the geometrical parameters of supershaped dielectric lens antennas yielding optimal antenna performance as well as to retrieve the dielectric response of lossy and dispersive materials. The performance comparison of the developed EWQPSO with conventional QPSO and WQPSO algorithms confirms that the proposed technique is faster and features improved accuracy.

The EWQPSO has been applied to solve the inverse problem consisting in the determination of unknown Gielis' parameters describing supershaped dielectric lens antennas with a four-beam main lobe at the frequency f=60 GHz. Numerical results prove that the presented approach is able to identify optimal solutions in a very effective way. Furthermore, the proposed algorithm is easy to implement, since it does not require the numerical evaluation of complicated evolutionary operators, and does not rely on a large number of synthesis parameters. This makes the developed technique an interesting alternative and an efficient tool to design and characterize the considered class of antennas.

Subsequently, the method has been used to map the nonlinear functional relationship between the physical/geometrical characteristics of a Raicu-like dispersive layered slab and the relevant reflected signal characteristics under plane wave excitation. By using the presented approach, the thickness and the dispersion parameters of the permittivity function have been calculated. The obtained results prove that the EWQPSO method is a useful tool for measuring the complex permittivity and to identify the inner layout of unknown multilayered dielectric materials, which cannot be directly measured.

REFERENCES

Bia, P., Caratelli, D., Mescia, L., & Gielis, J. (2013). Electromagnetic Characterization of Supershaped Lens Antennas for High-Frequency Applications. *Proceedings of the 10th European Radar Conference (EuRAD)*, 1679-1682.

Bia, P., Caratelli, D., Mescia, L., & Gielis, J. (2015). Analysis and Synthesis of Supershaped Dielectric Lens Antennas. IET Microwaves. *Antennas & Propagation, 9,* 1497–1504.

Bia, P., Caratelli, D., Mescia, L., Cicchetti, R., Maione, G., & Prudenzano, F. (2015). A novel FDTD formulation based on fractional derivatives for dispersive Havriliak–Negami media. *Signal Processing, 107,* 312-318.

Caratelli, D., Mescia, L., Bia, P., & Stukach, O. V. (2016). Fractional-Calculus-Based FDTD Algorithm for Ultrawideband Electromagnetic Characterization of Arbitrary Dispersive Dielectric Materials. *IEEE Transactions on Antennas and Propagation, 64*(8), 3533–3544. doi:10.1109/TAP.2016.2578322

Chantraine-Bars, B., Sauleau, R., & Coq, L. L. (2005). A new accurate design method for millimeter-wave homogeneous dielectric substrate lens antennas. *IEEE Transactions on Antennas and Propagation, 53*(3), 1069–1082. doi:10.1109/TAP.2004.842644

Ciuprina, G., Ioan, D., & Munteanu, I. (2002). Use of Intelligent-Particle Swarm Optimization in Electromagnetics. *IEEE Transactions on Magnetics, 38*(2), 1037–1040. doi:10.1109/20.996266

Clerc, M., & Kennedy, J. (2002). The particle swarm: Explosion, stability, and convergence in a multi-dimensional complex space. *IEEE Transactions on Evolutionary Computation, 6*(1), 58–73. doi:10.1109/4235.985692

del Valle, Y., Venayagamoorthy, G.-K., Mohagheghi, S., Hernandez, J.-C., & Harley, R. G. (2008). Particle swarm optimization: Basic concepts, variants and applications in power systems. *IEEE Transactions on Evolutionary Computation, 12*(2), 171–195. doi:10.1109/TEVC.2007.896686

dos Santos Coelho, L. (2008). A quantum particle swarm optimizer with chaotic mutation operator. *Chaos, Solitons, and Fractals, 37*(5), 1409–1418. doi:10.1016/j.chaos.2006.10.028

Eberhart, R. C., & Shi, Y. 2000. Comparing inertia weights and constriction factors in particle swarm optimization. *Proc. of Congress on Evolutionary Computing, 84*–89. doi:10.1109/CEC.2000.870279

Fang, Q., Meaney, P. M., & Paulsen, K. D. (2004). Microwave image reconstruction of tissue property dispersion characteristics utilizing multiple-frequency information. *IEEE Transactions on Microwave Theory and Techniques, 52*(8), 1866–1875. doi:10.1109/TMTT.2004.832014

Fhager, A., Gustafsson, M., & Nordebo, S. (2012). Image reconstruction in microwave tomography using a dielectric Debye model. *IEEE Transactions on Microwave Theory and Techniques, 59*, 156–166. PMID:21937340

Filipovic, D. F., & Rebeiz, G. M. (1993). Double-slot antennas on extended hemispherical and elliptical quartz dielectric lenses. *International Journal of Infrared and Millimeter Waves, 14*(10), 1905–1924. doi:10.1007/BF02096363

Fornarelli, G., & Mescia, M. (2013). *Swarm Intelligence for Electric and Electronic Engineering.* Hershey, PA: IGI Global. doi:10.4018/978-1-4666-2666-9

Fornarelli, G., Giaquinto, A., & Mescia, M. (2013). *Optimum design and characterization of rare earth-doped fibre amplifiers by means of particle swarm optimization approach.* Hershey, PA: IGI Global.

Fu, X., Liu, W., Zhang, B., & Deng, H. (2013). Quantum Behaved Particle Swarm Optimization with Neighborhood Search for Numerical Optimization. *Mathematical Problems in Engineering, 2013,* 469723. doi:10.1155/2013/469723

Hassanien, A. E., & Emary, E. (2015). *Swarm Intelligence: Principles, Advances, and Applications.* CRC Press. doi:10.1201/b19133

Huang, T., & Mohan, A. S. (2004). A hybrid boundary condition for robust particle swarm optimization. *IEEE Antennas and Wireless Propagation Letters, 4*(1), 112–117. doi:10.1109/LAWP.2005.846166

Iwasaki, N., Yasuda, K., & Ueno, G. (2006). Dynamic Parameter Tuning of Particle Swarm Optimization. *IEEJ Trans, 1,* 353–363.

Jaco, F., Schutte, F., & Groenwold, A. A. (2005). A study of global optimization using particle swarms. *Journal of Global Optimization, 31*(1), 93–108. doi:10.1007/s10898-003-6454-x

Jin, J., & Rahmat-Samii, Y. (2007). Advances in Particle Swarm Optimization for Antenna Designs: Real-Number, Binary, Single-Objective and Multiobjective Implementations. *IEEE Transactions on Antennas and Propagation, 55*(3), 556–567. doi:10.1109/TAP.2007.891552

Kennedy, J., & Eberhart, R. (1995). Particle Swarm Optimization. *Proc. of IEEE Int. Conf. on Neural Networks*, 1942-1948. doi:10.1109/ICNN.1995.488968

Lee, J., Yoo, M., & Lim, S. (2015). A Study of Ultra-Thin Single Layer Frequency Selective Surface Microwave Absorbers With Three Different Bandwidths Using Double Resonance. *IEEE Transactions on Antennas and Propagation, 63*(1), 221–230. doi:10.1109/TAP.2014.2365826

Mahanfar, A., Bila, S., Aubourg, M., & Verdeyme, S. (2007). Cooperative particle swarm optimization of passive microwave devices. *Int. J. Numer. Model., 21*(1-2), 151–168. doi:10.1002/jnm.655

Mescia, L., Bia, P., & Caratelli, D. (2014). Fractional Derivative Based FDTD Modeling of Transient Wave Propagation in Havriliak-Negami Media. *IEEE Transactions on Microwave Theory and Techniques, 62*(9), 1920–1929. doi:10.1109/TMTT.2014.2327202

Mescia, L., Bia, P., & Caratelli, D. (2015). Authors. *Reply. IEEE Trans. Microw. Theory Techn., 63*(12), 4191–4193. doi:10.1109/TMTT.2015.2495263

Mescia, L., Bia, P., Caratelli, D., Chiapperino, M. A., Stukach, O., & Gielis, J. (2016). Electromagnetic Mathematical Modeling of 3-D Supershaped Dielectric Lens Antennas. Mathematical Problems in Engineering.

Mescia, L., Bia, P., & Caratelli, D. (2015). Fractional-calculus-based FDTD method for solving pulse propagation problems. *International Conference on Electromagnetics in Advanced Applications (ICEAA)*, 460-463.

Omkar, S. N., Khandelwal, R., Ananth, T. V. S., Narayana Naik, G., & Gopalakrishnan, S. (2009). Quantum behaved Particle Swarm Optimization (QPSO) for multi-objective design optimization of composite structures. *Expert Systems with Applications, 36*(8), 11312–11322. doi:10.1016/j.eswa.2009.03.006

Parsopoulos, K. E., & Vrahatis, M. N. (2010). *Particle Swarm Optimization and Intelligence: Advances and Applications*. Hershey, PA: IGI Global. doi:10.4018/978-1-61520-666-7

Piro, G., Bia, P., Boggia, G., Caratelli, D., Grieco, L. A., & Mescia, L. (2016). Terahertz electromagnetic field propagation in human tissues: a study on communication capabilities. *Nano Communication Networks*.

Raicu, V. (1999). Dielectric dispersion of biological matter: Model combining Debye-type and universal responses. *Physical Review E: Statistical Physics, Plasmas, Fluids, and Related Interdisciplinary Topics, 60*(4), 4677–4680. doi:10.1103/PhysRevE.60.4677 PMID:11970331

Raman, S., Barker, N. S., & Rebeiz, G. M. (1998). AW-band dielectric lens-based integrated monopulse radar receiver. *IEEE Transactions on Microwave Theory and Techniques, 46*(12), 2308–2316. doi:10.1109/22.739216

Ratnaweera, A., Saman, K., & Watson, H. C. (2004). Self–Organizing Hierarchical Particle Swarm Optimizer with Time–Varying Acceleration Coefficients. *IEEE Transactions on Evolutionary Computation, 8*(3), 240–255. doi:10.1109/TEVC.2004.826071

Ravishankar, S., & Dharshak, B. (2014). A rapid direction of arrival estimation procedure for adaptive array antennas covered by a shaped dielectric lens. *Proc. IEEE Radio and Wireless Symposium (RWS '14)*, 124-126.

Robinson, J., & Rahmat-Samii, Y. (2004). Particle Swarm Optimization in Electromagnetics. *IEEE Transactions on Antennas and Propagation, 52*(2), 397–407. doi:10.1109/TAP.2004.823969

Roy, S., Roy, S. D., Tewary, J., Mahanti, A., & Mahanti, G. K. (2015). Particle Swarm Optimization for Optimal Design of Broadband Multilayer Microwave Absorber for Wide Angle of Incidence. *Progress in Electromagnetics Research, 62*, 121–135. doi:10.2528/PIERB14122602

Shi, Y., & Eberhart, R. (1998). A modified particle swarm optimizer. *Proc. IEEE International Conference on Evolutionary Computation (ICEC)*, 69-73.

Shi, Y., & Eberhart, R.C. (1999). Empirical Study of Particle Swarm Opimization. *Proc. IEEE Int. Conf. on Evolutionary Computation, 3*, 101–106.

Simeoni, M., Cicchetti, R., Yarovoy, A., & Caratelli, D. (2011). Plastic-based supershaped dielectric resonator antennas for wide-band applications. *IEEE Transactions on Antennas and Propagation, 59*(12), 4820–4825. doi:10.1109/TAP.2011.2165477

Skaar, J., & Haakestad, M. W. (2012). Inverse scattering of dispersive stratified structures. *Journal of the Optical Society of America. B, Optical Physics, 29*(9), 2438–2445. doi:10.1364/JOSAB.29.002438

Sun J., Lai, C-H., & Wu, X-J. (2011). *Particle Swarm Optimisation: Classical and Quantum Perspectives*. CRC Press, Inc.

Sun, J., Feng, B., & Xu, W. B. (2004). Particle swarm optimization with particles having quantum behavior. *Proc. IEEE Congress on Evolutionary Computation (CEC '04)*, 325–331. doi:10.1109/CEC.2004.1330875

Sun, J., Fang, W., Palade, V., Wua, X., & Xu, W. (2011). Quantum-behaved particle swarm optimization with Gaussian distributed local attractor point. *Applied Mathematics and Computation, 218*, 3763–3775,

van den Bergh, F., & Engelbrecht, A. P. (2006). A study of particle swarm optimization particle trajectories. *Information Sciences, 176*(8), 937–971. doi:10.1016/j.ins.2005.02.003

van den Bergh, F., & Engelbrecht, A. P. (2004). A Cooperative Approach to Particle Swarm Optimization. *IEEE Trans. on Evolutionary Computation, 8*, 225-239.

Woolfson, M. M., & Pert, G. J. (1999). *An Introduction to Computer Simulation*. New York, NY: Oxford University Press.

Xi, M., Sun, J., & Xu, W. (2008). An improved quantum-behaved particle swarm optimization algorithm with weighted mean best position. *Applied Mathematics and Computation, 205*(2), 751–759. doi:10.1016/j.amc.2008.05.135

Yasuda, K., Iwasaki, N., Ueno, G., & Aiyoshi, E. (2008). Particle Swarm Optimization: A Numerical Stability Analysis and Parameter Adjustment Based on Swarm Activity. *IEEJ Trans, 3*, 642–659.

Yumin, D., & Li, Z. (2014). Quantum Behaved Particle Swarm Optimization Algorithm Based on Artificial Fish Swarm. *Mathematical Problems in Engineering, 2014*, 592682. doi:10.1155/2014/592682

ADDITIONAL READING

Chien-Ching, C., Min-Hui, H., & Shu-Han, L. (2013). PSO and APSO for Optimizing Coverage in Indoor UWB Communication System. Int. *J. RF and Microwave Computer-Aided Engineering*, *23*(3), 300–308. doi:10.1002/mmce.20674

Huang, V. L., Suganthan, P. N., & Liang, J. J. (2006). Comprehensive Learning Particle Swarm Optimizer for Solving Multiobjective Optimization Problems. *International Journal of Intelligent Systems*, *21*(2), 209–226. doi:10.1002/int.20128

Jin, J., & Rahmat-Samii, Y. (2008). Particle Swarm Optimization for Antenna Designs in Engineering Electromagnetics. Hindawi. *Journal of Artificial Evolution and Applications*, *2008*, 728929. doi:10.1155/2008/728929

Mikki S. M., Kishk A.A., 2008. Particle Swarm Optimizaton: A Physics-Based Approach. Morgan & Claypool Publishers series.

Nakano, H., Taguchi, Y., Kanamori, Y., Utani, A., Miyauchi, A., & Yamamoto, H. (2012). A Competitive Particle Swarm Optimizer and Its Application to Wireless Sensor Networks. *IEEJ Trans*, *7*, S52–S58.

Schutte, J. F., Reinbolt, J. A., Fregly, B. J., Haftka, R. T., & George, A. D. (2004). Parallel global optimization with the particle swarm algorithm. *International Journal for Numerical Methods in Engineering*, *61*(13), 2296–2315. doi:10.1002/nme.1149 PMID:17891226

Semnani, A., & Kamyab, M. (2007). An enhanced method for inverse scattering problems using Fourier series expansion in conjunction with FDTD and PSO. *Progress in Electromagnetics Research*, *76*, 45–64. doi:10.2528/PIER07061204

Wilke, D. N., Kok, S., & Groenwold, A. A. (2007). Comparison of linear and classical velocity update rules in particle swarm optimization: Notes on diversity. *International Journal for Numerical Methods in Engineering*, *70*(8), 962–984. doi:10.1002/nme.1867

Ying-Nan, Z., & Hong-Fei, T. (2008). Detecting particle swarm optimization. *Concurrency and Computation*, *21*, 449–473.

Chapter 4
Parameter Settings in Particle Swarm Optimization

Snehal Mohan Kamalapur
K. K. Wagh Institute of Engineering Education and Research, India

Varsha Patil
Matoshree College of Engineering and Research Center, India

ABSTRACT

The issue of parameter setting of an algorithm is one of the most promising areas of research. Particle Swarm Optimization (PSO) is population based method. The performance of PSO is sensitive to the parameter settings. In the literature of evolutionary computation there are two types of parameter settings - parameter tuning and parameter control. Static parameter tuning may lead to poor performance as optimal values of parameters may be different at different stages of run. This leads to parameter control. This chapter has two-fold objectives to provide a comprehensive discussion on parameter settings and on parameter settings of PSO. The objectives are to study parameter tuning and control, to get the insight of PSO and impact of parameters settings for particles of PSO.

INTRODUCTION

Research in optimization is very active and different optimization algorithms are being proposed regularly. Kennedy and Eberhart (Kennedy & Eberhart, 1995; Eberhart & Kennedy, 1995) introduced an optimization technique named Particle Swarm Optimization (PSO) in 1995. PSO is from the category of algorithms named Swarm Intelligence and is motivated by social behavior patterns of organisms living and interacting within large groups. In particular, it incorporates swarming behavior observed in bird flocks and fish schools. Social sharing of information among individuals of a population is the core idea behind PSO.

The performance of PSO is sensitive to the parameter settings. The computational behavior of PSO is significantly affected by initialization of particles, velocity threshold, inertia weight, constriction coefficient, acceleration coefficient, neighborhood typologies and swarm size. The algorithm finds a solution which is near optimum efficiently depending on the values of these parameters. Assigning the

DOI: 10.4018/978-1-5225-2128-0.ch004

proper values to these parameters needs much effort. Hence it is necessary to analyze the PSO theoretically to tune the parameters. Particles change their position dynamically based on socio-cognition model.

MAIN FOCUS OF THE CHAPTER

The chapter has two-fold objectives, to provide an insight of PSO and to present a comprehensive discussion on the impact of parameters settings on the performance of PSO. The chapter provides a broad view in the field to help researchers. Particle swarm optimization algorithm is formulated and the parameters of PSO are listed down in the first section. Parameter settings for PSO algorithm influence the performance of the algorithm. The second section focuses on parameter tuning and control. The parameter tuning in PSO is based on the theoretical and empirical analysis. Theoretical analysis of PSO and the states of PSO are discussed in the third section. Parameters may or may not be independent and trying all combinations is practically impossible. In essence, tuning parameter values before the optimization process does not guarantee an optimal performance of the algorithm. Parameters can be controlled based on evidence such as generation number, fitness values or convergence and diversity of the population by fixed control without feedback or by adaptive control with feedback mechanism. Feedback can be fitness value or state of the swarm. PSO is a population based method and the evolutionary state reflects current population and fitness diversity. The search process can be accelerated by finding out the state of the swarm. The fourth section focuses on parameter tuning and control in PSO.

PARTICLE SWARM OPTIMIZATION

Swarm Intelligence (SI) is collective intelligence. It is simulation of social interaction between individuals. In SI, metaphors from successful behavior of animal or human societies are applied to problem solving. The social behavior of fish and birds has influenced scientists. Various interpretations of the movement of organisms in a bird flock or fish school are simulated by number of scientists. Natural flocks seem to consist of two balanced, opposing behaviors: a desire to stay close to the flock and a desire to avoid collisions within the flock.

The PSO is a population based approach (Engelbrecht, 2005) and follows swarm intelligence principles. The swarm consists of particles. These particles fly through the problem space. The velocity directs flying of the particles. The particles fly by following the current optimum of objective function. Social sharing of information among individuals of a population is the core idea behind PSO. The first version of the PSO was published by Kennedy and Eberhart (1995) and has rapidly progressed in recent years since then. Swarm of N particles is represented as

$$S = X_1, X_2, ..., X_N \tag{1}$$

Depending on the problem at hand each particle has d-dimensions. For a d-dimensional search space, the position of the ith particle is represented as-

$$X_i = \left(X_{i1}, Xi_2, ..., X_{id} \right)^T \tag{2}$$

The velocity of each particle is represented as

$$V_i = \left(V_{i1}, Vi_2, ..., V_{id} \right)^T \tag{3}$$

Where i = 1, 2, ..., N

The particles move iteratively within the search space. $X_i(t)$ and $V_i(t)$ denote current position and velocity of ith particle respectively at iteration t. The best position of particle is determined by pareto dominance (Eberhart & Kennedy, 1995).

PSO algorithm -

- Initialize the population of particles randomly
- Do
  - Calculate fitness values of each particle as per objective function
  - Update particles best position if the current fitness value is better than earlier best position
  - Determine the best fitness value in the swarm
  - For each particle calculate velocity of particle
  - For each particle calculate position of the particle depending on the velocity calculated
- While the maximum number of iterations or criterion is not attained

Two main versions of PSO namely global best version and local best version were introduced initially. A local best version of PSO has been proposed to improve the performance of global version of PSO. The particles move in the problem hyperspace.

The performance of the PSO is influenced by following parameters-

1. Swarm Size
   The swarm consists of particles. The Swarm size is a size of the population.
2. Acceleration Coefficients
   Acceleration coefficients c_1 and c_2 indicate cognitive and social influence values respectively.
3. Neighborhood Topology
   Neighborhood topology is a scheme to determine the neighbors of particles in a swarm. Information exchange among the particles is related to exploration capability of the swarm. Each particle may have set of other particles as neighbors.
4. Velocity
   The velocity of a particle is updated using equation (4) and (5) respectively for global and local version of PSO respectively

$$v_{id}(t+1) = v_{id}(t) + c_1 * r_1 * \left(p_{id} - x_{id} \right) + c_2 * r_2 * \left(p_{gd} - x_{id} \right) \tag{4}$$

$$v_{id}\left(t+1\right) = v_{id}\left(t\right) + c_1{}^*r_1{}^*\left(p_{id} - x_{id}\right) + c_2{}^*r_2{}^*\left(p_{ld} - x_{id}\right) \tag{5}$$

Where

c_1 and c_2 are acceleration coefficients,
r_1 and r_2 are random vectors,
P_{gd} and p_{ld} are the global and local best particle respectively

5. Inertia Weight

    The first version of PSO developed by Eberhart (1995) has no inertia weight. Velocity clamping was used in PSO to prevent particle's uncontrolled increase of magnitude from current position. As swarm was not able to converge towards the promising position by clamping the velocity, a new parameter inertia weight ω was introduced (Shi, 1998) as shown in equation (6)

$$v_{id}\left(t+1\right) = \omega * v_{id}\left(t\right) + c_1 * r_1 * \left(p_{id}\left(t\right) - x_{id}\left(t\right)\right) + c_2 * r_2 * \left(p_{gd}\left(t\right) - x_{id}\left(t\right)\right)$$
$$v_i\left(t+1\right) = \omega^*v_i\left(t\right) + c_1{}^*r_1{}^*\left(p_i - x_i\right) + c_2{}^*r_2{}^*\left(p_g - x_i\right)$$
$$v_i\left(t+1\right) = \omega^*v_i\left(t\right) + c_1{}^*r_1{}^*\left(p_i - x_i\right) + c_2{}^*r_2{}^*\left(p_g - x_i\right)$$
$$v_i\left(t+1\right) = \omega^*v_i\left(t\right) + c_1{}^*r_1{}^*\left(p_i - x_i\right) + c_2{}^*r_2{}^*\left(p_g - x_i\right) v_i\left(t+1\right) = \omega^*v_i\left(t\right) + c_1{}^*r_1{}^*\left(p_i - x_i\right) + c_2{}^*r_2{}^*\left(p_g - x_i\right)$$
$$\tag{6}$$

The inertia weight defines the impact of the previous velocity of each particle to the current one and controls the scope of search. Poli, Kennedy & Blackwell (2007) interpreted it as the fluidity of the medium in which particles move.

6. Constriction Factor

    An important variant of standard PSO is the constriction coefficient approach of Contemporary PSO (CPSO), which was proposed by Clerc and Kennedy (2002). The velocity of CPSO is updated by equation (7)

$$v_{id}\left(t+1\right) = \chi * \left(v_{id}\left(t\right) + \varphi_1\left(p_{id}\left(t\right) - x_{id}\left(t\right)\right) + \varphi_2\left(p_{gd}\left(t\right) - x_{id}\left(t\right)\right)\right) \tag{7}$$

PARAMETER TUNING AND CONTROL

In the literature of evolutionary computation parameter settings fall into two categories - parameter tuning and parameter control (Eiben, 1999). Parameters are configured prior to the process of implementation in parameter tuning. The approach of finding proper values before applying the optimization process is called parameter tuning. The optimal values of the parameters can be used for a wide range of optimization problems. The algorithm may have different parameters and every parameter can be tuned separately.

The following methods of parameter tuning are discussed in the literature-

- **ANOVA or Design of Experiments** Birattari, Stutzle, Paquete, & Varrentrapp, 2002; Yuan & Gallagher, 2004; Bartz-Beielstein, Lasarczyk, & Preuss, 2005; Nannen & Eiben 2007)
- **F-Race algorithm** (Birattari et al., 2002; Yuan & Gallagher, 2004) and **Random Sampling Design F-Race (RSD/F-Race)** (Balaprakash, Birattari, & Stutzle, 2007)
- **ANOVA or Design of Experiments**
  ANOVA is a rigorous approach used for parameter tuning. Consider algorithm with 3 parameters and each with 6 different values. Testing requires $3^6 = 729$ setups for one run. Each experimental setup has to be executed more than once to get reliable results. If we perform 30 independent runs for each setup, one has to perform 7290 steps. It is computationally extensive.
- **F-Race Algorithm** and **Random Sampling Design F-Race (RSD/F-Race)**
  F-Race uses the non-parametric Friedman's two-way analysis of variance by rank (Birattari et al., 2002). Parameter values are sampled initially. Birattari et al. (2002) used a full factorial design (FFD) on the parameter space. The Friedman's two-way analysis of variance by rank test is used to discard ranges that perform significantly worse than the best range. A drawback of a FFD is to select the levels of each parameter. Though computationally less expensive than ANOVA, F-Race still requires a large number of runs.

Balaprakash et al. (2007) proposed the random sampling design. The initial elements are sampled according to some probability model in random sampling. The smaller range increases complexity while the wider range decreases sampling accuracy.

Tuning each parameter separately is time consuming. Hence the parameters can be tuned together and different combinations of these parameters can be verified. This leads to vast experimentation for tuning all the parameters. Hence theoretical analysis of the algorithm can be used to tune the parameters. Theoretical analysis help to tune the parameter but the theoretical analysis in general is done after simplification of the algorithm or problem at hand. Theoretical analysis of PSO is discussed in the article.

The static parameter tuning may lead to poor performance as optimal values of parameters may be different at different stages of the run. This leads to parameter control. Optimization process starts with initial configuration and then the values are changed dynamically during the process.

Parameter control is classified based on update mechanism and level of adaptation by Angeline (1995). Population, individual and component levels were considered with absolute and empirical rules as update mechanism. Hinterding, Michalewicz, & Peachey (1996) extended the classification proposed by Angeline (1995) by considering the environment level as an additional level of adaptation. Smith and Fogarty (1996) considered what is being adapted in the classification. Essential features and terminology were presented by Eiben et. al.(1995). The parameter control can be used depending on how, when and what is changed. The scope/level of change may be at population-level or individual-level. Ursem (2003) proposed a taxonomy that basically distinguishes "non adaptive control" and "adaptive control".

The terminology proposed by Eiben (1999) became standards in the field. Parameter control is based on following:

- What is changed? (Parameters e.g., representation, evaluation function, population size etc.)
- When is the change made? (The evidence upon which the change is carried out e.g. diversity of the population, generation number etc.)
- How is the change made? (Mechanism e.g., deterministic, implicit adaptation or explicit adaption)

Parameters can be controlled using rules or adaptively. The deterministic rule is used to control the parameter value in the iteration. This gives better performance for some cases but not in all cases. Hence the parameter control can be done using current state of the search.

THEORETICAL ANALYSIS OF PSO

Theoretical analysis of PSO is an important area of research. A few theoretical studies of particle trajectories can be found, which concentrate on simplified PSO systems (Ozcan, 1998; Ozcan, 1999; Bergh, 2002; Trelea, 2003; Clerc & Kennedy, 2002; Yasuda, Ide, & Iwasaki, 2003; Eberhart & Shi, 2001). Kennedy (1998) studied particle trajectory by considering PSO without inertia weight and constriction coefficient.

Kennedy considered one dimensional PSO and φ is used as in Equation (10) using Equations (8), (9)

$$\varphi_1 = c_1 * r_1 \tag{8}$$

$$\varphi_2 = c_2 * r_2 \tag{9}$$

$$\varphi = \varphi_1 + \varphi_2 \tag{10}$$

The velocity is updated using equation (11) without inertia weight or constriction coefficient.

$$v_{id}(t+1) = v_{id}(t) + \varphi_1\left(p_{id}(t) - x_{id}(t)\right) + \varphi_2\left(p_{gd}(t) - x_{id}(t)\right) \tag{11}$$

The position of the particle is updated as in equation (12).

$$x_{id}(t+1) = x_{id}(t) + v_{id}(t) + \varphi_1\left(p_{id}(t) - x_{id}(t)\right) + \varphi_2\left(p_{gd}(t) - x_{id}(t)\right) \tag{12}$$

Each particle follows the mean of the best positions as in Equation (13)

$$\frac{\varphi_1 \times p_i + \varphi_2 \times p_g}{\varphi_1 + \varphi_2} \tag{13}$$

Kennedy further simplified the PSO model and considered the constant best position of a particle. Hence velocity and particle update equations are further simplified as in Equation (14):

$$v(t+1) = \left(v(t) + \varphi_1(p - x)\right) \tag{14}$$

The experiments were performed on this model for $\varphi = 4$. Thus it was a simplified model where the behavior of one particle in one dimension, in the absence of stochasticity, and during stagnation was considered. Inertia, velocity clamping, or constriction was not considered. Also personal and global best were assumed to coincide. The work was extended by Ozcan and Mohan (1999). Multi-dimensional particles were covered by the model. This model also considered personal and global best as different. Under these assumptions, solutions for the trajectories of the particle were derived. The work addressed how particle trajectories are changed with φ_1 and φ_2 and how the behavior of the PSO depends on the value of $\varphi = \varphi_1 + \varphi_2$. The model suggests that $\varphi > 4$ may eventually leave the region of interest in the search space as leads to growth in the oscillations of the particles. The model predicts that particles exhibit bounded periodic oscillations for $\varphi < 4$.

Clerc and Kennedy's model (2002) considered one particle, one dimension, deterministic behavior with stagnation. The particle is a discrete-time linear dynamical system. The Eigenvalues and Eigenvectors of the state transition matrix are used for the dynamics of the state of the particle. The model predicted that the particle will converge to equilibrium if the magnitude of the eigenvalues is smaller than 1. The Eigenvalues of the system are functions of the parameters specifically φ.

Bergh (2002) modeled one particle, with no stochasticity during stagnation, and considered PSO with an inertia weight. Model provided an explicit solution for the trajectory of the particle. The model highlighted on the particles are attracted towards a fixed point corresponding to the weighted sum of neighborhood best and personal best with weights φ_1 and φ_2. Arguments were also put forward as the analysis would be valid also in the presence of stochasticity.

A model using the multidimensional and multiparticle approach was proposed by Kamalapur & Patil (2012). The model considered PSO with constriction coefficient. The particle trajectory of initial PSO variant without inertia weight and without constriction coefficient was also considered for comparison. The model considered personal and global best. The particles surf on the wave. A derivation of the closed from of PSO with constriction coefficient was provided.

STATES OF PSO

Following four states are observed in PSO-

1. **Exploration:** During the initial stage of the run every particle should explore its own best (personal best), so the evolutionary state is an exploration state. Every particle follows its own best position and does not follow the current best in the neighborhood. This avoids a crowding about the current best and in turn avoids trapping in the local optima.
2. **Exploitation:** The particles interact with each other and use the information to update their own position. Thus, learning from the neighborhood and encouraging particle to follow the neighborhood's best may lead to the exploitation state. In this state the particles may be trapped into the local optima.
3. **Convergence:** Learning from the neighborhood and encouraging the particle to follow the neighborhood best may lead to the convergence state. This may lead it to find the global optimum.
4. **Jumping Out:** The current best particle may be moving away from the crowd already formed by the particles. This leads to jumping out of the local optima and going toward the global optima.

The state of the population can be viewed by the swarm diversity. There is a crowding of particles when the particles are converging towards either local or global optima and the diversity is less. Different techniques are used to find the diversity of the particles in the swarm. Diversity can be measured from the perspective of position of the particles, velocity of the particles as speed and direction of particles. Shi & Eberhart (2008) proposed different diversity measures for PSO.

PARAMETER TUNING AND CONTROL FOR PSO

Pedersen & Chipperfield (2010) have demonstrated that a satisfactory performance can be achieved with basic PSO when its parameters are tuned properly. Parameters setting plays an important role in the performance of the algorithm and different parameter settings are needed for a problem instance as well as for different optimization stages of that instance.

1. Swarm Size

An appropriate swarm size plays a key role in the performance of PSO (Tan, 2001). Theoretical studies shows large swarm size have emphasize on better exploration while small swarm size may lead to exploitation. Large swarm size increases computational cost. Swarm Size varies from 20 to 60 (Clerc (2006), Eberhart & Kennedy (1995)).

The swarm size is approximated using Equation (15)

$$s = 10 + \left[2* sqrt(D) \right] \tag{15}$$

As the number of dimensions increase swarm size increases which leads to increase in computational cost. To address this problem the swarm size can be controlled on-the-fly. The computational cost can be reduced by adjusting the swarm size dynamically. The swarm size can be controlled using deterministic approach or using state of the search. The swarm size can be set to a predefined value and then as per iteration, the number of particles in the swarm can be increased or decreased. The swarm size can be set to a predefined value and then as per the stated information, the number of particles in the swarm can be increased or decreased.

In PSO the particles are independent, so each particle will survive till the end of the search but the adaptive PSO proposed by Hu & Eberhart (2002) introduced re-randomization rate. There is death of the old particles and birth of new particles. Environment detection and response were added to PSO. Two environment detection methods were introduced changed-gBest-value method and fixed-gBest-value method. Both these methods successfully detected dynamic changes. The changed-gBestvalue method was fast but required extra time to re-evaluate the fitness while the fixed-gBest-value method was slow but capable of being used in any situation. The strategy of re-randomization with respect to response to the detection of environment changes was used. As per testing 10% re-randomization rate is a good choice for most cases. An alternative method used was to re-randomize the gBest particle.

2. **Inertia Weight**

The inertia weight defines the impact of previous velocity of each particle to the current one and controls the scope of search. Poli et al. (2007) interpreted it as the fluidity of the medium in which the particles move. Inertia weight can be tuned statically for fixed value. The analysis is done using discrete time dynamical system theory. Eberhart & Shi (2000) empirically evaluated an inertia weight of 0.729.

The performance degrades by keeping the inertia weight constant. Over the past few years, several inertia weight strategies have been proposed to improve the performance of PSO. Inertia weight value is dynamically adjusted based on with and without feedback.

Fixed Control of Inertia Weight as Per Generation Number Without Feedback

Researchers suggested that the inertia weight should be in the range [0.9, 1.2]. Many variations of PSO were proposed based on selecting value of inertia weight. These variations are briefly discussed here -

An inertia weight value starting from 0.9 linearly decreasing to 0.4 improves the performance (Shi, 1998; Shi 1999). Linearly decreasing inertia weight strategy (LDIW) is represented using Equation (16)

$$\omega\left(t\right) = \left(\omega_{max} - \omega_{min}\right)\left(\frac{T_{max} - t}{T_{max}}\right) + \omega_{min} \tag{16}$$

As the value of inertia weight linearly decreases with time, the searching varies from exploratory phase, towards the refinement of local search at the end. Though linearly decreasing inertia weight strategy has ability to converge it may fall into local optimum.

Linearly increasing inertia weight value was tested by Zheng (2003). Linearly increasing inertia weight improves convergence ability. Four standard test functions with asymmetric initial range settings were used for testing.

Adriansyah & Amin (2006) investigated the performance of the PSO algorithm with sigmoid decreasing. The sigmoid function has contributed in getting minimum fitness function. The quick convergence ability and aggressive movement narrowing towards the solution region is observed with different sigmoid constant in combination of sigmoid function and linear increasing inertia weight.

Inertia weight is adjusted according to the probability so that the PSO can be adapted for complex condition. This was done by Gao & Duan (2007) using random inertia weight.

A chaotic mapping was used to set the inertia weight coefficient for chaotic inertia weight (Feng et el. 2007). Logistic mapping used here is two strategies of chaotic descending inertia weight (CDIW) and chaotic random inertia weight (CRIW), proposed by Feng et al. (2007). It is a nonlinear dynamic system. Chaos is sensitive to the initial value of inertia weight. The aim of CDIW is to avoid trapping in local optimum which is observed in LDIW.

The inertia weight is calculated for each iteration as in Equation (17)

$$\omega\left(t\right) = \left(\omega_{max} - \omega_{min}\right)\left(\frac{T_{max} - t}{T_{max}}\right) + \omega_{min} \times z_{k+1} \tag{17}$$

Where z_k is k^{th} chaotic number. The two strategies alter the constant item of the linear descending inertia weight and the random inertia weight into "chaotic item" (Feng et el. 2007).

Three oscillating inertia weight functions of time were proposed by Kentzoglanakis & Poole (2009). Oscillating inertia weight provides periodical transition between exploration and exploitation state. A set of three oscillating inertia weight functions of time were proposed which periodically alternate between global and local search waves or exploitation and exploration. So there are periodical transitions of the swarm from exploratory to exploitation states of search

The logarithm decreasing inertia weight with chaos mutation operator was proposed by Gao et al. (2008) as shown in Equation (18). To improve the convergence speed, logarithmic decreasing inertia weight was introduced while chaos mutation was used to overcome the premature convergence as well to increase the diversity of the population.

$$\omega(t) = \omega_{max} + \left(\omega_{min} - \omega_{max}\right) \times \log_{10}\left(a + 10 \times t \times T_{max}\right) \tag{18}$$

Two natural exponent inertia weight strategies based on the basic idea of decreasing inertia weight(DIW) were proposed by Chen et al. (2006). These two new strategies as in Equation (19) and (20) converge faster than linear one during the early stage of the search process (Chen et al., 2006).

$$\omega(t) = \omega_{min} + \left(\omega_{max} - \omega_{min}\right) \times e^{\left|\dfrac{t/MAXITER}{10}\right|} \tag{19}$$

$$\omega(t) = \omega_{min} + \left(\omega - \omega_{min}\right) \times e^{\left|\dfrac{t/MAXITER}{4}\right|^2} \tag{20}$$

Li & Gao (2009a, 2009b) proposed exponent decreasing inertia weights with stochastic mutation. Exponent decreasing inertia weights is specified to improve the convergence speed while stochastic mutations is used to improve the diversity of the swarm in order to overcome premature convergence and oscillatory occurrences (Li & Gao, 2009a, 2009b).

Maca & Pech (2015) proposed inertia weight modifications based on random numbers generated using the beta distribution. The approach balances exploratory and exploitive search.

Figure 1 shows convergence observed using linearly decreasing inertia weight, linearly increasing inertia weight, non linear decreasing inertia weight, oscillating inertia weight and chaotic inertia weight strategies. Here r_1 and r_2 are considered as n dimensional vector while c_1 and c_2 are considered as constant 1.496. Rastrigin benchmark function is considered here for experimentation.

Particles converge faster in case of linearly increasing, chaotic, oscillating and random inertia weight strategies as compared to other strategies. This can be observed from Figure 2. Inertia weight variations are shown in Figure 2. Inertia weight values vary up and down in case of chaotic, oscillating and random inertia weight strategies during the iterations.

Figure 1. Particle position for different inertia weight strategies

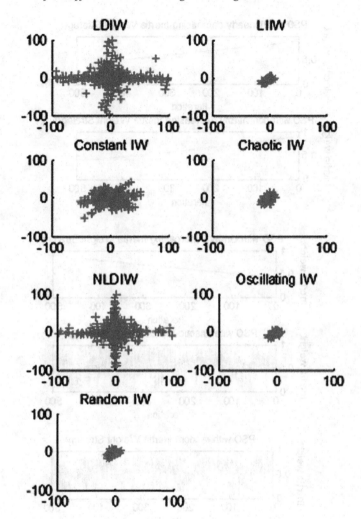

Generation number or iteration does not reflect state of the population or convergence hence strategies of adaptive control of inertia weight based on fitness value and population diversity as feedback mechanism were proposed by the researchers.

Adaptive Control of Inertia Weight Using Fitness Value as Feedback Mechanism

Shi & Eberhart (2001) proposed a fuzzy adaptive inertia weight method in which the range of best candidate solutions was used to adjust the inertia weight. Shi & Eberhart (2001) strongly believed that the convergence and dynamic performance could still be improved by elaborating more on incorporating fuzzy computations into it. Almost all inertia weight variations show poor performance on Rosenbrock function.

Figure 2. Inertia weight variations during 500 iterations

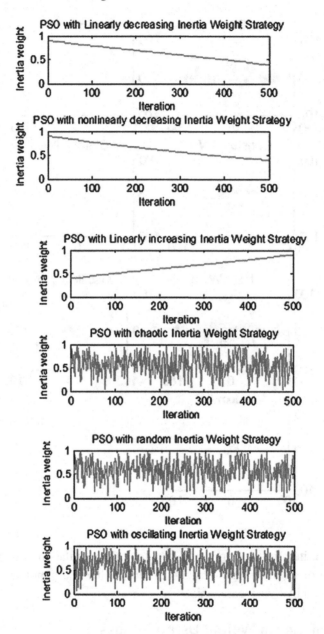

Adaptive Inertia Weight strategy was proposed by Nikabadi & Ebadzadeh (2008) to overcome the weakness of premature convergence to local minimum and to improve its searching capability. Population diversity was controlled by adaptive adjustment of Inertia Weight.

Adaptive threshold mutation PSO (AMPSO) proposed by Li and Gao (2009) aims at the phenomenon of premature convergence. AMPSO used the adaptive exponent decreasing inertia weight, a dynamic adaptive changing threshold and mutation of the particles satisfying threshold by average distance of the particle. Proposed AMPSO adaptively adjusts the threshold.

Though fitness values as feedback mechanism improve convergence this may lead to premature convergence. Strategies of adaptive control of inertia weight based on population distribution as feedback mechanism were proposed to maintain diversity and improve convergence.

Adaptive Control of Inertia Weight Using Diversity of the Population or Population Distribution as Feedback Mechanism

A novel self-adaptive particle swarm optimization algorithm (SAPSO) proposed by Li, Fu, & Zhang (2008) deals with premature convergence. The exploitative state and exploration state for each particle were considered in the SAPSO algorithm. A particle activity metrics was defined to reflect its current exploration capability. Activity threshold gets updated with time. Before updating a particle, its activity gets computed. Depending on activity metric and the activity threshold, particle stays in exploration state or the exploitative state. A self-adjusted inertia weight varies dynamically with each particle's evolution degree. Simulation and comparisons were based on non-noisy problems and noisy problems. It was verified that SAPSO is effective, efficient and robust.

Zhan, Zhang, Li & Chung (2009) proposed an adaptive particle swarm optimization (APSO). A real-time evolutionary state estimation procedure identifies one of the four defined evolutionary states exploration, exploitation, convergence and jumping out. During initial stage of the run every particle should explore its own best (personal best), so the evolutionary state is exploration state. Every particle follows its own best position and do not follow current best in the neighborhood. This avoids crowding about current best and in turn avoids trapping in local optima. APSO is based on evolutionary state estimation and elitist learning strategy using automatic control of inertia weight, acceleration coefficients.

Cheng, Shi, Qin, & Ting (2012) proposed two inertia weight strategies based on fitness value and population diversity. Inertia weight is randomly generated initially within the range [0.4, 0.9] for each particle. Inertia weight is not changed if there is improvement in global fitness value and changed in case of no improvement. The inertia weight is changed based on the distribution of particles. The inertia weight will be close to minimum if the global best particle is close to the centre of swarm, it will be close to maximum otherwise. The minimum increment in inertia weight in initial stages of search enhances the ability of exploration. The maximum decrement in inertia weight at the end of the search there by enhancing the ability of exploitation.

Particle swarm optimization with multiple adaptive methods (PSO-MAM) proposed by Hu, Wu, & Weir (2013) is based on the distance between each particle and global best particle. Li, Cheng, Chen (2014) proposed adaptive inertia weight feedback is based on iterative number, aggregation degree of swarm and the improved evolution speed of each particle. Chaotic disturbance is added to jump out of local optima.

Self regulating PSO (SRPSO) (Tanweer, Suresh, & Sundararajan, 2015) uses self regulating inertia weight in which the global best particle accelerates in same direction as it is in search of global optimum. All particles other than global best follow linearly decreasing inertia weight. Exploration improves because of self regulating inertia weight.

3. Acceleration Coefficients

Acceleration coefficients c_1 and c_2 indicate cognitive and social influence value respectively. Acceleration coefficients balance exploration and exploitation. Acceleration coefficients are essential to the success of PSO (Kennedy 1997). Eberhart & Shi (2000) empirically evaluated acceleration coefficients of 1.496 for convergence.

The search capability of PSO is affected by c_1 and c_2 values. The bias may occur towards personal best or social best. Figure 3 illustrates 500 positions generated by for current position (0, 0) considering different c_1 and c_2 values with one and n dimensional r_1 and r_2. If one dimensional r_1 and r_2 are random values, then particle positions are restricted in parallelepiped region as shown in Figure 1. In case of n dimensional r1 and r_2 values particle positions are in all directions. If c_1 and c_2 values are set to two then the particles are more scattered.

Exploration and exploitation of swarm are influenced by these values. By keeping these values constant affects convergence. Hence acceleration coefficient values are controlled based on the evidence upon which the change is carried out or adaptation evidences.

Fixed Control of Acceleration Coefficient Without Feedback as Per Generation Number

Kennedy (1997, 1998) suggested a fixed value 2.0 for acceleration coefficients. Suganthan (1999) tested a method of linearly decreasing acceleration coefficients c_1, c_2 with time and found that the fixed acceleration coefficients of value 2 generate better solutions.

A new parameter automation strategy of time varying acceleration coefficients for the PSO was proposed by Ratnaweera Halgamuge & Watson (2004). The cognitive component was reduced and the social component was increased with change in the acceleration coefficients c_1 and c_2 with time. With time varying acceleration the particles move around the search space with decreasing cognitive component and increasing social component and allowed the particles to converge to the global best with time. It has been identified from the results that the best range for c_1 and c_2 are 2.5 to 0.5 and 0.5 to 2.5, respectively (Ratnaweera et al., 2004).

Acceleration Coefficient Control Using Fitness Value as Feedback Mechanism

Acceleration coefficients are in general particle-independent. The convergence rate may be reduced as the personal best position is not used while controlling acceleration coefficients. Arumugam, Chandramohan, & Rao (2005) proposed PSO approaches in terms of the global and local best values and the standard PSO. The inertia weight and the acceleration coefficient were defined as a function of personal best and global best.

Cai, Cui, & Tan (2009) proposed a predicted modified particle swarm optimization with time-varying acceleration coefficients, in which acceleration coefficients are adjusted by exploring the velocity information.

Using best position to control acceleration coefficients leads to exploration or exploitation. Strategies to control acceleration coefficients are proposed based on population diversity to overcome this.

Acceleration Coefficient Control Using Diversity of the Population or Population Distribution as Feedback Mechanism

Zhan et al. (2009) proposed an adaptive particle swarm optimization (APSO). It consists of two main steps. First step is evaluation of the population distribution and particle fitness. Second step is to perform

Figure 3. Particle positions generated (a) c1 and c2=1 (b) c3=2 (c) c1 and c2=1.496

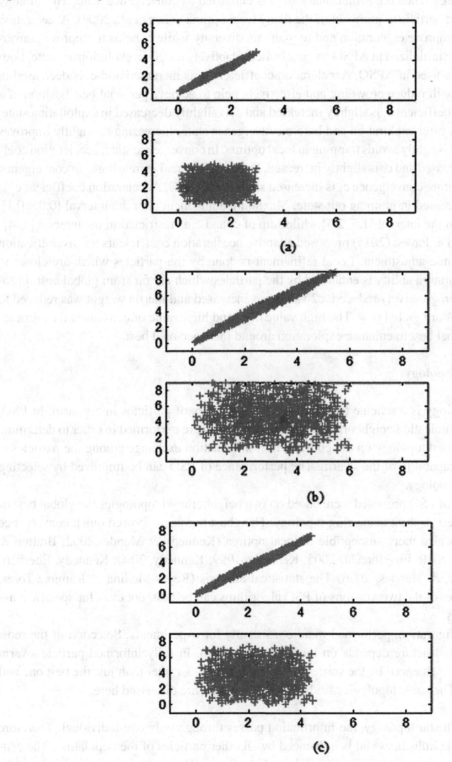

an elitist learning strategy when the evolutionary state is classified as convergence state. The strategy acts on the globally best particle to jump out of the likely local optima (Zhan et al., 2009). Acceleration coefficient c_1 helps to improve exploration and to maintain diversity while c_2 helps to improve convergence. Both c_1 and c_2 are initialized in APSO and controlled adaptively based on evolutionary state. Four different strategies were used in APSO. Acceleration coefficient c_1 is increased and c_2 is decreased in exploration state. This will reduce crowding and effectively help to achieve personal best position of a particle. Acceleration coefficient c_1 is slightly increased and c_2 is slightly decreased in exploitation state. Exploitation may occur after exploration and before convergence state. Increasing c_1 slightly improves search and decreasing c_2 slightly avoids trapping in local optima. In convergence state, acceleration coefficient c_1 is slightly increased and c_2 is slightly increased. Decreasing c_1 and increasing c_2 in convergence state may lead to premature convergence c_1 is increased slightly in APSO. Acceleration coefficient c_1 is decreased and c_2 is increased in jumping out state. Maximum adjustment is in the interval [0.05, 0.1]. c_1 and c_2 are clamped in the interval [1.5, 2.5] while sum of c_1 and c_2 is restricted in the interval [3, 4]

Ardizzon, Cavazzini & Pavesi (2015) proposed adaptive acceleration coefficients for diversification in PSO based on dynamic adjustment. Local refinement is done by the particles which are closer to global best while exploration ability is enhanced by the particles which are far from global best. In local refinement c_1 was progressively reduced, c2 value was increased and inertia weight was reduced to make more attracted toward global best. The high value of c_1 and high value of c_2 allowed the particles which are far from global best to enhance exploration around their personal best.

4. Neighborhood Topology

Neighborhood topology is a scheme to determine the neighbors of particles in a swarm. In PSO, each particle has communication neighborhood so several studies were performed in order to determine effect of the neighborhood topology on the convergence. Information exchange among the particles is related to exploration capability of the swarm. The performance of PSO can be improved by selecting proper neighborhood topology.

Initial two versions of PSO proposed were based on two neighborhood topologies the global best or gbest PSO and local best or lbest using ring topology. The gbest topology showed quick convergence than lbest, but gbest is also more susceptible to local optima (Kennedy & Mendes,2002; Bratton & Kennedy, 2007; Clerc, 2010; Engelbrecht, 2005; Kennedy, 1999; Kennedy, 2000; Kennedy, Eberhart, & Shi, 2001; Kennedy, & Mendes, 2006) The statistical analysis (Reyes-Medina & Ramirez-Tores, 2011) shows that neither of the two versions of PSO algorithms can be best, not even for specific class of benchmark problems.

Von Neumann configuration, performed more consistently for experiments. Selection of the most efficient neighborhood structure depends on the type of problem. In fully informed particle swarm (FIPS), each particle is influenced by the success of all its Neighbors, rather than just the best one and itself (Mendes, 2003).The static topologies studied in the literature are discussed here:

- **Star Topology:** In star topology, the information passes through only one individual. Therefore one central particle influences and is influenced by all other particles of the population. The central particle of the star topology can be selected randomly. The central particle compares the performance of every individual particle in the population and adjusts its own trajectory toward the best.

- **Ring or lbest Topology:** In the ring topology, the neighbors are closely connected. Kennedy & Mendes considered the ring topology to be the slowest, most indirect communication (Kennedy & Mendes, 2002). Each particle interacts only with its immediate neighbor, given a reasonably large population with uniform distribution. PSO algorithms using the ring topology are able to form stable niches across different local neighborhoods. This eventually locates multiple global/local optima (Engelbrecht, 2013a). "Wrap-around" ring topology was used by Xiaodong Li (2002) where the first particle is the neighbor of the last particle and vice versa. Ring or lbest shows slow convergence.
- **Mesh Topology:** In mesh topology one node is connected to several nodes. The particles on the mesh's center have four adjacent particles in the Neighborhood while the particles on the mesh's boundaries have three adjacent neighbors. There is redundancy because each particle has overlapping neighbors.
- **Tree or Hierarchical Topology:** Tree topology has a root node particle which is connected to one or more individuals that are one level below in the hierarchy which in turn connected to one level lower in the hierarchy. The tree topology is constructed as a binary tree.
- **Toroidal Topology:** The toroidal topology is modified mesh topology where all particles in the swarm have four adjacent Neighbors. The toroidal topology connects every corner particle with its symmetrical neighbor. The same occurs with the toroid boundaries.

Ring topology is simple and efficient. It shows good convergence rate. Toroidal topology also shows good convergence rate. Different neighborhood topologies have been proposed to improve the performance of PSO. The results show that PSO with a small neighborhood may achieve better performance for complex problems. Particles may get trapped in local optima in case of global best PSO. This is the reason the local best PSO model is preferred. But in case of local best PSO speed of convergence is reduced.

Neighborhood Control Without Feedback as Per Generation Number

Suganthan (1999) introduced gradual increase in neighborhood size of a particle till all particles in a swarm become neighbor. Suganthan (1999) suggested initial search with lbest ring lattice and then slowly increasing the size of the neighborhood. Hu and Eberhart (2002) suggested m-nearest particles in the neighborhood. Peram Veeramachaneni, & Mohan (2003) developed the fitness-distance-ratio-based PSO (FDR-PSO) which selects one particle having higher fitness value and is nearer to the particle being updated . Population diversity rapidly decreases in PSO while FDR-PSO maintains population diversity. Hence FDR-PSO is less likely to trap in local optima.

Lim and Isa (2014a) proposed variant of PSO with linearly increasing topology connectivity and shuffling mechanism. A new velocity update strategy was used with a new neighborhood search operator. Shuffling mechanism prevents particle to trap in local optima while linear increasing topology connectivity balances exploration and exploitation. This increasing topological connectivity performs better than PSO, Adaptive PSO, FIPSO, OLPSO, Self-organizing hierarchical PSO and modified PSO. PSO with adaptive time-varying topology connectivity (Lim and Isa, 2014b) vary topology connectivity based on searching performance. Adaptively varying topology connectivity with generation number improve exploration and exploitation search. These algorithms solve unconstrained optimization problems with continuous search space.

Neighborhood Control Using Fitness Value as Feedback Mechanism

Parsopoulos & Vrahatis (2004) recommended unified PSO (UPSO) by combining global and local version of PSO. Mendes et al introduced a fully informed PSO (Mendes, Kennedy, & Neves 2004) (FIPS) by considering fitness value of each particle to find the influence of neighbors.

Janson & Middendorf (2005) used dynamic hierarchy of particles. The particle moves upward in hierarchy with the best performance. Each particle is influenced by own best and the particle which is directly above it.

Clerc (2006) defined adaptive random topology in which each particle informs at random K (usually set to 3) particles. The graph of information link is modified at the beginning and after unsuccessful iteration. Clerc (2006) used TRIBES in which the neighborhood size evolves over time depending on the feedback. The population is divided into a subpopulation. Bad tribes get new members while good tribes may remove the weakest member from tribe to improve the convergence.

Beheshti, Shamsuddin, & Sulaiman (2013) employed both global and local topologies and proposed fusion global-local-topology to escape from the local optima.

5.   Velocity

The swarm explosion was the first issue addressed by researchers using velocity clamping. Velocity clamping prevents particles' uncontrolled increase of magnitude from current positions. There are various bound handling techniques discussed in literature to tune the parameter.

- Whenever the velocity goes beyond the threshold bound it is directly set to closest bound or threshold. Maximum velocity threshold (V_{max}) is used for clamping velocity. The velocity is bounded in -V_{max} to +V_{max}.
- Absorb or Zero

If velocity goes beyond threshold bound the velocity of the particle is set to 0.

Velocity of every particle is updated in iteration. Updated velocity may move the particle out of the search space. So velocity is restricted in the range as per search space.

- **Controlling Velocity Updates Using Generation Number as Fixed Control Without Feedback**
  Whenever the velocity goes beyond threshold bound then one of the following velocity bound handling method is used (Helwig, Branke, & Mostaghim, 2013) -
- **Nearest**
  The velocity is directly set to closest bound or threshold.
- **Absorb or Zero**
  The velocity of the particle is set to 0.
- **Deterministic Back**
  The velocity is set to feasible space depending on the distance of the particle from the boundary as in equation (21).

$$v_{id}\left(t+1\right) = -\lambda \times v_{id}\left(t+1\right) \qquad (21)$$

- **Random Back**
  The velocity is reversed back by multiplying with random value drawn from uniform distribution [0 1]
- **Adjust**
  The velocity is adjusted using position of the particle using Equation (22)

$$v_{id}(t+1) = x_{id}(t+1) - x_{id}(t) \qquad (22)$$

- **Hyperbolic**
  If velocity goes beyond threshold bound it is normalized using Equations (23), (24)

$$v_{id}(t+1) = \frac{v_{id}(t+1)}{1 + \frac{v_{id}(t+1)}{\max(x_{id}(t+1)) - x_{id}(t+1)}} \quad \text{if } v_{id}(t+1) > 0 \qquad (23)$$

$$v_{id}(t+1) = \frac{v_{id}(t+1)}{1 + \frac{v_{id}(t+1)}{x_{id}(t+1) - \min(x_{id}(t+1))}} \quad \text{if } v_{id}(t+1) < 0 \qquad (24)$$

FDR-PSO was proposed by Pearm et al (2003) based on relative fitness-distance-ratio. The velocity of the particle is updated not just by using personal and global best but also using nearest best particle in neighbor by introducing additional term in velocity update equation.

Jin Liang, Tian, & Zhuang (2013) proposed three variants of PSO, particle swarm optimization with random dimension selection, particle swarm optimization with heuristic dimension selection and particle swarm optimization with distance based dimension selection algorithm. Randomness from velocity update equation was removed in these variants. The first variant adds randomness for selecting the dimension, second variant used deterministic rule to select dimension and distance to global particle is used in third variant for dimensionality selection for velocity updation.

Enhanced leader PSO was proposed using a five staged successive mutation strategy by Jordehi (2015) to overcome premature convergence.

Velocity Updates Using Fitness Values as Feedback Mechanism

Li & Yang (2009) presented adaptive learning PSO (ALPSO) based on learning strategies for velocity updation. Each particle learns from the global best, personal best, and the personal best of the closest particle. Each particle adjusts the behavior using the above learning strategies and the random position generated around the particle. Selection ratio is assigned to these operators as per the reward value. Progress value and reward value is calculated to decide the operator. This work was extended and a self learning PSO (SLPSO) was proposed with four strategies of velocity updations. In SLPSO, each particle has a set of four strategies to cope with different situations. The co-operation of four strategies is implemented by an adaptive learning framework at the individual level. This enables particle to choose the optimal strategy according to its own local fitness. Some new features are introduced in SLPSO. Two strategies in ALPSO are replaced by two new strategies. A particle learns from only the particles whose personal bests are better than the particle's personal best using a biased selection method. The method of the frequency parameter updation in ALPSO is replaced by a new one. A super particle is introduced. Users do not need to tune the parameters in spite of introduction of new parameters. The experimental study on a set of 45 test functions and two real-world problems had been carried out. SLPSO enables a particle to adaptively adjust its search behavior during the search process for global optimization problems.

A cooperative particle swarm optimizer (CPSO-H) (Bergh & Engelbrecht, 2004) searches each dimension separately using one dimensional swarm to improve the performance. Particle learns from the experience of the other particle in different dimension in comprehensive learning PSO. This learning strategy proved effective to generate better quality solutions. Population manager varies size of neighborhood and the best information is shared among the particles using efficient population utilization strategy PSO.

The learning is probabilistically directed by the personal best of same particle or the personal best of other particles in CLPSO. The selection of exemplar is random in comprehensive learning PSO. So particle may not be guided properly. In a dynamic neighborhood learning based PSO (DNLPSO) (Nasir, Das, Maity, Sengupta, Halder, & Suganthan, 2012) the particle learns simultaneously from the best particle in the neighborhood, personal best of itself or the personal best of some other particle from its neighborhood. Though exemplar is random, neighborhood is changed periodically for proper exploration. DNLPSO improves the performance of CLPSO.

Lim & Isa (2014a, 2014b) proposed PSO with adaptive time-varying topology connectivity. Topology connectivity of a particle adaptively increases and randomly shuffles with time based on searching performance and location of particle in different sub-regions of search space. A new neighborhood search operator as searching strategy is used as alternative learning strategy to enhance the performance.

Two heterogeneous subpopulations of swarm are used in heterogeneous comprehensive learning PSO (Lynn & Suganthan, 2015). The subpopulations enhance either exploration or exploitation. Comprehensive learning strategy is used in both subpopulations to generate the exemplar using personal best experiences of the particle.

Self-Regulating PSO (SRPSO) (Tanweer et al, 2015) employed a self-regulated learning and self-perception strategies and velocity is updated using equation (25)

$$v_{id}\left(t+1\right) = v_{id}\left(t\right) + c_1 * r_1 * selfc * \left(p_{id} - x_{id}\right) + c_2 * r_2 * socialc * \left(p_{gd} - x_{id}\right) \tag{25}$$

Selfc is 0 for best particle otherwise 1.

Beheshti, Mariyam, & Shamsuddin (2014) introduced centripetal accelerated particle swarm optimization (CAPSO) using Newton's laws of motion. To deal with the problem of trapping in local optimum CAPSO uses median position of particle, current fitness of particle and worst fitness of swarm.

Velocity confinement methods and parameters such as inertia weight, neighborhood of the particle have major impact on PSO performance. Kamalapur & Patil (2014) tested variations of the PSO with adaptive random link neighborhood. The performance of adaptive random link PSO by geometrical updation of velocity with confinement methods was tested. Neighborhood of each particle is randomly varied based on the fitness value. If there is no improvement after threshold number of iterations then the neighborhood is randomly set. Positive correlation is observed in all proposed variations for adaptive random neighborhood PSO with varying link structure after ten unsuccessful iterations (Kamalapur & Patil, 2014).

Velocity Updates Using Diversity of the Population or Population Distribution as Feedback Mechanism

Riget & Vesterstrom (2002) explored attraction repulsion PSO (ARPSO) based on population diversity. ARPSO encourages high diversity and discourages premature convergence. Repulsion phase is introduced in case of drop of diversity below threshold. When diversity reaches threshold switches to attraction phase. Pant, Thangaraj & Singh (2007) modified ARPSO by positive conflict phase in between attraction and repulsion phase. Mutation is performed instead of repulsion phase to enhance diversity (Sun, Xu & Fang 2006). Though these strategies improve performance these are computationally expensive.

6. Position Updates

Researchers proposed probabilistic PSO algorithms by simulated trajectory of the particle using a random number generator, from a distribution. Popular among this is the bare bones particle swarm optimization (Kennedy, 2003).

Kennedy (2004) proposed bare bones particle swarm optimization (BBPSO) algorithm by adopting position updating using Gaussian distribution. The velocity update changes to Equation (26)

$$v_{id}\left(t+1\right) \sim N\left(\frac{y_{id}\left(t\right)+\hat{y}_{id}\left(t\right)}{2},\sigma\right), \sigma = \left|y_{id}\left(t\right)-\hat{y}_{id}\left(t\right)\right| \tag{26}$$

The position update changes to Equation (27)

$$x_{id}\left(t+1\right) = v_{id}\left(t+1\right) \tag{27}$$

BBPSO suffers of the premature while solving multimodal problems.

Quantum PSO (Sun, Feng & Xu (2004), Sun, Xu & Feng (2005)) was inspired by quantum mechanics and belongs to BBPSO family. Pant et al (2008, 2009) proposed variants using recombination operator based on interpolation and Sobal mutation operator.

Liu, Qin, Shi & Lu (2007) introduced center particle swarm optimization (CPSO) algorithm. A center particle guides search direction, its position is considered as the average of the other particles. Position updations of all other particles remain same.

Pant, Thangaraj & Abraham (2008) proposed two new variants of PSO called Adaptive Mutation Based PSO (AMPSO1 and AMPSO2). Both of these algorithms used adaptive mutation using Beta distribution. AMPSO1 mutates the personal best position of the swarm while AMPSO2 mutates the global best swarm position. The performance of AMPSO1 and AMPSO2 was evaluated on twelve unconstrained test problems and three real life constrained problems taken from the field of Electrical Engineering. AMPSO2 has shown good results for unconstrained test problems.

Krohling & Mendel (2009) proposed BBPSO with a jump strategy in case no improvement is observed on the value of the objective function. The jump strategy was applied using Gaussian or Cauchy distributions.

BBPSO with scale matrix adaptation (SMA-BBPSO) (Campos, Krohling & Enriquez, 2014) investigated a self-adaptive heavy-tailed distribution for selecting new positions and a deterministic rule for adaptation of the scale matrix to update the position of a particle. This balances exploration and exploitation.

Earlier PSO variants were biased and rotationally variant because of dimension by dimension method. Clerc (2012) proposed Standard PSO 2011 version to overcome the bias which modifies velocity in a geometrical way. Three Standard PSO algorithms have been defined so far SPSO2006, SPSO2007 and SPSO2011. PSO finds optimum value easily if it lies on axis or on the center of the system coordinate axis. SPSO 2011 improves the earlier system which was sensitive to the system of coordinates. For all three Standard PSO algorithms random position is initialized inside the search space for each particle according to uniform distribution. All three versions of SPSO use same inertia weight and acceleration coefficient value as 0.721 and 1.193 respectively. Clerc (2012) has defined adaptive random topology, which is used in all three versions of SPSO. SPSO uses Absorb or Zero confinement method for velocity when the position of the particle moves away from the boundary.

The positions of particles are updated synchronously in original PSO. An asynchronous update was introduced by Carlisle & Dozier (2001). Fitness of all particles is evaluated and sent in the neighborhood in synchronous PSO. Here velocity and position of the particle are updated only after receiving the best fitness value in the neighborhood. Velocity and position of the particle are updated based on current best value received in asynchronous PSO. Asynchronous PSO is considered as faster and less costly (Carlisle & Dozier, 2001).

Random asynchronous PSO (Rada-Vilela, Zhang & Seah, 2011a;2011b; 2012; 2013) selects the particle for evaluation and updation at random using uniform distribution in each iteration. Particles may get perfect information or imperfect information with varied degree of imperfectness. The quality of the result goes down with increasing neighborhood size in asynchronous PSO and random asynchronous.

There is no statistically significant difference between synchronous and asynchronous updates for all of the algorithms for most of the functions (Engelbrecht, 2013b).

7. Constriction Coefficient

Clerc (1999) indicates that use of a constriction coefficient may be necessary to insure convergence of the particle swarm algorithm. The performance of particle swarm optimization using an inertia weight and using a constriction coefficient was compared by Eberhart & Shi (2002).

Velocity updation using constriction coefficient as shown in Equation (10) and the constriction coefficient is calculated using equation (28).

$$\chi = \frac{2}{\left| 2 - \varphi - \sqrt{\varphi^2 - 4\varphi} \right|} \tag{28}$$

In all cases for which Clerc's (1999) constriction method was used, φ was set to 4.1 and the constant multiplier χ was calculated as 0.729. Eberhart & Shi (2002) pointed out that constriction coefficient is equivalent to inertia weight.

PSO VARIANT ANALYSIS

PSO variant analysis is shown in Table 1.

Table 1. PSO variant

PSO Variant	Remark
Adaptive PSO	Re-randomization rate
A modified PSO optimizer	Linearly decreasing inertia weight (IW) strategy
PSO with an increasing IW	Linearly increasing IW
PSO with sigmoid decreasing IW	Sigmoid IW
A new PSO with random IW	IW is adjusted according to the probability
Chaotic inertia weight in PSO	The two strategies alter the constant item of the linear descending IW and the random IW into "chaotic item
Chaotic PSO based on adaptive IW	Oscillating IW provides periodical transition between global search
Oscillating IW	velocity and position of the particle are updated only after receiving the best fitness value in the neighborhood
PSO with logarithmic decreasing inertia weight and Chaos Mutation	Improves the convergence speed, overcomes the premature convergence
Natural exponent decreasing IW strategy in PSO	Converge faster during the early stage of the search process
PSO with Exponent Decreasing IW and Stochastic Mutation	Improves the convergence speed and the diversity of the swarm
Fuzzy adaptive IW	The range of best candidate solutions was used to adjust the IW
PSO with adaptive Inertia Weight strategy	Overcomes the weakness of premature convergence
Adaptive threshold mutation PSO	Used adaptive exponent decreasing IW, a dynamic adaptive changing threshold and mutation of the particles
Self-adaptive PSO	A self-adjusted IW varies dynamically with each particle's evolution degree
Adaptive particle swarm optimization (APSO).	Based on evolutionary state estimation and elitist learning strategy using automatic control of IW, acceleration coefficients
Population Diversity Based IW Adaptation in PSO	IW is changed based on the distribution of particles
PSOMAM	Based on the distance between each particle and global best particle
Chaotic PSO based on adaptive IW	Chaotic disturbance is added to jump out of local optima
Self regulating PSO	Exploration improves because of self regulating inertia weight
PSO with time varying acceleration coefficients	With time varying acceleration the particles move around the search space with decreasing cognitive component and increasing social component
A predicted modified particle swarm optimization with time-varying acceleration coefficients	Acceleration coefficients are adjusted by exploring the velocity information
Adaptive acceleration coefficients for a new search diversification strategy in PSO	Adaptive acceleration coefficients for diversification in PSO based on dynamic adjustment
Fully informed particle swarm	Each particle is influenced by the success of all its neighbors
Niching Without Niching Parameters: PSO	"Wrap-around" ring topology
PSO with neighbourhood operator	Gradual increase in neighborhood size of a particle till all particles in a swarm become neighbor

continued on following page

Table 1. Continued

PSO Variant	Remark
Adaptive PSO	m-nearest particles in the neighborhood
FDR-PSO	Maintains population diversity
PSO with linearly increasing topology connectivity and shuffling mechanism	Shuffling mechanism prevents particle to trap in local optima while linear increasing topology connectivity balances exploration and exploitation
PSO with adaptive time-varying topology connectivity	Adaptively varying topology connectivity with generation number improve exploration and exploitation search
UPSO	Combining global and local version of PSO
A hierarchical PSO and its adaptive variant	Dynamic hierarchy of particles
PSO using dimension selection methods	Based on random dimension selection, heuristic dimension selection and distance based dimension selection algorithm
Enhanced leader PSO	A five staged successive mutation strategy
Adaptive learning PSO	Each particle adjusts the behavior using above learning strategies and random position generated around the particle.
SLPSO	Each particle has a set of four strategies to cope with different situations
A cooperative PSO	Searches each dimension separately using one dimensional swarm to improve the performance
Heterogeneous CLPSO	Comprehensive learning strategy is used in both subpopulations to generate the exemplar using personal best experiences of the particle
DNLPSO	The particle learn simultaneously from best particle in the neighborhood, personal best of itself or personal best of some other particle from its neighborhood
Self Regulating PSO	Employed self-regulated learning and self-perception strategies
Centripetal accelerated PSO	Uses median position of particle, current fitness of particle and worst fitness of swarm
PSO with adaptive random link neighborhood	Neighborhood of each particle is randomly varied based on the fitness value
Attraction repulsion PSO	Encourages high diversity and discourages premature convergence
Modified ARPSO	Positive conflict phase in between attraction and repulsion phase
Bare bones PSO	Adopt position updating using Gaussian distribution
Adaptive Mutation Based PSO	Used adaptive mutation using Beta distribution
BBPSO with a jump strategy	The jump strategy was applied using Gaussian or Cauchy distributions
BBPSO with scale matrix adaptation	Investigated a self-adaptive heavy-tailed distribution for selecting new positions and a deterministic rule for adaptation of the scale matrix to update the position of a particle
Quantum PSO	Inspired by quantum mechanics
Center PSO	A center particle guides search direction, its position is considered as average of the other particles
SPSO	Adaptive random topology
Asynchronous PSO	Velocity and position of the particle are updated only after receiving the best fitness value in the neighborhood
Random asynchronous PSO	Selects particle for evaluation and updation at random using uniform distribution in each iteration

APPLICATIONS OF PSO

According to the analysis of the applications of PSO (Poli [102]) applications range from biological and medical to electrical, electronic, problem solving to image analysis, signal processing and graphics to robotics. Electrical, electronic, mechanical, civil engineering, communication theory, operations research, medicine, chemistry, biology are main application categories of PSO as per Web of Science Core Collection.

FUTURE RESEARCH DIRECTIONS

Hybrid and adaptive PSO are active research trends in PSO. Exploring applications of modern technologies can be future research direction. Some challenges like effect of neighborhood topology as well as dynamics of PSO need to be focused. Issues such as search focus and spread, swarm stability and collapse can be explored with the adoption of new techniques. Very little research has been done on the initialization of the swarm and verification of initialization techniques can be direction of research.

CONCLUSION

PSO is a popular population based optimization algorithm. The initial PSO with the mathematical framework, PSO parameters and variants of PSO are discussed in this chapter. Different variants of PSO are proposed by researchers to improve convergence and performance of PSO. The performance of PSO depends on the parameter s though there very few parameters to set. The issue of setting the values of various parameters of an algorithm is vital as performance of the algorithm depends upon the values of parameters. Different values can be optimal at different phases of evolution. The computational behavior of PSO is significantly affected by initialization, velocity threshold, inertia weight, constriction coefficient, acceleration coefficient, neighborhood typologies and swarm size. Velocity clamping prevents particles uncontrolled increase of magnitude but particles may not converge towards roughly detected promising region. The convergence of particles towards best position is controlled by inertia weight. Acceleration coefficients c_1 and c_2 indicate cognitive and social influence value respectively. Social influence is more when $c_1 < c_2$ while $c_1 > c_2$ will bias towards self best. High values of c_1 and c_2 provide global exploration and smaller values of c_1 and c_2 provide refined local search. Neighborhood topology is a scheme to determine the neighbors of particles in a swarm. gbest, star, ring or lbest, Von Newman, pyramid, mesh, tree topologies are proposed in the literature. gbest is the standard topology where all particles communicate with each other through global best. Though it shows fast convergence it is more susceptible to local optima. Local best particle finds a good solution but has slow convergence rate. Von Newman neighborhood performs well consistently. Some topologies are good for global optimization while some topologies are good for local optimization. The best topology depends on the problem at hand. Dynamic topologies allow variation of the topology as the algorithm progresses. Parameter control can lead to optimal performance of the algorithm.

REFERENCES

Adriansyah, A., & Amin, S. (2006). Analytical and empirical study of particle swarm optimization with a sigmoid decreasing inertia weight. *Regional Conference on Engineering and Science*, Johor.

Angeline, P. (1995). Adaptive and self-adaptive evolutionary computations. Computational Intelligence: A Dynamic Systems Perspective. IEEE Press.

Ardizzon, G., Cavazzini, G., & Pavesi, G. (2015). Adaptive acceleration coefficients for a new search diversification strategy in particle swarm optimization algorithms*Information Sciences, 299*, 337–378..

Arumugam, M., Chandramohan, A., & Rao, M. (2005). Competitive Approaches to PSO Algorithms via New Acceleration Co-efficient Variant with Mutation Operators. *Sixth International Conference on Computational Intelligence and Multimedia Applications*, 225-230. doi:10.1109/ICCIMA.2005.18

Balaprakash, P., Birattari, M., & Stutzle, T. (2007). Improvement strategies for the F-race algorithm: Sampling design and iterative refinement. In *Lecture Notes in Computer Science: vol. 4771. Hybrid Metaheuristics, 4th International Workshop, Proceedings* (pp. 108-122). Berlin: Springer.

Bartz-Beielstein, T., Lasarczyk, C., & Preuss, M. (2005). Sequential parameter optimization. *IEEE Congress on Evolutionary Computation*, 773-780.

Beheshti, Z., Mariyam, S., & Shamsuddin, H. (2014). CAPSO: Centripetal accelerated particle swarm optimization. *Information Sciences, 258*, 54–79. doi:10.1016/j.ins.2013.08.015

Beheshti, Z., Shamsuddin, S., & Sulaiman, S. (2013). Fusion global-local-topology particle swarm optimization for global optimization problems. *Mathematical Problems in Engineering*.

Bergh, F. (2002). An Analysis of Particle Swarm Optimizers, PhD thesis. Pretoria, South Africa: Department of Computer Science, University of Pretoria. Retrieved from repository.up.ac.za/bitstream/handle/2263/24297/00thesis.pdf

Bergh, F., & Engelbrecht, A. (2004). A cooperative approach to particle swarm optimization. *IEEE Transactions on Evolutionary Computation, 8*(3), 225–239. doi:10.1109/TEVC.2004.826069

Birattari, M., Stutzle, T., Paquete, L., & Varrentrapp, K. (2002). A racing algorithm for configuring metaheuristics. In *GECCO 2002: Proceedings of the Genetic and Evolutionary Computation Conference*. Morgan Kaufmann Publishers.

Bratton, D., & Kennedy, J. (2007). Defining a Standard for Particle Swarm Optimization. *Proceedings of the IEEE Swarm Intelligence Symposium*, 120–127. doi:10.1109/SIS.2007.368035

Cai, X., Cui, Y., & Tan, Y. (2009). Predicted modified PSO with time-varying accelerator coefficients. *International Journal of Bio-inspired Computation, 1*(1-2), 50–60. doi:10.1504/IJBIC.2009.022773

Campos, M., Krohling, M., & Enriquez, I. (2014). Bare Bones Particle Swarm Optimization With Scale Matrix Adaptation. *IEEE Transactions on Cybernetics, 44*(9), 1567–1578. doi:10.1109/TCYB.2013.2290223 PMID:25137686

Carlisle, A., & Dozier, G. (2001) An off-the-shelf PSO. *Workshop on Particle Swarm Optimization*.

Chen, G. (2006). Natural exponential Inertia Weight strategy in particle swarm optimization. *Intelligent Control and Automation, WCICA, 1,* 3672–3675. doi:10.1109/WCICA.2006.1713055

Cheng, S., Shi, Y., Qin, Q., & Ting, T. (2012). Population Diversity Based Inertia Weight Adaptation in Particle Swarm Optimization. *IEEE International Conference on Advanced Computational Intelligence,* 395-403. doi:10.1109/ICACI.2012.6463194

Clerc, M. (1999). The swarm and the queen: towards a deterministic and adaptive particle swarm optimization. *Proc. 1999 ICEC,* 1951 – 1957. doi:10.1109/CEC.1999.785513

Clerc, M. (2006). *Particle Swarm Optimization.* International Scientific and Technical Encyclopedia. doi:10.1002/9780470612163

Clerc, M. (2010). From Theory to Practice in Particle Swarm Optimization. In *Handbook of Swarm Intelligence: Adaptation, Learning, and Optimization.* Springer.

Clerc, M. (2012). *Standard Particle Swarm Optimisation, Particle Swarm Central.* Technical Report. Retrieved from http://clerc.maurice.free.fr/pso/SPSOdescriptionspdf

Clerc, M., & Kennedy, J. (2002). The particle swarm explosion, stability and convergence in a multidimensional complex space. *IEEE Transactions on Evolutionary Computation, 6*(1), 58–73. doi:10.1109/4235.985692

Eberhart, R., & Kennedy, J. (1995). A new optimizer using particle swarm theory. *Proceedings of the Sixth International Symposium on Micro Machine and Human Science,* 39–43. doi:10.1109/MHS.1995.494215

Eberhart, R., & Shi, Y. (2000). Comparing inertia weights and constriction factors in particle swarm optimization. *Proceedings of the 2000 Congress on, IEEE evolutionary computation, 1,* 84–88. doi:10.1109/CEC.2000.870279

Eberhart, R., & Shi, Y. (2001). Particle swarm optimization: developments, applications and resources. *Proc. IEEE Int. Conf. on Evolutionary Computation,* 81-86. doi:10.1109/CEC.2001.934374

Eiben, A. E., Hinterding, R., & Michalewicz, Z. (1999). Parameter Control in Evolutionary Algorithms. *IEEE Transactions on Evolutionary Computation, 3*(2), 124–141. doi:10.1109/4235.771166

Engelbrecht, A. P. (2013a). Particle swarm optimization: Global best or local best? *2013 BRICS Congress on Computational Intelligence and 11th Brazilian Congress on Computational Intelligence,* 124-135.

Engelbrecht, A. P. (2013b). Particle Swarm Optimization: Iteration Strategies Revisited. *BRICS Congress on Computational Intelligence & 11th Brazilian Congress on Computational Intelligence.*

Engelbrecht, P. (2005). *Fundamentals of Computational Swarm Intelligence.* John Wiley & Sons Ltd.

Feng, Y., Teng, G., Wang, A., & Yao, Y. (2007). Chaotic Inertia Weight in Particle Swarm Optimization. *Innovative Computing, Information and Control, ICICIC'07. Second International Conference on,* 475.

Gao, Y., An, X., & Liu, J. (2008). A Particle Swarm Optimization Algorithm with Logarithm Decreasing Inertia Weight and Chaos Mutation. *Computational Intelligence and Security, International Conference on, 1,* 61-65.

Gao, Y., & Duan, Y. (2007). A New Particle Swarm Optimization Algorithm with Random Inertia Weight and Evolution Strategy. *International Conference on Computational Intelligence and Security Workshops*, 199-203.

Helwig, S., Branke, J., & Mostaghim, S. M. (2013). Experimental Analysis of Bound Handling Techniques in Particle Swarm Optimization. *Evolutionary Computation. IEEE Transactions*, *17*(2), 259–271.

Hinterding, R., Michalewicz, Z., & Peachey, T. (1996). Self-adaptive genetic algorithm for numeric functions. *Lecture Notes in Computer Science*, *1141*, 420–429. doi:10.1007/3-540-61723-X_1006

Hu, M., Wu, T., & Weir, J. (2013). An Adaptive Particle Swarm Optimization With Multiple Adaptive Methods. *IEEE Transactions On Evolutionary Computation, VOL.*, *17*(5), 705–720. doi:10.1109/TEVC.2012.2232931

Hu, X., & Eberhart, R. (2002). Adaptive Particle Swarm Optimization: Detection And Response to Dynamic Systems. *Proceedings of the IEEE Congress on Evolutionary Computation, CEC2002*, 1666-1670.

Janson, S., & Middendorf, M. (2005). A hierarchical particle swarm optimizer and its adaptive variant. *IEEE Transactions on Systems, Man, and Cybernetics. Part B, Cybernetics*, *35*(6), 1272–1282. doi:10.1109/TSMCB.2005.850530 PMID:16366251

Jin, X., Liang, Y., Tian, D., & Zhuang, F. (2013). Particle swarm optimization using dimension selection methods. *Applied Mathematics and Computation*, *219*(10), 5185–5197. doi:10.1016/j.amc.2012.11.020

Jordehi, A. (2015). Enhanced leader PSO (ELPSO): A new PSO variant for solving global optimisation problems. *Applied Soft Computing*, *26*, 401–417. doi:10.1016/j.asoc.2014.10.026

Ju, L., Du, Q., & Gunzburger, M. (2001). *Probabilistic methods for centroidal Voronoi tessellations and their parallel implementations*. Penn State Department of Mathematics Report No. AM250

Kamalapur, S., & Patil, V. (2012). Analysis of particle trajectories and monitoring velocity behaviour in particle swarm optimization. *International Conference on Hybrid Intelligent Systems*, 4-7.

Kamalapur, S., & Patil, V. (2014). Adaptive Random Link PSO with Link Change Variations and Confinement Handling. *International Journal of Intelligent Systems and Applications*, *7*(1), 62–72. doi:10.5815/ijisa.2015.01.06

Kennedy, J. (1997). The particle swarm social adaptation of knowledge. *Proc. IEEE Int. Conf. Evolutionary Computation*, 303–308. doi:10.1109/ICEC.1997.592326

Kennedy, J. (1999). Small Worlds and Mega-Minds: Effects of Neighborhood Topology on Particle Swarm Performance. *Proceedings of the IEEE Congress on Evolutionary Computation*, 1931–1938. doi:10.1109/CEC.1999.785509

Kennedy, J. (2000). Stereotyping: Improving Particle Swarm Performance with Cluster Analysis. *Proceedings of the IEEE Congress on Evolutionary Computation*, *2*, 1507–1512. doi:10.1109/CEC.2000.870832

Kennedy, J. (2003). Bare bones particle swarms. *Swarm Intelligence Symposium, SIS '03. Proceedings of the 2003 IEEE*, 80-87.

Kennedy, J., Eberhart, R., & Shi, Y. (2001). *Swarm Intelligence*. Morgan Kaufmann.

Kennedy, J., & Eberhart, R. C. (1995). Particle swarm optimization. *Proceedings of the IEEE International Conference on Neural Networks*, 4, 1942 – 1948. doi:10.1109/ICNN.1995.488968

Kennedy, J., & Mendes, R. (2002). Population structure and particle swarm performance. *Proc. 2002 Cong. Evol. Comput.*, 1671-1675.

Kennedy, J., & Mendes, R. (2006). Neighborhood topologies in fully informed and best-of-neighborhood particle swarms. *IEEE Transactions on Systems, Man and Cybernetics. Part C, Applications and Reviews*, 36(4), 515–519. doi:10.1109/TSMCC.2006.875410

Kentzoglanakis, K., & Poole, M. (2009). Particle swarm optimization with an oscillating Inertia Weight. *Proceedings of the 11th Annual conference on Genetic and evolutionary computation*, 1749-1750. doi:10.1145/1569901.1570140

Krohling, R., & Mendel, E. (2009). Bare bones particle swarm optimization with Gaussian or Cauchy jumps. *Proceeding of IEEE Congress of Evolutionary Computation*, 3285–3291. doi:10.1109/CEC.2009.4983361

Li, C., & Yang, S. (2009). An Adaptive Learning Particle Swarm Optimizer for Function Optimization. *Proceeding of IEEE Congress on Evolutionary Computation*, 381-388. DOI doi:10.1109/CEC.2009.4982972

Li, H., & Gao, Y. (2009a). Particle Swarm Optimization Algorithm with Adaptive Threshold Mutation. *Proceeding of International Conference on Computational Intelligence and Security*, 129-132.

Li, H., & Gao, Y. (2009b). Particle Swarm Optimization Algorithm with Exponent Decreasing Inertia Weight and Stochastic Mutation. *Second International Conference on Information and Computing Science*, 66-69. doi:10.1109/ICIC.2009.24

Li, J. W., Cheng, Y. M., & Chen, K. Z. (2014). Chaotic particle swarm optimization algorithm based on adaptive inertia weight. *The 26th Chinese Control and Decision Conference*, 1310-1315. doi:10.1109/CCDC.2014.6852369

Li, X. (2010). Niching Without Niching Parameters: Particle Swarm Optimization Using a Ring Topology. *IEEE Transactions on Evolutionary Computation*, 14(1), 150–169. doi:10.1109/TEVC.2009.2026270

Li, X., Fu, H., & Zhang, C. (2008). A self-adaptive particle swarm optimization algorithm. *Proceeding of International Conference on Computer Science and Software Engineering*, 186-189. DOI doi:10.1109/CSSE.2008.142

Liao, & Wang, J. (2011). Nonlinear, Inertia Weight Variation for Dynamic Adaptation in Particle Swarm Optimization ICSI, Part I. *LNCS, 6728*, 80-85.

Lim, W., & Isa, N. (2014a). Particle swarm optimization with increasing topology connectivity. *Engineering Applications of Artificial Intelligence*, 27, 80–102. doi:10.1016/j.engappai.2013.09.011

Lim, W., & Isa, N. (2014b). Particle swarm optimization with adaptive time-varying topology connectivity. *Applied Soft Computing*, 24, 623–642. doi:10.1016/j.asoc.2014.08.013

Liu, H., Su, R., Gao, Y., & Xu, R. (2009). Improved Particle Swarm Optimization Using Two Novel Parallel Inertia Weights. *Second International Conference on Intelligent Computation Technology and Automation*, 185-188 doi:10.1109/ICICTA.2009.53

Liu, Y., Qin, Z., Shi, Z., & Lu, J. (2007). Center particle swarm optimization. *Neurocomputing, 70*(4-6), 672–679. doi:10.1016/j.neucom.2006.10.002

Lynn, N., & Suganthan, P. (2015). Heterogeneous comprehensive learning particle swarm optimization with enhanced exploration and exploitation. *Swarm and Evolutionary Computation, 24*, 11–24. doi:10.1016/j.swevo.2015.05.002

Maca, P., & Pech, P. (2015). The Inertia Weight Updating Strategies in Particle Swarm Optimisation Based on the Beta Distribution. *Mathematical Problems in Engineering, 2015*, 790465. doi:10.1155/2015/790465

Mendes, R., Kennedy, J., & Neves, J. (2003). Watch thy Neighbor or How the Swarm can Learn from its Environment. *Proceedings of the IEEE Swarm Intelligence Symposium*, 88–94. doi:10.1109/SIS.2003.1202252

Mendes, R., Kennedy, J., & Neves, J. (2004). The Fully Informed Particle Swarm: Simpler, Maybe Better. *IEEE Transactions on Evolutionary Computation, 8*(3), 204–210. doi:10.1109/TEVC.2004.826074

Nannen, V., & Eiben, A. (2007).Relevance estimation and value calibration of evolutionary algorithm parameters. *Proceedings of the 20th International Joint Conference on Artificial Intelligence*, 975-980. doi:10.1109/CEC.2007.4424460

Nasir, M., Das, S., Maity, D., Sengupta, S., Halder, U., & Suganthan, P. (2012). A dynamic neighborhood learning based particle swarm optimizer for global numerical optimization. *Information Sciences, 209*, 16–36. doi:10.1016/j.ins.2012.04.028

Nikabadi, A., Ebadzadeh, M. (2008). Particle swarm optimization algorithms with adaptive Inertia Weight: A survey of the state of the art and a Novel method. *IEEE Journal of Evolutionary Computation*.

Ozcan, E., & Mohan, C. (1998). Analysis of a Simple Particle Swarm Optimization System. *Intelligent Engineering Systems Through Artifocial Neural Networks, 8*, 253–258.

Ozcan, E., & Mohan, C. K. (1999). Particle swarm optimization: surfing the waves. In *Evolutionary Computation, 1999. CEC 99. Proceedings of the 1999 Congress on (Vol. 3)*. IEEE

Pant, M., Thangaraj, R., & Abraham, A. (2008). A new quantum behaved particle swarm optimization. *Proceedings of the 10th Annual Conference on Genetic and Evolutionary Computation*, 87–94. doi:10.1145/1389095.1389108

Pant, M., Thangaraj, R., & Singh, V. (2007). A simple diversity guided particle swarm optimization. *Proceedings of IEEE Congress Evolutionary Computation*, 3294–3299. doi:10.1109/CEC.2007.4424896

Pant, M., Thangaraj, R., & Singhl, V. P. (2009). Sobal mutated quantum particle swarm optimization. *International Journal of Recent Trends in Engineering, 1*(1), 95–99.

Parsopoulos, K., & Vrahatis, M. (2004). UPSO: a Unified Particle Swarm Optimization Scheme. *Lecture Series on Computational Sciences*, 868–873.

Peram, T., Veeramachaneni, K., & Mohan, C. (2003). Fitness-distance-ratio based particle swarm optimization. *Proceedings of the IEEE Swarm Intelligence Symposium*, 174–181.

Poli, R., Kennedy, J., & Blackwell, T. (2007). Particle swarm optimization. *Swarm Intelligence, 1*(1), 33–57. doi:10.1007/s11721-007-0002-0

Rada-Vilela, J., Zhang, M., & Seah, W. (2011a). Random asynchronous PSO. *5th international conference on automation, robotics and applications*, 220–225. doi:10.1109/ICARA.2011.6144885

Rada-Vilela, J., Zhang, M., & Seah, W. (2011b). A performance study on synchronous and asynchronous updates in particle swarm optimization. Genetic and evolutionary computation conference, 21–28. doi:10.1145/2001576.2001581

Rada-Vilela, J., Zhang, M., & Seah, W. (2012). A performance study on the effects of noise and evaporation in particle swarm optimization. IEEE congress on evolutionary computation, 873–880. doi:10.1109/CEC.2012.6256451

Rada-Vilela, J., Zhang, M., & Seah, W. (2013). performance study on synchronicity and neighborhood size in particle swarm optimization. *Soft Computing, 17*(6), 1019–1030. doi:10.1007/s00500-013-1015-9

Ratnaweera, A., Halgamuge, S., & Watson, H. (2004). Self-Organizing Hierarchical Particle Swarm Optimizer With Time-Varying Acceleration Coefficients. *IEEE Transactions on Evolutionary Computation, 8*(3), 240–255. doi:10.1109/TEVC.2004.826071

Reyes-Medina, T., & Ramirez-Tores, J. (2011). A Statistical Study of the Effects of Neighborhood Topologies in Particle Swarm Optimization. *Studies in Computational Intelligence, 343*, 179–192.

Riget, J., & Vesterstrom, J. (2002). *A Diversity Guided Particle Swarm Optimizer- the ARPSO*. EVALife Technical Report no. 2002-02.

Shi, Y., & Eberhart, R. (1998). A modified particle swarm optimizer. *Evolutionary Computation Proceedings, 1998. IEEE World Congress on Computational Intelligence*, 69 – 73.

Shi, Y., & Eberhart, R. (1999). Empirical study of particle swarm optimization. *Proceedings of the 1999 Congress on Evolutionary Computation*, 1945-1950. doi:10.1109/CEC.1999.785511

Shi, Y., & Eberhart, R. (2001). Fuzzy adaptive particle swarm optimization, Evolutionary Computation. *Proceedings of the 2001 Congress*, 1, 101-106. doi:10.1109/CEC.2001.934377

Shi, Y., & Eberhart, R. (2008). Population diversity of particle swarms, Evolutionary Computation, 2008. *CEC 2008. IEEE World Congress on Computational Intelligence*, 1063 – 1067.

Smith, J., & Fogarty, T. (1996). Self adaptation of mutation rates in a steady state genetic algorithm. *International Conference on Evolutionary Computation*, 318-323. doi:10.1109/ICEC.1996.542382

Suganthan, P. (1999). Particle swarm optimizer with neighbourhood operator. *IEEE Congress on Evolutionary Computation*, 3, 1958-1962.

Sun, J., Feng, B., & Xu, W. (2004). Particle swarm optimization with particles having quantum behavior. *Proceedings of Congress on Evolutionary Computation*, 326–331. doi:10.1109/CEC.2004.1330875

Sun, J., Xu, B., & Fang, W. (2006). A diversity-guided quantum-behaved particle swarm optimization algorithm. *International Conference on Simulated Evolution and Learning*, 497–504. doi:10.1007/11903697_63

Sun, J., Xu, W., & Feng, B. (2005). Adaptive parameter control for quantum-behaved particle swarm optimization on individual level. *Proceedings of IEEE International Conference on Systems, Man, and Cybernetics*, 3049–3054. doi:10.1109/ICSMC.2005.1571614

Tanweer, M. R., Suresh, S., & Sundararajan, N. (2015). Self regulating particle swarm optimization algorithm. *Information Sciences*, *294*, 182–202. doi:10.1016/j.ins.2014.09.053

Trelea, I. C. (2003). The particle swarm optimization algorithm: Convergence analysis and parameter selection. *Information Processing Letters*, *85*(6), 317–325. doi:10.1016/S0020-0190(02)00447-7

Ursem, R. (2003). *Models for evolutionary algorithms and their applications in system identification and control optimization* (Ph.D. thesis). Univ. Aarhus, Denmark. Retrieved from www.brics.dk/DS/03/6/BRICS-DS-03-6.pdf

Yasuda, K., Ide, A., & Iwasaki, N. (2003). Adaptive particle swarm optimization. *Proceedings of the IEEE International Conference on Systems, Man, and Cybernetics*, 1554-1559.

Yuan, B., & Gallagher, M. (2004). Statistical racing techniques for improved empirical evaluation of evolutionary algorithms. In Lecture Notes in Computer Science: Vol. 3242. Parallel Problem Solving from Nature - PPSN VIII (pp. 172-181). Springer-Verlag. doi:10.1007/978-3-540-30217-9_18

Zhan, Z., & Zhang, J. (2009). Adaptive Particle Swarm Optimization. *IEEE Transactions on Systems, Man, and Cybernetics. Part B, Cybernetics*, *39*(6), 1362–1381. doi:10.1109/TSMCB.2009.2015956 PMID:19362911

Zhang, W., Wei, D., & Liang, H. (2014). A parameter selection strategy for particle swarm optimization based on particle positions. *Expert Systems with Applications*, *41*(7), 3576–3584. doi:10.1016/j.eswa.2013.10.061

Zheng, Y. (2003). Empirical study of particle swarm optimizer with an increasing inertia weight. *Proceeding of the IEEE Congress on Evolutionary Computation*, 221-226.

KEY TERMS AND DEFINITIONS

Adaptability: Ability to change dynamically based on external factor.

Particle: Individual in population.

Proximity: Ability of performing time and space computations.

Swarm: Population of potential solutions.

Swarm Intelligence: Branch of artificial intelligence which studies collective behavior.

Chapter 5
A Survey of Computational Intelligence Algorithms and Their Applications

Hadj Ahmed Bouarara
Dr. Tahar Moulay University of Saida, Algeria

ABSTRACT

This chapter subscribes in the framework of an analytical study about the computational intelligence algorithms. These algorithms are numerous and can be classified in two great families: evolutionary algorithms (genetic algorithms, genetic programming, evolutionary strategy, differential evolutionary, paddy field algorithm) and swarm optimization algorithms (particle swarm optimisation PSO, ant colony optimization (ACO), bacteria foraging optimisation, wolf colony algorithm, fireworks algorithm, bat algorithm, cockroaches colony algorithm, social spiders algorithm, cuckoo search algorithm, wasp swarm optimisation, mosquito optimisation algorithm). We have detailed each algorithm following a structured organization (the origin of the algorithm, the inspiration source, the summary, and the general process). This paper is the fruit of many years of research in the form of synthesis which groups the contributions proposed by various researchers in this field. It can be the starting point for the designing and modelling new algorithms or improving existing algorithms.

INTRODUCTION

Background

The algorithms play an important role in IT and for several real applications. It delivers an objective is to find answers, which are probably best likened to the runtime environment. In late years, engineers and decision makers are confronted daily with complex problems (NP-hard) that generally involve all sectors. Historically, researchers have attempted to resolve these problems as efficiently as possible. For many years ago, research has been conducted towards the proposition of exact algorithms for polynomial special problems. Afterwards, the appearance of heuristic algorithms allowed generally finding solutions

DOI: 10.4018/978-1-5225-2128-0.ch005

with good quality but often solutions for small instances, so why the need to find new types of algorithms that can lead to a major breakthrough for the practical resolution these problems became paramount.

Today, a huge success was achieved through modelling of organic and natural intelligence resulting in what is called "computational intelligence algorithms". This class of algorithms (include artificial neural networks, evolutionary computations, collective intelligence, artificial immune systems, human organ systems and fuzzy systems) constitutes a part of meta-heuristic and bio-mimicry areas. They have demonstrated their strength face to different complex issues where they are even attempting to determine the optimal solution from a finite number of existing solutions and offer a high performance results in experimental studies. It is frequently hard to understand why they perform well in a particular context. Another significant advantage is that these algorithms can often be applied without much knowledge about the problem, which makes them very suitable for various applications.

The conception of such algorithm requires the presence of the three characteristics to facilitate the implementation of these algorithms on a new problem:

- Choose a representation of possible solutions.
- Determine a function to measure the quality of a solution.
- Define the operators producing from a current set of solutions a new set of solutions.

It is no overstatement to state that this type of algorithm is everywhere, from design engineering to business planning and from routing of network to travel planning. In all these actions, we strain to reach some goals or optimize something like the quality of performance and the execution time. The delegation of this paper is a very important way to consolidate a number of new algorithms inspired by nature and have been offered in the literature. It is composed from more than 20 algorithms that were unionised in 2 parts classified by the biological source of inspiration of each one of them as illustrated in the next Figure 1.

The Organization of Our Work

We describe the algorithm following the next structure:

- **The Origin of the Algorithm:** It describes the start and the first appearance of this algorithm with references regarding the creator or developer of the algorithm.
- **The Inspiration Source:** It traces the inspiration phenomenon of the algorithm that can be natural, biological, physical or social.
- **The Summary of the Algorithm:** It summarizes the general cognitive process and the primary goal of the algorithm.
- **The General Process of the Algorithm:** It describes in more detail the various steps of the algorithm and the architecture, in the form of the figure.
- **The Procedure:** It is the structured image of the algorithm which describes its arrangement in terms of the necessary parameters, the input/output, the stopping criterion, and the intercourse between the different calculations performed by the constituents of the algorithm.

Figure 1. Taxonomy of different bio-inspired algorithms existed in literature

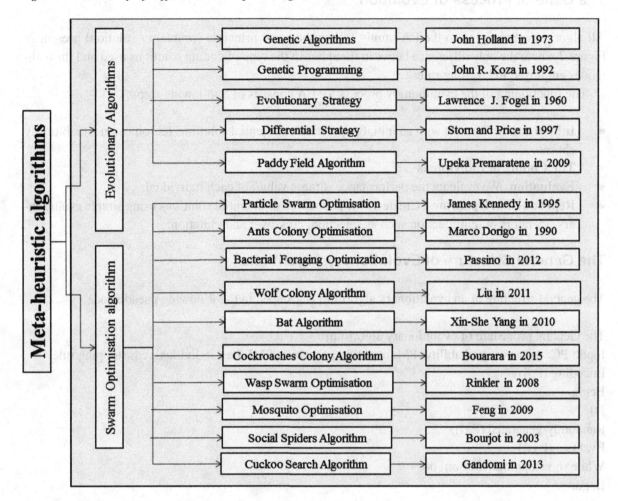

EVOLUTIONARY ALGORITHMS (EA)

In the 1950s until 1960, several computer scientists have studied independently scalable systems with the idea that evolution could be used as an optimization tool for engineering problems. Evolutionary algorithm (EA) is a family of stochastic and probabilistic algorithms that mimic the metaphor of biological evolution to solve several known problems in the computer area. These algorithms are established on the mechanisms of the theory of evolution proposed by Darwin in 1860 and published in his book "The Origin of Species by means of Natural Selection, or the struggle for existence in nature" (Darwin, 1859). They accept as input a population of individuals (set of potential answers) that will evolve from one generation to another following a set of reproduction rules (selection, mutation, crossing, and replacement) until the optimal solution satisfies the targets set in advance (stopping criterion). This process leads to the evolution of a population of individuals that are better adapted to their environment; as, the natural life, iteratively a new population of individuals will be created (Pohlheim, 2005).

The General Process of Evolution

All algorithms belonging to the EA family follow the same principle (problem / solution) present in Figure 2 where the only difference between them lies in the type of coding solutions used and the techniques employed in breeding rules.

The functioning of the evolutionary process for EA consists of 5 following steps:

- **Initialisation:** We start with an initial population of potential solutions (chromosomes) arbitrarily chosen.
- **The Coding of Individuals**
- **Evaluation:** We evaluate the performance (fitness value) of each individual.
- **Reproduction Operators:** Create a new population of potential solutions using simple evolutionary operators of reproduction such as selection, crossover and mutation.

The General Structure of Evolutionary Algorithms

The general structure of an evolutionary algorithm is grouped in the following pseudo code:

The General procedure of evolutionary algorithm
Input: PC: crossover probability; PM: mutation probability; MI: best individual; cd; stopping rule
Encoding (P (i))
Begin
I 0
Randomly-generated (P (i))
Evaluate (P (i))
While (no stopping criterion) do
Begin
i ← i + 1
Select P (i) from P (i-1)
Cross (P (i))
Mutate (P (i))
M_i ← evaluate (P (i))
P (i) ← Replace (P (i))
End
End
Output: M_i

Figure 2. The process (problem / solution) for an evolutionary algorithm

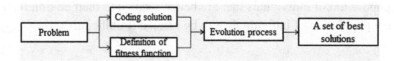

The EA are computationally expensive and do not guarantee the optimality of the results where it is difficult to implement them. Among all the EAs existed in literature, we have found:

GENETIC ALGORITHMS (GAS)

The Origin of the Algorithm

The commencement of genetic algorithms can be delineated to the early 1950s, when several biologists use computers to simulate biological systems (Goldberg, 1989). Nevertheless, in the 1960s, John Holland studied the evolutionary systems during his doctorate at the University of Michigan, USA and in 1975 he introduced the first formal model of GAs called the canonical genetic algorithms (CGA) in his book "adaptation in natural and artificial systems" (Holland, 1962; Holland, 1973).

The Inspiration Source

The GAs is a meta-heuristic algorithm optimization based on the principle of Neo-Darwinism derived from the Mendelian genetics (including heredity, the frequency of genes, chromosomes and alleles) and the natural evolution of Darwin mechanisms such as crossing, mutation, and natural selection (Holland, 1975).

The Summary of the Algorithm

The GAs is the best known evolutionary algorithms that provide solutions to problems that do not have calculable solutions in reasonable time, analytically or algorithmically. They accept as input a population of N solutions represented by individuals (named the parent population) that will evolve iteratively using genetic operators based on a fitness function to get the best solutions. The foundation of a new generation is achieved by creating new individual and destroying other (natural selection mechanism), allowing the renewal of the population and for each generation only a subset of individuals is able to reproduce and transmit the characters to the future generations. The original goal of Holland was not to design algorithms to solve specific problems, but rather to formally study the phenomenon of adaptation as it occurs in nature and to develop means by which natural coping mechanisms could be imported into computer systems (Reeves, 2003).

The General Process

The universal architecture of genetic algorithms is shown in Figure 2 (Section on The General Process of Evolution) and follows the same mathematical process as the process demonstrated in the old part. Each step in the functioning of GAs is detailed in the next:

Initialization

The foremost stride in the implementation of GAs is to create an initial population of individuals that should contain chromosomes distributed in all search space. The easiest way is to randomly generate N individuals. This step can condition the speed of the algorithm and the quality of the outcome.

Coding

The encoding is a delicate and vital step in designing a genetic algorithm because it permits the representation of individual in the contour of a chromosome for the carrying out of the reproduction operators. There are three types of coding techniques: binary, real and grey coding (Mitchell, 1998).

The Evaluation Function

The evaluation function (fitness) allows to measure the performance of each individual and to evaluate whether an individual is better suited than another to its environment. This feature, directly related to the problems is often simple to define it when there are few parameters. Unluckily, when there are lots of objectives, it becomes more difficult to fix it. In this case, the function is a weighted sum of several functions (multi-objective function).

Reproduction Operators

These operators play a key role in the success of AGs that can assure the passage from one generation to another in order to improve the population:

- **The Selection Process:** Natural selection proposed by Darwin (1859) and Wallace (1870) in the nineteenth century, is based on the principle that individuals tend to make more children and cannot be reproduced all (Wallace, 1870). This operator may be the most important because it allows to individuals in a population to survive, reproduce or die (identify the individuals to be crossed). In general, the probability of survival of an individual will be directly connected to its relative effectiveness within the population and the best individuals can be selected several times for the next generation, while the less able will have less chance of being.
- **Crossover Operator:** The crossover operator allows the institution of new individuals through exchanging of information between chromosomes (individuals). A cross is envisaged with two parents selected and generates one or two children who inherit some characteristic of their parents. To do this task we need a crossover probability fixed in advance MP after selecting two individuals we generate a random number $A \in [0, 1]$. If $A \leq PC$ then a crossing will be done along these two parents individuals. The intersection zone is generally chosen randomly. We can distinguish several techniques to realise the crossing.
  - **The Cross in a Point:** Both parents will be separated into two sections with a single break point. The cutoff position is randomly chosen and will be the same for both parents to transmit an information exchange.

- ○ **The Cross in Two Points:** Both parents will be divided into 3 parts with two break points. The cutoff areas will be randomly selected and will be the same for both parents to perform the interchange of data between them.
- ○ **Uniform Crosses:** It is based on the same principle of previous cross types, but the points of the cross can be multiple and randomly chosen.
- • **Mutation Operator:** It is an operator that provides exploration of the search space and ensures the diversity of the population with the general principle is to change a gene in a chromosome to another. For instance, in the binary encoding, we change a bit with its opposite. This is applied with a mutation probability (MP) fixed in advance which has usually a very low value between 0.001 and 0.01. We must randomly choose a variable A and if this variable is less than MP then the mutation will realized.
- • **Replacement:** This operator is to reintroduce children obtained by the successive application of the production operators (selection, crossover and mutation) on the population of the iteration me into the population of their parents (the population of iteration I + 1).

The Procedure

The general structure of genetic algorithms is grouped in the following pseudo code:

Genetic Algorithms (GAs)
CP: crossover probability; MP: mutation probability, CA: stopping criterion; Ni: the size of the population P; A: real variable; M_i: best individual (solution).
Input: PC, PM, CA, Ni, A
Begin
Initialization and encoding of the initial population P:
Evaluate (P)
While (No CA) do
P '= Selection of Parents in P
If rand (A) <PC then P '=Apply Crossing operator (P ')
If rand (A) <PM then P '= Apply Mutation operator (P ')
P ← Replace the elders of P by their Descendants P '.
M_i ← Evaluate (P)
End while
End
Output: M_i

GENETIC PROGRAMMING (GP)

The Origin of the Algorithm

The GP was proposed by John Koza in (Koza, 1992), as a particular class of evolutionary algorithms used for the development of computer programs. Koza has developed the GP by combining between the study released by Cramer in 1985 on the wooded-health structure for the representation of individual programs as well as the crossing under the parent trees (Cramer, 1985) and the study by Hicklin in 1986 on selecting and combining under trees (Hicklin, 1986).

The Inspiration

The Genetic Programming has the same inspiration source as genetic algorithms (selection mechanism and natural evolution) but it concentrates a lot along the evolution of genotypes. It has been handled as a subset of genetic algorithms, but the conflict is that the genotype is actually presented as a tree rather than a string or vector.

Summary of the Algorithm

Genetic programming (GP) is the last algorithm from the AE family that have emerged. It can automatically solve problems without the specification of the form or construction of the solution in advance by the user. At the most abstract level, GP is an independent systematic approach in the sphere because it provides information processing systems that can resolve problems automatically from a high-level statement of what must be done. Since its origin, the GP has attracted the interest of the myriad of people round the globe.

The objective of the GP is to use induction to design a computer program with the principle of evolving a set of computer programs from one generation to another with a tree structure for coding programs (individuals) to improve the fit between the candidate population programs and an objective function. The GP is a random procedure that does not guarantee the optimality of the results (Poole, 2008).

The General Process

The basic steps of GP are indicated in the next Figure 3, initially it discovers each program of the initial population by running and comparing their behaviour with another ideal. We might be interested, for

Figure 3. The general functioning of genetic programming algorithm

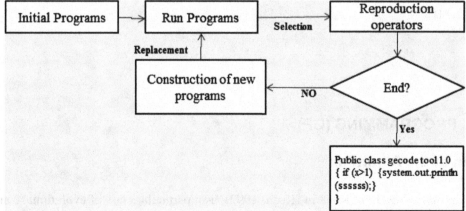

example, how a program includes a series of time or controls an industrial operation. This comparison is carried out using a fitness function (evaluation) set in advance according to the desired objective. The programs with the best fitness function (parent programs) will be selected to breed and produce new programs (children's program) for the next generation using the primary genetic operations (selection, crossover and mutation) (Koza, 1994).

Initial Programs Population

Like other evolutionary algorithms, in GP the programs of the first population must be generated randomly. There's a number of different approaches to generate this population as the global method and ramped method (KOZA 1992).

Coding Programs

In GP, each individual is a computer program represented as a nested list, which can be directly mapped into a syntax tree constituting from:

- Variables and constants that represent the leaves of the tree or terminals.
- Arithmetic operations are called internal nodes function.
- The functions and terminals from the primitive set of a PG system.

The Selection Operator

Genetic operators GP are applied to programs that are selected according to their fitness. In other words the best programs are liable to have more children programs. The most used selection method by GP, is the tournament technique (for more details see Section on The General Process under Genetic Algorithms).

Reproduction Operators

PG differs significantly from other evolutionary algorithms in the implementation of crossover and mutation operators.

- **The Crossover Operator:** The creation of new children programs by combining two random parts from two sub trees of selected parent programs. For this purpose a method called the cross in a sub-tree structure is used.
- **The Mutation Operator:** Creating a new child program, by modifying randomly a selected part of a sub father tree. The replacement step in GP will remain the same as the replacement method of GAs (more detail in the section on The General Process under Genetic Algorithms).

The Procedure

The general structure of the GP is grouped in the next pseudo code:

Genetic programming procedure

AM: Random Variable crossover [0-1] MP: best program; MP: mutation probability; CP: cross probability; AM: random mutation variable [0-1]; AM: Random Variable crossover [0-1], Pi{}: size list of Npg programs initially generated from the set of primitives available, NG{}: set of programs (parent and son) that will be built after each generation, Npg: the size of the list Pi{} and NG{}, PGi: program number I of population programs, Sp{}: the list of selected programs, SPGi: program number I from the selected programs.

Input: CP, MP, Pi

For each PGi from Pi do

Execute and evaluate the program i.

end

while (no sttoping cretirien) do

selection operator

SP ← tournament-selection (PGi) (for more detail see the section on The General Process under Genetic Algorithms)

The cross operator

For each (PGi and PGj) selected randomly from Sp do

Generat-randomly (AC)

If AC<PC then NG{} ← interbreed (SPGi, SPGj) (i must be different to j)

else NG{} ← do-not-cross(SPGi, SPGj)

end

mutation operator

For each PGi from NG do

Generate-randomly(AM)

if AM<PM then NG{} ← mutation(SPGi)

else do-not-mutation(SPGi)

end

for each PGi from NG do evaluate (PGi)

M_p ← best of (PGi)

end

output: M_p

EVOLUTIONARY STRATEGY (ES)

The Origin of the Algorithm (ES)

Evolutionary Strategy (SE) is chronologically the first of all the evolutionary algorithms. It dates back to the 1960s and is the most commonly applied as a black box in optimization problems in continuous search spaces, discrete and also in the case of the multi-objective constraints. The algorithm of the SE was born in Germany in the 60s and the first work was presented in (Fogel, 1962) to solve numerical optimization problems. It was later developed by Ingo Rechenberg, Hans-Paul Schwefel and colleagues in 1964 to resolve an aerodynamic design problem (Rechenberg, 1989).

The Inspiration

Evolutionary strategy is an optimization technique based on ideas of adaptation and evolution. It is animated by the theory of adaptation and evolution by natural selection and the macro level in the process of species evolution (phenotype, hereditary variation) unlike the genetic algorithm that trait the micro level at the genomic (genomic, chromosomes, genes, alleles).

The Summary of the Algorithm

The ES algorithm called evolutionary programming is particularly a suitable paradigm for nonlinear optimization spots. Like other evolutionary algorithms, genetic operators are applied in a loop. An iteration of the loop is called a generation. The sequence of generations is continued until a stopping criterion is reached. A very important feature of SE is the use of self-adaptive mechanisms to control the application of a mutation. These mechanisms are designed to optimize the research progress, by changing not only the solutions to the problem to study, but also some settings to mutate these solutions.

The General Process

The algorithm of evolution strategies is a specific instance of evolutionary algorithms and its operation is characterized by the following four properties:

1. The selection of individuals for recombination is impartial, that is based solely on fitness rankings.
2. The selection is a deterministic process.
3. The mutation operator is parameterized and therefore it can change its properties during optimization.
4. Individuals consist of decision parameters and Strategy Settings.

The operation of this algorithm is based on coding individuals, usually by a vector where each individual component of the vector is a real number, a deterministic selection, a cross (discreet for the parameters of the strategy and means for decision parameters) and mutation for the strategy and for the decision. Some forms of selection and sampling in the SE are as follows:

- SE - (1 + 1): This is a simple selection mechanism in which works by creating a vector of real value of the object variable from its parents by applying a mutation with a standard deviation identical to each variable object. Then, the individual results are evaluated and compared to their parents and if it has a greater fitness relative to those parents then it becomes a parent for the next generation.
- SE - ($\mu + \lambda$): μ in this case the parents are selected from the current generation and generate λ offspring through recombination operators and / or mutation where the best μ will be kept for the next generation.
- SE - (μ, λ) is the most used where μ parents will be selected from the current generation and used to generate λ children (with $\lambda > = \mu$) and only the best individuals descendants of μ construct the next generation by destroying completely the parents.

The Procedure

The general structure of the SE algorithm - (μ, λ) is shown in the following pseudo-code

Evolutionary algorithm strategy SE -(μ, λ)
Mi: best individu ; NG{ }: the list of children individus: CP: cross pobability; MP: mutation probability;
    P: population;
Input: μ: the number of candidate solutions in the parent generation.
λ: is the number of candidate solutions generated from the parent generation
P ← generate-randomly (μ solutions potentiel)
For each individu Ni ∈ P do
Evaluat(Ni)
End
Mi ← return-best-individu(P)
while (no-stopping-cretirien) do
NG{ } ← ∅
for i=0 à λ do
PRi ← return-parents (P, i)
Si A<P_M alors NG { } ← crossover (discret-coss, intermediate-coss)
If A<P_C then NG { } ← mutation (mutation (strategy parametes), mutation (décision-parametes))
endfor
Evaluation(NG)
Mi ← return-best-individu (NG, Mi)
P ← selection (P, NG, μ)
end
output: Mi

DIFFERENTIAL EVOLUTION (DE)

Another paradigm in the family of EA is the differential evolution (DE) proposed by Storn and Price in 1997 (Storn, 1997). The DE algorithm is similar to genetic algorithms since it is grounded on a population of individuals to research an optimal solution. The main difference is that in the GAs, the mutation is the result of small disturbances to the genes of an individual, but in the DE the mutation is the result of arithmetic combinations of individuals.

The DE is easy to implement that requires less adjustment parameters such as the weighting factor. It is considered as a reliable optimization technique, precise, robust and fast. Unfortunately, according to Crick & al in 2004, noise can interfere with the performance of DE because of its greedy nature of the DE and self-adaptation can eliminate the need for manual adjustment of control settings.

The General Process

The Differential Evolution algorithm involves maintaining a population of candidate solutions subjected to iterations of recombination, evaluation, and selection. The recombination approach involves the creation of new candidate solution components based on the weighted difference between two randomly selected population members added to a third population member. This perturbs population members relative to the spread of the broader population. In conjunction with the selection, the perturbation effect self-organizes the sampling of the problem space, bending it to known areas of interest.

The Procedure

The general structure of the DE algorithm is exhibited in the next pseudo-code:

```
Differential Evolution (DE) algorithm
Input: Population_size, P roblem_size, Weighting_factor, Crossover_rate
Population ← InitializePopulation(Population_size, Problem_size);
EvaluatePopulation(Population);
Sbest ← GetBestSolution(Population);
while:not StopCondition() do
NewPopulation ← ∅
For each Pi ∈ Population do
Si ← NewSample(Pi, Population, Problem_size, Weighting_factor, Crossover_rate);
if Cost(Si) ≤ Cost(Pi) then NewPopulation ← Si;
else NewPopulation ← Pi;
end
end
Population ← NewPopulation;
EvaluatePopulation(Population);
S_best ← GetBestSolution(Population);
end
Return: S_best;
```

PADDY FIELD ALGORITHM (PFA)

It is a new algorithm proposed by Premaratne & al in 2009 (Premaratne, 2009), which works on a principle of reproduction depends on the proximity of the overall solution and a population density similar to the plant populations. Unlike evolutionary algorithms, it does not use a combined behaviour or cross between individuals, it uses the pollination and dispersal steps. The PFA consists of five basic steps (seed, selection, planting, pollination, dispersion). It has a lower cost of computing.

The Procedure

The general structure of the PFA is exhibited in the next pseudo-code:

```
Paddy Field Algorithm (PFA)
Input: population_size, Problem_size
Initial population ← randomlly scattering seeds (plants)
```

While not stopping cretirion do
Selection ← select-best-plant(population)
For each plant ∈ population do
Seeding (population)
Pollination population)
End
Best$_{solution}$ ← evaluation population
Population ← dispersion (population)
Return:best$_{solution}$

ANALYTIC COMPARISON BETWEEN EVOLUTIONARY ALGORITHMS

This section presents a comparative analysis of the evolutionary algorithms (EAs) seen so far in terms of the representation, operators, areas of application and control parameters.

Table 1. The analytic comprison between evolutionary algorithms

	Steps	Parameters	Input and Coding	Application Domains
Gas	• Initialisation of population. • Reproduction operators (selection, crossover (1-point, 2-points, uniform), and mutation (exchange)), • Replacement.	• Number of iteration. • Size of the population. • Crossover probability, mutation probability • Size of the chromosome.	• -Individuals (potential solution) • - Binary, real or matrix.	Information retrieval, classification, clustering, Traveling salesmen problem, Business intelligence, data mining problem, network planning, scheduling problem, image segmentation, electromagnetism and mechanics computational fluid.
GP	• Population of initial program, • Tournament selection. • Tree crossing. • Mutation (change under a tree of a program) • Replacement	• Number of iteration. • The population size. • Crossover probability. • Mutation probability	• -Nested list (syntax tree with leaves or terminals, internal nodes called function).	Automatic discovery of reusable subroutines, classification, rules of associations, image processing, medical knowledge extraction, object detection, soccer robot problem
ES	• Mutation parameter • Selection (deterministic process). • Discrete crossover for strategic parameters. • Intermediate crossing for the decision parameters.	• Stopping criterion. • Probability of crossover. • Probability of mutation. • Selection and form of sampling used.	• -Individuals (strategic parameter, decision parameter) • -Vector with real components	Machine vision system, image processing, decision support system, scheduling problem, the problem of wireless mobile networks.
DS	• Selection. • Crossover. • Mutation (arithmetic combination between individuals). • Replace.	• The size of the population. • The size of the problem. • crossover probability.	• -Vectors of real values.	Unsupervised image classification, clustering, digital filter design, optimization of nonlinear functions.
PFA	• The dissemination of seeds. • Planting, selection. • Seeding, dispersion.	• Number of initial seed. • Seed size • Selection threshold. • the initial value of number of • Seed	• -Individuals (potential solutions) • -Linear=[x1,x2..x]	Optimization of neural network parameters, adjustment parameters in the PID controller, the optimization of the continuous function.

SWARM INTELLIGENCE ALGORITHM (SIAS)

The swarm intelligence (SI) is a phrase introduced firstly by Gerardo Beni and Jing Wang in 1989, as part of cellular robotic systems (Beni, 1993). The SI is a new paradigm emerging in bio-inspired computing that allows the implementation of adaptive algorithms inspired by the collective behaviour of natural swarms as a tool for solving complex problems. It can be seen in groups of birds, schools of fish, as well as insects like mosquitoes and gnats. As has mentioned in the previous section the EAs are based on the genetic adaptation of organisms, but SIAs are based on social behaviour and collective intelligence of organisms.

Generally, An SIA is composed of a population of simple autonomous agents interacting locally between them and with their environment. Agents are subsystems that follow very simple local rules, and although there is no centralized control structure dictating how individual agents should behave. The local interaction between these agents led to the emergence of a complex global behaviour that achieves a goal. One type of self-organization emerges from the set of actions of the group. This class of algorithms can produce solutions that are fast, robust and with less cost to more complex problems.

Since 1990, several algorithms inspired collective behaviour (such as social insects, flocking birds) have been proposed in the literature, and applied successfully in many application in real life (like the traveling salesman problem, routing network, classification, data mining, scheduling tasks, and collective robotics ...... .etc. In this section we discuss in detail a set of (SIAs):

PARTICLES SWARM OPTIMIZATION (PSO) ALGORITHM

The Origin of the Algorithm

The PSO is an SI stochastic algorithm that was proposed by the psychologist James Kennedy and the electrical engineer Russell Elberhart in 1995 (Kennedy, 1995). These two researchers used the studies of Craig Reynolds in the late 1987 about the foraging of a birds group (Reynolds, 1987). This algorithm was originally used for solving nonlinear optimization and continuous problems, but more recently it has been applied to many problems of real life, such as dynamic monitoring systems (Eberhart, 2001), control collective power (Yoshida, 2000), and the composition of music (Blackwell, 2002).

The Inspiration Source

The PSO is inspired by a sociological phenomenon associated to the flocking of birds and precisely the foraging behaviour. Naturally the birds fly in a group without collision and making use of their efforts to maintain an optimal distance between them and their neighbours as well as a local interaction to achieve the common objective of the group.

The phenomenon of flocking is clearly defined in the following scenario: Initially, a group of birds is looking randomly for food in a zone. There is only a piece of food in the desired area. The birds do not know where is the food, but they know how far away and the positions of their neighbours. So, what is the best strategy to find food? An effective strategy is to follow the bird that is the nearest food.

Summary of the Algorithm

The PSO is a global optimization algorithm generally used to deal with problems where a better solution can be represented as a point or a surface in an N-dimensional space. It is based on a population of solutions (particles) random (each solution is like a bird) and each particle is associated with a velocity and position. As time goes, the particles move through the search space with dynamically adjusted speeds based on their performance and updating each solution to direct the research process. Therefore the particles tend to fly in an optimal search area where they are evaluated according to certain fitness criteria after each step in time and also through simple rules following the particles with the best solutions (best fitness value) to be gradually converging to a local minimum.

The General Process

Each particle is characterized by its position, its best position found, the best position funded by its neighbors and its velocity. During the research process, each particle adjusts its position in the search space basing on his best position finding (Pbest) and the best position found by his neighbors (g_{best}). The general process of PSO is presented in the following figure:

As shown in previous figure each step will be detailed in the next:

The Initial Population

The generating of N initial solutions is based on the random generation of the velocity and position of each particle.

Evaluation

This step evaluates the quality of each solution by evaluating the position of each particle to detect the best position.

Figure 4. The various steps of the operation of particle swarm optimization algorithm (PSOA)

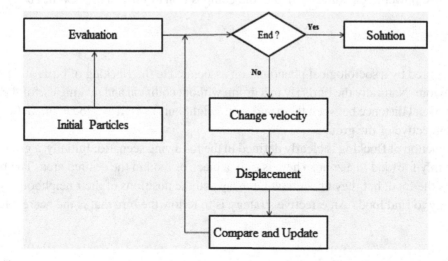

Change Velocity

Iteratively, each particle changes its speed depending on its current position and the better position of its neighbourhood using the following equation:

$$V^i_{K+1} = V^i_K + C_1 r_1 (P^i_K - X^i_K) + C_2 r_2 (P^g_K - X^i_K)$$

- P^i_K : The best position X^i_K of the particle i in the iteration K.
- P^g_K : The best position among all the positions of the particles.
- C_1, C_2: Two learning factors that control the influence of social and cognitive components.
- r_1, r_2: two random numbers generated independently in the range [0,1].

Displacement

The movement of each particle from one position to another is based on the current position and its speed of displacement. The next position of each particle is calculated through the following equation:

$$X^i_{K+1} = X^i_K + V^i_{K+1}$$

- X^i_K : The position of the particle i in the iteration K.
- V^i_K : Velocity of the particle i at iteration K.

Compare and Update

We compare the current position of each particle X^i_{K+1} with his best position found in the previous steps P^i_K. if $P^i_K \leq X^i_{K+1}$ then $P^i_{K+1} = X^i_{K+1}$.

Procedure

The general structure of the particle swarm optimization algorithm is presented in the following pseudo code:

Particles swarm optimisation

P best: best solution

Input:
- N:the number of particles of the initial population
- The fitness function

P ← generate-randomly (N, Vi, Xi)

For each Pi do

$\quad\quad P^g_0 \quad\quad$ ← Evaluat (pi)

```
end
```
$P_0^i \leftarrow X_0^i$

$K \leftarrow 0$

While (no stopping cetirien) do

For each particle pi of the population do

Change-velocity (pi)

Displacement (pi)

$\qquad P_{K+1}^i \leftarrow$ Comparer $(P_K^i, \ X_{K+1}^i)$

Mise à jour (P_{K+1}^i)

```
end
```

$\qquad P_{K+1}^g \leftarrow$ Evaluat(Pi)

$P_{best} \leftarrow \ P_{K+1}^g$

$K \leftarrow k+1$

```
end
```

output: P_{best}

ANT COLONY OPTIMIZATION ALGORITHM

The Origin of the Algorithm

The ACO algorithm is a meta-heuristic probabilistic SI which was introduced by an Italian Marco Dorigo around the 1990 during his doctoral thesis on the optimization and natural algorithms (Dorigo, 1992). This algorithm was firstly proposed for solving a discrete optimization problem at the end of 1991, and also used for solving the traveling salesman problem in (Dorigo, 1997). Several versions of this algorithm have been proposed in the literature as the minimisation algorithm proposed by -maximum Stützle and Hoos in 1997 (Stützle, 1997), and the ant system algorithm proposed in (Dorigo, 1996).

The Inspiration Source

The ACO was inspired by the behavior of ant colonies that are social insects with the ability to find the shortest path between their nest and the food source as well as the phenomenon of stegmergy introduced in 1959 by fat in (Grasse, 1967) which refers to the indirect communication between ants using pheromone trails that allows them to find the most current paths.

Ants first start by randomly explore the environment around their nest. When moving, ants leave a chemical pheromone trail on their way, the movement of ants is guided by the smell of pheromone Ants first start by randomly explore the environment around their nest. The movement of ants is guided by the smell of pheromone. Ants tend to choose the ways marked by the concentration of the stronger pheromone. In return, the amount of pheromone that leaves the ant on its way depends on the quality and quantity of food wear.

Summary of the Algorithm

The main idea of the algorithm is to model the problem to be solved as a research problem of an optimal path in a weighted graph by using artificial ants to find the quality paths among all the paths that exist. The ants move from one node to the next following a transition rule based on a probability of displacement. Each solution built is evaluated according to a fitness function in order to detect the shortest path (the nodes of the graph which corresponds to the components of the solution).

General Process

The general operation of ACO is presented in the following figure and each step is detailed in the next:

Figure 5. The functioning of the ant colony algorithm (ACO)

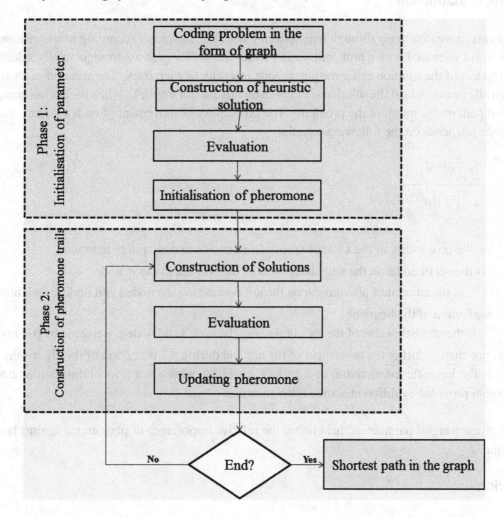

Coding Solutions

The solutions space of the problem is represented as a graph where each solution is a path.

Creation of Heuristic Solutions

The creation of N initial solutions using heuristics based on external resources. This step will generate values for the arcs that connect the nodes.

Pheromone Initialization

Initially, the traces of all tracks of the graph pheromone are initialized with a small constant value.

Solutions Construction

Artificial ants move iteratively through neighbouring nodes of the graph according to a transition rule. This movement is carried with a probability rule, which allows for each ant to sequentially select components (nodes) of the solution using the pheromone intensity of each track. The solution of each ant is built when all components of the solution are chosen by this ant (for example, when the ant has completed a tour / full path on the graph of the problem). The probability of movement of each ant from the node i to the node j depends on the following equation:

$$P_{ij}^{K}(t) = \frac{[\tau_{ij}(t)]^{\propto} * [\mu_{ij}]^{\beta}}{\sum_{l \in N_i^k}[\tau_{il}(t)]^{\propto} * [\mu_{il}]^{\beta}}$$

- P_{ij}^{K} : is the probability of the kth ant to move from node i to node j in t[th] iteration.
- N_i^k : is the set of nodes in the neighbourhood of the Nth ant in the ith node.
- $\tau_{ij}(t)]^{\propto}$: is the amount of pheromone on the arc connecting the node i and node j, weighted by α (the confession of the heuristic).
- $[\mu_{ij}]^{\beta}$: is the heuristic value of the arc connecting the node i and node j, weighted by β. This value does not change during the movement of the ant and during the execution of the algorithm.
- μ : is the heuristic information, or a path of visibility, which is a priori information about the problem provided by different source other than ants.

$\propto$ et β are weights parameters that control the relative importance of pheromone against heuristic information.

Evaluation

Once a solution (path) is built, it will be evaluated using a fitness function to determine the amount of pheromone deposited on each track.

Update Pheromone

Once complete solutions have been built, the pheromones slopes must be updated. This step also includes the evaporation of pheromone (the pheromone potentials are reduced) in order to help the ants to forget the bad solutions that were previously learned. The values of the pheromone of the visited arcs are increased, with quantities proportionally inverse to the cost of their tours.

$$\tau_{ij}\left(t+1\right) \leftarrow (1\text{-}P)^* \, \tau_{ij}(t) + \sum_{K=1}^{m} \Delta\tau_{ij}^{k}\left(t\right)$$

$$\Delta\tau_{ij}^{k}\left(t\right) = \begin{cases} \dfrac{Q}{C^{k}\left(t\right)} & , \; if \; arc\left(i,j\right) \in T^{k}(t) \\ else & 0 \end{cases}$$

- Q: is a specific constant.
- M: is the number of ants.
- A: is the set of arcs of the graph.
- P: the evaporation rate of pheromone.
- $C^{k}\left(t\right)$: is the function of the overall cost of the tour $T^{k}(t)$ built by the kth ant at iteration t..
- $T^{k}(t)$: is the set of arcs visited by ant k at iteration t.

Procedure

The following pseudo code summarizes the general structure and the different stages of the ACO algorithm

Ant Colony optimisation procedure
SH: heuristic solution.
Input: N: the size of the population, m, P, α, β
Coding problem (representation of solutions in the form of weighting graph)
Sh ← creation of heuristic solution
F(c_{best}) ← Evaluate (Sh)
c_{best} ← Sh
Pheromone ← initialisation of pheromone
While (no stopping criterion) do
S ← ∅
For i=1 to m do
Si ← probability (pheromone, α, β)
F(si) ← evaluate(Si)
If (f(Si) ≤ f(c_{best})) then
f(c_{best}) ← f(Si)
c_{best} ← Si

```
end if
S ← Si
End
Evaporation-of-pheromone(pheromone, P)
For each Si ∈ S do
Updating-pheromone(pheromone, Si,f(Si))
end
Output: c_best
```

BACTERIAL FORAGING OPTIMIZATION (BFO)

The Origin of the Algorithm

The bacteria are characterized by diverse behaviours like (foraging, reproduction and movement) that summers the inspiration of many computer scientists for a long time for the development of optimization algorithms. In 2012 an algorithm called bacterial foraging optimization (BFO) was introduced by Passino & al in (Pasino, 2012) where they are used studies conducted by biologists on the chemotactic movement of E.coli bacteria. This algorithm represents a promising new branch in bio mimicry that can bridge the gap between microbiology and engineering.

The Inspiration

The BFO is the first algorithm based on the foraging and moving of a bacteria colony (such as E. coli). The bacteria are always looking for the nutrients to maximize the energy obtained per unit of time and communicate by sending signals. The movement of bacteria is called chemotaxis, which represents the key idea of this algorithm.

The Summary of the Algorithm

The input of the BFO is a set of artificial bacteria that will be displaced in the solution space simultaneously taking into account their performance and their proximity with others bacteria. Following successive stages (moving, swarming, reproduction, disposal and dispersal) the population of bacteria searches the best solution to a problem from iteration to another until it reaches the stop criterion.

The General Process

The basic functioning of BFO is shown in the following figure:

Figure 6 shows the general functioning of BFO and the role of each step in this process are detailed as follows:

Figure 6. The general process of the bacterial foraging optimisation algorithm (AOBB)

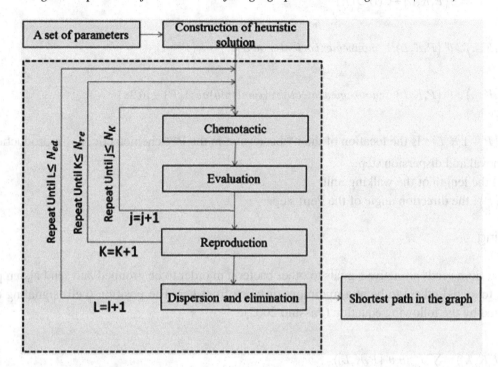

Initialization of Locations

Initially the location of each bacterium must be initialized randomly based on the number of artificial bacteria and the problem to be optimized.

Chemotaxis

The movement of E. Coli bacteria is guided by two characteristics: they are unable to choose the direction in which they move and they are also unable to follow the same direction a long time because they easily forget the directions in which they are going. For this reason there are two different types of motions:

- **The Oriented Movement (Swimming):** It is the movement of bacteria in the same direction. The presence of a chemical guardian (place of food) allows bacteria to react with the phenomenon of chemotactic and they will direct their movements in the direction of such guardian. In the case where a bacterium feels that it moves in the right direction (towards the chemical caretaker) then it continues straight as for a long time before tumbling phase.
- **The Random Motion (Tumbling):** It is the movement in a random direction where if a bacterium forgets the direction in which it goes and if she feels that she is not going in the right direction, it will follow a new direction chosen randomly. The movement of the i[em] bacterium after each step is given by the following two equations (Passino 2002):

$$\delta\left(P+1,K,L\right)=\delta\left(P,K,L\right)+\text{C(i)}\,\varnothing\left(P\right)$$

$$\theta^i\left(P+1,K,L\right)>\theta^i\left(P,K,L\right)\quad mouvement\,orienter\,où\,\varnothing\left(P\right)=\varnothing\left(P-1\right)$$

$$\theta^i\left(P+1,K,L\right)>\theta^i\left(P,K,L\right)\quad mouvement\,aléatoire\left(tumbling\right)où\,\varnothing\left(P\right)\in\left[0,2\pi\right]$$

- $\theta^i\left(P+1,K,L\right)$: Is the location of the i^{em} bacterium in the P^{eme} chemotactic, K^{em} reproduction, the removal and dispersion step.
- C(i) the length of the walking unit.
- $\varnothing\left(P\right)$: the direction angle of the Pem step.

Swarming

Each bacterium sends attractive signals to other bacteria in order to be grouped and send also repellent products to signal others to be at a minimum distance from her. The position (cell) signaling can be represented by the following equation (Passino 2002):

$$\text{J}_{cc}(\theta,P\left(J,K,L\right))=\sum_{i=1}^{s}J_{cc}^{\;i}(\theta,\theta^i\left(P,K,L\right))$$

$$=\sum_{i=1}^{s}[d_{atraction}\exp(-\omega_{attraction}\sum_{m=1}^{P}\left(\theta_m-\theta_m^{\;i}\right)^2)]$$

$$+\sum_{i=1}^{s}[h_{repoussant}\exp(-\omega_{repoussant}\sum_{m=1}^{P}\left(\theta_m-\theta_m^{\;i}\right)^2)]$$

- $\text{J}_{cc}(\theta,P\left(J,K,L\right))$: the objective function
- S: the total number of bacteria (number of cell in a population)
- P: the number of variables to be optimized which are present in each bacterium
- $\theta=\left[\theta_1,\theta_2,\ldots\ldots\ldots,\theta_P\right]^T$: refers to a point in the dimension of the search area
- $d_{atraction}$: the depth of the bait released by the cell
- $\omega_{attraction}$: a measure of the width of the attraction signal
- $h_{repoussant}$: the height of the repellent effect
- $\omega_{repoussant}$: the measurement of the width of repulsive

Reproduction

After the NC steps of chemotactic, the reproducing step must be done and the performances (fitness function values) of bacteria will be stored in an ascending order. The functioning principle is that the bacteria with less healthy eventually die and the remaining bacteria (i.e. healthy bacteria) will be divided into two identical and placed in the same place.

Dispersion and Elimination

In order to avoid local optima, a process of dispersion and removal is done after the REN phases of reproduction. Depending on a probability (ped), a bacterium is selected to be scattered and moved to another position within the environment.

Procedure

The general structure of BFO is grouped in the following pseudo code:

Bacterial foraging optimisation (BFO)

N_{um} the size of the population ; Ned: the number of elimination and dispertion step; REN: the number of reproduction step ; N_c is the number of steps of chemotactic; Ped: the probability of a cell being subjected to the removal and dispersion.

Input:

Num, Ned, REN, Nc, Ped,

P ← initialize the location of each bacterium

For l=0 to Ned do

for K=0 to REN do

for j=0 to NC do

P ← chemotaxis (p)

For i=1 to N_{um} do

Calculate the fitness function for each bacterium f(i)

If B_{best} ≤ f(i) then B_{best} ← f(i)

end

end

P ← reproduction(P)

end

for each bacterium i from the popualtion P do

If A ≤ Ped then

P(i) ← Dispersion and elimination (I)

end

end

output: Bbest

Other Bacteria Algorithms

In the literature others algorithms have been proposed by mimicking the biological characteristics of bacteria such as:

- The algorithm of bacterial chimiotaxis (BCC) proposed by Li & al in 2005 (Li, 2005).
- The algorithm Superbag Algorithm (SUA) has been proposed by (Anandarman, 2012) which is based on the findings of the epidemic and antiviral research. The operation of the SUA is comprised from the following operators (initialization of the population, inversion mutation with inter changes for each pair of bacteria, transfer genes between bacteria to improve the level of fitness).
- The Bacterial Optimization Algorithm (BOA) was proposed by Niu and Wang in 2012 (Niu, 2012). The functioning of the BOA consists of the following steps: chemotaxis, communication, elimination, reproduction and migration.

WOLF COLONY ALGORITHM (WCA)

The Origin of the Algorithm

The WCA was firstly introduced by Liu & al in 2011 (Liu, 2011) which is based on the studies conducted by Macdonald in (Macdonald, 2004) and Fuller in (Fuller, 2003).

The Inspiration Source

The wolf colony algorithm (WCA) is inspired by the natural social life of wolves and intra-specific phenomenon of social hunting. It mimics the operation from intelligent predatory of the northern gray wolves as (seeking food, besieging behaviour and the behaviour of the division food).

The Summary of the Algorithm

In the WCA each artificial wolf is a solution. Initially a set of artificial wolves are generated for searching in the field activity of a prey flock (the solutions search space). When the artificial search wolves discovered that herd, they inform other artificial wolves of this position by the howling (the solutions will be improved iteratively). Other artificial wolves get closer to that flock and besiege. The wolf colony is updated iteratively. The performance of the WCA is discussed based on the objective of the optimization problem.

General Process

The operation of the WCA is shown in the following figure:

Figure 7 describes the relationship between the different steps involved in the operation of the WCA, which will be detailed in the next:

Initialisation of Wolf Colony

D is the size of the search space, n is the number of individual; Xi represents the position of artificial i^{eme} wolf, so we have the following equation to represent the position vector of each wolf (Liu, 2011):

$$X_i = X_{i1}, \ldots \ldots X_{id}, \ldots \ldots X_D \qquad \qquad 1.$$

Figure 7. The functioning of the wolf colony algorithm (WCA)

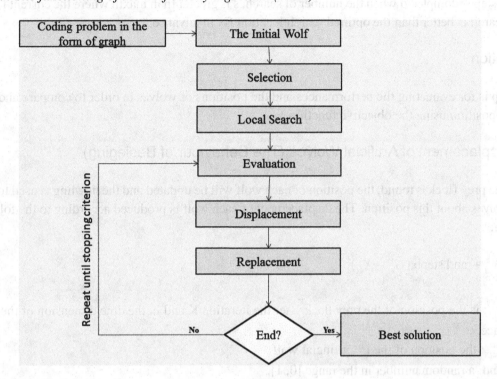

with $1 \leq i \leq n$ et $1 \leq d \leq D$

This step allows the initializes of N artificial wolves by randomly generating the position Xi of each one of them.

Selection

This operator selects from N wolves, q most optimum artificial wolves (called Scouts wolves that are closer to the prey flock) designated for research to detect the potential activities of the prey flock in order to increase the probability of discovering their positions.

The Local Search (Besiege the Flock of Prey)

Each search wolf selected is moved using the following equation:

$Yj = XX_i + randn \ .stepa$

- Maxdh: denotes the number of maximum research
- XXI: Is the location of the ith Scout wolf (totally h locations are created around the candidate wolf).
- Yj: the j^{eme} position of research.
- Rand: A random number in the range [-1, 1].
- Stepa: the search step

This step is completed when the number of searches is greater than maxth where the current location of the search is better than the optimal search location fix in advance.

Evaluation

This step is for evaluating the performances and the positions of wolves in order to compare and detect the best position using the objective function.

The Displacement of Artificial Wolves (The Behaviour of Besieging)

When the prey flock is found, the position of each wolf will be updated and the howling is used to notify other wolves about this position. The displacement of each wolf is produced according to the following equation:

$$X_{id}^{k+1} = X_{id}^k + \text{rand.stepb.}(G_d^k - X_{id}^k)$$

- G_d^k : is the position of the prey flock after the iteration K and in the dme dimension of the search space.
- X_{id}^k : the position of the i^{eme} artificial wolf
- Rand: a random number in the range [0, 1].
- Stepb: the search step.
- K: the iteration number.
- The range [XMIN$_d$, XMAX$_d$] is used for the representation of the dth position.

Replacement (Division of Food)

The food is eaten first by the strongest wolves, then by other wolves. In this colony, the m (parameter set in advance) wolves with the worst performance will be replaced with new artificial wolves created randomly and will be integrated into the next iteration of the colony. This mechanism can prevent the algorithm falling into local optimum.

Procedure

The general structure of the wolf colony algorithm (ACL) and the relationship between these function is present in the pseudocode:

Wolf colony algorithm (WCA)
L$_{best}$: best solution ; CL: wolf colony ; LR{}: the list of search wolf generated.
Input:
N, q, h:the direction of research, maxdh, stepa, stepb, m: the number of wolves having the best performances which will be kept for the next iteration.
CL ← initialisation (N, Xi)

For each wolf Li do

$L_{best} \leftarrow$ evaluation (Xi)

While (no-stopping cretirien) do

For each wolf Li $\in$ CL do

LR{} $\leftarrow$ Select(q)

end

for each wolf Li$\in$ LR{} do

Displacement following: Yj = XXi + randn .stepa

Li $\leftarrow$ new position

end

$L_{best} \leftarrow$ evaluation(Xi)

For each Li $\in$ CL

displace (Li) using

$$X_{id}^{k+1} = X_{id}^k + \text{rand.stepb.}(G_d^k - X_{id}^k)$$

end

Replacement (m)

end

output: L_{best}

WOLF PACKS SEARCH (WPS)

There are other algorithms inspired by the social life of wolves such as wolf pack search (WPS) which is introduced in 2007 by Yang in (Yang, 2007). The WPS is composed of 4 main steps: initialization parameters ii) random generation of a set of packs of artificial wolf ii) evaluating the performance of each artificial wolf to determine the best solution using a a fitness function iiii) the circulation and update step.

BAT ALGORITHM (BA)

The Origin of the Algorithm

The bat algorithm (BA) was proposed by Xin-She Yang in 2010 (Yang, 2010). It was firstly applied on the benchmark functions, and it gets better results compared to genetic algorithms and PSO.

The Source Inspiration

The bats have mysterious behaviours that have a long time ago attracted the attention of human. They emit a very loud noise pulse and listen to the echo that bounces from surrounding objects. Their impulses vary according to their hunting strategies. This behaviour is called echolocation, which allows to bats to find their prey and discriminate different types of insects even in complete darkness. The inspiration of the BA is summarized in the Bat movement for foraging and the behaviour of echolocation.

The Summary of the Algorithm

The input of the BA is a population of N bats (possible solutions) that uses echolocation to detect the distance. The artificial bats fly through a random search space by conducting the update of their positions Xi and velocities vi from one step to another. Each solution $b_i = b_{i2} + b_{i2} + \ldots\ldots + b_{id}$ is evaluated by a fitness function $F\left(b_i\right)$. The goal is to find food / prey (best solutions).

The General Process

The operation of the BA is shown in the following figure. Initially, some numerical parameters associated with bats foraging behaviour are defined such as the velocity (vi) at the position (xi) with a fixed minimum frequency (f_{min}), a wavelength variable (λ) and intensity (Ao).

The previous figure demonstrated the various steps of the BA that will be detailed in the next:

Initial Displacement

Initially a population of N bats (potential solutions) must be initialized by the random generation of the positions and velocities of each bat.

Displacement

After the random displacement of bats in the previous step, the displacement of bats in the next step will be realized through the adjustment of their frequencies and updating of their velocities and positions. New locations / solutions (xit) and velocities (Vit) over time and step t are given by the following equation.

Figure 8. The general functioning of the bat algorithm (BA)

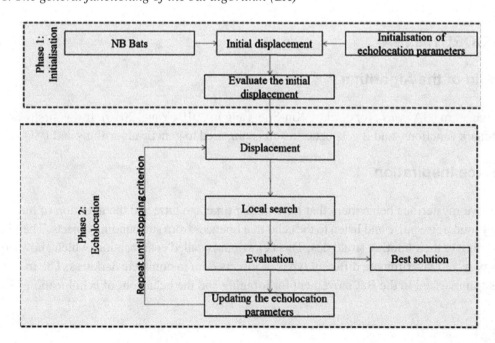

$$F_i = f_{min} + (f_{max} - f_{min}) \cdot \beta ,$$

$$V_i^t = V_i^{t-1} + (x_i^t - x_*) \cdot F_i$$

$$x_i^t = x_i^{t-1} + V_i^t$$

- $\beta \in [0, 1]$: is a random vector drawn from the uniform distribution
- F_i: is the speed increment
- F_{min}, f_{max}: are the lower and upper bounds imposed for the frequency range of virtual bats.
- x_*: the best global position.

The Local Search

In this local search step a new solution is generated for each artificial bat of the current population according to the next equation

$$X_{nv} = X_{anc} + \varepsilon A^t$$

- ε : a random number.
- A^t: is the average intensity of all bats.

Evaluation

The evaluation of each artificial bat using the fitness function and the solutions were ranke in order to find the best solution $X *$.

Updating the Echolocation Parameters

The general rule is that the intensity decreases as the pulse emission rate increases, when a bat found his prey. The intensity and the pulsing rate are updated through the following equation:

$$A_i^{t+1} = \propto A_i^t$$

$$R_i^{t+1} = r_i^0 [1 - exp(-^\gamma t)]$$

- A_i^t, A_i^{t+1}: the previous and current intensity of the ith bat.
- $\propto$ et γ : constants with $0 < \propto < 1$ and $\gamma > 0$.
- R_i^{t+1}: is the pulse rate of the i^{me} bat at the iteration t+1.

The Procedure

The general structure of the bat algorithm is shown in the following pseudo-code:

Bat algorithm (BA)
PCS: population of artificiel bats
Entré: Ai, Fi, Ri, NB: the number of generated bats
Initial displacement
PCS ← initialisation of the population(Xi, Vi, NB)
Evaluat(PCS)
While (no-stopping criterien) do
PCS ← displacement(PCS)
PCS ← local-seach(PCS)
Evaluate (PCS)
updating echolocation parameters (Ai, Ri, fi)
X* ← Evaluat(PCS)
End
Output: X*

COCKROACHES COLONY ALGORITHM (CCA)

The Origin of the Algorithm

The CCA was introduced the first time by Bouarara & al in 2015 (Bouarara, 2015) where they have used the studies carried out by Bell & al on social life and behaviour of cockroaches proposed in (Bell, 2007).

The Inspiration Source

The CCA is inspired by the natural behaviour of cockroaches and the phenomenon of seeking the most attractive and secure place (shelter) for hiding. We can identify different types of cockroaches in our work, we are interested by the cockroaches that live in apartments, which are fertile and they are never isolated.

This phenomenon is well detailed in an experiment conducted by French biologists when they met a group of cockroaches in a basin where there's light everywhere, and they built two artificial shelters (shelter is a place with less brightness as shown in the figure) using two red circles because cockroaches do not observe the color red as shown in the following figure.

Figure 9. Description of the experience

a- two Shelters   b-exploration phase   c- the experience environment

Figure 10. The groping of cockroaches under the same place
Source: Bouarara, 2015

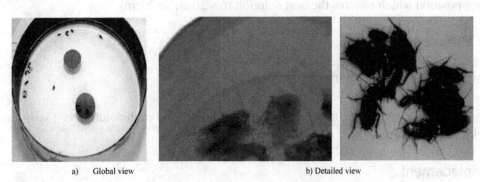

a) Global view   b) Detailed view

From previous experience it was observed that cockroaches have a choice of two shelters to hide where they always choose the most secure shelter. A biological model explaining this phenomenon is presented by the following:

Random Displacement of Cockroaches

Initially cockroaches will move randomly in all directions (exploration phase) as demonstrated in Figure 5.b. When a cockroach finds an attractive shelter, it hides and sends pheromones as smell to its congeners. The movement of cockroaches is guided by a set of displacement rules:

The Darkness Shelters

Cockroaches are attracted by the darkest places like corners and shelters with less brightness. The degree of darkness plays a very important role for the quality security of each shelter.

The Congener's Attraction

Each cockroach seeks shelter where there are more of its congeners (cockroaches from the same colony) to hide it.

The Security Quality

Cockroaches positioned in the middle of the shelter have a higher safety compared with cockroaches positioned at the border of the shelter.

Summary of the Algorithm

Initially a set of cockroaches will be assigned randomly to N shelters (initial solutions). Iteratively these solutions going to be improved using the displacement process following a set of rules (the darkness of each shelter, the attraction of congeners, permutation, and quality safety) until a stopping criterion.

The main objective is that every cockroach should be hidden in the shelter where he feels secure (find cockroaches position which ensures the best solution to a given problem).

General Processes

Representation of the Problem

Initially the problem must be transformed as a set of solutions and each solution is a position (shelter) where cockroaches is hidden.

Initial Displacement

The initial displacement of artificial cockroaches is carried according to a random generation of their positions (shelter Xi where each cockroach was hidden).

Seeking Operators

After the random displacement initially performed, cockroaches begin to change their current shelter according to the following rules:

- **Shelter Darkness:** The darkness of each shelter Xi for the cockroach Ck is calculated following the next equation:

Figure 11. The general functioning of cockroaches colony algorithm (CCA)

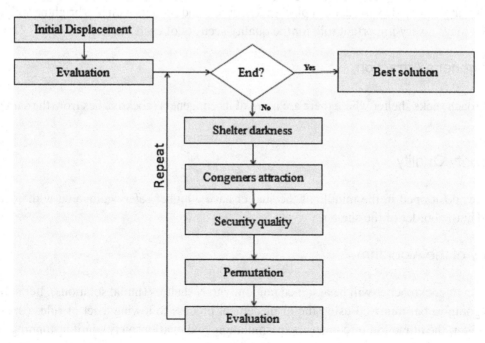

$$O_t(X_i) = O_t + \frac{C\left(Xi\right)_T}{N}$$

- **N: The Cockroaches Number**
- $C\left(Xi\right)_T$: the number of cockroaches in the shelter Xi in the iteration T
- $O_t(X_i)$: the darkness rate of the shelter Xi in the iteration T.
- **The Attraction Congeners:** In each iteration, the attraction of the neighbourhood (congeners) for each cockroach in each shelter changes depending on its positions and the best position of its neighbourhood.

$$AC_{T+1}^K \left(Xi\right) = AC_T^K + V_1(M_t^K - QS_T^K) + V_2(M_T - QS_T^K)$$

- M_t^K : the best security quality of the cockroach K among all the shelters where it was hidden previously.
- $AC_T^K \left(Xi\right)$: the rate of attraction of the neighbourhood (congeners) for the cockroach K hiding in the shelter Xi at iteration T.
- QS_T^K : the secuity cuality of the cockoach K in the iteration T.
- M_T: the best quality security among all security quality of cockroaches in all positions at time T.
- V_1, V_2: [0,1].
- **The Security Quality:** The security quality of each cockroach K in shelter Xi is calculated through the following equation:

$$QS_{T+1}^K \left(X_i\right) = QS_T^K + \alpha * O_{t+1}(X_i) + \beta * AC_{T+1}^K \left(Xi\right)$$

Evaluation

This step evaluates the position of each cockroach and the content of each shelter following an objective function fixed in advance in order to detect the best solution.

Permutation of Shelters

This step is used to avoid the local optimum and maintain the diversity of results. Firstly, a permutation probability (PP) is fixed and a random variable B is generated if B <M MP then cockroaches are randomly selected (one per shelter) and we permute them.

Displacement

Iteratively, each cockroach leaves his shelter to look for another place with more security. The displacement of cockroaches is achieved following a transition rule that allows for each cockroach to choose the direction and the next shelter that it will join. This choice is made via the following equation using the amount of security and external information that must be fixed in advance (e.g. in the traveling salesman problem that information is 1 / distance).

$$P_{ij}^{K}(T) = \frac{QS_T^K(j) * \mu_{ij}}{\sum_{l \in N_l^k} QS_{il}((t) * \mu_{il})}$$

- P_{ij}^{K} : Is the probability of the kth cockroach to pass from the shelter i to the shelter j in the iteration t.
- N_l^k : Is the set of shelters in the neighbourhood of the Kth cockroach in the ith shelter.
- $QS_T^K(j)$: The security quality of the Kth if it moves to the shelter j at iteration t.
- μ_{ij} : Is the value of external information of the path that connects the shelter i and shelter j. This value does not change during the movement of the cockroach and during the execution of the algorithm.

Updating of Shelter

For each cockroach, we compare the security quality of its current position X_{K+1}^i with its best position found in the previous steps P_K^i. If the security quality of its current shelter is better than the security quality of its shelters previously visited, its position X_{K+1}^i will be defined as the best position $M_t^K = X_{K+1}^i$.

Procedure

The next pseudo code summarizes the general structure and the different steps of the CCA algorithm:

Cockroaches colony algorithm (CCA)
Coding the problem
P ← generate-randomly ($X_i^K(t=0)$, AC_0^K)
M$_{position}$ ← evaluation (P)
T ← 0
While (no stopping criterion) do
P ← Ot+1(Xi)
P ← $AC_{T+1}^K(Xi)$
P ← QS_{T+1}^K (Xi)
if A≤PP then
choose randomly two cockroaches from two different shelters
P ← permute ($C_T^K(X_i)$, $C_T^G(X_j)$)
End if
M$_{position}$ ← evaluation (P)
For each cockoach of the population do
    C_T^K ← P_{ij}^K (T)
End
P ← displacement (C_T^K)
P ← update ($X_i^K(T)$, AC_T^K)

T ← T+1
End
output: M$_{position}$

MOSQUITO OPTIMIZATION ALGORITHM (MPA)

In (Feng, 2009), the traveling salesman problem is solved by the Mosquito Host Seeking Algorithm (MHSA) derived from the mosquito hunting behaviour.

WASP SWARM OPTIMIZATION (WSO):\

In 2008 Rinkler & al imitated the behaviour of wasps for the development of a new algorithm called Wasp Swarm Optimization proposed in (Runkler, 2008).

SOCIAL SPIDERS' ALGORITHM (SSA)

Social spiders also served as inspiration for example for the detection in images (Bourjot 2003) or securing wireless networks (Benahmed, 2012).

THE CUCKOO SEARCH ALGORITHM (CSA)

The behaviour of social animals such as cuckoos (birds of the family Cuculidae) has also been imitated by researchers. The cuckoos have as particularity to parasitize the nests of other species by laying their eggs. Other birds have two options: they perceive the trickery and destroy eggs, or they did not perceive them. To ensure the survival of their offspring, cuckoos are seeking to place them in the nests where they have the greatest chance of survival. Gandomi & al have developed The Cuckoo Search algorithm that was directly inspired by this parasitism in (Gandomi, 2013).

FIREWORKS ALGORITHM (FWA)

Since its creation, the FWA has been developed, and many extensions have seen the light. It was proposed for the first time in 2010 by Tan and Zhu in (Tan, 2010). This first algorithm was designed for function optimization which consists of local search space. However, in 2011 the FWA algorithm was used by Janecek and Tan in (Janecek, 2011) for the improvement of multiplicative update of non-negative matrix factorization algorithm. They put the FWA in confrontation with four other approaches using nature inspired algorithms (Genetic algorithms, Particle Swarm Optimization, Differential Evolution, and Fish School Search). Meanwhile, the FWA was studied many times. In (Pei, 2012), the authors presented an empirical study about the effect of approximation approaches for the enhancement of FWA. The first improvement that the algorithm has seen was in 2013 when an improvement was presented in (Liu,

2013) in which authors presented a new improvement of FWA. The improvement touched the way that the algorithm uses to compute the number of sparks and fireworks by designing a transfer function in order to control the exploration and exploitation of fireworks.

In (Zheng, 2013), an enhanced firework algorithm was proposed. The enhancement was designed to cover up some of the disadvantages of the original algorithm on shiftig functions, and the high computational cost per iteration. They proved five adaptations: a minimal explosion check, a new operator for generation of sparks, a new mapping way that could hold the problem of sparks that are out of the space, a new operator for the generation of Gaussian sparks, and finally, a new operator for selections of locations.

Later, in 2014, two extensions of firework algorithm were published in the CEC' 2014. One of them is a dynamic firework algorithm that was presented in (Zheng, 2014). They built a model in order to deal with the limitations of the previous enhanced firework algorithm (EFWA) by integrating a dynamic explosion mechanism for the fireworks. Also, they proved that the computational efficiency of EFWA could be improved by removing one of its operators. The other is presented (Li, 2014), in which the amplitude computation is changed by an adaptive one in purpose of dealing with the lack of adaptability of the EFWA.

The Procedure

The next pseudo code summarises the general structure and the different steps of the FWA:

Fireworks algorithm (FWA)
Input: Randomly select N locations for fireworks
while not stopping cretiriendo
Set off N fireworks respectively at the N locations:
for all fireworks xi do
Calculate the number of sparks as Si
Calculate the amplitude of sparks as Ai
end
//m is the number of sparks generated
for k =1 to m do
Randomly select a firework xi and generate a spark
end
select the best spark and the other sparks according to selection strategy
end
Return: best spark

ANALYTIC COMPARISON BETWEEN SWARM INTELLIGENCE ALGORITHMS

The next Table 2 summarises a comparative analysis of the swarm intelligence algorithms (SIAs) seen so far in terms of the representation, operators, areas of application and control parameters.

Table 2. Summary of a comparative study between the swarm intelligence algorithms

	Steps	Parameters	Input/Coding	Application Domains
PSO	• Particle initialization (speed and position of each particle) • Change in velocity • Particle displacement • Evaluation • Compare and Update	• Best position of each particle • Best position in the neighbourhood • Two random numbers generated independently • Two learning factors	• -The positions and velocities of the particles. • -Binary coding, Real, speed	Clustering, Classification in the multi-class databases, feature selection, composition of Web services, extraction of fuzzy neural network rules, the integration of planning and scheduling
ACO	• Initialization of parameters, • Coding the problem as a graph, Construction of heuristic solutions, Evaluation, • Initialisation of pheromone • Updating and evaporation of pheromone	• displacement probability of each ant at each node • The weights of the arcs that connect the nodes. • Evaporation rate	• -Graph weighted binary -Matrice	Traveling salesman problem, problem backpack, vehicle routing problem, detecting intrusion, problems of knowledge extraction, coloration of graphs, project scheduling, water distribution systems design.
BFO	• Initialise the positions of bacteria. • chemotaxis • The oriented movement • Random motion • Swarming. • Reproduction. • Dispersion.	• Number of bacteria. • The length of the walk unit. • Size of the search space. • Number of steps of chemotactic. • Number of disposals and dispersion steps. • Number of reproductive steps. • Probability of elimination.	• A set of i artificial bacteria	Extracting fuzzy rules, traveling salesman problem, classification, information retrieval, image segmentation, the resolution of the dynamic economic problem of distribution, applications on multi-objective optimization.
WCA	• Initialisation the positions of wolves. • Selecting scout wolf. • Local Search. • Evaluation. • The behaviour of besieging (displacement of the wolves).	• The number of scouts' wolves selected. • h: the search direction, maxdh, stepa, STEPB, • m: number of wolves that have better performance. • N: number of artificial wolves	• -A set of artificial wolfs. • -Integer, real, binary and matrix	The global optimization problems without constraints, the knowledge extraction tasks, Vehicle routing problems, combinatorial optimization problems, the detection of anomaly, the image segmentation.
FWA	• Selection of N locations • Explosions of N fireworks • Get the location of sparks • Evaluating the position of the sparks • Calculate the amplitude • Mapping • selecting the best fireworks for the next generation.	• N: number of locations • Number of iteration • Number of generating sparks	• -A set of location of fireworks. • -Binary, real, integer, structured tree	Business intelligence, data mining problem, network planning, scheduling problem, image segmentation, and electromagnetism and mechanics computational fluid.
CCA	• Initial displacement • Shelter darkness • Congeners attraction • The security quality • Permutation • Evaluation • Displacement and updating	• Number of initial cockroaches • Iteration number • Probability of changing shelter • Best quality security of each cockroaches in each shelter previously visited • The attraction rate of the neighbourhood	• -Vector (binary, real, matrix) Structured tree	Spam detection, plagiarism detection, unsupervised classification, information retrieval, traveling salesman problem, knapsack problem, airéin routing problem, optemisation of multi-objective problem.
BA	• Initialization of echolocation parameters • initial displacement • Movement • local Search • Evaluation • Updating the parameters of echolocation	• The velocity (v_i). • The position (x_i). • A fixed minimum frequency (f_{min}). • A wavelength variable (⅂). • intensity (Ao), At: is the average intensity of all bats.	• -A set of artificial bats. • -Vector (binary, real, matrix)	Machine vision system, image processing, decision support system, scheduling problem, the problem of wireless mobile networks.

CONCLUSION

The bio-inspired methods, or more generally meta-heuristics, will be a new revolution in computer science. The scope of this field is really wide, which open a new area in the next generation of computing, modelling and engineering of the algorithm. Unfortunately, we must keep in mind that the imitation of a biological mechanism does not necessarily provide an advantage, especially when the technology cannot match the biology, or because the desired objective may be different from that of biological mechanisms. The correct practice of bio-inspired artificial intelligence requires effort to extract the scientific principles of organic intelligence from data and theories provided by biologists and engineering efforts to translate these principles into algorithms and technologies.

This paper offers a trip on the theory and applications of meta-heuristic algorithms where we have compiled a comprehensive literature review on a range of natural computing algorithms. These are drawn from an evolutionary metaphor or natural and biological phenomena, including evolutionary algorithms (GAs, PG, SE, SD, CA), and swarm intelligence algorithms (PSO, ACO, BFA, WCA,CCA, BA, and FWA). The description of each algorithm is structured in 4 concepts (originally the inspiration, the summary, the general process). This work has allowed us to better understand the functioning of existing methods to help researchers to design a new bio-inspired method.

As just see throughout this paper, nature is a rich source of inspiration for solving real problems. Applications and the growth of these algorithms in recent years is very drastic summers when they applied to many optimization problems in computer networks, control systems, bioinformatics, game theory, biometrics systems power, image processing, industrial and engineering, parallel and distributed computing, robotics, economics and finance, forecasting problems, applications involving computer security.

REFERENCES

Anandaraman, C., Sankar, A. V. M., & Natarajan, R. (2012). A new evolutionary algorithm based on bacterial evolution and its applications for scheduling a flexible manufacturing system. *Jurnal Teknik Industri*, *14*(1), 1–12. doi:10.9744/jti.14.1.1-12

Bell, W. J., Roth, L. M., & Nalepa, C. A. (2007). *Cockroaches: ecology, behavior, and natural history*. JHU Press.

Benahmed, K., Merabti, M., & Haffaf, H. (2012). Inspired social spider behavior for secure wireless sensor networks. *International Journal of Mobile Computing and Multimedia Communications*, *4*(4), 1–10. doi:10.4018/jmcmc.2012100101

Beni, G., & Wang, J. (1993). *Swarm intelligence in cellular robotic systems. In Robots and Biological Systems: Towards a New Bionics?* (pp. 703–712). Springer Berlin Heidelberg. doi:10.1007/978-3-642-58069-7_38

Blackwell, T., & Bentley, P. J. (2002). Improvised music with swarms. *Proceedings of the 2002 Congress on Evolutionary Computation CEC 2002*, 1462–1467.

Bouarara, H. A., & Bouarara, Y. (2016). Swarm Intelligence Methods for Unsupervised Images Classification: Applications and Comparative Study. *International Journal of Organizational and Collective Intelligence*, 6(2), 50–74. doi:10.4018/IJOCI.2016040104

Bouarara, H. A., Hamou, R. M., & Amine, A. (2014). Text Clustering using Distances Combination by Social Bees: Towards 3D Visualisation Aspect. *International Journal of Information Retrieval Research*, 4(3), 34–53.

Bouarara, H. A., Hamou, R. M., & Amine, A. (2015). New Swarm Intelligence Technique of Artificial Social Cockroaches for Suspicious Person Detection Using N-Gram Pixel with Visual Result Mining. *International Journal of Strategic Decision Sciences*, 6(3), 65–91. doi:10.4018/IJSDS.2015070105

Bouarara, H. A., Hamou, R. M., & Amine, A. (2015). Novel Bio-Inspired Technique of Artificial Social Cockroaches (ASC). *International Journal of Organizational and Collective Intelligence*, 5(2), 47–79. doi:10.4018/IJOCI.2015040103

Bouarara, H. A., Hamou, R. M., & Amine, A. (2015). A Novel Bio-Inspired Approach for Multilingual Spam Filtering. *International Journal of Intelligent Information Technologies*, 11(3), 45–87. doi:10.4018/IJIIT.2015070104

Bouarara, H. A., Hamou, R. M., Rahmani, A., & Amine, A. (2015). Boosting Algorithm and Meta-Heuristic Based on Genetic Algorithms for Textual Plagiarism Detection. *International Journal of Cognitive Informatics and Natural Intelligence*, 9(4), 65–87. doi:10.4018/IJCINI.2015100105

Bourjot, C., Chevrier, V., & Thomas, V. (2003). A new swarm mechanism based on social spiders colonies: From web weaving to region detection. *Web Intelligence and Agent Systems: An International Journal*, 1(1), 47–64.

Bremermann, H. (1974). Chemotaxis and optimization. *Journal of the Franklin Institute*, 297(5), 397–404. doi:10.1016/0016-0032(74)90041-6

Colorni, A., Dorigo, M., Maniezzo, V., & Trubian, M. (1994). Ant System for Job-shop Scheduling. Belgian Journal of Operations Research. *Statistics and Computer Science*, 34(1), 39–53.

Cramer, N. L. (1985, July). A representation for the adaptive generation of simple sequential programs. *Proceedings of the First International Conference on Genetic Algorithms*, 183-187.

Darwin, C. (1859). *On the origin of species by means of natural selection, or the preservation of favoured races in the struggle for life*. New York, NY: D. Appleton and Company.

Darwin, C. (1991). *On the origin of species by means of natural selection*. London: Murray.

Darwin, C. (2009). *The origin of species by means of natural selection: or, the preservation of favored races in the struggle for life*. Academic Press.

Dorigo, M. (1992). *Optimization, learning and natural algorithms* (Ph.D. Thesis). Dipartimento diElettronica, Politecnico di Milano, Italy. (in Italian)

Dorigo, M., & Gambardella, L. M. (1997). Ant colony system: A cooperative learning approach to the traveling salesman problem. Evolutionary Computation. *IEEE Transactions on*, 1(1), 53–66.

Dorigo, M., & Gambardella, L. M. (1997). Ant colonies for the travelling salesman problem. *Bio Systems*, *43*(2), 73–81. doi:10.1016/S0303-2647(97)01708-5 PMID:9231906

Dorigo, M., & Gambardella, L. M. (1997). Ant colony system: A cooperative learning approach to the traveling salesman problem. Evolutionary Computation. *IEEE Transactions on*, *1*(1), 53–66.

Dorigo, M., Maniezzo, V., & Colorni, A. (1996). Ant System: Optimization by a colony of cooperating agents. *IEEE Transactions on Systems, Man, and Cybernetics. Part B, Cybernetics*, *26*(1), 29–41. doi:10.1109/3477.484436 PMID:18263004

Dorigo, M., Maniezzo, V., & Colorni, A. (1996). Ant system: optimization by a colony of cooperating agents. Systems, Man, and Cybernetics, Part B: Cybernetics. *IEEE Transactions on*, *26*(1), 29–41.

Dorigo, M., Maniezzo, V., & Colorni, A. (1991). *Positive feedback as a search strategy*. Tech. Report 91-016, Dipartimento di Elettronica, Politecnico di Milano, Italy.

Eberhart, R. C., & Shi, Y. (2001). Tracking and optimizing dynamic systems with particle swarms. *Proc. Congress on Evolutionary Computation 2001*. doi:10.1109/CEC.2001.934376

Engelbrecht, A. P. (2007). *Computational intelligence: an introduction*. John Wiley & Sons. doi:10.1002/9780470512517

Feng, X., Lau, F. C., & Gao, D. (2009). A new bio-inspired approach to the traveling salesman problem. In *Complex Sciences* (pp. 1310–1321). Springer Berlin Heidelberg. doi:10.1007/978-3-642-02469-6_12

Fuller, T. K., Mech, L. D., & Cockrane, J. F. (2003). Wolf population dynamics. In L. D. Mech & L. Boitani (Eds.), *Wolves: Behavior, Ecology and Conservation* (pp. 161–191). Chicago: University of Chicago Press.

Gandomi, A. H., Yang, X. S., & Alavi, A. H. (2013). Cuckoo search algorithm: A metaheuristic approach to solve structural optimization problems. *Engineering with Computers*, *29*(1), 17–35. doi:10.1007/s00366-011-0241-y

Grassé, P. P. (1967). Nouvelles experiences sur le termite de Müller (Macrotermes mülleri) et considerations sur la théorie de la stigmergie. *Insectes Sociaux*, *14*(1), 73–101. doi:10.1007/BF02222755

Hicklin, J. F. (1986). *Application of the genetic algorithm to automatic program generation*. Academic Press.

Hofstadter, D. (2013). *Alan Turing: Life and legacy of a great thinker* (C. Teuscher, Ed.). Springer Science & Business Media.

Holland, J. H. (1975). *Adaptation in natural and artificial systems*. Ann Arbor, MI: The University of Michigan Press.

Janecek, A., & Tan, Y. (2011, July). Iterative improvement of the multiplicative update nmf algorithm using nature-inspired optimization. In *Natural Computation (ICNC), 2011 Seventh International Conference on* (Vol. 3, pp. 1668-1672). IEEE. doi:10.1109/ICNC.2011.6022356

Kennedy, J., & Eberhart, R. C. (1995). Particle Swarm Optimization. *Proceedings of IEEE International Conference on Neural Networks*, 1942–1948. doi:10.1109/ICNN.1995.488968

Koza, J. R. (1992). *Genetic programming: on the programming of computers by means of natural selection* (Vol. 1). MIT Press.

Koza, J. R. (1992). *Genetic programming: on the programming of computers by means of natural selection* (Vol. 1). MIT Press.

Koza, J. R. (1994). Genetic programming II: Automatic discovery of reusable subprograms. Cambridge, MA: Academic Press.

Li, J., Zheng, S., & Tan, Y. (2014, July). Adaptive Fireworks Algorithm. In *Evolutionary Computation (CEC), 2014 IEEE Congress on* (pp. 3214-3221). IEEE. doi:10.1109/CEC.2014.6900418

Li, W.-W., Wang, H., & Zou, Z. J. (2005). Function optimization method based on bacterial colony chemotaxis. *Journal of Circuits and Systems, 10*, 58–63.

Liu, C., Yan, X., Liu, C., & Wu, H. (2011). The wolf colony algorithm and its application. *Chinese Journal of Electronics, 20*, 212–216.

Liu, J., Zheng, S., & Tan, Y. (2013). The improvement on controlling exploration and exploitation of firework algorithm. In *Advances in swarm intelligence* (pp. 11–23). Springer Berlin Heidelberg; doi:10.1007/978-3-642-38703-6_2

Macdonald, D. W., Creel, S., & Mills, M. G. L. (2004). Society: Canid society. In D. W. Macdonald & C. Sillero-Zubiri (Eds.), *Biology and Conservation of Wild Carnivores* (pp. 85–106). Oxford, UK: Oxford University Press. doi:10.1093/acprof:oso/9780198515562.003.0004

Mitchell, M. (1998). *An introduction to genetic algorithms*. MIT Press.

Niu, B., & Wang, H. (2012). Bacterial colony optimization. *Discrete Dynamics in Nature and Society, 2012*, 1–28.

Passino, K. M. (2012). Bacterial foraging optimization. *Innovations and Developments of Swarm Intelligence Applications, 219*.

Pei, Y., Zheng, S., Tan, Y., & Takagi, H. (2012, October). An empirical study on influence of approximation approaches on enhancing fireworks algorithm. In *Systems, Man, and Cybernetics (SMC), 2012 IEEE International Conference on* (pp. 1322-1327). IEEE. doi:10.1109/ICSMC.2012.6377916

Pohlheim, H. (2005). Evolutionary algorithms: overview, methods and operators. *GEATbx: Gentic & Evolutionary AlgorithmToolbox for Matlab.*

Poli, R., Langdon, W. B., McPhee, N. F., & Koza, J. R. (2008). *A field guide to genetic programming.* Lulu.com.

Premaratne, U., Samarabandu, J., & Sidhu, T. (2009, December). A new biologically inspired optimization algorithm. In *Industrial and Information Systems (ICIIS), 2009 International Conference on* (pp. 279-284). IEEE. doi:10.1109/ICIINFS.2009.5429852

Rechenberg, I. (1989). *Evolution strategy: Nature's way of optimization. In Optimization: Methods and applications, possibilities and limitations* (pp. 106–126). Springer Berlin Heidelberg. doi:10.1007/978-3-642-83814-9_6

Reeves, C. (2003). *Genetic algorithms*. Springer, US. doi:10.1007/0-306-48056-5_3

Reynolds, C. W. (1987, August). Flocks, herds and schools: A distributed behavioral model. *Computer Graphics*, *21*(4), 25–34. doi:10.1145/37402.37406

Runkler, T. A. (2008). Wasp swarm optimization of the c-means clustering model. *International Journal of Intelligent Systems*, *23*(3), 269–285. doi:10.1002/int.20266

Storn, R., & Price, K. (1997). Differential evolution–a simple and efficient heuristic for global optimization over continuous spaces. *Journal of Global Optimization*, *11*(4), 341–359. doi:10.1023/A:1008202821328

Stützle, T., & Hoos, H. (1997, April). MAX-MIN ant system and local search for the traveling salesman problem. In *Evolutionary Computation, 1997., IEEE International Conference on* (pp. 309-314). IEEE. doi:10.1109/ICEC.1997.592327

Wallace, A. R. (1870). *Contributions to the theory of natural selection: A series of essays*. Macmillan and Company.

Yang, C., Tu, X., & Chen, J. (2007). Algorithm of marriage in honey bees optimization based on the wolf pack search. In *IEEE International Conference on Intelligent Pervasive Computing (IPC)* (pp. 462–467). doi:10.1109/IPC.2007.104

Yoshida, H., Kawata, K., Fukuyama, Y., Takayama, S., & Nakanishi, Y. (2000). A particle swarm optimization for reactive power and voltage control considering voltage security assessment. *IEEE Transactions on Power Systems*, *15*(4), 1232–1239. doi:10.1109/59.898095

Zheng, S., Janecek, A., Li, J., & Tan, Y. (2014, July). Dynamic search in fireworks algorithm. In *Evolutionary Computation (CEC), 2014 IEEE Congress on* (pp. 3222-3229). IEEE. doi:10.1109/CEC.2014.6900485

Zheng, S., Janecek, A., & Tan, Y. (2013, June). Enhanced fireworks algorithm. In *Evolutionary Computation (CEC), 2013 IEEE Congress on* (pp. 2069-2077). IEEE. doi:10.1109/CEC.2013.6557813

Chapter 6
Optimization of Process Parameters Using Soft Computing Techniques:
A Case With Wire Electrical Discharge Machining

Supriyo Roy
Birla Institute of Technology, India

Kaushik Kumar
Birla Institute of Technology, India

J. Paulo Davim
University of Aveiro, Portugal

ABSTRACT

Machining of hard metals and alloys using Conventional machining involves increased demand of time, energy and cost. It causes tool wear resulting in loss of quality of the product. Non-conventional machining, on the other hand produces product with minimum time and at desired level of accuracy. In the present study, EN19 steel was machined using CNC Wire Electrical discharge machining with pre-defined process parameters. Material Removal Rate and Surface roughness were considered as responses for this study. The present optimization problem is single and as well as multi-response. Considering the complexities of this present problem, experimental data were generated and the results were analyzed by using Taguchi, Grey Relational Analysis and Weighted Principal Component Analysis under soft computing approach. Responses variances with the variation of process parameters were thoroughly studied and analyzed; also 'best optimal values' were identified. The result shows an improvement in responses from mean to optimal values of process parameters.

DOI: 10.4018/978-1-5225-2128-0.ch006

INTRODUCTION

Requests for deciding items have turned out to be progressively perplexing as clients expect improved execution over an assortment of differing and changing framework working conditions. Reconfigurable frameworks are having the limit and usefulness keeping in mind the end goal to meet complex destinations and capacity viably in changing working conditions with competent to convey esteem in element economic situations. They are intended to keep up an abnormal state of execution by changing their design to meet the numerous capacity necessities or a change in working conditions inside worthy reconfiguration time and cost.

Wire Electrical discharge machining (WEDM) is a non-traditional, thermo-electric procedure which disintegrates material from the work piece by a progression of discrete sparkles between a work and instrument terminal submerged in a fluid dielectric medium. Schematic representation is represented underneath in Figure 1.

These electrical discharges melt and vaporize minute amounts of the work material, which are then ejected and flushed away by the dielectric (Tosun et al. 2004, Tosun and Cogun 2003). A wire of diameter ranging from 0.05 to 0.25 mm is used as the tool electrode (Kozak et al. 1994). The wire is persistently supplied from the supply spool through the work-piece, which is clasped on the table by the wire footing rollers. A crevice of 0.025 to 0.05 mm is kept up always between the wire and work-piece (Spedding and Wang 1997a). The wires once utilized can't be reused because of the variety in dimensional exactness (Scott et al. 1991). Recently, WEDM is being used to perform machining operation on a wide variety of miniature and micro-parts made of metals, alloys, sintered materials, cemented carbides, ceramics and silicon (Muttamara et al. 2003, Mohri et al. 2002, Weng and Her 2002, Yeo and Yap 2001 etc.). Here, investigation of optimum combination of machining process parameters for large value of MRR and minimum value of surface roughness were carried out by using soft computing techniques like Taguchi Analysis, Grey Analysis and Weighted Principal Component Analysis. Sensitivity analysis is proposed to show the efficacy of one method over other methods.

Figure 1. Schematic representation of Wire EDM process

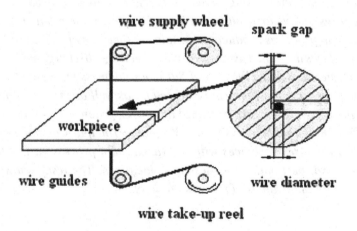

LITERATURE REVIEW

Wire electrical release machining (WEDM) is the second most prominent non-customary machining process, after EDM, broadly utilized for producing part of the aviation, vehicles and therapeutic commercial enterprises and in addition in essentially all territories of conductive material machining. In this procedure, material is disintegrated from the work-piece by a progression of release sparkle between the work-piece and wire cathode isolated by a dainty film of dielectric liquid which is consistently introduced to the machining zone to flush away the dissolved particles. As a fundamental prerequisite, the machining operation ought to create the product with least time and at wanted level of surface texture. Machining time is subject to the material removal rate (communicated in mass per unit time and also volume per unit time) of the procedure. For mechanical practice, MRR ought to be greatest from financial perspective. Then again, surface texture or roughness assumes a vital part for the tribological operation of any segment. It has substantial effect on the mechanical properties like fatigue behavior, corrosion resistance, creep life and so forth. It additionally influences other useful characteristics of machine parts like friction, wear, light reflection, heat transmission, lubrication, electrical conductivity and so on.

Analysts have endeavored to optimize the performance of WEDM procedure by various methodologies. Tarng et al. (1995) have defined ANN model and Simulated Annealing Algorithm with a specific end goal to foresee and streamline surface roughness and cutting speed of the WEDM procedure in machining of SUS-304 stainless steel material. Spedding and Wang (1997b) have concentrated on ideal blend of procedure parameters utilizing RSM and ANN for greatest cutting rate, ensuring surface roughness and waviness within the required limits in WEDM of AISI 420. Lok and Lee (1997) have worked on the machining execution terms of MRR and surface finish through perceptions acquired by handling of two advanced ceramics (Sialon and AI203-TiC) under various machining conditions utilizing WEDM. Huang et al. (1999) have explored experimentally the impact of machining parameters on the gap width, surface roughness, and the depth of white layer on the machined work piece surface in WEDM of SKD11 steel utilizing Taguchi strategy and numerical investigation. It is found that the pulse-on time and the distance between the wire periphery and the work piece surface are two critical elements influencing machining output. Huang and Liao (2003) have exhibited the utilization of Grey Relational Analysis for deciding the ideal parameters setting of WEDM procedure. The outcomes demonstrate that MRR and Surface Roughness are effectively impacted by table feed rate and pulse on time. Liao et al. (2004) have demonstrated that the machining voltage, current-restricting resistance, pulse-generating circuit and capacitance are most noteworthy parameters influencing Surface Roughness in machining procedure of WEDM. Kuriakose and Shunmugam (2004) have done analyses with titanium 15 composites (Ti-6Al-4V) and utilized a Data-Mining Technique to concentrate on the impact of different salient parameters of WEDM procedure on the Cutting Speed and Surface Roughness. Tosun et al. (2004) have explored the impact and optimization of machining parameters on the kerf (cutting width) and MRR in WEDM operations. It is seen that gap voltage and spark on-time duration affects both kerf and MRR. Miller et al. (2004) have researched the impact of spark on-time span and ratio on MRR and surface properties of four sorts of cutting edge material; porous metal foams, metal bond diamond grinding wheels, sintered Nd-Fe-B magnets and carbon-carbon bipolar plates. Kuriakose and Shunmugam (2005) have enhanced the cutting speed and Surface Roughness of WEDM procedure utilizing the Non Dominated Sorting Genetic Algorithm in WEDM of titanium alloy (Ti-6Al-4V). Hewidy et al. (2005) have created scientific models for correlating inter relationships of various WEDM machining parameters of Inconel 601 material such as Peak Current, Duty Factor, Wire Tension and De-ionized Water Pressure on MRR, wear ratio and surface roughness using RSM. Manna and Bhattacharyya (2006) have set up scientific models identifying with the machining execution criteria like MRR, Surface Roughness, Spark Gap and Gap Current utilizing the Gauss elimination technique for successful machining of Al/SiC-MMC. Sarkar et al. (2005) have built up a model for anticipating cutting velocity; Surface Roughness and offset of wire in WEDM operation of γ titanium aluminide utilizing ANN. Ozdemir and Ozek (2006) have explored the machinability of standard G40 nodular cast iron by WEDM. Ramakrishnan and Karunamoorthy (2006) have streamlined multiple responses viz. MRR, Surface Roughness, and wire wear ratio in WEDM process performed on heat-treated tool steel considering pulse-on-time, wire tension, delay time, wire feed velocity and ignition current intensity as process parameters. Mahapatra and Patnaik (2006) have created connections between different procedure parameters like discharge current, pulse duration, pulse frequency, wire speed, wire tension and dielectric flow rate and responses like MRR, Surface Roughness and kerf by method for non-linear regression analysis and after that utilized genetic algorithm to optimize the WEDM process with multi-objectives. Chiang and Chang (2006) have exhibited a methodology for advancement of WEDM procedure of composite material with Al2O3 reinforcement with two output characteristics, i.e. surface Roughness and MRR, in light of grey relational analysis. Kanlayasiri and Boonmung (2007) have explored impacts of machining parameters on surface roughness in WEDM of DC 53 grade steel. Han et al. (2007) have examined the impact of machining parameters on surface roughness in WEDM of composite steel (Cr12) and found that surface harshness is enhanced by diminishing both pulse-off-time and discharge current. Mahapatra and Patnaik (2007) have connected Taguchi technique and Genetic Algorithm (GA) to acquire an ideal parametric blend to accomplish coveted nature of machined item. Ramakrishnan and Karunamoorthy (2008) have created ANN models and multi response optimization technique to anticipate and select best cutting parameters of WEDM procedure of Inconel 718 as work material and found that the pulse-on-time, delay time and ignition current have more impact than wire feed speed on MRR and surface quality. Saha et al. (2008) have built up a second order multi-variable regression model and a feed-forward back-propagation neural network model using pulse on-time, pulse off-time, peak current, and capacitance as process parameters for foreseeing cutting rate and surface roughness in WEDM of tungsten carbide-cobalt (WC-Co) composite material. Esme et al. (2009) have built up a surface roughness forecast model in WEDM of AISI 4340 steel utilizing ANN and regression analysis utilizing four input parameters viz. open voltage, wire speed, pulse span and pressure of dielectric flushing. Singh and Garg (2009) have researched the impacts of different procedure parameters of WEDM like pulse-on-time, pulse-off-time, gap voltage, peak current, wire feed and wire tension to uncover their effect on MRR of steel (H-11) and optimized the procedure parameters for ultimate MRR. Rao and Sarcar (2009) have examined the impacts of procedure parameters on machining attributes viz. cutting rate, spark gap and MRR in WEDM of brass work pieces. Dey and Tripathi (2013) have concentrated on impacts of procedure parameters viz. pulse-on-time, pulse-off-time, spark gap, set voltage, peak current, wire tension and wire feed on output attributes viz. cutting rate, surface roughness, hole present and dimensional deviation in WEDM. Gauri and Chakraborty (2009) have optimized various process parameters for maximization of MRR and surface finish and minimization of wire wear ratio in WEDM using WPCA. Datta and Mahapatra (2010) have built up a numerical model for forecast of MRR, surface roughness and kerf in WEDM of D2 steel utilizing RSM. Lin and Wang (2010) have optimized different machining parameters for greatest MRR and least surface roughness in WEDM of magnesium composite parts utilizing Taguchi based grey analysis. Shah et al. (2011) have concentrated on the impacts of machining parameters on the machining responses, for example, MRR, kerf, and surface roughness of tungsten carbide material in WEDM and reasoned that the material thickness has a minimal impact as far as surface roughness is concerned. Jangra et al. (2011) have optimized few procedure parameters for maximum MRR and minimum surface roughness during intricate machining of a carbide block using grey relational analysis. Alias et al. (2012) have concentrated on the significance of kerf width, MRR, average surface roughness (Ra) and surface topography and their solid reliance on the input parameters in WEDM of Titanium Ti-6Al-4V material. Ghodsiyeh et al. (2012) have contemplated the impact of different parameters viz. pulse on time, pulse off time and peak current on MRR and surface roughness and built up a scientific model for machining parameters utilizing RSM for WEDM of titanium compound (Ti6Al4V). Mukherjee et al (2012) have optimized pulse duration, pulse frequency, duty factor, peak current, dielectric flow rate, wire speed and wire tension with of single and multi-response outputs including MRR, cutting width (kerf), surface roughnesss and dimensional deviation using various optimization tools such as genetic algorithm, particle swarm optimization, sheep flock algorithm, ant colony optimization, ABC and biogeography-based optimization in WEDM of Inconel 601. Kumar et al. (2012) have examined on WEDM of immaculate titanium material with six machining parameters viz. and they proposed a quadratic mathematical model and optimized procedure parameters for machining rate and surface roughness. Henceforth analyst have utilized WEDM for machining of various materials (Gao et al (2013), Khanna and Singh (2013), Kumar et al. (2013), Sharma et al. (2013), Sharma et al. (2014), Khan et al. (2014), Ravindranadh et al. (2015), Nayak and Mahapatra (2016)) and individuals (Garg et al. (2012), Sadeghi et al. (2011), Sharma et al. (2013)) have also used different soft computing techniques for the optimization and indentification of the optimal values of the different input parameters. Kapoor et al. (2012) have contemplated the impact of cryogenic treated metal wire terminal on material removal rate rather than the wire utilized by most of the other reasearchers.

The literature review indicated that researchers have taken one or two surface roughness parameters as responses. In this work five roughness parameters have been considered individually and collectively along with Material removal rate for optimization.

DESIGN OF EXPERIMENTS

Modern physicists can no more bear to direct analysis in an experimentation way, transforming one element at once, the way Edison did in building up the light. A significantly more viable technique is to apply a computer-enhanced, orderly way to deal with experimentation, one that considers all variables together. That methodology is called Design of Experiments (DOE), and enterprises worldwide are receiving it as a financially savvy approach to take care of difficult issues burdening their operations. DOE gives data about the collaboration of components and the way the aggregate framework works, something not possible through testing one variable at once while holding different elements steady. Another preferred standpoint of DOE is that it demonstrates how interconnected elements react over an extensive variety of qualities, without requiring the testing of every single conceivable esteem specifically. This idea has been being used since Fisher's work in agricultural experimentation, over 60 years back. Fisher (1951) effectively composed examinations to decide ideal medicines for area to accomplish most extreme yield. When all is said in done, a framework or procedure can be imagined as a mix of machines, techniques, individuals and different assets that changes some info (machining process parameters, electrode, machines, instruments, equipments, energy, manpower, and so on) into a yield (material removal rate, surface roughness) that has one or more recognizable reactions as appeared in Figure 2.

Figure 2. General model of procedure/framework

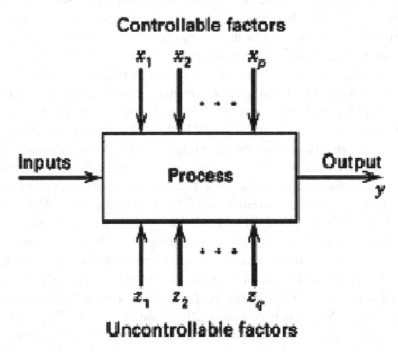

A portion of the procedure variables (x1, x2,..., xp) are controllable (current, voltage, duty factor, dielectric, feed rate, inter-electrode gap, and so forth) i.e. they can be reasonably changed to control the procedure reaction, while different variables (z1, z2, ..., zq) are wild (mistakes in measuring instrument and cathodes, machines, human blunders, and so on.) i.e. they are outside the ability to control of anyone.

An outlined analysis is a test or arrangement of tests where pre-arranged changes are made to the controllable variables of a procedure or framework so that the purpose behind changes in the reaction can be watched and distinguished. This sort of factual methodology is required to test outline, on the off chance that we wish to reach a significant inference from the watched information. Likewise, DOE alludes to the way toward arranging, planning and breaking down the investigation so that substantial and target conclusion can be drawn adequately and effectively. DOE can be exceedingly compelling (Montgomery, 2001) when it is important to optimize item and procedure plans, examine the impacts of numerous components on the execution, take care of generation issues by equitably laying out the analyses, and so forth. There are a few techniques exist in the writing of configuration of trials; most conspicuous amongst them is Orthogonal Array.

Orthogonal Array

Orthogonal Arrays (OA) are usually used for the experimentation in Taguchi analysis (Taguchi 1990, Ross 1996). These are special matrices used as the design matrices in the fractional factorial design for the estimation of the effect of several factors in a highly efficient way. These designs are applicable even when the factors have more than two levels and for mixed level experiments where all factors do not have same number of levels. In general, when the number of process parameter increases, large number of experiments has to be carried out for factorial design. But using orthogonal array, carrying out small number of experiments in the specified range and effects of process parameters can be studied.

In the present study, four factors are taken with three levels, which have 20 degree of freedom. Hence, as per basic rule, L27 OA is used in the study. An L27 OA has 27 rows corresponding to the number of tests (26 degrees of freedom) with columns. The 1st, 2nd, 3rd and 4th column is assigned to parameter A, B, C and D respectively.

TAGUCHI ANALYSIS

Dr. Genichi Taguchi built up this strategy in light of orthogonal array (OA) which gives abundantly lessened difference for the analysis with ideal settings of control parameters. It is known as Robust Design strategy due to its ability of deciding those mixes of controllable variables that minimizes the impact of the wellsprings of experimentation variability (Roy, 1990). Taguchi strategy is likewise a capable instrument for outline of fantastic frameworks. It presents a coordinated methodology that is basic and productive to locate the best scope of outlines for quality, execution and computational expense. To accomplish alluring nature of the item, Dr. Taguchi suggests that procedure or item ought to be done in a three - stage approach, for example, system design, parameter design and tolerance design. Parameter design is utilized to acquire the element levels that create the best execution of the item or procedure. The ideal condition is chosen so that the impact of the uncontrolled or clamor components causes least variety of framework execution. The parameter design has the key part in the Taguchi technique to accomplish high caliber without expanding the cost variable. Resilience configuration is utilized to tweak the ideal blends proposed by parameter plan by fixing the resistance of the components with huge impact on the finished product.

S/N Ratio

The customary strategy for ascertaining normal component impacts and accordingly deciding the attractive variable levels (ideal condition) includes taking a gander at the straightforward midpoints of the outcomes. Albeit normal estimation is moderately straightforward, it doesn't catch the variability of results inside a trial condition. A superior approach to contrast the populace conduct is with utilize the mean squared deviation (MSD), which joins impact of both normal and standard deviation of the outcomes. For comfort of linearity and to suit far reaching information, a logarithmic change of MSD, called the signal-to-noise (S/N) ratio is prescribed for the examination of the outcomes. In this way, when S/N proportion is utilized for result examination, the ideal condition distinguished from such investigation will probably deliver steady execution. Taguchi technique utilizes the S/N proportion to quantify the quality attributes. The three classifications of value qualities utilized are: smaller-the-better (minimize), larger–the–better (expand) and nominal-the-best. In Taguchi technique, the expression "signal" speaks desirable value (mean) for the output response and the expression "noise" represents the undesirable value (Standard Deviation) for the output response. The S/N proportion is utilized to quantify the quality trademark going astray from the craved worth. The sign to-commotion proportion details for the three classifications of quality charecteristics are as per the following:

S/N ratio for larger–the–better (maximize),

$$S/N_L = -10log\left(\frac{1}{n}\sum_{i=1}^{n}\frac{1}{y_i^2}\right)$$ (1)

S/N ratio for smaller-the-better (minimize),

$$S/N_s = -10log\left(\frac{1}{n}\sum_{i=1}^{n}y_i^2\right)$$ (2)

S/N ratio for nominal-the-best,

$$S/N_T = 10log\left(\frac{\bar{y}}{s_y^2}\right)$$ (3)

where y is the data, n is the number of observations, $\bar{y}$ is the mean of the observed data and s_y^2 is the variance of y. S/N ratios are usually expressed on a decibel (dB) scale. Taguchi technique utilizes OA to diminish the quantity of trials for deciding the ideal procedure parameters. Taguchi has classified a few standard orthogonal clusters. The decision of an appropriate OA is basic for the achievement of the analysis and relies on upon the aggregate degrees of opportunity required to think about the principle and cooperation impacts, the objective of the trial, assets and spending plan accessible and time imperatives. Orthogonal Array permits one to process the fundamental and communication impacts by means of least number of exploratory trials (Ross, 1996). Factor level that amplifies the proper S/N proportion is optimal. A statistical analysis of variance (ANOVA) is then used to discover the impacts of the procedure parameters on the framework reaction under thought.

Taguchi technique is utilized with the accompanying system keeping in mind the end goal to upgrade the procedure parameters for various machining operation consecutively: recognize execution attributes and select procedure parameters to be assessed, decide the quantity of levels for the procedure parameters and conceivable connections between the procedure parameters, select the fitting OA and task of procedure parameters to the same, lead the analyses taking into account the course of action of the OA, compute the aggregate total loss function and the S/N proportion, analyze the test results utilizing the S/N proportion and ANOVA, select the optimal levels of procedure parameters, lastly check the performance of the optimal procedure parameters through affirmation test.

Analysis of Variance (ANOVA)

Analysis of variance is a statistical tool to distinguish and measure sources of variation inside a set of data. This is finished by separating the aggregate variety in the data into its segment parts and contrasting every part and the aggregate variety. ANOVA additionally helps in figuring out if the varieties are due to variability between techniques or inside strategies. The inside technique varieties are varieties because of individual variety inside treatment bunches, while the between-strategy varieties are because of contrasts between the strategies (Bass, 2007).

Confirmation Test

To check the precision of the investigation, a confirmation test should be conveyed subsequent to setting the optimal level of machining parameters. The assessed S/N proportion $\bar{\gamma}$ utilizing the optimal level of the procedure parameters can be ascertained as:

$$\bar{\gamma} = \gamma_m + \sum_{i=1}^{0} \left(\bar{\gamma}_i - \gamma_m \right) \tag{4}$$

where γ_m is the total mean S/N Ratio, γ_i is the mean S/N Ratio at the optimal level and 0 is the number of the main design parameters.

GREY RELATIONAL ANALYSIS

Taguchi strategy is known as a disconnected quality control technique and is more appropriate for optimization of single output issues. In any case, Taguchi strategy alone can't improve various output issues as and when all things considered a component, which could be imperative to one quality trademark, might be immaterial to the next quality attributes or at the end of the day the higher S/N proportion for one execution attributes may relate to a lower S/N proportion for another. Along these lines, a general assessment of the S/N proportion is required for the enhancement of various execution qualities. To wipe out such issue Gray technique comes into the situation. This strategy joined with Taguchi technique can without much of a stretch face any different reaction issues and turn out decisively. The Gray hypothesis was started by (Deng 1982) and has been ended up being helpful for managing poor, deficient and unverifiable data.

Implementing Grey Relational Analysis

Grey Relational Analysis is utilized for improving various reaction issues and in such cases the confounded numerous execution qualities are changed over into optimizing a solitary Grey Relational Grade. The stepwise contribution in Grey Relational Analysis is:: Normalize the responses of the quality characteristics, calculate grey relational grade, analyze grey relational grade, and conduct confirmation tests (Figure 3).

Normalization of Experimental Results

Grey relational analysis begins with grey relational generation where in results of the experiments are normalized in the range between zero to one. The normalization can be done on three objectives including:

(1) Normalization using higher-the-better criterion and is expressed as:

$$x_i\left(k\right) = \frac{y_i\left(k\right) - \min y_i\left(k\right)}{\max y_i\left(k\right) - \min y_i\left(k\right)} \tag{5}$$

Figure 3. Schematic representation of the steps involved in grey relational analysis

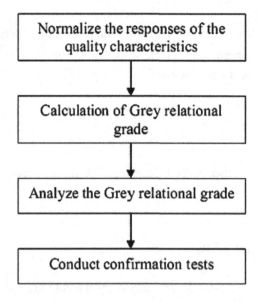

(2) Normalization using lower-the-better criterion and is expressed as:

$$x_i(k) = \frac{\max y_i(k) - y_i(k)}{\max y_i(k) - \min y_i(k)}$$

(6)

(3) Normalization using objective value or nominal the best criterion and is expressed as:

$$x_i(k) = \frac{\| y_i(k) - y_0 \|}{\max y_i(k) - y_0}$$

(7)

where $x_i(k)$ is the post grey relational generation value, $\min y_i(k)$ being the smallest value of $y_i(k)$ for the kth response, and $\max y_i(k)$ being highest value of $y_i(k)$ for the kth response. An ideal sequence would be $x_0(k)$ (k=1,2,3,........,27) for the response. By definition of grey relational grade, in this case, in the grey relational analysis is to indicate the relational degree between the twenty seven sequences [0 x (k) and ix (k), i 1,2,......,27;k 1,2,......27].

Grey Relational Coefficient

Grey relational coefficients are evaluated to elaborate the relationship between the ideal (best = 1) and the real experimental results. The grey relational coefficient $\xi_i(k)$ is evaluated as:

$$\xi_i(k) = \frac{\Delta_{min} + \Psi\Delta_{max}}{\Delta_{0i}(k) + \Psi\Delta_{max}}$$

(8)

where $\Delta_{min} + \Psi\Delta_{max}$ is difference of the absolute value between x0(k) and xi(k), Δ_{min} and Δ_{max} are respectively the smallest and largest values of the absolute differences (Δ0i) of all comparing sequences. Ψ is a distinguishing coefficient, $0 \leq \psi \leq 1$, the utility of which is to weaken the effect of Δ_{max} when it gets too large, and thus enlarges the difference significance of the relational coefficient. The most reasonable suggested value of the distinguishing coefficient, Ψ, is 0.5, due to the average distinguishing effects and better stability of outcomes. Therefore, Ψ is adopted as 0.5 for further analysis in the present work.

Generation of Grey Relational Grade

In the grey relational analysis, the grey relational grade is instrumental in elaborating the relationship among the series. The overall multiple response characteristics evaluation is based on grey relational grade which in turn is just the average of the grey relational coefficients generated in the earlier step.

$$\gamma_i = \frac{1}{n} \sum_{k=1}^{n} \xi_i\left(k\right)$$

(9)

Grey Relational Ordering

In GRA, the practical meaning of the numerical values of grey relational grade between elements is not absolutely important, whereas grey relational ordering between them yields better information. The combination giving the largest grey relational grade is allotted an order of 1 while the combination yielding the smallest grade is allotted the lowest order i.e.0.

WEIGHTED PRINCIPAL COMPONENT ANALYSIS (WPCA)

Conventional Taguchi approach neglects to tackle a multi-reaction optimization issue. It is in this way important to join these different targets into a comparable single target capacity which will be dealt as representative of overall quality index for multi-quality characteristics. The technique is useful to dispense with reaction relationship, on the off chance that it exists. This methodology changes over connected reactions into an equivalent or less number of uncorrelated quality records which are called individual principal components. The principal component which has the maximum accountability proportion (AP) is generally treated as overall performance index. In any case, when more than one principal component part has impressive estimation of responsibility extent which can't be disregarded; the issue of figuring composite principal component emerges. Writing demonstrates that distinctive scientists recommended diverse ways to deal with compute this composite main segment (Huang and Lin 2008, Datta et al. 2009). Be that as it may, those methodologies are not dependable dependably and in the meantime there is no physical elucidation of the said composite primary part. Estimations of individual vital parts increased by their need weight are added to ascertain composite principal component defined as Multi-response Performance Index (MPI). MPI is then optimized (maximized) using Taguchi method.

Implementing WPCA

By a linear combination of the original variables, principal component analysis (PCA) (Johnson 1998) can be used to elaborate the variance-covariance structure of a group of variables. The PCA technique can estimate most of the variation of the original p variables using q uncorrelated principal components, where $q \leq p$.

Considering Taguchi's design of experiments, if there are m iterations and for each iteration, quality loss of p performance characteristics (response variables) are determined, then the data set can be written as $(L)_{m \times p}$. Taguchi (Phadke 1989) categorized the performance characteristics (response variables) into three different groups, e.g. lesser-the-better, higher-the-better and nominal-the-best. The formulae for evaluation of quality loss (Lij) for jth value of response corresponding to ith iteration (i=1, 2,..., m; j=1, 2,..., p) are distinctive for various sorts of response variables, and these are as follows:

For higher-the-better (HB),

$$L_{ij} = \frac{1}{n} \sum_{k=1}^{n} \frac{1}{y_{ijk}^2}$$
(10)

For lower-the-better (LB),

$$L_{ij} = \frac{1}{n} \sum_{k=1}^{n} y_{ijk}^2$$
(11)

For nominal-the best (NB),

$$L_{ij} = \left(\frac{\mu^2}{\sigma^2} \right)$$
(12)

where,

$$\mu = \frac{1}{n} \sum_{k=1}^{n} y_{ijk} , \ \sigma^2 = \frac{1}{n} \sum_{k=1}^{n} \left(y_{ijk} - \mu \right)^2$$

where, n represents the number of iterative experiments, y_{ijk} is the experimental value of jth response variable in ith iteration at kth test and L_{ij} is the evaluated quality loss for jth response in ith trial. Through the PCA, the deviation in the original p response variables corresponding to ith trial can be further elaborated by the following q uncorrelated linear combinations:

$$\Omega_1^i = a_{l1} L_{i1} + a_{l2} L_{i2} + a_{l3} L_{i3} \ldots \ldots \ldots a_{lp} L_{ip} ; (l = 1, 2, \ldots \ldots q)$$
(13)

where, $a_{l1}^2 + a_{l2}^2 + \ldots \ldots \ldots \ldots a_{lp}^2 = 1$. Here Ω_1^i is first principal component, Ω_2^i is second principal component and so on. The coefficients of the l th component, i.e. $a_{l1} + a_{l2} + \ldots \ldots \ldots \ldots a_{lp}$ are the components of the eigenvector corresponding to the l th eigen value of the correlation matrix or the covariance matrix of the response variables. The eigen values for the q components and the eigenvector corresponding to each eigen value can be obtained by subjecting the experimental data set, (L)m×p, to principal component analysis using SAS, SPSSX and STATISTICA software.

An estimate of the variance of the original variables can be obtained from higher eigen value of a principal component, which shows a significant contribution in elaborating overall variation. According to Su and Tong (1997) and Antony (2000), the components with eigen values greater than 1 may be chosen to replace the original responses. They further elaborated in their case studies that eigen value for the first principal component is only larger than 1 and hence they considered only the first principal component. The first principal component 1 corresponding to a trial is observed to be the weighted average of the original p response variables. The weights are analytically decided and not on engineer's judgment providing a unbiased value. This first principal component was considered as an index by them to optimize the process settings. But when more than one eigen value becomes 1, problem arises. In such cases trade-offs are necessary (Su and Tong 1997) to select an unknown feasible solution. In the weighted principal component (WPC) based procedure (Liao 2006) for optimization, to completely explain the overall variation of multi responses, all the principal components are considered irrespective of their eigen values.

In this approach, the extent of general variety clarified by every segment is dealt with as the weight to consolidate all principal components in order to form a multi-response performance index (MPI). From the optimum value of MPI, the optimized setting of parameters is obtained. The WPC method was applied by Liao (2006) considering quality losses as the experimental data i.e. (L)m×p. But in the present study, signal-to-noise (S/N) ratio, a logarithmic transformation of the quality loss function, is suggested. This improves the additive effect of two or more control factors (Ross 1996) and hence this logarithmic transformation is done. On the other hand, if the real value of some performance characteristic, e.g. defect count is used for creating the additive model, it is quite likely that the predicted value of the defect count for optimal conditions will become negative (Phadke 1989). This is highly undesirable as in the logarithmic scale, negative counts can never be evaluated and should not exist. The S/N ratio is usually expressed in decibel (dB) unit. The maximization of S/N ratio leads to the minimization of the quality loss since log being a monotone function.

So in case of a multi-response optimization, the WPC method can, thus, be described in following six steps:

Step 1: Evaluate the signal-to-noise (S/N) ratio for each response. Based on the type of quality characteristic, the quality loss (Lij) of the jth response corresponding to ith iteration has been calculated using equation (10) or (11) or (12), and then, the S/N ratio (ijα) value for jth response corresponding to ith iteration is evaluated using equation (14):

$$\alpha_{ij} = -10 log_{10} L_{ij} \qquad (14)$$

Step 2: The S/N ratio value for each response is transformed into (0, 1) interval using the following equation:

$$Y_{ij} = \frac{\alpha_{ij} - \alpha_j^{\min}}{\alpha_j^{\max} - \alpha_j^{\min}} \qquad (15)$$

where, Y_{ij} =scaled S/N ratio value for jth response at ith iteration, $\alpha_j^{\min} = \min\{ \alpha_{1j}, \alpha_{2j}, ...\alpha_{mj} \}$ and $\alpha_j^{\max} = \max\{ \alpha_{1j}, \alpha_{2j}, ...\alpha_{mj} \}$

Step 3: Checking for correlation between two response using Pearson correlation coefficient. The correlation coefficient amongst two response variables is calculated by the following equation:

$$\rho_{ij} = \frac{Cov(Q_j, Q_k)}{\sigma_{Qj} * \sigma_{Qk}} \qquad (16)$$

where, ρ_{ij} is the correlation coefficient between response variables j and k, $Cov(Q_j, Q_k)$ is the covariance of response variables j and k, σ_{Qj} and σ_{Qk} are the standard deviation of response variables j and k respectively. Finally, the correlation is verified by testing the hypothesis. There will be no correlation between the responses, if $\rho_{ij} = 0$; and the correlation exist, if $\rho_{ij} \neq 0$

Step 4: PCA on the computed data is performed, and the principal components are obtained. The PCA is performed using STATISTICA software. The principal components of q number of responses corresponding to i trials are evaluated as follows:

$$Z_1^i = a_{l1}Y_{i1} + a_{l2}Y_{i2} + ... + a_{lp}Y_{ip}; (l = 1,2,....., q) \qquad (17)$$

$a_{l1}, a_{l2}, ..., a_{lp}$ are elements of eigenvector, $Y_{i1}, Y_{i2}, ..., Y_{ip}$ are normalized values of response.

Step 5: Multi-response performance index (MPI) is computed corresponding to each iteration. As MPI is weighted sum of all principal components, hence for ith trial, it can be evaluated using the following equation:

$$MPI^i = \sum_{l=1}^{q} W_l Z_l^i \qquad (18)$$

where, W_l is the proportion of overall variance of the response obtained by lth principal component, Z_l^i is the evaluated value of lth principal component corresponding to ith iteration and $\sum_{l=1}^{q} W_l = 1$. It might be noticed that since all the principal components are autonomous of each other, the additive model is proper here and a higher value of MPI will imply better quality.

Step 6: The optimal factor or level combination is determined and ascertained. ANOVA on MPI values for identification of significant factors is undertaken and average MPI values at different levels of the control factors are computed. Larger MPI value implies better process performance. Eventually, a confirmation experiment is performed to certify the obtained value.

EXPERIMENTATION

Material

A 0.25 mm diameter zinc coated brass wire and circular block of EN 19 tool steel are selected as tool electrode and work piece respectively for experimentation.

Machine and Instrument

CNC WEDM (Electronica Machine Tools Ltd) has been used as the machine (Figure 4). For the surface roughness and weight measurement Talysurf (Make – Taylor Hobson, UK) (Figure 5) and Mettle Toddler electronic balance (Figure 6) are used respectively.

Input Process Parameters Considered

In this work four controllable factors such as discharge current, Gap voltage, pulse on time and pulse off time are used as process parameters. Three equally spaced levels of each Process parameter were selected (Table 1). The control factors were identified and selected on the basis of extensive review literature, research experience, and few preliminary investigations. Few different elements, which can also affect the measures of execution viz. Wire speed, Wire tension, Dielectric flow rate etc. are held constant.

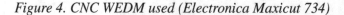

Figure 4. CNC WEDM used (Electronica Maxicut 734)

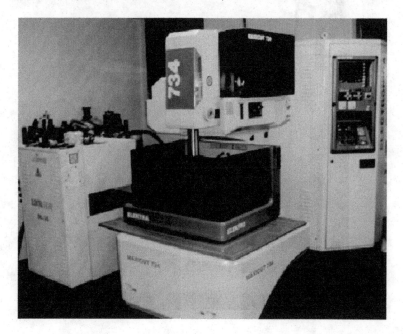

Figure 5. Roughness measuring instrument

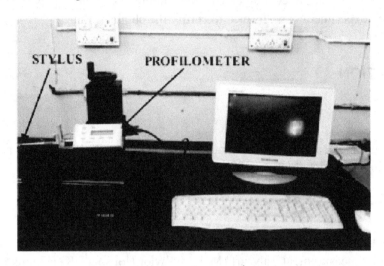

Figure 6. Mettle Toddler electronic balance

Table 1. Different variables used in the experiment and their levels (L27 OA)

Variable	Coding	Level		
		1	2	3
Discharge current (Ip) in A	A	4	6	8
Voltage (V) in V	B	45	50	55
Pulse on time (Ton) in µs	C	2	3	4
Pulse off time (Toff) in µs	D	2	3	4

Output Considered

Material Removal Rate (MRR)

The parameter MRR is selected as response variable, which refers to the machining efficiency of any machining process and defined as follows:

$$MRR = \frac{W_i - W_f}{t} \tag{21}$$

where, Wi, Wf are masses (in gm) of the work material before and after machining, respectively, and 't' is the time of machining in minutes or seconds. An electronic weighing machine with an accuracy of 0.01 mg is used in this work.

Surface Roughness (Ra, Rq, Rsk, Rku and Rsm)

There are many parameters present for defining surface roughness. Many of them have been formulated due to some specific purposes. The roughness parameters used in this work are:

Center Line Average (Ra)

Center line average, Ra is the arithmetic mean value of the deviation of the profile from the centre line along the sampling length calculated by the formula:

$$R_a = \frac{1}{L} \int_0^L Z(x)dx \tag{22}$$

where, Z (x) is the height of the surface above mean line at a distance x from the origin and L is the measured length of the profile as shown in Figure 7. Ra is usually expressed in µm.

Figure 7. Center line average of a surface over sampling length L (Sahoo 2005)

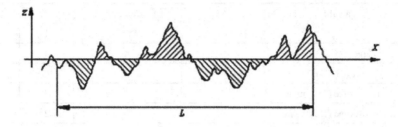

Root Mean Square Roughness (R_q)

It represents the standard deviation of the distribution of surface heights. Its unit is also μm. It is defined as the root mean square deviation of the profile from the mean line and is evaluated as:

$$R_q = \sqrt{\frac{1}{L} \int_0^L [Z(x)]^2 \, dx} \qquad (23)$$

Skewness (R_{sk})

It is a measure of the deviation of a distribution curve from its symmetry as in Gaussian distribution and may be expressed in the form:

$$R_{sk} = \frac{1}{R_q^3} \int_0^L [Z(x)]^3 \, dx \qquad (24)$$

It is a non-dimensional number, and $R_{sk} = 0$ for a symmetrical distribution for example a Gaussian distribution. A surface with positive skewness has a wider range of peak heights, higher than the mean (peak type profile). In contrary a surface with negative skewness has more peaks, closer to the mean as compared to a Gaussian distribution (valley type profile).

Kurtosis (R_{ku})

It is measure of the hump on a distribution curve and may be expressed in the form:

$$R_{ku} = \frac{1}{R_q^3 L} \int_0^L [Z(x)]^4 \, dx \qquad (25)$$

It is also non-dimensional, and for a symmetrical i.e. Gaussian distribution, $R_{ku} = 3$. $R_{ku} > 3$ implies that the peaks are sharper than Gaussian and vice versa.

Mean Line Peak Spacing (R_{sm})

It is defined as the mean gap between peaks, with a peak defined relative to the mean line (a peak like a sinusoidal curve is required to move across the mean line both above and below it). This parameter may be expressed:

$$R_{sm} = \frac{1}{m} \sum_{n=1}^{m} S_n \tag{26}$$

where m is the number of peak spacing and S is the spacing between two consecutive peaks. As per the definition values of Rs_m are higher than the earlier discussed parameters hence it is generally expressed in millimeters.

Surface Roughness Measurement

The surface roughness parameters on the machined surfaces were measured utilizing Talysurf (Make–Taylor Hobson, UK) appearing in Figure 5. The Talysurf instrument (Surtronic 3+) is an independent instrument for the estimation of surface roughness. The profilometer was set to a cut-off length of 0.8 mm, Gaussian filter, and transverse speed 1 mm/sec and 4 mm cross length. Roughness estimations, in the transverse direction, on the work pieces were performed five times and mean of five estimations of surface roughness parameter qualities was recorded. The deliberate profile was digitized and prepared through the dedicated and advanced surface finish analysis software Talyprofile.

Design of Experiment

As discussed earlier experimentation was conducted as per the DOE table and the results of MRR (gm/min), Ra (μm), Rq (μm), Rsk, Rku, Rsm (mm) were tabulated in Table2

RESULT AND DISCUSSION

Optimization of Responses Using Taguchi Method

S/N Ratio

With the aid of MINITAB 16, the experimental observations were further converted into signal-to-noise (S/N) ratio. There are many (S/N) ratios available based on objective of optimization of the response. MRR was maximized representing better machining performance (higher-the better (HB)) whereas surface roughness (Ra, Rq, Rsk, Rku and Rsm) was minimized indicating better surface finish (lower-the better (LB)) and are depicted in Table 3.

Table 2. Experimental results for response parameters

Exp. No.	A	B	C	D	MRR (gm /min)	Ra (µm)	Rq (µm)	Rsk	Rku	Rsm (mm)
1	4	45	2	2	0.039	5.862	7.183	0.105	3.540	0.115
2	4	45	3	3	0.060	5.500	6.850	0.526	4.113	0.118
3	4	45	4	4	0.041	5.055	6.423	0.147	2.681	0.112
4	4	50	2	3	0.029	5.708	7.098	0.301	4.023	0.145
5	4	50	3	4	0.055	5.313	6.555	0.399	4.005	0.109
6	4	50	4	2	0.059	4.983	6.193	0.143	3.640	0.163
7	4	55	2	4	0.051	5.216	6.382	0.259	3.143	0.107
8	4	55	3	2	0.046	6.150	7.588	0.087	2.853	0.114
9	4	55	4	3	0.049	5.335	6.558	0.174	2.900	0.098
10	6	45	2	3	0.048	2.498	3.195	0.254	4.115	0.119
11	6	45	3	4	0.039	4.623	5.680	0.088	3.738	0.108
12	6	45	4	2	0.033	5.535	6.860	0.297	3.250	0.131
13	6	50	2	4	0.027	5.653	6.883	0.047	2.643	0.108
14	6	50	3	2	0.051	6.353	7.858	0.086	3.155	0.125
15	6	50	4	3	0.047	3.326	4.133	0.086	3.578	0.140
16	6	55	2	2	0.046	4.897	6.017	0.147	3.050	0.118
17	6	55	3	3	0.040	3.123	3.880	0.117	4.048	0.116
18	6	55	4	4	0.053	5.535	6.843	0.236	3.215	0.120
19	8	45	2	4	0.048	5.700	7.013	0.113	2.773	0.110
20	8	45	3	2	0.059	5.463	6.800	0.132	3.390	0.128
21	8	45	4	3	0.058	5.335	6.593	0.013	2.900	0.106
22	8	50	2	2	0.054	6.703	8.361	0.077	2.985	0.118
23	8	50	3	3	0.058	6.498	8.000	0.131	2.817	0.112
24	8	50	4	4	0.055	5.425	6.698	0.044	3.403	0.122
25	8	55	2	3	0.065	5.643	6.910	0.080	2.915	0.116
26	8	55	3	4	0.052	6.130	6.653	0.123	2.713	0.110
27	8	55	4	2	0.062	5.424	6.343	0.168	4.591	0.118

The graphical representation of the main effects of four control factors on MRR, Ra, Rq, Rsk, Rku and Rsm are shown in Figure 8, Figure 9, Figure 10, Figure 11, Figure 12 and Figure 13 respectively.

In order to investigate the effect of input parameters on the responses, response tables were developed and it was observed that parameter A indicates most noteworthy delta value and hence has the greatest influence over MRR, Ra, Rq, Rsk, Rku and Rsm. The rank of each of the parameters can be viewed in tables 4, 5, 6, 7, 8 and 9 respectively.

Table 3. S/N Ratio Value for Responses

Exp. No.	S/N Ratio					
	MRR	Ra	Rq	Rsk	Rku	Rsm
1	-28.220	-15.362	-17.126	19.576	-10.980	18.786
2	-24.443	-14.807	-16.714	5.580	-12.282	18.540
3	-27.645	-14.074	-16.154	16.654	-8.566	18.996
4	-30.637	-15.129	-17.022	10.421	-12.090	16.773
5	-25.195	-14.506	-16.332	7.991	-12.052	19.242
6	-24.573	-13.950	-15.838	16.881	-11.222	15.774
7	-25.917	-14.347	-16.099	11.734	-9.945	19.398
8	-26.801	-15.778	-17.602	21.224	-9.104	18.900
9	-26.245	-14.543	-16.335	15.189	-9.248	20.191
10	-26.387	-7.952	-10.089	11.896	-12.287	18.520
11	-28.146	-13.298	-15.087	21.144	-11.452	19.332
12	-29.663	-14.862	-16.727	10.552	-10.238	17.671
13	-31.443	-15.045	-16.755	26.493	-8.440	19.332
14	-25.849	-16.059	-17.906	21.272	-9.980	18.062
15	-26.526	-10.438	-12.324	21.272	-11.072	17.062
16	-26.730	-13.798	-15.587	16.627	-9.686	18.562
17	-27.951	-9.890	-11.777	18.636	-12.144	18.711
18	-25.552	-14.862	-16.704	12.549	-10.144	18.453
19	-26.424	-15.118	-16.918	18.960	-8.857	19.156
20	-24.543	-14.748	-16.650	17.621	-10.604	17.839
21	-24.706	-14.543	-16.381	37.873	-9.248	19.473
22	-25.381	-16.525	-18.445	22.234	-9.499	18.544
23	-24.747	-16.255	-18.062	17.670	-8.996	19.029
24	-25.160	-14.688	-16.518	27.161	-10.636	18.308
25	-23.789	-15.029	-16.790	21.944	-9.293	18.730
26	-25.589	-15.749	-16.460	18.217	-8.667	19.196
27	-24.174	-14.686	-16.045	15.494	-13.238	18.562

Analysis of Variance (ANOVA)

As discussed earlier ANOVA was performed for the experimental data and tables for the analysis of influence of process parameters for the responses were generated using MINITAB 16. Here SOV is Source of Variation, DOF stands for Degrees of freedom, SS for Sum of Squares and MS is for Mean Square. For the selected levels and values in WEDM process, Tables 10, 11, 12, 13, 14, 15 respectively show influence of input parameters on responses (MRR, Ra, Rq, Rsk, Rku and Rsm) with percentage contribution of each parameter towards the response.

Figure 8. Main effects plot for S/N ratios of MRR

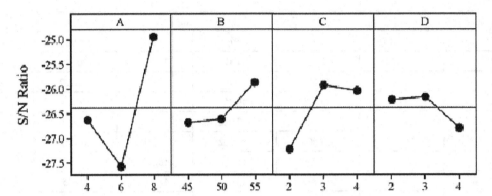

Figure 9. Main effects plot for S/N ratios of Ra

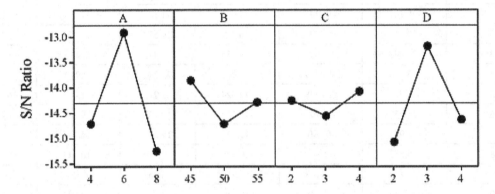

Figure 10. Main effects plot for S/N ratios of Rq

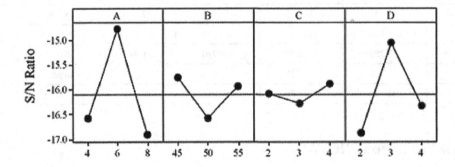

Confirmation Test

To validate the analysis, confirmation tests were carried out. Tables 16, 17, 18, 19, 20 and 21 show the results for the estimated responses and the actual responses using the optimal parameters for MRR, Ra, Rq, Rsk, Rku and Rsm. It is seen that there is a good correlation between the estimated and actual responses. The improvements of S/N ratios from initial to optimal condition for all the responses are shown in Table 22.

Figure 11. Main effects plot for S/N ratios of Rsk

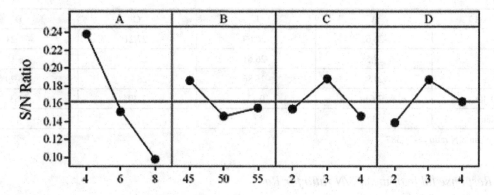

Figure 12. Main effects plot for S/N ratios of Rku

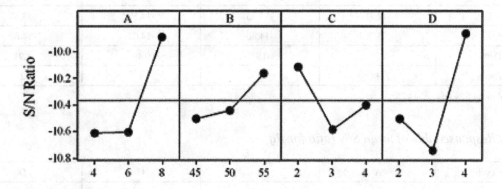

Figure 13. Main effects plot for S/N ratios of Rsm

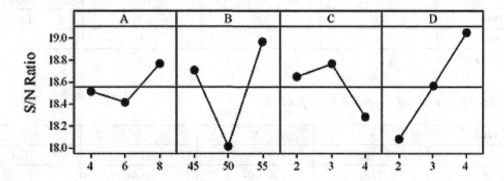

Multi Objective Optimization of Responses Using Grey Relational Analysis

For grey relational analysis, the experimental results are normalized and for this, higher-the-better (HB) criterion is selected for MRR (Equation 5) and lower-the-better (LB) criterion is selected for surface roughness (Equation 6). The normalized data (grey relational generation) is shown in Table 23. As a next step, the difference of the absolute value (Δoi) was calculated (shown in Table 24). After that Grey Relational Coefficients were calculated using Equation 8 and presented in Table 25.

Table 4. Response table of mean S/N ratio for MRR

Level	A	B	C	D
1	-26.63	-26.69	-27.21	-26.21
2	-27.58	-26.61	-25.92	-26.16
3	-24.95	-25.86	-26.03	-26.79
Delta	2.64	0.83	1.30	0.63
Rank	1	3	2	4

The total mean S/N ratio = -26.387

Table 5. Response table of mean S/N ratio for Ra

Level	A	B	C	D
1	-14.72	-13.86	-14.26	-15.09
2	-12.91	-14.73	-14.57	-13.18
3	-15.26	-14.30	-14.07	-14.63
Delta	2.35	0.87	0.49	1.91
Rank	1	3	4	2

The total mean S/N ratio = -14.298

Table 6. Response table of mean S/N ratio for Rq

Level	A	B	C	D
1	-16.58	-15.76	-16.09	-16.88
2	-14.77	-16.58	-16.29	-15.05
3	-16.92	-15.93	-15.89	-16.34
Delta	2.15	0.82	0.40	1.83
Rank	1	3	4	2

The total mean S/N ratio = -16.090

Table 7. Response table of mean S/N ratio for Rsk

Level	A	B	C	D
1	13.92	17.76	17.76	17.94
2	17.83	19.04	16.60	17.83
3	21.91	16.85	19.29	17.88
Delta	7.99	2.20	2.70	0.11
Rank	1	3	2	4

The total mean S/N ratio = 17.884

Table 8. Response table of mean S/N ratio for Rku

Level	A	B	C	D
1	-10.61	-10.50	-10.12	-10.51
2	-10.61	-10.44	-10.59	-10.74
3	-9.89	-10.16	-10.40	-9.86
Delta	0.72	0.34	0.47	0.88
Rank	2	4	3	1

The total mean S/N ratio = -10.514

Table 9. Response table of mean S/N ratio for Rsm

Level	A	B	C	D
1	18.51	18.70	18.64	18.08
2	18.41	18.01	18.76	18.56
3	18.76	18.97	18.28	19.05
Delta	0.35	0.95	0.48	0.97
Rank	4	2	3	1

The total mean S/N ratio = 18.561

Table 10. Results of ANOVA for MRR

SOV	DOF	SS	MS	F-ratio	% Contribution
A	2	32.099	16.049	5.63*	32.55
B	2	3.756	1.878	0.66	3.8
C	2	9.302	4.651	1.63	9.43
D	2	2.166	1.083	0.38	2.19
AXB	4	0.719	0.18	0.06	0.72
AXC	4	5.349	1.337	0.47	5.42
BXC	4	28.079	7.02	2.46	28.48
Error	6	17.115	2.853		17.36
Total	26	98.585			100

Note: *Significant at 95% confidence level ($F_{0.05,2,6}$=5.14)

Subsequent to averaging the grey relational coefficients, the grey relational grade (γi) is ascertained utilizing Equation 9. Table 26 shows the results for the grey relational grade and their order. The grey relational grade represents the overall characteristics of MRR and surface roughness performance. In this way, the multi-objective optimization situation has been transformed into a single objective optimization situation using the association of Taguchi method and grey relational analysis.

Table 11. Results of ANOVA for Ra

SOV	DOF	SS	MS	F-ratio	% Contribution
A	2	27.25	13.62	3.69*	27.98
B	2	3.41	1.70	0.46	3.49
C	2	1.12	0.56	0.15	1.15
D	2	17.91	8.95	2.43	18.39
AXB	4	3.33	0.83	0.23	3.42
AXC	4	3.93	0.98	0.27	4.03
BXC	4	18.28	4.57	1.24	18.77
Error	6	22.15	3.69		22.74
Total	26	97.36			100

Note: *Significant at 90% confidence level ($F_{0.1,2,6}$=3.4633)

Table 12: Results of ANOVA for Rq

SOV	DOF	SS	MS	F-ratio	% Contribution
A	2	23.96	11.98	3.61*	26.41
B	2	3.34	1.67	0.50	3.68
C	2	0.71	0.35	0.11	0.77
D	2	15.82	7.91	2.38	17.43
AXB	4	3.79	0.95	0.29	4.17
AXC	4	4.06	1.02	0.31	4.48
BXC	4	19.11	4.78	1.44	21.07
Error	6	19.92	3.32		21.95
Total	26	90.704			100

Note: *Significant at 95% confidence level ($F_{0.1,2,6}$=3.4633)

Table 13. Results of ANOVA for Rsk

SOV	DOF	SS	MS	F-ratio	% Contribution
A	2	287.41	143.71	3.07*	25.6
B	2	21.94	10.97	0.23	1.95
C	2	32.91	16.46	0.35	2.93
D	2	0.06	0.03	0	0.01
AXB	4	189.36	47.34	1.01	16.86
AXC	4	171.99	43	0.92	15.32
BXC	4	137.9	34.47	0.74	12.28
Error	6	281	46.83		25.03
Total	26	1122.57			100

Note: *Significant at 90% confidence level ($F_{0.1,2,6}$=3.4633)

Table 14. Results of ANOVA for Rku

SOV	DOF	SS	MS	F-ratio	% Contribution
A	2	3.061	1.53	1.25	6.32
B	2	0.588	0.294	0.24	1.31
C	2	0.995	0.498	0.41	2.06
D	2	3.718	1.859	1.52	7.68
AXB	4	12.282	3.07	2.5	25.4
AXC	4	10.659	2.665	2.17	22.02
BXC	4	9.683	2.421	1.97	20.01
Error	6	7.355	1.226		15.2
Total	26	48.339			100

Note: *Significant at 90% confidence level ($F_{0.1,2,6}$= 3.4633)

Table 15. Results of ANOVA for Rsm

SOV	DOF	SS	MS	F-ratio	% Contribution
A	2	0.579	0.2895	0.66	2.62
B	2	4.3547	2.1773	4.96*	19.72
C	2	1.1499	0.5749	1.31	5.2
D	2	4.216	2.108	4.8*	19.09
AXB	4	3.8296	0.9574	2.18	17.34
AXC	4	1.649	0.4123	0.94	7.47
BXC	4	3.6631	0.9158	2.09	16.59
Error	6	2.6332	0.4389		11.92
Total	26	22.0745			100

Table 16. Confirmation Test for MRR

Level	Initial parameter combination	Optimum parameter combination	
	A2B2C2D2	A3B3C2D2	
		Prediction	Experimental
MRR	0.051528		0.05987
S/N ratio (dB)	-25.7085	-24.95	-24.4558
Note: Improvement of S/N ratio = 1.2527dB. (4.87%)			

Analysis of Signal-To-Noise (S/N) Ratio

Taguchi technique utilizes S/N ratio to change over the test results into a value for the assessment characteristics in the optimal parameter investigation. Here, S/N ratio evaluation is performed with grey relational grade as the performance index. As grey relational grade is to be enhanced, the S/N ratio is

Table 17. Confirmation Test for Ra

Level	Initial parameter combination	Optimum parameter combination		
	A2B2C2D2	A2B1C3D2		
		Prediction		Experimental
Ra	5.940			3.356
S/N ratio (dB)	-15.4757	-12.91		-10.5164
Note: Improvement of S/N ratio = 4.9593dB. (32%)				

Table 18. Confirmation Test for Rq

Level	Initial parameter combination	Optimum parameter combination		
	A2B2C2D2	A2B1C3D2		
		Prediction		Experimental
Rq	7.065			5.0123
S/N ratio (dB)	-16.9822	-14.77		-14.0007
Note: Improvement of S/N ratio = 2.9815dB. (18%)				

Table 19. Confirmation Test for Rsk

Level	Initial parameter combination	Optimum parameter combination	
	A2B2C2D2	A3B3C2D2	
		Prediction	Experimental
Rsk	0.085		0.082
S/N ratio (dB)	21.41162		16.97474
Note: Improvement of S/N ratio = 4.9593dB. (32%)			

Table 20. Confirmation Test for Rku

Level	Initial parameter combination	Optimum parameter combination		
	A2B2C2D2	A3B3C1D3		
		Prediction		Experimental
Rku	3.435			2.893
S/N ratio (dB)	-10.7185	-10.5141		-9.2269
Note: Improvement of S/N ratio = 1.4916dB. (14%)				

Table 21. Confirmation Test for Rsm

Level	Initial parameter combination	Optimum parameter combination	
	A2B2C2D2	A3B3C2D3	
		Prediction	Experimental
Rsm	0.115		0.10
S/N ratio (dB)	18.786	19.46	20
Note: Improvement of S/N ratio = 1.214dB. (7%)			

Table 22. Optimum combinations with improvements in S/N ratios for MRR, Ra, Rq, Rsk, Rku and Rsm

Level	Initial parameter combination	Optimum parameter combination	Improvement of S/N ratio (dB)
MRR	A2B2C2D2	A3B3C2D2	1.252
Ra	A2B2C2D2	A2B1C3D2	4.959
Rq	A2B2C2D2	A2B1C3D2	2.982
Rsk	A2B2C2D2	A3B3C2D2	4.437
Rku	A2B2C2D2	A3B3C1D3	1.492
Rsm	A2B2C2D2	A3B3C2D3	1.214

calculated using greater-the-better (HB) criterion. The response table for the mean of grey relational grade is tabulated in Table 27. The response table evaluates the relative magnitude of the effects which includes ranks based on delta statistics. The delta statistic is the largest average for each factor less the lowest average for the same and ranks are designated on the basis of delta values.

From the response table it was observed that parameter A (current) is the most prominent factor in controlling MRR and surface roughness characteristics of WEDM. Figure 14 shows the main effects plots between the process parameters. It can be easily observed from the main effects plot that parameter discharge current (A) is the most significant parameter while parameter pulse off time (D) also has a quite substantial effect on the response. Thus from the present analysis it is quite evident that the discharge current (A) is the most affecting parameters for controlling the multiple responses of WEDM process. Hence, the optimal combination of parameters is found to be A3B1C1D2 for maximum MRR and minimum roughness characteristics.

Analysis of Variance (ANOVA)

Table 28 shows ANOVA result for overall grey relational grade of MRR and roughness parameters. It is clear from the table that parameter current (A) is the most influential factor affecting MRR and roughness at the confidence level of 90% within the chosen test range. Similarly, interaction between voltage (B) and pulse on time (C) has some influence on MRR and surface roughness characteristics.

Table 23. Normalized values of experimental data

Exp. No.	MRR	Ra	Rq	Rsk	Rku	Rsm
1	0.318	0.200	0.228	0.821	0.540	0.990
2	0.876	0.286	0.292	0.000	0.246	0.986
3	0.388	0.392	0.375	0.739	0.980	0.993
4	0.069	0.237	0.245	0.438	0.292	0.955
5	0.745	0.331	0.350	0.249	0.301	0.997
6	0.853	0.409	0.420	0.746	0.488	0.935
7	0.629	0.354	0.383	0.521	0.744	0.999
8	0.500	0.132	0.150	0.856	0.892	0.991
9	0.580	0.325	0.349	0.686	0.868	0.000
10	0.559	1.000	1.000	0.530	0.244	0.985
11	0.327	0.495	0.519	0.855	0.438	0.998
12	0.161	0.278	0.291	0.447	0.688	0.971
13	0.000	0.250	0.286	0.933	1.000	0.998
14	0.639	0.083	0.098	0.857	0.737	0.978
15	0.539	0.803	0.819	0.857	0.520	0.961
16	0.510	0.430	0.454	0.738	0.791	0.986
17	0.350	0.852	0.867	0.797	0.279	0.989
18	0.686	0.278	0.294	0.566	0.706	0.984
19	0.553	0.239	0.261	0.806	0.934	0.995
20	0.858	0.295	0.302	0.769	0.617	0.975
21	0.829	0.325	0.342	1.000	0.868	1.000
22	0.714	0.000	0.000	0.875	0.824	0.986
23	0.822	0.049	0.070	0.770	0.911	0.993
24	0.751	0.304	0.322	0.940	0.610	0.982
25	1.000	0.252	0.281	0.870	0.860	0.989
26	0.680	0.136	0.331	0.786	0.964	0.995
27	0.926	0.304	0.391	0.698	0.000	0.986

Confirmation Test

The comparison between estimated grey relational grade and actual grey relational grade using the optimal parameters has been tabulated in Table 29. It indicates that there is a fairly good agreement between them. The improvement of grey relational grade from initial to optimal condition is 0.17077 that means improved by 21%.

Table 24. Table for Δoi values

Exp. No.	MRR	Ra	Rq	Rsk	Rku	Rsm
1	0.682	0.800	0.772	0.179	0.460	0.010
2	0.124	0.714	0.708	1.000	0.754	0.014
3	0.612	0.608	0.625	0.261	0.020	0.007
4	0.931	0.763	0.755	0.562	0.708	0.045
5	0.255	0.669	0.650	0.751	0.699	0.003
6	0.147	0.591	0.580	0.254	0.512	0.065
7	0.371	0.646	0.617	0.480	0.256	0.001
8	0.500	0.869	0.850	0.144	0.108	0.009
9	0.421	0.675	0.651	0.314	0.132	1.000
10	0.442	0.000	0.000	0.470	0.756	0.015
11	0.673	0.505	0.481	0.146	0.562	0.002
12	0.839	0.722	0.709	0.553	0.312	0.029
13	1.000	0.750	0.714	0.067	0.000	0.002
14	0.361	0.917	0.903	0.143	0.263	0.022
15	0.462	0.197	0.181	0.143	0.480	0.039
16	0.490	0.570	0.546	0.262	0.209	0.014
17	0.650	0.149	0.133	0.203	0.721	0.011
18	0.314	0.722	0.706	0.434	0.294	0.016
19	0.447	0.762	0.739	0.194	0.066	0.005
20	0.142	0.705	0.698	0.231	0.383	0.025
21	0.171	0.675	0.658	0.000	0.132	0.000
22	0.286	1.000	1.000	0.125	0.176	0.014
23	0.178	0.951	0.930	0.230	0.089	0.007
24	0.249	0.696	0.678	0.060	0.390	0.018
25	0.000	0.748	0.719	0.131	0.140	0.011
26	0.320	0.864	0.669	0.214	0.036	0.005
27	0.074	0.696	0.609	0.302	1.000	0.014

Multi Objective Optimization of Responses Using Weighted Principal Component Analysis (WPCA)

The experimental results for MRR and five surface roughness parameters (Ra, Rq, Rsk, Rku and Rsm) was evaluated, using the WPCA method with the target to determine the machining parameters combination for optimum MRR and surface roughness. For MRR, higher-the-better criterion and for all surface roughness parameters lower-the-better criterion has been employed. Then, the S/N ratios are scaled into (0, 1) interval using equation 15. The scaled S/N ratios values are shown in Table 30.

Table 25. Table for grey relational coefficient

Exp. No.	MRR	Ra	Rq	Rsk	Rku	Rsm
1	0.423	0.385	0.393	0.736	0.521	0.980
2	0.801	0.412	0.414	0.333	0.399	0.973
3	0.450	0.451	0.445	0.657	0.962	0.987
4	0.349	0.396	0.398	0.471	0.414	0.918
5	0.662	0.428	0.435	0.400	0.417	0.993
6	0.772	0.458	0.463	0.663	0.494	0.885
7	0.574	0.436	0.448	0.510	0.661	0.998
8	0.500	0.365	0.370	0.776	0.823	0.982
9	0.543	0.426	0.434	0.614	0.791	0.333
10	0.531	1.000	1.000	0.515	0.398	0.971
11	0.426	0.497	0.510	0.775	0.471	0.995
12	0.373	0.409	0.413	0.475	0.616	0.946
13	0.333	0.400	0.412	0.882	1.000	0.995
14	0.581	0.353	0.357	0.778	0.656	0.958
15	0.520	0.718	0.734	0.778	0.510	0.928
16	0.505	0.467	0.478	0.656	0.705	0.973
17	0.435	0.771	0.790	0.712	0.410	0.978
18	0.614	0.409	0.415	0.535	0.630	0.969
19	0.528	0.396	0.404	0.720	0.883	0.991
20	0.779	0.415	0.417	0.684	0.566	0.952
21	0.745	0.426	0.432	1.000	0.791	1.000
22	0.636	0.333	0.333	0.800	0.740	0.973
23	0.737	0.345	0.350	0.685	0.848	0.987
24	0.667	0.418	0.425	0.893	0.562	0.965
25	1.000	0.401	0.410	0.793	0.782	0.978
26	0.610	0.367	0.428	0.700	0.933	0.991
27	0.871	0.418	0.451	0.623	0.333	0.973

After data normalization, to ascertain correlation between responses, a check has to be made using Pearson's correlation coefficient (equation 16). It is observed that all the correlation coefficient have non-zero value hence it can be concluded that all the responses are correlated to one another (Table 31). Eigen value, Eigen vector, accountability proportion (AP) and cumulative accountability proportion (CAP) are shown in Table 32 using STATISTICA 8.0 software, which represents results of PCA.

Applying equation 17, the 6 principal components corresponding to a trail (i) are then evaluated as follows:

Table 26. Grey relational grades and their orders

Exp. No.	Grade	Order	Exp. No.	Grade	Order
1	0.573	22	17	0.682	5
2	0.555	24	18	0.595	21
3	0.658	9	19	0.654	11
4	0.491	27	20	0.636	14
5	0.556	23	21	0.732	2
6	0.623	16	22	0.636	13
7	0.604	20	23	0.659	8
8	0.636	12	24	0.655	10
9	0.524	26	25	0.727	3
10	0.736	1	26	0.671	6
11	0.612	18	27	0.612	19
12	0.539	25			
13	0.670	7			
14	0.614	17			
15	0.698	4			
16	0.631	15			

Table 27. Response table for grey relational grade

Level	A	B	C	D
1	0.580	0.633	0.636	0.611
2	0.642	0.622	0.625	0.645
3	0.665	0.632	0.626	0.631
Delta	0.085	0.011	0.011	0.034
Rank	1	4	3	2

Total mean grey relational grade = 0.62885

Figure 14. Main effects plot for mean grey relational grade

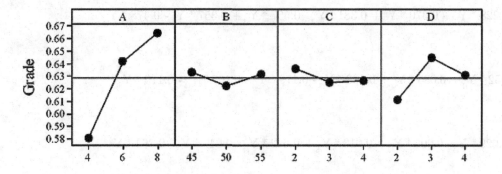

Table 28. Response table for grey relational grade

SOV	DOF	SS	MS	F-ratio	% Contribution
A	2	0.034	0.017	4.810*	34.18
B	2	0.001	0.000	0.080	0.58
C	2	0.001	0.000	0.090	0.65
D	2	0.005	0.003	0.740	5.22
AXB	4	0.005	0.001	0.320	4.61
AXC	4	0.010	0.003	0.700	9.99
BXC	4	0.024	0.006	1.650	23.40
Error	6	0.022	0.004		
Total	26	0.101			100.00

Note: *Significant at 90% confidence level ($F_{0.1,2,6}$= 3.4633)

Table 29. Confirmation Test for Rsm

Level	Initial parameter combination	Optimum parameter combination	
	A2B2C2D2	A3B1C1D2	
		Prediction	Experimental
MRR	0.052		0.059
Ra	5.940		3.942
Rq	7.065		4.523
Rsk	0.085		0.045
Rku	3.135		2.733
Rsm	0.115		0.107
Grade	0.633	0.665	0.804
Note: Improvement of S/N ratio = 0.17077 (21%)			

$$Z_1^i = - 0.069 * Y_{i1} + 0.563 * Y_{i2} + 0.559 * Y_{i3} + 0.257 * Y_{i4} - 0.486 * Y_{i5} + 0.254 * Y_{i6} \tag{27}$$

$$Z_2^i = - 0.228 * Y_{i1} + 0.370 * Y_{i2} + 0.381 * Y_{i3} - 0.557 * Y_{i4} + 0.357 * Y_{i5} - 0.478 * Y_{i6} \tag{28}$$

$$Z_3^i = 0.952 * Y_{i1} + 0.085 * Y_{i2} + 0.103 * Y_{i3} - 0.179 * Y_{i4} - 0.107 * Y_{i5} - 0.179 * Y_{i6} \tag{29}$$

$$Z_4^i = - 0.029 * Y_{i1} - 0.005 * Y_{i2} + 0.013 * Y_{i3} + 0.642 * Y_{i4} - 0.047 * Y_{i5} - 0.764 * Y_{i6} \tag{30}$$

Table 30. Scaled S/N ratio of multiple responses

Exp. No.	MRR	Ra	Rq	Rsk	Rku	Rsm
1	0.421	0.136	0.158	0.567	0.471	0.318
2	0.914	0.200	0.207	1.000	0.199	0.374
3	0.496	0.286	0.274	0.657	0.974	0.271
4	0.105	0.163	0.170	0.850	0.239	0.774
5	0.816	0.235	0.253	0.925	0.247	0.215
6	0.898	0.300	0.312	0.650	0.420	1.000
7	0.722	0.254	0.281	0.809	0.686	0.180
8	0.607	0.087	0.101	0.516	0.862	0.292
9	0.679	0.231	0.253	0.702	0.832	0.000
10	0.660	1.000	1.000	0.804	0.198	0.378
11	0.431	0.376	0.402	0.518	0.372	0.195
12	0.233	0.194	0.206	0.846	0.625	0.571
13	0.000	0.173	0.202	0.352	1.000	0.195
14	0.731	0.054	0.065	0.514	0.679	0.482
15	0.642	0.710	0.733	0.514	0.452	0.708
16	0.616	0.318	0.342	0.658	0.740	0.369
17	0.456	0.774	0.798	0.596	0.228	0.335
18	0.770	0.194	0.208	0.784	0.645	0.394
19	0.656	0.164	0.183	0.586	0.913	0.234
20	0.901	0.207	0.215	0.627	0.549	0.533
21	0.880	0.231	0.247	0.000	0.832	0.162
22	0.792	0.000	0.000	0.484	0.779	0.373
23	0.875	0.031	0.046	0.626	0.884	0.263
24	0.821	0.214	0.231	0.332	0.542	0.426
25	1.000	0.174	0.198	0.493	0.822	0.331
26	0.765	0.090	0.237	0.609	0.953	0.225
27	0.950	0.215	0.287	0.693	0.000	0.369

$$Z_5^i = 0.188 * Y_{i1} + 0.194 * Y_{i2} + 0.183 * Y_{i3} + 0.424 * Y_{i4} + 0.789 * Y_{i5} + 0.302 * Y_{i6} \tag{31}$$

$$Z_6^i = 0.009 * Y_{i1} + 0.708 * Y_{i2} - 0.706 * Y_{i3} - 0.003 * Y_{i4} - 0.004 * Y_{i5} - 0.019 * Y_{i6} \tag{32}$$

where Yi1, Yi2, Yi3, Yi4, Yi5 and Yi6 are the scaled S/N ratio values of MRR and Surface roughness respectively, for ith trial. Finally, multi-response performance index (MPI) for each trail (shown in Table 33) computed using equation 18 and equation 33.

Table 31. Correlation among quality characteristics

Sl. No.	Correlation between	Responses	Pearson correlation
1	MRR and Ra	0.9918	Both are correlated
2	MRR and Rq	-0.0994	Both are correlated
3	MRR and Rsk	-0.0388	Both are correlated
4	MRR and Rku	-0.0654	Both are correlated
5	MRR and Rsm	-0.0362	Both are correlated
6	Ra and Rq	0.9917	Both are correlated
7	Ra and Rsk	0.1124	Both are correlated
8	Ra and Rku	-0.4738	Both are correlated
9	Ra and Rsm	0.1436	Both are correlated
10	Rq and Rsk	0.1062	Both are correlated
11	Rq and Rku	-0.4689	Both are correlated
12	Rq and Rsm	0.3559	Both are correlated
13	Rsk and Rku	-0.4519	Both are correlated
14	Rsk and Rsm	0.1803	Both are correlated
15	Rku and Rsm	-0.3929	Both are correlated

Table 32. Eigen values, Eigen vectors, Accountability proportion (AP) and cumulative accountability proportion (CAP) computed

	MRR	Ra	Rq	Rsk	Rku	Rsm
Eigen values	2.523	1.281	1.001	0.822	0.367	0.008
Eigenvector	-0.070	0.563	0.559	0.257	-0.486	0.254
	-0.228	0.370	0.381	-0.557	0.357	-0.478
	0.952	0.085	0.103	-0.179	-0.107	-0.179
	-0.029	-0.005	0.013	0.642	-0.047	-0.764
	0.188	0.194	0.183	0.424	0.789	0.302
	0.009	0.708	-0.706	-0.003	-0.004	-0.019
AP	0.420	0.213	0.167	0.137	0.061	0.001
CAP	0.420	0.634	0.801	0.938	0.999	1.000

$$\text{MPI}^i = 0.4204 * Z_1^i + 0.2134 * Z_2^i + 0.1667 * Z_3^i + 0.1369 * Z_4^i + 0.0611 * Z_5^i + 0.0013 * Z_6^i \tag{33}$$

The level average of MPI for all levels of each parameter is tabulated in Table 34. Higher value of MPI indicates better quality. Figure 15 shows the main effects plots of MPI. From the plots, it is observed that parameter pulse off time (D) and current (A) have got the most significant effect on MRR and surface roughness. Optimal combination of machining process parameters can be obtained for maximum MRR and minimum surface roughness as A2B1C3D2.

Table 33. Scaled S/N ratio of multiple responses

Exp. No.	A	B	C	D	MPI	Exp. No.	A	B	C	D	MPI	Exp. No.	A	B	C	D	MPI
1	1	1	1	1	0.095	10	2	1	1	2	0.742	19	3	1	1	3	0.099
2	1	1	2	2	0.231	11	2	1	2	3	0.283	20	3	1	2	1	0.154
3	1	1	3	3	0.153	12	2	1	3	1	0.091	21	3	1	3	2	0.137
4	1	2	1	2	0.075	13	2	2	1	3	0.029	22	3	2	1	1	0.018
5	1	2	2	3	0.258	14	2	2	2	1	0.018	23	3	2	2	2	0.028
6	1	2	3	1	0.182	15	2	2	3	2	0.464	24	3	2	3	3	0.146
7	1	3	1	3	0.215	16	2	3	1	1	0.211	25	3	3	1	2	0.130
8	1	3	2	1	0.033	17	2	3	2	2	0.563	26	3	3	2	3	0.100
9	1	3	3	2	0.191	18	2	3	3	3	0.152	27	3	3	3	1	0.266

Table 34. Level average on MPI

Level	A	B	C	D
1	0.159	0.220	0.179	0.119
2	0.284	0.135	0.185	0.285
3	0.120	0.207	0.198	0.159

Figure 15. Main effects plot for MPI

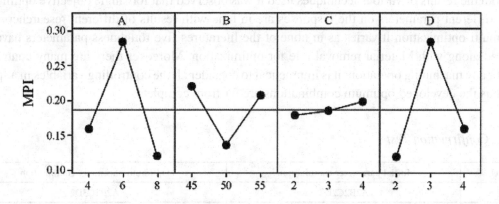

Analysis of Variance (ANOVA)

Table 35 shows ANOVA result for MPI of MRR and surface roughness in WEDM. From this table, it is seen that individual parameter current and pulse off time and also, among the interaction between voltage and pulse on time are significant parameters contributing to control MRR and surface roughness in WEDM.

Table 35. Results of ANOVA for MPI

SOV	DOF	SS	MS	F-ratio	% Contribution
A	2	0.132	0.066	1.780	17.890
B	2	0.038	0.019	0.510	5.120
C	2	0.002	0.001	0.020	0.220
D	2	0.134	0.067	1.820	18.230
AXB	4	0.043	0.011	0.29	5.81
AXC	4	0.033	0.008	0.23	4.53
BXC	4	0.133	0.033	0.9	18.05
Error	6	0.222	0.037		30.12
Total	26	0.737			100

Confirmation Test

To validate the results obtained, a confirmatory test is carried out and comparison between the initial parameter combination and optimum combination is provided in Table 36.

From the table, it is evident that the total S/N ratio at optimum combination is greater than the initial parameter combination. The enhancement of the S/N ratio is found to be about 5.58166dB (21%). It is obvious that regardless of the category of the performance characteristics, a larger S/N ratio always corresponds to a better performance. Hence, the result of confirmatory test ascertains better performance at the optimum design.

So from the results of various techniques used it was observed that for single objective optimization effect of different parameters on the responses are in tune with results of different researchers but in case of multi-optimization it varies as in none of the literatures five roughness parameters have been considered along with Material removal rate for optimization. Moreover there are many controllable factors for any machining operation; it is impractical to consider all the controlling variables in a specific study. Thus the developed optimum combinations are far from complete.

Table 36. Confirmation Test

Level	Initial parameter combination	Optimum parameter combination
	A2B2C2D2	A2B1C3D2
		Experimental
MRR	0.05183	0.05881
Ra	5.94	5.535
Rq	7.065	6.86
Rsk	0.085	0.067
Rku	3.135	2.613
Rsm	0.106	0.103
S/N Ratio	-26.9039	-21.3326
Note: Improvement of S/N ratio = 5.58166 dB (21%)		

Since EN19 material has been used in this work which contains lower percentage of carbon (0.35% - 0.45%) and also due to the higher localized and concentrated spark energy produces in WEDM, more material melts and erodes from the work piece as a result Ra is having a higher value than other researchers working with high carbon materials and using other non conventional machining techniques.

CONCLUSION

Wire Electrical discharge machining (WEDM) is a non-traditional, thermo-electric procedure which disintegrates material from the work piece by a progression of discrete sparkles between a work and instrument terminal submerged in a fluid dielectric medium.; currently being employed to perform machining operation on a wide variety of miniature and micro-parts made of metals, alloys, sintered materials, cemented carbides, ceramics and silicon

CNC WEDM operations are carried out on EN 19 steel for different levels of discharge current (A), voltage (B), pulse on time (C) and pulse off time (D). The experiments were performed based on Taguchi L27 orthogonal array. The experimental results are further analyzed using three optimization soft computing tools.

Taguchi analysis yields the optimum combination of process parameters for maximum MRR and minimum surface roughness. From this analysis, it is observed that discharge current is the most significant factor affecting MRR and surface roughness parameters. This is quite natural as increase in discharge current would erode the material more and hence MRR would increase and so will be the surface roughness parameters.

Regarding the multi response optimization it is observed that with the aid of Grey Relation Analysis, the optimal combination of process parameters for improved responses was obtained as A3B1C1D2 (Improvement of S/N Ration of 0.17 dB) where as in case of WPCA, same was found to be A2B1C3D2 (Improvement of S/N Ration of 5.58 dB). The difference can be attributed to the variation in weightage used for the responses in the two different techniques.

These optimal combinations of parameters can be directly employed by industrial sector (depending on the requirement i.e. single objective / multi-objective etc.) for enhancement of overall productivity and profitability.

REFERENCES

Alias, A., Abdullah, B., & Abbas, N. M. (2012). Influence of machined feed rate in WEDM of titanium Ti-6Al-4V with constant current (6A) using brass wire. *Procedia Engineering*, *41*, 1806–1811. doi:10.1016/j.proeng.2012.07.387

Antony, J. (2000). Multi-response optimization in industrial experiments using Taguchis quality loss function and principal component analysis. *Quality and Reliability Engineering International*, *16*(1), 3–8. doi:10.1002/(SICI)1099-1638(200001/02)16:1<3::AID-QRE276>3.0.CO;2-W

Bass, I. (2007). *Six Sigma Statistics with Excel and Minitab*. McGraw Hill.

Chiang, K. T., & Chang, F. P. (2006). Optimization of the WEDM process of particle-reinforced material with multiple performance characteristics using grey relational analysis. *Journal of Materials Processing Technology*, *180*(1-3), 96–101. doi:10.1016/j.jmatprotec.2006.05.008

Datta, S., & Mahapatra, S. S. (2010). Modeling, simulation and parametric optimization of wire EDM process using response surface methodology coupled with grey-Taguchi technique. *International Journal of Engineering Science and Technology*, *2*(5), 162–183. doi:10.4314/ijest.v2i5.60144

Datta, S., Nandi, G., Bandyopadhyay, A., & Pal, P. K. (2009). Application of PCA based hybrid Taguchi method for multi-criteria optimization of submerged arc weld: A case study. *International Journal of Advanced Manufacturing Technology*, *45*(3-4), 276–286. doi:10.1007/s00170-009-1976-0

Deng, J. (1989). Introduction to Grey System. *Journal of Grey System*, *1*, 1–24.

Dey, S., & Tripathi, B. (2013). Analyzing the effects of process variables (cutting rate surface roughness and gap current) of the wire electric discharge machining (WEDM)-a study. *International Journal of Engineering and Science Research*, *3*, 168–172.

Durairaj, M., Sudharsun, D., & Swamynathan, N. (2013). Analysis of Process Parameters in Wire EDM with Stainless Steel Using Single Objective Taguchi Method and Multi Objective Grey Relational Grade. *Procedia Engineering*, *64*, 868–877. doi:10.1016/j.proeng.2013.09.163

Esme, U., Sagbas, A., & Kahraman, F. (2009). Prediction of surface roughness in wire electrical discharge machining using design of experiments and neural networks, *Iranian Journal of Science and Technology, Transaction B, Engineering*, *33*, 231-240.

Fisher, R. A. (1951). *Design of experiments, Edinburgh*. Oliver and Boyd.

Gao, C., Zhan, Z., Wang, S., He, N., & Li, L. (2013). Research on WEDM Process Optimization for PCD Micro Milling Tool. *Procedia CIRP*, *6*, 209–214. doi:10.1016/j.procir.2013.03.035

Garg, M. P., Jain, A., & Bhushan, G. (2012). Modelling and multi-objective optimization of process parameters of wire electrical discharge machining using non-dominated sorting genetic algorithm-II. *Proceedings of the IMechE, Part B: Journal of Engineering Manufacture.*, *226*(12), 1986–2001. doi:10.1177/0954405412462778

Gauri, S. K., & Chakraborty, S. (2009). Multi-response optimisation of WEDM process using principal component analysis. *International Journal of Advanced Manufacturing Technology*, *41*(7-8), 741–748. doi:10.1007/s00170-008-1529-y

Ghodsiyeh, D., Lahiji, M. A., Ghanbari, M., Golshan, A., & Shirdar, M. R. (2012). Optimizing rough cut in WEDMing titanium alloy (Ti6Al4V) by brass wire using the Taguchi method. *Journal of Basic and Applied Scientific Research*, *2*, 7488–7496.

Han, F., Jiang, J., & Yu, D. (2007). Influence of machining parameters on surface roughness in finish cut of WEDM. *International Journal of Advanced Manufacturing Technology*, *34*(5-6), 538–546. doi:10.1007/s00170-006-0629-9

Hewidy, M. S., El-Taweel, T. A., & El-Safty, M. F. (2005). Modelling the machining parameters of wire electrical discharge machining of Inconel 601 using RSM. *Journal of Materials Processing Technology, 169*(2), 328–336. doi:10.1016/j.jmatprotec.2005.04.078

Huang, J. T., & Liao, Y. S. (2003). Application of grey relational analysis to machining parameter determination of wire electrical discharge machining. *International Journal of Production Research, 41,* 1244–1256. doi:10.1080/13528160310000074973

Huang, J. T., Liao, Y. S., & Hsue, W. J. (1999). Determination of finish-cutting operation number and machining-parameters setting in wire electrical discharge machining. *Journal of Materials Processing Technology, 87*(1-3), 69–81. doi:10.1016/S0924-0136(98)00334-3

Huang, M. S., & Lin, T. Y. (2008). Simulation of a regression-model and PCA based searching method developed for setting the robust injection molding parameters of multi-quality characteristics. *International Journal of Heat and Mass Transfer, 51*(25-26), 5828–5837. doi:10.1016/j.ijheatmasstransfer.2008.05.016

Jangra, K., Grover, S., & Aggarwal, A. (2011). Simultaneous optimization of material removal rate and surface roughness for WEDM of WCCo composite using grey relational analysis along with Taguchi method. *International Journal of Industrial Engineering Computations, 2*(3), 479–490. doi:10.5267/j.ijiec.2011.04.005

Johnson, D. E. (1998). *Applied multivariate methods for data analysis.* Pacific Grove, CA: Duxbury.

Kanlayasiri, K., & Boonmung, S. (2007). Effects of wire-EDM machining variables on surface roughness of newly developed DC 53 die steel: Design of experiments and regression model. *Journal of Materials Processing Technology, 192-193,* 59–464. doi:10.1016/j.jmatprotec.2007.04.085

Kapoor, J., Singh, S., & Khamba, J. S. (2012). Effect of cryogenic treated brass wire electrode on material removal rate in wire electrical discharge machining, *Proc. Inst. Mech. Eng. Part C. Journal of Mechanical Engineering Science, 226*(11), 2750–2758. doi:10.1177/0954406212438804

Khan, N. Z., Khan, Z. A., Siddiquee, A. N., & Chanda, A. K. (2014). Investigation on the effect of wire EDM process parameters on surface integrity of HSLA: A multi-performance characteristics optimization. *Prod. Manuf. Res, 2*(1), 501–518.

Khanna, R., & Singh, H. (2013). Performance analysis for D-3 material using response surface methodology on WEDM. *Int. J. Machining and Machinability of Materials, 14*(1), 45–65. doi:10.1504/IJMMM.2013.055120

Kozak, J., Rajurkar, K. P., & Wang, S. Z. (1994). Material removal in WEDM of PCD Blanks. *Journal of Manufacturing Science and Engineering, 116,* 363–369.

Kumar, A., Kumar, V., & Kumar, J. (2012). Prediction of surface roughness in wire electrical discharge machining (WEDM) process based on response surface methodology. *IACSIT International Journal of Engineering and Technology, 2,* 708–719.

Kumar, A., Kumar, V., & Kumar, J. (2013). Multi-response optimization of process parameters based on response surface methodology for pure titanium using WEDM process. *International Journal of Advanced Manufacturing Technology, 68*(9-12), 2645–2688. doi:10.1007/s00170-013-4861-9

Kuriakose, S., & Shunmugam, M. S. (2004). Characteristics of wire-electro discharge machined Ti6Al4V surface. *Materials Letters*, *58*(17-18), 2231–2237. doi:10.1016/j.matlet.2004.01.037

Kuriakose, S., & Shunmugam, M. S. (2005). Multi-objective optimization of wire-electro discharge machining process by non-dominated sorting genetic algorithm. *Journal of Materials Processing Technology*, *170*(1-2), 133–141. doi:10.1016/j.jmatprotec.2005.04.105

Liao, H. C. (2006). Multi-response optimization using weighted principal component. *International Journal of Advanced Manufacturing Technology*, *2006*(7-8), 720–725. doi:10.1007/s00170-004-2248-7

Liao, Y. S., Huang, J. T., & Chen, Y. H. (2004). A study to achieve a fine surface finish in Wire EDM. *Journal of Materials Processing Technology*, *149*(1-3), 165–171. doi:10.1016/j.jmatprotec.2003.10.034

Lin, K. W., & Wang, C. C. (2010). Optimizing multiple quality characteristics of wire electrical discharge machining via Taguchi method-based gray analysis for magnesium alloy. *Journal of C.C.I.T.*, *39*, 23–34.

Lok, Y. K., & Lee, T. C. (1997). Processing of advanced ceramics using the wire-cut EDM process. *Journal of Materials Processing Technology*, *63*(1-3), 839–843. doi:10.1016/S0924-0136(96)02735-5

Mahapatra, S. S., & Patnaik, A. (2006). Optimization of wire electrical discharge machining (WEDM) process parameters using genetic algorithm. *Indian Journal of Engineering and Materials Science*, *13*, 494–502.

Mahapatra, S. S., & Patnaik, A. (2007). Optimization of wire electrical discharge machining (WEDM) process parameters using Taguchi method. *International Journal of Advanced Manufacturing Technology*, *34*(9-10), 911–925. doi:10.1007/s00170-006-0672-6

Manna, A., & Bhattacharyya, B. (2006). Taguchi and Gauss elimination method: A dual response approach for parametric optimization of CNC wire cut EDM of PRAlSiCMMC. *International Journal of Advanced Manufacturing Technology*, *28*(1-2), 67–75. doi:10.1007/s00170-004-2331-0

Miller, S. F., Shih, A. J., & Qu, J. (2004). Investigation of the spark cycle on material removal rate in wire electrical discharge machining of advanced materials. *International Journal of Machine Tools & Manufacture*, *44*(4), 39–400. doi:10.1016/j.ijmachtools.2003.10.005

Mohri, N., Fukuzawa, Y., Tani, T., & Sata, T. (2002). Some considerations to machining characteristics of insulating ceramics towards practical use in industry. *Ann CIRP*, *51*(1), 112–116. doi:10.1016/S0007-8506(07)61490-5

Montgomery, D. C. (2001). *Design and Analysis of Experiments*. New York: Wiley.

Mukherjee, R., Chakraborty, S., & Samanta, S. (2012). Selection of wire electrical discharge machining process parameters using non-traditional optimization algorithms. *Applied Soft Computing*, *12*(8), 2506–2516. doi:10.1016/j.asoc.2012.03.053

Muttamara, A., Fukuzawa, Y., Mohri, N., & Tani, T. (2003). Probability of precision micro-machining of insulating Si3N4 ceramics by EDM. *Journal of Materials Processing Technology*, *140*(1-3), 243–247. doi:10.1016/S0924-0136(03)00745-3

Nayak, B.B. and Mahapatra, S.S. (2016). Optimization of WEDM process parameters using deep cryo-treated Inconel 718 as work material. *Engineering Science and Technology, an International Journal, 19*(1), 161–170.

Ozdemir, N., & Ozek, C. (2006). An investigation on machinability of nodular cast iron by WEDM. *International Journal of Advanced Manufacturing Technology, 28*(9-10), 869–872. doi:10.1007/s00170-004-2446-3

Phadke, M. S. (1989). *Quality engineering using robust design.* Englewood Cliffs, NJ: Prentice Hall.

Ramakrishnan, R., & Karunamoorthy, L. (2006). Multi response optimization of wire EDM operations using robust design of experiments. *International Journal of Advanced Manufacturing Technology, 29*(1-2), 105–112. doi:10.1007/s00170-004-2496-6

Ramakrishnan, R., & Karunamoorthy, L. (2008). Modeling and multi-response optimization of Inconel 718 on machining of CNC WEDM process. *Journal of Materials Processing Technology, 207*(1-3), 343–349. doi:10.1016/j.jmatprotec.2008.06.040

Rao, C. V. S. P., & Sarcar, M. M. M. (2009). Evolution of optimal parameters for machining brass with wire cut EDM. *Journal of Scientific and Industrial Research, 68,* 32–35.

Ravindranadh B. R., Madhu, V. & Gogia, A.K. (2015). Multi response optimization of wire-EDM process parameters of ballistic grade aluminium alloy. *Engineering Science and Technology, an International Journal, 18*(4), 720–726.

Ross, P. J. (1996). Taguchi Techniques for Quality Engineering (2nd ed.). New York: McGraw Hill.

Roy, R. K. (1990). *A primer on the Taguchi method.* Dearborn, MI: Society of Manufacturing Engineers.

Sadeghi, M., Razavi, H., Esmaeilzadeh, A., & Kolahan, F. (2011). Optimization of cutting conditions in WEDM process using regression modelling and Tabu-search algorithm. *Proceedings of the Institution of Mechanical Engineers. Part B, Journal of Engineering Manufacture, 225*(10), 1825–1834. doi:10.1177/0954405411406639

Saha, P., Singha, A., Pal, S. K., & Saha, P. (2008). Soft computing models based prediction of cutting speed and surface roughness in wire electro-discharge machining of tungsten carbide cobalt composite. *International Journal of Advanced Manufacturing Technology, 39*(1-2), 74–78. doi:10.1007/s00170-007-1200-z

Sahoo, P. (2005). *Engineering Tribology.* New Delhi: Prentice Hall of India.

Sarkar, S., Mitra, S., & Bhattacharyya, B. (2005). Parametric analysis and optimization of wire electrical discharge machining of γ-titanium aluminide alloy. *Journal of Materials Processing Technology, 159*(3), 286–294. doi:10.1016/j.jmatprotec.2004.10.009

Sharma, N., Khanna, R., & Gupta, R. D. (2013). Multi Quality Characteristics Of WEDM Process Parameters With RSM. *Procedia Engineering, 64,* 710–719. doi:10.1016/j.proeng.2013.09.146

Sharma, N., Khanna, R., Gupta, R. D., & Sharma, R. (2013). Modeling and multiresponse optimization on WEDM for HSLA by RSM. *International Journal of Advanced Manufacturing Technology*, *67*(9-12), 2269–2281. doi:10.1007/s00170-012-4648-4

Sharma, N., Singh, A., Sharma, R., & Deepak, . (2014). Modelling the WEDM Process Parameters for Cryogenic Treated D-2 Tool Steel by Integrated RSM and GA. *Procedia Engineering*, *97*, 1609–1617. doi:10.1016/j.proeng.2014.12.311

Singh, H., & Garg, R. (2009). Effects of process parameters on material removal rate in WEDM. *Journal of Achievements in Materials and Manufacturing Engineering*, *32*, 70–74.

Spedding, T. A., & Wang, Z. Q. (1997a). Parametric optimization and surface characterization of wire electrical discharge machining process. *Precision Engineering*, *20*(1), 5–15. doi:10.1016/S0141-6359(97)00003-2

Spedding, T. A., & Wang, Z. Q. (1997b). Study on modeling of wire EDM process. *Journal of Materials Processing Technology*, *69*(1-3), 18–28. doi:10.1016/S0924-0136(96)00033-7

Su, C. T., & Tong, L. I. (1997). Multi-response robust design by principal component analysis. *Total Quality Management*, *8*(6), 409–416. doi:10.1080/0954412979415

Taguchi, G. (1990). *Introduction to Quality Engineering*. Tokyo: Asian Productivity Organization.

Tarng, Y. S., Ma, S. C., & Chung, L. K. (1995). Determination of optimal cutting parameters in wire electrical discharge machining. *International Journal of Machine Tools & Manufacture*, *35*(12), 1693–1701. doi:10.1016/0890-6955(95)00019-T

Tosun, N., & Cogun, C. (2003). An investigation on wire wears in WEDM. *Journal of Materials Processing Technology*, *134*(3), 273–278. doi:10.1016/S0924-0136(02)01045-2

Tosun, N., Cogun, C., & Tosun, G. (2004). A study on kerf and material removal rate in wire electrical discharge machining based on Taguchi method. *Journal of Materials Processing Technology*, *152*(3), 316–322. doi:10.1016/j.jmatprotec.2004.04.373

Weng, F., & Her, M. (2002). Study of the batch production of micro parts using the EDM process. *International Journal of Advanced Manufacturing Technology*, *19*(4), 266–270. doi:10.1007/s001700200033

Chapter 7
Augmented Lagrange Hopfield Network for Combined Economic and Emission Dispatch with Fuel Constraint

Vo Ngoc Dieu
Ho Chi Minh City University of Technology, Vietnam

Tran The Tung
Ho Chi Minh City University of Technology, Vietnam

ABSTRACT

This chapter proposes an augmented Lagrange Hopfield network (ALHN) for solving combined economic and emission dispatch (CEED) problem with fuel constraint. In the proposed ALHN method, the augmented Lagrange function is directly used as the energy function of continuous Hopfield neural network (HNN), thus this method can properly handle constraints by both augmented Lagrange function and sigmoid function of continuous neurons in the HNN. For dealing with the bi-objective economic dispatch problem, the slope of sigmoid function in HNN is adjusted to find the Pareto-optimal front and then the best compromise solution for the problem will be determined by fuzzy-based mechanism. The proposed method has been tested on many cases and the obtained results are compared to those from other methods available the literature. The test results have shown that the proposed method can find good solutions compared to the others for the tested cases. Therefore, the proposed ALHN could be a favourable implementation for solving the CEED problem with fuel constraint.

NOMENCLATURE

a_i, b_i, c_i emission coefficients for thermal unit i
d_i, e_i, f_i fuel cost coefficients for thermal unit i
B_{ij}, B_{0i}, B_{00} transmission loss formula coefficients
F_{ik} fuel delivery for thermal unit i during subinterval k, in tons

DOI: 10.4018/978-1-5225-2128-0.ch007

F_i^{min}, F_i^{max} lower and upper fuel delivery limits for thermal unit i, in tons

M number of subintervals of scheduled period

N total number of thermal units;

P_{Dk} load demand of the system during subinterval k, in MW

P_{Lk} transmission loss of the system during subinterval k, in MW

P_{ik} output power of thermal unit i during subinterval k, in MW

P_i^{min}, P_i^{max} lower and upper generation limits of thermal unit i, in MW

Q_{ik} fuel consumption function of thermal unit i in subinterval k, in tons/h

t_k duration of subinterval k, in hours

X_{i0} initial fuel storage for unit i, in tons

X_{ik} fuel storage for unit i during subinterval k, in tons

X_i^{min}, X_i^{max} lower and upper fuel storage limits for thermal unit i, in tons

$V_{p,ik}$ output of continuous neuron representing for output power P_{ik}

$V_{f,ik}$ output of continuous neuron representing for fuel delivery F_{ik}

$V_{x,ik}$ output of continuous neuron representing for fuel storage X_{ik}

$V_{\lambda,k}$ output of multiplier neuron associated with power balance constraint

$V_{\gamma,k}$ output of multiplier neuron associated with fuel delivery constraint

$V_{\eta,ik}$ output of multiplier neuron associated with fuel storage constraint

$U_{p,ik}$, $U_{f,ik}$, $U_{x,ik}$ inputs of continuous neurons corresponding to the outputs $V_{p,ik}$, $V_{f,ik}$ and $V_{x,ik}$, respectively

$U_{\lambda,k}$, $U_{\gamma,k}$, $U_{\eta,ik}$ inputs of multiplier neurons corresponding to the outputs $V_{\lambda,k}$, $V_{\gamma,k}$ and $V_{\eta,ik}$, respectively

ΔP_k power balance constraint error in sub-interval k, in MW

ΔF_k fuel delivery constraint error in subinterval k, in tons

ΔX_{ik} fuel storage constraint error for unit i during subinterval k, in tons

$\Delta V_{p,ik}$, $\Delta V_{f,ik}$, $\Delta V_{x,ik}$ iterative errors of continuous neurons

σ slope of sigmoid function of continuous neurons

α_p, α_f, α_x updating step sizes for continuous neurons

α_λ, α_γ, α_η updating step sizes for multiplier neurons

φ_{0i}, φ_{1i}, φ_{2i} fuel consumption coefficients for thermal unit i

λ_k, γ_k, η_{ik} Lagrangian multipliers associated with power balance, fuel delivery and fuel storage constraints, respectively

$\beta_{\lambda,k}$, $\beta_{\gamma,k}$, $\beta_{\eta,sk}$ penalty factors associated with power balance, fuel delivery and fuel storage constraints, respectively

INTRODUCTION

Economic dispatch with fuel constraint is an important part of utility for operation and planning since it is a complex problem with a long range of time periods and a large set of constraints and variables. The fuel used by a thermal generating unit may be obtained from different contracts at different prices. The fuel contracts are generally under a take-or-pay agreement including both maximum and minimum limits on delivery of fuel to generating units over life of the contract. The fuel storage for units is usually within a specified limit to allow for inaccurate load forecasts and the inability to deliver on time of suppliers (Asgarpoor, 1994). On the other hand, thermal generating units generate toxic gases during power production due to fossil fuels and this is also considered as a source of environment pollution

(Rau & Adelman, 1995). With recently increasing concern on environment impact of power generation, the power generation dispatch is required to reduce the emission level while meeting load demand (El-Keib, Ma & Hart 1994). However, both the fuel cost and emission level conflict together since the pollution minimization will lead to maximizing the fuel cost and vice versa. Therefore, they both must be simultaneously considered to attain a practical compromise operation and this is termed combined economic and emission dispatch (CEED) problem. For solving this problem, one usually finds a set of compromise solutions by simultaneously optimizing all objectives to form a Pareto-optimal front which represents the tradeoffs among conflicting objective functions.

The objective of the CEED problem with fuel constraint is to minimize both total fuel cost and emission from thermal units while satisfying power balance, fuel delivery, fuel storage constraints together with fuel delivery, fuel storage, and generator operating limits. The schedule time horizon for this problem can be decomposed into long-term (weeks to year) (Kumar *et al.*, 1986), short-term (days to week) (Kumar *et al.*, 1984), daily (hours to day) (Kumar *et al.*, 1985), and real-time (minutes to hour) (Parikh & Chattopadhyay, 1996) problems. In the long-term schedule problem, the schedule time is divided into sub-periods (months or weeks) to obtain optimal fuel use strategy.

The economic dispatch with fuel constraint for thermal units have been investigated in (Parikh & Chattopadhyay, 1996) using linear programming (LP) and network flow programming (NFP). In the LP method (Wood & Wollenberg, 2012), the total time period is divided into discrete time increments and the objective function is made up a sum of linear functions where each of function is a function of one or more variables from one step time. In the NFP method (Zhu & Momoh, 2001), the input/output characteristics of generating units can be linear or non-linear which will form linear or non-linear network. For the non-linear network, the problem is solved as a sequence of linear networks with artificial limits calculated from the current solution of the linear network and used for calculating the next solution of the linear network. Nonetheless, these methods suffer difficulties in solving optimization problems. The computation efforts in the NFP will drastically increase when there exist some convex branches in the flow network whereas LP requires linearization of objectives and constraints. On the other hand, the CEED problem has been attracted several researchers. Conventional methods have been applied for solving the problem such as Newton-Raphson (NR) method (Dhillon, Parti & Kothari, 1993), linear programming (LP) (Jabr, Coonick & Cory, 2000), Lagrangian relaxation (LR) method (Sashirekha *et al.*, 2013), etc. The advantage of these methods is that they can quickly find optimal solution for a problem. However, they suffer some difficulties when dealing with complex and large-scale nonlinear problems such as matrix inversion in NR method, linearization in LP method and duality gap in LR method. For dealing with more complicated problems, several artificial intelligent based methods have been used such as genetic algorithm (GA) (Song *et al.*, 1997), evolutionary programming (EP) (Qu *et al.*, 2010), differential evolution (DE) (Lu *et al.*, 2011), and particle swarm optimization (PSO) (Cai *et al.*, 2009; Cai *et al.*, 2010). These population based search methods are suitable for finding near optimal solution for non-convex complicated problems. However, for large-scale problems, these methods become very slow in finding solution and the near optimal solution is not always obtained. Neural networks are also popular for solving the CEED problem (Kulkarni *et al.*, 2000; Basu, 2002). Hopfield neural network (HNN) is the most popular neural network applied to optimization problems and has been successfully applied to the CEED dispatch problem with fuel constraint (Basu, 2002). Though the HNN can easily handle maximum and minimum constraints for continuous variables based on a sigmoid function, its formulation still suffers some difficulties such as constraint linearization, parameter selection associated with energy function that may lead to local optima if they are not precisely chosen, and map from the problem to the HNN.

In this chapter, an augmented Lagrange Hopfield network (ALHN) is proposed for solving combined economic dispatch with fuel constraint. In the proposed ALHN method, the augmented Lagrange function is directly used as the energy function of continuous Hopfield neural network (HNN), thus this method can properly handle constraints by both augmented Lagrange function and sigmoid function of continuous neurons in HNN. For dealing with the bi-objective economic dispatch problem, the slope of sigmoid function in HNN is adjusted to find the Pareto-optimal front and then the best compromise solution for the problem will be determined by fuzzy-based mechanism. The proposed method has been tested on three systems with many cases considered and the obtained results are compared to those from other methods available the literature including recursive approach (RA) (Muralidharan, Srikrishna & Subramanian, 2006), simplified recursive approach (SRA) (Balamurugan & Subramanian, 2007), Newton Raphson (NR) (Dhillon, Parti & Kothari, 1993), fuzzy logic controlled genetic algorithm (FCGA) (Song *et al.*, 1997), analytical strategy (AS) (Palanichamy & Babu, 2008), multi-objective chaotic particle swarm optimization (MOCPSO) (Cai *et al.*, 2009), multi-objective chaotic ant swarm optimization (MOCASO) (Cai *et al.*, 2010), and HNN (Babu, 2008).

The remaining organization of this paper is follows. Section 2 addresses the formulation of the combined economic dispatch problem with fuel constraint. Augmented Lagrange Hopfield neural network implement for the problem is described in Section 3. Numerical results are presented in Section 4. Finally, the conclusion is given.

ALHN FOR COMBINED ECONOMIC AND EMISSION DISPATCH WITH FUEL CONSTRAINT

Problem Formulation

Assuming that the entire schedule time horizon is divided into M subintervals each having a constant load demand P_{Dk} and that all generating units are available and remain on-line for M subintervals. The objective is to simultaneously minimize generation cost F_1 and emission level F_2 of generating units over the M subintervals such that the constraints for power balance, fuel delivery and fuel storage for any given subinterval as well as maximum-minimum fuel delivery, fuel storage, and generator operating constraints for each generating unit are satisfied.

Mathematically, the problem formulation for a system having N thermal generating units scheduled in M subintervals is as follows (Babu, 2008):

$$\text{Min } \{F_1, F_2\} \tag{1}$$

where F_1 and F_2 respectively representing the total fuel cost and emission functions are defined based on the quadratic function as follows:

$$F_1 = \sum_{k=1}^{M} \sum_{i=1}^{N} t_k \left(a_i + b_i P_{ik} + c_i P_{ik}^2 \right) \tag{2}$$

$$F_2 = \sum_{k=1}^{M} \sum_{i=1}^{N} t_k \left(d_i + e_i P_{ik} + f_i P_{ik}^2 \right) \tag{3}$$

subject to

- **Power balance Constraints**

The total power supply from the generating units must be sufficient supplying to forecasted load demand of the system and power transmission loss for the whole schedule time horizon:

$$\sum_{i=1}^{N} P_{ik} - P_{Lk} - P_{Dk} = 0; k = 1,..., M \tag{4}$$

where system power loss is determined by the Kron's formula [8] as follows:

$$P_{Lk} = \sum_{i=1}^{N} \sum_{j=1}^{N} P_{ik} B_{ij} P_{jk} + \sum_{i=1}^{N} B_{0i} P_{ik} + B_{00} \tag{5}$$

- **Fuel delivery Constraint**

The total fuel delivery to the generating units must satisfy their demand during the considered schedule time horizon:

$$\sum_{i=1}^{N} F_{ik} - F_{Dk} = 0; k = 1, ..., M \tag{6}$$

- **Fuel storage Constraint**

The fuel storage for the generating units must be sufficient for their consumption during the considered schedule time horizon:

$$X_{ik} = X_{ik-1} + F_{ik} - t_k Q_{ik}; i = 1, ..., N; k = 1, ..., M \tag{7}$$

where the fuel consumption of generating units are expressed as a function of power generation:

$$Q_{ik} = \varphi_{0i} + \varphi_{1i} P_{ik} + \varphi_{2i} P_{ik}^2 \tag{8}$$

- **Generator Operating Limits**

The power outputs from the generators are limited by their capacity of generation:

$$P_i^{\min} \leq P_{ik} \leq P_i^{\max} \, ; i = 1, ..., N, \, k = 1, ..., M \tag{9}$$

- **Fuel Delivery Limits**

The fuel delivery to generating units is limited by the capacity of suppliers:

$$F_i^{\min} \leq F_{ik} \leq F_i^{\max} \, ; i = 1, ..., N; \, k = 1, ..., M \tag{10}$$

- **Fuel Storage Limits**

The fuel storage for generating units is limited by the capacity of the storages:

$$X_i^{\min} \leq X_{ik} \leq X_i^{\max} \, ; i = 1, ..., N; \, k = 1, ..., M \tag{11}$$

The fuel storage at subinterval k in (7) can be rewritten in terms of initial fuel storage as follows:

$$X_{ik} = X_{i0} + \sum_{l=1}^{k} \left(F_{il} - t_l Q_{il} \right) \tag{12}$$

in which, the initial fuel storage X_{i0} is given.

Augmented Lagrange Hopfield Network Implementation

For implementation of the bi-objective problem in ALHN, the two objectives are combined in the Lagrangian function which is used as energy function in HNN. By adjusting the sigmoid slope of continuous neurons the obtained corresponding solutions will form a Pareto-optimal front and then the best compromise solution will be determined by fuzzy-based mechanism (Niimura & Nakashima, 2003). The principle of multi-objective optimization and the fuzzy-based mechanism are given in Appendix.

The augmented Lagrange function L of the problem is formulated as follows

$$
\begin{aligned}
L = &\sum_{k=1}^{M} \sum_{i=1}^{N} t_k \left[\left(a_i + b_i P_{ik} + c_i P_{ik}^2 \right) + \left(d_i + e_i P_{ik} + f_i P_{ik}^2 \right) \right] \\
&+ \sum_{k=1}^{M} \left[\lambda_k \left(P_{Lk} + P_{Dk} - \sum_{i=1}^{N} P_{ik} \right) + \frac{1}{2} \beta_{\lambda,k} \left(P_{Lk} + P_{Dk} - \sum_{i=1}^{N} P_{ik} \right)^2 \right] \\
&+ \sum_{k=1}^{M} \left[\gamma_k \left(\sum_{i=1}^{N} F_{ik} - F_{Dk} \right) + \frac{1}{2} \beta_{\gamma,k} \left(\sum_{i=1}^{N} F_{ik} - F_{Dk} \right)^2 \right] \\
&+ \sum_{k=1}^{M} \sum_{i=1}^{N} \left[\eta_{ik} \left(X_{ik} - X_{i0} - \sum_{l=1}^{k} \left(F_{il} + t_l Q_{il} \right) \right) + \frac{1}{2} \beta_{\eta,ik} \left(X_{ik} - X_{i0} - \sum_{l=1}^{k} \left(F_{il} + t_l Q_{il} \right) \right)^2 \right]
\end{aligned}
\tag{13}
$$

To represent in augmented Lagrange Hopfield neural network, *3NxM* continuous neurons and *(N+2)* x*M* multiplier neurons are required. The energy function *E* of the problem is formulated based on the augmented Lagrangian function in terms of neurons as follows.

$$
\begin{aligned}
E = &\sum_{k=1}^{M}\sum_{i=1}^{N} t_k \left[\left(a_i + b_i V_{ik} + c_i V_{p,ik}^2 \right) + \left(d_i + e_i V_{p,ik} + f_i V_{p,ik}^2 \right) \right] \\
&+ \sum_{k=1}^{M} \left[V_{\lambda k} \left(P_{Lk} + P_{Dk} - \sum_{i=1}^{N} V_{p,ik} \right) + \frac{1}{2} \beta_{\lambda k} \left(P_{Lk} + P_{Dk} - \sum_{s=1}^{N} V_{p,ik} \right)^2 \right] \\
&+ \sum_{k=1}^{M} \left[V_{\gamma k} \left(\sum_{i=1}^{N} V_{f,ik} - F_{Dk} \right) + \frac{1}{2} \beta_{\gamma,k} \left(\sum_{s=1}^{N} V_{f,ik} - F_{Dk} \right)^2 \right] \\
&+ \sum_{k=1}^{M}\sum_{i=1}^{N} \left[V_{\eta,ik} \left(V_{x,ik} - X_{i0} - \sum_{l=1}^{k} \left(V_{f,il} + t_l Q_{il} \right) \right) + \frac{1}{2} \beta_{\eta,ik} \left(V_{x,ik} - X_{i0} - \sum_{l=1}^{k} \left(V_{f,il} + t_l Q_{il} \right) \right)^2 \right] \\
&+ \sum_{k=1}^{M}\sum_{i=1}^{N} \left[\int_0^{V_{p,ik}} g^{-1}(V) dV + \int_0^{V_{f,ik}} g^{-1}(V) dV + \int_0^{V_{x,ik}} g^{-1}(V) dV \right]
\end{aligned}
\tag{14}
$$

In (14), the sums of integral terms are Hopfield terms where their global effect is a displacement of solutions toward the interior of the state space (Berg & Bioch, 1993).

The dynamics of augmented Lagrange Hopfield network for updating neuron inputs are defined as follows.

$$
\begin{aligned}
\frac{dU_{p,ik}}{dt} &= -\frac{\partial E}{\partial V_{p,ik}} \\
&= -\left\{
\begin{array}{l}
t_k \left(b_i + 2 c_i V_{p,ik} \right) + t_k \left(e_i + 2 f_i V_{p,ik} \right) \\
+ \left[V_{\lambda k} + \beta_k \left(P_{Dk} + P_{Lk} - \sum_{i=1}^{N} V_{p,ik} \right) \right] \left(\frac{\partial P_{Lk}}{\partial V_{p,ik}} - 1 \right) \\
+ \left[V_{\eta,ik} + \beta_{ik} \left(V_{x,ik} - X_{i0} - \sum_{l=1}^{k} \left(V_{f,il} + t_l Q_{il} \right) \right) \right] \times t_k \frac{dQ_{ik}}{dV_{p,ik}} + U_{p,ik}
\end{array}
\right\}
\end{aligned}
\tag{15}
$$

$$
\begin{aligned}
\frac{dU_{f,ik}}{dt} &= -\frac{\partial E}{\partial V_{f,ik}} \\
&= -\left\{
\begin{array}{l}
\left[V_{\gamma,k} + \beta_{\gamma,k} \left(\sum_{i=1}^{N} V_{f,ik} - F_{Dk} \right) \right] \\
- \left[V_{\eta,ik} + \beta_{\eta,ik} \left(\begin{array}{c} V_{x,ik} - X_{i0} \\ - \sum_{l=1}^{k} \left(V_{f,il} + t_l Q_{il} \right) \end{array} \right) \right] + U_{f,ik}
\end{array}
\right\}
\end{aligned}
\tag{16}
$$

$$\frac{dU_{x,ik}}{dt} = -\frac{\partial E}{\partial V_{x,ik}}$$
$$= -\left\{ V_{\eta,ik} + \beta_{\eta,ik} \left(V_{x,ik} - X_{i0} - \sum_{l=1}^{k} \left(V_{f,il} + t_l Q_{il} \right) \right) + U_{x,ik} \right\} \tag{17}$$

$$\frac{dU_{\lambda,k}}{dt} = +\frac{\partial E}{\partial V_{\lambda,k}} = P_{Dk} + P_{Lk} - \sum_{i=1}^{N} V_{p,ik} \tag{18}$$

$$\frac{dU_{\gamma,k}}{dt} = +\frac{\partial E}{\partial V_{\gamma,k}} = \sum_{i=1}^{N} V_{f,ik} - F_{Dk} \tag{19}$$

$$\frac{dU_{\eta,ik}}{dt} = +\frac{\partial E}{\partial V_{\eta,ik}} = V_{x,ik} - X_{i0} - \sum_{l=1}^{k} \left(V_{f,il} + t_l Q_{il} \right) \tag{20}$$

where,

$$\frac{\partial P_{Lk}}{\partial V_{p,ik}} = 2\sum_{j=1}^{N} B_{ij} V_{p,jk} + B_{i0} \tag{21}$$

$$\frac{\partial Q_{ik}}{\partial V_{p,ik}} = \varphi_{1i} + 2\varphi_{2i} V_{p,ik} \tag{22}$$

The inputs of neurons are updated based on their dynamics as follows:

$$U_{p,ik}^{(n)} = U_{p,ik}^{(n-1)} - \alpha_p \frac{\partial E}{\partial V_{p,ik}} \tag{23}$$

$$U_{f,ik}^{(n)} = U_{f,ik}^{(n-1)} - \alpha_f \frac{\partial E}{\partial V_{f,ik}} \tag{24}$$

$$U_{x,ik}^{(n)} = U_{x,ik}^{(n-1)} - \alpha_x \frac{\partial E}{\partial V_{x,ik}} \tag{25}$$

$$U_{\lambda,k}^{(n)} = U_{\lambda,k}^{(n-1)} + \alpha_{\lambda} \frac{\partial E}{\partial V_{\lambda,k}} \qquad (26)$$

$$U_{\gamma,k}^{(n)} = U_{\gamma,k}^{(n-1)} + \alpha_{\gamma} \frac{\partial E}{\partial V_{\gamma,k}} \qquad (27)$$

$$U_{\eta,ik}^{(n)} = U_{\eta,ik}^{(n-1)} + \alpha_{\eta} \frac{\partial E}{\partial V_{\eta,ik}} \qquad (28)$$

The outputs of continuous neurons representing for output power, fuel delivery and fuel storage of power plants are calculated from on their inputs by a sigmoid function (Park *et al.*, 1993)

$$V_{p,ik} = g(U_{p,ik}) = \left(\frac{P_i^{\max} - P_i^{\min}}{2} \right) \left[1 + \tanh\left(\sigma U_{p,ik} \right) \right] + P_i^{\min} \qquad (29)$$

$$V_{f,ik} = g(U_{f,ik}) = \left(F_i^{\max} - F_i^{\min} \right) \left(\frac{1 + \tanh\left(\sigma U_{f,ik} \right)}{2} \right) + F_i^{\min} \qquad (30)$$

$$V_{f,ik} = g(U_{f,ik}) = \left(F_i^{\max} - F_i^{\min} \right) \left(\frac{1 + \tanh\left(\sigma U_{f,ik} \right)}{2} \right) + F_i^{\min} \qquad (31)$$

where σ determines the shape of the sigmoid function. The shape of the sigmoid function is shown in Figure 1.

The outputs of multiplier neurons representing Lagrangian multipliers are determined by a transfer function:

$$V_{\lambda,k} = g(U_{\lambda,k}) = U_{\lambda,k} \qquad (32)$$

$$V_{\gamma,k} = g(U_{\gamma,k}) = U_{\gamma,k} \qquad (33)$$

$$V_{\eta,ik} = g(U_{\eta,ik}) = U_{\eta,ik} \qquad (34)$$

Figure 1. Sigmoid function with different slopes

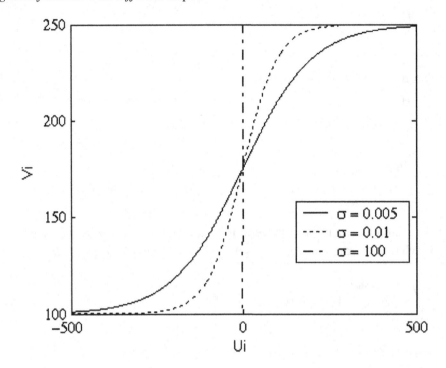

The proof of convergence of the ALHN method is given Appendix.

Selection of Parameters

All positive parameters in the ALHN model have to be selected in advance including slope of sigmoid function and updating step sizes for neurons and penalty factors associated with constraints. These parameters are selected by experiments and the proper parameters will lead to fast convergence of the network. Among the parameters, the value of σ has directly effect on the priority of objectives in the problem. If σ is greater than 1, the fuel objective is more important than the emission one. In contrast, if σ is smaller than 1, the emission objective is more important. Therefore, the non-dominated solutions for the problem will be obtained by adjusting the value of σ from smaller than 1 to very large values. The penalty factors associated with all constraints are equally chosen and usually fixed to a small value. The other parameters including α_p, α_x, α_γ and α_η will be tuned depending on the considered problem. It is observed that the larger the values of these parameters, the closer the system act to being a discrete system, producing values at the upper and lower limits of each neuron. On the contrary, the smaller the values of them, the slower the convergence of the network. For simplicity, the values of α_f and α_x can be equally chosen. It is similar manner for α_γ and α_η.

Initialization

The algorithm requires initial conditions for inputs and outputs of all neurons. In this paper, the initial outputs of neurons are selected as follows.

For the continuous neurons representing for power output and fuel delivery of units, their outputs are initiated by "mean distribution" (Lin & Viviani, 1984).

$$V_{p,ik}^{(0)} = P_{Dk} \frac{P_i^{max}}{\sum\limits_{i=1}^{N} P_i^{max}} \tag{35}$$

$$V_{f,ik}^{(0)} = F_{Dk} \frac{F_i^{max}}{\sum\limits_{i=1}^{N} F_i^{max}} \tag{36}$$

For the neurons representing for fuel storage of power plants, their outputs are initiated at the medium value between the maximum and minimum values of fuel storage:

$$V_{x,ik}^{(0)} = \left(X_i^{max} + X_i^{min} \right) / 2 \tag{37}$$

For the multiplier neurons associated with power balance constraint, their outputs are initialized by mean values as follows:

$$V_{\lambda k}^{(0)} = \frac{1}{N} \sum\limits_{i=1}^{N} \frac{t_k \left(b_i + 2c_i V_{p,ik}^{(0)} \right) + t_k \left(e_i + 2f_i V_{p,ik}^{(0)} \right)}{1 - \dfrac{\partial P_{Lk}}{\partial V_{p,ik}}} \tag{38}$$

The outputs of other multiplier neurons are initiated from zeros. The inputs of all neurons are calculated corresponding to their outputs via the inversion of corresponding sigmoid and transfer functions.

Stopping Criteria

The algorithm of the ALHN will be terminated when either the maximum error Err_{max} including both constraint and iterative errors is lower than a predefined tolerance ε or maximum number of iterations N_{max} is reached.

The constraint and iterative errors at iteration n are calculated as follows.

$$\Delta P_k^{(n)} = \left| P_{Dk} + P_{Lk} - \sum\limits_{i=1}^{N} V_{p,ik}^{(n)} \right| \tag{39}$$

$$\Delta F_k^{(n)} = \left| \sum\limits_{i=1}^{N} V_{f,ik}^{(n)} - F_{Dk} \right| \tag{40}$$

$$\Delta X_{ik}^{(n)} = \left| V_{x,ik}^{(n)} - X_{i0} - \sum_{l=1}^{k} \left(V_{f,il}^{(n)} + t_l Q_{il} \right) \right| \tag{41}$$

$$\Delta V_{p,ik}^{(n)} = \left| V_{p,ik}^{(n)} - V_{p,ik}^{(n-1)} \right| \tag{42}$$

$$\Delta V_{f,ik}^{(n)} = \left| V_{f,ik}^{(n)} - V_{f,ik}^{(n-1)} \right| \tag{43}$$

$$\Delta V_{x,ik}^{(n)} = \left| V_{x,ik}^{(n)} - V_{x,ik}^{(n-1)} \right| \tag{44}$$

The maximum error of the model is determined:

$$Err_{\max}^{(n)} = \max \left\{ \Delta P_k^{(n)}, \Delta F_k^{(n)}, \Delta X_{ik}^{(n)}, \Delta V_{p,ik}^{(n)}, \Delta V_{f,ik}^{(n)}, \Delta V_{x,ik}^{(n)} \right\} \tag{45}$$

Overall Procedure

Overall procedure of ALHN for solving the CEED problem with fuel constraint is as follows:

Step 1: Select parameters for the network and choose stopping criteria.
Step 2: Initialize inputs and outputs for all neurons
Step 3: Set number of iteration $n = 1$.
Step 4: Calculate dynamics of neurons from equations (15) - (20).
Step 5: Update inputs of neurons from equations (23) - (28).
Step 6: Calculate outputs of neurons from equations (29) - (34).
Step 7: Calculate maximum error.
Step 8: If $Err_{max} > \varepsilon$ and $n < N_{max}$, $n = n + 1$ and return to Step 4.
Step 9: Calculate total cost and emission, and stop.

Numerical Results

The proposed ALHN is tested on six-unit and three-plant systems without fuel constraint and a five-unit system with fuel constraint. The algorithm of ALHN is coded in Matlab platform and run on a 2.1 GHz with 2 GB RAM PC. For stopping criteria, the maximum tolerance ε is set to 10^{-4}.

Case 1: Six-Unit System Neglecting Fuel Constraint

The test system from (Muralidharan *et al.*, 2006) includes six units supplying to a load demand of 900 MW. The unit data is given in Table 1.

The B-matrix coefficient for calculation of transmission loss is given:

Table 1. Data for the six-unit system in Case 1

Unit	1	2	3	4	5	6
a_i ($/h)	756.800	451.325	1050.000	1243.530	1658.570	1356.660
b_i ($/MWh)	38.540	46.160	40.400	38.310	36.328	38.270
c_i ($/MW²h)	0.1525	0.1060	0.0280	0.0355	0.0211	0.0180
d_i (kg/h)	13.86	13.86	40.267	40.267	42.9	42.9
e_i (kg/MWh)	0.3300	0.3300	-0.5455	-0.5455	-0.5112	-0.5112
f_i (kg/MW²h)	0.00420	0.00420	0.00683	0.00683	0.00460	0.00460
$P_{i,max}$ (MW)	125	150	225	210	325	315
$P_{i,min}$ (MW)	10	10	35	35	130	125

$$B_{ij} = \begin{bmatrix} 0.002022 & -0.000286 & -0.000534 & -0.000565 & -0.000454 & -0.000103 \\ -0.000286 & 0.003243 & 0.000016 & -0.000307 & -0.000422 & -0.000147 \\ -0.000533 & 0.000016 & 0.002085 & 0.000831 & 0.000023 & -0.000270 \\ -0.000565 & -0.000307 & 0.000831 & 0.001129 & 0.000113 & -0.000295 \\ -0.000454 & -0.000422 & 0.000023 & 0.000113 & 0.000460 & -0.000153 \\ 0.000103 & -0.000147 & -0.000270 & -0.000295 & -0.000153 & 0.000898 \end{bmatrix}$$

Case 1a: Neglecting Power Loss

When power loss is neglected, the total power generation is balanced to load demand. Three cases are considered in this cases including best economic dispatch, best emission dispatch and combined economic and emission dispatch.

The obtained results from best economic dispatch and best emission dispatches are compared to those from recursive approach (RA) method (Muralidharan *et al.,* 2006) given in Table 2. Table 3 shows a comparison of best compromise solution from ALHN to that from RA method and simplified RA (SRA)

Table 2. Comparison of best economic and emission dispatches for Case 1a

	Best economic dispatch		Best emission dispatch	
	RA (Muralidharan, 2006)	ALHN	RA (Muralidharan, 2006)	ALHN
P_1 (MW)		32.5300		115.3908
P_2 (MW)		10.9402		116.1375
P_3 (MW)		143.8057		135.8819
P_4 (MW)		142.8481		135.8150
P_5 (MW)		287.1910		198.4285
P_6 (MW)		282.6850		198.3464
Fuel cost ($/h)	**45,465.50**	**45,465.48**	48,027.70	47,987.89
Emission (kg/h)	793.571	793.263	**646.162**	**646.171**

Table 3. Comparison of best compromise solution for Case 1a

	RA (Muralidharan, 2006)	SRA (Balamurugan, 2006)	ALHN
P_1 (MW)		66.894	73.5021
P_2 (MW)		69.952	87.3043
P_3 (MW)		154.466	139.9281
P_4 (MW)		145.647	131.6449
P_5 (MW)		235.084	237.6909
P_6 (MW)		227.957	229.9295
Fuel cost ($/h)	46,131.80	46,131.80	46,449.27
Emission (kg/h)	679.241	679.241	669.807
Emission PPF ($/kg)	44.7880	44.7880	44.7880
Equiv. cost of emission ($/h)	30,421.85	30,421.85	29,999.32
Total equiv. cost ($/h)	**76,554.65**	**76,554.65**	**76,448.59**

method (Balamurugan *et al.,* 2006). To find the best compromise solution by ALHN, a Pareto-optimal front is obtained first as shown in Figure 2 and then the fuzzy-based mechanism is used. For comparison of the best compromise solution among the methods, a price penalty factor (PPF) method (Kulkarni *et al.,* 2000) is used as in Table 3. The explanation and calculation of PPF are given Appendix.

For the cases with single objective optimization, the total cost and emission amount by the proposed method are closed to those from RA method. However, for the case of best compromise solution, the total equivalent cost from the proposed ALHN is less than that from RA method.

Case 1b: Considering Power Loss

When power loss is included, the total power generation is balanced to load demand plus power loss. In this case, three load demands are considered including 500 MW, 700 MW, and 900 MW. The total costs and emissions obtained from the proposed ALHN for best economic dispatch and best emission dispatch are compared to those from fuzzy logic controlled genetic algorithm (FCGA) method (Song *et al.,* 1997) given in Table 4. Table 5 shows the comparison of best compromise solutions from the proposed method to those from NR (Jabr *et al.,* 2000) and FCGA methods. The Pareto-optimal fronts for fuel cost and emission corresponding to the load demands are given in Figures 3-5. For all the compared cases in Tables 4 and 5, the proposed method can find better solutions in terms of less total costs and emission levels for single objective problems and less total equivalent costs for CEED than the others.

Case 2: Three-Plant System Neglecting Fuel Constraint

The test system has three plants with six generating units supplying to a total load demand of 900 MW as shown in Figure 6. The unit data is from (Palanichamy & Babu, 2008) and also given in Table 1.

The power loss coefficients for this system are given:

Figure 2. Pareto-optimal front for fuel cost and emission from Case 1a

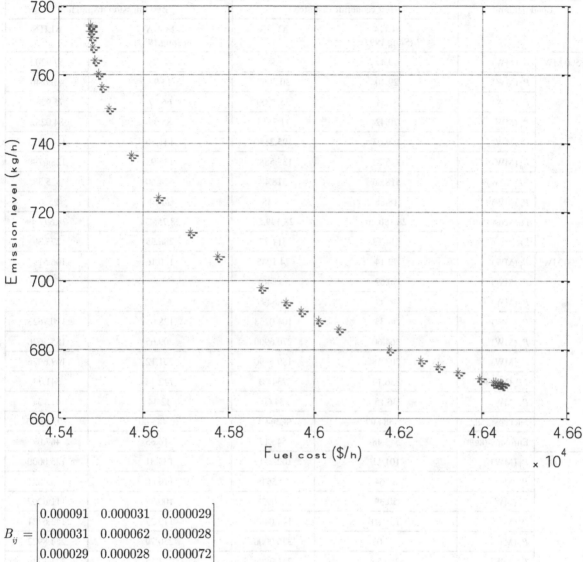

$$B_{ij} = \begin{bmatrix} 0.000091 & 0.000031 & 0.000029 \\ 0.000031 & 0.000062 & 0.000028 \\ 0.000029 & 0.000028 & 0.000072 \end{bmatrix}$$

In calculation, the system power loss in terms of load demand and B-matrix coefficients is derived out in (Palanichamy & Babu, 2008). The total costs, emission amount, and equivalent costs obtained from the ALHN method for best economic dispatch, bet emission dispatch and CEED are compared to those from AS method (Palanichamy & Babu, 2008), MOCPSO (Cai *et al.*, 2009), and MOCASO (Cai *et al.*, 2010) in Tables 6, 7, and 8, respectively. The Pareto-optimal front obtained by the ALHN for this case is shown in Figure 7. In all cases, the total cost in best economic dispatch, total emission in best emission dispatch, and total equivalent cost in CEED from the proposed method are less than those from the others. For the computational time, the proposed method also obtains solution faster than the others for best economic dispatch and best emission dispatch. Note the computational times obtained in AS,

Table 4. Comparison of best fuel cost and emission dispatch for Case 1b

Load demand		Best economic dispatch		Best emission dispatch	
		FCGA (Song,1997)	**ALHN**	**FCGA (Song,1997)**	**ALHN**
500 MW	P_1 (MW)	49.47	50.5882	81.08	57.9202
	P_2 (MW)	29.40	30.3067	13.93	43.9240
	P_3 (MW)	35.31	35.0000	66.37	75.9281
	P_4 (MW)	70.42	71.7814	85.59	84.0282
	P_5 (MW)	199.03	195.2150	141.70	134.8973
	P_6 (MW)	135.22	135.5882	135.93	128.6799
	ΣP_i (MW)	518.86	518.48	524.60	525.38
	P_L (MW)	18.86	18.48	24.61	25.38
	Fuel cost ($/h)	**28,150.80**	**28,149.26**	28,756.71	28,697.49
	Emission (kg/h)	314.53	311.77	**286.59**	**275.39**
700 MW	P_1 (MW)	72.14	74.1085	120.16	106.5193
	P_2 (MW)	50.02	50.3461	21.36	77.5669
	P_3 (MW)	46.47	45.8499	62.09	93.6306
	P_4 (MW)	99.33	104.0253	128.05	110.7623
	P_5 (MW)	264.60	270.6900	209.65	185.5626
	P_6 (MW)	203.58	189.5790	201.12	167.6926
	ΣP_i (MW)	736.14	734.60	742.44	741.73
	P_L (MW)	36.15	34.60	42.44	41.73a
	Fuel cost ($/h)	**38,384.09**	**38,364.44**	39,455.00	39,666.95
	Emission (kg/h)	543.48	543.17	**516.55**	**467.09**
9000 MW	P_1 (MW)	101.11	102.2117	133.31	125.0000
	P_2 (MW)	67.64	72.5648	110.00	113.4621
	P_3 (MW)	50.39	62.0938	100.38	111.6207
	P_4 (MW)	158.80	144.0449	119.27	143.6121
	P_5 (MW)	324.08	325.0000	250.79	254.8923
	P_6 (MW)	256.56	251.2909	251.25	221.1249
	ΣP_i (MW)	958.58	957.21	965.00	969.71
	P_L (MW)	58.58	57.21	65.00	69.71
	Fuel cost ($/h)	**49,655.40**	**49,615.22**	53,299.64	51,381.13
	Emission (kg/h)	877.61	856.21	**785.64**	**759.92**

Table 5. Comparison of best compromise solution for Case 1b

	Load demand	NR (Dhillon,1993)	FCGA (Song,1997)	ALHN
500 MW	P_1 (MW)	59.873	65.23	43.0446
	P_2 (MW)	39.651	24.29	30.1950
	P_3 (MW)	35.000	40.44	55.2104
	P_4 (MW)	72.397	74.22	68.4095
	P_5 (MW)	185.241	187.75	174.0563
	P_6 (MW)	125.000	125.48	152.4054
	ΣP_i (MW)	517.162	517.41	523.3211
	P_L (MW)	17.162	17.41	23.3211
	Fuel cost ($/h)	28,550.15	28,231.06	28,263.87
	Emission (kg/h)	312.513	304.90	294.84
	Emission PPF ($/kg)	43.8983	43.8983	43.8983
	Equiv. cost of emission ($/h)	13,718.7894	13,384.5917	12,942.9748
	Total equiv. cost ($/h)	**42,268.9394**	**41,615.6517**	**41,206.8448**
700 MW	P_1 (MW)	85.924	80.16	70.2056
	P_2 (MW)	60.963	53.71	56.2767
	P_3 (MW)	53.909	40.93	83.4104
	P_4 (MW)	107.124	116.23	103.6340
	P_5 (MW)	250.503	251.20	229.3945
	P_6 (MW)	176.504	190.62	200.5139
	ΣP_i (MW)	734.927	732.85	743.44
	P_L (MW)	34.927	32.85	43.44
	Fuel cost ($/h)	39,070.74	38,408.82	38,663.47
	Emission (kg/h)	528.447	527.46	496.43
	Emission PPF ($/kg)	44.7880	44.7880	44.7880
	Equiv. cost of emission ($/h)	23,668.0842	23,623.8785	22,234.1068
	Total equiv. cost ($/h)	**62,738.8242**	**62,032.6985**	**60,897.5768**
900 MW	P_1 (MW)	122.004	111.40	102.6409
	P_2 (MW)	86.523	69.33	83.5040
	P_3 (MW)	59.947	59.43	103.6490
	P_4 (MW)	140.959	143.26	140.9162
	P_5 (MW)	325.000	319.40	288.1489
	P_6 (MW)	220.063	252.11	249.1925
	ΣP_i (MW)	954.498	954.92	968.05
	P_L (MW)	54.498	54.92	68.05
	Fuel cost ($/h)	50,807.24	49,674.28	50,136.23
	Emission (kg/h)	864.060	850.29	798.35
	Emission PPF ($/kg)	47.8222	47.8222	47.8222
	Equiv. cost of emission ($/h)	41,321.2501	40,662.7384	38,178.8534
	Total equiv. cost ($/h)	**92,128.4901**	**90,337.0184**	**88,315.0834**

Figure 3. Pareto-optimal front for fuel cost and emission from Case 1b with load demand of 500 MW

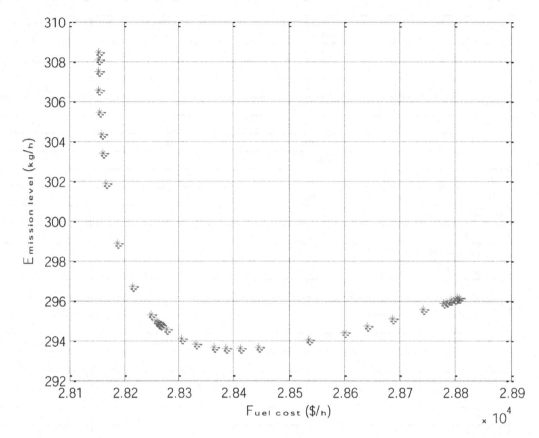

Table 6. Comparison of best fuel cost dispatch for Case 2

	AS (Palanichamy, 2008)	MOCPSO (Cai, 2009)	MOCASO (Cai, 2010)	ALHN
P_1 (MW)	33.77	33.71	33.77	33.8001
P_2 (MW)	12.65	12.65	12.65	12.7532
P_3 (MW)	150.56	150.56	150.56	150.6051
P_4 (MW)	148.50	148.50	148.50	148.4971
P_5 (MW)	296.29	296.30	296.29	296.1497
P_6 (MW)	293.68	293.72	293.67	293.4774
ΣP_i (MW)	935.45	935.44	935.44	935.28
P_L (MW)	35.45	35.44	35.44	35.28
Fuel cost ($/h)	**47,188.29**	**47,549.87**	**47,187.41**	**47,179.72**
Emission (kg/h)	857.74	823.36	857.74	857.11
CPU time (s)	0.189	12.03	10.45	0.031

Figure 4. Pareto-optimal front for fuel cost and emission in Case 1b with load demand of 700 MW

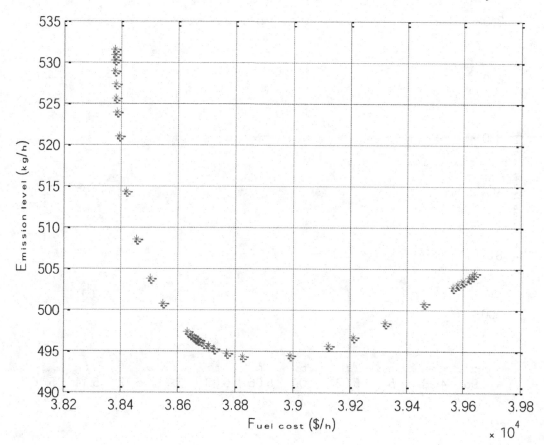

Table 7. Comparison of best emission dispatch for Case 2

	AS (Palanichamy, 2008)	MOCPSO (Cai, 2009)	MOCASO (Cai, 2010)	ALHN
P_1 (MW)	124.51	124.51	124.51	122.7077
P_2 (MW)	124.51	124.51	124.51	124.1467
P_3 (MW)	140.31	140.31	140.31	140.6565
P_4 (MW)	140.31	140.31	140.31	140.4737
P_5 (MW)	204.15	204.14	204.14	204.8772
P_6 (MW)	204.15	204.14	204.14	204.7960
ΣP_i (MW)	937.94	937.92	937.92	937.66
P_L (MW)	37.92	37.91	37.90	37.66
Fuel cost ($/h)	50,217.62	50,217.56	50,217.56	50,141.53
Emission (kg/h)	**696.99**	**696.92**	**696.92**	**696.58**
CPU time (s)	0.189	9.84	10.45	0.035

Figure 5. Pareto-optimal front for fuel cost and emission in Case 1b with load demand of 900 MW

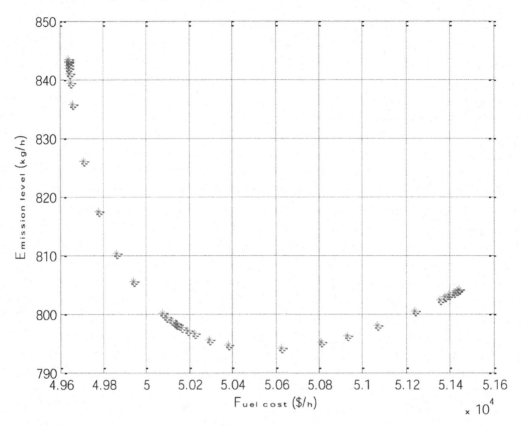

Figure 6. Test system for Case 2

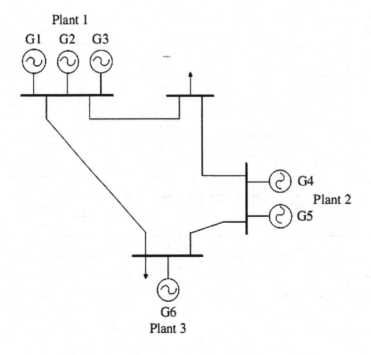

Table 8. Comparison of best compromise solution for Case 2

Method	AS (Palanichamy, 2008)	MOCPSO (Cai, 2009)	MOCASO (Cai, 2010)	ALHN
P_1 (MW)	51.82	51.82	51.81	75.6664
P_2 (MW)	38.64	32.66	38.66	89.9414
P_3 (MW)	248.73	208.79	248.73	159.9137
P_4 (MW)	122.14	128.12	122.12	134.9283
P_5 (MW)	252.01	291.95	252.01	241.3487
P_6 (MW)	223.57	223.57	223.57	233.4936
ΣP_i (MW)	936.91	936.91	936.90	935.2921
P_L (MW)	36.90	39.90	36.89	35.29
Fuel cost ($/h)	47,804.55	47,549.87	47,804.59	48,218.21
Emission (kg/h)	843.42	823.36	843.41	721.50
Emission PPF ($/kg)	47.8222	47.8222	47.8222	47.8222
Equiv. cost of emission ($/h)	40,334.1999	39,374.8866	40,333.7217	34,503.7173
Total cost ($/h)	**88,138.7499**	**86,924.7566**	**88,138.3117**	**82,721.9273**

Figure 7. Pareto-optimal front for fuel cost and emission in Case 2

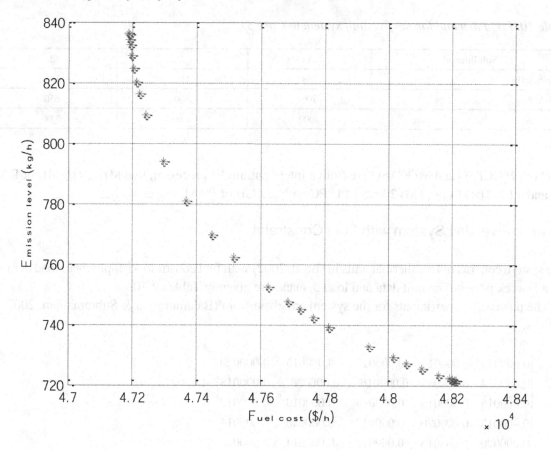

Table 9. Data for the five-unit system in Case 3

Unit	1	2	3	4	5
a_i ($/h)	25	60	100	120	40
b_i ($/MWh)	2.0	1.8	2.1	2.2	1.8
c_i ($/MW²h)	0.0080	0.0030	0.0012	0.0040	0.0015
d_i (lb/h)	80	50	70	45	30
e_i (lb/MWh)	-0.8050	-0.5550	-0.9550	-0.6000	-0.5550
f_i (lb/MW²h)	0.0180	0.0150	0.0115	0.0080	0.0120
φ_{0i} (tons/h)	0.83612	2.00669	3.34448	4.01338	1.33779
φ_{1i} (tons/MWh)	0.066889	0.060200	0.070234	0.073578	0.060200
φ_{2i} (tons/MW²h)	0.00026756	0.00010033	0.00004013	0.00013378	0.00005017
$P_{i,max}$ (MW)	75	125	175	250	300
$P_{i,min}$ (MW)	20	20	30	40	50
$F_{i,max}$ (tons)	1000	1000	2000	3000	3000
$F_{i,min}$ (tons)	0	0	0	0	0
$X_{i,max}$ (tons)	10000	10000	20000	30000	30000
$X_{i,min}$ (tons)	0	0	0	0	0

Table 10. Load demand for the five-unit system in Case 3

Sub-interval	1	2	3
Duration (h)	168	168	168
P_{Dk} (MW)	700	800	650
F_{Dk} (tons)	7000	7000	7000

and both MOCPSO and MOCASO are from a Intel Pentium III processor, 996 MHz, 416 MB of RAM PC and a Intel (R) Core (TM) 2 Duo CPU PC with 2.2 GB of RAM, respectively.

Case 3: Five-Unit System with Fuel Constraint

The system consists of five thermal units in (Basu, 2002) with fuel constraints supplying to load demand for a 3-week period. The unit data and load demand are given in Tables 9-10.

The power loss coefficients for the system are given from (Balamurugan & Subramanian, 2007) as follows:

$$B_{ij} = \begin{bmatrix} 0.000049 & 0.000014 & 0.000015 & 0.000015 & 0.000020 \\ 0.000014 & 0.000045 & 0.000016 & 0.000020 & 0.000018 \\ 0.000015 & 0.000016 & 0.000039 & 0.000010 & 0.000012 \\ 0.000015 & 0.000020 & 0.000010 & 0.000040 & 0.000014 \\ 0.000020 & 0.000018 & 0.000012 & 0.000014 & 0.000035 \end{bmatrix}$$

Three sub-cases with differently initial fuel storage are considered for this system. The initial values of fuel storage are given in Table 11.

Case 3a: Neglecting Power Loss

When system power loss is neglected, the total costs and total emission amount for best economic dispatch and best emission dispatch obtained by the proposed ALHN are given in Table 12 and the comparison of best compromise solutions obtained by the proposed method to those from conventional HNN (Basu, 2002) are shown in Table 13. The Pareto-optimal fronts for this case are depicted in Figures 8-10. Based on the compared results in Table 13, the ALHN method dominates the HNN method for all sub-cases.

Table 11. Initial storage for the five-unit system in Case 3

Sub-case	Unit	1	2	3	4	5
1	$X_i^{(0)}$ (tons)	2000	5000	5000	8000	8000
2	$X_i^{(0)}$ (tons)	2000	5000	5000	500	8000
3	$X_i^{(0)}$ (tons)	2000	2500	2500	8000	500

Figure 8. Pareto-optimal front for fuel cost and emission in Sub-case 1 of Case 3a

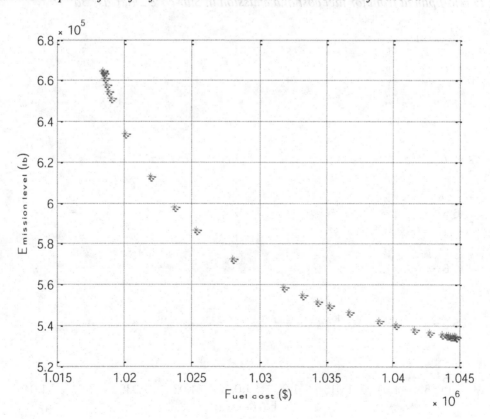

Table 12. Best fuel cost and emission dispatch results for Case 3a by ALHN

Sub-case	Best economic dispatch			Best emission dispatch		
	1	**2**	**3**	**1**	**2**	**3**
Fuel cost ($)	1,002,551.43	1,002,551.43	1,003,047.70	1,072,673.57	1,057,999.29	1,072,683.93
Emission (kg)	756,288.67	756,290.24	741,033.64	521,793.47	531,822.70	521,793.48

Table 13. Comparison of best compromise solutions for five-unit system in Case 3a

Method	Sub-case 1		Sub-case 2		Sub-case 3	
	HNN (Basu, 2002)	**ALHN**	**HNN (Basu, 2002)**	**ALHN**	**HNN (Basu, 2002)**	**ALHN**
Fuel cost ($)	1046893.5	1044733.66	1028321.9	1044733.74	1059194.2	1045198.27
Emission (kg)	547128.86	534482.85	582051.34	534483.24	538379.22	534060.83
Emission PPF ($/kg)	2.3291	2.3291	2.3291	2.3291	2.3291	2.3291
Equiv. cost of emission ($)	1274317.83	1244864.01	1355655.78	1244864.91	1253939.04	1243881.08
Total cost ($)	**2321211.33**	**2289597.67**	**2383977.68**	**2289598.65**	**2313133.24**	**2289079.35**

Figure 9. Pareto-optimal front for fuel cost and emission in Sub-case 2 of Case 3a

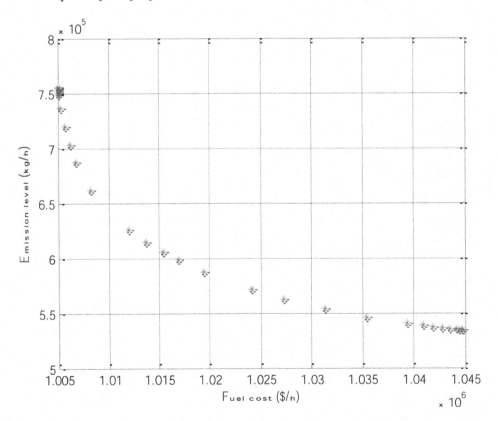

Figure 10. Pareto-optimal front for fuel cost and emission in Sub-case 3 of Case 3a

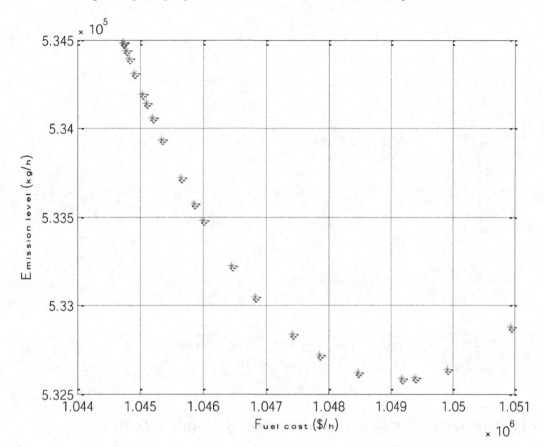

Table 14. Results for Case 3b by ALHN

Sub-case		Best economic dispatch	Best compromise	Best emission dispatch
1	Fuel cost ($)	1,019,015.50	1,060,811.32	1,087,044.04
	Emission (kg)	768,070.66	551,449.20	539,030.43
2	Fuel cost ($)	1,019,015.50	1,060,811.55	1,071,453.61
	Emission (kg)	768,072.24	551,449.06	552,832.49
3	Fuel cost ($)	1,019,894.04	1,060,811.55	1,087,054.81
	Emission (kg)	750,973.95	551,449.06	539,030.48

Case 3b: Considering Power Loss

When the system power loss is considered, the obtained results from the ALHN method are given in Table 14 and Pareto-optimal fronts for the sub-cases are shown in Figures 11-13.

Figure 11. Pareto-optimal front for fuel cost and emission in Sub-case 1 of Case 3b

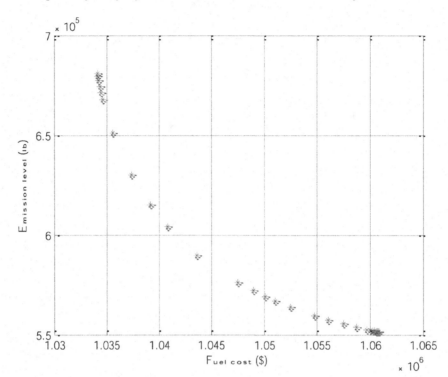

Figure 12. Pareto-optimal front for fuel cost and emission in Sub-case 2 of Case 3b

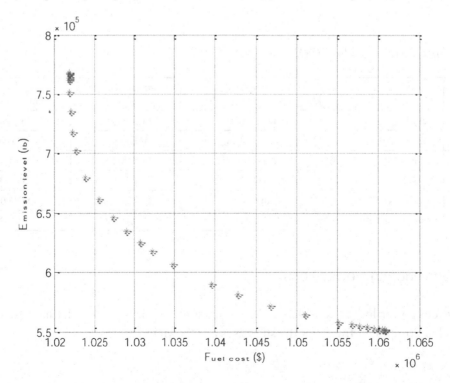

Figure 13. Pareto-optimal front for fuel cost and emission in Sub-case 3 of Case 3b

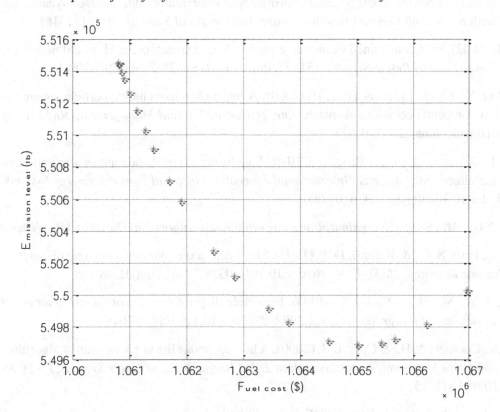

CONCLUSION

In this chapter, the ALHN method has been efficiently implemented for solving the CEED problem with fuel constraint. By directly using the augmented Lagrange function as the energy function for Hopfield network together with sigmoid function of continuous neurons, the problem constraints are properly handled. Moreover, ALHN is a recurrent neural network with parallel processing which leads to quick convergence to the optimal solution for the optimization problems. For obtaining different non-dominated solutions of a multi-objective optimization problem, the slope of sigmoid function of continuous neurons is adjusted from very small to very large values. The result comparisons from the many tested cases have shown that the proposed ALHN can obtain better optimal solutions than many other methods. Therefore, ALHN could be a favourable implementation for solving the CEED with complicated constraints.

REFERENCES

Asgarpoor, S. (1994). Comparison of linear, nonlinear, and network flow programming techniques in fuel scheduling. *Electric Power Systems Research*, *30*(3), 169–174. doi:10.1016/0378-7796(94)00851-5

Balamurugan, R., & Subramanian, S. (2007). A simplified recursive approach to combined economic emission dispatch. *Electric Power Components and Systems*, *36*(1), 17–27. doi:10.1080/15325000701473742

Balamurugan, R., & Subramanian, S. (2007). An improved differential evolution based dynamic economic dispatch with nonsmooth fuel cost function. *Journal of Electrical Systems*, *3*(3), 151–161.

Basu, M. (2002). Fuel constrained economic emission load dispatch using Hopfield neural networks. *Electric Power Systems Research*, *63*(1), 51–57. doi:10.1016/S0378-7796(02)00090-1

Cai, J., Ma, X., Li, Q., Li, L., & Peng, H. (2009). A multi-objective chaotic particle swarm optimization for environmental/economic dispatch. *Energy Conversion and Management*, *50*(5), 1318–1325. doi:10.1016/j.enconman.2009.01.013

Cai, J., Ma, X., Li, Q., Li, L., & Peng, H. (2010). A multi-objective chaotic ant swarm optimization for environmental/economic dispatch. *International Journal of Electrical Power & Energy Systems*, *32*(5), 337–344. doi:10.1016/j.ijepes.2010.01.006

Deb, K. (2001). *Multi-objective optimization using evolutionary algorithms* (Vol. 16). John Wiley & Sons.

Dhillon, J., Parti, S. C., & Kothari, D. P. (1993). Stochastic economic emission load dispatch. *Electric Power Systems Research*, *26*(3), 179–186. doi:10.1016/0378-7796(93)90011-3

El-Keib, A. A., Ma, H., & Hart, J. L. (1994). Economic dispatch in view of the clean air act of 1990. *IEEE Transactions on Power Systems*, *9*(2), 972–978. doi:10.1109/59.317648

Jabr, R. A., Coonick, A. H., & Cory, B. J. (2000). A homogeneous linear programming algorithm for the security constrained economic dispatch problem. *IEEE Transactions on Power Systems*, *15*(3), 930–936. doi:10.1109/59.871715

Kulkarni, S., Kothari, AG, & Kothari, DP, P. (. (. (2000). Combined economic and emission dispatch using improved backpropagation neural network. *Electric Machines &Power Systems*, *28*(1), 31–44. doi:10.1080/073135600268496

Kumar, A. B., Vemuri, S., Ebrahimzadeh, P., & Farahbakhshian, N. (1986). Fuel resource scheduling-The long-term problem. *IEEE Transactions on Power Systems*, *1*(4), 145–151. doi:10.1109/TP-WRS.1986.4335030

Kumar, A. B., Vemuri, S., Gibbs, L. A., Hackett, D. F., & Eisenhauer, J. T. (1984). Fuel Resource Scheduling, Part III: The Short-Term Problem. Power Engineering Review, IEEE, (7), 25-26.

Kumar, A. B., Vemuri, S., & Imah, A. H. (1985). Fuel Resource Scheduling The Daily Scheduling Problem. *IEEE Transactions on Power Apparatus and Systems*, *PAS-104*(2), 313–320. doi:10.1109/TPAS.1985.319045

Lin, C. E., & Viviani, G. L. (1984). Hierarchical economic dispatch for piecewise quadratic cost functions. *IEEE Transactions on Power Apparatus and Systems*, *PAS-103*(6), 1170–1175. doi:10.1109/TPAS.1984.318445

Lu, Y., Zhou, J., Qin, H., Wang, Y., & Zhang, Y. (2011). Chaotic differential evolution methods for dynamic economic dispatch with valve-point effects. *Engineering Applications of Artificial Intelligence*, *24*(2), 378–387. doi:10.1016/j.engappai.2010.10.014

Muralidharan, S., Srikrishna, K., & Subramanian, S. (2006). Emission constrained economic dispatch—A new recursive approach. *Electric Power Components and Systems, 34*(3), 343–353. doi:10.1080/15325000500241225

Niimura, T., & Nakashima, T. (2003). Multiobjective tradeoff analysis of deregulated electricity transactions. *International Journal of Electrical Power & Energy Systems, 25*(3), 179–185. doi:10.1016/S0142-0615(02)00076-5

Palanichamy, C., & Babu, N. S. (2008). Analytical solution for combined economic and emissions dispatch. *Electric Power Systems Research, 78*(7), 1129–1137. doi:10.1016/j.epsr.2007.09.005

Parikh, J., & Chattopadhyay, D. (1996). A multi-area linear programming approach for analysis of economic operation of the Indian power system. *IEEE Transactions on Power Systems, 11*(1), 52–58. doi:10.1109/59.485985

Park, J. H., Kim, Y. S., Eom, I. K., & Lee, K. Y. (1993). Economic load dispatch for piecewise quadratic cost function using Hopfield neural network. *IEEE Transactions on Power Systems, 8*(3), 1030–1038. doi:10.1109/59.260897

Qu, B. Y., Suganthan, P. N., Pandi, V. R., & Panigrahi, B. K. (2010, December). Multi objective evolutionary programming to solve environmental economic dispatch problem. In *11th International Conference on Control, Automation, Robotics and Vision, ICARCV 2010, Proceedings*. IEEE. doi:10.1109/ICARCV.2010.5707926

Rau, N. S., & Adelman, S. T. (1995). Operating strategies under emission constraints. *IEEE Transactions on Power Systems, 10*(3), 1585–1591. doi:10.1109/59.466484

Sakawa, M., Yano, H., & Yumine, T. (1987). An interactive fuzzy satisficing method for multiobjective linear-programming problems and its application. *IEEE Transactions on Systems, Man, and Cybernetics, 17*(4), 654–661. doi:10.1109/TSMC.1987.289356

Sashirekha, A., Pasupuleti, J., Moin, N. H., & Tan, C. S. (2013). Combined heat and power (CHP) economic dispatch solved using Lagrangian relaxation with surrogate subgradient multiplier updates. *International Journal of Electrical Power & Energy Systems, 44*(1), 421–430. doi:10.1016/j.ijepes.2012.07.038

Song, Y. H., Wang, G. S., Wang, P. Y., & Johns, A. T. (1997, July). Environmental/economic dispatch using fuzzy logic controlled genetic algorithms. In *Generation, Transmission and Distribution, IEE Proceedings* (Vol. 144, No. 4, pp. 377-382). IET.

Tapia, C. G., & Murtagh, B. A. (1991). Interactive fuzzy programming with preference criteria in multiobjective decision-making. *Computers & Operations Research, 18*(3), 307–316. doi:10.1016/0305-0548(91)90032-M

van den Berg, J., & Bioch, J. C. (1993). *Constrained optimization with a continuous Hopfield-Lagrange model*. Technical report EUR-CS-93-10, Erasmus University Rotterdam.

Wood, A. J., & Wollenberg, B. F. (2012). *Power generation, operation, and control*. John Wiley & Sons.

Zhu, J., & Momoh, J. A. (2001). Multi-area power systems economic dispatch using nonlinear convex network flow programming. *Electric Power Systems Research*, *59*(1), 13–20. doi:10.1016/S0378-7796(01)00131-6

APPENDIX

Proof of Convergence for ALHN

In the ALHN, the neurons associated with continuous variables are called *continuous neurons* and the neurons associated with Lagrangian multipliers are called *multiplier neurons*.

To explain how the dynamics of neurons cause the energy function (14) to be minimized with respect to continuous neurons and maximized with respect to multiplier neurons, the effects from the status changes of neurons on the energy function are considered.

Considering the effect of the change in continuous neuron $V_{p,ik}$ representing on energy function E:

$$\frac{dE}{dt} = \frac{\partial E}{\partial V_{p,ik}} \frac{dV_{p,ik}}{dt} \tag{46}$$

Substituting (29) into (46):

$$\frac{dE}{dt} = \frac{\partial E}{\partial V_{p,ik}} \frac{dg\left(U_{p,ik}\right)}{dt} = \frac{\partial E}{\partial V_{p,ik}} \frac{dg\left(U_{p,ik}\right)}{dU_{p,ik}} \frac{dU_{p,ik}}{dt} \tag{47}$$

Substituting (15) into (47):

$$\frac{dE}{dt} = -\frac{dg\left(U_{p,ik}\right)}{dU_{p,ik}} \left(\frac{dU_{p,ik}}{dt}\right)^2 \tag{48}$$

Since $g(U_{p,ik})$ is a monotonically increasing function, the value of dE/dt is always negative. Thus, the energy function of Hopfield network (14) is minimized with respect to continuous neuron $V_{p,ik}$ when this neuron changes its status. It is similar to other continuous neurons $V_{f,ik}$ and $V_{x,ik}$. Therefore, the energy function of Hopfield neuron (14) is always minimized with respect to status changes of continuous neurons.

On the other hand, considering the effect of the change in multiplier neuron $V_{\lambda,k}$ on energy function:

$$\frac{dE}{dt} = \frac{\partial E}{\partial V_{\lambda,k}} \frac{dV_{\lambda,k}}{dt} \tag{49}$$

Substituting (32) into (49):

$$\frac{dE}{dt} = \frac{\partial E}{\partial V_{\lambda,k}} \frac{dg\left(U_{\lambda,k}\right)}{dt} = \frac{\partial E}{\partial V_{\lambda,k}} \frac{dU_{\lambda,k}}{dt} \tag{50}$$

Substituting (18) into (50):

$$\frac{dE}{dt} = \left(\frac{dU_{\lambda,k}}{dt}\right)^2 \tag{51}$$

It is obvious that *dE/dt* is always positive, that means the energy function (14) is always maximized with respect to the change of multiplier neuron $V_{\lambda,k}$. Similarly, the energy function is also maximized with the change of other multiplier neurons $V_{\gamma,k}$ and $V_{\eta,ik}$. Therefore, the energy function (14) is always maximized with respect to status change of multiplier neurons.

Principle of Multi-Objective Optimization

In a multi-objective optimization problem, there often exists a conflict among the objectives. For dealing the problem, a set of optimal solutions is found instead of only one optimal solution since no objective can be considered to be better than any others. The obtained set of solutions known as Pareto-optimal solutions is a collection of non-dominated solutions where there is a trade-off among the objectives [28].

Generally, a multi-objective optimization problem is formulated as follows:

$$\text{Min } F_i(x); i = 1, ..., N_{obj} \tag{52}$$

subject to

$$g_j(x) = 0; j = 1, ..., J \tag{53}$$

$$h_k(x) \leq 0; j = 1, ..., K \tag{54}$$

where

$F_i(x)$ the objective function i
x vector of variables
N_{obj} the number of objectives
$g_j(x)$ equality constraint j
$h_k(x)$ inequality constraint k
J number of equality constraints
K number of inequality constraints

For any two solutions x_1 and x_2 from the above problem, there is always two possibilities whether a solution dominates the other or not dominate the other. For example, the solution x_1 dominates x_2 if one of the following conditions is satisfied:

1. $\forall i \in \{1, 2,..., N_{obj}\}: F_i(x_1) \leq F_i(x_2)$
2. $\exists j \in \{1, 2,..., N_{obj}\}: F_j(x_1) < F_j(x_2)$

If one of the above conditions is violated, the solution x_1 does not dominate the solution x_2. If x_1 dominates x_2 in a set of two solutions $\{x_1, x_2\}$, x_1 is called the non-dominated solution of the set of solution. The set of non-dominated solutions entire the search space of the problem is known as *Pareto-optimal front*. The concept of Pareto-optimal front for a multi-objective optimization problem is explained in Figure 14.

Best Compromise Solution by Fuzzy-Based Mechanism

The Pareto-optimal front of a multi-objective optimization problem provides decision maker (DM) several options for decision making. However, it does not help the DM to choose the best solution among the provided options since there is always a trade-off among the objectives and the best solution has to satisfy a fair trade-off among the objectives. One of the methods to find the best compromise solution from the Pareto-optimal front of a multi-objective optimization problem is fuzzy satisfying method [20]. This method determines the distance from the value of each objective in the obtained solutions to its maximum value using a linear membership function. A solution is considered the best if the sum of the distances from all objectives in that solution is greater than the sums of the distances from any other solutions.

The fuzzy goal is represented in linear membership function as follows (Sakawa, Yano & Yumine, 1987):

$$\mu_j = \begin{cases} 1 & \text{if } F_j \leq F_j^{\min} \\ \dfrac{F_j^{\max} - F_j}{F_j^{\max} - F_j^{\min}} & \text{if } F_j^{\min} < F_j < F_j^{\max} \\ 0 & \text{if } F_j \geq F_j^{\max} \end{cases} \tag{55}$$

where μ_j is membership value of objective j, and $F_j^{\max}$ and $F_j^{\min}$ are maximum and minimum values of objective j, respectively. The shape of the membership function is depicted in Figure 15.

Figure 14. Pareto-optimal front for a multi-objective optimization problem

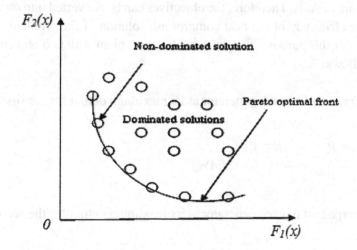

Figure 15. Linear fuzzy membership function

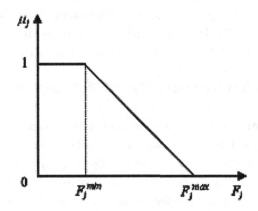

For each non-dominated solution, the membership function is normalized as follows [30]:

$$\mu^k = \frac{\sum\limits_{j=1}^{N_{obj}} \mu_j}{\sum\limits_{k=1}^{N_P}\sum\limits_{j=1}^{N_{obj}} \mu_j} \tag{56}$$

where μ^k is membership function of non-dominated solution k; N_{obj} is the number of objective functions; and N_p is the number of Pareto-optimal solutions.

The solution with maximum membership function μ^k can be chosen as the best compromise solution for the problem.

Price Penalty Factor Calculation

In a multi-objective optimization problem, the objectives are represented for different factors which lead different measurement units. Therefore, the objectives can be converted into one measurement unit system to estimate the efficiency of the best compromise solution of the problem and PPF method is one of the approaches for this purpose. For the considered problem with two objectives, the method to calculate PPF is as follows:

1. Evaluate the average cost of each generator at its maximum output for the first objective

$$\frac{F_{1i}(P_i^{\max})}{P_i^{\max}} = \frac{\sum\limits_{k=1}^{M} t_k \left[a_i + b_i P_i^{\max} + c_i (P_i^{\max})^2 \right]}{P_i^{\max}} \quad (\$/MW) \tag{57}$$

2. Evaluate the average cost of each generator at its maximum output for the second objective

$$\frac{F_{2i}(P_i^{\max})}{P_i^{\max}} = \frac{\sum\limits_{k=1}^{M} t_k \left[d_i + e_i P_i^{\max} + f_i (P_i^{\max})^2 \right]}{P_i^{\max}} \text{ (kg/MW)} \tag{58}$$

3.   Divide the average cost of the first objective to that of the second one

$$\frac{F_{1i}(P_i^{\max})/P_i^{\max}}{F_{2i}(P_i^{\max})/P_i^{\max}} = \frac{\sum\limits_{k=1}^{M} t_k \left[a_i + b_i P_i^{\max} + c_i (P_i^{\max})^2 \right]/P_i^{\max}}{\sum\limits_{k=1}^{M} t_k \left[d_i + e_i P_i^{\max} + f_i (P_i^{\max})^2 \right]/P_i^{\max}} \text{ (\$/kg)} \tag{59}$$

This ratio is called PPF and denoted by

$$h_i = \frac{F_{1i}(P_i^{\max})/P_i^{\max}}{F_{2i}(P_i^{\max})/P_i^{\max}} ; i = 1, 2, \ldots, N \text{ (\$/kg)} \tag{60}$$

4.   Note each h_i is associated with corresponding generator i. Arrange h_i in ascending order and calculate the accumulation of maximum capacity of generators starting from the lowest h_i until the following condition is satisfied:

$$\sum_{i=1}^{N} P_i^{\max} \geq P_D' \tag{61}$$

where P_D' is the average load demand for the whole schedule time horizon.

5.   The value of h_i associated with the last unit in the accumulation sum is chosen as PPF for the given load demand.

Chapter 8

Speaker Recognition With Normal and Telephonic Assamese Speech Using I–Vector and Learning–Based Classifier

Mridusmita Sharma
Gauhati University, India

Rituraj Kaushik
Tezpur University, India

Kandarpa Kumar Sarma
Gauhati University, India

ABSTRACT

Speaker recognition is the task of identifying a person by his/her unique identification features or behavioural characteristics that are included in the speech uttered by the person. Speaker recognition deals with the identity of the speaker. It is a biometric modality which uses the features of the speaker that is influenced by one's individual behaviour as well as the characteristics of the vocal cord. The issue becomes more complex when regional languages are considered. Here, the authors report the design of a speaker recognition system using normal and telephonic Assamese speech for their case study. In their work, the authors have implemented i-vectors as features to generate an optimal feature set and have used the Feed Forward Neural Network for the recognition purpose which gives a fairly high recognition rate.

INTRODUCTION

Speaker or voice recognition is the task of automatically recognizing the identity of the person speaking. The task of speaker recognition considers the individual behavior as well as the characteristics of the vocal cord as features to identify a speaker. Speaker recognition is however very much different from speech

DOI: 10.4018/978-1-5225-2128-0.ch008

recognition. In speech recognition, the speech signals which convey much information to the listeners are being detected with the help of the features that has the ability to represent the speech content. The primary level of speech recognition is to recognize the speech content spoken by the speaker. But at a higher level, the spoken utterances or speech samples contains the information regarding the gender, emotions and also the individuality of the speaker speaking (Reynolds, 2002).

With the rapid growth of techniques in the signal processing and model building and empowerment of computing devices, significant progress has been made in the speech recognition area. Research in the field of speaker recognition has also evolved at par with speech recognition and speech synthesis because of the similar characteristics and challenges associated with it. Research and development in the field of speaker recognition dates back to over four decades and this area is still an active topic for research. The application of speaker recognition technology has been continually growing in various fields of application such as forensic applications, dynamic signatures, gait, keystroke recognition, data encryption purpose, user validation in contact centers, etc (Beigi, 2011).

From the literature, it has been found that recent speaker recognition tasks have implemented i-vector based features for their purpose. The characteristics of a voice sample or about the speaker can be obtained by the features extracted from the speech sample. Recently the i-vector paradigm is widely used for the speaker recognition systems. The i-vector based feature extraction is based on Joint Factor Analysis (JFA) approach which provides an elegant way to convert the Mel Frequency Cepstral Coefficient (MFCC) feature vector of a variable length utterance into a low dimensional vector representation (Dehak et. al., 2011). I-vectors are one example of subspace modeling approaches that can be used to reduce the dimensionality of data before training and applying to classifiers for recognition purpose. The dimensionality reduction should make training of the classifier less computationally expensive which could enable us to train the system with more data. In this work, we have considered Assamese speech for our experimental work as the number of work done in this language is relatively less. Also, Assamese language has a very rich and diverse phonological content which shows notable variations from region to region as well as speaker to speaker. The diversity and variations present in this language increases the need to develop a language specific tool for speech and speaker recognition system (Sharma & Sarma, 2015).

The organization of the chapter is as follows. The second section provides an overview of the basic considerations and theoretical background that are associated with various speaker recognition tasks. A detailed literature survey of the previous work done related to speaker recognition problems and the features used for the purpose is presented in the third section. The fourth section gives the proposed system model, the speech database and the basic algorithm used for our proposed work. Experimental details and results derived from our work is shown in Section five. Section six concludes the chapter.

THEORETICAL CONSIDERATIONS

The study of the basic theoretical considerations of speaker recognition and other such related topics gives a proper understanding of the speaker recognition problems. In this section a brief overview of the basic theoretical considerations related to speaker recognition problem, features used and the soft computing technique implemented for the recognition purpose is provided.

1. **Speaker Recognition Basics:** Speaker recognition is the process of recognition of the person speaking on the basis of the uttered speech. The history of speaker recognition dates back to the

mid twentieth century and the acoustic features of speech signals were used to distinguish the individuals. Some of the most used modeling techniques for speaker recognition have been the Gaussian Mixture Models (GMMs) and the Support Vector Machines (SVMs) in addition to the use of Artificial Neural Networks (ANN) and other such classifiers (Beigi, 2012). The characteristics of speech signals are a speaker dependent feature which helps us to identify the speaker speaking. With the rapid growth of techniques in the signal processing and model building and empowerment of computing devices, significant progress has been made in the speech recognition area. Research in the field of speaker recognition has also evolved at par with speech recognition and speech synthesis because of the similar characteristics and challenges associated with it. Research and development in the field of speaker recognition area is still an active topic. The application of speaker recognition technology has been continually growing in various fields of application such as forensic applications, dynamic signatures, gait, keystroke recognition, data encryption purpose, user validation in contact centers, etc. The retinal image scans and fingerprints are considered to be the reliable means of identification, however speech can also be considered as a biometric modality that can be collected over phone or by various other means. Speech based password are more convenient because it is unlikely to be stolen and also ones voice cannot be forgotten (Beigi, 2011).

Speech consists of acoustic pressure waves created by the voluntary movements of the anatomical structure in the human speech production system. The speaker produces a speech signal in the form of pressure waves that travels from the speaker's head to the listener's ear. The generation of speech signal is the result of many biological activities which comprises the coordinated muscle action of the vocal cord, larynx, pharynx, diaphragm, etc. For each sound there is a particular position for each of the vocal tract articulators such as vocal folds, tongue, lips, teeth, velum and jaw (Sukor, 2012). It has also been mentioned that because of the shape of the vocal tract, larynx size and other speech production organs, no two individuals sounds alike. Also, the physical differences and the manner of speaking of an individual along with the rhythm, pronunciations, style of intonation and other such parameters greatly influences the speaker characteristics (Kinnunen & Li, 2010). Figure 1 shows the speech production organs.

The speech signal production is a result of several transformations occurring at the levels of semantics, acoustics, linguistics and articulatory. The differences present in these transformations are the differences present in the acoustic properties of the speech signal. The differences in the acoustic features and the individual characteristics of the vocal tract and the speaking habit of each speaker are used to differentiate the speakers from one another. The speaker recognition system makes an attempt to identify the speaker based on the trained model and matching the characteristics of the given speech. Speaker recognition comprises of two fundamental divisions namely Speaker verification and Speaker identification (Rajsekhar. G, 2008).

Speaker identification is the task of determining who is speaking from the set of known voices and speakers. On the other hand, speaker verification is the task of verifying the person who claims to be the one who has spoken. Automatic speaker verification can be termed as the authentication of one's identity claim. Speaker identification is further divided into two sub-categories which are text-dependent and text independent speaker identification.

Text-dependent speaker identification is performed on a voiced instance of a specific word uttered by the speaker, whereas in text-independent speaker identification the speaker can say anything. Figure 2. shows the classification diagram of the speaker recognition types.

Figure 1. Organs for speech production

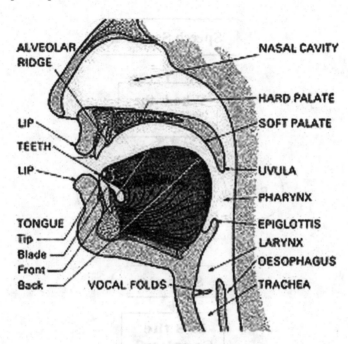

Figure 2. Classification of Speaker Recognition

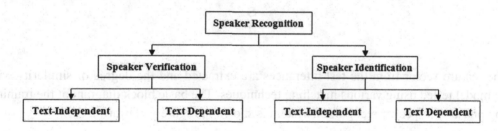

As mentioned earlier, speaker recognition problem deals with the automatic recognition of the person who is speaking on the basis of the individual characteristics present in the speech samples. It is carried out in two sessions. The first phase is the training session in which input speech samples from each registered speaker is collected so as to build or train a reference model for the speakers. The second session is referred to as the testing phase or the operational phase where the input sample is matched with the database present in the reference model and recognition decision is made subsequently. This technique makes it possible to use the speaker's voice to verify their identity and control access to various services such as voice dialing, telephone banking, shopping by telephone, voice mail, remote access to computer, etc. The differences between speaker verification and speaker identification are shown diagrammatically in Figure 3 (Rajsekhar. G, 2008).

The training and the testing phase of the speaker recognition system is similar to any other pattern recognition system. The feature that represents the speaker characteristics is extracted from the speech samples of the training utterances which are used for building the reference model. Similarly, during

Figure 3. a) Speaker Identification. b) Speaker Verification

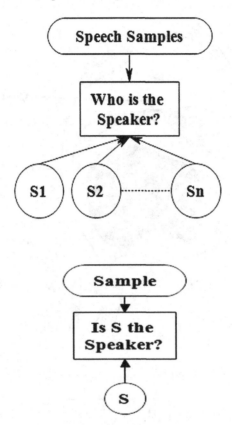

testing the feature vector from the test utterances are extracted and the degree of similarity with the reference model tested using various matching techniques. The basic block diagram of the training and the testing phase of a speaker recognition system is shown in Figure 4 (Tiwari, 2010).

2. **I-Vector Extraction:** The i-vector or identity vector based feature extraction technique was originally proposed by Dehak et. al. in the year 2010. The concept was initially used for speaker recognition tasks but later gained popularity in various other speech related problems like verification, speaker diarization, language identification, etc. The i-vector extraction technique is a dimensionality reduction technique which provides an elegant approach to reduce rough input speech utterances to a corresponding low dimensional vector space representation whereas retaining the important information that were present in the original input speech samples. The i-vector representation is used as a data driven approach for feature extraction which consist of mapping a number of frames of a speech utterances into a dimensionally reduced speech representation super vector based on high dimensional linear Gaussian Mixture Model (GMM) and traditional low dimensional Mel Frequency Cepstral Coefficient (MFCC) features. The design of these intermediate-sized vectors or i-vectors was motivated by the existing super-vector based Joint Factor Analysis (JFA) approach. While the i-vectors are formed by modeling a low dimensional total variability space that considers both the speaker and channel variability, the JFA approach models the speaker and the channel

Figure 4. a) Training phase of a speaker recognition system. b) Testing phase of a speaker recognition system

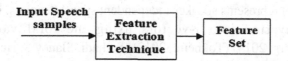

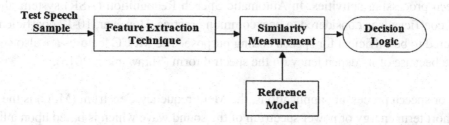

variability space separately. With this approach Dehak et. al. found that the i-vector do not lose any important information that is useful for speaker discrimination unlike the JFA where some of the speaker discriminant information is lost in the channel space. In i-vector extraction, the channel variability is included in the total variability sub-space which includes many standard channel compensation techniques such as Linear Discriminant Analysis (LDA), Within Class Covariance Normalization (WCCN) and Nuisance Attribute Projection (NAP) to attenuate channel variability in the i-vector extraction. The variations in channel may include mismatch between enrolment and verification utterance, arising from the differences in microphones, acoustic environments, transmission channels and the variations in individual speaker's voices. A speaker and channel dependent GMM super-vector, s, can be represented as follows-

$$s = m + Tw \tag{1}$$

where, m is the speaker and the channel independent Universal Background Model (UBM) super vector, T is the total variability subspace which is a low rank matrix that represents the represents the primary directions for variations across a large collection of data to be developed. w is normally distributed with parameters $N(0;1)$, and is the i-vector representation of a particular utterance. The basic block diagram representation of i-vector extraction is shown in Figure 5.

Figure 5. Basic block diagram of i-vector extraction

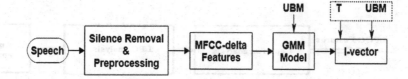

The speech samples are pre-processed in the first step with silence part removal and then the MFCC features are extracted. The sequence of feature vectors extracted is then represented by their UBM distribution which is a GMM that represents speaker-independent speech features. Later on these distribution parameters are converted into i-vectors using the total variability matrix T (Dehak, et.al, 2011) (Greenberg, 2014) (Tokheim, 2012) (Sadjadi, Slaney & Heck, 2013).

3. **MFCC Extraction:** Various literatures listed numerous method of parametric representation of the acoustic signals among which MFCC is considered to be the most popular and widely used technique. The use of MFCC can be used as the standard method for feature extraction related to speech processing activities. In Automatic Speech Recognition (ASR) system, the use of 20 MFCC coefficients is considered to be a common practice. However, 10-12 coefficients are often considered to be sufficient for speech coding purpose. The MFCC features are also very sensitive to noise because of its dependency on the spectral form (Shrawankar, 2013).

In sound or speech processing applications, the Mel Frequency Cepstrum (MFC) is the representation of the short term energy or power spectrum of the sound wave which is based upon a linear cosine transform of a log power spectrum or a nonlinear Mel scale of frequency. The extensive use of MFCC is due to the fact that in Mel scale cepstrum the frequency bands are equally distributed on the Mel scale which represents approximately the human auditory system's response than the linearly spaced bands used in the normal cepstrum. The steps involved in MFCC feature extraction is diagrammatically represented in Figure 6.

As mentioned earlier, the computation of MFCC features is based on the short term analysis of the speech signal in order to maintain the periodicity of the signal. Since speech signals are quasi-periodic, in MFCC extraction the discontinuities present in the signal are removed by applying Hamming window in a frame by frame pattern over the speech sample and the MFCC coefficients are calculated from each frame. Spectral distortions created by overlapping by this process are also decreased by this manner. Then Discrete Fourier Transform (DFT) operation is carried out to generate the Mel filter bank. The width of the triangular filter varies according to the Mel frequency warping and so the log total energy in a critical band around the centre frequency is included. After the frequency warping, the number of coefficients is obtained. Later on, the inverse DFT (IDFT) is used for the calculation of the cepstral coefficients. For phonetically important characteristics speech signal is expressed in Mel frequency scale. The general formula for the calculation of MFCC is given below (Sharma & Sarma, 2015)-

Figure 6. Steps involved in MFCC feature extraction

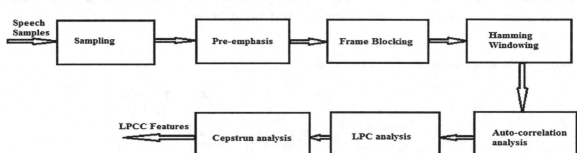

$$Mel(f) = 2595 * \log 10(1 + f / 700) \hspace{3cm} (2)$$

4. **Background to Assamese Phonology:** Assamese which is the anglicized form of the word Asamiya, is a major language of the state of Assam. It was accorded the status of one of the official language of the state in India along with English by the state's Official Language Act in the year 1960. Assamese is the eastern most Indo-Aryan language which is found in the entire northeastern part of India and is considered to be the lingua-franca of the whole North-East India. It is also the eastern most member of the Indo-European family tree and is spoken in the state of Assam, Meghalaya, Nagaland and Arunachala. The history of Assamese language can be traced back to very early times. The birth of the Assamese language is from Sanskrit language, which is an ancient language of the Indian subcontinent. It was basically found along the Brahmaputra valley and has certain similarities with the Bengali language in terms of alphabets used. The vocabulary, phonology and grammar of the Assamese language have been greatly influenced by the original inhabitants if Assam namely the Bodos and the Kacharis. The development of Assamese is from Magadhi Prakrit which is the eastern branch of apabhramas that followed Prakrit. Assamese has been a borrowing language, and during its long history of evolution from the Vedic dialects, it has enriched its vocabulary by acquisition from all the non-aryan languages. It has also been found in the literature that Hindi and other such north Indian languages have contributed to the greater development of the Assamese language. Many words from the foreign languages have also found to have influenced the language to a certain extent. Assamese is a rich language with diverse ethnographic contents and dialectical variations. It typically consists of various regional dialects which are primarily based on the morphology and the phonology. A renowned linguist of Assam, Banikanta Kakati, has divided the Assamese language into two major dialects namely Eastern Assamese and Western Assamese. However, recent study reveals that the modern day linguists have grouped the Assamese language into four major dialects namely Eastern Dialect, Central Dialect, Goalpariya Dialect and Kamrupi Dialect (Sharma, Sarma & Sarma, 2013) (Sharma & Sarma, 2015). Figure 7. shows the Indo-European family tree.

The map of Assam outlining the various dialects of the regions is depicted in Figure 8.

5. **Multi-Layer Feed Forward Neural Network (MLFNN):** Artificial Neural Networks (ANN) or simply Neural Networks (NN) are made up of smallest building blocks called the neurons. The neurons are sometimes called nodes or units. The basic design of the ANN was motivated by the structure of the human brain where the neurons operates on the local data and communicates with the other elements.

The basic operation of different types of NNs are similar to each other where each neurons in the network is able to receive input signals and processes them and send as output signals. Each neuron is connected to a minimum of one neuron and each connection of neurons is evaluated by a real number called the weight coefficient that reflects the degree of importance of the given connection in the neural network. The NN is also considered as the universal approximator i.e. it can realize an arbitrary mapping of one vector space to another vector space. The main advantage of NN is its ability to retain the learning which can be subsequently used in further processing. In mathematical terms, to learn means to adjust weight coefficients in such a way that some conditions are fulfilled.

Figure 7. Indo-European family Tree

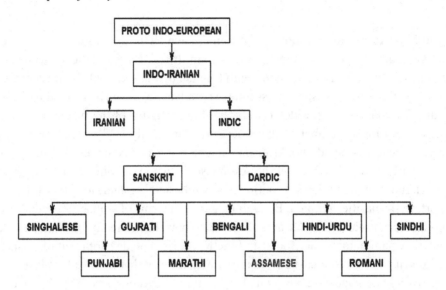

Figure 8. Various dialects of the state of Assam

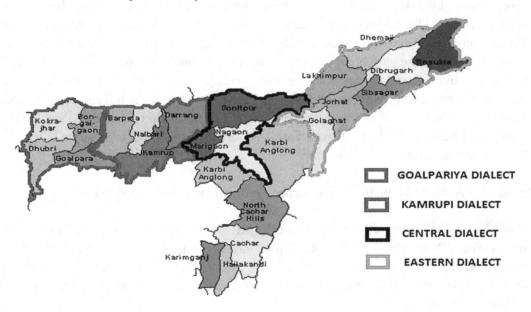

There are two types of training processes namely supervised and unsupervised training. In supervised training the NN already knows the desired output and it adjusts the weight coefficients in such a way that the calculated and the desired outputs are as close as possible. But in unsupervised training, the output is not known and the system is provided with a group of patterns. Based upon the patterns the system is left to itself to settle down to a stable state and learn in some number of iterations. NNs are basically used for classification problems and regression problems. The objective of the classification problem is to determine which class an input belongs to.

An MLFNN also consists of neurons that are structured into layers. The first layer is called the input layer and the last layer is called the output layer. In between the input and the output layer, one or more units of hidden layers are present. A NN that has no hidden layer is called a perceptron. However, a perceptron can only represent linear functions and so is considered not powerful enough for solving sophisticated applications. On the other hand, an MLFNN can represent non-linear functions which are very useful in practice. An MLFNN got its name multilayer because of the fact that it has a layer of processing unit along with the output layer. These networks are also called feed forward because the output from one layer of neurons feeds forward to the next layer of neurons. In this type of network, there are no backward connections and the connections never skips a layer of neurons. The algorithm for training the MLFNN is the back-propagation algorithm which is the most popular one. In back-propagation algorithm, the error of the output propagates from the output layer through the hidden layers to the input layer. The derivatives of the objective function for the output layer and then the hidden layers can be recurrently calculated in case of MLFNN.

The modes of operation of MLFNN are training and prediction modes. For training and prediction using the MLFNN separate data sets are used for both the modes of operation, training set and the test set respectively. The operation of the training mode starts with arbitrary adjustment of the weight values and proceeds iteratively. Each iteration of the complete training set is called an epoch. The adjustment of the weights in the network in each epoch is done in such a way that the error is reduced. As the iterative process of the weight adjustment continues the weight values reaches a local optimal sets of values. Many epochs are usually required for the successful completion of the training process.

The use of MLFNN has certain advantages and disadvantages. The MLFNN application offers the following useful properties and capabilities such as in case of learning the ANNs are able to adapt the user interference. Non-linearity is another very important characteristic of the NN. Since the neuron is a non-linear device so is the NN. In case of supervised learning, to every input signal there is a corresponding desired output response. The training of the network is repeated for many examples of the training set until it reaches a stable state. In this manner the network learns from the examples by constructing an input-output mapping for the problem. Another advantage of using MLFNN is its robustness toward noise, i.e. its performance degrades gracefully in the presence of noise. Amidst the advantages there are also certain disadvantages of ANNs too. One of the problems in ANN is the fact that it cannot explain the prediction process taking place during the training of the network (Mitchell, 1997) (Alpaydin, 2004) (Svozil, Kvasnicka, & Pospichal, 1997).

Figure 9. Shows a typical Multilayer Feed-forward Neural Network

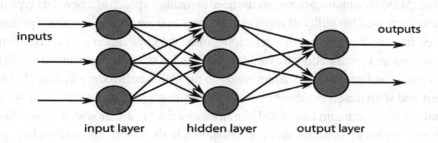

LITERATURE SURVEY OF VARIOUS WORKS DONE RELATED TO OUR TOPICS OF DISCUSSION

The i-vector framework, which has a very recent history, for speaker recognition has gained much popularity in the research field. A number of works across the world has been carried out by the scientist in the last few year that deals speaker recognition tasks using i-vector framework.

Review of the Literature for Speaker Recognition Problems Using I-Vectors and Other Features

The following section provides a detailed survey on the study of the literature that deals with the work related to speaker recognition and also the use of i-vector framework.

McLaren and Leeuwen (2011), in their paper have mentioned that the development of the i-vector framework for speaker recognition has set the standard of performance in the research field to a new level. They have explained i-vector to be the compact representation of the speaker utterances that is extracted from a low dimensional total variability subspace. In their work, the authors have proposed a novel source normalized and weighted LDA algorithm developed to improve the robustness of the i-vector based speaker recognition system under mismatched evaluation condition and conditions where limited speech resources are available for adequate system development. They have evaluated their proposed algorithm on the NIST 2008 and 2010 Speaker Recognition Evaluation (SRE) dataset. From their experimental findings, they have found that the proposed technique gives an improved result of 31% in minimum DCF and EER under mismatched and sparsely available resource condition.

Dehak, Dehak, Reynolds and Torres-Carrasquillo (2011), in their work have presented a new Language Identification (LID) system based on the total variability approach which was previously developed in the field of speaker identification. The authors here have continued to borrow different techniques that were developed for speaker recognition and have applied them to the language identification task. They have employed various techniques to extract the salient features in the lower dimensional i-vector space and have obtained excellent performance on the Language Recognition Evaluation (LRE) 2009 dataset without the need for post processing. These approaches are namely Linear Discriminant Analysis (LDA), Neighborhood Component Analysis (NCA) and their combination with Within Class Covariance Normalization (WCCN). From the experimental results, the authors have concluded that the proposed system gives a very competitive result in comparison with state-of-the-art LID systems and have also mentioned that the system shows additional performance when combined with the state-of-the-art systems.

The emerging use of telephony and computers as well as the growing use of speech as input means in man-to-machine (M2M) communications and the need to manage speech as a new data type in multimedia applications have increased the utility of recognizing a person from his or her voice. Speaker recognition can be classified into two main categories depending upon the application performed, namely, Speaker verification and Speaker identification. Reynolds (1995), in his work have presented a high performance speaker identification and verification system based on the Gaussian Mixture Speaker Models (GMSM) based on robust and statistical representations of speaker identity. The identification system proposed here by the authors is a maximum likelihood classifier and the verification system is a likelihood ratio hypothesis tester using background speaker normalization. In their work, the authors have presented and evaluated identification and verification systems for text-independent speaker recognition using Gaussian Mixture speaker models. They have mentioned that the Gaussian Mixture Model (GMM) provides a simple yet effective speaker representation which is computationally inexpensive and provides high recognition accuracy. The authors have evaluated the proposed system on four publically available speech databases namely TIMIT, NTIMIT, Switchboard and YOHO. The experimental results obtained by the authors on the TIMIT and NTIMIT databases were 99.5% and 60.7% respectively and on a 113 speaker population from the switchboard database the identification result was 82.8%. From the experimental results, the authors have concluded that transmission degradation including noise and microphone variability is the major limiting factor.

In their paper, Kinnunen & Li (2010), gives an overview of the automatic speaker recognition technology with an emphasis on the text-independent recognition. They have also stated that the accuracy of the current speaker recognition system under controlled conditions is high and that the accuracy degrades in the practical situations as many negative factors are encountered including mismatched handsets for training and testing, limited training data, unbalanced text, background noise and non-co-operative users. The authors have also mentioned the necessity of the robust feature extraction techniques, feature normalization, model-domain compensation and score normalization methods.

Sparse representation methods have of late shown promises for the speaker recognition systems. Kua, Epps and Ambikairajah (2013), in their paper have investigated and developed an i-vector based sparse representation and classification (SRC) as an alternative classifier to Support Vector Machine (SVM) and Cosine Distance Scoring (CDS) classifier. They have termed the approach as i-vector sparse representation classification (i-SRC). The authors have explained that unlike SVM, which fixes the support vectors for each target examples, SRC allows the supports which are the sparse coefficient vectors, to be adapted to test signal being characterized. Furthermore, unlike the CDS, the SRC does not require a training phase. The authors have also investigated different types of sparseness methods and dictionary composition of SRC for speaker verification using i-vector from total variability model. From the experimental results, the authors have observed that the inclusion of the identity matrix in the dictionary results in the relative reduction of the error rate. They have also found that the sparse representation method can outperform the best performance achieved by CDS and SVM.

Kanagasundaram, et. al. (2014) has proposed techniques to improve the performance of i-vector based speaker verification techniques when only short utterances are available. The authors have mentioned that short length utterance i-vectors vary with speaker, session variations and the phonetic contents of the utterance. They have identified the variability introduced by phonetic content due to utterance variations as an additional source of degradation when short duration utterances are used. In order to compensate for utterance variations in short i-vector speaker verification systems using Cosine Similarity Scoring (CSS), the authors have introduced a short utterance variance normalization (SUVN) technique and a Short Utterance Variance (SUV) modeling approach at the i-vector feature level. The authors have found that the combination of SUVN with LDA and SN-LDA is shown to provide improvement in performance over the traditional approach of using LDA and/or SN-LDA followed by WCCN. They have also introduced an alternative approach using Probabilistic Linear Discriminant Analysis (PLDA) to directly model the SUV. They have concluded saying that the combination of SUVN, LDA and SN-LDA followed by SUV-PLDA modeling provides improved performance over the baseline PLDA approach.

Kanagasundaram, et. al. (2014) , in their proposed work has investigated the advanced channel compensation techniques for the purpose of improving the performance of i-vector speaker verification in the presence of high intersession variability using the NIST 2008 and 2010 SRE corpora. They have investigated the performance of four channel compensation technique namely Weighted Maximum Margin criterion (WMMC), Source Normalized WMMC (SN-WMMC), Weighted Linear Discriminant

Analysis (WLDA) and Source Normalized WLDA (SN-WLDA). From their experimental results they have reported that by extracting the discriminatory information between pairs of speakers as well as capturing the source variation information in the development if i-vector space, the SN-WLDA system based on the Cosine Similarity Scoring (CSS) i-vector system provides a 20% improvement in the EER for the NIST 2008 interview and microphone verification task and over 10% improvement in the telephone verification of NIST 2008. They have also analyzed the score-level fusion techniques to combine the best channel compensation approach which provides over 8% improvement in DCF over the best single approach, SN-WLDA, for NIST 2008 interview/telephone enrolment verification task.

Tiwari (2010), in her work have mentioned the use of speech processing in various fields such as speaker recognition, verification, etc. They have also mentioned that the objective of the automatic speaker recognition is to extract, characterize and recognize the information about speaker identity. In this work, the authors have used Mel frequency Cepstral Coefficients (MFCC) features for designing a text dependent speaker identification system as MFCC can describe the signal characteristics, relative to the speaker discriminative vocal tract properties. They have also mentioned about some of the modifications that can be done to the MFCC features which will improve the speaker recognition accuracy.

Sonmez, Heck, Weintraub and Shriberg (1997), in their work have mentioned that the statistics of pitch have been used successfully in speaker recognition system. It has also been proven that the uses of pitch parameters are more robust than cepstra to acoustic environment mismatch. In this work the authors have developed a statistical model of pitch that is based upon unbiased estimation of pitch statistics from pitch tracks which are subjected to doubling or halving. They have used the obtained pitch statistics as features in speaker verification on the March 1996 NIST speaker Recognition Evaluation (SRE) database and have reported the results on the "one session" condition with males only for both the claimant and the imposter speakers. The experimental results of their work showed 22% reduction in false alarm rate at 1% miss rate and 11% reduction in false alarm rate at 10% miss rate over the cepstrum-only system.

Kanagasundaram, Vogt, Dean and Sridharan (2012), in their work have investigated the effects of limited speech data in the context of speaker verification using Probabilistic Linear Discriminant Analysis (PLDA) approach. The development of automatic speaker verification system in real world applications largely depends upon the reduction of the length of required speech data. From the literature, the authors have found that the Heavy Tailed PLDA (HTPLDA) modeling of speakers in the i-vector space provides state-of-the-art performance when sufficient speech is available. In this paper, the authors have analyzed the speaker verification problem with respect to the duration of utterance used for both speaker evaluation and score normalization during the development. The authors have investigated two different approaches to total variability representation within the PLDA approach to show improved performance in short utterance mismatched evaluation conditions and also for the condition where insufficient speech resources are available for adequate system development. From the experimental findings using the NIST 2008 SRE dataset, the authors have suggested that the HTPLDA system provides better performance than Gaussian PLDA (GPLDA) as the evaluation utterance lengths are reduced. They have also stated that better performance can be achieved by a pooled total variability approach than the traditional total variability approach for short utterances and insufficient speech data condition.

Revathi, Ganapathy and Venkataramani (2009), in their reported work have presented the effectiveness of perceptual features and iterative clustering approach for performing both speech and speaker recognition. The authors have mainly emphasized on the utilization of clustering models developed for the training data using Mel Frequency Linear Predictive Cepstrum. They have found that these features produced 9% low Equal Error Rate (EER) which is used as the performance measure for the speaker recognition tasks.

Nijhawan and Soni (2014), in their paper have discussed the usefulness of real time speaker recognition in various voice controlled applications. It is mentioned that background noise influences the overall efficiency of the speaker recognition system. The authors in their work have used MFCC along with Vector quantization- Linde, Buzo and Gray (VQLBG) algorithm for designing the speaker recognition system. They have also used Voice Activity Detector to discriminate between the silence and the voiced part. They have concluded that the proposed method gives a significantly good performance for limited speaker database.

Jeng, Lee, Tsao and Wang (2014), in their paper have reformulated the derivation of the i-vector scheme which is considered to be the state-of-the-art representation for speaker verification obtained from the Universal background Model (UBM) based mixtures of factor analyzers (UMFA) and then proposed a clustering based UMFA method called the CMFA. The authors have explained that in UMFA each analyzer is characterized by a subspace, and the same projection of the coordinate of a utterance into individual subspaces is called the i-vector. They have also mentioned that in CMFA, each utterance is represented by multiple i-vectors, each of which is represented by similar subspaces associated with same cluster. The authors have also investigated two strategies for merging these i-vectors into a single one to be applied in the classifier. The database used for the experiment part was the male portion of the core task in the NIST 2005 Speaker Recognition Evaluation. The normalized decision cost function (min DCF) and Equal Error Rate (EER) defines the performance of merit of the new i-vector method over the conventional i-vector method.

In automatic speaker recognition, robust speaker verification on short utterances remains a key consideration as many real world applications often have access to only limited duration speech data. The authors in this paper, Kanagasundaram, et. al. (2011), have explored the popularity of the total variability modeling when the length of the training and the testing utterances are reduced. In the result part, the authors have provided a comparison of Joint Factor Analysis (JFA) and i-vector based systems including various compensation techniques such as Within Class Covariance Normalization (WCCN), Linear Discriminant Analysis (LDA), Scatter Difference Nuisance Attribute Projection (SDNAP) and Gaussian Probabilistic Linear Discriminant Analysis (GPLDA). They have presented a speaker verification performance for utterances with 2 seconds of data taken from the NIST Speaker Recognition Evaluations which provides a clear picture of the current performance characteristics of the techniques in short speech utterance condition.

Rajan, Kinnunen and Hautamaki (2013), in their work have mentioned that the i-vector representation and the PLDA classifier have shown state-of-the-art performance for speaker recognition systems. They have stated that the availability of more than one enrollment utterance for a speaker creates a variety of configurations which can further be used to enhance robustness to noise. They have explored the technique of multi condition training that can be utilized at different stages of the system which included enrollment and classifier training. They have also studied the effect of mismatched training, average and length normalization. Their study indicates that multi condition training of the PLDA model and the enrollment i-vectors plays the key role in achieving good performance in noisy evaluation data.

A mathematical algorithm for automatic speaker recognition system using MFCC and Vector quantization technique is proposed in the paper by Bharti and Bansal (2015). From the experimental results, the authors have found that by using 120 speakers with TIDIGIT database provides 91% of accuracy under normal environmental condition at 20dB SNR. The system proposed by the authors recognizes real time speaker with the help of stored database that can further be increased with more number of users and can be used with other statistical matching techniques such as Hidden Markov Model (HMM).

Reynolds, Quatieri and Dunn (2000), in their proposed work have stated that the Gaussian Mixture Model (GMM) based speaker verification system, which is the major component of the MIT Lincoln laboratory, was successfully used in several NIST speaker recognition evaluations. They have mentioned that the system was built across the likelihood ratio test for verification purpose using effective and simple GMM for likelihood functions, a Universal Background Model (UBM) for alternative speaker representation and a form of Bayesian adaptation for deriving the speaker models from the UBM. The authors have also discussed the development and use of a handset detector and score normalization technique which can improve the verification performance to a large extent. The authors have finally presented the representative performance benchmarks and system behavior experiments on NIST SRE corpora.

Reynolds and Rose (1995), in their work have introduced and motivated the use of Gaussian Mixture Model (GMM) for robust text-independent speaker recognition. They have mentioned that the individual Gaussian components of a GMM represent some general speaker dependent spectral shapes which can be used for modeling speaker identity. In their work the authors have focused on the applications which requires high accuracy rate using short utterances from constrained conversational speech. They have also considered the robustness to degradations produced by transmission over a telephone channel. The authors have conducted the experimental evaluation of the Gaussian Mixture speaker model taking into consideration 49 speakers and conversational telephone speech database. The experimental evaluations consisted of examining algorithmic issues, performance of large population, spectral variability robustness technique and comparisons of other speaker modeling technique. The experimental findings gave an accuracy rate of 96.8% using 5 seconds clean speech utterances and 80.8% accuracy for 15 seconds telephone speech utterance. The authors have also commented that the proposed Gaussian Mixture speaker model is shown to outperform other speaker modeling techniques on a similar task consisting of 16 speakers with telephone speech utterances.

In Senoussaoui, Kenny, Dehak and Dumouchel (2010), the authors have proposed a new architecture for text independent speaker verification system that was trained with limited amount of data that are application specific and was supplemented with a sufficient amount of training data that were taken from some other context. The authors have mentioned that the architecture is based on the extraction of i-vector parameters from the low dimensional total variability space proposed by Dehak. The authors aimed at extending Dehak's work to speaker recognition on sparse microphone data. The main challenge, as mentioned by the authors, is to overcome the condition of insufficient application specific data to accurately estimate the total variability covariance matrix. They have proposed a method based on the Joint factor Analysis (JFA) to estimate sparse microphone Eigen channels with sufficient telephone Eigen channel data. For the classification purpose, they have used the Support Vector Machines (SVMs) and cosine distance based Cosine Distance Scoring (CDS) classifier. They have concluded saying that the proposed system gives best performance when the system is fused with the state-of-the-art JFA.

Stolcke (2005) in his work have mentioned the use of adaptation transforms as features for speaker recognition system. This system normalizes the choice of spoken words in text-independent speaker verification. They have computed affine transforms for the Gaussian means of the acoustic models used in a recognizer using Maximum Likelihood Linear Regression (MLLR). The high dimensional vectors that are formed by the transform coefficients are then modeled as features for the speakers using Support

Vector Machines (SVMs). The authors have concluded that the resulting speaker verification system is competitive and sometimes significantly more accurate than state-of-the-art cepstral GMM and SVM system.

Table 1 provides the summary of the various works found in the literature that have dealt with the identification, verification and recognition of Speakers using i-vectors and various other speech related features.

Table 1. Summary of the works depicting the use of various features for Speaker recognition tasks

Sl. No.	Authors	Feature Parameters	Task Performed	References
1	McLaren, Leeuwen	i-vector	Speaker recognition	(McLaren and Leeuwen, 2011)
2	Dehak, Dehak, Reynolds, Torres-Carrasquillo	i-vectors and total variability space	Language identiffication	(Dehak, et. al., 2011)
3	Reynolds	MFCC	Speaker identification and verification	(Reynolds, 1995)
4	Kinnunen, Li	Short-term spectral features, prosodic features, spectro-temporal features, voice source features.	Speaker recognition	(Kinnunen and Li, 2010)
5	Kua, Epps, Ambikairajah	i-vector	Speaker verification	(Kua, Epps, and Ambikairajah, 2013)
6	Kanagasundaram, Dean, Sridharan, Gonzalez-Dominguez, Gonzalez-Rodriguez, Ramos,	i-vector	Speaker Verification	(Kanagasundaram, et. al., 2014)
7	Kanagasundaram, Dean, Sridharan, McLaren, Vogt	i-vector	Speaker Verification	(Kanagasundaram, et. al., 2014)
8	Tiwari	MFCC	Speaker identification	(Tiwari, 2010),
9	Sonmez, Heck, Weintraub, Shriberg	Pitch statistics	Speaker verification	(Sonmez, Heck, Weintraub and Shriberg, 1997)
10	Kanagasundaram, Vogt, Dean, Sridharan	HTPLDA, i-vector	Speaker verification	(Kanagasundaram, Vogt, Dean and Sridharan, 2012)
11	Revathi, Ganapathy, Venkataramani	Mel Frequency Linear Predictive Cepstrum	Speaker recognition	(Revathi, Ganapathy and Venkataramani, 2009),
12	Nijhawan, Soni	MFCC	Speaker recognition	(Nijhawan and Soni, 2014),
13	Jeng, Lee, Tsao, Wang	Clustering based i-vector	Speaker verification	(Jeng, Lee, Tsao and Wang, 2014)
14	Kanagasundaram, Vogt, Dean, Sridharan, Mason	i-vector	Speaker verification	(*Kanagasundaram, et. al., 2011*),
15	Rajan, Kinnunen, Hautamaki	i-vector	Speaker recognition	(*Rajan, Kinnunen and Hautamaki, 2013*),
16	Bharti, Bansal	MFCC	Speaker recognition	(Bharti and Bansal, 2015).
17	Reynolds, Quatieri, Dunn	GMM-UBM	Speaker verification	(Reynolds, Quatieri and Dunn, 2000),
18	Reynolds, Rose	Maximum likelihood parameters	Speaker identification	(Reynolds and Rose, 1995)
19	Senoussaoui, Kenny, Dehak, Dumouchel	i-vector	Speaker verification	(Senoussaoui, Kenny, Dehak and Dumouchel, 2010)
20	Stolcke	Maximun Likelihood Linear Regression	Speaker verification	(Stolcke, 2005),

SYSTEM MODEL AND SPEECH DATABASE

For any speech or speaker related task, the foremost step is the collection of the database. The raw speech database used for our experimental findings is collected from the native speakers of the state of Assam. The speech signal consists of a fixed length long Assamese sentence. We have considered 15 speakers of both male and female gender for collecting the samples for our proposed text-dependent speaker recognition model. In our work, we have concentrated on use of i-vectors as our feature parameters which is calculated from the total variability subspace. As previously mentioned, the calculation of Total Variability Matrix (TVM) comprises of both the speaker and channel variability, therefore the recorded samples consist of four channels which comprises of telephonic recording and high quality normal recordings and the results are calculated considering both the normal and telephonic recordings. The speech samples collected are preprocessed by using the silence removal algorithm before any further processing. Table 2 provides an overview of the speech database used for our work.

For our proposed work, the feature vectors used are the i-vector parameters. An audio signal is first preprocessed to find the location of the voiced part and then the acoustic features are extracted that conveys the speaker information. The first step in the formation of the i-vectors is the extraction of the MFCC features from the sample utterance considering a frame of 20 ms. This feature vector is then represented by their distribution related to a Universal Background Model (UBM) which is a GMM distribution that characterizes the speaker-independent speech features. The parameters of the distribution are then transformed into i-vectors using a TVM that comprises of the speaker and channel variability. The database for the work consists of a 17-word sentence repeated by fifteen speakers (5 females and 10 males) recorded with normal and telephonic modes of speaking. The sentence is recorded while it is spoken continuously by the speaker in normal environment. The same is repeated with telephonic recording. The speakers include male and female volunteers with all showing distinct native orientation. In the present work, the emotion aspect is not considered. The experiments are performed only for validating the proposed text-dependent approach.

The work can be summarized by the following two phase of formulating the classifier:

1.   Steps of Implementation and Training the Multi Layer Feed Forward Neural Network (MLFNN):

Recording of the sample speech from the native speakers of Assam. The native Assamese speakers are asked to utter a fixed length long Assamese sentence in a low noise environment which is used as the

Table 2. Overview of the database used

Parameters	Remarks
Language used	Assamese
No. of speakers	15 (10 males, 5 females)
Speaker's age	22-35 years
Sentence length	17 words
No. of recordings	120 (15 speakers x 4 sessions x 2 utterances)
Types of recording	Normal and telephonic

samples for the text-dependent speaker recognition model. With the help of a pre-processing and silence removal algorithm, the voiced part of the sample utterances is found out thereafter.

From the preprocessed utterances, MFCC features are extracted from all the speech utterances with a 20 ms frame. The following steps are involved in the extraction of MFCC features. First the pre-emphasis is done on the speech signal by silence removal. The speech signal is then segmented into 20 ms frame with 50% overlapping between two adjacent frames. Each frame is then multiplied with a Hamming window of size same as that of the frame. FFT of 512 point is taken on the windowed signal. The first 256 values are considered and the power spectrum is calculated by squaring each of the values. the result is then filtered with Mel filter bank of size 22 and logarithm of the value is calculated. The DCT of these 22 values are computed and the first 13 values are considered which are the required MFCC coefficients for each frame.

For the extraction of i-vector from a particular speech utterance, computation of Universal Background Model (UBM) is carried out using all the MFCC vectors extracted from the database. The UBM is a GMM of 256 Gaussian components. After the UBM computation the following steps are performed to extract the i-vectors.

Computation of i-vectors: Computation of i-vector initially consists of computation of the 0th and 1st order Baum-Welch statistics using the UBM and the MFCC feature of that speech utterance. Computation of the Total variability matrix from all the speech samples, considering all the speaker and channel variations. Calculation of the i-vector from the Total variability subspace.

Linear Discriminant Analysis (LDA) is performed on the i-vectors to project them on a 14-dimensional space.

Training the MLFNN with the feature vectors of the training samples and finally storing the trained network.

2.   Steps for Testing Phase:

Preprocessing of the test samples is carried out using a silence removal algorithm to find out the audio part of the speech signal.

Extraction of the MFCC features with a 20 ms frame from the preprocessed sample is carried out.

Extraction of i-vectors: Computation of the 0th and 1st order Baum-Welch statistics using the already computed UBM. Computation of the i-vector from the already calculated Total variability matrix.

LDA on the i-vectors to project them on the 14-dimensional space.

Testing the samples with the stored network for getting the recognition accuracy of the text-dependent speaker recognition model.

The proposed system model is shown in the Figure 10.

The working of the model is dependent on training the classifier, validating and subsequently testing it.

EXPERIMENTAL RESULTS AND DISCUSSIONS

For a particular case,

Figure 10. a) Training phase of our system model. b) Testing phase of our system model

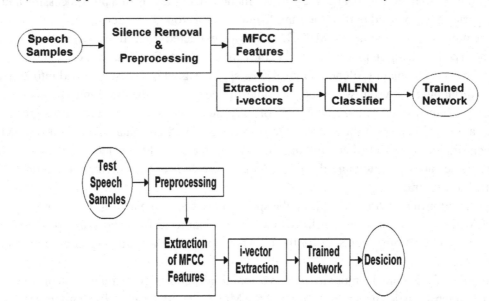

The sentence recorded for an individual speaker is of duration 8 seconds i.e. 8000 milliseconds. Sampling rate is taken to be 8 KHz which is 8000 samples/sec. As mentioned earlier, the first step in the formation of i-vectors is the creation of MFCC feature vector from the sample utterance considering 20 ms frame.

In 1 ms, we have 8 samples, therefore in 20 ms we have 8 x 20 samples i.e. 160 samples per frame. The length of the MFCC feature vector considered for our purpose is 13 per frame.

The time required for pre-processing using silence removal algorithm is 1.39 seconds. We have also calculated the accuracy of silence removal of the speech sample. For calculating the accuracy we have first found out the error percentage for silence removal by computing the size of the signals after manually removing the silence part with the help of speech analysis software as well as automatically removing the silence part by silence removal algorithm. Here, for a particular case,

The size of the original signal is 87851 samples. The size of the signal after manually removing the silence part using speech analysis software is 53471 samples. The size of the speech sample after removing the silence part automatically = 57920 samples.

Therefore, the formula for calculating the error percent is given by,

$$\left|\frac{manual-automatic}{manual}\right| X100\% \tag{3}$$

Therefore, from equation (3) we get,

$$\left|\frac{53471-57920}{53471}\right| X100\% = 8.32\%$$

Table 3. Summary of the various parameters of the speech sample for a particular case

Duration of the sentence	8000 ms
Samples per 20ms frame	160
Length of MFCC vector	13 per frame
Time taken for MFCC extraction for a given case	1.75 sec
Size of a particular sample	87851 samples
Accuracy of silence removal	91.68%

$$Accuracy = (100 - 8.32)\% = 91.68\%$$

This is achieved during silence removal processing.

Table 3 provides a summary of the considerations about the size of speech sample, MFCC feature length and various other parameters related to a particular case.

The experimental findings of our proposed text-dependent speaker recognition system involve trained system. We have used MLFNN classifier for the recognition purpose because of its robustness to noise and non-linear characteristics. The proposed model gives a maximum recognition rate of 98.8% with a Total Variability matrix of dimension 50 and 256 Gaussian Mixture components and 30.84 seconds computational time. The MLFNN is trained using the Scaled Conjugate Gradient (SCG) training algorithm and low dimensional i-vector. The MLFNN consist of 3 hidden layers, one input layer and one output layer. The input layer consists of 14 neurons, the 3 hidden layers consists of 100, 100 and 50 neurons respectively and the output layer consists of 15 neurons which is equal to the number of speakers. The parameters of the MLFNN are listed in Table 4.

For training the system we have divided the Assamese speaker database in to two parts. Here, 70% of the database is used for training the classifier and the remaining 30% is used for testing purpose.

In Table 5 the recognition rate and the training time of the proposed system with respect to the corresponding TVM dimension is presented.

From Table 5 considering the TVM dimension of 50 we get a recognition rate of 98.8% with a computational time of 30.84 seconds. The corresponding recognition rate and computational time considering TVM dimension of 120 is 63.8% and 38.08 seconds respectively.

Therefore, with $\frac{98.8-63.8}{98.8} X100\%$ i.e. 35.42% percentage gain in recognition rate, there is a $\frac{30.84-38.08}{38.08} X100\%$ i.e. 19.01% fall in computational time during training.

Table 6 shows the variation of recognition rate and training time with Gaussian mixture components for total variability dimension 50.

Table 4. Specifications of MLFNN

Hidden layers	3 (tansig, tansig, tansig)
Maximum Epochs	8000
Goal	.005
Training Algorithm	Scaled Conjugate Gradient

Table 5. The variation of training time and recognition rate with total variability space dimension for 256 Gaussian Mixture components

Total Variability Matrix Dimension	Recognition Rate	Training Time (Seconds)
20	93.5%	29.77
40	97.3%	29.34
50	98.8%	30.84
60	93.5%	32.28
80	86.8%	31.56
100	72.5%	35.07
120	63.8%	38.08

Table 6. The variation of recognition rate and training time with Gaussian mixture components for total variability dimension 50

No. of GM components	Recognition Rate	Training Time (Seconds)
8	87.5%	5.56
16	92.5%	6.27
32	92.5%	7.52
64	93.5%	11.68
128	96.2%	16.25
256	98.8%	29.28

Table 6 shows that the recognition rate is maximum for 256 GM components with a training time of 29.28 seconds.

The variation of recognition rate with change in number of GM components is shown in Figure 11.

From the Figure 11, it can be concluded that the recognition rate increases with the increasing GM components and a maximum recognition rate of 98.8% is obtained for 256 GM components.

In Figure 12 the variation of the recognition rate with respect to the increasing Total Variability matrix dimension is shown. The highest recognition rate is obtained with Total Variability matrix dimension of 50.

Figure 11. GMM components Vs Recognition rate

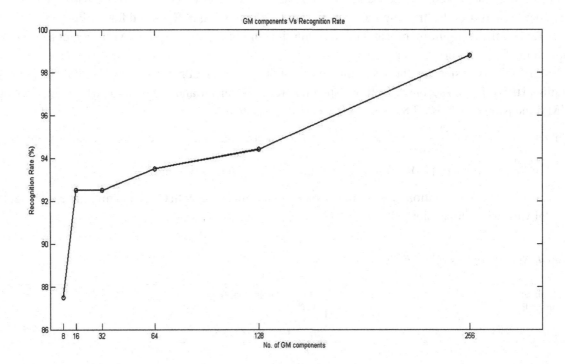

Figure 12. Total Variability Dimension Vs Recognition rate

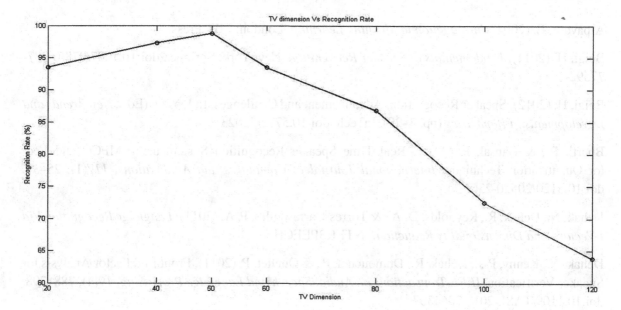

A work (Bharti & Bansal, 2015), uses MFCC and Vector quantization for developing automatic speaker recognition system under normal environmental conditions at 20 dB SNR and achieved a success rate of 91%. Compared to that, our proposed approach achieves a success rate between 87% to 98% using i-vector and MLFNN in case of telephonic conversation involving Assamese speech and the advantage is obvious.

CONCLUSION

In this chapter, we have described the design of a text-dependent speaker recognition model using Assamese speech. The work considers speakers with native orientation and the features used for our work is based on the i-vector framework which is considered to be one of the state-of-the-art techniques. We have used MLFNN which is non-linear and robust to noise. In this work, we have used Assamese normal and telephonic speech. The linguistic diversity and phonetic richness of Assamese language is best captured by the i-vector MLFNN combination. From the experimental results we have found that the recognition rate of the system is very high even though the speaker database contains session variations among the speakers. we have also seen that the dimension of the Total variability matrix is an important parameter for the high performance rate of the system. We have also seen that the number of Gaussian components in UBM model also has significant impact on the recognition rate of the system. The proposed system gives a satisfactory recognition rate of 98.8% with a computational time of 30.84 seconds with Total variability matrix dimension of 50 and Gaussian components of 256, despite of certain limitations. One of the limitations is the limited dataset which needs to be increased further. Despite of the limitations, the performance accuracy and the computational time together makes the proposed system a suitable one for speaker recognition for a rich language like Assamese.

REFERENCES

Alpaydin, E. (2004). *Introduction to Machine Learning*. London: MIT Press.

Beigi, H. (2011). *Fundamentals of Speaker Recognition*. New York: Springer. doi:10.1007/978-0-387-77592-0

Beigi, H. (2012). Speaker Recognition: Advancement and Challenges. In J. Yang (Ed.), *New Trends and Developments in Biometrics* (pp. 3–29). InTech. doi:10.5772/52023

Bharti, R., & Bansal, P. (2015). Real Time Speaker Recognition System using MFCC and Vector Quantization Technique. *International Journal of Computers and Applications*, *117*(1), 25–31. doi:10.5120/20520-2361

Dehak, N., Dehak, R., Reynolds, D. A., & Torres-Carrasquillo, P. A. (2011). *Language Recognition Via I-Vectors And Dimensionality Reduction*. INTERSPEECH.

Dehak, N., Kenny, P. J., Dehak, R., Dumouchel, P., & Ouellet, P. (2011). Front End Factor Analysis for Speaker Verification. *IEEE Transactions on Audio. Speech and Language Processing*, *19*(4), 788–798. doi:10.1109/TASL.2010.2064307

Furui, S. (1997). Recent Advances in Speaker Recognition. In *Proceedings of first International Conference on Audio and Video based Biometric Person Authentication*, *1206*, 235-252. doi:10.1007/BFb0016001

Greenberg, C. S., et al. (2014). The NIST 2014 Speaker Recognition i-vector Machine Learning Challenge. *Odyssey- The Speaker and Language Recognition Workshop*, 224-230.

Jeng, S., Lee, H., Tsao, Y., & Wang, H. (2014). Clustering-based i-vector formulation for speaker recognition.*Proceedings of INTERSPEECH*, 1101-1105.

Kanagasundaram, A., Dean, D., Sridharan, S., Gonzalez-Dominguez, J., Gonzalez-Rodriguez, J., & Ramos, D. (2014). Improving Short Utterance i-vector Speaker Verification using Utterance Variance Modeling and Compensation Techniques. *Speech Communication*, *59*, 69–82. doi:10.1016/j.specom.2014.01.004

Kanagasundaram, A., Dean, D., Sridharan, S., McLaren, M., & Vogt, R. (2014). I-vector Based Speaker Recognition using Advanced Channel Compensation Techniques.*Speech Communication*,*28*(1), 121–140.

Kanagasundaram, A., Vogt, R., Dean, D., & Sridharan, S. (2012). PLDA Based Speaker Recognition on Short Utterances. Odyssey: The Speaker and Language Recognition Workshop.

Kanagasundaram, A., Vogt, R., Dean, D., Sridharan, S., & Mason, M. (2011). i-vector Based Speaker Recognition on Short Utterances.*Proceedings of the 12th Annual Conference of the International Speech Communication Association (ISCA)*, 2341-2344.

Kinnunen, T., & Li, H. (2010). An Overview of Text-independent Speaker Recognition: From Features to Super-vectors. *Speech Communication*, *52*(1), 12–40. doi:10.1016/j.specom.2009.08.009

Kua, J. M. K., Epps, J., & Ambikairajah, E. (2013). i-vector with Sparse Representation Classification for Speaker Verification. *Speech Communication*, *55*(5), 707–720. doi:10.1016/j.specom.2013.01.005

McLaren, M., & Leeuwen, D. V. (2011). Source Normalized and Weighted LDA for Robust Speaker Recognition using i-vector. In *Proceedings of IEEE International Conference on Acoustics, Speech and Signal Processing (ICASSP)* (pp.5456-5459). Prague: IEEE.

Mitchell, T. (1997). *Machine Learning*. Maidenhead, UK: McGraw Hill.

Nautsch, A. (2014). *Speaker Verification using i-vector*. Hochschule Darmstadt, Germany: University of Applied Science.

Nijhawan, G., & Soni, M. K. (2014). Speaker Recognition using MFCC and Vector Quantization. *International Journal on Recent Trends in Engineering and Technology*, *11*(1), 211–218.

Rajan, P., Kinnunen, T., & Hautamaki, V. (2013). *Effect of Multicondition Training on i-vector PLDA Configurations for Speaker Recognition*. INTERSPEECH.

Rajsekhar, A. G. (2008). *Real Time Speaker Recognition using MFCC and VQ*. Rourkela, India: National Institute of Technology.

Revathi, A., Ganapathy, R., & Venkataramani, Y. (2009). Text Independent Speaker Recognition and Speaker Independent Speech Recognition using Iterative Clustering Approach. *International Journal of Computer Science and Information Technology*, *1*(2), 31–42.

Reynolds, D. A. (1995). Speaker Identification and Verification using Gaussian Mixture Speaker Models. *Speech Communication*, *17*(1-2), 91–108. doi:10.1016/0167-6393(95)00009-D

Reynolds, D. A. (2002). An Overview of Automatic Speaker Recognition Technology. In *Proceedings of IEEE International Conference on Acoustics, Speech and Signal Processing (ICASSP)* (pp.4072-4075). Orlando, FL: IEEE. doi:10.1109/ICASSP.2002.5745552

Reynolds, D. A., Quatieri, T. F., & Dunn, R. B. (2000). Speaker Verification Using Adapted Gaussian Mixture Models. *Digital Signal Processing*, *10*(1-3), 19–41. doi:10.1006/dspr.1999.0361

Reynolds, D. A., & Rose, R. C. (1995). Robust Text-Independent Speaker Identification using Gaussian Mixture Speaker Models. *IEEE Transactions on Speech and Audio Processing*, *3*(1), 72–83. doi:10.1109/89.365379

Sadjadi, S. O., Slaney, M., & Heck, L. (2013). *MSR Identity Toolbox v1. 0: a MATLAB Toolbox for Speaker-Recognition Research*. Speech and Language Processing Technical Committee Newsletter.

Senoussaoui, M., Kenny, P., Dehak, N., & Dumouchel, P. (2010). *An i-vector Extractor suitable for Speaker Recognition with both Microphone and Telephone Speech*. Odessey.

Sharma, M., & Sarma, K. K. (2015). Dialectal Assamese Vowel Speech Detection using acoustic Phonetic Features, KNN and RNN. In *Proceedings of 2nd International Conference on Signal Processing and Integrated Networks (SPIN)* (pp.674-678). New Delhi, India: SPIN. doi:10.1109/SPIN.2015.7095270

Sharma, M., & Sarma, K. K. (2015). Soft-Computational Techniques and Spectro-Temporal Features for Telephonic Speech Recognition: an overview and review of current state of the art. In S. Bhattacharyya, P. Banerjee, D. Majumdar, & P. Dutta (Eds.), Handbook of Research on Advanced Hybrid Intelligent Techniques and Applications (pp. 161–189). Academic Press.

Sharma, M., Sarma, M., & Sarma, K. K. (2013). Recurrent Neural Network Based Approach to Recognize Assamese Vowels using Experimentally Derived Acoustic Phonetic Features. In *Proceedings of IEEE 1st International Conference on Emerging Trends and Applications in Computer Science (ICETACS)* (pp.140-143). Shillong, India: IEEE. doi:10.1109/ICETACS.2013.6691411

Shrawankar, U., & Thakare, V. (2013). *Techniques for Feature Extraction in Speech Recognition System: A Comparative Study*. CoRR, abs/1305.1145.

Sonmez, M. K., Heck, L., Weintraub, M., & Shriberg, E. (1997). A Lognormal Tied Mixture Model of Pitch for Prosody-Based Speaker Recognition. *Proceedings of Eurospeech*, *3*, 1391–1394.

Stolcke, A., Ferrer, L., Kajarekar, S., Shriberg, E., & Venkataraman, A. (2005). MLLR Transforms as Features in Speaker Recognition. In *Proceedings of the 9th European Conference on Speech Communication and Technology*, *4*, 2424-2427.

Sukor, A. S. (2012). Speaker Identification System using MFCC procedure and Noise Reduction method. University Tun Hussein Onn, Malaysia.

Svozil, D., Kvasnicka, V., & Pospichal, J. (1997). Introduction to Multi Layer Feed Forward Neural Network. *Chemo-Metrics and Intelligent Laboratory Systems, 39*(1), 43-62.

Tiwari, V. (2010). MFCC and its applications in Speaker Recognition. *International Journal of Emerging Technologies*, *1*(1), 19–22.

Tokheim, A. E. H. (2012). i-vector Based Language Recognition. Norwegian University of Science and Technology.

Chapter 9
A New SVM Method for Recognizing Polarity of Sentiments in Twitter

Sanjiban Sekhar Roy
VIT University, India

Rohan Kumar
VIT University, India

Marenglen Biba
University of New York – Tirana, Albania

Rahul Kumar
VIT University, India

Pijush Samui
NIT Patna, India

ABSTRACT

Online social networking platforms, such as Weblogs, micro blogs, and social networks are intensively being utilized daily to express individual's thinking. This permits scientists to collect huge amounts of data and extract significant knowledge regarding the sentiments of a large number of people at a scale that was essentially impractical a couple of years back. Therefore, these days, sentiment analysis has the potential to learn sentiments towards persons, object and occasions. Twitter has increasingly become a significant social networking platform where people post messages of up to 140 characters known as 'Tweets'. Tweets have become the preferred medium for the marketing sector as users can instantly indicate customer success or indicate public relations disaster far more quickly than a web page or traditional media does. In this paper, we have analyzed twitter data and have predicted positive and negative tweets with high accuracy rate using support vector machine (SVM).

INTRODUCTION

There has been a colossal surge in user generated opinion-rich data since the Web 2.0 era. Millions of people post opinions on all aspects of life every day. Social networks such as Facebook, LinkedIn and the microblogging website Twitters are the mainstays of this massive, continuous stream of user-generated content on a wide range of topics. Easy availability of such data via APIs or publicly available data

DOI: 10.4018/978-1-5225-2128-0.ch009

sets has led to new opportunities in the field of Sentiment Analysis and Opinion Mining. Sentiment Analysis is the process of computationally identifying and extracting opinions in natural language texts. Furthermore, known as Opinion Mining, Sentiment analysis uses Natural Language Processing and text data mining (text analysis) to understand opinions expressed in the text. It is not only applied to social media data but also to product reviews, news articles and other public opinion texts. Given the direct applicability to real-world problems such as understanding customer opinion, financial prediction and disaster management, it is imperative that Sentiment Analysis prevails as one of the most researched topics today. There are three different classification levels in sentiment analysis: document level, sentence level and aspect level. The character limitation on Twitter posts may suggest sentence-level classification as the most suited classification; however, given the informal nature of tweets, we expect the sentiment to be compact and explicit. Hence, our paper focuses on the document-level approach to Sentiment Analysis. Twitter is considered one of the best sources of opinion-rich data because a large number of people share and discuss their thoughts and opinions on the platform. That is to say, we focus on Tweets from Twitter in this paper. Polarity classification is the fundamental task in Sentiment Analysis. It can be achieved through multiple approaches. Lexicon-based methods decide the polarity of the document based on polarities of individual words and phrases in the document. Machine Learning based methods aim at building classifiers to resolve polarity and identify which category a document belongs to. We focus on the Machine Learning based approach. Over the years, a large amount of wide-reaching research has been carried out in the area of sentiment classification on large texts as explained by Pang and Lee(2008). There has been research on effects of machine learning techniques such as Naive Bayes, Maximum Entropy, and Support Vector Machines in the specific domains. More recently, similar techniques have been applied to the Twitter microblogging platform as stated by Go and Huang(2009).Machine learning techniques like support vector machine is getting popularity in recent time as stated by Roy and Viswanatham(2016),Roy et al.(2015),Basu et al.(2015), Mittal et al.(2015) and Das et al(2014).Challenges include a wide range of topics to be classified, use of informal language on social media platforms, and the message length limitation of 140 characters per tweet imposed by Twitter. In our experiments, we transact a 2-way classification into positive and negative labels, unlike other approaches such as multi-label or multi-class classification as stated by Liu and Chen(2015). Support Vector Machines are a group of associated learning methods that aim to recognize inherent patterns in data as stated by Boser et al.(1992) . They are one of the several kernel-based techniques of machine learning algorithms. SVMs have been successfully applied to varied fields. SVMs can be used for both classification and regression analysis. However, given our focus on sentiment analysis on microblogging data, we limit our investigation to classification techniques.

In this paper, we use Support Vector Machines (with radial kernel) to categorise tweets based on their inherent sentiment, effectively. For the purposes of our research, we define sentiment to be "a personal positive or negative feeling" as stated by Go et al.(2009).

RELATED WORK

Sentiment Analysis began as classification of reviews into two categories: positive and negative as stated by Turney(2002). This was followed by additional work focusing on analysis of movie reviews by overall sentiment of everyone's document as explained by Pang and Lee(2008). However, these were both early approaches applied to large-sized documents. Sentiment Analysis yielded different results when applied

Figure 1. Flowchart of the complete process

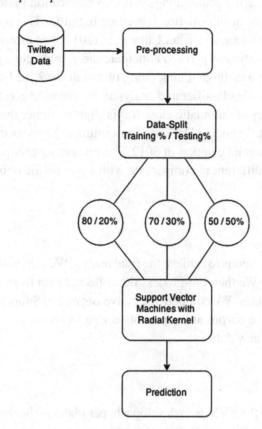

on a sentence-level and on the aspect-level as explained by Agarwal(2009). All these methods would not apply directly to the character-limited, informal nature of text from the Twitter platform. There are tweets on a greatly large range of topics, which is different from typical sentiment analysis data sets consisting of text from specific genres. Go and Huang.(2009) devised a method specifically catered to Tweet classification, which used distant learning.Experimental observations indicate unigrams as the best approach to Sentiment Analysis for movie reviews as stated by Pang et al.(2002) whereas additional research indicated that bigrams and trigrams produced better results for product reviews as explained by Dave et al.(2003)

Given the nature of Tweets, we applied the unigram approach to argue that the R programming platform is easily the best-suited platform for Sentiment Analysis of Tweets owing to the breath of topics in Twitter documents. They highlight the merits of the R programming language and how it simplifies the task of Sentiment Analysis by effectively mining opinion forms the Tweets of NHL hockey teams.

A multinomial logistic expression has been applied to Tweets in the form of Maximum Entropy Classifiers for feature selection as stated by Mansour et al.(2015). This model focuses on ensemble classification contrary to earlier approaches such as unigrams or bigrams to achieve similar classification accuracy as the state-of-the-art NRC system Mohammad et al.(2013) from the SemEval competition. Tang (2015) concludes that feature engineering using hand-coded features don't capture the semantics of texts. He proposes semantic representation of documents into specific constitutes: word representation, sentence structure, sentence composition and document composition. Sarlam et al. (2014) reports on the design of Sentiment Analysis using prototyping on a web application system. Zaman et al.(2010) has proposed a predictive model for of information spreading in twitter.This model finds the future tweets by adopting a probabilistic collaborative filter.Choy et al.(2011) has discussed about using weighting techniques related to online sentiment parts to anticipate the vote percentage for any person. Mohammad et al.(2015) has proposed a method of annotating tweets in the 2012 US presidencial election.This work also developed an automatic classifier and analysed the tweets in great detail.The disadvantage of their model is that the accuracy of automatic classifier is slightly higher than 55%. Many issues related with sentiment analysis are still existing.Data used in sentiment analysis can be very poor I quality.It happens during the US presidential election in 2012.The supporting group of Obama and Roomney in social media was completely different in comparison with a real public opinion.

PROPOSED METHOD

We perform a sequence of operations to achieve the final results. We start with the collection of data from MPQA Subjectivity Lexicon. We then pre-process the collected data from the Subjectivity Lexicon by removal of unnecessary attributes. We compare the Naive Bayes and Support Vector Machines methods for analysis of the data from the corpus and report observations on the same. The model is then trained and used for classification of new data.

Basic Sketch of SVM

The very motive behind using the SVM is to develop a hyper plane as the decision surface in such a way, so that the margin of separation between the positive and negative samples is maximized in an appropriate feature space as stated by Cortes and Vapnik(1995). As most of the pattern recognition problems to be solved in practice are of nonlinear nature, kernel functions are employed to perform the nonlinear mapping, which computes the inner product matrix, the so-called kernel matrix, on pairs of samples in the transformed feature space commonly called as the Z space as stated by Meyer et al.(2003).SVM is used for many practical problems which are related to uncertainty.It usually adopted for text and image classification.SVM can also be used for hand-written recognition and biological science.

Linear SVM

The training set of vectors can be linearly separated into two classes as stated by Schölkopf, et al.(1998), as (x_i, y_i), where, x_i refers to R^n, and the values of y_i can vary between {-1,+1}, where, $i= 1,...,n$
(1)

Here, x_i represents real number and has n-dimension and y_i is label of the class x_i. The hyper plane separation can be done with a vector **w** which is orthogonal by nature and b represents the *bias* for satisfying the equation

$$\mathbf{w}.\mathbf{x} + b = 0 \qquad (2)$$

The problem of minimization is given as

Minimize $\frac{1}{2}(\mathbf{w}.\mathbf{w})$ (3)

Which subject to

$y_i(\mathbf{w}.\mathbf{x}_i + b) \geq 1$ for $i = 1,2,..,n$ (4)

Now with the introduction of the slack variable $\xi_i \geq 0$, $i = 1,2,\ldots,n$ equation(4) takes the form as,

$y_i(\mathbf{w}.\mathbf{x}_i + b) \geq 1 - \xi_i$, $i = 1,2,\ldots,n.$ (5)

The minimization problem takes the form as,

Minimize $\frac{1}{2}(\mathbf{w}.\mathbf{w}) + C\sum_{i=0}^{n}\xi_i$ (6)

C is represented as a constant quantity and the newly formed optimization problem can be explained from the Lagrange function, given as,

$L(\mathbf{w},b,\xi,\alpha,\beta) = \frac{1}{2}(\mathbf{w}.\mathbf{w}) + C\sum_{i=0}^{n}\xi_i - \sum_{i=0}^{n}\alpha_i\left[y_i(\mathbf{w}.\mathbf{x}_i + b) - 1 + \xi_i\right] - \sum_{i=0}^{n}\beta_i\xi_i$ (7)

Non-Linear SVM

When linear separability is not possible, the input vector is mapped into a larger dimensional space. The definition of non-linearity is given as,

$\phi : X \ Z$ (8)

where Z is the higher dimensional space.

This transformation from X to Z space can be done using a kernel function, i.e.

$\mathbf{z}.\mathbf{z}' = K(\mathbf{x},\mathbf{x}')$ (14)

As a result, the equation becomes

Maximize $\sum_{i=0}^{n}\alpha_i - \frac{1}{2}\left(\sum_{i=0}^{n}y_iy_j\alpha_i\alpha_jK(\mathbf{x}_i,\mathbf{x}_j)\right)$ (9)

The kernel function can be any symmetric function satisfying the Mercer's condition. The most commonly used kernels are the RBF kernel, polynomial kernel, and the sigmoid kernel.

RBF Kernel Based SVM

For our work, we have adopted Radial Base Function (RBF) kernel for SVM,

$$K\left(\mathbf{x}, \mathbf{x}'\right) = \exp\left(-\gamma\mathbf{x} - \mathbf{x}'^2\right) \tag{10}$$

where γ, d and r are the kernel parameters.

In case, of Gaussian radial basis function the related features space is called Hilbert Space and these space infinite dimensions. Classifiers with maximum margin are very much regularized, and in the past it was believed that infinite dimension don't ruin the outcomes. On the other hand, it has been demonstrated that higher measurements do build the generalization error, in spite of the fact that the quantity is limited.

EXPERIMENTS AND OBSERVATIONS

Data Selection

We focus on messages obtained from Twitter for prototyping, but the system can be extended to achieve similar results using other sources as well. We used text corpus that has been downloaded from the website (https://github.com/maxluk/tweet-sentiment/blob/master/tweet-sentiment/StormTopology/data/dictionary.tsv).In the data set, percentage sharing of strong and weak subjects is 70% and 30% .Also, emotions of the tweets in terms of percentage sharing in the data set are 57% and 43%.

Experimental Result and Analysis

The data are divided into two sets; the first one is used for training the classifier and the other is used for testing. We have used different combinations of percentages for training and test data: 80/20, 30/70 and 50/50%. We divide the data into two attributes positive and negative. Prediction on test cases gives the accuracy. We have compared our result to n Naive Bayes and SVM classifiers with linear kernel. Upon applied SVM with radial basis kernel, on all the test sets(70%-30%,80%-20%,50%-50%) the accuracies of classifying negative and positive tweet have not varied, rather it was same for all the three splits and that been shown in Figure 2.

Table 1. Percentage of different emotions of strong and weak subjects

Subjects	Emotions
Strongsubj: 70% Weak Subject:30%	negative:57% positive: 43%

Figure 2. Accuracy graph on test dataset

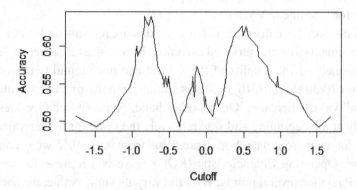

On dividing the dataset into multiple splits we get similar accuracy graphs for all the splits.
We make use of the following evaluation measures:

$$Accuracy = \frac{TP + TN}{P + N}$$

$$Error\ Rate = \frac{FP + FN}{P + N}$$

$$Precision = \frac{TP}{TP + FP}$$

$$Recall = \frac{TP}{P}$$

Here, TP is True Positive, TN is True Negative, FP is False Positive, P refers to positive samples, N refers to negative samples. In the below table,(Table 2) have shown that, when applied to training tweeter data, the value of the objective function keeps changing on the basis of varying sigma values. In the experiment we kept cost function c value as 10. The accuracy, precision, recall and error formulas are given above. Tweets are the favoured medium for the marketing tool .These tweets help getting customer success or indicate public relations disaster far more quickly than a webpage or traditional media does.

Table 2. Obtained Sigma Values, no of support vectors and objective functions

Sigma value	No of Support Vectors	Objective Function Value
0.1	608	-1555.096
0.5	611	-298.8966
1.5	612	-298.5381
2	612	-290.9768

This paper analyses twitter data and have predicted positive and negative tweets with high accuracy rate using this support vector machine (SVM).

Precision refers to the portion of documents retrieved that are relevant and useful. Recall refers to the portion of relevant documents that are retrieved currently. Both impart a degree of relevance. Precision-recall graphs are generated for the 3 splits of the dataset and have found that precision recall for the 80/20 (Figure 3(a)) and 70/30 (Figure 3(b)) splits is similar. Initially precision is high in both cases but it declines as the recall values increases. On the other hand, precision-recall values for the 50-50 split increase exponentially at the beginning and stay relatively the same for higher values of recall. We see in the 70/30 split that for an approximate drop in precision from 0.8 to 0.55 we get an approximate recall value of 0.35.Receiver Operating Characteristic (ROC) curve is a representation created by plotting recall (TP rate) and FP rate for several points. With the varying sigma value, number of support vectors and the objective function value also gets change. RBF kernel is a general kernel and is applied when no additional previous knowledge exists on data.

Comparison With Other Classifiers

In comparison with other classifiers SVM with RBF kernel has produced better accuracy in in terms of positive tweet and negative tweets when applied to test data set. Comparison of performance of SVM with RBF kernel has been done with SVM polynomial kernel and Naïve Bayes classifier; both the case proposed method has outperformed the two methods.

Figure 3. (a) Precision-Recall for 80% of train dataset. (b) Precision-Recall for 70% train dataset. (c) Precision-Recall for the 50% (train) split of the dataset (d) ROC Curve for the 70% of the train dataset

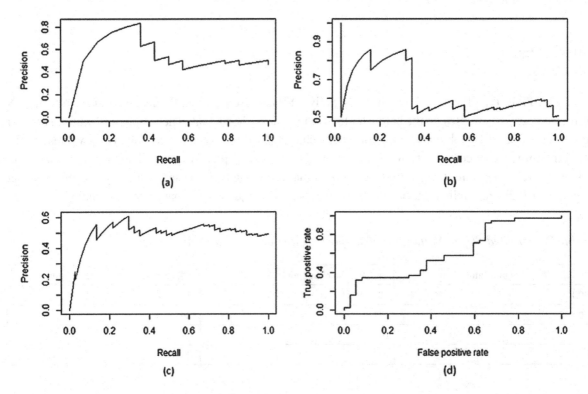

Table 3. Accuracy on test set

Radial Basis Kernel		Polynomial Kernel		Naive Bayes	
Positive	Negative	Positive	Negative	Positive	Negative
0.89805865	0.1019413	0.8787855	0.1212145	0.6512805	0.3487195
0.89806147	0.1019385	0.8789067	0.1210933	0.6512805	0.3487195
0.09907419	0.9009258	0.1290510	0.8709490	0.8400497	0.1599503
0.09913631	0.9008637	0.1290337	0.8709663	0.8400497	0.1599503
0.89804356	0.1019564	0.8789316	0.1210684	0.8400497	0.1599503
0.09911407	0.9008859	0.1291611	0.8708389	0.6512805	0.3487195

CONCLUSION

Twitter has increasingly become a significant social networking platform where people express themselves. It permits its clients to post messages of up to 140 characters; known as 'Tweets'. Tweets have become the preferred medium for the marketing as user the user instantly indicate customer success or indicate public relations disaster far more quickly than a web page or traditional media does. In this paper, we have analyzed twitter data and predicted positive and negative tweets with high-accuracy using machine learning methods based on support vector machines. We present several experimental settings with interesting insights on the prediction accuracy. In future, new methods of hybrid models can be developed to detect the polarity of the sentiments.

REFERENCES

Agarwal, A., Biadsy, F., & Mckeown, K. R. (2009). Contextual phrase-level polarity analysis using lexical affect scoring and syntactic n-grams. In *Proceedings of the 12th Conference of the European Chapter of the Association for Computational Linguistics*, (pp. 24-32). Association for Computational Linguistics. doi:10.3115/1609067.1609069

Basu, A., Roy, S. S., & Abraham, A. (2015). A Novel Diagnostic Approach Based on Support Vector Machine with Linear Kernel for Classifying the Erythemato-Squamous Disease. In *Computing Communication Control and Automation (ICCUBEA),2015International Conference on*, (pp. 343-347). IEEE. doi:10.1109/ICCUBEA.2015.72

Boser, B. E., Guyon, I. M., & Vapnik, V. N. (1992). A training algorithm for optimal margin classifiers. In *Proceedings of the fifth annual workshop on Computational learning theory*, (pp. 144-152). ACM. doi:10.1145/130385.130401

Choy, Cheong, Laik, & Shung. (2011). *A sentiment analysis of Singapore Presidential Election 2011 using Twitter data with census correction.* arXiv preprint arXiv:1108.5520

Cortes, C., & Vapnik, V. (1995, September). Support-vector networks. *Machine Learning, 20*(3), 273–297. doi:10.1007/BF00994018

Das, T. K., Acharjya, D. P., & Patra, M. R. 2014, January. Opinion mining about a product by analyzing public tweets in Twitter. In *Computer Communication and Informatics (ICCCI), 2014 International Conference on* (pp. 1-4). IEEE. doi:10.1109/ICCCI.2014.6921727

Dave, K., Lawrence, S., & Pennock, D. M. (2003). Mining the peanut gallery: Opinion extraction and semantic classification of product reviews. In *Proceedings of the 12th international conference on World Wide Web*, (pp. 519-528). ACM. doi:10.1145/775152.775226

Go, A., Bhayani, R., & Huang, L. (2009). *Twitter sentiment classification using distant supervision.* CS224N Project Report, Stanford. Retrieved from https://github.com/maxluk/tweet-sentiment/blob/master/tweet-sentiment/StormTopology/data/dictionary.tsv

Liu, S. M., & Chen, J.-H. (2015). A multi-label classification based approach for sentiment classification. *Expert Systems with Applications*, *42*(3), 1083–1093. doi:10.1016/j.eswa.2014.08.036

Meyer, D., Leisch, F., & Hornik, K. (2003, September). The support vector machine under test. *Neuro-computing*, *55*(1), 169–186. doi:10.1016/S0925-2312(03)00431-4

Mittal, D., Gaurav, D., & Roy, S. S. (2015, July). An effective hybridized classifier for breast cancer diagnosis. In *2015 IEEE International Conference on Advanced Intelligent Mechatronics (AIM)* (pp. 1026-1031). IEEE. doi:10.1109/AIM.2015.7222674

Mohammad, S. M., Kiritchenko, S., & Zhu, X. (2013). NRC-Canada: Building the state-of-the-art in sentiment analysis of tweets.*Proceedings of the Second Joint Conference on Lexical and Computational Semantics (SEMSTAR'13)*.

Mohammad, S. M., Zhu, X., Kiritchenko, S., & Martin, J. (2015). Sentiment, emotion, purpose, and style in electoral tweets.*Information Processing & Management*, *51*(4), 480–499. doi:10.1016/j.ipm.2014.09.003

Pang & Lee. (2008). Opinion mining and sentiment analysis. *Foundations and Trends in Information Retrieval, 2*(1-2), 1-135.

Pang, B., Lee, L., & Vaithyanathan, S. (2002). Thumbs up? Sentiment classification using machine learning techniques. In *Proceedings of the ACL-02 conference on Empirical methods in natural language processing (vol. 10,* pp. 79-86). Association for Computational Linguistics. doi:10.3115/1118693.1118704

Riham, M., Abdel Hady, M. F., Hosam, E., Amr, H., & Ashour, A. (2015). Feature Selection for Twitter Sentiment Analysis: An Experimental Study. In Computational Linguistics and Intelligent Text Processing, (pp. 92-103). Springer International Publishing.

Roy, S. S., Mittal, D., Basu, A., & Abraham, A. (2015). Stock market forecasting using LASSO linear regression model. In *Afro-European Conference for Industrial Advancement* (pp. 371–381). Springer International Publishing. doi:10.1007/978-3-319-13572-4_31

Roy & Viswanatham. (2016). Classifying Spam Emails Using Artificial Intelligent Techniques. *International Journal of Engineering Research in Africa, 22*.

Sarlan, A., Nadam, C., & Basri, S. (2014). Twitter sentiment analysis. In *Information Technology and Multi-media (ICIMU), 2014 International Conference on*, (pp. 212-216). IEEE. doi:10.1109/ICIMU.2014.7066632

Schölkopf, B., Simard, P., Vapnik, V., & Smola, A. J. (1997). Improving the accuracy and speed of support vector machines. *Advances in Neural Information Processing Systems, 9*, 375–381.

Tang, D. (2015). Sentiment-Specific Representation Learning for Document-Level Sentiment Analysis. In *Proceedings of the Eighth ACM International Conference on Web Search and Data Mining*, (pp. 447-452). ACM. doi:10.1145/2684822.2697035

Turney, P. D. (2002). Thumbs up or thumbs down?: semantic orientation applied to unsupervised classification of reviews. In *Proceedings of the 40th annual meeting on association for computational linguistics*, (pp. 417-424). Association for Computational Linguistics. doi:10.3115/1073083.1073153

Zaman, T. R., Herbrich, R., Van Gael, J., & Stern, D. (2010). Predicting information spreading in twitter. *Workshop on computational social science and the wisdom of crowds, nips, 104*(45), 17599-601.

Chapter 10

Automatic Generation Control of Multi–Area Interconnected Power Systems Using Hybrid Evolutionary Algorithm

Omveer Singh
Maharishi Markandeshwar University, India

ABSTRACT

A new technique of evaluating optimal gain settings for full state feedback controllers for automatic generation control (AGC) problem based on a hybrid evolutionary algorithms (EA) i.e. genetic algorithm (GA)-simulated annealing (SA) is proposed in this chapter. The hybrid EA algorithm can take dynamic curve performance as hard constraints which are precisely followed in the solutions. This is in contrast to the modern and single hybrid evolutionary technique where these constraints are treated as soft/hard constraints. This technique has been investigated on a number of case studies and gives satisfactory solutions. This technique is also compared with linear quadratic regulator (LQR) and GA based proportional integral (PI) controllers. This proves to be a good alternative for optimal controller's design. This technique can be easily enhanced to include more specifications viz. settling time, rise time, stability constraints, etc.

INTRODUCTION

Electric power systems are operating with huge number of interconnected control areas or regions exhibiting well organized set of generators. The transmission lines interconnecting these areas are named as tie-lines. Tie-lines facilitate prefixed energy transactions between areas and supply inter-area real power help in case of abnormal situations. AGC is a fundamental control function in power systems to regulate the real power production of generators within a defined area to maintain the system frequency and transmission line power within predetermined limits (Elgerd, 2011; Dhar, 1982).

DOI: 10.4018/978-1-5225-2128-0.ch010

AGC is being an important key idea in operation and control of power systems for providing adequate and reliable electrical energy. AGC controls the power systems with a hierarchy of multi-level control. The prime motive of AGC is to control the electric power production of generating plants, its regularly varying according user power requirement. AGC gives much more operational facility and interconnected functional movement within a control center.

A lot of work has been done for the designing of optimal AGC controllers of interconnected power systems (Bevrani & Hiyama, 2011; Ibraheem, Kumar, & Kothari, 2005). The most of the investigations with using PI control strategies have been carried out. A variety of control strategies have been deployed in the sketch of AGC regulators in order to get much greater passionate characteristic (Fujita, Shirai, & Yokoyama, 2002; Ibraheem, Kumar, & Ahmad, 2004; Nanda, Kothari & Satsangi, 1983; Ibraheem, Kumar, & Khatoon, 2005).

This chapter presents the modeling of multi-area interconnected reheat type power systems including (i) alternating current (AC) transmission line only (ii) parallel with AC/DC (direct current) transmission lines as an area interconnection between control regions. The EAs i.e. GA and SA based optimal AGC controllers are designed for power system models under investigation. Moreover, dynamic responses obtained with EA based AGC regulators to investigate the effect of using AC/DC links parallel for 0.01 per unit load perturbation. The effect of nominal parameter variation is also investigated.

EVOLUTIONARY ALGORITHMS

Evolutionary algorithm is a gradually enhancing research discipline taking soft computing techniques that are motivated by idea of natural evolution. The three prime mechanisms that move evolution forward are reproduction, mutation, and natural identification (i.e., survival of the fittest theory which is published in the Darwinian principle). In the biological practice, these mechanisms reflect life frameworks to a special environment over successive productions. EAs take these mechanisms of natural evolution in simple paths and breed progressively better results to a wide variety of complex optimization and design issues. An EA uses some mechanisms motivated by biological evolution: regeneration, mutation, recombination and selection. Further, EA categorizes in GA, genetic programming and evolutionary programming etc. However, GA technique is more probabilistic methodology than the other EA strategies.

J. H. Holland was the first to introduce GA (Holland, 1992) and its Pseudo-code is represented in the below.

GA procedure
begin
completion:=worse
Initialisation *{initial population}*
while (No completion) **do**
Evaluation
if (No termination condition) (*fitness functionperformedon chromosomes*)
then
Selection *{intermediatepopulation}*
Crossover & mutation operation (*nextpopulation*)
else

```
completion:=good
end
end
```

It manages a population of encoded parent solutions to a present optimization issue. A development of a simple GA initiates with the creation of a primary population which composed of randomly produced chromosomes. An assessment of chromosomes is activated to upcoming position. Every chromosome string is partitioned into substrings which are utilized as the inputs to a fitness objective. The substrings numbers relies on the difficulty to be resolved and is also unbounded. The fitness function amount achieved for a specified chromosome is presented to the fitness values achieve for other members of the population, and is fixed to calculated chromosome structure as its fitness value. In the upcoming state, an intervening occupant is created. This population is the outcome of a selection criterion which can be operated in many ways. One of them is a stochastic sampling with renewal.

In this methodology, the population is traced into a rank based selection strategy where each parent is represented by a position that proportionally refers to its fitness value. Parents of the intermediate population are identified by a clock work selection of the ranking. At the end, upcoming population is yielded using the crossover and mutation operations. Crossover is implemented to the randomly grouped chromosomes from the intermediate population with a probability (P_c). The chromosomes of each group (pair) are divided into two parts at the randomly created crossover point and recombined. In the process of mutation, all bits in substrings are changed with a mutation probability (P_m). At this point the GA backs to the exercise of evaluation (Goldberg, 1989; Deb, 2005; Lansberry, Wozniak, & Goldberg, 1992). All these paces are repeated number of times, and every iteration is known as a generation.

SIMULATED ANNEALING

Simulated annealing is a capable tool for resolving combinatorial optimization hassles (Milani & Mozafari, 2011). It has ability to get away from local optimum by adding a probability function in acquiring or refusing recent solutions. It is also a global search technique based on a local search method. The main cause for its global search capability is that it can choose ill-groomed result of the local search with specific probability. The annealing process requires adequate time so as to obtain the global optimal solution.

On the other hand, many EA workers agree that GAs normally cannot fight with more innovatory optimization algorithms. These algorithms are ruled towards a precise problem and exploit convinced qualities of it. This headed to the growth of many hybrid approaches; GA was joined with problem specific changing operators and intelligent encodings (Kirkpatrick, Gelatt, & Vecchi, 1983). In fact, GA based techniques for significant practical problems are relatively complicated and dependent on the problem.

Present time, hybrids of GA which are universally involved with these techniques i.e. SA, particle swarm optimization, ant colony optimization, bacteria foraging, fuzzy logic algorithm and artificial neural network etc. are used (Bevrani & Hiyama, 2011; Ibraheem, Kumar, & Kothari, 2005), and for many hard combinatorial optimization problems, such schemes are today's optimistic algorithms for evolving superior solutions to large problem occurrences.

GA joined with SA which pertains with SA to check the members of the new population created by the reproduction, crossover and mutation of GA. GASA can keep away from entrapment in local optimum to some area since the solution diversity becomes greater. However, with the temperature becoming towards the bottom, the probability of trapping in local optimum reduces.

The notable benefits of the hybrid GASA technique over the optimal method based on Matrix of Riccati (MR) expression (Yip & Pao, 1995) incorporated the following:

1. Straight forward presentation of constraints on transient characteristic provisions.
2. Care of constraints as hard constraints.
3. Potential to manage the non-linear and time changing systems.

In this chapter, the hybridization of SA with GA is utilized which is called as hybrid stochastic search algorithm. The sketch of optimal state feedback regulators for AGC in power systems is finalized using hybrid EA. A hybrid EA technique, taking into account a synergistic combination of GA and SA is applied to achieve the optimal state feedback gains of the controllers. A penalty function based strategy for satisfying the transient response specifications on systems frequency, generation and tie-lines is also used. These controllers are investigated with different type of control area interconnections and also with parametric variations. Moreover, these regulators are compared with MR expression based LQR and GA based regulators.

POWER SYSTEM MODELS UNDER INVSTIGATION

The AGC regulators are sketched and developed considering the successive few case studies based on the different power system models. These models are described by following case studies.

Case Study-1

Power systems model-1 is a multi-area interconnected power systems comprising of three power units with reheat thermal turbines and is interconnected through AC tie-line only. The transfer function model is shown in Figure 1.

Case Study-2

Power systems model-2 is a multi-area interconnected power systems comprising of three power units with reheat thermal turbines and is interconnected through parallel AC/DC lines. The transfer function model is given in Figure 2.

Case Study-3

In this section, both case studies are considered with variations of parameters in the power systems. Case studies investigations are operated with the variation of ±30% value of the tie-line parameters of the power systems (Ibraheem, Kumar, & Khatoon, 2005). The parametric variations considered for this case study are as follows:

Figure 1. Transfer function model of multi-area interconnected power systems consisting reheat turbines

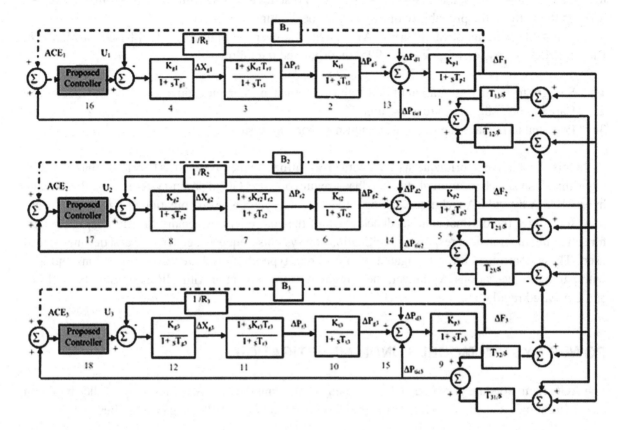

- Case Study-3 (a) Diversification in synchronizing coefficient (T_{ij}) of case study-1
- Case Study-3 (b) Diversification in DC link time constant (T_{dc}) of case study-2

The sketch of optimal AGC controllers for the power system model under investigation is carried out using hybrid EA technique. This technique is implemented using state space model of the power system.

OPTIMAL CONTROL STRATEGY

The realistic model of multi-area interconnected power systems has all the operating levels. This type of model can be easily operated and controlled by modern optimal control concept. One of the most basic needs of modern optimal control theory to the application of AGC regulator design is the growth of vital system model in state variable formation.

The exact presentation of power system dynamics involves a set of large number of non-linear differential equations. The optimal AGC regulator design with non-linear system models poses computationally difficult problems when dealing with higher order complex systems. To cope with this problem, the design engineers discover linearization of system equations about an operating point for optimal

Figure 2. Transfer function model of multi-area interconnected power systems consisting reheat turbines with parallel AC/DC links

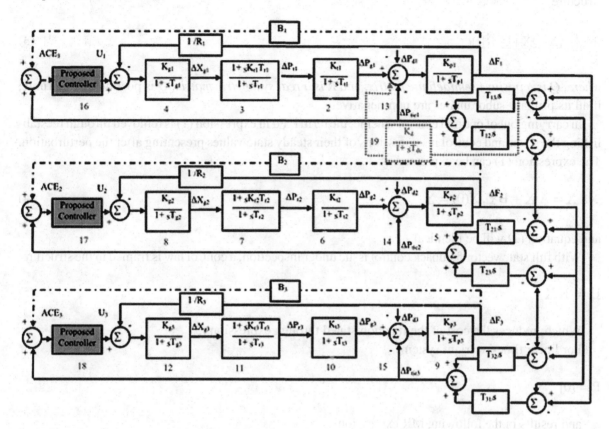

systems controller designs and apply the linear state controller theory to obtain the desired control law. The control strategies resulting from the application of linear state regulator theory depend on the availability of whole state variables directly or via state reestablishment plan taking either an observer or a filter in power systems practice of state variables being inaccessible for their measurement. However, this involves higher cost of AGC regulators and complexity in design problems.

Optimal Control Design Algorithm

Consider multi-area interconnected power systems with state space exhibition provided by the following differential expressions (1) and (2).

$$\dot{X} \dot{X} X = A X + B U + \Gamma Pd \tag{1}$$

$$Y = C X \tag{2}$$

Obtain the control law $\underline{U}$, so as to keep down the worth of quadratic performance index (J) of the structure

$$J = \int_0^\infty (\underline{X}^T Q \underline{X} + \underline{U}^T R \underline{U}) dt \tag{3}$$

where, Q is a positive semidefinite matrix, and R is a real symmetric matrix. Q is positive semidefinite, if all its primary subordinates are non-negative.

In carrying out of optimal control scheme, the term $\Gamma \underline{P}d$ in expression (1) is removed through reestablishing the states and control in expressions of their steady state values presenting after the perturbation. The expression (1) can be expressed as:

$$\dot{X}\dot{X} \underline{X} = A \underline{X} + B \underline{U}, \underline{X}(0) = \underline{X}_0 \tag{4}$$

and equation (2) will be identical.

With full state vector feedback control issue under inspection, a control law is framed in the structure:

$$\underline{U} = -K \underline{X} \tag{5}$$

Which; reduces the cost of the function stated through expression (3)
For linear time-invariant systems,

$$P = [0]$$

and results in the following MR expression.

$$PA + A^T P + Q - P B R^{-1} B^T P = 0 \tag{6}$$

The result of expression (6) creates a positive definite symmetric matrix P and the optimal control law is specified by

$$\underline{U}^* = -R^{-1} B^T P \underline{X}^* \tag{7}$$

and the desired optimal feedback gain matrix is presented by

$$K = -R^{-1} B^T P \tag{8}$$

The derivation of the equation (8) based on optimal control theory for the design of AGC controllers is described (Ibraheem & Singh, 2010).

For drawing up the state variable model for this justification the optimal feedback gain loops are untied and every time constant is expressed by a single block. State variables are explained as outcomes of all the blocks having either an integrator or a time constant. By observing the block diagrams examine that system has state variables i.e. eighteen for model-1 and nineteen for model-2.

Different variables have been selected as;

Power System Model-1

System State Vector

$[X_I] = [\Delta F_1 \; \Delta P_{g1} \; \Delta P_{r1} \; \Delta X_{g1} \; \Delta F_2 \; \Delta P_{g2} \; \Delta P_{r2} \; \Delta X_{g2} \; \Delta F_3 \; \Delta P_{g3} \; \Delta P_{r3} \; X_{g3} \; \Delta P_{tie12} \; \Delta P_{tie23}$

$\Delta P_{tie31} \; \int ACE_1 dt \; \int ACE_2 dt \; \int ACE_3 dt]^T$

Control Vector

$[U_I] = [\Delta P_{c1} \; \Delta P_{c2} \; \Delta P_{c3}]^T = [U_1 \; U_2 \; U_3]^T$

Disturbance Vector

$[P_{d\,I}] = [P_{d1} \; P_{d2} \; P_{d3}]^T$

From the transfer function blocks labelled from 1 to 18 (From Figure 1). The power systems dynamic expressions in state space for this model can be evaluated as;

For Block 1:

$\Delta F_1 + T_{p1} \; \dot{\Delta F_1} \; \Delta F_1 = K_{p1} (\Delta P_{g1} - \Delta P_{tie1} - \Delta P_{d1})$

i.e., $\quad \dot{\Delta F_1} \; \Delta F_1 = -\dfrac{1}{T_{p1}} \Delta F_1 + \dfrac{K_{p1}}{T_{p1}} \Delta P_{g1} - \dfrac{K_{p1}}{T_{p1}} \Delta P_{tie1} - \dfrac{K_{p1}}{T_{p1}} \Delta P_{d1}$
$\hfill (9)$

For Block 2:

$\Delta P_{g1} + T_{t1} \dot{\Delta P_{g1}} \; \Delta P_{g1} = \Delta P_{r1}$

i.e., $\quad \dfrac{d}{dt} \Delta P_{g1} = -\dfrac{1}{T_{t1}} \Delta P_{g1} + \dfrac{1}{T_{t1}} \Delta P_{r1}$
$\hfill (10)$

For Block 3:

$\Delta P_{r1} + T_{r1} \dot{\Delta P_{r1}} \; \Delta P_{r1} = \Delta X_{g1} + K_{r1} T_{r1} \dot{\Delta X_{g1}} \; \Delta X_{g1}$

i.e., $\quad \dot{\Delta P_{r1}} \; \Delta P_{r1} = (\dfrac{1}{T_{r1}} + \dfrac{K_{r1} T_{r1}}{T_{r1}}) \Delta X_{g1} - \dfrac{1}{T_{r1}} \Delta P_{r1}$
$\hfill (11)$

For Block 4:

$$\Delta \dot{X}_{g1} + T_{g1} \, \Delta \dot{X}_{g1} \, \Delta X_{g1} = -\frac{1}{R_1} \Delta F_1 + \Delta P_{c1}$$

i.e., $\Delta \dot{X}_{g1} \, \Delta X_{g1} = -\dfrac{1}{R_1 T_{g1}} \Delta F_1 - \dfrac{1}{T_{g1}} \Delta X_{g1} + \dfrac{1}{T_{g1}} \Delta P_{c1}$ \hfill (12)

Similarly other differential expressions are obtained as;

For Block 5:

$$\Delta \dot{F}_1 \, \Delta F_1 = -\frac{K_{p2}}{T_{p2}} \Delta P_{tie2} - \frac{1}{T_{p2}} \Delta F_2 + \frac{K_{p2}}{T_{p2}} \Delta P_{g2} - \frac{K_{p2}}{T_{p2}} \Delta P_{d2} \tag{13}$$

For Block 6:

$$\frac{d}{dt} \Delta P_{g2} = -\frac{1}{T_{t2}} \Delta P_{g2} + \frac{1}{T_{t2}} \Delta P_{r2} \tag{14}$$

For Block 7:

$$\Delta \dot{P}_{r1} \, \Delta P_{r1} = \left(\frac{1}{T_{r2}} + \frac{K_{r2} T_{r2}}{T_{r2}} \right) \Delta X_{g2} - \frac{1}{T_{r2}} \Delta P_{r2} \tag{15}$$

For Block 8:

$$\Delta \dot{X}_{g1} \, \Delta X_{g1} = -\frac{1}{R_2 T_{g2}} \Delta F_2 - \frac{1}{T_{g2}} \Delta X_{g2} + \frac{1}{T_{g2}} \Delta P_{c2} \tag{16}$$

For Block 9:

$$\Delta \dot{F}_1 \, \Delta F_1 = -\frac{K_{p3}}{T_{p3}} \Delta P_{tie3} - \frac{1}{T_{p3}} \Delta F_3 + \frac{K_{p3}}{T_{p3}} \Delta P_{g3} - \frac{K_{p3}}{T_{p3}} \Delta P_{d3} \tag{17}$$

For Block 10:

$$\frac{d}{dt} \Delta P_{g3} = -\frac{1}{T_{t3}} \Delta P_{g3} + \frac{1}{T_{t3}} \Delta P_{r3} \tag{18}$$

For Block 11:

$$\Delta \dot{P}_{r1} \, \Delta P_{r1} = \left(\frac{1}{T_{r3}} + \frac{K_{r3} T_{r3}}{T_{r3}} \right) \Delta X_{g3} - \frac{1}{T_{r3}} \Delta P_{r3} \tag{19}$$

For Block 12:

$$\Delta \dot{X}_{g1} \ \Delta X_{g1} = - \frac{1}{R_3 T_{g3}} \Delta F_3 - \frac{1}{T_{g3}} \Delta X_{g3} + \frac{1}{T_{g3}} \Delta P_{c3} \qquad (20)$$

For Block 13:

$$\Delta \dot{P}_{tie1} \ \Delta P_{tie1} = (2 \pi T_{13} + 2 \pi T_{12}) \Delta F_1 - 2 \pi T_{12} \Delta F_2 - 2 \pi T_{13} \Delta F_3 \qquad (21)$$

For Block 14:

$$\Delta \dot{P}_{tie2} \ \Delta P_{tie2} = (2 \pi T_{21} + 2 \pi T_{23}) \Delta F_2 - 2 \pi T_{21} \Delta F_1 - 2 \pi T_{23} \Delta F_3 \qquad (22)$$

For Block 15:

$$\Delta \dot{P}_{tie3} \ \Delta P_{tie3} = (2 \pi T_{32} + 2 \pi T_{31}) \Delta F_3 - 2 \pi T_{32} \Delta F_2 - 2 \pi T_{31} \Delta F_1 \qquad (23)$$

To comprise the integral function in the sketch of optimal AGC controllers, the integrals of area control errors (IACE) of both areas are calculated as below;

For Block 16:

$$\dot{IACE}_1 \ IACE_1 = B_1 \Delta F_1 + \Delta P_{tie12} \qquad (24)$$

For Block 17:

$$\dot{IACE}_2 \ IACE_2 = B_2 \Delta F_2 + \Delta P_{tie23} \qquad (25)$$

For Block 18:

$$\dot{IACE}_3 \ IACE_3 = B_3 \Delta F_3 + \Delta P_{tie31} \qquad (26)$$

Above expressions are managed in vector matrix form known as the 'state expression':

$$\dot{X} \ddot{X} \underline{X} = A \underline{X} + B \underline{U} + \Gamma \underline{P}d$$

where; A(18×18) is state matrix, B(18×3) is control matrix and Γ (3×18) is disturbance matrix.

Power Systems Model-2

System State Vector

$$[X_{II}] = [\Delta F_1 \ \Delta P_{g1} \ \Delta P_{r1} \ \Delta X_{g1} \ \Delta F_2 \ \Delta P_{g2} \ \Delta P_{r2} \ \Delta X_{g2} \ \Delta F_3 \ \Delta P_{g3} \ \Delta P_{r3} \ X_{g3} \ \Delta P_{tie12} \ \Delta P_{tie23}$$

$$\Delta P_{tie31} \ \int ACE_1 dt \ \int ACE_2 dt \ \int ACE_3 dt \ \Delta P_{dc}]^T$$

Control Vector

$$[U_{II}] = [\Delta P_{c1} \ \Delta P_{c2} \ \Delta P_{c3} \ \Delta P_{dc}] = [U_1 \ U_2 \ U_3 \ \Delta U_{dc}]^T$$

Disturbance Vector

$$[P_{dII}] = [P_{d1} \ P_{d2} \ P_{d3}]^T$$

Most of the differential expressions for this model are similar to power systems model-1. But few expressions are different due to incorporation of DC link in parallel with AC transmission link between areas-1 and 3 in Figure 2. These expressions are mentioned below;

For Block 1:

$$\Delta \dot{F}_1 \ \Delta F_1 = -\frac{1}{T_{p1}} \Delta F_1 + \frac{K_{p1}}{T_{p1}} \Delta P_{g1} - \frac{K_{p1}}{T_{p1}} \Delta P_{tie1} - \frac{K_{p1}}{T_{p1}} \Delta P_{d1} - \frac{K_{p1}}{T_{p1}} \Delta P_{dc} \tag{27}$$

For Block 9:

$$\Delta \dot{F}_1 \ \Delta F_1 = -\frac{K_{p3}}{T_{p3}} \Delta P_{tie3} - \frac{1}{T_{p3}} \Delta F_3 + \frac{K_{p3}}{T_{p3}} \Delta P_{g3} - \frac{K_{p3}}{T_{p3}} \Delta P_{d3} - \frac{K_{p3}}{T_{p3}} a_{31} \Delta P_{dc} \tag{28}$$

For Block 13:

$$\Delta \dot{P}_{tie1} \ \Delta P_{tie1} = (2 \pi T_{13} + 2 \pi T_{12} - \frac{K_{dc}}{T_{dc}}) \Delta F_1 - 2 \pi T_{12} \Delta F_2 - (2 \pi T_{13} + \frac{K_{dc}}{T_{dc}}) \Delta F_3 + \frac{1}{T_{dc}} \Delta P_{tie13} \tag{29}$$

For Block 15:

$$\Delta \dot{P}_{tie1} \ \Delta P_{tie1} \ \Delta P_{tie3} \ \Delta P_{tie3} = (2 \pi T_{32} + 2 \pi T_{31} + \frac{K_{dc}}{T_{dc}}) \Delta F_3 -$$

$$2 \pi T_{32} \Delta F_2 - (2 \pi T_{31} + \frac{K_{dc}}{T_{dc}}) \Delta F_1 - \frac{1}{T_{dc}} \Delta P_{tie31} \tag{30}$$

For Block 19:

$$\Delta \dot{P}_{tie1} \ \Delta \dot{P}_{tie1} \ \Delta \dot{P}_{tie1} = \frac{K_{dc}}{T_{dc}} \Delta F_1 - \frac{K_{dc}}{T_{dc}} \Delta F_3 - \frac{1}{T_{dc}} \Delta P_{dc} \qquad (31)$$

The matrices A_I, B_I and Γ_I for power systems model-1 and A_{II}, B_{II} and Γ_{II} for power systems model-2 are;

$$[B_{II}{}^T] = \begin{bmatrix} B_I{}^T \\ \Delta P_{dc} \end{bmatrix} \text{ and } [\Gamma_{II}{}^T] = [\Gamma_I{}^T]$$

In model-2, A_{II} (19×19) is state matrix, B_{II} (19×3) is control matrix and Γ_{II} (3×19) is disturbance matrix. All the matrices are similar in case study-3 (a) as case study-1 and case study-3 (b) as case study-2. But transmission line parameters are changed (disturbed) from its nominal values in the studies.

Matrices A_I
Matrices A_{II}
Matrices $\Gamma_I{}^T$
Matrices $\Gamma_I{}^T$

Measurement/Output Matrix 'C'

Normally, the matrix 'C' is chosen a matrix of nx1 dimensions for each power systems model study.

State Cost Weighting Matrix 'Q'

Normally, the matrix 'Q' is chosen as a diagonal matrix of suitable dimensions for each power systems model study.

Control Cost Weighting Matrix 'R'

It is chosen as an identity matrix. It has the dimensions of 3x3 for model-1 and 4x4 for model-2.

All the dimension of the matrices are shown in Table 1 which is represent the matrices of the system 'C', 'Q' and 'R'.

Table 1. Dimensions of the Matrices

Power Systems Case Study	Dimension of Matrix 'C'	Dimension of Matrix 'Q'	Dimension of Matrix 'R'
1	18x1	18x18	3x3
2	19x1	19x19	4x4
3 (a)	18x1	18x18	3x3
3 (b)	19x1	19x19	4x4

OPTIMAL HYBRID EA DESIGN TECHNIQUE

Modern control theory is implemented to sketch a LQR for a multi-area power systems model. In accordance with modern terminology, ΔP_{c1}, ΔP_{c2} and ΔP_{c3} will be referred to as control outputs U_1, U_2 and U_3 for model-1 and U_1, U_2, U_3 and U_{dc} for model-2. These were included by the integral of ACEs in the PI approach. Creation of these control outputs are done by optimal state feedback gains of the regulator. The performance of the AGC is completely depending upon value of these state feedback gains. These state feedback gains are in the range of local optima. So, this optimal controller dynamic response has large number of oscillations in the operating condition whenever perturbations are occurred. These state feedback gains can achieve the near global or global optimum values by any type of EA. Single GA can develop only near to global optimum solutions. Therefore, finding of global optimum solutions can be furnished through hybrid evolutionary algorithm. So, hybrid EA technique utilized for getting global range of the state feedback gains of the regulators.

Hybrid EA can be presented as an accommodation with appropriate alterations of the assigned evolutionary SA heuristic for function optimization (Kirkpatrick, Gelatt, & Vecchi, 1983). It has been outlined with a real coded string appearance of the chromosomes on which the genetic blend crossover operator is practiced in (Milani & Mozafari, 2011). This scheme includes SA in the selection operation of GA variables. This strategy supports in handling diversity in the search criteria and keep away from attaining glued in local optimum.

The state feedback gains are refined by a linear composition of whole systems states by hybrid EA technique. This design technique used PI structure of AGC regulators to minimize error criteria in the each iteration. The performance index integral square error (ISE) is used to define the PI controller's error criteria. At first, power systems models are represented as a set of differential equations. Then, these equations are used to evaluate the system dynamic responses. Initially, error minimization criterion is done by GA (Goldberg, 1989; Deb, 2005; Lansberry, Wozniak, & Goldberg, 1992; Milani & Mozafari, 2011) and then applied SA (Kirkpatrick, Gelatt, & Vecchi, 1983). In the each iteration, the regulators gains are going to be in the global range (fitness values) of the AGC problem. These fitness values are used to select best parents from population.

In this segment, the novel characteristics of this scheme are summarized in the execution procedure which exhibited is in the flow chart. The execution information that needs to be completed for the AGC is also shown in this part.

FLOW CHART OF HYBRID GASA TECHNIQUE

Certain implementation issues need to be settled before any successful implementation of hybrid EA (Ibraheem & Singh, 2010). The issues for the AGC are discussed below with the flowchart in Figure 3.

Representation of the Systems

As all the state feedback gains of the LQR are continuing floating point integers, it has been build appropriate to encode the state feedback gains as a pattern of floating point integers. Every constituent of the string presents the feedback gains (K) of the state.

Figure 3. Flowchart of a GASA technique

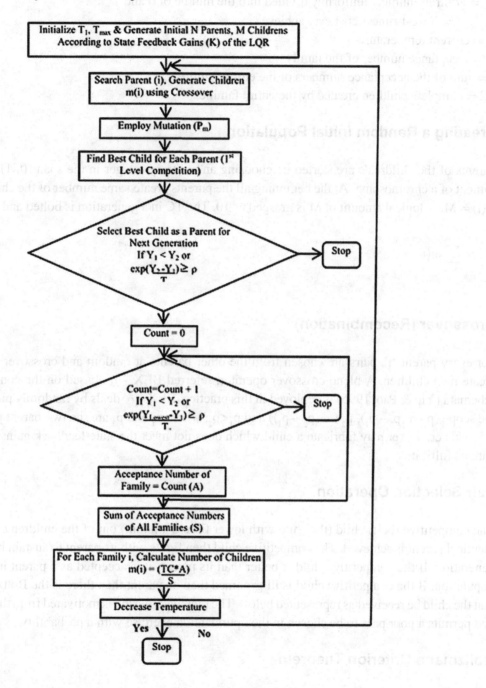

Where T^1 = initial temperature and T^{MAXIT} = final temperature

N = parent strings and M = children strings

Y_1 = fitness cost of best child

Y_2 = fitness cost of its parent

T = temperature coefficient

ρ = arbitrary number uniformly divided into the middle of 0 and 1

Y_{LOWEST} = lowest fitness cost ever achieve

T_c = current temperature

A = acceptance number of the family

S = sum of the acceptance numbers of the entire families

TC = complete children created by the entire families

Creating a Random Initial Population

Parents of the children's are started by choosing an arbitrary integer in the span (0, 1) for every constituent of a chromosome. At the beginning all the parents create same number of the children stated by m(i) = M. A logical amount of M is grasped as 10. The TC in a generation is bolted and is presented by

$$TC = \sum_{i=1}^{N} m(i) \tag{32}$$

Crossover (Recombination)

For every parent 'i', pairs are chosen from the other parents at random and crossover is employed to create m(i) children. A blend crossover operator, referred BLX - α, based on the concept of interim schemata (Yip & Pao, 1995) is deployed in this practice. BLX - α deals by randomly picking a point in the scope $(p_1 - \alpha (p_2 - p_1), p_2 + \alpha (p_2 - p_1))$ and $p_1 < p_2$, where p_1 and p_2 are the two parent points, and $\alpha =$ 0.5. This crossover may fabricate a child which does not meet the state feedback gains even when the parents fulfil it.

Pair Selection Operation

The competitive (best) child (the child with lower fitness amount) out of the children created from the identical parent is achieved. The competitive child then fights with its parent to sustain in the upcoming generation. If the competitive child is better than its parent, it is accepted as a parent in the upcoming population. If the competitive child is ill-groomed than its parent then there is the Boltzmann standard that the child be received as represented below. The picking criterion is motivated from the SA procedure and permits a poor pass to be chosen in the optimization exercise with a probability.

Boltzmann Criterion Theorem

As in SA, the choice of temperatures is such that essentially the probable event of acceptance of a poor pass, i.e., receiving the best child as the parent for upcoming generation when it is ill-groomed than the current parent, is prominent (approximately ≈ 1) but as the temperatures are progressively down this probability is declined till at the end of the process, the probability of receiving a poor pass is negligible (approximately ≈ 0) (Kirkpatrick, Gelatt, & Vecchi, 1983). The initial and final temperatures are evaluated as given below:

A poor pass is received as claimed to the Boltzmann criterion. At first the probability of receiving a poor pass is near about one, i.e.

$$\exp(-\frac{\Delta X_{average}}{T^1}) = 0.99 \tag{33}$$

and finally

$$\exp(-\frac{\Delta X_{average}}{T^{MAXIT}}) = 0.0001 \tag{34}$$

Therefore;

$$T^1 = -\frac{\Delta X_{average}}{\log(0.99)}$$

$$T^{MAXIT} = -\frac{\Delta X_{average}}{\log(0.0001)} \tag{35}$$

where; $\Delta X_{average}$ = average variation between the fitness X for any two neighborhood points in the explore area. This average is evaluated over a digit of chromosomes.

Cooling Event

Temperature is cooled towards a lower position with the iterations as explained (Ibraheem & Singh, 2010);

$$T^{k+1} = \frac{T^k}{1+^2.T^k} \tag{36}$$

where; $\beta = \frac{T^1 - T^{MAXIT}}{T^1.T^{MAXIT}.(MAXIT - 1)}$

Signification of superscript k presents the iteration count.

Creation of Acceptance Number

The digit of children created in the upcoming generation is proportional to the specification known as the acceptance number. This number delivers a scale of the goodness of the solutions in the neighborhood of the latest parent. This scheme provides the algorithm to the concentration on seeking the better areas in the search domain.

Selection on Control Parameter in Hybrid EA Technique

In the first instance, the effect of population size for divergent experimental tests was analysed. Distinct populations (100, 120, 140, 160, 180 and 200) were review and it has been seen that a population size of 200 was adequate. After choosing the size of population, the effect of mutation and crossover probabilities was observed. It has been examined that the appropriate matching of mutation and crossover probabilities providing best productions change with the investigations. Different matches of mutation probabilities (0.1, 0.2, 0.3 and 0.4) and the crossover probabilities (0.6, 0.8, 0.9 and 1.0) were examined and it was achieved that $P_c = 0.6$ and $P_m = 0.4$ provide the best results for all the case studies. It is valuable suggestion here that throughout the optimization procedure higher and lower boundaries of all the gain settings were chosen as -5 and 5 respectively, and the starting temperature and final temperature is in the span of 0.99 and 0.0001.

RESULTS DISCUSSION

The power system models are simulated at MATLAB 13.1 platform to obtain optimal feedback gains of EA based AGC regulators. The performance of EA based AGC regulators are compared with LQR and GA based regulators.

To the performance of the GASA based optimal AGC controllers, the simulation study is completed in wake of 1% step load disturbance in area-1. The frequency deviations (ΔF_1, ΔF_2 and ΔF_3), deviations in power generation (ΔP_{g1}, ΔP_{g2} and ΔP_{g3}) and tie-line power flow deviations (ΔP_{tie12}, ΔP_{tie23} and ΔP_{tie31}) are shown by Figures 4-12. Referring to these figures which are drawn for PI, LQR, GA and EA based controllers for power systems model-1. It is seen that better dynamic system responses are obtained with

Figure 4. Dynamic response of ΔF_1 for 1% load disturbance in area-1

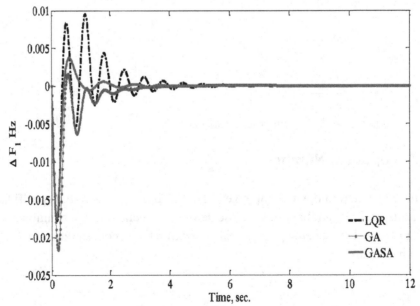

Figure 5. Dynamic response of ΔF_2 for 1% load disturbance in area-1

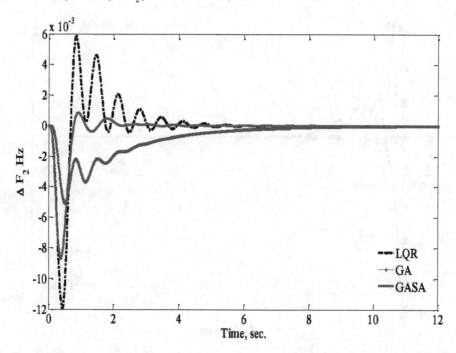

Figure 6. Dynamic response of ΔF_3 for 1% load disturbance in area-1

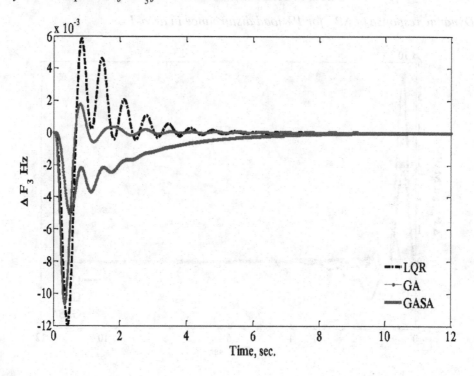

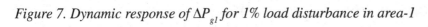

Figure 7. Dynamic response of ΔP_{g1} for 1% load disturbance in area-1

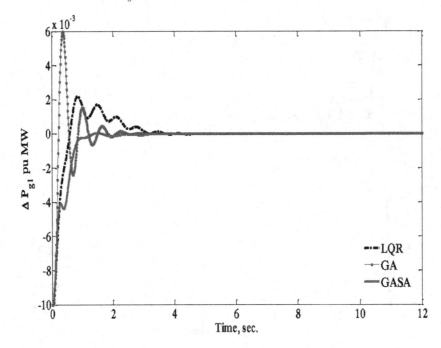

Figure 8. Dynamic response of ΔP_{g2} for 1% load disturbance in area-1

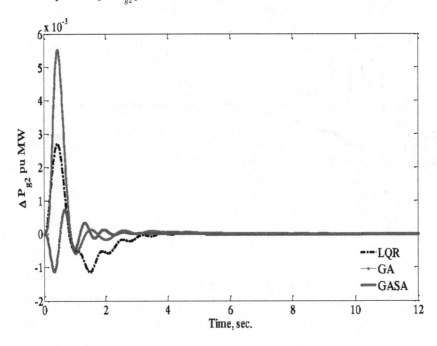

Figure 9. Dynamic response of ΔP_{g3} for 1% load disturbance in area-1

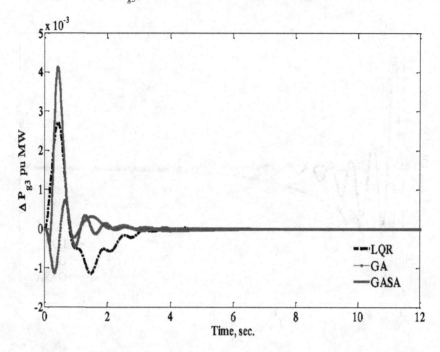

Figure 10. Dynamic response of ΔP_{tie12} for 1% load disturbance in area-1

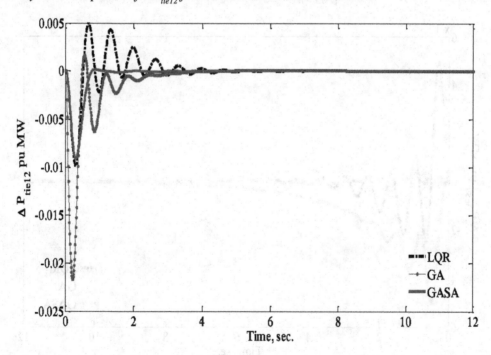

Figure 11. Dynamic response of ΔP_{tie23} for 1% load disturbance in area-1

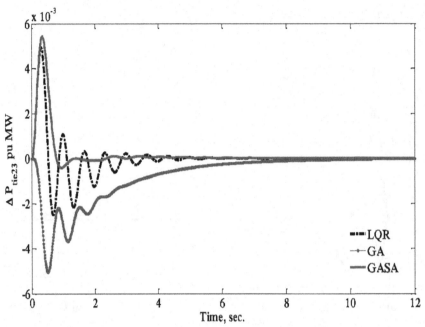

Figure 12. Dynamic response of ΔP_{tie31} for 1% load disturbance in area-1

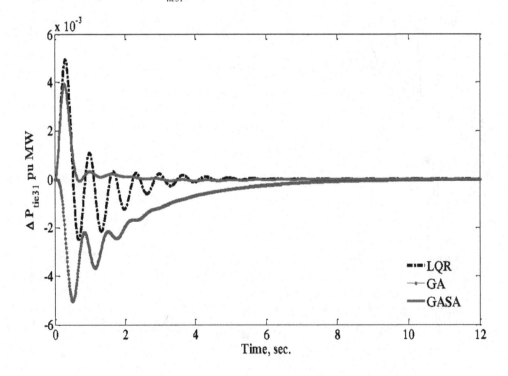

the EA based optimal controllers than LQR and GA based optimal AGC regulators as well as frequency, power generations and tie-line power flow responses are very smooth.

Responses of the optimal GASA based AGC regulators are presented with AC link only and parallel AC/DC links as area interconnection between control areas in Figures 13-15. It is seen power system model-2 having region interconnection as AC/DC links.

Table 2 shows that the optimal state feedback gains of the power systems for LQR and EA based controllers.

In the case study-3, the power systems model-1 and model-2 considering variations in EHV AC tie-line and HVDC link time constant parameters. The effect of $\pm 30\%$ variations is investigated in T_{ij} & T_{dc} from its nominal values.

Figures 16-18 demonstrate the effect of variations in transmission line parameters in time response curves of ΔP_{tie12}, ΔP_{tie23} and ΔP_{tie31}. These plots show that due to the variations in T_{ij}. The transmission power flow response of the disturbed area is so much affected. The performance of the transmission line deteriorates its performance. These response plots shows that oscillations and settling time will be more whenever off-nominal parameters of tie-line time constants are involving in the systems.

The effect of $\pm 30\%$ variations in time constant of DC transmission line while functioning in parallel with EHV AC transmission line as systems interconnection is investigated with the response curves of Figures 19-21. The presence of off-nominal parameters involves the more oscillations and increases settling time of the transmission line power flow (ΔP_{tie12}, ΔP_{tie23} and ΔP_{tie31}) in the systems.

In nut shell, power systems response characteristics investigation is reported in Table 3 which shows that system realistic performance in different scenarios. The present work also includes a comparative

Figure 13. Dynamic response of ΔF_1 for 1% load disturbance in area-1

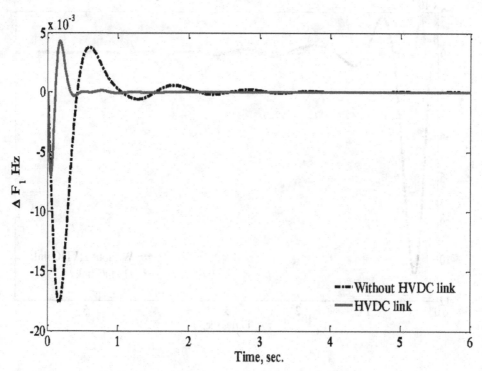

Figure 14. Dynamic response of ΔF_2 for 1% load disturbance in area-1

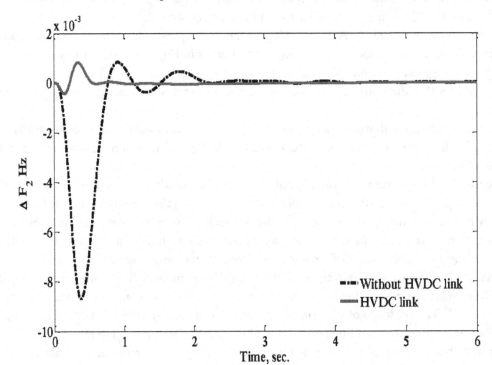

Figure 15. Dynamic response of ΔF_3 for 1% load disturbance in area-1

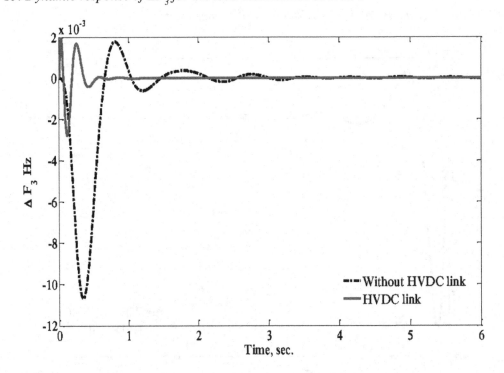

Table 2. Optimal feedback gain matrix

Case Studies	Algorithm	Optimal Feedback Gain Matrix (K)
1.	LQR	[0.3389 6.0196 1.0420 0.5983 0.5556 1.3433 0.1372 0.0227 0.5556 1.3433 0.1372 0.0227 -3.2837 -1.1587 -1.1587 1.0000 -0.0000 -0.0000; 0.5556 1.3433 0.1372 0.0227 0.3389 6.0196 1.0420 0.5983 0.5556 1.3433 0.1372 0.0227 -1.1587 -3.2837 -1.1587 -0.0000 1.0000 -0.0000; 0.5556 1.3433 0.1372 0.0227 0.5556 1.3433 0.1372 0.0227 0.3389 6.0196 1.0420 0.5983 -1.1587 -1.1587 -3.2837 -0.0000 -0.0000 1.0000];
	GASA	[0.4917 7.3582 1.0934 0.0660 3.0213 3.7492 0.0168 0.0972 0.1919 5.7580 0.3175 0.6623 0.0979 2.6834 1.2636 0.6294 0.5904 0.8487; 1.0101 1.3135 0.0194 -0.0891 -0.0410 2.4152 0.0364 -0.0655 0.1240 0.6513 0.1094 0.1267 0.7530 0.3560 1.2985 0.0614 0.3688 0.0519; 0.7153 0.5058 -0.9892 0.4925 0.7852 -0.2833 -0.4099 -0.0774 0.9816 2.4982 1.3598 -0.2366 0.8229 0.7912 0.4077 0.1086 -0.4967 0.2060];
2.	LQR	[0.0416 1.8743 0.5337 0.5113 0.0010 0.1503 0.0190 0.0033 0.0384 0.9478 0.1266 0.0223 -0.0001 -0.1568 -0.1234 0.5753 0.0002 0.4260 -0.0014; 0.0132 0.1596 0.0191 0.0033 0.0829 5.1926 0.9571 0.5844 0.0242 0.1842 0.0209 0.0035 -0.0655 -2.6972 -0.3084 0.0752 0.9939 -0.0790 0.0102; 0.0360 0.9166 0.1257 0.0223 -0.0107 0.1479 0.0200 0.0035 0.0390 1.8631 0.5322 0.5111 -0.0154 -0.1761 -0.0996 0.4760 -0.0047 0.5198 0.0219; 0.0551 0.9549 0.0181 -0.0016 0.3372 0.7020 0.0430 0.0053 2.6146 1.7806 0.0434 0.0014 -1.8027 -0.3984 -0.7500 -0.6609 0.1099 0.7363 0.6567];
	GASA	[1.2164 1.0441 0.1824 -0.4254 1.8256 -0.9343 -0.2329 0.2173 -1.0119 0.6440 0.7183 0.4861 1.2777 3.6224 0.6929 0.4553 0.9890 0.7321 1.2606; 1.3514 0.9247 0.2542 0.3472 0.1173 2.1193 0.9501 0.3914 0.9531 0.6822 0.1537 0.0210 1.3179 0.8563 -0.0118 0.5506 0.9975 0.6549 0.4429; 2.3120 0.2058 -0.3250 0.5859 -2.1011 -0.4514 1.2553 0.4392 -1.9306 0.8461 1.3565 0.6089 0.3786 0.4402 0.8446 0.8378 0.1921 -0.4809 1.6609; 0.0551 0.9549 0.0181 -0.0016 0.3372 0.7020 0.0430 0.0053 2.6146 1.7806 0.0434 0.0014 -1.8027 -0.3984 -0.7500 -0.6609 0.1099 0.7363 0.6567];

Figure 16. Dynamic response of ΔP_{tie12} incorporating variations in tie-line time constants

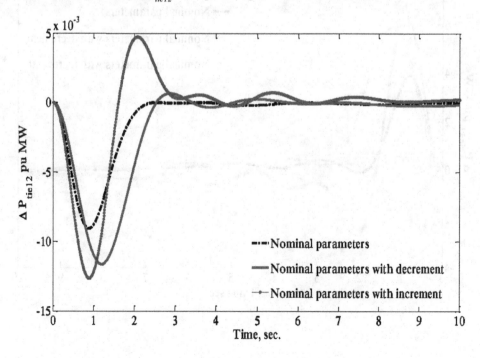

Figure 17. Dynamic response of ΔP_{tie23} incorporating variations in tie-line time constants

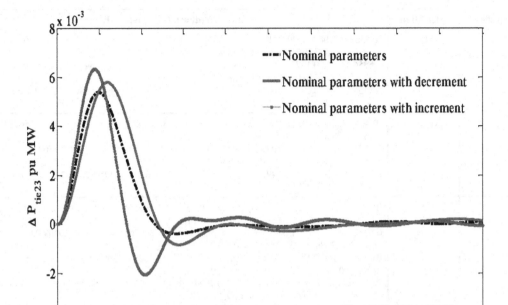

Figure 18. Dynamic response of ΔP_{tie31} incorporating variations in tie-line time constants

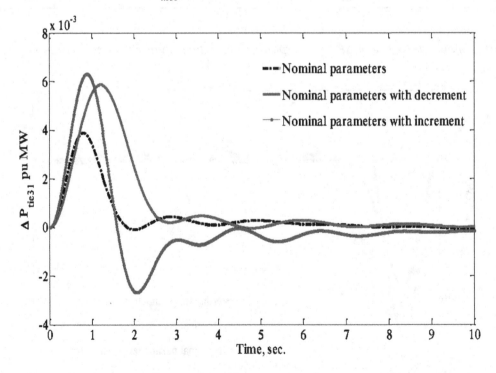

Figure 19. Dynamic response of ΔP_{tie12} incorporating variations in DC time constants

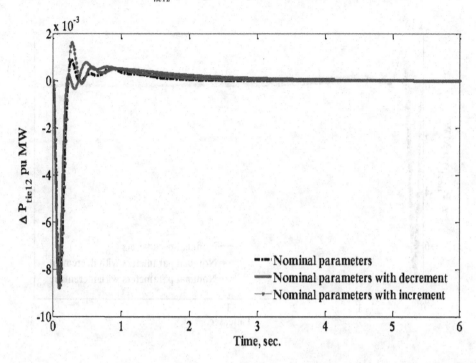

Figure 20. Dynamic response of ΔP_{tie23} incorporating variations in DC time constants

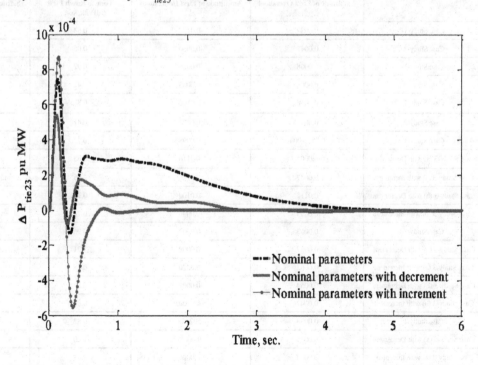

Figure 21. Dynamic response of ΔP_{tie31} incorporating variations in DC time constants

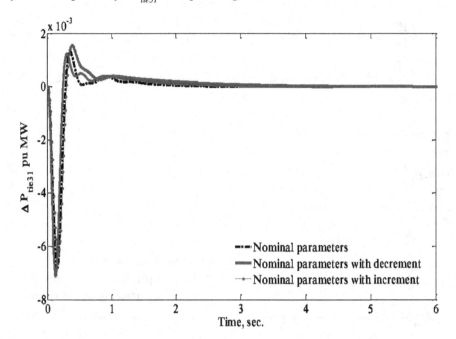

Table 3. System response characteristics

System States	Case Studies	System Response Parameters			
		Amplitude of First Overshoot	Amplitude of First Undershoot	Time to Reach First Peak, sec.	Settling Time, sec.
ΔF_1	Case Study-1	0.0037	-0.0173	0.64	5.96
	Case Study-2	0.0042	-0.0060	0.05	0.81
ΔF_2	Case Study-1	0.0008	-0.0086	0.92	5.64
	Case Study-2	0.0008	-0.0003	3.42	0.79
ΔF_3	Case Study-1	0.0018	-0.0106	0.82	5.57
	Case Study-2	0.0019	-0.0027	0.41	0.84
ΔP_{tie12}	Case Study-1	0.845e-004	-0.0098	0.72	3.46
	Case Study-3 (a) with Decrement	0.0006	-0.0116	2.85	more than 10
	Case Study-3 (a) with Increment	0.0047	-0.0126	2.05	more than 10
	Case Study-3 (b) with Decrement	0.0112	-0.0100	0.97	6.84
	Case Study-3 (b) with Increment	0.0099	-0.0096	0.74	3.82
ΔP_{tie23}	Case Study-1	0.0053	-0.0003	0.96	10.15
	Case Study-3 (a) with Decrement	0.0057	-0.0008	1.21	more than 10
	Case Study-3 (a) with Increment	0.0063	-0.0020	0.88	more than 10
	Case Study-3 (b) with Decrement	0.0054	-0.0002	0.87	8.30
	Case Study-3 (b) with Increment	0.0047	5.61e-005	0.82	8.52
ΔP_{tie31}	Case Study-1	0.0038	-7.502e-005	0.82	9.51
	Case Study-3 (a) with Decrement	0.0058	0.0001	1.20	9.90
	Case Study-3 (a) with Increment	0.0063	-0.0026	0.87	9.87
	Case Study-3 (b) with Decrement	0.0080	-0.0165	0.39	6.71
	Case Study-3 (b) with Increment	0.0085	-0.0145	0.29	3.61

Table 4. Matrices A_I

0	0	0	0	0	0	0	0	0	0	0	0	0	0	0	0	0	0
0	0	0	0	0	0	0	0	0	0	0	0	0	0	0	0	0	0
0	0	0	0	0	0	0	0	0	0	0	0	0	0	0	0	0	0
0	0	0	0	0	0	0	0	$\dfrac{-K_{p3}}{T_{p3}}$	0	0	0	0	0	0	0	0	a_{31}
0	0	0	0	$\dfrac{-K_{p2}}{T_{p2}}$	0	0	0	0	0	0	0	0	0	0	0	a_{23}	0
$\dfrac{-K_{p1}}{T_{p1}}$	0	0	0	0	0	0	0	0	0	0	0	0	0	0	a_{12}	0	0
0	0	0	0	0	0	0	0	0	0	$\dfrac{(1/T_{t3})+K_{r3}\cdot T_{r3}}{T_{t3}}$	$\dfrac{-1}{T_{g3}}$	0	0	0	0	0	0
0	0	0	0	0	0	0	0	0	$\dfrac{1}{T_{t3}}$	$\dfrac{-1}{T_{t3}}$	0	0	0	0	0	0	0
0	0	0	0	0	0	0	0	$\dfrac{K_{p3}}{T_{p3}}$	$\dfrac{-1}{T_{t3}}$	0	0	0	0	0	0	0	0
0	0	0	0	0	0	0	0	$\dfrac{-1}{T_{p3}}$	0	0	$\dfrac{-1}{R_3 T_{g3}}$	$-2\pi T_{13}$	$-2\pi T_{23}$	$2\pi T_{32}+2\pi T_{31}$	0	B_3	0
0	0	0	0	0	$\dfrac{(1/T_{t2})+K_{r2}\cdot T_{r2}}{T_{t2}}$	$\dfrac{-1}{T_{g2}}$	0	0	0	0	0	0	0	0	0	0	0
0	0	0	0	$\dfrac{1}{T_{t2}}$	$\dfrac{-1}{T_{t2}}$	0	0	0	0	0	0	0	0	0	0	0	0
0	0	0	0	$\dfrac{K_{p2}}{T_{p2}}$	$\dfrac{-1}{T_{t2}}$	0	0	0	0	0	0	0	0	0	0	0	0
0	0	0	0	$\dfrac{-1}{T_{p2}}$	0	0	$\dfrac{-1}{R_2 T_{g2}}$	0	0	0	0	$-2\pi T_{12}$	$2\pi T_{21}+2\pi T_{23}$	$-2\pi T_{32}$	B_2	0	0
0	0	$\dfrac{(1/T_{t1})+K_{r1}\cdot T_{r1}}{T_{t1}}$	$\dfrac{-1}{T_{g1}}$	0	0	0	0	0	0	0	0	0	0	0	0	0	0
0	$\dfrac{-1}{T_{t1}}$	$\dfrac{-1}{T_{t1}}$	0	0	0	0	0	0	0	0	0	0	0	0	0	0	0
$\dfrac{K_{p1}}{T_{p1}}$	$\dfrac{-1}{T_{t1}}$	0	0	0	0	0	0	0	0	0	0	0	0	0	0	0	0
$\dfrac{-1}{T_{p1}}$	0	0	$\dfrac{-1}{R_1 T_{g1}}$	0	0	0	0	0	0	0	0	$2\pi T_{13}+2\pi T_{12}$	$-2\pi T_{21}$	$-2\pi T_{31}$	B_1	0	0

Table 5. Matrices A_{II}

1	2	3	4	5	6	7	8	9	10	11	12	13	14	15	16	17	18	19
$\frac{-K_{p1}}{T_{p1}}$	0	0	0	0	0	0	0	$\frac{-a12\cdot K_{p3}}{T_{p3}}$	0	0	0	0	0	0	0	0	0	$\frac{-1}{T_{dc}}$
0	0	0	0	0	0	0	0	0	0	0	0	0	0	0	0	0	0	0
0	0	0	0	0	0	0	0	0	0	0	0	0	0	0	0	0	0	0
0	0	0	0	0	0	0	0	0	0	0	0	0	0	0	0	0	0	0
0	0	0	0	0	0	0	0	$\frac{-K_{p3}}{T_{p3}}$	0	0	0	0	$\frac{-1}{T_{dc}}$	0	0	a_{31}	0	0
0	0	0	0	$\frac{-K_{p2}}{T_{p2}}$	0	0	0	0	0	0	0	0	0	0	a_{23}	0	0	0
$\frac{-K_{p1}}{T_{p1}}$	0	0	0	0	0	0	0	0	0	0	0	0	0	0	a_{12}	0	0	0
0	0	0	0	0	0	0	0	$\frac{(1/T_{r3})+K_{r3}\cdot T_{r3}}{T_{r3}}$	$\frac{-1}{T_{g3}}$	$\frac{1}{T_{dc}}$	0	0	0	0	0	0	0	0
0	0	0	0	0	0	0	$\frac{1}{T_{r3}}$	$\frac{-1}{T_{r3}}$	0	0	0	0	0	0	0	0	0	0
0	0	0	0	0	0	0	$\frac{K_{p3}}{T_{p3}}$	$\frac{-1}{T_{13}}$	0	0	0	0	0	0	0	0	0	0
0	0	0	0	0	0	0	$\frac{-1}{T_{p3}}$	0	0	$\frac{-1}{R_3\,T_{g3}}$	$\frac{K_{dc}-2\pi T_{13}}{T_{dc}}$	$\frac{2\pi T_{32}+2\pi T_{31}+K_{dc}}{T_{dc}}$	0	0	B_3	0	$\frac{-K_{dc}}{T_{dc}}$
0	0	0	0	0	$\frac{(1/T_{r2})+K_{r2}\cdot T_{r2}}{T_{r2}}$	$\frac{-1}{T_{g2}}$	0	0	0	0	0	0	0	0	0	0	0	0
0	0	0	0	$\frac{1}{T_{r2}}$	$\frac{-1}{T_{r2}}$	0	0	0	0	0	0	0	0	0	0	0	0	0
0	0	0	0	$\frac{K_{p2}}{T_{p2}}$	$\frac{-1}{T_{r2}}$	0	0	0	0	0	0	0	0	0	0	0	0	0
0	0	0	0	$\frac{-1}{T_{p2}}$	0	0	$\frac{-1}{R_2\,T_{g2}}$	0	0	0	$-2\pi T_{12}$	$2\pi T_{21}+2\pi T_{23}$	$-2\pi T_{32}$	0	0	B_2	0	0
0	0	$\frac{(1/T_{r1})+K_{r1}\cdot T_{r1}}{T_{r1}}$	$\frac{-1}{T_{g1}}$	0	0	0	0	0	0	0	0	0	0	0	0	0	0	0
0	$\frac{1}{T_{l1}}$	$\frac{-1}{T_{r1}}$	0	0	0	0	0	0	0	0	0	0	0	0	0	0	0	0
$\frac{K_{p1}}{T_{p1}}$	$\frac{-1}{T_{l1}}$	0	0	0	0	0	0	0	0	0	0	0	0	0	0	0	0	0
$\frac{-1}{T_{p1}}$	0	0	$\frac{-1}{R_1\,T_{g1}}$	0	0	0	0	0	0	0	$\frac{-K_{dc}+2\pi T_{13}+2\pi T_{12}}{T_{dc}}$	$-2\pi T_{21}$	$\frac{-2\pi T_{31}-K_{dc}}{T_{dc}}$	0	0	B_1	0	$\frac{K_{dc}}{T_{dc}}$

Table 6. Matrices B_I^T

0	0	0	$\frac{1}{T_{g1}}$	0	0	0	0	0	0	0	0	0	0	0	0	0	0
0	0	0	0	0	0	0	$\frac{1}{T_{g2}}$	0	0	0	0	0	0	0	0	0	0
0	0	0	0	0	0	0	0	0	0	0	$\frac{1}{T_{g3}}$	0	0	0	0	0	0

Table 7. Matrices Γ_I^T

$\frac{-K_{p1}}{T_{p1}}$	0	0	0	0	0	0	0	0	0	0	0	0	0	0	0	0	0
0	0	0	0	$\frac{-K_{p2}}{T_{p2}}$	0	0	0	0	0	0	0	0	0	0	0	0	0
0	0	0	0	0	0	0	0	$\frac{-K_{p3}}{T_{p3}}$	0	0	0	0	0	0	0	0	0

study of parallel AC/DC links interconnection and merits of additional DC tie-line as presented in the Figures. While considering different controllers designs studied here, the better dynamic response of ΔF_i, ΔP_{gi} and ΔP_{tieij} with optimal AGC controllers is obtained with GASA AGC regulators for multi-area interconnected power systems with HVDC tie-line commissioned in parallel to EHVAC inter-tie by considering HVDC link power flow as a control variable with turbine controllers only.

CONCLUSION

A new hybrid EA based optimal AGC controllers are sketched and applied on a multi-area interconnected power system. A GASA technique based notable method of determining optimal gain settings for full state feedback controllers for AGC problem is introduced. The hybrid EA scheme has been investigated on a number of case studies and gives competent solutions. The performance of EA based AGC controllers are compared with LQR and GA based optimal AGC controllers. This proves to be a good revolutionary method for optimal controller's design. Experimental results demonstrate the efficacy of the hybrid EA approach in optimizing the state variable feedback gains to provide a fairly better controller characteristic.

Furthermore, there is an appreciable improvement in the dynamic performance of the power system incorporating AC/DC links as area interconnection rather than using AC link only.

REFERENCES

Bevrani, H., & Hiyama, T. (2011). *Intelligent Automatic Generation Control*. CRC Press.

Deb, K. (2005). *Multi-Objective Optimization using Evolutionary Algorithms*. Willey Eastern Limited.

Dhar, R. N. (1982). *Computer Aided Power System Operation and Analysis*. Tata McGraw-Hill Publishing Company Ltd.

Elgerd, O. I. (2001). *Electric Energy Systems Theory* (2nd ed.). Tata: McGraw-Hill.

Fujita, G., Shirai, G., & Yokoyama, R. (2002). Automatic Generation Control for DC Link Power System. *IEE Proceedings on Transmission and Distribution Conference and Exhibition: Asia Pacific, 3*, 1584-1588.

Goldberg, D. E. (1989). *Genetic Algorithms in Search, Optimization and Machine Learning*. Addison-Wesley Publishing Company Inc.

Holland, J. H. (1982). *Adaption in Natural and Artificial Systems: An Introductory Analysis with Applications to Biology, Control, and Artificial Intelligence*. MIT Press.

Ibraheem & Ahmad. (2004). Dynamic Performance Enhancement of Hydro-power Systems with Asynchronous Tie-lines. *Journal Institution of Engineers, 85*.

Ibraheem, K., Kumar, P., & Kothari, D. P. (2005, February). Recent Philosophies of Automatic Generation Control Strategies in Power Systems. *IEEE Transactions on Power Systems, 20*(1), 346–357. doi:10.1109/TPWRS.2004.840438

Ibraheem, K. P., & Khatoon, S. (2005). Effect of Parameter Uncertainties on Dynamic Performance of an Interconnected Power System with AC/DC Links. *International Journal of Power and Energy Systems, 25*(3).

Ibraheem & Singh. (2010). Hybrid GA-SA based Optimal AGC of a Multi-area Interconnected Power System with Asynchronous Tie-lines. *International Journal of Electrical and Power Engineering, 4*(2), 78-84.

Kirkpatrick, S., Gelatt, C. D., & Vecchi, M. P. (1983). Optimization by Simulated Annealing. *Science New Series, 220*, 671–680. PMID:17813860

Lansberry, J. E., Wozniak, L., & Goldberg, D. E. (1992). Optimal Hydro-generator Governor Tuning with a Genetic Algorithm. *IEEE Transactions on Energy Conversion, 7*(4), 623–630. doi:10.1109/60.182643

Milani, A. E., & Mozafari, B. (2011, June). Genetic Algorithm based Optimal Load Frequency Control in Two-area Interconnected Power Systems. *Transactions on Power System Optimization, 2*, 6–10.

Nanda, J., Kothari, M. L., & Satsangi, P. S. (1983, January). Automatic Generation Control of an Interconnected Hydro-thermal System in Continuous and Discrete Modes Considering Generation Rate Constraints. *IEE Proceedings. Control Theory and Applications, 130*(1), 17–27. doi:10.1049/ip-d.1983.0004

Yip, P. P. C., & Pao, Y. H. (1995, March). Combinational Optimization with Use of Guided Evolutionary Simulated Annealing. *IEEE Transactions on Neural Networks, 6*(2), 290–295. doi:10.1109/72.363466 PMID:18263313

APPENDIX

List of Symbols

The various symbols have the following descriptions for power systems models shown in Tables 8 and 9 respectively.

Table 8. A. Power System Models

Power Systems Parameters	Power Systems Model of Figure 1	Power Systems Model of Figure 2
Incremental Change in frequency	ΔF_i	ΔF_i
Subscript Referring to Area	(i=1,2,3)	(i=1,2,3)
Incremental Change in Load Demand (p.u.MW/Hz)	ΔP_{di}	ΔP_{di}
Incremental DC Power Flow		ΔP_{dc}
Incremental Change in Governor Valve Position	ΔXg_i	
Incremental Change in Speed Changer Position	ΔP_{ci}	ΔP_{ci}
Speed Governor Gain Constants	K_{gi}	K_{gi}
Speed Governor Time Constant, sec.	T_{gi}	T_{gi}
Reheat Thermal Turbine Gain Constant	K_{ti}	K_{ti}
Turbine Time Constants, sec.	T_{ti}	T_{ti}
Reheat Coefficient's & Reheat Time's, sec.	K_{ri}, T_{ri}	K_{ri}, T_{ri}
Electric System Gain Constants	K_{pi}	K_{pi}
Electric System Time Constants, sec.	T_{pi}	T_{pi}
Frequency Bias Constant (p.u.MW/Hz)	B_i	B_i
Speed Regulation Parameter, Hz/p.u.MW	R_i	R_i
Area Control Error's	ACE_i	ACE_i
Outputs of the Controller	U_i	U_i
Synchronizing Coefficient of AC Tie-line	$T_{ij\,(i \neq j)}$	$T_{ij\,(i \neq j)}$
Time Constant of HVDC Link, sec.		T_{dc}
Gain associated with DC link		K_{dc}

Table 9. B. Optimal Control Theory

Γ	n x m	Disturbance Matrix
A	n x n	System Matrix
B	n x m	Control Matrix
C	l x n	Measurement/Output Matrix
J		Performance Index Value
K	mxn	Optimal Feedback Gain Matrix
n, m, l		Dimensions of State, Control and Output Vectors
P	n x n	Positive Definite Symmetric Matrix
Pd	m x 1	Disturbance Vector
Q	n x n	Positive semi-Definite Symmetric State Cost Weighting Matrix
R	mx m	Positive Definite Symmetric Control Cost Weighting Matrix
U	m x 1	Control Vector
X	n x 1	State Vector
Y	l x 1	Output Vector

Chapter 11
Mathematical Optimization by Using Particle Swarm Optimization, Genetic Algorithm, and Differential Evolution and Its Similarities

Shailendra Aote
Ramdeobaba College of Engineering and Management, India

Mukesh M. Raghuwanshi
Yeshwantrao Chavan College of Engineering, India

ABSTRACT

To solve the problems of optimization, various methods are provided in different domain. Evolutionary computing (EC) is one of the methods to solve these problems. Mostly used EC techniques are available like Particle Swarm Optimization (PSO), Genetic Algorithm (GA) and Differential Evolution (DE). These techniques have different working structure but the inner working structure is same. Different names and formulae are given for different task but ultimately all do the same. Here we tried to find out the similarities among these techniques and give the working structure in each step. All the steps are provided with proper example and code written in MATLAB, for better understanding. Here we started our discussion with introduction about optimization and solution to optimization problems by PSO, GA and DE. Finally, we have given brief comparison of these.

1. INTRODUCTION

Problem solving is one of the most complicated intellectual activities of the human brain. The process of problem solving deals with finding the solution in the presence of the constraints. An exact solution to some problems might simply be infeasible, especially if it has larger dimensionality. In those problems, solution near to the exact value might be deemed very good and sufficient. Knapsack problem, linear

DOI: 10.4018/978-1-5225-2128-0.ch011

programming problem is an example of an optimization problem. Another example of an optimization problem is to arrange the transistors on a computer chip, so that it will occupy the smallest area and the number of components it will used are as few as possible. Optimization is generally used in many problems like Scheduling Problems, Resource Allocation, Decision Making, and Industrial Planning. Furthermore, these optimization techniques cover large application areas in business, industry, and engineering and computer science. Due to simplicity, involvement of less parameter and fast convergence, Many real world problems like Economic Dispatch (Selvakumar & Thanushkodi, 2007), Scheduling Problems (Pongchairerks, 2009), Textual Entailment Recognition (Mehdad & Magnini, 2009), Term Extraction (Mehdad & Magnini, 2009), Intelligent Web Caching (Syafrullah & Salim, 2010), Text Feature Selection (Sulaiman, Shamsuddin, Forkan, & Abraham, 2008) etc. are solved using these algorithms.

1.1. Basic Concepts

Optimization means problems solving in which one tries to find a minimum or maximum value of the given function by systematically choosing the values of real or integer variables from given set. The representation of an optimization problem is as follows,

Given: Consider a function f, which maps from set X to the real numbers.

If an element x_i in X such that $f(x_i) \geq f(x)$ for all other x in X is called maximization or such that $f(x_i) \leq f(x)$ for all other x in X is called minimization. And our aim is to find x_i.

Let, R is the Euclidean space and X is a subset of R. Every member of X has to satisfy the set of constraints, equalities or inequalities. The search space is defined as the domain X of f, while the elements of X are represented as feasible solutions. The function f is called as an objective function. An optimal solution is a feasible solution that minimizes (or maximizes) the value of the objective function.

In case of an optimization of a single objective function f, an optimum value is either its maximum or minimum. This is depended on the nature of the problem. This optimum must satisfy the constraints. Consider the process of manufacturing plant: we have to assign incoming orders to machines, so that it minimizes the time needed to complete them. On the other hand, we will arrange the employment of staff, the placing of commercials and the purchase of raw materials in a way that maximizes our profit. In global optimization, the optimization problems are mostly defined as minimization problems. A global optimum is a value, which is the best among all the values in whole domain X while a local optimum is an optimum of only a subset of X. If anyone wants to minimize the solution, then it tries to get a global minimum point in the search space. It is possible to get local minimum during the search, which diverts the pointer from achieving a better solution. This problem is referred as local minima in Artificial Intelligence (AI). AI also defines the problems in the optimization as plateau and ridge.

Optimization problems are mainly classified as a single objective optimization (SOO) and multiobjective optimization (MOO). Here our aim is to deal with the single objective optimization problems. SOO Problems are further classified as Unimodal and Multimodal Optimization, whereas other types of classes are Single dimensional and multidimensional problems. Difficulty in solving the problems increases from unimodal to multimodal as well as from single dimensional to multidimensional problems. If the problem is multimodal and multidimensional, then optimum solution is presently far away from the real solution.

1.2. Classical Methods

Different methods to solve optimization problems are as follows.

1. Traditional Optimization algorithms use the exact method to find the best available solution (Selvakumar & Thanushkodi, 2007). The idea is that if the problem can be solved, then the algorithm must find the global best solution. Brute force method is an example of an exact method, which tries every solution in the search space. But as the search space increases, the cost of brute force method also increases. Therefore the brute force method is not appropriate for the NP-hard problems. Another method includes Linear Programming, Divide and Conquer, Dynamic Programming and Greedy etc.

2. Stochastic Optimization methods try to find the near-optimal solution for NP-Hard problems in polynomial time. It considers any random initial solution in the search space, and goes about finding an optimal solution in a number of iterations. Hill Climbing algorithm, Simulated Annealing, Tabu search etc are known as stochastic optimization methods.

3. Evolutionary algorithm is also one of the stochastic optimization methods, which differs with others in the fact that EAs maintains a population of the probable solutions to a problem. Different types of Evolutionary algorithms are Genetic Algorithm, Differential Evolution, Genetic programming, etc. The Evolutionary algorithm works as follows: A population of individuals is initialized in the search space, where each individual has its potential solution. The quality of each solution is evaluated by using the given fitness function. It starts with selection process, which is used to give next population. Mutation and Crossover is performed to alter the individuals and the higher order transformation respectively. This process is repeated for several numbers of iterations or till the optimal solution is obtained. Figure 1 shows the working principle of evolutionary algorithms.

4. Particle swarm optimization, Ant colony optimization, Cuckoo Search, etc. are the swarm intelligence techniques in optimization.

2. LITERATURE REVIEW

The first evolutionary algorithms that were purposefully designed to obtain an approximation set were proposed in the mid-1980s (Kursawe, 1990; Schaffer, 1985; Fourman, 1985). In these schemes, a proportion of the population was selected according to each individual objective. The main difficulty with this approach is that it often creates a phenomenon known as speciation, in which solutions arise in the population that are particularly strong in a single objective and particularly poor in others. Thus, important compromise solutions remain undiscovered, since the recombination of solutions from different extreme regions of the tradeoff surface cannot usually be assumed to generate an „intermediate" compromise. In the weighted-sum approach to MO, performance is captured in a single objective, calculated as a weighted-sum of individual performance in each of the original individual objectives. The well-known drawbacks of this approach are the difficulty in setting values for the weights, and the necessary condition for convexity of the trade-off surface that is required to obtain all Pareto optimal solutions. Thus, no combination of weights exists that can generate solutions in non-convex regions of the trade-off surface, as shown geometrically by Fleming and Pashkevich (1985). However, MOEAs based on weighted-sums schemes have also been proposed. Haleja and Lin (1992) included the weight

Figure 1. A flowchart of working principle of evolutionary algorithms

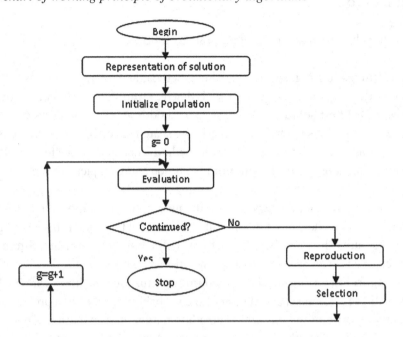

vector in the solution genotype and allowed multiple weight combinations to be propagated through the population during evolution. Jin, Okabe and Sendhoff (2001) varied the weight vector over the evolution, and have also provided theoretical justification for the method (Jin, Okabe, & Sendhoff, 2001a; 2001b). Unlike these early attempts, the majority of modern MOEAs are based on the concept of Pareto dominance (Coello, 2002). The use of Pareto dominance as a basis for solution comparison in Goldberg first suggested EAs in (Goldberg, 1989), together with the use of a niching technique to encourage solution distribution across the trade-off surface. In the early-1990s, three much-cited techniques emerged based on Goldberg"s ideas: Fonseca and Fleming"s (1993) multi-objective genetic algorithm (MOGA), Horn and Nafpliotis"s (1993) niched Pareto genetic algorithm (NPGA) and Srinivas and Deb"s nondominated sorting genetic algorithm (NSGA) (Srinivas & Deb, 1994), although early less well-known implementations by Ritzel and Cieniawski have also been reported (Horn & Nafpliotis, 1993; Fonseca & Fleming, 1995). The techniques differ slightly in the way in which fitness is derived from Pareto comparisons of solutions. MOGA, NPGA, and NSGA all use fitness sharing for diversity promotion (Goldberg & Richardson, 1987).

Lots of PSO variants are proposed from its formation to till date. Efforts are put towards increase in efficiency and convergence speed. Both the things are rarely achieved in a single algorithm. Low dimensional problems are easier to solve, where as complexity increase as the increase in dimensions and modality. A niching method is introduced in EAs to locate multiple optimal solutions (Li & Deb, 2010). Distance based LIPS model (Qu, Suganthan, & Das, 2013), a memetic PSO (Wang, Moon, Yang, & Wang, 2012), Adaptive PSO (Zhan, Zhang, Li, & Chung, 2009), Fractional PSO (Kiranyaz, Ince, Yildirim, & Gabbouj, 2010), AGPSO (Mirjalili, Lewis, & Sadiq, 2014), CSO (Cheng & Jin, 2015) and many other techniques are proposed to handle higher dimensional and multimodal problems. In spite of these techniques, trapping in local minima and the rate of convergence are two unavoidable problems in PSO and all other EAs. Though the PSO is nature inspired algorithm, a lot of issues can still be modeled to improve the performance. Different techniques to deal with the stagnation are studied in Bonyadi, Reza, Michalewicz, and Li (2014), Li and Yao (2012), and Bonyadi, Reza, Michalewicz, and Li (2014). They control the parameters involved in velocity update equation. To remove the problem of stagnation and to get the better performance, lot of techniques like GCPSO (Bergh, 2002) which uses a different velocity update equation for the best particle since its personal best and global best both lie at the same point. OPSO (Wang et al., 2007) employs opposition based learning for each particle and applies dynamic Cauchy mutation on the best particle. QPSO (Yang, Wnag, & Jiao, 2004) proposed a new discrete particle swarm optimization algorithm based on quantum representation of individuals, which in turn causes faster convergence. In the new method called H-PSO (Janson & Middendorf, 2005), the particles are arranged in a dynamic hierarchy that is used to define a neighborhood structure. Depending on the quality of their so-far best found solution, the particles move up or down the hierarchy. This gives good particles that move up in the hierarchy a larger influence on the swarm. George I. Evers proposed a RegPSO (Evers & Ghalia, 2009), where the problem of stagnation is removed by automatically triggering the swarm regrouping. Efforts are taken to solve multimodal problems. To solve higher dimensional problems, variants cooperative co evolution strategies like CPSO-SK and CPSO-HK (Bergh & Engelbrecht, 2004), CCPSO (Yang, Tang, & Yao, 2008), CCPSO2 (Cui, Zeng, & Yin, 2008) are proposed.

3. PARTICLE SWARM OPTIMIZATION

Scientists and engineers from all disciplines often have to deal with the classical problem of search and optimization. Optimization means the action of finding the best-suited solution of a problem within the given constraints and flexibilities. While optimizing performance of a system, we aim at finding out such a set of values of the system parameters, for which the overall performance of the system will be the best under some given conditions. Usually, the parameters governing the system performance are represented in a vector x= [x1, x2, x3 ....xD] . For real parameter optimization, each parameter xi is a real number. To measure how far the "best" performance we have achieved, an objective function (or fitness function) is designed for the system. Let us consider the following simple objective function named sphere function.

$$F(x) = \sum_{i=1}^{n} z_i^2 \; where \; x \; \varepsilon \; [-100, \, 100]$$

Particle Swarm Optimization (PSO) is a simple real parameter optimization algorithm. It works through simple cycle of stages as shown in Figure 3.

3.1. Representation of Solution

There are different methods for representing solution/point in search space (variable space). The use of proper data structure (like list, tree etc.) plays very important role in processing of solutions. Particles are the basic building blocks in particle swarm optimization. Particle movement in the search space leads to the solution. The movement depends on velocity (v) and displacement (x) of the particle. When particle moves, they adjust their velocity, so that no collision should occur between them. Velocity of the

Figure 2. Objective function – sphere

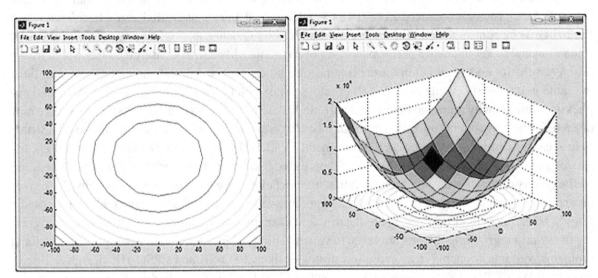

(a): Contour of Sphere function   **(b): 3-D Sphere function**

Figure 3. Stages in PSO working

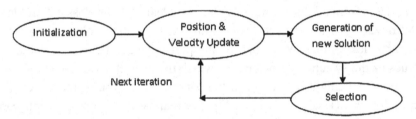

particle depends on certain factors like current velocity & personal best and social best of the swarm. After finding the velocity, the new displacement vector of each particle is find out.

Generally in PSO, variables and objectives are represented separately

```
NP = 10;
x = zeros(NP,D);
v = zeros(NP,D);
pbest = x ;
fit = fun(x);
gbest = x(min(fit));
```

3.2. Initialization

Particle Swarm Optimization algorithm (PSO) begins its process by randomly initializing the NP number of particles in D dimension vectors within the search space. These vectors act as a candidate solution for a given objective function. Every cycle in PSO can be considered as a generation, G= 1, 2, 3 ….. Gmax. Any candidate solution at any generation can be denoted as:

$$x_{i,g}=[x_{1,g},x_{2,g},x_{3,g}\ldots\ldots\ldots x_{D,g}]$$

There exists a lower and upper bound within search space for each parameter in the problem, it can be denoted as:

$$X_{min}=[X_{1,min},X_{2,min}\ldots\ldots X_{d,min}] \text{ and } X_{max}=[X_{1,max},X_{2,max}\ldots\ldots X_{d,max}]$$

To consider the effect of normal distribution, the initial population at G=0 must cover the maximum range between the lower and upper bound. This can be achieved by following equation:

$$X_{j,i,0}= X_{j,min}+ \text{rand } [0,1] (X_{j,max}- X_{j,min})$$

whereas $x_{j,i,0} = $ j[th] component of ith member of the population at 0th generation and $x_{j,min}$ and $x_{j,min}$ are its respective lower and upper value. This type of initialization is called symmetric initialization, where the search is being performed in given range only. This range varies as per the fitness function.

Let us consider NP=8, D=2, then the initial population for above mentioned objective function with fitness value will be as shown in Table 1.

3.2.1. Random Initialization (Symmetric)

Code:

```
function [pop]=init_pop(pop,NP,D,xl,xu)
for i=1:NP
        for j=1:D
                xMin=xl(j);
                xMax=xu(j);
                % Random real number between xMin and xMax
```

Table 1. Initial population with fitness value

SN	Initial Population		Fitness Value
1	49.2214	4.6626	2444.48605672000
2	92.3987	-93.9459	17363.3518885000
3	-13.9432	78.0072	6279.53607808000
4	-54.05976	-77.8154	8977.69412841760
5	30.3994	-74.9137	6536.18596805000
6	76.0132	51.1828	8397.68559008000
7	56.6531	95.7127	12370.4946809000
8	-89.8707	-14.8693	8297.83880098000
9	-87.9401	80.6312	14234.8516014500
10	-40.3144	2.7629	**1632.88446377000**

Figure 4. Distribution of initial population in search space

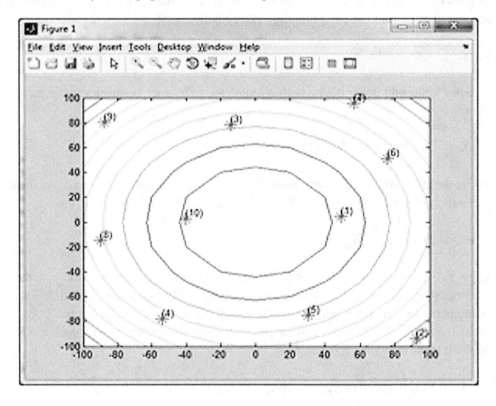

```
        x(i,j) = xMin+rand*(xMax-xMin); %Initialize Position
v(i,j) = xMin+rand*(xMax-xMin);
        end
end
end
```

Function *init_pop* randomly initializes a population of size NP. There are D numbers of decision variables in each solution of population. Each variable is having lower (*xl*) and upper (*xu*) bound. Each variable is randomly initialized between the lower & upper bound. If lower and upper bounds for all variables are same (for ex. xl=-100 &xu=100) then

```
For i=1:NP
        for j=1:D
                x(i,j) = xl+rand*(xu-xl);
                v(i,j) = xl+rand*(xu-xl);
        end
end
```

3.2.2. Information Based Initialization

In most real-world problems, the knowledge of the exact optimum is usually not available. Symmetric initialization creates population around the optimal solution whereas skewed initialization creates population away from the actual optimum. Performance of PSO on symmetric initialization may not represent the PSO's true performance in solving the same problem with a different initialization or other problem. The initialization of population away from global basin makes sure that an algorithm must overcome a number of local minima to reach global basin. Hence it is always better to use either mix initialization scheme or test the performance of algorithm on both types of initialization schemes.

After initialization of population it is further tuned to ensure well and uniform distribution over search space. There are various techniques like opposition based learning (OBL), k-means clustering, Chaotic methods *etc* can be used for tuning. After initialization of population, next job is to calculate fitness or objectives of each solution.

For example: sphere function (*fun=1*) is single objective function.

```
function fit = func(x,func_num)
% Sphere Function
If func_num==1
        fit = sum(x.*x, 2);
end
for i = 1:1:N
    f(i) = func(x(i,:),fun);       % Function value for initial position
end
```

Other variables are defined as shown in Table 2.

3.3. Generation of New Solution

In a particle swarm optimizer, individuals are "evolved" by cooperation and competition among the individuals themselves through generations. Each particle adjusts its flying according to its own flying experience and its companions' flying experience. Each individual is named as a "particle" which, in fact, represents a potential solution to a problem. Each particle is treated as a point in a D dimensional space. The ith particle is represented as

Table 2.

Variables	Formula / Values
pbest	pbest = x;
gbest	p_f = f; [gbest, g] = min(p_f);
w	0.72
c1, c2	1.49

$$X_i = (X_{i1}, X_{i2}, \ldots\ldots\ldots, X_{iD})$$

The best previous position (the position giving the best fitness value) of any particle is recorded and represented as

$$P_i = (P_{i1}, P_{i2}, \ldots\ldots, P_{iD})$$

The index of the best particle among all the particles in the population is represented by the symbol g. The rate of the position change (velocity) for particle i is represented as

$$V_i = (V_{i1}, V_{i2}, \ldots\ldots\ldots, V_{iD})$$

The Particle are manipulated according to equation

$$V_{iD} = w \times V_{iD} + c1 \times rand() \times (P_{iD} - X_{iD}) + c2 \times rand() \times (P_{gD} - X_{iD}) \qquad \text{(a)}$$

$$X_{iD} = X_{iD} + V_{iD} \qquad \text{(b)}$$

rand() is a random function which generates value in the range[0,1]. The second part of the equation (a) is the "cognition' part, which represents the private thinking of the particle itself. The third part is the "social" part, which represents the collaboration among the particles. The equation (a) is used to calculate the particle's new velocity according to its previous velocity and the distances of its current position from its own best experience (position) and the group's best experience. Then the particle flies toward a new position according to equation (b).

w = Inertia weight used to explore and exploit the search space
c1= Cognitive constant i.e. learning factor for personal movement
c2 = Social Constant i.e. learning factor for group movement

Let us consider w=0.7, c1=c2=1.49, then

Vid = w * Vid + c1 * rand() * (Pid - Xid) + c2 * rand() * (Pgd - Xid)

Figure 5. Particle's position change

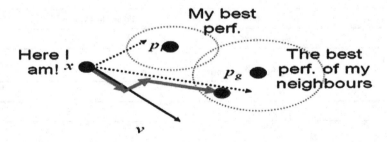

Table 3. Values at 1ˢᵗ generation

V			V		P		X		G	
-15.0702	2.2853		49.2214	4.6626	49.2214	4.6626	49.2214	4.6626	-40.3144	2.7629
-38.8352	9.1370		92.3987	-93.9459	92.3987	-93.9459	92.3987	-93.9459	-40.3144	2.7629
-46.9353	-49.1100		-13.9432	78.0072	-13.9432	78.0072	-13.9432	78.0072	-40.3144	2.7629
-27.6555	10.0255		-54.0597	-77.8154	-54.0597	-77.8154	-54.0597	-77.8154	-40.3144	2.7629
-39.9655	14.0055	=	30.3994	-74.9137	30.3994	-74.9137	30.3994	-74.9137	-40.3144	2.7629
2.5150	15.1180		76.0132	51.1828	76.0132	51.1828	76.0132	51.1828	-40.3144	2.7629
7.4889	-18.4958		56.6531	95.7127	56.6531	95.7127	56.6531	95.7127	-40.3144	2.7629
25.1628	-5.5890		-89.8707	-14.8693	-89.8707	-14.8693	-89.8707	-14.8693	-40.3144	2.7629
25.6015	-19.1241		-87.9401	80.6312	-87.9401	80.6312	-87.9401	80.6312	-40.3144	2.7629
-29.0263	1.9892		-40.3144	2.7629	-40.3144	2.7629	-40.3144	2.7629	-40.3144	2.7629

X			X			V	
34.1511	6.9479		49.2214	4.6626		-15.0702	2.2853
53.5634	-84.8088		92.3987	-93.9459		-38.8352	9.1370
-60.8785	28.8971		-13.9432	78.0072		-46.9353	-49.1100
-81.7152	-67.7898		-54.0597	-77.8154		-27.6555	10.0255
-9.5661	-60.9081	=	30.3994	-74.9137	+	-39.9655	14.0055
78.5282	66.3008		76.0132	51.1828		2.5150	15.1180
64.1420	**100**		56.6531	95.7127		7.4889	-18.4958
-100	-20.4583		-89.8707	-14.8693		25.1628	-5.5890
-100	**100**		-87.9401	80.6312		25.6015	-19.1241
-69.3407	4.7521		-40.3144	2.7629		-29.0263	1.9892

Code:

```
function [x,v]=generation(x,v,pbest,g,c1,c2,w,LB,UB,D,N)
    gbest = repmat(x(g,:),N, 1);
    %Update Velocity & Position
    for i=1:N
        v(i,:) = w*v(i,:) + c1*rand()*(pbest(i,:) -
x(i,:))+c2*rand()*(gbest(i,:)-x(i,:)); % Update the velocity
        x(i,:) = x(i,:) + v(i,:); %Update Position
    end
    %Initialize the particle in range if they move outside the range
    for i=1:N
        for j = 1:1:D
            xMin=LB(j);
            xMax=UB(j);
            if x(i,j) > xMax
```

```
                    x(i,j) = xMax;
                    v(i,j) = -0.5*v(i,j);
                end
                if x(i,j) < xMin
                    x(i,j) = xMin;
                    v(i,j) = -0.5*v(i,j);
                end
            end %j
        end
end
```

3.4. Selection of Solutions to Generate New Solutions

When particles move outside, those should be reinitialized on the boundary. It is shown in above table by bold values (having values -100 or 100). It is necessary to change the value pbest for next generation. To do so, calculate the fitness value of newly calculated position vector. Those fitness values are then compared with old fitness value of position vector. If new fitness value is better than old, then make corresponding position as pbest otherwise it remains as it is. This process is continuing until the stopping criterion is met or up to end of number of iterations.

Code:

```
[pbest p_f g]=selection(x,f,p_f,N,pbest);
function [pbest,p_f,g]=selection(x,f,p_f,N,pbest)
%Change personal best
    for i=1:1:N
        if f(i) <= p_f(i)
            pbest(i,:) = x(i,:);
            p_f(i) = f(i);
        end

    end

    [gbest, g] = min(p_f);
End
```

3.5. Generation of Next Generation Population

All the values calculated newly i.e. x, v, pbest, gbest are taken for next generation.

3.6. Criteria for Termination

This generational process is repeated until a termination condition has been reached. Common terminating conditions are:

Table 4. New pbest in next generation after selection

Old Positions		Fitness value of old Position	New Positions		Fitness Value new Position	Pbest for next Generation	
49.2214	4.6626	2444.48605672000	**34.1511**	**6.9479**	**1214.57626957250**	34.1511	6.9479
92.3987	-93.9459	17363.3518885000	**53.5634**	**-84.8088**	**10061.5888734928**	53.5634	-84.8088
-13.9432	78.0072	6279.53607808000	**-60.8785**	**28.8971**	**4541.24653749198**	-60.8785	28.8971
-54.0597	**-77.8154**	8977.69412841760	-81.7152	-67.7898	11272.8411887860	-54.0597	-77.8154
30.3994	-74.9137	6536.18596805000	**-9.5661**	**-60.9081**	**3801.30857959820**	-9.5661	-60.9081
76.0132	**51.1828**	**8397.68559008000**	78.5282	66.3008	10562.4814334842	76.0132	51.1828
56.6531	**95.7127**	**12370.4946809000**	64.1420	100	14114.2012432503	56.6531	95.7127
-89.8707	**-14.8693**	**8297.83880098000**	-100	-20.4583	10418.5442021252	-89.8707	-14.8693
-87.9401	**80.6312**	**14234.8516014500**	-100	100	20000	-87.9401	80.6312
-40.3144	**2.7629**	**1632.88446377000**	-69.3407	4.7521	4830.72539761717	-40.3144	2.7629

Bold values in each row indicate selected values of positions for next generation. These values are taken as pbest values.

Figure 6. Particle's movements in different iterations
Here representations are, 25th iter: Blue 'o', 50th iter: Green 'o', 75th iter: Red '+', 100th iter: Blue '+'

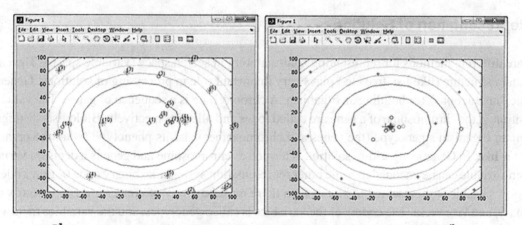

a): 2ⁿᵈ Generation movements on Contour (b): Particle movements after every 25ᵗʰ Generation

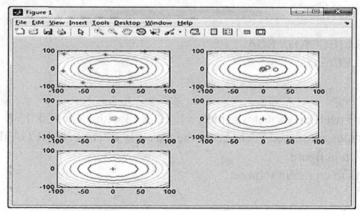

(c) : Particle's trajectories in different iterations

- A solution is found that satisfies minimum criteria
- Fixed number of generations reached
- Allocated budget (computation time/money) reached
- The highest ranking solution's fitness is reaching or has reached a plateau such that successive iterations no longer produce better results
- Manual inspection
- Combinations of the above

4. GENETIC ALGORITHM

Genetic Algorithms (GAs) are adaptive heuristic search algorithm based on the evolutionary ideas of natural selection and genetics. Some fundamental ideas of genetics (for data representation) and natural evolutionary process (for data processing) are borrowed and used artificially to construct search algorithm that are robust and required minimum problem information. GAs exploits historical information to direct the search into the region of better performance within the search space. They use natural reproduction mechanisms that work exclusively with one (asexual reproduction) or more parents (sexual reproduction). They use natures rule of "survival of the fittest". GA is flexible enough to incorporate many such principles and rules of nature to model search strategy.

4.1. Representation of Solution

There are different methods for representing solution/point in search space (variable space). The use of proper data structure (like list, tree etc.) plays very important role in processing of solutions. Genes are the basic "instructions" for building an organism. A chromosome is a sequence of genes. The value and the position in the chromosome of a gene are called locus and allele, respectively. Biologists distinguish between an organism's genotype (the genes and chromosomes) and its phenotype (what the organism actually is like. In Genetic algorithm solution is termed as chromosome and gene is a decision variable. Decision variable can be encoded in some other representation system like binary code 0r gray code etc. if decision variable is represented in binary then there must be a way of converting continuous values into binary, and vice versa. The coding of the variables is called genotypes, and the variables themselves are called phenotypes.

There are two types of Gas:

1. Binary coded GA (BCGA) or BGA.
2. Real coded GA (RCGA).

For Example:

Let solution x has 3 decision variables namely x1, x2 & x3 with values 20, 15 & 10 respectively. In RCGA decision variables are placed in chromosome x as it is where as in BCGA they are encoded in binary system as shown in figure.

There are two ways to represent solution:

1. Decision variables and objective are place together to form chromosome that is represented by a single entity.
    NP = 10;
    pop=zeros(NP,D+m);
2. Decision variables and objectives are represented separately in two different entities
    NP = 10;
    pop=zeros(NP,D);
    obj=zeros(NP,m);

4.2. Creation of Initial Population

Evolutionary algorithms work on set of solutions (i.e. population) rather than single solution. Evolution begins with an initial population where solutions are (usually) randomly generated. The population size depends on the nature of the problem, but typically contains several hundreds or thousands of possible solutions. Traditionally, the population is generated randomly, allowing the entire range of possible solutions (the search space). Occasionally, the solutions may be "seeded" in areas where optimal solutions are likely to be found. In either case it is essential that solutions must be well and uniformly distributed over the search space.

4.2.1. Random Initialization

This is same as the information discussed in section 3.2.1

4.2.2. Information Based Initialization

Population can be initialized with set of known values rather than random values. This can be done based on the past experience of solving similar types of problem or based on some information about the possible solutions. In following example population is initializing with known values,

Ex. pop = [
49.22 4.66;
92.39 -93.95
-13.94 78.00;
-54.06 -77.82
30.39 -74.91;
76.01 51.18
56.65 95.71;
-89.87 -14.87
-87.94 80.63;
-40.31 2.76];

In most the real-world problems, the knowledge of the exact optimum is usually not available. Symmetric initialization creates population around the optimal solution whereas skewed initialization creates population away from the actual optimum. Performance of GA on symmetric initialization may not represent the GA's true performance in solving the same problem with a different initialization or other problem. The initialization of population away from global basin makes sure that an algorithm must overcome a number of local minima to reach global basin. Hence it is always better to use either mix initialization scheme or test the performance of algorithm on both types of initialization schemes. After initialization, population can be further tuned to ensure well and uniform distribution over search space. There are various techniques like opposition based learning (OBL), k-means clustering, Chaotic methods *etc.*, can be used for tuning. After initialization of population, next job is to calculate fitness or objectives of each solution. For example: Sphere function (*fun=1*) is single objective function.

Code:

```
function fit = func(x,func_num)
% Sphere Function
If func_num==1
     fit = sum(x.*x, 2);
end
for i=1:NP
     [pop(i,D+1)] = func(pop(i,1:D),fun);
End
```

4.3. Generation of New Solution

Let x(x1, x2,....,xD) is a vector (that stores group of values). There are two ways to generate new vector from x;

a. $x \pm \delta$, δ is some value that is added or subtracted from x
b. $(x1 \pm \delta, x2 \pm \delta, x3 \pm \delta......... xD \pm \delta)$, where δ may have different value

Generation of new solution is a two steps process

a.   Generation of new value for variable from existing value
b.   Making or formation of new solution from values

These two steps may be perform separately or may be integrated.

In multi-variable crossover, for each variable that undergo crossover (depends upon the Crossover probability). Let X_i^1 and X_i^2 are two values of xi gene in two different chromosomes.

Let y_i is a new value (offspring) generated.

$$y_{i=} x_i^1 \pm \left(\beta_i \times D\right)$$

Here δ is β_i and d is a distance,

$$D = \left(\left| x_i^1 - x_i^2 \right| / 2 \right) \text{ or } D = \left(\sqrt{\left(x_i^1 - x_i^2 \right)} / 2 \right)$$

β_i is calculated as

$$\beta i = \begin{cases} \left(2u_i \right)^{1/(n+1)} & \text{if } u_i \leq 0.5 \\ \left[1 / 2 \left(1 - u_i \right) \right]^{1/(n+1)} & \text{otherwise} \end{cases}$$

Choose a random number u_i between 0 and 1 and from the polynomial probability distribution function with index η, find the ordinate β_i, so that the area under the probability curve from 0 to β_i is equal to the u_i. The change is $\partial_i = \left(\beta_i \times D \right)$, where β_i (known as spread factor) is calculated from polynomial probability distribution. β_i depends upon probability distribution index η (variable *mu* in code) and contracting or expanding crossover. Spread factor β_i, *for* contracting crossover $(u_{i \leq 0.5})$ is $0 <= \beta <= 1$ and for expanding crossover $(u_i > 0.5)$ is $\beta_i > 1$. The β_i is calculated by equating the area under the probability distribution curve to *u* (in code variable *rnd*). D is a Euclidian distance among solutions. Since $\beta_i > 0$ and distance is also positive hence δ_i is also positive.

Code:

```
p=2; xl=5.0; xu=30.0; x(1)=9.7;
x(2)=20.1;
mu=2.0;
fprintf('No of parents:%d\tDistribution index:%d\n', p, mu);
for i=1:p
        fprintf('x%1d:%f\t', i,x(i));
end
fprintf('\n');
alpha = 2.0;
rnd = rand(1);
if rnd<= 1.0/alpha
% contracting crossover
alpha = alpha*rnd;
expp = 1.0/(mu+1.0);
betaq = alpha.^expp;
else
% expanding crossover
alpha = alpha*rnd;
alpha = 1.0/(2.0-alpha);
expp = 1.0/(mu+1.0);
if (alpha < 0.0) fprintf('ERRRORRR \n'); return;
```

```
end
betaq = alpha.^expp;
end
%generating two children
dist=0.0;
for k=1:p
dist=dist + (abs(x(1)-x(k))* abs(x(1)-x(k)));
end
dist=sqrt(dist)/p;
fprintf('rnd:%f\tbetaq:%f\tDist:%f\n', rnd,betaq, dist);
y(1) = x(1) - betaq * dist;
y(2) = x(1) + betaq * dist;
fprintf('y1:%f\ty2:%f\n', y(1),y(2));
Output:
```

a.   Expanding crossover (_rnd_   > 0.5 then _betaq_>1**)**

```
No of parents:2        Distribution index:2
x1:9.700000              x2:20.100000
rnd:0.959492            betaq:2.311060   Dist:5.200000
y1:-2.317513             y2:21.717513


No of parents:2        Distribution index:2 x1:9.700000
x2:20.100000
rnd:0.505957            betaq:1.004003   Dist:5.200000
y1:4.479183             y2:14.920817
```

b.   Contracting Crossover (rnd <= 0.5 then 0 <=betaq<=1)

```
No of parents:2        Distribution index:2
x1:9.700000              x2:20.100000
rnd:0.498364            betaq:0.998908   Dist:5.200000
y1:4.505677             y2:14.894323


No of parents:2        Distribution index:2
x1:9.700000              x2:20.100000
rnd:0.035712            betaq:0.414903 Dist:5.2000
y1:7.542504             y2:11.857496
```

In parent-centric crossover, contracting crossover generates children(i.e. new values) near the parent (i.e. variable) and expanding crossover generates children faraway from parent. In mean- centric crossover, contracting crossover generates children between the parents (parents enclose the children) and expanding crossover generates children faraway from parent(children enclose the parents). Contracting and expanding crossover is also possible with other probability distributions. Following is a code for log-normal probability distribution.

Code:

```
alpha = 2.0;
rnd = rand(1);
if rnd<= 1.0/alpha
% contracting crossover
z1=logninv(1-rnd);
betaq = exp(-z1*mu);
else
% expanding crossover z1=logninv(rnd);
betaq = exp(z1*mu);
end
Output:
```

a. Expanding crossover (*rnd* > 0.5 then *betaq* > 1**)**

```
  No of parents:2  Log-N Distn index:2
   x1:9.700000          x2:20.100000
   rnd:0.996135         betaq:2901261705651.418900    Dist:5.200000
   y1:-15086560869377.682000          y2:15086560869397.080000


No of parents:2       Log-N Distn      index:2
x1:9.700000            x2:20.100000
rnd:0.546882           betaq:9.487806    Dist:5.200000
y1:-39.636592          y2:59.036592
```

b   Contracting Crossover (rnd <= 0.5   then 0 <=betaq<=1)

```
No of parents:2       Log-N Distn index:2
x1:9.700000            x2:20.100000
rnd:0.485376           betaq:0.125595    Dist:5.200000
y1:9.046906            y2:10.353094

No of parents:2       Log-N Distn index:2
x1:9.700000            x2:20.100000
rnd:0.011902           betaq:0.000000    Dist:5.200000
y1:9.700000            y2:9.700000
```

For polynomial probability distribution, its ability to generate children away from the parent decreases as the value of distribution index increases. For log-normal probability distribution, its ability to generate children faraway from parent increases as the value of distribution index increases. Operator with polynomial distribution is good for exploitation of search space whereas log-normal distribution is better for exploration of search space.

Figure 7. Probability distribution of contracting and expanding crossovers for the lognormal distribution

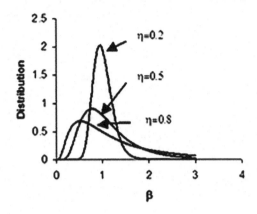

Variations:

1.   Choose different probability distribution (like polynomial, lognormal, normal etc.)
2.   Choose different distribution index
3.   Generate offspring around the parents or around the mean of parents.
4.   Instead of Euclidean distance take normal average distance.

Use more than two parents then D becomes

$$D = \left(\sum_{k=1}^{\mu} \left(\sum_{i=1}^{\mu} \left| x_i^j - x_i^k \right| \right) / \mu \right) / \mu$$

4.4. Making of Solution From Values

One can generate δ as discuss above and use this δ to bring variation in decision variables. Or generate δ_i for each decision variable and then take decision to use that δ_i to change value of ith decision variable. The processes of generation of δ and then bringing variation in decision variable may be done separately or may be put together. It is not mandatory to change all variables in solution. The decisions of choosing variable for change and whether to add or subtract δ from variable are very decisive. Probability of crossover (p_c) decides how many variables (out of D variables) in solution will change their value. For example if p_c=0.9 then only 90% variables will change their value and 10% will remain unchanged.

Code:

```
p=2;
xl=5.0;
xu=30.0;
D=3;
pc=0.9;
```

```
fprintf('No of parents: %d\t No of var: %d\tCrossProb: %f\n', p, D,pc);
for i=1:p
par(i,1:D)=xl+(xu-xl).*rand(1,D);
end
for i = 1: p
fprintf('Par%d:\t',i);
for j=1:D
fprintf('x%1d: %f\t', j,par(i,j));
end fprintf('\n'); end
for j = 1: D for k=1:p x(k)=par(k,j); end rnd=rand(1);
%variable is selected for crossover or not ifrnd<= pc
        y=MPX_p11(x,p);
        child_1(j) = y(1);
        child_2(j) = y(2);
else% no recombination
        child_1(j) = x(1);
        child_2(j) = x(2);
end
end%end of j
fprintf('Child-1:\t');
for j=1:D
fprintf('x%1d: %f\t', j,child_1(j));
end
fprintf('\n');
fprintf('Child-2:\t');
for j=1:D
fprintf('x%1d: %f\t', j,child_2(j));
end
fprintf('\n');
Output:
No of parents: 2        No of var: 3          Cross Prob: 0.900000


Par1:      x1: 19.380215    x2: 6.494489     x3: 10.869498
Par2:      x1: 13.828964    x2: 25.529851    x3: 5.385086
Child-1:   x1: 17.766576    x2: -6.498945    x3: 8.265344
Child-2:   x1: 20.993854    x2: 19.487922    x3: 13.473651


No of parents: 2        No of var: 3          Cross Prob: 0.900000


Par1:      x1: 18.675222    x2: 12.408020    x3: 23.617320
Par2:      x1: 9.723875     x2: 22.169386    x3: 9.587779
Child-1:   x1: 13.502892    x2: 10.442059    x3: 23.617320
Child-2:   x1: 23.847552    x2: 14.373982    x3: 23.617320
```

```
No of parents: 2        No of var: 3        Cross Prob: 0.900000

Par1:      x1:  9.869107   x2: 10.648045   x3:  9.267701
Par2:      x1: 10.691607   x2: 15.892467   x3: 12.777557
Child-1:   x1:  9.869107   x2:  9.053808   x3:  9.267701
Child-2:   x1:  9.869107   x2: 12.242281   x3:  9.267701
```

The decision of applying crossover operator on variable is taken by random number (rnd=rand(1)<= pc).

4.5. Selection of Solutions to Generate New Solutions

Selection is the process of choosing individuals from the current generation to move into the breeding pool. Selection usually favors the fitter individuals. The selection pressure can be control by varying the level of emphasis the process assigns to fitter individuals. A more stringent selection process that is more biased towards the fitter solutions will lead to exploitation while a less stringent selection process will put less pressure lead to exploration of population. There are various selection methods to form breeding or mating pool. Some of the state-of-the art methods for selection of parents for reproduction are random selection, proportionate selection tournament selection Rank-based selection

1. *Random selection*

Here out of two parents required to form mating pool, one parent is selected sequentially from population and other parent is selected randomly from population. Both the parents are distinct.

Code:

```
parent(1)=p;
for i=2:nPar
          % select other parents randomly
    while(1)
    j=randi(NP,1);
    if (ismember(j,parent(1:i-1))== 0)
    break;
    end
    end parent(i)=j;
    end %i
```

2. *Tournament selection*

The basic idea of tournament selection scheme is quite straightforward. A group of individuals is selected randomly from the population. The individuals in this group are then compared with each other, with the fittest among the group becoming the selected individual.

Code:

```
% select first parent sequentially parent(1)=p;
for i=2:nPar
while(1)
        j=randi(NP,1);
if (ismember(j,parent(1:i-1))== 0)
break;
end end
while(1)
        k=randi(NP,1);
if (ismember(j,parent(1:i-1))== 0)
if(j ~= k)
break;
end
end
end
    % play tournament (winner selected)
if (pop(j,D+1) <= pop(k,D+1)) parent(i)=j;
else
parent(i)=k;
end
end%i
```

3. *Proportionate selection*

In proportionate selection (Roulette Wheel Selection or Spinning Wheel Selection) each individual is assigned a selection probability based on its fitness over the total fitness of the entire population. Once this is done, individuals are concatenated with each other to form a spinning wheel, with each portion of the wheel representing an individual and the size of each portion representing the corresponding selection probabilities.

4. *Rank-based selection*

Rank-based selection schemes first sort individuals in the population according to certain criteria (usually according to their fitness). A function is then used to map the indices of individuals in the sorted list to their selection probabilities. All these methods can be applied directly to single objective problem but for multi-objective problem they need a single scalar fitness assignment method

Despite the great diversity of life on earth, natural reproduction mechanisms work exclusively with one (asexual reproduction) or two parents (sexual reproduction). The majority of the species reproduce in an asexual manner, showing the viability of asexual reproduction. However, species that are higher in the evolutionary hierarchy use sexual production, suggesting that sexual reproduction is more advanced. In Genetic Algorithm (GA) variation is carried out through crossover (sexual reproduction) and mutation (asexual reproduction) operations. The purpose of a crossover operator is twofold, Initial random strings representing the problem variables must be searched thoroughly in order to create good strings_ Thereafter, good portions of these strings must be combined together to form better strings. The search power of a crossover operator is defined here as a measure of how flexible the operator is to create an arbitrary point in the search space. The search power of a crossover operator is the probability of creating an arbitrary point in the search space from two given parent points. Thus the polynomial distribution has probability of creating children points closer to the parent points is larger than that of points far away from the parents. Whereas, the lognormal distribution has ability to create children points far away from the parents. Ideally a good search algorithm must have a broad search in early generations and as the generations proceed the search must be focused on to a narrow region. Ideally search must be explorative in nature in the beginning and slowly as generation progress it must be *exploitative* in nature. Crossover may occur at *chromosome-level* or it may be *gene-wise* crossover.

4.6. Construction of Next Generation Population

Generational GA and steady-state GA are two strategies for reproducing the population members in GA. In generational GA, each iteration creates a complete set of NP (population size) new offspring. For preserving elite solutions, both the parent and the offspring populations are compared and the best NP solutions are retained. Each member in current population may or may not get chance to reproduce children. Its participation in reproduction process depends on fitness of a member. If concept of mating pool is used then fitter solutions get more privilege and chances to reproduce solutions. In the simplest strategy each solution in current population get chance to reproduce solutions. The members in current population are called parents and the solutions reproduces by them are called offspring or children.

Here first parent is selected sequentially from population and other parent is selected by using tournament selection. One can select both the parents by using tournament selection. Also one can also use multi-level tournament selection.

Table 5. Parent population and offspring population

Parent or Current Population					Offspring Population			
SN	x	x	O		SN	x_1	x_2	Obj
1	49.22	4.66	2444.		1	49.22	-49.58	4880.84
2	92.39	-93.95	17362.		2	93.17	37.97	10122.97
3	-	78	6278.		3	-19.86	36.68	1739.52
4	-	-77.82	8978.		4	-1.52	39.82	1588.28
5	30.39	-74.91	6535.		5	30.39	-74.91	6535.06
6	76.01	51.18	8396.		6	76.01	51.18	8396.91
7	56.65	95.71	12369.		7	52.06	78.46	8865.54
8	-	-14.87	8297.		8	-36.75	1.03	1351.82
9	-	80.63	14234.		9	-38.75	115.64	14874.88
10	-	2.76	1632.		10	-15.64	17.71	558.13

Reproduction and Selection

Figure 8. Parent population and offspring population

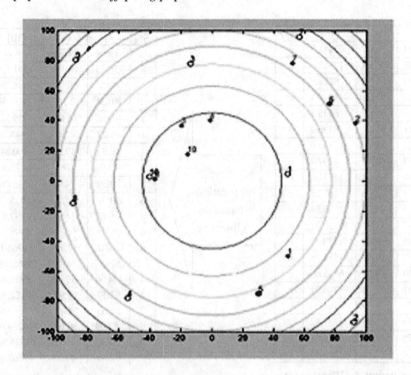

In order to form population for next generation, put together members of parent population and offspring population (size is 2NP). Then, select first NP better solutions from combined population as member of next generation.

Code:

```
for i=1:NP
        % copy parent Population temp(i,1)=1; %for parent
temp(i,2)=i; %parent number temp(i,3)=pop(i,D+1);
end
for i=1:NP
        % copy offspring population
temp(NP+i,1)=0; %for child temp(NP+i,2)=i;
%child number
temp(NP+i,3)=pop_off(i,D+1); end
temp=sortrows(temp,3);

%select first NP better solution from sorted combined populations
for i=1:NP
if(temp(i,1) == 1)
```

Table 6. Selection of better solution

SN	x₁	x₂	Obj	p/c
1	49.22	4.66	2444.3	p
2	92.39	-93.95	17362.5	p
3	-13.94	78	6278.3	p
4	-54.06	-77.82	8978.4	p
5	30.39	-74.91	6535.1	p
6	76.01	51.18	8396.9	p
7	56.65	95.71	12369.6	p
8	-89.87	-14.87	8297.7	p
9	-87.94	80.63	14234.6	p
10	-40.31	2.76	1632.5	p
1	49.22	-49.58	4880.84	c
2	93.17	37.97	10122.97	c
3	-19.86	36.68	1739.52	c
4	-1.52	39.82	1588.28	c
5	30.39	-74.91	6535.06	c
6	76.01	51.18	8396.91	c
7	52.06	78.46	8865.54	c
8	-36.75	1.03	1351.82	c
9	-38.75	115.64	14874.88	c
10	-15.64	17.71	558.13	c

Combined Parent & Offspring (or children) populations

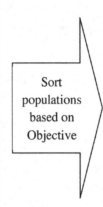

Sort populations based on Objective

SN	x₁	x₂	Obj	p/c
10	-15.64	17.71	558.13	c
8	-36.75	1.03	1351.82	c
4	-1.52	39.82	1588.28	c
10	-40.31	2.76	1632.5	p
3	-19.86	36.68	1739.52	c
1	49.22	4.66	2444.3	p
1	49.22	-49.58	4880.84	c
3	-13.94	78	6278.3	p
5	30.39	-74.91	6535.06	c
5	30.39	-74.91	6535.1	p
8	-89.87	-14.87	8297.7	p
6	76.01	51.18	8396.9	p
6	76.01	51.18	8396.91	c
7	52.06	78.46	8865.54	c
4	-54.06	-77.82	8978.4	p
2	93.17	37.97	10122.97	c
7	56.65	95.71	12369.6	p
9	-87.94	80.63	14234.6	p
9	-38.75	115.64	14874.88	c
2	92.39	-93.95	17362.5	p

Sorted combined population

SN	x₁	x₂	Obj
1	-15.64	17.71	558.13
2	-36.75	1.03	1351.82
3	-1.52	39.82	1588.28
4	-40.31	2.76	1632.5
5	-19.86	36.68	1739.52
6	49.22	4.66	2444.3
7	49.22	-49.58	4880.84
8	-13.94	78	6278.3
9	30.39	-74.91	6535.06
10	30.39	-74.91	6535.1

```
    next_pop(i,:)= pop(temp(i,2),:);
else
next_pop(i,:)= pop_off(temp(i,2),:);
end
end
```

Table 7. Finding Next Generation population

Parent Population			Offspring Population			Next Generation		
49.22	4.66	2444.3	49.22	-49.58	4880.84	-15.64	17.71	558.13
92.39	-93.95	17362.5	93.17	37.97	10122.9	-36.75	1.03	1351.82
-13.94	78	6278.3	-19.86	36.68	1739.52	-1.52	39.82	1588.28
-54.06	-77.82	8978.4	-1.52	39.82	1588.28	-40.31	2.76	1632.51
30.39	-74.91	6535.1	30.39	-74.91	6535.06	-19.86	36.68	1739.52
76.01	51.18	8396.9	76.01	51.18	8396.91	49.22	4.66	2444.32
56.65	95.71	12369.6	52.06	78.46	8865.54	49.22	-49.58	4880.84
-89.87	-14.87	8297.7	-36.75	1.03	1351.82	-13.94	78.00	6278.32
-87.94	80.63	14234.6	-38.75	115.6	14874.8	30.39	-74.91	6535.06
-40.31	2.76	1632.5	-15.64	17.71	558.13	30.39	-74.91	6535.06

In steady state GAs, each iteration creates a set of offspring solutions. For preserving elite solutions a separate archive of elite solutions is maintained or elite solutions are marked in main population.

The term generation gap is used to describe the size of the population overlap in steady state GAs. The selection pressure is more in steady-state GAs but its memory requirement is less as compare to generational GAs. Steady-state GAs having small population size normally looses diversity very fast and large population size increases the cost of computation and slows down the speed of convergence.

4.7. Criteria for Termination

This generational process is repeated until a termination condition has been reached. Common terminating conditions are:

- A solution is found that satisfies minimum criteria,
- Fixed number of generations reached,
- Allocated budget (computation time/money) reached,
- The highest ranking solution's fitness is reaching or has reached a plateau such that successive iterations no longer produce better results,
- Manual Inspection,
- Combination of the above.

5. DIFFERENTIAL EVOLUTION

Differential evolution (DE) performs same as GA in initializing, representing the solution. It differs with GA in generation of solution.

5.1. Generation of New Value

5.1.1. Mutation

Each point (individual) can be represented as vector in search space. In DE each parent vector of current generation is known as *target vector*. All individuals in current generation get a chance to become a *target vectors*. The resultant vector obtain through mutation is known as *donor vector*. DE generates a *donor vector* by adding the weighted difference between two population vectors to a third vector. For each target vector $X_{i,G}$, $i = 1, 2, \ldots NP$, a mutant vector is generated as follows

$$v_{i,G+1} = x_{r1,G} + F * (x_{r2,G} - x_{r3,G})$$

Whereas r1, r2, r3 ϵ 1. . . NP are mutually different integers and F > 0 ϵ [0, 2] known as scaling factor. The integer r1, r2 and r3 are randomly chosen. That to be different from the running index i. F is a real and constant factor which controls the amplification of the differential variation ($x_{r2,G}$ - $x_{r3,G}$).

Hence δ in DE is δ=F*($X_{r2,G}$-$X_{r3,G}$).

Consider three points' r1, r2, r3 in two-dimension space as shown in Figure 9. The vector directing from origin to this points r1, r2, r3 are $\vec{r1}, \vec{r2}, \vec{r3}$. The vector directed from point r1 to r2 represented by ($\vec{r2} - \vec{r1}$) scaling by some factor (F=scaling factor) either can increase or decrease the magnitude of it but in same direction. When the scaled difference is added with $\vec{r3}$. It gives a new vector U in a search space.

Let us consider F=0.5 and r1,r2,r3 as follows than the donor vectors will be:

Code:

```
rot = (0:1:NP-1); % rotating index array (size NP) [ui,popold]= mutation (NP,p
op,F,strategy,rot,bestmemit);
```

Figure 9. Finding new vector in search space

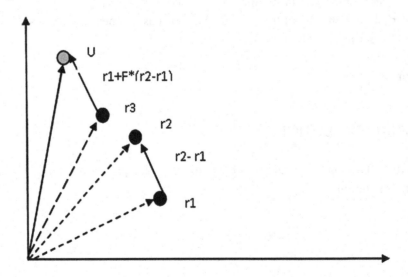

Table 8. Three different vectors

r_1			r_2		r_3	
56.6531	95.7127		-40.3144	2.7629	-13.9432	78.0072
30.3994	-74.9137		-54.0598	-77.8154	56.6531	95.7127
49.2214	4.6626		92.3987	-93.9459	30.3994	-74.9137
-87.9401	80.6312		-13.9432	78.0072	49.2214	4.6626
-89.8707	-14.8693		56.6531	95.7127	-87.9401	80.6312
76.0132	51.1828		30.3994	-74.9137	-89.8707	-14.8693
-40.3144	2.7629		49.2214	4.6626	76.0132	51.1828
-54.0598	-77.8154		-87.9401	80.6312	-40.3144	2.7629
92.3987	-93.9459		-89.8707	-14.8693	-54.0598	-77.8154
-13.9432	78.0072		76.0132	51.1828	92.3987	-93.9459

Donor vectors will be:

V_i		=	r_1		F	r_2		-	r_3	
43.4675	58.0906	=	56.6531	95.7127	0.5	-40.3144	2.7629	-	-13.9432	78.0072
-24.9570	-161.6778		30.3994	-74.9137		-54.0598	-77.8154		56.6531	95.7127
80.2211	-4.8535		49.2214	4.6626		92.3987	-93.9459		30.3994	-74.9137
-119.5224	117.3035		-87.9401	80.6312		-13.9432	78.0072		49.2214	4.6626
-17.5741	-7.3286		-89.8707	-14.8693		56.6531	95.7127		-87.9401	80.6312
136.1482	21.1606		76.0132	51.1828		30.3994	-74.9137		-89.8707	-14.8693
-53.7103	-20.4972		-40.3144	2.7629		49.2214	4.6626		76.0132	51.1828
-77.8726	-38.8812		-54.0598	-77.8154		-87.9401	80.6312		-40.3144	2.7629
74.4932	-62.4728		92.3987	-93.9459		-89.8707	-14.8693		-54.0598	-77.8154
-22.1360	150.5716		-13.9432	78.0072		76.0132	51.1828		92.3987	-93.9459

```
function [ui,popold]= mutation (NP,pop,F,strategy,rot,bestmemit)
    popold = pop;
    ind = randperm(4); % index pointer array

    a1 = randperm(NP); % shuffle locations of vectors
    rt = rem(rot+ind(1),NP); % rotate indices by ind(1) positions
    a2 = a1(rt+1); % rotate vector locations
    rt = rem(rot+ind(2),NP);
    a3= a2(rt+1);
    rt= rem(rot+ind(3),NP);
    a4= a3(rt+1);
    rt= rem(rot+ind(4),NP);
    a5= a4(rt+1);

pm1 = popold(a1,:); % shuffled population1 pm2 = popold(a2,:); % shuffled
population 2 pm3 = popold(a3,:); % shuffled population 3 pm4 = popold(a4,:); %
shuffled population 4 pm5 = popold(a5,:); % shuffled population 5

    for i=1:NP % population filled with the best member bm(i,:) = bestmemit; %
of the last iteration
        end
```

```
        if (strategy > 5)
st = strategy-5; % binomial crossover
else
        st = strategy;
        end
    if (st == 1) % DE/best/1
        ui = bm + F*(pm1 - pm2); % differential variation
elseif (st == 2) % DE/rand/1
        ui = pm3 + F*(pm1 - pm2); % differential variation
        elseif (st == 3) % DE/rand-to-best/1
        ui = popold + F*(bm-popold) + F*(pm1 - pm2);
    elseif (st == 4) % DE/best/2
        ui = bm + F*(pm1 - pm2 + pm3 - pm4); % differential variation
    elseif (st == 5) % DE/rand/2
        ui = pm5 + F*(pm1 - pm2 + pm3 - pm4); % differential variation

    end
end
```

5.2. Making of Solution From Values

5.2.1. Crossover

Each chromosome or solution in a population is a set or vector of D decision variables. In DE, $\delta = F *$ $(X_{r2,G} - X_{r3,G})$. This δ brings variation in decision variables. Or generate δ_i for i^{th} decision variable (x_i) that one want to change. Or generate δ_i for each decision variable and then take decision to use that δ_i to change value of ith decision variable. The processes of generation of δ and then bringing variation in decision variable may be done separately or may be put together. It is not mandatory to change all variables in solution. The decisions of choosing variable for change are very decisive. Probability of crossover (*CR*) decides how many variables (out of D variables) in solution will change their value. For example if CR=0.6 then only 60% variables will change their value and 40% will remain unchanged.

It increases the diversity of the population. The parameters of mutated vector are mixed with the parameters of another predetermined vector, the target vector, to yield the so-called trial vector. This parameter mixing is referred as crossover. In crossover trial vector u $_{i;G+1}$ = (u $_{1i,G+1}$, u $_{2i,G+1}$ $\cdots$ u $_{Di;G+1}$) is formed . DE provides the two different types of crossovers *binomial crossover* and *exponential crossover*. The binomial crossover can be defined as:

$$U_{ji;G+1} \begin{cases} V_{ji,G+1} & if\left(randb\left(j\right) \leq CR\right)or j = rnbr\left(i\right) \\ X_{ji,G} & if(randb\left(j\right) > CR)and j \neq rnbr\left(i\right); \end{cases}$$

$j = 1, 2 \ldots$ D. randb(j) is the jth evaluation of a uniform random number generator ϵ [0, 1].CR is the crossover constant ϵ [0,1]. rnbr(i) is a randomly chosen index ϵ 1,2....D which ensures that $U_{i,G+1}$ gets at least one parameter from $v_{i,G+1}$.

5.3. Construction of Next Generation Population

5.3.1. Selection

To decide whether or not new vector should become a member of generation G+1, the trial vector $U_{i,G+1}$ is compared to the target vector $X_{i,G}$ using the greedy criterion. If vector $U_{i,G+1}$ yields a smaller cost function value than $X_{i,G}$, then $X_{i,G+1}$ is set to $U_{i,G+1}$; otherwise, the old value $X_{i,G}$ is retained.

$$X_{i,G+1} = \begin{cases} U_{i,G} & if f\left(U_{i,G}\right) \leq f\left(X_{i,G}\right) \\ X_{i,G} & else \end{cases}$$

Criteria for termination are same as PSO and GA.

6. RESEARCH DIRECTIONS

A lot of variants are suggested to improve the performance of algorithms. Most of them have some limitations in terms of convergence speed, dimensional space, memory requirement, premature convergence, etc. Based on the literature, some of the research gaps are identified as follows;

1. Premature convergence is always the problem with any evolutionary algorithms.
2. The difficulty is achieving the solution increases with respect to the number of dimensions.
3. Cooperative strategies are used to deal with multidimensional problems. But, the main difficulty in designing an effective strategy to group the swarm along the dimensions.
4. Tradeoff between optimal solution and the convergence speed.
5. Initial distribution of particle plays very important role in achieving better performance.
6. Parameter adjustment is always the issue. A lot of work is carried out to solve this problem, but still there is scope to find optimum parameter value.

7. CONCLUSION

PSO, GA and DE are nature inspired techniques. All these techniques perform same kind of task but are having different working structure but share some commonalities. Here it has been tried to make the readers understand about the working of all these algorithms and their behavior. All these methods follow same procedure but differ in their equation. The detail working in each step and their performance is shown here. To better understand the working and behavior in each step, MATLAB code is also given with each step.

This chapters helps the beginners, who want to start the research in EA's.

REFERENCES

Bonyadi, M. R., & Michalewicz, Z. (2014). A locally convergent rotationally invariant particle swarm optimization algorithm. *Swarm Intelligence*, *8*(3), 159–198. doi:10.1007/s11721-014-0095-1

Bonyadi, M. R., Michalewicz, Z., & Li, X. (2014). An analysis of the velocity updating rule of the particle swarm optimization algorithm. *Journal of Heuristics*, *20*(4), 417–452. doi:10.1007/s10732-014-9245-2

Cheng, R., & Jin, Y. (2015, February). A Competitive Swarm Optimizer for Large Scale Optimization. *IEEE Transactions On Cybernetics*, *45*(2), 191–204. doi:10.1109/TCYB.2014.2322602 PMID:24860047

Coello, C. A. C. (2002). Theoretical and numerical constraint-handling techniques used with evolutionary algorithms: A survey of the state of the art. *Computer Methods in Applied Mechanics and Engineering*, *191*(11–12), 1245–1287. doi:10.1016/S0045-7825(01)00323-1

Cui, Z., Zeng, J., & Yin, Y. (2008). An improved PSO with time-varying accelerator coefficients. *Eighth International conference on intelligent systems design and applications*, 638–643. doi:10.1109/ISDA.2008.86

Evers, G. I., & Ben Ghalia, M. (2009). Regrouping Particle Swarm Optimization: A New Global Optimization Algorithm with Improved Performance Consistency Across Benchmarks. *IEEE International Conference on Systems, Man and Cybernetics*, 3901-3908. doi:10.1109/ICSMC.2009.5346625

Fleming, P. J., & Pashkevich, A. P. (1985). Computer aided control system design using a multiobjective optimization approach. *Proceedings of the IEE Control 85 Conference*, 174–179.

Fonseca, C. M., & Fleming, P. J. (1993). Genetic algorithms for multiobjective optimization: Formulation, discussion and generalization. In S. Forrest (Ed.), *Proceedings of the Fifth International Conference on Genetic Algorithms*. Morgan Kauffman Publishers.

Fonseca, C. M., & Fleming, P. J. (1995). Multiobjective genetic algorithms made easy: Selection, sharing, and mating restriction. In A. M. S. Zalzala (Ed.), *Proceedings of the First International Conference on Genetic Algorithms in Engineering Systems: Innovations and Applications (GALESIA 95)*. Institution of Electrical Engineers.

Fourman, M. P. (1985). Compaction of symbolic layout using genetic algorithms. In J. Grefenstette (Ed.), *Proceedings of the First International Conference on Genetic Algorithms*. Lawrence Erlbaum Associates.

Goldberg, D. E. (1989). *Genetic Algorithms in Search, Optimization and Machine Learning*. Pearson Education Asia.

Goldberg, D. E., & Richardson, J. (1987). Genetic algorithms with sharing for multimodal function optimization. In J. Grefenstette (Ed.), *Proceedings of the Second International Conference on Genetic Algorithms*. Lawrence Erlbaum Associates.

Haleja, P., & Lin, C.-Y. (1992). Genetic search strategies in multicriterion optimal design. *Structural Optimization*, *4*(2), 99–107. doi:10.1007/BF01759923

Horn, J., & Nafpliotis, N. (1993). Multiobjective optimization using the niched Pareto genetic algorithm. In *IlliGAL Report 93005*. Urbana, IL: University of Illinois at Urbana-Champaign.

Immanuel Selvakumar, A., & Thanushkodi, K. (2007, February). A New Particle Swarm Optimization Solution to Nonconvex Economic Dispatch Problems. *IEEE Transactions on Power Systems*, *22*(1), 42–51. doi:10.1109/TPWRS.2006.889132

Janson, S., & Middendorf, M. (2005, December). A Hierarchical Particle Swarm Optimizer and Its Adaptive Variant. *IEEE Transactions on Systems, Man, and Cybernetics. Part B, Cybernetics*, *35*(6), 1272–1282. doi:10.1109/TSMCB.2005.850530 PMID:16366251

Jin, Y., Okabe, T., & Sendhoff, B. (2001). Adapting weighted aggregation for multiobjective evolutionary optimization. *Proceedings of the Genetic and Evolutionary Computation Conference (GECCO 2001)*, 1042–1049.

Jin, Y., Okabe, T., & Sendhoff, B. (2001). Dynamic weighted aggregation for evolutionary multi-objective optimization: Why does it work and how?. In *Proceedings of the 2001enetic and Evolutionary Computation Conference (GECCO 2001)*. Morgan Kaufmann Publishers.

Kiranyaz, S., Ince, T., Yildirim, A., & Gabbouj, M. (2010, April). AlperYildirim, and Moncef Gabbouj, "Fractional Particle Swarm Optimization in Multidimensional Search Space. *IEEE Transactions on Systems, Man, and Cybernetics. Part B, Cybernetics*, *40*(2), 298–319. doi:10.1109/TSMCB.2009.2015054

Kursawe, F. (1990). A variant of evolution strategies for vector optimization. In Parallel Problem Solving from Nature. Berlin, Germany: Springer-Verlag. doi:10.1007/BFb0029752

Li, X., & Yao, X. (2012, April). Cooperatively Coevolving Particle Swarms for Large Scale Optimization. *IEEE Transactions on Evolutionary Computation*, *16*(2), 210–224. doi:10.1109/TEVC.2011.2112662

Li & Deb. (2010). Comparing lbest PSO Niching algorithms Using Different Position Update Rules. *WCCI 2010 IEEE World Congress on Computational Intelligence*, 1564-1571.

Mehdad, Y., & Magnini, B. (2009). Optimizing Textual Entailment Recognition Using Particle Swarm Optimization. *Proceedings of the 2009 Workshop on Applied Textual Inference*, 36–43. doi:10.3115/1708141.1708148

Mirjalili, S., Lewis, A., & Sadiq, A. S. (2014). Autonomous Particles Groups for Particle Swarm Optimization. *Arab J Sci Eng*, *39*(6), 4683–4697. doi:10.1007/s13369-014-1156-x

Pongchairerks, P. (2009). Particle swarm optimization algorithm applied to scheduling problems. *ScienceAsia*, *35*(1), 89–94. doi:10.2306/scienceasia1513-1874.2009.35.089

Qu, Suganthan, & Das. (2013). A Distance-based Locally Informed Particle Swarm Model for Multimodal Optimization. *IEEE Transactions on Evolutionary Computation*, *17*(3), 387-402.

Schaffer, J. D. (1985). Multiple objective optimization with vector evaluated genetic algorithms. In J. Grefenstette (Ed.), *Proceedings of the First International Conference on Genetic Algorithms*. Lawrence Erlbaum Associates.

Srinivas, N., & Deb, K. (1994). Multiobjective Optimization Using Nondominated Sorting in Genetic Algorithms". *Evolutionary Computation*, *2*(3), 221–248. doi:10.1162/evco.1994.2.3.221

Sulaiman, S., Shamsuddin, S. M., Forkan, F., & Abraham, A. (2008). Intelligent Web Caching Using Neurocomputing and Particle Swarm Optimization Algorithm. *AMS, 2008, Asia International Conference on Modelling & Simulation, Asia International Conference on Modelling & Simulation*, 642-647. doi:10.1109/AMS.2008.40

Syafrullah & Salim. (2010). Improving Term Extraction Using Particle Swarm Optimization Techniques. *Journal of Computing, 2*(2), 116-120.

van den Bergh, F. (2002). *An analysis of particle swarm optimizers* (Ph.D. dissertation). Dept. Comput. Sci., Univ. Pretoria, Pretoria, South Africa.

van den Bergh, F., & Engelbrecht, A. (2004, June). A cooperative approach to particle swarm optimization. *IEEE Transactions on Evolutionary Computation, 8*(3), 225–239. doi:10.1109/TEVC.2004.826069

Wang, H. (2007). Opposition-based particle swarm algorithm with Cauchy mutation. *Proceedings of the IEEE Congress on Evolutionary Computation*, 4750-4756.

Wang, H., Moon, I., Yang, S., & Wang, D. (2012). A memetic particle swarm optimization algorithm for multimodal optimization problems. *Information Sciences, 197*, 38–52. doi:10.1016/j.ins.2012.02.016

Yang, Wang, & Jiao. (2004). A Quantum Particle Swarm Optimization. *Proceedings of the IEEE Congress on Evolutionary Computation (CEC 2004)*, 320 – 324.

Yang, Z., Tang, K., & Yao, X. (2008, August). Large scale evolutionary optimization using cooperative coevolution. *Inform. Sci., 178*(15), 2986–2999. doi:10.1016/j.ins.2008.02.017

Zhan, Z.-H., Zhang, J., Li, Y., & Chung, H. S.-H. (2009, December). Adaptive Particle Swarm Optimization. *IEEE Transactions on Systems, Man, and Cybernetics. Part B, Cybernetics, 39*(6), 1362–1381. doi:10.1109/TSMCB.2009.2015956 PMID:19362911

Chapter 12
GA_SVM:
A Classification System for Diagnosis of Diabetes

Dilip Kumar Choubey
Birla Institute of Technology Mesra, India

Sanchita Paul
Birla Institute of Technology Mesra, India

ABSTRACT

The modern society is prone to many life-threatening diseases which if diagnosis early can be easily controlled. The implementation of a disease diagnostic system has gained popularity over the years. The main aim of this research is to provide a better diagnosis of diabetes. There are already several existing methods, which have been implemented for the diagnosis of diabetes. In this manuscript, firstly, Polynomial Kernel, RBF Kernel, Sigmoid Function Kernel, Linear Kernel SVM used for the classification of PIDD. Secondly GA used as an Attribute selection method and then used Polynomial Kernel, RBF Kernel, Sigmoid Function Kernel, Linear Kernel SVM on that selected attributes of PIDD for classification. So, here compared the results with and without GA in PIDD, and Linear Kernel proved better among all of the noted above classification methods. It directly seems in the paper that GA is removing insignificant features, reducing the cost and computation time and improving the accuracy, ROC of classification. The proposed method can be also used for other kinds of medical diseases.

1. INTRODUCTION

In this era, one of the needs of this generation is healthcare and diabetes is one of the chronic diseases. Diabetes is the problem used to describe a metabolic condition of having higher than normal blood sugar levels. This is also called hyperglycemia. Diabetes occurs when insulin is not being properly produced or responded by the body, which is needed to maintain the rate of sugar. Diabetes can be controlled with the help of insulin injections, taking oral medications (pills), a controlled diet (changing eating habits), and exercise programs, but no entire cure is available.

DOI: 10.4018/978-1-5225-2128-0.ch012

Diabetes can be categorized into four types: Type 1 (Juvenile or Insulin Dependent or Brittle or Sugar) diabetes and Type 2 (Adult onset or Non Insulin Dependent) diabetes, Pre diabetes and Gestational diabetes.

Type 1 diabetes mostly occurs to children and young adults but can affect at any age, 5-10% of diabetes have Type 1 diabetes. The body does not produce or make insulin. Insulin helps the body to use sugar from food as a source of energy. People with type-1 diabetes need insulin therapy. There is a destruction of insulin secreting cells (β cells) of pancreas in our body. The cause is immune-mediated or idiopatic. It usually requires external insulin therapy hence known as Insulin Dependent Diabetes Mellitus (IDDM).

Type 2 diabetes is the most common type of diabetes, in which people are suffering at least 90-95% of all the diabetes cases. Type 2 diabetes symptoms often develop slowly. This type mostly occurs to the people more than forty years old but can also be found in younger classes. Type 2 diabetes symptoms are usually the same for men and women however, urological problems such as erectile dysfunction (ED). This is asymptomatic for many years. Body does not produce enough insulin (Insulin Deficiency) or the body cells do not respond to insulin (Insulin Resistance) or both. It can be controlled or often need lifestyle modification, taking oral medications (pills) or if required insulin therapy but no entire cure for diabetes is available.

Pre diabetes is a milder form of diabetes that is sometimes called Impaired Glucose Tolerance. It can be diagnosed with a simple blood test.

Gestational diabetes occurs during pregnancy. It raises mother's risk of getting diabetes for the rest of her life. It also raises the child's risk of being overweight and getting diabetes. It displays a high blood sugar level during pregnancy, usually occurs at around 28 weeks or later, and affects about 4% of all pregnant women. This type of diabetes usually goes away after pregnancy and causes are unknown.

In this chapter, for the analysis to diagnose of diabetes, the proposed method is implemented and evaluated by GA as an Attributes selection and used Polynomial Kernel, RBF Kernel, Sigmoid Function, Linear Kernel SVM for classification. By using GA method, 4 attributes obtained among 8 attributes. The mentioned methods have been implemented on Pima Indian Diabetes Dataset (PIDD). Here, used dataset is precise, no missing value have found, noisy free dataset.

The rest of the paper is organized as follows: Brief description of Attribute Selection, GA, Classification, and SVM are in section 2, Problem Specification is introduced in section 3, Related work is presented in section 4, Proposed methodology is discussed in section 5, Results and Discussion of proposed methodology are present in section 6, Conclusion and Work are devoted to section 7.

2. BRIEF DESCRIPTION OF ATTRIBUTE SELECTION, GA, CLASSIFICATION, AND SVM

2.1. Attribute Selection

It is a process of selecting important attributes or best subset of attributes by removing the redundant and irrelevant attributes, which will save resources while improving the classification accuracy.

In particular, the utmost aim of attribute selection is to deduce the number of attributes used in classification, while sustaining the considerable ROC and classification accuracy. However, reduction in the number of attributes or dimensionality helps us is critical in statistical learning. Notably, the attribute selection process helps us to preserve the storage capacity or memory, computation time (shorter training time and test time), computation cost, Processor requirements, and increases classification rate. As we know that classification method may not scale up to the size of full attribute set in either sample or time. It allows us to better understand the domain, cheaper and safer to collect a reduced set of predictors. The problem of attribute selection is to search for a subset of relevant or important attributes introduces an additional layer of complexity in the modeling task, additional time for learning. There are broadly two methods for attribute selection: (a) Wrapper method (b) Filter method

2.1.1. Wrapper Method

It uses a subset evaluator, which will create all possible subsets from your feature vector. To find a subset the evaluator will use a search method (Random search, Breadth First Search (BFS), Depth First Search (DFS)) for a good subset using the learning algorithm. The using wrapper method provide interaction between attribute subset search and model selection, and the ability to take into account attribute dependencies and the problem of Wrapper method is the higher risk of over fitting then filter methods and are very computationally intensive, especially if building the classifier has a high computational cost.

2.1.2. Filter Methods

They try to evaluate the merits of attributes from the data, ignoring the effects of the selected attributes subset on the performance of the learning algorithm. for e.g., PCA or Clustering. Filter method provides easily scale to very high-dimensional datasets, computationally simple and fast, and independent of the classification algorithm.

Filter method ignores the interaction with the classifier, they are often univariate or low variate, this means that each attribute is considered separately, thereby ignoring attribute dependencies, which may lead to worse classification performance when compared to other types of attribute selection methods.

WEKA provides an attribute selection tool. The process is separated into two parts i.e., Attribute Evaluator, Search Method.

- **Attribute Evaluator:** The method by which attribute subsets are evaluated or estimated. for e.g., Cfs Subset Eval, Classifier Subset Eval, Wrapper Subset Eval.
- **Search Method:** The method by which the space of possible subsets is searched. for e.g., BFS, Exhaustive, GA.

So, In this paper GA used as an attribute selection method. In the section 2.2, brief description of GA has been given.

2.2. GA

John Holland is known as the father of the original GA who introduced this 1970 at University of Michigan (US). GA is robust heuristic or unorthodox searching and optimization algorithms based on the progressive ideas of natural selection and genetics (Sivanandam & Deepa, 2007) inspired by the biological evolutionary process. GA may be also defined as an adaptive heuristic search algorithms based on the evolutionary ideas of natural selection and genetics, which is inspired by Darwin's theory (Darwin, 1859) about survival of the fittest. GA enacts the natural evolution process given by the Darwin i.e., in GA the next population is evolved through simulating operators of selection, crossover and mutation.

John Holland first familiarizes selection, crossover, and mutation operators in (Holland, 1975). Goldberg (1989) and Michalewicz (1996) later improved these operators. The advantages in GA (Choubey et al., 2014; Choubey & Paul, 2016) Concepts are easy to understand, Solves problems with multiple solutions, Global search methods, Blind search methods, GAs can be easily used in parallel machines, Modular: separate from application, Supports multi–objective optimization, Good for "noisy" environment, Inherently parallel, Easily distributed. and the limitation are Certain optimization problems, No absolute assurance for a global optimum, Cannot assure constant optimization response times, cannot find the exact solution. GA can be applied in Artificial creativity, Bioinformatics, Chemical kinetics, Gene expression profiling, Control engineering, Software engineering, Traveling salesman problem, Mutation testing, Quality Control, Business. Mainly, the GA utilizes certain rules, i.e. selection, crossover, and mutation, at each step to build the next generation from the current population. The GA are more briefly illustrated in Choubey and Paul (2015) and Choubey and Paul (2016), also selection, crossover, mutation.

2.2.1. Selection

Selection is also called reproduction phase whose first objective is to promote good solutions and terminate bad solutions in the current population, while keeping the population size constant. This is done by distinguishing good solutions (in terms of fitness) in the current population and make identical copies of these. Now in order to maintain the population size constant, eliminate some bad solutions from the populations so that multiple copies of good solutions can be placed in the population. There are several methods available for selection like Roulette–wheel selection, Boltzmann selection, Tournament selection, Rank selection, Steady–state selection, etc., but the most commonly used selection method is Roulette wheel. Fitness value of individuals plays an important role in these all selection procedures.

2.2.2. Crossover

As it may be seen in selection phase that the prime objective of selection operator is to make only multiple copies of better solutions than the others but it does not generate any new solution. So in the crossover phase, the new solutions are generated. First two solutions from the new population are selected either haphazardly or by applying any presumptive rule and bring them in the mating pool in order to create two off springs. So the parents have good bit strings combinations which will be carried over to offsprings. Even if the newly generated off springs are not better in terms of fitness then we should not be bothering about because they will be evicted in next selection phase. In this phase, new off springs are made from those parents, which were selected in the selection phase. There are several crossover methods available like single-point crossover, two-point crossover, Multi-point crossover, uniform crossover, Matrix crossover, etc.

2.2.3. Mutation

Mutation to an individual takes part with a very low probability. If any bit of an individual is selected to be muted then it is flipped with a possible alternative value for that bit. For example, possible substituted value for 0 is 1 in binary string representation case i.e. 0 is flipped with 1 and 1 is flipped with 0. The mutation phase is applied next to crossover to keep diversity in the population. Again, it is not always to get better offsprings after mutation but it is done to search few solutions in the neighborhood of original solutions.

2.3. Classification

The grouping together of similar things into different segments based on common qualities or attributes. Classification is a supervised learning method, i.e., the training data has to specify what we are trying to learn (i.e., the classes). Since a training set exists, we call to this method as supervised learning. In classification, the dataset partition between training dataset (generally 70%, may be any %) and testing dataset (i.e., here 30%). The training data set is used for training the system and testing data set is used to measure the performance of the system. Generally, in classification a set of predefined classes and the goal is to find in which class a new object belongs to. It enables us to retrieve a particular thing or information, which we need without too much time consuming. It helps us easier to organize things or easier to locate, retrieve, maintain things and information which make our life easier. Classification also provide a guide for treatment and prognosis, help in streamlining data collection, help in clinicians to compare efficacy and efficiency of treatments, reduce victim blaming. So, here Polynomial Kernel, RBF Kernel, Sigmoid Function Kernel, Linear Kernel SVM used as a classification method. In the section 2.4, brief description of SVM has been introduced.

2.4. SVM

Vladimir N. Vapnik (1995) firstly proposed SVM in the 1995. SVM is supervised learning approach, which operates on the finding of hyper plane, which uses an interclass distance or margin width for the separation of positive and negative samples. For the unequal misclassification, cost a coefficient factor of $C+$ & $C-$ denoted as 'J' is used for the generation of errors can be outweighs both positive and negative examples (Morik et al., 1998). Hence, the optimization problem of SVM becomes (Kennedy & Eberhart, 1995):

$$minimize \frac{1}{2} \| w \|^2 + C_+ + \sum_{i|y_i=1} \aleph_i + C_- \sum_{j|y_j=-1} \aleph_j \tag{1}$$

This satisfies the condition,

$$y_k \left(wx_k + b \right) \geq 1 - \aleph_k, \aleph_k \geq 0 \tag{2}$$

SVM is fulfilled in linear and non-linear way, the non-linear form or Radial bias kernel are used for the non-linearly separable data with language multiplier α_i,

Hence optimization problem becomes:

$$minimize\ w(\alpha) = \sum_{i=1}^{l} \alpha_i - \frac{1}{2} \sum_{i=1,j=1}^{l} \alpha_i y_i \alpha_j y_j K \left(x_i . y_j \right) \tag{3}$$

Table 1. Various notations used

Parameters	Explanation
y_i	Class labels used in the training dataset
W	Normal to the hyper plane
$\lvert b \rvert\, l\, \lVert w \rVert$	Perpendicular distance from origin (b) to the hyper plane (w)
$\lVert w \rVert$	Euclidean norm of w
C	Regularization parameter used to find the tradeoff between training error and margin width d
$\aleph_i$	Slack variable that allows error in classification (Aslam, Waqar., Zhu, Zhechen., Nandi, & Kumar, 2013).

where,

$$C \geq \alpha_i \geq 0 \forall_i, \sum_{i=1}^{l} \alpha_i y_i = 0 \tag{4}$$

Due to the chance of non-linearity and error SVM is based on black box models. For the classification of medical diabetes mellitus, a final decision is crucial requirement by the end users (Chen et al., 2007). Hence, Feature Extraction is executed for the exact working of the SVM (Barakat, 2007).

Figure 1 represent the basic architecture of Linear SVM. SVM contains a hyper plane of the form $\text{wo.p} + \text{bs} = 0$, where '$p$' is the dynamic point lying on the considered hyper plane and 'bs' denotes the

Figure 1. Basic architecture of linear SVM

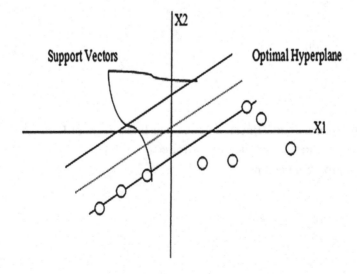

bias value of the distance of hyper plane from origin and 'wo' denotes orientation of hyper plane. The advantages of SVM are (Choubey et al., 2014; Choubey & Paul, 2016): Training is relatively easy, Scales well to high dimensional data, Error can be controlled explicitly and disadvantages are: Need for a good kernel function, Not able to provide comprehensible justification for the classification decisions they make and the application are: Pattern recognition problems, Hand writing analysis, Face analysis, Text and hypertext categorization, Classification of images.

3. PROBLEM SPECIFICATION

It is well known that before some year's physicians, diagnoses the disease with experience and clinical data of the patient's means with laboratory tests reports. The people laboratory test report may vary depending on meals, exercise, sickness, stress, due to small changes in temperature, different equipment used, and way of sample handling. So, this kind of diagnosis the disease is time consuming because It is entirely dependent up on the availability and the experience of physicians who deal with imprecise and uncertain clinical of the patients. So, to improve the decision making with clinical data and to reduce time consumption, A good (intelligent) diagnosis system is needed, and here we just analyses the input data (patient's data i.e., PIDD) and to develop an accurate description or model for each class using the attributes in the dataset by which further easily based on the same concept, diagnosis system may be developed. Researchers said that even the experience physicians are not able to detect the disease quickly and accurately. It is always the problem for physicians to find disease more accurately with speedily. He may require feedbacks from the several patient for diagnose of a particular disease. It is always the problem for physicians to find disease more accurately and speedy manner.

4. RELATED WORK

Dogantekin et al. (2010) used Linear Discriminant Analysis (LDA) and ANFIS for diagnosis of diabetes. LDA is used to separate feature variables between healthy and patient (diabetes) data, and ANFIS is used for classification on the result produced by LDA. The methods used provide good accuracy then the existing results. So, physicians can perform very accurate decisions by using such an efficient tool.

Polat and Gunes (2007) used Principal Component Analysis (PCA) and Adaptive Neur–Fuzzy Inference System (ANFIS) in which PCA is used to reduce the dimensions of diabetes and ANFIS apply classification on that reduced features of diabetes datasets.

Seera and Lim (2014) introduced Fuzzy Min-Max neural network, Classification and Regression Tree (CART), Random Forest (RF) for the classification of medical data. The methodology is implemented on various datasets i.e., Breast Cancer Wisconsin, PIDD, and Liver Disorders and performs better as compared to other existing methods.

Orkcu and Hasan (2011) used Backpropagation neural network, binary-coded genetic algorithms, real coded genetic algorithm for the classifications of medical datasets.

Luukka (2011) used Fuzzy entropy measure, similarity classifier for the classification of diabetic disease. Fuzzy entropy used as a feature selection and similarity classifier used for the classification on that selected features.

Temurtas et al. (2009) stated Levenberg-Marquardt (LM) algorithm and Probabilistic neural network (PNN) were used to train a multilayer neural network, Ten fold cross validation technique was used for estimation of result. The used techniques LM, PNN, 10-Fold cross validation provide better correct training pattern than conventional validation method.

Aslam et al. (2013) implemented an expert system for the classification of diabetes data using Genetic Programming (GP). The methods implemented here consists of three stages: the first stage includes feature selection using t-test and kolmogorov-smirnov test and kulback-Leibler divergence test, the next stage uses GP, which is used for the non-linear combination of selected attributes from the first stage. At the final stage the generated features using GP is compared with K-nearest neighbor (KNN) and SVM. The classification is done on PIDD consists of 768 instance values in the dataset and 8 attributes and one output variable (class variable) which have either a value '1' or '0' available in the dataset. The selected features are then used for the classification of diabetes patients with high accuracy of classification.

Goncalves et al. (2006) also implemented a new neuro-fuzzy model for the classification of diabetes patients. Here in this paper an inverted hierarchical neuro-fuzzy based system is implemented which is based on binary space partitioning model and it provided embodies for the continue recursive of the input space and automatically generates own structure for the classification of inputs provided. The method implemented finally generates a series of rules extraction on the basis of which classification can be done.

Selvakuberan et al. (2011) used Ranker search method, K star, REP tree, Naive bayes, Logisitic, Dagging, Multiclass in which Ranker search approach is used for attribute selection and K star, REP tree, Naive bayes, Logisitic, Dagging, Multiclass are used for classification. The methods implemented here provide a reduced feature set with higher classification accuracy.

Kayaer and Yildirim (2003) used General Regrssion Neural Network (GRNN) to classify a medical data in which the optimum spread values were found by trial and error and used for training and the classification of test data.

Polat et al. (2008) stated a Generalized discriminant analysis (GDA) and Least square support vector machine (LS–SVM) for the classification of diabetes. Here the methodology is implemented in two stages: in the first stage pre-processing of the data is done using the GDA such that the discrimination between healthy and patient disease can be done. In the second stage LS-SVM method is applied for the classification of Diabetes disease patient's. The methodology implemented here provides accuracy about 78.21% based on 10 fold-cross validation from LS-SVM and the obtained accuracy for classification is about 82.05%.

Choubey and Paul (2015) used GA_J48graft DT for the classification of PIDD. The method J48graft Decision Tree (J48graft DT) for the classification of data, and GA used as a feature selection and then have performed once again classification on the selected feature.

Kahramanli and Allahverdi (2008) used Artificial Neural Network (ANN) and Fuzzy Neural Network (FNN) for the classification of heart and diabetes disease. The method applied on PIDD and Cleveland heart disease dataset and achieved the accuracy 84.24%, 86.8% respectively better then several existing technique.

Wang et al. (2007) implemented an ontology based fuzzy interface for the classification of diabetes dataset. The ontology based fuzzy interface implemented here provides and utilizes the diabetes ontology of the diabetes patients to perform the diabetes data classification of PIDD. The ontology contains all the required knowledge of personal diabetes ontology repository from which an expert system is implemented for the classification of diabetes disease.

Lee (2011) used Fuzzy Ontology (FO), Fuzzy Diabetes Ontology (FDO), Semantic Decision Support Agent (SDSA) for the diagnosis of diabetes disease.

Ephzibah (2011) used GA and Fuzzy Logic (FL) for diagnosis of diabetes in which GA has been used as a attribute selection and FL is used for classification.

Qasem and Shamsuddin (2011) introduced a Time Variant Multi– Objective Particle Swarm Optimization (TVMOPSO) of Radial basis function (RBF) network for diagnosing the medical disease. RBF networks training to determine whether RBF networks can be developed using TVMOPSO, and the performance is validated based on accuracy and complexity.

T and A (2010) introduced an ANN method for the classification of diabetes in which classification accuracy improved.

Choubey and Paul (2016) introduced GA_MLP NN for the classification of PIDD. This work consists in two stages firstly GA has been used as a feature selection then Multi Layer Perceptron Neural Network (MLP NN) has been used for classification on the selected features by GA and on all the features. The authors have compared the result with MLP NN and GA_MLP NN to assure that the benefit of feature selection.

Barakat et al. (2010) worked on the classification of diabetes using a machine learning approach such as SVM. The authors stated Sequential Covering Approach (SQRex-SVM) for rule extraction and Electic method also for rule extraction to enable SVMs to be more intelligible.

Choubey and Paul (2016) analyzed and compared the several existed work on diabetes with their advantages, issues, technique, tool used, existed work, future work. The used technique, tool has also been discussed on basis of following parameter i.e., advantages, issues, application.

Choubey and Paul (2017) used GA as an attribute selection and Radial Basis Function Neural Network (RBF NN) for the classification on PIDD. GA is removing insignificant features, reducing the cost, computation time and improving the accuracy, ROC of the classification.

Patil et al. (2010) implements an association rule based method for the classification of type -2 diabetic patients. The classification is implemented for PIDD containing an eight number of attributes and one class. The methodology provides the generation of rules using Apriori algorithm on the basis of some support and confidence. In the first stage the numeric attributes are converted into categorical form which is based on the input parameters. Lastly generated the association rules which are useful to identify general associations in the data, to understand the relationship between the measured fields whether the patient goes on to develop diabetes or not. The authors presented step-by-step approach to help the physicians to explore their data and to understand the discovered rules better.

Palivela and Thotadara (2007) used K-means clustering, SMO, Fuzzy "C" mean, Random Forest, Rotation Forest, Bagging, AdaBoost M1, Naive Bayes, J48 algorithm, Cross–validation methods for the prediction of diabetes by clustering and classification approach.

Kumar et al. (2016) and Kumar and Mishra (2015) used functional link artificial neural network (FLANN) for medical image denoising. They optimize the FLANN filters weights through evolutionary method i.e., Cat Swarm Optimization (CSO), Particle Swarm Optimization (PSO).

Suraj, Ghosh, and Sinha (2015) used GA, PSO, hybrid GA-PSO and K means clustering to distinguish two class motor imagery (MI) tasks. Here, K means clustering is distinguishing the two class MI and GA, PSO, hybrid GA-PSO is helping to optimize the two class MI.

5. PROPOSED METHODOLOGY

In the proposed approach, GA is implemented and evaluated as an Attribute selection and Polynomial Kernel, RBF Kernel, Sigmoid Function Kernel, Linear Kernel SVM for Classification on PIDD which is obtained from the UCI repository of machine learning databases.

In the Figure 2, It may be seen that the proposed work of the manuscript. The proposed algorithm and approach of this manuscript are mentioned below.

5.1. Proposed Algorithm

Step1: Start
Step2: Load PIDD
Step3: Initialize the parameters for the GA
Step4: Call the GA
Step5.1: Construction of the first generation
Step5.2: Selection

While stopping criteria not met do

Figure 2. Block Diagram of Proposed Work

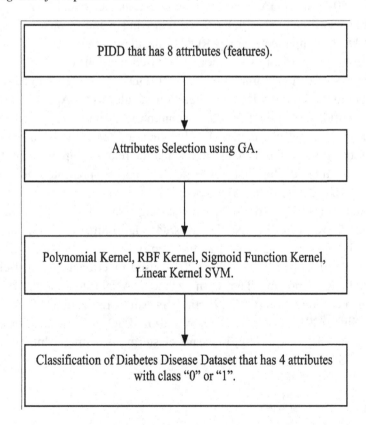

Step5.3: Crossover
Step5.4: Mutation
Step5.5: Selection

End

Step6: Apply Polynomial Kernel, RBF Kernel, Sigmoid Function Kernel, Linear Kernel SVM
Step7: Training Dataset
Step8: Calculation of error and accuracy
Step9: Testing Dataset
Step10: Calculation of error and accuracy
Step11: Stop

The proposed approach works in the following phases:

1.   The PIDD obtained from the UCI repository of machine learning databases.
2.   Used GA as an Attribute Selection on PIDD.
3.   Do the Classification by using Polynomial Kernel, RBF Kernel, Sigmoid Function Kernel, Linear Kernel SVM on all attributes and selected attributes in PIDD.

5.1.1. Used Diabetes Disease Dataset

The PIDD was obtained from the UCI Repository of Machine Learning Databases (n.d.). The same dataset used in the reference (Dogantekin et al., 2010; Plat & Gunes, 2007; Seera & Lim, 2014; Orkcu & Hasan, 2011; Luukka, 2011; Temurtas, Yumusak, & Temurtas, 2009; Aslam et al., 2013; Goncalves et al., 2006; Selvakuberan, Kayathiri, Harini, & Devi, 2011; Kayaer & Yildirim, 2003; Polat, Gunes, & Arslan, 2008; Ganji & Abadeh, 2010; Coubey & Paul, 2015; Kahramanli & Allahverdi, 2008; Wang et al., 2007; Lee, 2011; Karatsiolis & Schizas, 2012; Ephzibah, 2011; Kalaiselvi & Nasira, 2014; Qasem & Shamsuddin, 2011; Karegowda, Manjunath, & Jayaram, 2011; T & A, 2010; Choubey & Paul, 2016; Barakat, Bradley, & Barakat, 2010; Barakat & Bradley, 2007; Choubey & Paul, 2014; Barakat, 2007; Choubey & Paul, 2016; Choubey & Paul, 2016; Patil, Joshi, & Toshniwal, 2010; Palivela & Thotadara, 2007; Daho et al., 2013; Choubey et al., 2016). The National Institute of Diabetes and Digestive and Kidney Diseases originally owned this data and received in 9 May 1990. All patients in this database are Pima Indian Woman at least 21 years old and living near Phoenix, Arizona, USA. The features of this database are given in below:

*   Number of instances: 768
*   Number of attributes: 8
*   Attributes:
    1.   Number of times pregnant
    2.   Plasma glucose concentration a 2 hours in an oral glucose tolerance test
    3.   Diastolic blood pressure (mm Hg)
    4.   Triceps skin fold thickness (mm)
    5.   2 – hour serum insulin (mu U/ml)

Box 1. Class distribution (class value 1 is interpreted as "tested positive for diabetes")

Class Value	Number of Instances
0	500 (65.1%)
1	268 (34.9%)

6. Body mass index (weight in kg/ (height in m)2)
7. Diabetes pedigree function
8. Age (years)
9. Class variable (0 or 1)

There are eight all numeric-valued attributes and one output variable (class variable) which has either a value '1' or '0'.

5.1.2. GA for Attributes Selection

The GA is a ceaseless process of selection, crossover, and mutation with the population of individuals in each iteration called a generation. Each chromosome or individual is encoded in a linear string (generally of 0s and 1s) of fix length in genetic analogy. In search space, first, the individual members of the population are randomly initialized. After initialization each population member is evaluated with respect to objective function being solved and is assigned a number (value of the objective function) which represents the fitness for survival for the corresponding individual. The GA maintains a population of a fix number of individuals with the corresponding fitness value. In each generation, the more fit individuals (selected from the current population) go in the mating pool for crossover to generate new off springs, and there upon individuals with high fitness are provided more chance to generate off springs. Now, each new offspring is modified with a very low mutation probability to maintain the diversity in the population. Now, the parents and off springs together forms the new generation based on the fitness which will treated as parents for next generation. In this way, the new generation and hence successive generations of individual solutions is expected to be better in terms of average fitness. The algorithms stop forming new generations when either a maximum number of generations have been formed or a satisfactory fitness value is achieved for the problem.

The flowchart of GA is given below. In the below Figure 3 flowchart of GA, It may be seen that How the GA used as an attribute selection method. It is already discussed in section 2.2, and 5.1.2. However, here also just discussed the indication about the figure. Firstly after start the parameter have to configure, and then initialize the randomly population and set generation counter = 0 and then check generation counter = max gen? If yes, then end neither evaluate of fitness value, for this may be also assign fitness value your own, and apply roulette wheel reproduction or selection operator . By using this operator highly or fitted strings placed in mating pool, then from mating pool randomly chosen two chromosomes and apply the crossover operator. For this, assign some random value, If random value greater then crossover rate (Pc), the offspring's equal to parents neither apply one-point crossover operator.

After this check enough new generation if no then once again choose two fitted offspring's from mating pool, if yes then perform mutation operator. For this, assign a random value, if yes random value greater than mutation rate (Pm) then perform no mutation, if no then perform mutation and now after

Figure 3. Flowchart of GA

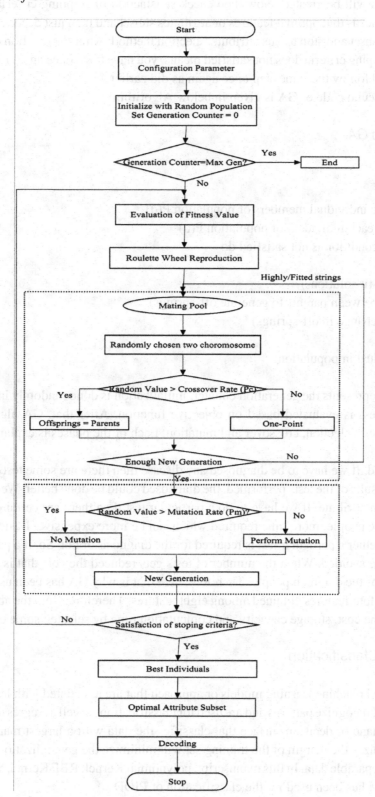

this new generation will be created. Now then check satisfaction of stopping criteria, if yes then best individuals occur means that optimal features or attributes subset and then just decode to this and get the original attribute subset and stop to this attribute selection method. After the creation of new generation if satisfaction of stoping criteria does not satisfied means, you have to go once again from the evaluation of fitness value and follow the same step once again as did earlier.

The standard pseudo code of GA is given in below Algorithm:

5.1.2.1. Algorithm GA

Begin
$q = 0$
Randomly initialize individual members of population P(q)
Evaluate fitness of each individual of population P(q)
while termination condition is not satisfied do
$q = q + 1$
selection (of better fit solutions)
crossover (mating between parents to generate off-springs)
mutation (random change in off-springs)
end while
Return best individual in population;

In Algorithm 1, q represents the generation counter, initialization is done randomly in search space and corresponding fitness is evaluated based on objective function. After that, GA algorithm requires a cycle of three phases: selection, crossover and mutation. Each of the phases is explained in section 2.2 GA part.

In medical world, If we have to be diagnosed any disease then there are some tests to be performed. After getting the results of the tests performed, the diagnosed could be done better. We can consider each and every test as an attribute. If we have to do a particular test then there are certain set of chemicals, equipments, may be people, more time required which can be more expensive. Basically, Attribute selection informs whether a particular test is required for the diagnosis or not. So, if a particular test is not required that can be avoided. When the number of tests gets reduced the cost that is required also gets reduced which helps the common people. Therefore, here that is why GA has been used as an Attribute selection by which four features obtained among eight features. Therefore, from the above it is clear that GA is shortening the cost, storage capacity and computation time by selected some of the attributes.

5.1.3. SVM for Classification

SVM are supervised machine learning models or approach that are associated with learning algorithms which analyze data, recognize patterns and are used for classification as well as regression analysis. SVM constructs hyper plane or decision surface that classifies the data with a largest margin. The decision surface that maximizes the margin of the training set will minimize the generalization error. SVM classifies the linearly separable data. In this manuscript, polynomial Kernel, RBF Kernel, Sigmoid Function, Linear Kernel SVM has been used for the classification of PIDD.

5.1.3.1. Linear SVM

Linear SVM was developed to separate the two classes that belong to either one side of the margin of hyper plane or the other side. Given labeled training data as data points of the form:

$$M = \left\{ \left(x_1, y_1\right), \left(x_2, y_2\right), \ldots\ldots\ldots\ldots\ldots\ldots\ldots\ldots\ldots, \left(x_n, y_n\right) \right\} \tag{5}$$

where $y_n = 1 / -1$, this constant denotes the class which will belongs to the point x_n, n = Number of data sample. Each x_n, is a p-dimensional real vector or is a set of training tuples with associated class labels y_n. The SVM classifier first maps the input vectors into a decision value, and then performs the classification using an appropriate threshold value.

To view the training data, we divide or separate the hyper plane, which can be defined as:

Mapping: $w^T.x + b = 0$ (6)

where w is a p-dimensional vector or weight vector and b is a scalar. The vector w points perpendicular to the separating hyper plane. The problem of finding best hyper plane among the number of separating hyper planes can be solved by maximal marginal hyper plane. The offset parameter b allows to increase the margin. As we know that the training data is linearly separable, we constructs hyper planes, and try to maximize the distance between hyper planes. The distance between two hyper plane is, $2 / |w|$ thus we need to minimize $|w|$ by ensuring that for all i either

$$w.x_i - b \geq 1 \text{ or } w.x_i \leq -1 \tag{7}$$

To calculate the margin, two parallel hyper planes are constructed, one on each side of the separating hyper plane, which are "pushed up amongst" the two classes. A good separation is achieved by the hyper plane that has the largest distance to the neighboring data points of both classes, since in general the larger the margin the lower the the generalization error of the classifier. The hyper plane is found by using support vectors and margins.

5.1.3.2. Non-Linear

If the data is non-linear, SVM do not achieve classification tasks. To overcome this limitation, these support vectors are transformed into higher dimensional feature space, which is introduced by kernel functions (Chen, Li, & Wei, 2007). Here by support vectors we mean the training points that are nearest to the separating function are called support vectors. For a domain expert a kernel is a similarity function provide to a machine-learning algorithm. Kernel makes linear models in non linear settings. Kernel is used for non-separable problem in to separable and map data into better representational space. A Kernel function is defined as a function that corresponds to a dot product of two feature vectors in some expanded feature space:

$$K\left(x_i, x_j\right) = D(x_i)^T D\left(x_j\right) \tag{8}$$

The motivation for this extension is that a SVM with non linear decision surface can classify non linear separable data.

5.1.3.2.1. SVM Algorithm

1. Pick out a kernel function.
2. Pick out a value for c (Classification error).
3. Solve the Quadratic Programming (QP) problem.
4. Construct the discriminant function from the support vectors.

5.1.3.2.1.1. Polynomial Kernel

The polynomial kernel is a non–stationary kernel. This kernel has degree d, gamma, r parameters. Polynomial kernels are well suited for problems where all the training data is normalized. For a degree- d polynomials, the polynomial kernel is defined as:

$$K\left(x_i, x_j\right) = (x_i^T x_j + c)^d \tag{9}$$

where x and y are vectors in the input space, i.e. vectors of features computed from training or test samples and $c \geq 0$ is a free parameter trading off the influence of higher-order versus lower-order terms in the polynomial. When $c = 0$, the kernel is called homogeneous. As a kernel, k corresponds to an inner product in a feature space based on some mapping:

$$K\left(x_i, x_j\right) = \left(D\left(x_i\right), D\left(x_j\right)\right) \tag{10}$$

The nature of D can be seen from an example. Let $d = 2$, So we get the special case of the quadratic kernel.

$$K\left(x, y\right) = (\sum_{i=1}^{n} x_i y_i + c)^2 = \sum_{i=1}^{n}\left(x_i^2\right)\left(y_i^2\right) + \sum_{i=2}^{n}\sum_{j=1}^{i-1}\left(\sqrt{2}x_i x_j\right)\left(\sqrt{2}y_i y_j\right) + \sum_{i=1}^{n}\left(\sqrt{2c}x_i\right) + \left(\sqrt{2c}y_i\right) + c \tag{11}$$

From this, it follows that the feature map is given by:

$$D\left(x\right) = \left(x_n^2, \ldots, x_1^2, \sqrt{2}x_n x_{n-1,\ldots,} \sqrt{2}x_n x_{1,} \sqrt{2}x_{n-1} x_{n-2,\ldots,} \sqrt{2}x_{n-1} x_{1,\ldots,} \sqrt{2}x_2 x_{1,} \sqrt{2c}x_n, \sqrt{2c}x_n, c\right) \tag{12}$$

5.1.3.2.1.2. RBF Kernel

RBF kernel is also known as the Gaussian kernel. The non-linear RBF Kernel SVM is also used for classifier to analyze higher dimensional data. RBF kernel has gamma parameter. RBF Kernel is a more popular and commonly used in SVM classification than the polynomial Kernel. The output of the RBF Kernel is dependent on Euclian distance i.e. from x_i to x_j (Among all, one will be the support vector and rest or other will be the testing data point). The support vector will be lie on the centre of the RBF and γ will determine the area of influence this support vector has over the data space.

$$K\left(x_i, x_j\right) = \exp(-\gamma \parallel x_i - x_j \parallel^2), \gamma > 0 \tag{13}$$

where, x_i is the training vector, γ is a kernel parameter where,

$$\gamma = \frac{1}{2\sigma^2} \tag{14}$$

A larger value of γ will give a smoother decision surface and more regular decision boundary. This is because a RBF with larger ³ will allow a support vector to have a strong influence over a larger area.

The RBF kernel on two samples x_i, and x_j, represented as feature vectors in some input space, is defined as:

$$K\left(x_i, x_j\right) = \exp\left(-\frac{\parallel x_i - x_j \parallel^2}{2\sigma^2}\right) \tag{15}$$

$\parallel x_i - x_j \parallel^2$ may be recognized as the squared Euclidean distance between the two feature vectors, σ stands for a window width or may say is a free parameter.

5.1.3.2.1.3. Sigmoid Function

Sigmoid kernel has gamma, r parameters. Most often, sigmoid function is a special case of the logistic function and defined by the formula i.e.

$$S\left(t\right) = \frac{1}{1 + e^{-t}} \tag{16}$$

For e.g., besides the logistic function, sigmoid functions include the ordinary arctangent, the hyperbolic tangent, and gudermannian function, and the error function, but also the generalized logistic function and algebraic functions like

$$f\left(x\right) = \frac{x}{\sqrt{1 + x^2}} \tag{17}$$

The integral of any smooth, positive, "bump-shaped" function will be sigmoid, thus the cumulative distribution functions (CDF) of a normal distribution such as error function for many common probability distributions are sigmoid.

$$K\left(x_j, x_j\right) = \tanh\left(\beta_0 x_i^T x_j + \beta_1\right) \tag{18}$$

With user $^2{}_0$ defined parameter and $^2{}_1$. It does not satisfy the mercer condition on all $^2{}_0$ and $^2{}_1$. It is originated from neural network works and has similar feature like MLP.

5.1.3.2.1.4 Linear Kernel

Linear kernel has no parameter.

$$K\left(x_i, x_j\right) = x_i^T x_j \tag{19}$$

The training of the linear kernel is faster than other kernel such as RBF, Polynomial, and Sigmoid because this kernel does not perform any mapping, we need to optimize the c regularization parameter and also may be using a dedicated library such as Liblinear. Linear kernel never be more accurate than a properly tuned RBF kernel because linear kernel is a degenerate version of RBF. Linear kernel tends to perform very well when the number of features is large because there is no need to map to an even higher dimensional feature space and only searches for the parameter c. for e.g., Document classification, with thousands of dimensions in input space.

6. RESULTS AND DISCUSSION OF PROPOSED METHODOLOGY

In this manuscript, the experimental result have been performed on i3 processor with 2.30GHz speed, 2 GB RAM, 320 GB external storage and software used JDK 1.8.2 (Java Development Kit), NetBeans 8.0 IDE and have done the coding in Java. For the computation of SVM, WEKA library, etc. are used. In Experimental studies, the dataset has been partition 70-30% (538-230) for training & test of GA_SVM, SVM method for diagnosis of diabetes. The studies have been performed on PIDD mentioned in section 5.1.1. The results have been compared the proposed system i.e. GA_SVM, SVM with the previous results reported by earlier methods (Seera & Lim, 2014; Choubey & Paul, 2016). According to the Table 6, GA method provides 4 features among 8 features. It means that reduced the cost to s(x) = 4/8 = 0.5 from 1 and have obtained an improvement on the training and classification by a factor of 2.

Classification Accuracy: Classification accuracy is the ratio of total number of correctly diagnosed cases to the total number of cases.

$$\text{Classification accuracy}\left(\%\right) = \left(\text{TP} + \text{TN}\right) / \left(\text{TP} + \text{FP} + \text{TN} + \text{FN}\right) \tag{20}$$

TP (True Positive): Diabetic people correctly detected as diabetic people.
FP (False Positive): Healthy people incorrectly detected as diabetic people.
TN (True Negative): Healthy people correctly detected as healthy people.
FN (False Negative): Diabetic people incorrectly detected as healthy people.

Precision: Precision may be defined as the measures of the rate of correctly classified samples that are predicted as diabetic samples or precision is the ratio of true positive to the sum of true positive and false positive.

or Precision = TP / TP + FP   (21)

Recall: Recall may be defined as the measures of the rate of correctly classified samples that are actually diabetic samples or recall is the ratio of true positive to the sum of true positive and false negative.

or Recall = TP / TP + FN   (22)

Fallout: The term fallout is used to check true negative of the dataset during classification.

F - Measure: The F – Measure computes some average of the information retrieval precision and recall metrics. The F – Measure (F – Score) is calculated based on the precision and recall. It is a trade-off between precision and recall. It is the harmonic – mean of precision and recall. The calculation is as follow:

$$F - Measure = \frac{2*Precision*Recall}{Precision + Recall}$$ (23)

Area Under Curve (AUC): It is defined as the metric used to measure the performance of classifier with relevant acceptance. It is calculated from area under curve (ROC) based on true positives and false positives.

$$AUC = \frac{1}{2}\left(\frac{TP}{TP + FN} + \frac{TN}{TN + FP}\right)$$ (24)

ROC (Receiver Operating Curve Graph) is an effective method of evaluating the performance of diagnostic tests. ROC is defined as a plot of test or relationship between Sensitivity or True Positive Rate (TPR) as the Y coordinate and 1-Specificity or False Positive Rate (FPR) as the X coordinate

Confusion Matrix: A confusion matrix (Polat & Gunes, 2007; Polat et al., 2008) contains information regarding actual and predicted classifications done by a classification system.

Kappa Statistics: It is defined as performance to measure the true classification or accuracy of the algorithm.

$$K = \frac{T_0 - T_C}{1 - T_C}$$ (25)

where, T_0 is the total agreement probability and T_C is the agreement probability due to change.

Mean Absolute Error (MAE): MAE means the average of the absolute errors. MAE is a quantity used to measure how close forecasts or predictions are to the eventual outcomes. MAE is a common measure of forecasts errors. MAE can be compared between models whose errors are measured in the same units. It is usually similar in magnitude to RMSE, but slightly smaller.

It is defined as:

$$MAE = \frac{\left|t_1 - q_1\right| + ... + \left|t_n - q_n\right|}{n} \tag{26}$$

Root Mean-Squared Error (RMSE): The square root of the mean /average of the square of all of the error. RMSE is used to assess how well a system learns a given model. RMSE can be compared between models whose errors are measured in same units.

It is defined as:

$$RMSE = \sqrt{\frac{\left(t_1 - q_1\right)^2 + ... + \left(t_n - q_n\right)^2}{n}} \tag{27}$$

Relative Absolute Error (RAE): Like RSE, RAE can be compared between models whose errors are measured in the different units.

It is defined as:

$$RAE = \frac{\left|t_1 - q_1\right| + ... + \left|t_n - q_n\right|}{\left|\overline{q} - q_1\right| + ... + \left|\overline{q} - q\right|} \tag{28}$$

Relative Squared Error (RSE): Unlike RMSE, RSE can be compared between models whose errors are measured in different units.

It is defined as:

$$RSE = \frac{\left(t_1 - q_1\right)^2 + ... + \left(t_n - q_n\right)^2}{\left(\overline{q} - q_1\right)^2 + ... + \left(\overline{q} - q_n\right)^2} \tag{29}$$

where, $q_1, q_2, ...q_n$ are the actual target values and $t_1, t_2, ...t_n$ are the predicted target values.

The time taken to build model training set evaluation= 196.67 seconds, and time taken to build model testing set evaluation = 190.4 seconds for Polynomial Kernel method. The Table 2 shows the results

Table 2. Results of Polynomial Kernel SVM for PIDD

Measure	Training Set Evaluation	Testing Set Evaluation
Precision	0.656	0.614
Recall	0.677	0.648
F-Measure	0.64	0.613
Accuracy	67.658%	64.7826%
ROC	0.586	0.554
Kappa statistics	0.1947	0.121
Mean absolute error	0.3234	0.3522
Root mean–squared error	0.5687	0.5934
Relative absolute error	70.9346%	77.6358%
Root relative squared error	119.1302%	124.9502%

of both the training set and testing set evaluation by using Polynomial Kernel SVM method for PIDD based on some parameters, which are noted in Box 2 and Box 3.

Figure 4 is the ROC graph for tested positive class by using Polynomial Kernel SVM method on PIDD, achieved 0.5537 ROC. The figure generating more error rate, and ratio between FPR vs TPR is also not good.

The time taken to build model training set evaluation= 0.44 seconds, and time taken to build model testing set evaluation = 0.41 seconds for RBF Kernel SVM method. The Table 3 shows the results for both the training set and testing set evaluation by using RBF Kernel SVM method for PIDD based on some parameters, which are noted in Box 4 and Box 5.

Figure 5 is the ROC graph for tested_positive class by using RBF Kernel SVM method on PIDD, achieved 0.5 ROC. Figure 5 generating more error rate, and ratio between FPR vs TPR is also not good.

The time taken to build model training set evaluation= *0.18* seconds, and time taken to build model testing set evaluation = *0.16* seconds for Sigmoid Function Kernel method. The Table 4 shows the results for both the training set and testing set evaluation by using Sigmoid Function Kernel method for PIDD based on some parameters, which are noted in Box 6 and Box 7.

Figure 6 is the ROC graph for tested_positive class by using Sigmoid Function Kernel SVM methodology on PIDD, achieved 0.5 ROC. It may be seen in the figure that generating more error rate, and ratio between FPR vs TPR is also not good.

The time taken to build model training set evaluation= 0.40 seconds, and time taken to build model testing set evaluation = 0.38 seconds for Linear Kernel SVM method. The Table 5 shows the results for

Box 2. Cofusion Matrix for Training set

a	b	<--classified as
311	38	a = tested_ negative
136	53	b = tested_ positive

Box 3. Cofusion Matrix for Testing set

a	b	<--classified as
129	22	a = tested_ negative
59	20	b = tested_ positive

Figure 4. ROC graph for tested positive class by using Polynomial Kernel SVM methodology on PIDD

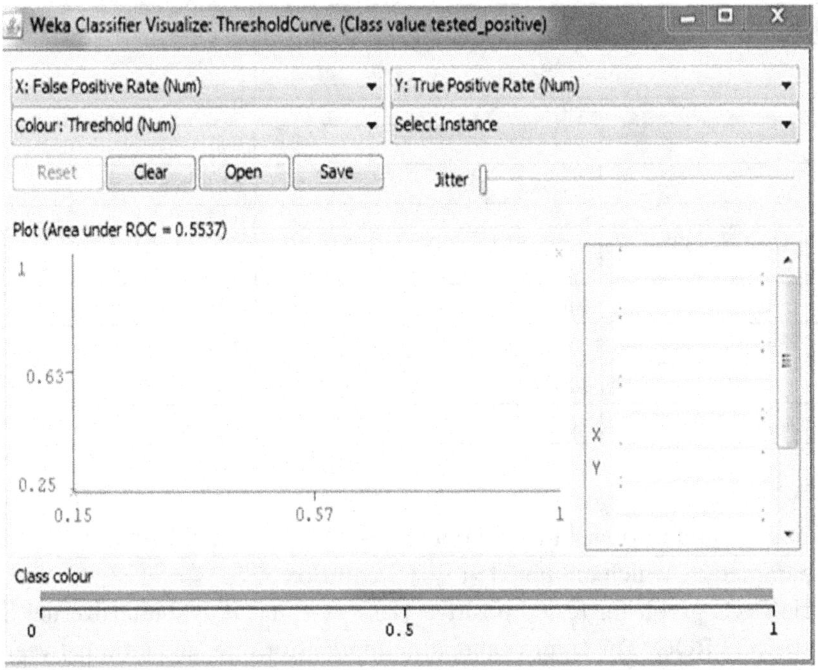

Table 3. Results of RBF Kernel SVM for PIDD

Measure	Training Set Evaluation	Testing Set Evaluation
Precision	1	0.431
Recall	1	0.657
F – Measure	1	0.52
Accuracy	100%	65.6522%
ROC	1	0.5
Kappa statistics	1	0
Mean absolute error	0	0.3435
Root mean – squared error	0	0.5861
Relative absolute error	0%	75.7188%
Root relative squared error	0%	123.3979%

Box 4. Cofusion Matrix for Training set

a	b	<--classified as
349	0 I	a = tested_ negative
0	189 I	b = tested_ positive

Box 5. Cofusion Matrix for Testing set

a	b	<--classified as
151	0 I	a = tested_ negative
79	0 I	b = tested_ positive

Figure 5. ROC graph for tested positive class by using RBF Kernel SVM methodology on PIDD

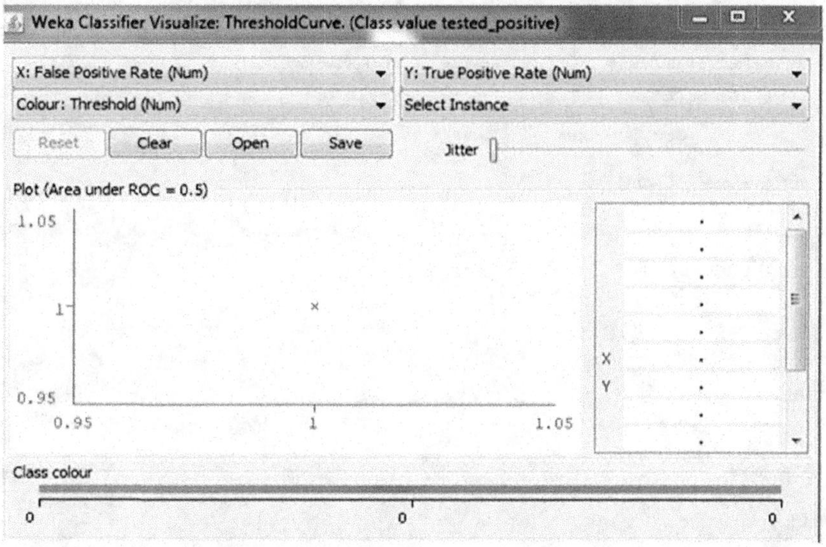

Table 4. Results of Sigmoid Function SVM for PIDD

Measure	Training Set Evaluation	Testing Set Evaluation
Precision	0.421	0.431
Recall	0.649	0.657
F – Measure	0.51	0.52
Accuracy	64.8699%	65.6522%
ROC	0.5	0.5
Kappa statistics	0	0
Mean absolute error	0.3513	0.3435
Root mean – squared error	0.5927	0.5861
Relative absolute error	77.0497%	75.7188%
Root relative squared error	124.159%	123.3979%

Box 6. Cofusion Matrix for Training set

a	b	<--classified as
349	0 I	a = tested_ negative
189	0 I	b = tested_ positive

Box 7. Cofusion Matrix for Testing set

a	b	<--classified as
151	0 I	a = tested_ negative
79	0 I	b = tested_ positive

both the training set and testing set evaluation by using Linear Kernel SVM method for PIDD based on some parameters, which are noted in Box 8 and Box 9.

Figure 7 is the ROC graph for tested positive class by using Linear Kernel SVM methodology on PIDD, achieved 0.7162. So, from all i.e., Polynomial Kernel, RBF Kernel, Sigmoid Function Kernel, and

Figure 6. ROC graph for tested positive class by using Sigmoid Function SVM methodology on PIDD

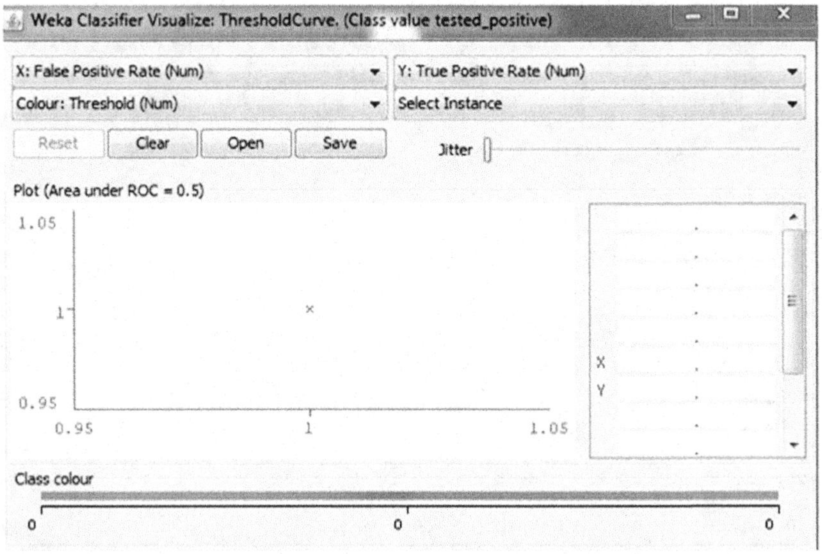

Table 5. Results of Linear Kernel SVM for PIDD

Measure	Training Set Evaluation	Testing Set Evaluation
Precision	0.769	0.769
Recall	0.773	0.774
F – Measure	0.765	0.763
Accuracy	77.3234%	77.3913%
ROC	0.723	0.716
Kappa statistics	0.4731	0.4631
Mean absolute error	0.2268	0.2261
Root mean – squared error	0.4762	0.4755
Relative absolute error	49.7358%	49.8403%
Root relative squared error	99.7533%	100.1143%

Box 8. Cofusion Matrix for Training set

a	b	<--classified as
311	38	a = tested_ negative
84	105	b = tested_ positive

Box 9. Cofusion Matrix for Testing set

a	b	<--classified as
136	15	a = tested_ negative
37	42	b = tested_ positive

Figure 7. ROC graph for tested positive class by using Linear Kernel SVM methodology on PIDD

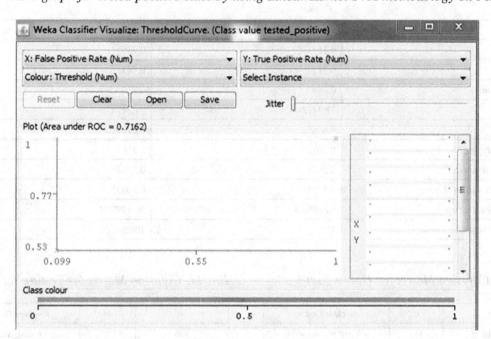

Linear Kernel SVM, It may be seen that Linear Kernel SVM generates less error rate and ratio between FPR vs TPR is good as shown in Figure 7.

The Table 6 shows the Attribute selection by using GA on PIDD, which is noted as follows.

The time taken to build model training set evaluation= *133.9* seconds, and time taken to build model testing set evaluation = *129.26* seconds for GA_Polynomial Kernel SVM methodology. The Table 7 shows the results for both the training set and testing set evaluation by using Polynomial Kernel SVM method for PIDD on the selected attributes by using GA based on some parameters, which is noted in Box 10 and Box 11.

Table 6. GA for attributes selection

Data Set	Number of Attributes	Name of Attributes	No. of Instances	No. of Classes
PIDD (Without GA)	8	1. Number of times pregnant 2. Plasma glucose concentration a 2 hours in an oral glucose tolerance test 3. Diastolic blood pressure 4. Triceps skin fold thickness 5. 2 – hour serum insulin 6. Body mass index 7. Diabetes pedigree function 8. Age (years)	768	2
PIDD (With GA)	4	2. Plasma glucose concentration a 2 hours in an oral glucose tolerance test 5. 2 – hour serum insulin 6. Body mass index 8. Age (years)	768	2

Table 7. Results of GA_Polynomial Kernel SVM for PIDD

Measure	Training Set Evaluation	Testing Set Evaluation
Precision	0.711	0.736
Recall	0.717	0.743
F – Measure	0.689	0.726
Accuracy	71.7472%	74.3478
ROC	0.635	0.672
Kappa statistics	0.3042	0.3767
Mean absolute error	0.2825	0.2565
Root mean – squared error	0.5325	0.5065
Relative absolute error	61.9659%	56.5495%
Root relative squared error	111.3446%	106.6401%

Box 10. Cofusion Matrix for Training set

a	b	<--classified as
318	31 I	a = tested_ negative
121	68 I	b = tested_ positive

Box 11. Cofusion Matrix for Testing set

a	b	<--classified as
136	15 I	a = tested_ negative
44	35 I	b = tested_ positive

Figure 8 is the ROC graph for tested_positive class by using GA_Polynomial Kernel SVM methodology on PIDD, achieved 0.6719. The figure generating not so more error rate, and ratio between FPR vs TPR is also not bad.

The time taken to build model training set evaluation = *0.63* seconds, and time taken to build model testing set evaluation = *0.38* seconds for GA_RBF Kernel SVM methodology. The Table 8 shows the results for both the training set and testing set evaluation by using RBF Kernel SVM method on the selected attributes by using GA based on some parameters, which is noted in Box 12 and Box 13.

Figure 9 is the ROC graph for tested_positive class by using GA_RBF Kernel SVM methodology on PIDD, achieved 0.4868. It may be seen in the figure, that generating more error rate, and ratio between FPR vs TPR is also not good.

The time taken to build model training set evaluation= 5.18 seconds, and time taken to build model testing set evaluation = 0.16 seconds for GA_Sigmoid Function Kernel SVM methodology. The Table 9 shows the results for both the training set and testing set evaluation by using Sigmoid Function Kernel SVM method on the selected attributes by using GA based on some parameters, which is noted in Box 14 and Box 15.

Figure 10 is the ROC graph for tested_positive class by using GA_Sigmoid Function Kernel SVM methodology on PIDD, achieved 0.5. It may be seen in the figure, that generating more error rate, and ratio between FPR vs TPR is also bad.

The time taken to build model training set evaluation= 5.51 seconds, and time taken to build model testing set evaluation = 6.61 seconds for GA_Linear Kernel SVM methodology. The Table 10 shows the results for both the training set and testing set evaluation by using Linear Kernel SVM method on the selected attributes by using GA based on some parameters, which is noted in Box 16 and Box 17.

Figure 8. ROC graph for tested_positive class by using GA_Polynomial Kernel SVM methodology on PIDD

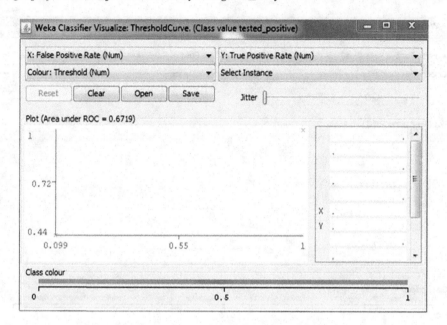

Table 8. Results of GA_RBF Kernel SVM for PIDD

Measure	Training Set Evaluation	Testing Set Evaluation
Precision	0.998	0.427
Recall	0.998	0.639
F – Measure	0.998	0.512
Accuracy	99.8141%	63.913%
ROC	0.997	0.487
Kappa statistics	0.9959	-0.0342
Mean absolute error	0.0019	0.3609
Root mean – squared error	0.0431	0.6007
Relative absolute error	0.4077%	79.5527%
Root relative squared error	9.0312%	126.4834%

Box 12. Cofusion Matrix for Training set

a	b	<--classified as
349	0|	a = tested_ negative
1	188|	b = tested_ positive

Box 13. Cofusion Matrix for Testing set

a	b	<--classified as
151	0		a = tested_ negative
79	0		b = tested_ positive

Figure 9. ROC graph for tested_positive class by using GA_RBF Kernel SVM methodology on PIDD

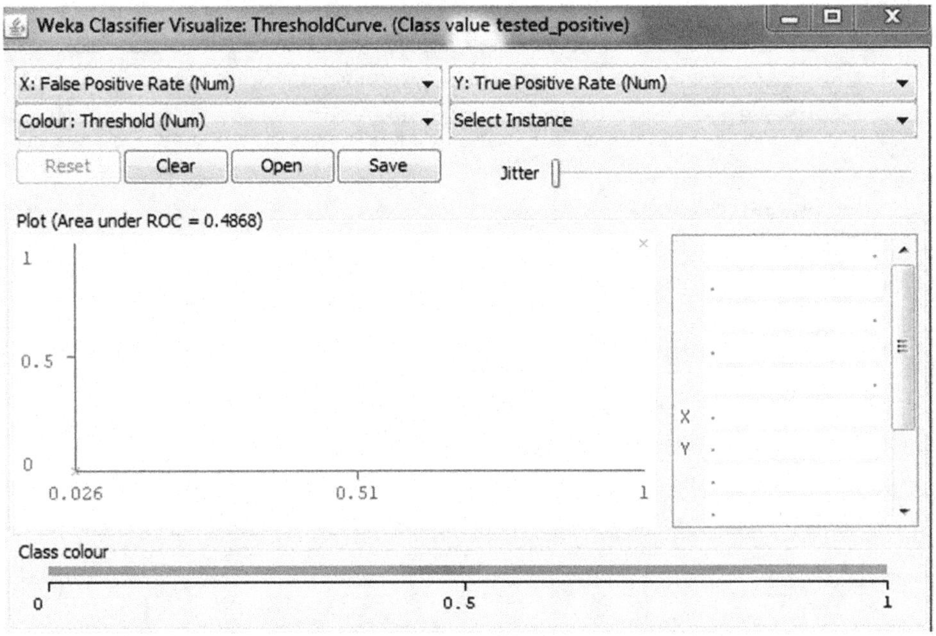

Table 9. Results of GA_Sigmoid Function Kernel SVM for PIDD

Measure	Training Set Evaluation	Testing Set Evaluation
Precision	0.421	0.431
Recall	0.649	0.657
F – Measure	0.51	0.52
Accuracy	64.8699	65.6522%
ROC	0.5	0.5
Kappa statistics	0	0
Mean absolute error	0.3513	0.3435
Root mean – squared error	0.5927	0.5861
Relative absolute error	77.0497%	75.7188%
Root relative squared error	124.159%	123.3979%

Box 14. Cofusion Matrix for Training set

a	b	<--classified as
349	0	a = tested_ negative
189	0	b = tested_ positive

Box 15. Cofusion Matrix for Testing set

a	B	<--classified as
151	0	a = tested_ negative
79	0	b = tested_ positive

Figure 10. ROC graph for tested_positive class by using GA_Sigmoid Function Kernel SVM methodology on PIDD

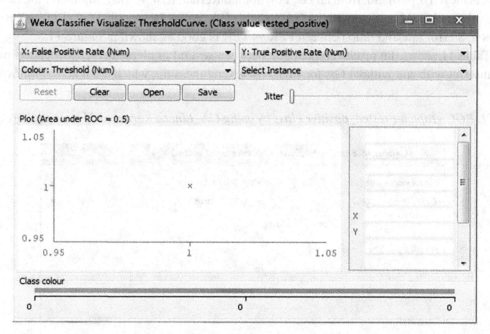

Table 10. Results of GA_Linear Kernel SVM for PIDD

Measure	Training Set Evaluation	Testing Set Evaluation
Precision	0.759	0.792
Recall	0.764	0.796
F – Measure	0.754	0.789
Accuracy	76.3941%	79.5652%%
ROC	0.711	0.748
Kappa statistics	0.4493	0.5224
Mean absolute error	0.2361	0.2043
Root mean – squared error	0.4859	0.452
Relative absolute error	51.7741%	45.0479%
Root relative squared error	101.7769%	95.1795%

Box 16. Cofusion Matrix for Training set

a	b	<--classified as
314	35 I	a = tested_ negative
92	97 I	b = tested_ positive

Box 17. Cofusion Matrix for Testing set

a	b	<--classified as
136	15 I	a = tested_ negative
32	47 I	b = tested_ positive

Figure 11 is the ROC graph for tested_positive class by using GA_Linear Kernel SVM methodology on PIDD, achieved 0.7478. So, from all i.e., Polynomial Kernel, RBF Kernel, Sigmoid Function Kernel, and Linear Kernel SVM method without GA and also GA, It may be seen that GA_Linear Kernel SVM generates less error rate and ratio between FPR vs TPR is good as shown in Figure 11.

The Table 11 shows the results comparison between several implemented classification method in this manuscript with and without GA for PIDD by several measure, which are noted as follows.

Figure 11. ROC graph for tested_positive class by using GA_Linear Kernel SVM methodology on PIDD

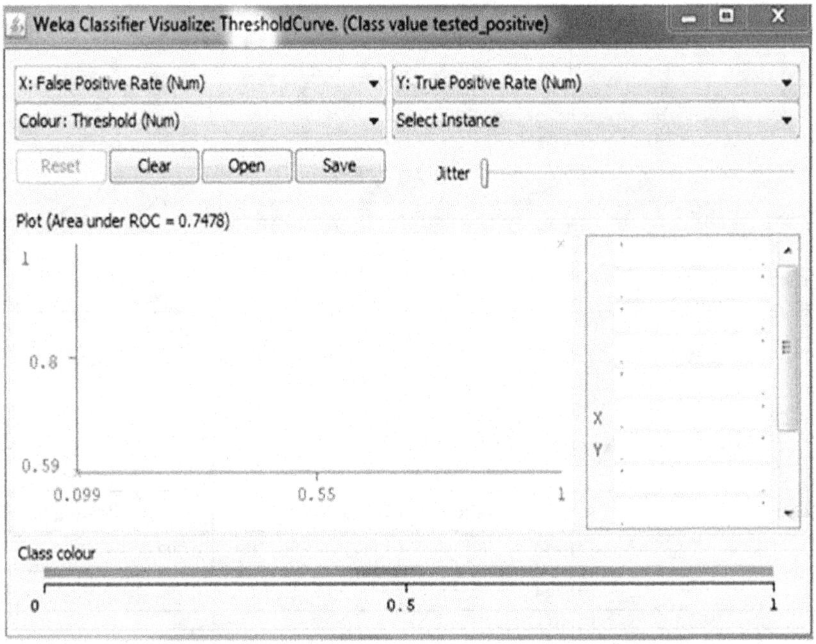

Table 11. Results comparison between several implemented classification method with and without GA for PIDD

Measure	Polynomial Kernel SVM	GA_ Polynomial Kernel SVM	RBF Kernel SVM	GA_RBF Kernel SVM	Sigmoid Function Kernel	GA_Sigmoid Function Kernel	Linear Kernel SVM	GA _ Linear Kernel SVM
Precision	0.614	0.736	0.431	0.427	0.431	0.431	0.769	0.792
Recall	0.648	0.743	0.657	0.639	0.657	0.657	0.774	0.796
F – Measure	0.613	0.726	0.52	0.512	0.52	0.52	0.763	0.789
Accuracy	64.7826%	74.3478%	65.6522%	63.913%	65.6522%	65.6522%	77.3913%	79.5652%
ROC	0.554	0.672	0.5	0.487	0.5	0.5	0.716	0.748
Kappa statistics	0.121	0.3767	0	-0.0342	0	0	0.4631	0.5224
MAE	0.3522	0.2565	0.3435	0.3609	0.3435	0.3435	0.2261	0.2043
RMSE	0.5934	0.5065	0.5861	0.6007	0.5861	0.5861	0.4755	0.452
RAE	77.6358%	56.5495%	75.7188%	79.5527%	75.7188%	75.7188%	49.8403%	45.0479%
RRSE	124.9502%	106.6401%	123.3979%	126.4834%	123.3979%	123.3979%	100.1143%	95.1795%

In the Table 11, it may be seen that with GA the improvement has occurred in the case of classification method except RBF kernel SVM method. May be this is an exceptional classification method for this dataset which is not achieving even the same result with GA. Among all classification method in this table, Linear Kernel SVM, GA_ Linear Kernel SVM providing the good result, which is useful, and in the rest classification method just experimental work has been performed but not useful for this work because existed method already providing good results for this dataset. So, now it may be seen to individual analysis to every classification method in table 11. In the case of polynomial kernel SVM, with GA the improvement has occurred in every measure. Now come in the case of RBF Kernel SVM, with GA not improvement but poor result in every measure. In the Sigmoidal Kernel SVM with GA achieving the same result in every measure as in Sigmoidal Function Kernel SVM. So now come in last i.e., Linear Kernel SVM also may be seen that with GA the improvement has occurred in every measure, which will be the also proposed method for this work.

The figure shown below is the analysis of comparison result with and without GA on several methods i.e., Polynomial Kernel, RBF Kernel, Sigmoid Function Kernel, and Linear Kernel SVM for PIDD.

The Figure 12 is representing the above Table 11 measures in chart graphical or histogram form and this is indicating the difference in more precise form between several methods as already mention in the table.

The Table 12 shows the analysis of comparison result with and without GA on SVM for PIDD by several measures along with several methods i.e., noted in table.

Figure 12. Evaluation of Polynomial Kernel, GA_Polynomial Kernel, RBF Kernel, GA_RBF Kernel, Sigmoid Function Kernel, GA_Sigmoid Function Kernel, Linear Kernel SVM and GA_Linear Kernel SVM Performance for PIDD

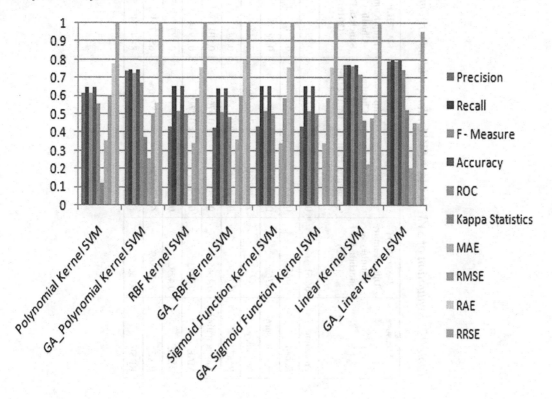

Table 12. Evaluation of SVM & GA _ SVM, along with several method Performance for PIDD

Measure	J48graft DT Dilip Kumar & Sanchita Paul (2015)	GA_J48graft DT Dilip Kumar Choubey & Sanchita Paul (2015)	MLP NN Dilip Kumar Choubey & Sanchita Paul (2016)	GA_MLP NN Dilip Kumar Choubey & Sanchita Paul (2016)	RBF NN Dilip Kumar Choubey & Sanchita Paul (2017)	GA_RBF NN Dilip Kumar Choubey & Sanchita Paul (2017)	NBs Dilip Kumar Choubey & Sanchita Paul (2017)	GA_NBs Dilip Kumar Choubey & Sanchita Paul (2017)	Linear Kernel SVM	GA_ Linear Kernel SVM
Precision	0.761	0.789	0.781	0.79	0.756	0.768	0.766	0.782	0.769	0.792
Recall	0.765	0.748	0.783	0.791	0.761	0.774	0.77	0.787	0.774	0.796
F – Measure	0.762	0.754	0.77	0.78	0.757	0.767	0.767	0.78	0.763	0.789
Accuracy	76.5217%	74.7826%	78.2609	79.1304%	76.087%	77.3913%	76.9565%	78.6957%	77.3913%	79.5652%
ROC	0.765	0.786	0.853	0.842	0.813	0.848	0.846	0.844	0.716	0.748
Kappa statistics	0.4665	0.4901	0.4769	0.5011	0.455	0.4733	0.478	0.5021	0.4631	0.5224
MAE	0.3353	0.3117	0.2716	0.2984	0.3337	0.3108	0.2768	0.295	0.2261	0.2043
RMSE	0.4292	0.4114	0.387	0.387	0.4057	0.3871	0.3973	0.3919	0.4755	0.452
RAE	73.9186%	68.7038%	59.8716%	65.7734%	73.5706%	68.522%	61.0206%	65. 0317%	49.8403%	45.0479%
RRSE	90.3686%	86.6146%	81.4912%	81.4774%	85.4247%	81.5054%	83.654%	82.5241%	100.1143%	95.1795%

In the Table 12, It may be seen that among all classification method Linear Kernel SVM, GA_ Linear Kernel SVM provides the approximate good result. With attribute selection method i.e., here GA on every classification method achieving a good result, as already discussed the merit of this method in section 2.2. and here also achieved.

Figure 13 is the analysis of comparison result with and without GA on several methods i.e., J48graft DT, MLP NN, RBF NN, NBs and Linear Kernel SVM for PIDD.

The Figure 13 is representing the above Table 12 measures in chart graphical or histogram form and this is indicating the difference in more precise form between several methods as already mention in the table.

In the Table 13, it may be seen that there is already several existed method for PIDD. The Table 13 shows the result comparison in terms of accuracy on PIDD for the diagnosis of diabetes. The method i.e., GA_Linear Kernel SVM provides the highest accuracy from all other existing method.

The Table 14 shows the result comparison in terms of ROC on PIDD for the diagnosis of diabetes. The method i.e., here GA_Linear Kernel SVM provides not so bad ROC than other all existing method.

Figure 13. Evaluation of J48graft DT, GA_J48graft DT, MLP NN, GA_MLP NN, RBF NN, GA_RBF NN, NBs, GA_NBs Linear Kernel SVM and GA_Linear Kernel SVM Performance for PIDD

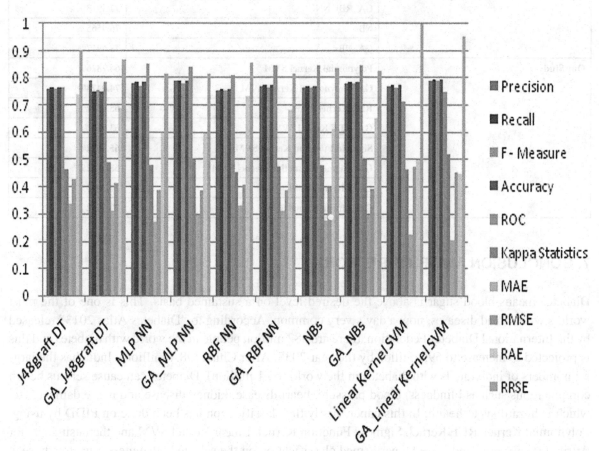

Table 13. Results and comparison with other existing methods for the PIDD

Source	Method	Accuracy
Pasi Luukka (2011)	Sim	75.29%
	Sim + F1	75.84%
	Sim + F2	75.97%
H. Hasan Orkcu et al. (2011)	Binary – coded GA	74.80%
	BP	73.80%
	Real – coded GA	77.60%
Manjeevan Seera et al. (2014)	FMM	69.28%
	FMM – CART	71.35%
	FMM-CART – RF	78.39%
Dilip Kumar Choubey & Sanchita Paul (2015)	J48graft DT	76.5217%
	GA_J48grft DT	74.7826 %
Dilip Kumar Choubey & Sanchita Paul (2016)	MLP NN	78.2609%
	GA_MLP NN	79.1304%
Dilip Kumar Choubey & Sanchita Paul (2017)	RBF NN	76.087 %
	GA_RBF NN	77.3913%
	NBs	76.9565 %
	GA_NBs	78.6957 %
Our Study	**Polynomial Kernel SVM**	**64.7826%**
	GA _Polynomial Kernel SVM	**74.3478%**
	RBF Kernel SVM	**65.6522%**
	GA_RBF Kernel SVM	**63.913%**
	Sigmoid Function Kernel SVM	**65.6522%**
	GA_ Sigmoid Function Kernel SVM	**65.6522%**
	Liner Kernel SVM	**77.3913%**
	GA_Linear Kernel SVM	**79.5652%**

7. CONCLUSION AND FUTURE WORK

Diabetes means blood sugar is above the desired level on a sustained basis. This is one of the most world's widespread diseases, now a day's very common. According to "Diabetes Atlas 2013" released by the International Diabetes Federation, there are 382 million people in the world with diabetes and this is projected to increase to 592 million by the year 2035. After China (98.4 million), India has the largest numbers of individuals with diabetes in the world (65.1 million). Diabetes can cause serious health complications such as blindness, blood pressure, heart disease, kidney disease and nerve damage, etc. which is hazardous to health. In this paper, firstly the classification has been done on PIDD by using, Polynomial Kernel, RBF Kernel, Sigmoid Function Kernel, Linear Kernel SVM and then using GA for Attributes selection, and there by performed classification on the selected attributes. It is already seen in Section 6 i.e., Results and Discussion of proposed methodology that only Linear Kernel SVM, GA_

Table 14. Results of ROC for PIDD

Source	Method	ROC
Pasi Luukka (2011)	Sim	0.762
	Sim + F1	0.703
	Sim + F2	0.667
Manjeevan Seera et al. (2014)	FMM	0.661
	FMM – CART	0.683
	FMM-CART – RF	0.732
Dilip Kumar Choubey & Sanchita Paul (2015)	J48graft DT	0.765
	GA_J48grft DT	0.786
Dilip Kumar Choubey & Sanchita Paul (2016)	MLP NN	0.853
	GA_MLP NN	0.842
Dilip Kumar Choubey & Sanchita Paul (2017)	RBF NN	0.813
	GA_RBF NN	0.848
	NBs	0.846
	GA_NBs	0.844
Our Study	**Polynomial Kernel SVM**	**0.554**
	GA _Polynomial Kernel SVM	**0.672**
	RBF Kernel SVM	**0.5**
	GA_RBF Kernel SVM	**0.487**
	Sigmoid Function Kernel SVM	**0.5**
	GA_ Sigmoid Function Kernel SVM	**0.5**
	Liner Kernel SVM	**0.716**
	GA_Linear Kernel SVM	**0.748**

Linear Kernel SVM provides the good results and rest of the classification method do not achieve the good result. So here considered Linear Kernel SVM as proposed classification method for this dataset i.e., PIDD which is very useful. If we discuss for the same method, then with attribute selection method the improvement has occurred in every measure i.e., precision, recall, f-measure, classification accuracy, ROC, kappa statistics, MAE, RMSE, RAE, RRSE. Therefore, attribute selection method once again proved that preserve the storage capacity or memory, computation time (shorter training time and test time), computation cost, processor requirements, and increases classification rate. The proposed method by further working in the manuscript may help physicians to improve, or take accurate decisions to do work speedily for this particular dataset.

For the future research work, we suggest to develop an expert system of diabetes disease, which will provide good ROC, classification accuracy, precision, recall, F - Measure, Kappa statistics, MAE, RMSE, RAE, RRSE, and this is possible to achieve only by using different Attribute selection and classification method which, could significantly decrease healthcare costs via early prediction and diagnosis of diabetes disease. The proposed method can also be used for other kinds of diseases but not sure that in all the medical diseases either same or greater than the existing results. Results that are more interesting may also happen for the exploration of the dataset also.

REFERENCES

Aslam, M. W., Zhu, Z., & Nandi, A. K. (2013). Feature generation using genetic programming with comparative partner selection for diabetes classification. *Expert Systems with Applications, Elsevier, 40*(13), 5402–5412. doi:10.1016/j.eswa.2013.04.003

Barakat, N. (2007). *Rule extraction from support vector machines: Medical diagnosis prediction and explanation* (Ph.D. thesis). School Inf. Technol. Electr. Eng. (ITEE), Univ. Queensland, Brisbane, Australia.

Barakat, N. H., & Bradley, A. P. (2007). Rule Extraction from Support Vector Machines: A Sequential Covering Approach. *IEEE Transactions on Knowledge and Data Engineering, 19*(6), 2007. doi:10.1109/TKDE.2007.190610

Barakat, N. H., Bradley, A. P., & Barakat, M. N. H. (2010). Intelligible Support Vector Machines for Diagnosis of Diabetes Mellitus. *IEEE Transactions on Information Technology in Biomedicine, 14*(4), 1114–1120. doi:10.1109/TITB.2009.2039485 PMID:20071261

Chen, Z., Li, J., & Wei, L. (2007). A multiple kernel support vector machine scheme for feature selection and rule extraction from gene expression data of cancer tissue. *Artificial Intelligence in Medicine, 41*(2), 161–175. doi:10.1016/j.artmed.2007.07.008 PMID:17851055

Choubey & Sanchita. (2016). GA_MLP NN: A Hybrid Intelligent System for Diabetes Disease Diagnosis. *International Journal of Intelligent Systems and Applications, 8*(1), 49-59.

Choubey, D. K., Paul, S., & Bhattacharjee, J. (2014). Soft Computing Approaches for Diabetes Disease Diagnosis: A Survey. *International Journal of Applied Engineering Research, 9*, 11715-11726.

Choubey, D. K., & Sanchita. (2015). GA_J48graft DT: A Hybrid Intelligent System for Diabetes Disease Diagnosis. *International Journal of Bio-Science and Bio-Technology, 7*(5), 135–150.

Choubey, D. K., & Paul, S. (2016). Classification Techniques for Diagnosis of Diabetes Disease: A Review. *International Journal of Biomedical Engineering and Technology, 21*(1), 15-39.

Choubey, D. K., & Paul, S. (2017). GA_RBF NN: A Classification System for Diabetes. *International Journal of Biomedical Engineering and Technology, 23*(1), 71-93.

Choubey, D. K., Paul, S., Kuamr, S., & Kumar, S. (2017). Classification of Pima Indian Diabetes Dataset using Naive Bayes with Genetic Algorithm as an Attribute Selection. In *Communication and Computing Systems: Proceedings of the International Conference on Communication and Computing System (ICCCS 2016)*, pp. 451-455. CRC Press Taylor Francis.

Daho, M. E. H., Settouti, N., Lazouni, M. E. A., & Chikh, M. A. (2013). Recognition Of Diabetes Disease Using A New Hybrid Learning Algorithm For Nefclass. *8th International Workshop on Systems, Signal Processing and their Applications (WoSSPA)*.

Darwin, C. (1859). *On the origins of species by means of natural selection*. London: Murray.

Dogantekin, E., Dogantekin, A., Avci, D., & Avci, L. (2010). An Intelligent Diagnosis System For Diabetes On Linear Discriminant Analysis and Adaptive Network Based Fuzzy Inference System: LDA–ANFIS. *Digital Signal Processing, Elsevier*, 20(4), 1248–1255. doi:10.1016/j.dsp.2009.10.021

Ephzibah, E. P. (2011). Cost Effective Approach on Feature Selection using Genetic Algorithms and Fuzzy Logic for Diabetes Diagnosis. International Journal on Soft Computing, 2(1).

Ganji, M. F., Abadeh, M. S. (2010). Using fuzzy Ant Colony Optimization for Diagnosis of Diabetes Disease. *Proceedings of ICEE*.

Goldberg, D. E. (1989). Genetic algorithms in search, optimization, and machine learning. *NN Schraudolph and J.*, *3*, 1.

Goncalves, L. B., Bernardes, M. M., & Vellasco, R. (2006). Inverted Hierarchical Neuro–Fuzzy BSP System: A Novel Neuro-Fuzzy Model for Pattern Classification and Rule Extraction in Databases. IEEE Transactions on Systems, Man, and Cybernetics—Part C: Applications and Reviews, 36(2).

Hemant & Pushpavathi. (2007). *A novel approach to predict diabetes by Cascading Clustering and Classification*. Academic Press.

Holland, J. H. (1975). *Adaptation in natural and artificial systems*. Ann Arbor, MI: The University of Michigan Press.

Jayalakshmi, T., & Santhakumaran, A. (2010). A Novel Classification Method for Diagnosis of Diabetes Mellitus Using Artificial Neural Networks. *International Conference on Data Storage and Data Engineering*, 159-163. doi:10.1109/DSDE.2010.58

Kahramanli, H., & Allahverdi, N. (2008). Design of a hybrid system for the diabetes and heart diseases. *Expert Systems with Applications, Elsevier*, 35(1-2), 82–89. doi:10.1016/j.eswa.2007.06.004

Kalaiselvi & Nasira. (2014). A New Approach for Diagnosis of Diabetes and Prediction of Cancer using ANFIS. *World Congress on Computing and Communication Technologies*. IEEE. doi:10.1109/WCCCT.2014.66

Karatsiolis, S., & Schizas, C. N. (2012). Region based Support vector machine algorithm for Medical Diagnosis on PIMA Indian Diabetes Dataset. *Proceedings of the IEEE 12th International Conference on Bioinformatics& Bioengineering (BIBE)*, 11-13.

Karegowda, A. G., Manjunath, A.S., & Jayaram, M.A. (2011). Application Of Genetic Algorithm Optimized Neural Network Connection Weights For Medical Diagnosis Of Pima Indians Diabetes. International Journal On Soft Computing, 2(2).

Kayaer, K., & Yildirim, T. (2003). Medical Diagnosis on Pima Indian Diabetes Using General Regression Neural Networks. IEEE.

Kumar, M., & Mishra, S. K. (2015). Particle swarm optimization-based functional link artificial neural network for medical image denoising. In *Computational Vision and Robotics* (pp. 105–111). Springer India. doi:10.1007/978-81-322-2196-8_13

Kumar, M., Mishra, S. K., & Sahu, S. S. (2016). *Cat Swarm Optimization Based Functional Link Artificial Neural Network Filter for Gaussian Noise Removal from Computed Tomography Images*. Applied Computational Intelligence and Soft Computing, Hindawi.

Lee, C.-S. (2011). A Fuzzy Expert System for Diabetes Decision Support Application. Transactions on Systems, Man, and Cybernetics—Part B: Cybernetics, IEEE, 41(1).

Luukka, P. (2011). Feature selection using fuzzy entropy measures with similarity classifier. *Expert Systems with Applications, Elsevier, 38*(4), 4600–4607. doi:10.1016/j.eswa.2010.09.133

Michalewicz, Z. (1996). *Genetic algorithms + data structures = evolution programs*. Springer. doi:10.1007/978-3-662-03315-9

Orkcu, H., & Bal, H. (2011). Comparing performances of backpropagation and genetic algorithms in the data classification. *Expert Systems with Applications, Elsevier, 38*(4), 3703–3709. doi:10.1016/j.eswa.2010.09.028

Patil, B. M., Joshi, R. C., & Toshniwal, D. (2010). Association rule for classification of type -2 diabetic patients. *Second International Conference on Machine Learning and Computing*. IEEE. doi:10.1109/ICMLC.2010.67

Polat, K., & Güneş, S. (2007). An expert system approach based on principal component analysis and adaptive neuro-fuzzy inference system to diagnosis of diabetes disease. *Digital Signal Processing, Elsevier, 17*(4), 702–710. doi:10.1016/j.dsp.2006.09.005

Polat, K., Güneş, S., & Arslan, A. (2008). A cascade learning system for classification of diabetes disease: Generalized Discriminant Analysis and Least Square Support Vector Machine. *Expert Systems with Applications, Elsevier, 34*(1), 482–487. doi:10.1016/j.eswa.2006.09.012

Qasem, S. N., & Shamsuddin, S. M. (2011). Radial basis function network based on time variant multi objective particle swarm optimization for medical diseases diagnosis. *Applied Soft Computing, Elsevier, 11*(1), 1427–1438. doi:10.1016/j.asoc.2010.04.014

Seera, M., & Lim, C. P. (2014). A hybrid intelligent system for medical data classification. *Expert Systems with Applications, Elsevier, 41*(5), 2239–2249. doi:10.1016/j.eswa.2013.09.022

Selvakuberan, K., Kayathiri, D., Harini, B., & Devi, M. I. (2011). An efficient feature selection method for classification in Health care Systems using Machine Learning Techniques. IEEE.

Suraj, T. P., Ghosh, S., & Sinha, R.K. (2015). Classification of two class motor imagery tasks using hybrid GA-PSO based K-means Clustering. Computational Intelligence and Neuroscience.

Temurtas, H., Yumusak, N., & Temurtas, F. (2009). A Comparative Study On Diabetes Disease Diagnosis Using Neural Networks. *Expert Systems With Applications, Elsevier, 36*(4), 8610–8615. doi:10.1016/j.eswa.2008.10.032

UCI Repository of Bioinformatics Databases. (n.d.). Available: http://www.ics.uci.edu./~mlearn/ML Repository.html

Vapnik, V. N. (1995). *The nature of statistical learning theory*. New York, NY: Springer-Verlag New York, Inc. doi:10.1007/978-1-4757-2440-0

Wang, M.-H., Lee, C–S., Li, H–C., & Ko, W–M. (2007). Ontology-based Fuzzy Inference Agent for Diabetes Classification. IEEE.

Chapter 13
The Insects of Nature-Inspired Computational Intelligence

Sweta Srivastava
B.I.T. Mesra, India

Sudip Kumar Sahana
B.I.T. Mesra, India

ABSTRACT

The desirable merits of the intelligent computational algorithms and the initial success in many domains have encouraged researchers to work towards the advancement of these techniques. A major plunge in algorithmic development to solve the increasingly complex problems turned out as breakthrough towards the development of computational intelligence (CI) techniques. Nature proved to be one of the greatest sources of inspiration for these intelligent algorithms. In this chapter, computational intelligence techniques inspired by insects are discussed. These techniques make use of the skills of intelligent agent by mimicking insect behavior suitable for the required problem. The diversities in the behavior of the insect families and similarities among them that are used by researchers for generating intelligent techniques are also discussed in this chapter.

INTRODUCTION

The term "computational intelligence" was coined by Bezdek (1994) based on the intelligent behavior of computer motivated by the nature. Computational Intelligence (CI) (Bezdel, 1994) is the study of the design of intelligent agents based system. The agents can be a brainwave from insects, worms, animals, airplane, human, organizations, society and many more. It utilizes the skills of intelligent agents for required results as illustrated in Figure 1. CI had opened numerous brand new dimensions of the scientific research in past two decades.

Computational intelligence can be grouped into several families depending on its functionality and the source of inspiration. It can be inspired by physics (Karaboga & Akay, 2009) like Central Force Optimization (CFO), Big Bang-Big Crunch (BBC), and Particle Collision Algorithm (PCA). There are several techniques inspired by chemistry (Karaboga & Akay, 2009) like Artificial Chemical Process

DOI: 10.4018/978-1-5225-2128-0.ch013

Figure1. Computational intelligence agents and the driving skills

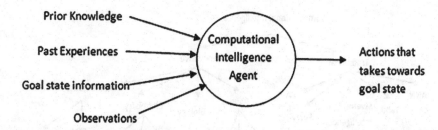

(ACP), Chemical Reaction Algorithm (CRA), and Gases Brownian Motion Optimization (GBMO). Techniques inspired by mathematics are Base Optimization Algorithm (BOA) and Matheuristics.

There are several biological inspirations for innovative CI. These can be further grouped into multiple classes like animals, birds, tribes, plants, etc. depending upon the nature of the problem (Karaboga & Akay, 2009). There are many algorithms bagged into each category like techniques motivated from animal includes Cat Swarm Optimization (CSO), Monkey Search, Wolf Pack Search (WPS). Artificial Fish Swarm Algorithm (AFSA), Fish School Search (FSS), Shark-Search Algorithm (SSA) and many more techniques are based on aquatic animals. Techniques like Cuckoo Optimization Algorithm (COA), Dove Swarm Optimization (DSO), and Migrating Birds Optimization (MBO) are inspired by birds. Bacterial Foraging Algorithm (BFA), Amoeboid Organism Algorithm (AOA) and several others are inspired by microorganisms. Frog Calling Algorithm (FCA). Shuffled Frog Leaping Algorithm (SFLA) is inspired by amphibians. Plants inspired algorithms include Paddy Field Algorithm (PFA), Invasive Weed Optimization (IWO). Saplings Growing Up Algorithm (SGUA).

Over the past two decades from the evidence of the promising results of many researches, technologies inspired by insects have enjoyed widely acceptance and an extraordinary attractiveness that had opened brand new aspects for scientific research. The primary focus of this chapter is on families of insects contributing towards the development of Computational Intelligence. Figure 2 shows the family tree of the computational intelligence leading to insects.

The word insect came into existence from a Latin word 'insectum' (Chapman, 2006). Insects are among the most assorted collection of animals in the world, including more than millions of species. Their body is divided into three-parts (head, thorax and abdomen). They have three pairs of jointed legs, a pair of compound eyes and two antennae. Insects habitually live in solitude, but some, like bees, ants, termites, etc. are found in large and well organized colonies. These small living beings had always inspired researchers with their fascinating organizational, food foraging, mating and reproductive behaviors. They communicate (Karaboga & Akay, 2009; Wedde & Farooq, 2006; Bitam & Mellouk, 2013; Krishnanand et al., 2006; Krishnanand & Ghose, 2005; Karaboga & Basturk, 2007) with each other in a variety of ways like different variations of sound, light, smell, waggle dance or by rubbing wings. Food foraging (Karaboga & Akay, 2009; Pan, 2012; Karaboga & Basturk, 2007; Feng, Lau & Gao, 2009) is another major attraction for researchers. The insects strive hard to explore promising food sources, inform the colony members and exploit it in an optimal manner. They often divide nest mates into several groups for different jobs such as mending of the nest, finding a site or exploitation of food source. The selection of a partner for mating of some insects can also be framed by computational intelligence scientists (Abbass, 2001a). The queen selects fittest partner from the nest for mating in order to build a better next generation. Another major attribute found in insects are a division of the colony depending on its size

Figure 2. Family of computational intelligence

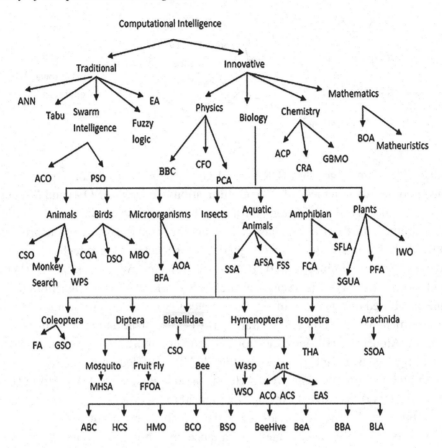

and resource availability. In families like bees, they can have only one queen (Zungeru, and & Seng, 2007; Karaboga & Basturk, 2007).

Chapter Organization

This chapter is grouped into nine sections. Section 2 shows progress towards the development of CI based on insects. This section also groups the insects according to their family. Section 3 to 8 describes the members of each family and algorithm based on them. This section also highlights the important similarities, differences, suitability and limitation of each of the techniques. Lastly, section 9 gives an overview of all the techniques and their implementations.

INSECT ORIENTED ALGORITHM MODEL

The growth of insect inspired techniques in the last two decades is shown in Figure 3. It can be clearly interpreted from the techniques discussed here that gradually the growth in innovative techniques inspired from insects is stepping up.

Figure 3. The growth of insect inspired techniques in last two decades

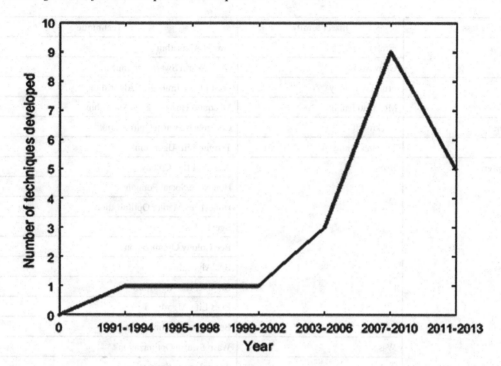

The insect families can be grouped into several classes (Hölldobler & Wilson, 2009; Xing & Gao, 2014). The classes along with techniques inspired are mentioned below in Table 1 (Bezdek, 1994; Chapman, 2009; Xing & Gao, 2014).

All the above mentioned classes and the insect families along with the techniques inspired by them are described in the coming sections.

Coleoptera Family

The insect order Coleoptera consists of the beetles and weevils. It is the largest order of insects, representing about 40 percent of the known insect species (Chapman, 2009; Bouchard, 2014). Some of the members are beetles, firefly and glow worms.

Firefly Algorithm

Firefly algorithm is inspired by the communication skill and attraction of luminous insects towards each other by the flashing lights (Yang, 2008, 2010a, 2010b, 2013). These insects carry a bio- luminescent quality called luciferin. Fireflies are attracted towards the bright glow of the neighboring insects. The glow of insects reduces with the distance. FA uses the three idealized rules which simplify its search process to reach an optimal solution (Yang, 2010b):

1. Fireflies are unisex so there is no mutation operation alter the attractiveness fireflies have for each other.

Table 1. Classification of the insects' families

Class	Insect family	Technique
Coleoptera	Firefly	Firefly Algorithm
	Glow worm	Glow Worm Swarm Optimization
Diptera	Fruit Fly Family	Fruit Fly Optimization Algorithm
	Mosquito Family	Mosquito Host-Seeking Algorithm
Blatellidae	Cockroach	Cockroach Swarm Optimization
Isopetra	Termites family	Termite-hill Algorithm
Hymenoptera	Bee	Artificial Bee Colony
		Honeybee Social Foraging
		Honeybees Mating Optimization
		BeeHive
		Bee Colony Optimization
		Bee Algorithm
		Bumblebees Algorithm
		Bees Life Algorithm
		Bee Swarm Optimization
	Wasp	Wasp Swarm Optimization
	Ant	Ant colony optimization
		Ant Colony System
		Elitist ant System
Arachnida	Spider family	Social Spider Optimization Algorithm

2. The distribution of information or food between the fireflies is proportional to the attractiveness. The attractiveness increases with a decreasing distance between them. For any two flashing fireflies, the one which is less bright will move towards the brighter one. If there is no brighter firefly than that particular firefly, it will move randomly.
3. The brightness intensity of a firefly is determined by the landscape of the objective function. Normally for the minimization problems, the light intensity is taken inversely proportional to the value of the objective function.

There are two important issues in the FA that are the variation of light intensity or brightness and formulation of attractiveness.

Variation in the light intensity: For a swarm of n fireflies, with fitness value f(xi), i= 1,2...n, represents a solution state for a firefly i which is initially positioned randomly in the space (Yang, 2010b). The light intensity Ir varies with the distance r monotonically and exponentially as shown in equation 1.

$$I = I0e^{\gamma r_{ij}} \tag{1}$$

where, I0 is the original light intensity, γ is the light absorption coefficient, and r is the distance between i^{th} and j^{th} firefly.

Movement in the direction of attractive firefly: Attractiveness is proportional to the light intensity as seen by adjacent fireflies (Yang, 2010b). Each firefly has its own distinctive attractiveness β which tells how strongly it attracts the other members. Attractiveness function $\beta(r)$ of the firefly is determined by equation 2

$$\beta = \beta_0 e^{-\gamma r^2_{ij}} \tag{2}$$

The movement of firefly i at location xi attracted to another more attractive (brighter) firefly j at location xj is determined as given in equation 3.

$$Xi(t+1) = Xi(t) + \beta_0 e^{-\gamma r^2_{ij}} \,(xj\text{-}xi) + \alpha \varepsilon i \tag{3}$$

where εi is Gaussian distribution function and α is random parameter.

The Firefly algorithm is explained as follows:

Step 1: Generate the initial population of fireflies placed at random positions within the n-dimensional search space.
Step 2: Initialize the parameters, such as the light absorption coefficient (γ).
Step 3: Define the light intensity (Ii) of each firefly (xi) as the value of the cost function f(xi)
Step 4: For each firefly xi, compare the light intensity.
Step 5: If Ij> Ii, move firefly xi towards xj in n-dimensions.
Step 6: Compute the new values of the cost function for each of firefly and update the new light intensity.
Step 7: Rank the fireflies based on new values and determine the current best.
Step 8: Repeat Steps 3–7 until the termination criteria is satisfied.

Firefly algorithm is based on the global communication among the swarm of fireflies. The firefly algorithm uses real random numbers, thus it seems more effectual in multi-objective optimization. An additional advantage of the firefly algorithm is that the fireflies will work almost independently, hence it is particularly suitable for parallel implementation. It is found to be better than genetic algorithm and particle swarm optimization because fireflies aggregate more closely around each optimum state (Xing & Gao, 2014).

Glow Worm Swarm Optimization Algorithm

The glowworm swarm optimization (GlSO) algorithm is inspired by luminous insects. This algorithem deal with the multimodal problems (Krishnanand et al, 2006; Krishnanand & Ghose, 2005). Each of the iterations of GlSO algorithm have two phases.

1.   Luciferin-update phase.
2.   Movement phase.

Additionally, for GlSO, there is a dynamic decision range update rule which is used to alter the glow-worms' adaptive neighborhoods.

- **The Luciferin-Update Phase (Krishnanand & Ghose, 2006):** It is the method by which the luciferin quantities are tailored. The value of luciferin can either raise, as glowworms deposit luciferin on the current position, or it can decrease, because of luciferin decay. It is given by equation 4:

$$Li (t+1)= (1-\rho). Li (t)+ \gamma J \{xi (t+1)\} \tag{4}$$

where Li denotes the luciferin level associated with the glowworm i at time t, ρ is the luciferin decay constant, γ is the luciferin enhancement constant, J (xi (t)) stands for the value of the objective function at the glowworm i at the time t.

- **Movement Phase** (Krishnanand & Ghose, 2006): During the movement phase, the glowworm i chooses a new position j to move using a bias, i.e., probabilistic decision rule, toward the good-quality individual which has better luciferin value than its own as shown in equation 5.

$$Pij(t) = \frac{l_j(t) - l_i(t)}{\sum_{k \in Ni(t)} l_j(t) - l_i(t)} \tag{5}$$

where j ϵNi(t), the set of neighbors of the glowworm i at time t.

GlSO algorithm can be summarized as given as follows:

Step 1: Initialize the parameters.
Step 2: Initialize the population of N candidate solution which is randomly generated in the search space.
Step 3: Calculate the fitness function value corresponding to each candidate solution.
Step 4: Perform iteration procedures that includes both luciferin update phase, movement phase. Update the decision range in each iteration.
Step 5: Check if the termination criterion is reached, else go to step 3.
Step 6: If the specified termination criteria are satisfied, stop and return the best solution.

Observations on Coleoptera Family

- Both Firefly and Glowworms use their luminosity to communicate. The insects are attracted to the member with higher luminosity.
- Fireflies of equal brightness, moves randomly in the search space, they may not form clusters like GlSO.
- Ranking of solution is observed in Firefly algorithm.
- GlSO converge to a state where all the glowworms construct an optimal solution time and again.
- The fireflies can automatically subdivide into subgroups and hence they can find multiple global solutions simultaneously. Though, in GlSO, there is no insight limit based on distance, but the swarm splits into sub-groups and converge to a high function value point.

Diptera Family

Flies and mosquitoes belong to the family of Diptera (Zungeru, Ang & Seng, 2012; Marshall, 2012). These are minute aerial insects with extremely variable colors with soft bodies and compound eyes that occupy most of their heads. Most of the flies eat liquid food like water or decomposing matter, animal and plant secretions, flower nectars, animal tissue fluid, vertebrate blood, etc. In this section we are going to discuss about Mosquito Host-Seeking Algorithm and Fruit fly optimization algorithm.

Fruit Fly Optimization Algorithm

Fruit flies are the small flies with dark red compound eyes that are often attracted to ripened food in the kitchen (Yang, 2010a). These flies have an amazing sense of smell. They can get the aroma food source from approximately 40 Km away. They exploit food sources with extraordinary smelling capacity and vision which is equivalent to 760 units of eyes (Chapman, R.F., 2013). It smells the food source by osphresis organ, and then it flies towards that locality (Chapman, R.F., 2013). After it gets close to the food source, it uses the sensitive vision to locate the food. The algorithm Fruit fly optimization algorithm (FFOA) is described below (Pan, 2012).

Step 1: Initialize the Optimization process.

$$Xi = X\_axis + Random\ Value,$$

$$Yi = Y\_axis + Random\ Value \tag{6}$$

where "random value" is random vector sampled from a uniform distribution.

Step 2: Construct the oath based on distance and smell concentration value for each fruit fly.

$$Dist_i = \sqrt{X_i^2 + Y_i^2} \tag{7}$$

$$S_i = \frac{1}{Dist_i} \tag{8}$$

where, Disti is the distance between i[th] individual and the food source.

Si is the smell concentration.

Step 3: Define fitness function

Smelli = Function (Si),   (9)

[BestSmell, BestIndex] =max(smelli)   (10)

where *Smelli* is smell concentration of individual fruit fly, *BestSmell, BestIndex* represents the largest elements of smell vector.

Step 4: Find out the fruit fly with maximum smell concentration among the swarm.

SmellBest= Best Smell.

X_axis=X(BestIndex)

Y_axis= Y(BestIndex)   (11)

Step 5: Rank the solution
Step 6: Repeat from Step 2 till stopping criteria is reached.

Mosquito Host-Seeking Algorithm

In the actual world, both male and female mosquitoes feed on nectar, but the female of many species is also capable of drinking blood. Only female mosquitoes search the host to attack by detecting carbon dioxide (CO_2) and 1-octen-3-ol ($C_8H_{16}O$) from a distance. Mosquito Host-Seeking algorithm (MHSA) is based on these behaviors of the mosquitoes (Feng, Lau, & Gao, 2009):

1.   The mosquitoes search for smell of host.
2.   It distinguishes the smell of the hosts and then seeks towards a high-concentration location.
3.   It makes a crash when it feels the radiated heat of the host.

    The steps of MHSA are given below.

Step 1: Initialize the population and parameters.
Step 2: Calculate the distance between artificial mosquitoes and the host at time t.
Step 3: Compute the motion of the mosquitoes to find the shortest path between destinations.
Step 4: For each of the artificial mosquito calculate its strength. The better the strength of mosquitoes, more chances are there to attack the host.
Step 5: Update the value of distance and strength.
Step 6: If termination criteria are reached, stop. Else go to step 2.

    This algorithm was designed for travelling salesperson problem [28]. The computed result showed that the algorithm could jump out of local optimal values.

Observations on Diptera Family

- FFOA is simple to compute, easy to understand and have simple implementation.
- MHSA was designed and implemented for travelling salesperson problem.
- FFOA was found to be more convenient and with time it is gaining popularity in problem areas like data mining, power load forecasting and other optimization problems. The applications will be discussed in section 9.

Blatellidae Family

This family contains many of the smaller common household pests, cockroaches (Chapman, 2006). In the earlier times, termites were considered as a separate order, Isoptera, but genetic and molecular indications suggest a close relationship between the two, both cockroaches and termites having evolved from a common ancestor.

Cockroach Swarm Optimization Algorithm

Cockroach Swarm Optimization Algorithm (CSOA) is based on the chase swarming, dispersing and ruthless manners of cockroaches (Chen & Tang, 2010, 2011). A swarm of N cockroaches is positioned in a D dimensional search space R^D. Each member i represents a D dimensional vector $X(i) = (Xi1, Xi2, \ldots\ldots\ldots XiD)$ for (i= 1,2........N). The location of each individual member is a potential solution.

Chase-swarm behavior: Each individual cockroach (Xi) will chase other cockroach (Pi) which carries the local optimum. This behavior can be modeled as given in equation 12.

$$x'(i) = \begin{cases} X(i) + step.rand.[P(i) - X(i)] & ; \text{if} X(i) \neq P(i) \\ X(i) + step.rand.[P_g - X(i)] & ; \text{if } X(i) = P(i) \end{cases} \qquad (12)$$

Pg indicates the global optimum individual cockroach, P(i) denotes a fixed value, and rand stands for a random number within the interval of [0,1].

Dispersing behavior of cockroaches: During a definite time interval, each of the cockroach will be randomly dispersed for the purpose of keeping the assortment of the current swarm. This behavior can be modeled as shown in equation 13.

$$x'(i) = x(i) + rand(1, D), \qquad i = 1, 2\ldots\ldots, N \qquad (13)$$

where rand(1,D) is a D-dimensional random vector which falls within a certain interval.

Ruthless behavior: At a certain time interval, the cockroach, which carries the current best value substitute another cockroach in a randomly selection manner. This behavior can be modeled as given in equation 14:

$$X(k) = Pg \qquad (14)$$

where k is a random integer within the interval of [1, N]

CSOA algorithm can be summarized into the following steps.

Step 1: Set parameters and initialize population;
Step 2: Search P(i) and Pg;
Step 3: Perform chase-swarming and update Pg;
Step 4: Execute dispersing behavior and update Pg;
Step 5: Execute the ruthless behavior and update Pg;
Step 6: Check if stopping criteria are met. If not, go to step 2.

Isopetra Family

Termites belong to the family of Isopetra. This family is said to have close ancestral links the family of Blattodea, to which cockroaches belong (Cranshaw, 2013). Like the family of Hymenoptera, termites also divide labors among themselves based on castes. The sterile male and females form the works and soldiers. The fertile members belong to the royal family. They are also said to be good architects and form well organized societies (Keller & Gordon, 2009). They feed on dead plants and cellulose.

Termite-Hill Algorithm

The powerful colonies of termites always inspire the researchers. This algorithm is based on hill building ability of termites [27]. This algorithm was developed for network routing problem in wireless sensor network. This algorithm can be summarized as given bellow.

Step 1: Initialize the termites on nodes.
Step 2: Pheromone update

$$T'rs= Trs +\gamma \tag{15}$$

$$\gamma = \frac{N}{E - \left(\frac{E_{min} - N_j}{E_{av} - N_j}\right)} \tag{16}$$

where, E denotes the initial energy of the nodes.

Step 3: Rout Selection: Each node is initialized by uniform probability distribution.

$$P_{s,d} = \frac{1}{N_k} \tag{17}$$

where, Nk denotes number of nodes in the network.

Step 4: Repeat till termination criteria are reached.

Observation on Blatellidae and Isopetra Families

Both the families of Blatellidae and Isopetra share ancestral links and thus many similar attribute. Both the algorithms are robust; produce good results for many optimization problems. Although there are limitations on work in both the areas, some extension on CSO can be sited in the literature (Pham & Castellani, 2009). Implementation of both the algorithm is mentioned in section 9 of this chapter.

Hymenoptera Family

Hymenoptera is the third-largest category of insects, comprising the bees, wasps, and ants. This group range in a size from extremely small to large insects, which usually have two pairs of wings. It has a variety of social insects with diverse attributes. This group had always been researchers favored one. There are many CI algorithms based on this family mushrooming with time.

Artificial Bee Colony Algorithm

The ABC algorithm was proposed by Karaboga in the year 2005, and the performance of ABC was analyzed in the year 2007 (Karaboga, 2005; Karaboga & Basturk, 2007). The ABC algorithm inspects the behavior such as food foraging, sharing information with nest mates, of the real bees. In the ABC, the artificial agents are defined and classified into three types- the employed bee, the onlooker bee, and the scout based on their specific roles. The employed bee stays on a food source and provides collects nectar and keeps the location in its memory; the onlooker gets the information about food sources from the employed bees and select the best available food source; and the scout is responsible for finding new food sources. The process of the ABC algorithm is presented as follows:

Step 1 – Initialization: Spray η percentage of the population into the solution space randomly, and then calculate the fitness values, where η represents the ratio of employed bees to the total population of the bees. Once these populations of the bees are placed into the solution space, they are called the employed bees.

Step 2 – Move the Onlookers Bees: Calculate the probability of selecting a food source using the equation (18). The food source is selected by roulette wheel for every onlooker bees. Determine the nectar amounts of them. The movement of the onlookers follows the equation (19).

$$P_i = \frac{F(\theta i)}{\sum_{k=1}^{s} F(\theta k)} \tag{18}$$

where θi denotes the position of the ith employed bee, S represents the number of employed bees, and Pi is the probability of selecting i^{th} employed bee.

$$(t + 1) = \theta i j + ((t) - \theta(t)) \tag{19}$$

where xi denotes the position of the ith Onlooker bee, t denotes the iteration number, θk is the randomly chosen employed bee, represents the dimension of the solution.

Step 3 – Move the Scout Bees: If the fitness values of the employed bees are not enhanced by a continuous predetermined number of iterations, then food sources are discarded, and these employed bees become the scouts bees. The scouts are moved by the equation 20.

$$\theta ij = \theta ijmin + r \cdot (\theta ijmax - \theta ijmin) \tag{20}$$

*where r is a random num*ber and $r \in [0, 1]$.

Step 4 – Update the *Best* **Food Source Found so Far:** Memorize the best fitness value and the location discovered by the bees.

Step 5 – Termination Checking: If the termination condition is satisfied, conclude the; otherwise go back to the Step 2.

Honeybee Social Foraging Algorithm

Modeling of a social foraging for nectar involves representation of the environment, activities during bee expeditions, dance strength decisions, explorer allocation, unloading nectar, recruitment on the dance floor, and accounting for interactions with other hive functions. These are the elements of Honeybee Social Foraging Algorithm (HSFA) (Quijano & Passino, 2010). The major steps of the algorithm are given bellow.

Step 1: Set the parameter values
Step 2: Compute the total nectar profitability, and the total nectar influx.

$$s_j(k) = \frac{a_j}{x_j(k)} \tag{21}$$

$s_j(k)$ is the number of honey bees at site j.

$$F^i(k) = \begin{cases} 1 & \text{if } J_f(\theta^i(k) + w^i_f(k) \geq \varepsilon_n \\ J_f(\theta^i(k) + w^i_f(k) & \text{if } 1 > J_f(\theta^i(k) + w^i_f(k) > \varepsilon_n \\ 0 & \text{if } J_f(\theta^i(k) + w^i_f(k) \leq \varepsilon_n \end{cases} \tag{22}$$

where, $w^i_f(k)$ is the profitability assessment of noise and $F^i(k)$ is the amount of nectar gathered. .

Step 3: Determine the strength of employed foragers and successful forager dance based on sampling of profitability as given in equation 23.

$$F_{tq}(k) = \sum_{i=1}^{B} F^i_q(k) = \alpha F_t(k) \tag{23}$$

Step 4: Bee becomes an explorer. Set location for explorer to go to on the next expedition as shown in equation 24.

$$P_i(k) = \frac{L_f^i(k)}{\sum_{i=1}^{B_f(k)} L_f^i(k)} \tag{24}$$

To estimate the effectiveness of the HBSF algorithm, an engineering application, namely, "dynamic resource allocation for multi-zone temperature control problem" was taken on by Quijano and Passino (2010).

Honeybees Mating Optimization

The honeybees mating optimization (HBMO) algorithm were proposed in Abbass (2001a, 2001b) to simulate the mating behavior found among honeybees. A colony may contain one or more queen during its life-cycle, which are named as monogamous and/or polygamous colonies, respectively. The queen bees' are bigger in size than the rest of its nest mate. There are several hundreds of drones that live with the queen and worker bees. The queen mate during their mating flights far-off from the nest. A mating flight starts with a dance performed by the in which the drones follow the queen and mate with her in the air. At the beginning of the flight, the queen is initialized with some energy content and returns to her nest when this energy is lost.

HBMO algorithm can be constructed with the five main stages:

Step 1: Mating flight, where the queen (best solution) selects drones probabilistically for the creation of broods as shown in equation 25 (Niknam, 2009, 2011)..

$$\Pr(D) = \exp\left(\frac{-\Delta(F)}{V_{Queen}(t)}\right) \tag{25}$$

where $\Pr(D)$ denotes probability of a drone D to fertilize the queen, $\Delta(F)$ is the absolute difference between the fitness of drones and $V_{Queen}(t)$ is velocity of queen at time t.

$$V_{Queen}(t+1) = \alpha V_{Queen}(t)$$
$$E_{Queen}(t+1) = \alpha E_{Queen}(t) \tag{26}$$

where α denotes decreasing factor which lies between the interval [0, 1].

Step 2: Creation of new broods, (trial solutions) by crossover operation of the drone's genotypes with the queens as shown in equation 27 (Niknam, 2009, 2011).

$$X_{brood,j} = X_{Queen} + \beta(X_{Queen} - D_i) \tag{27}$$

where D_i represents the ith drone, $\beta \in [0,1]$ refers to the mating factor.

Step 3: Use of workers to conduct a local search on broods (trial solutions).
Step 4: An adaptation of worker's fitness, based on the amount of improvement achieved on the broods.
Step 5: Replacement of the weaker queens by flittered broods.
Step 6: Termination

Bee Hive Algorithm

Bee Hive algorithm is a technique for the network routing algorithm which is inspired by the dance language and food foraging behavior of the honeybees (Wedde & Farooq, 2006; Wedde, Farooq & Zhang, 2004; Farooq, 2006). Bee- Hive algorithm can be summarized as follows:

Step 1: All the nodes in the networks begin with a foraging region formation process. The first generation of the short distance bees is launched for propagation of their nomination in the neighborhood.
Step 2: By comparing the received information from the short distance bees, the nodes will determine whether to resign as a representative node or to join the foraging region.
Step 3: Once the old representative nodes are removed, the other nodes will activate an election mechanism.
Step 4: The nodes continues to introduce the new generations of shorter distance bees by following the pre-decided steps till the network splits into disjoint foraging regions, and overlaps with the foraging zones.
Step 5: After the execution of Step 4, the Bee Hive algorithm gets into a regular phase.
Step 6: When a copy of the specific bee reaches a site, it will update its locally stored routing information.
Step 7: Representative nodes generate long distance bees that could be received by the neighbors.
Step 8: Bees employ a priority queue mechanism with the intention of swift routing of information dissemination.
Step 9: Each node carries the present routing information for the reaching nodes within its foraging zone and the representative nodes of the foraging regions.
Step 10: Choose the next hop for data packets in a stochastic manner.
Step 11: The goodness of a neighbor j of node i for arriving at the destination d is denoted by equation 28

$$g_{jd} = \frac{\dfrac{1}{p_{jd} + q_{jd}}}{\displaystyle\sum_{k=1}^{N} \dfrac{1}{p_{jd} + q_{jd}}} \tag{28}$$

where the propagation delay and the queuing delays are denoted by pjd and qjd, respectively.

Bee Colony Optimization

The BCO is a metaheuristic technique capable of solving complicated combinatorial optimization problems (Tasgetiren, Pan, Suganthan & Chen, 2010; Teodorovic, 2009a, 2009b; Teodorovic & Dell'Orco, 2005). The artificial bee colony behaves partially the same, and partially in a different way from bee colonies in nature. In BCO, when the foragers return back to the hive, a waggle dance is performed by each forager. The other bees based on a probability of the dance, follow the foragers. In order to implement BCO, the following procedures need to be followed (Teodorovic, 2009a, 2009b)

Step 1: Initialization: Assigning an empty solution state to each of the bee within the colony.

Step 2: For each bee, perform a forward pass mechanism, (a) Set k=1; (b) Evaluate all possible constructive movements; (c) Select one movement using the roulette wheel strategy, (d) k = k+1. If k≤NC, repeat the subtask (b).

Step 3: All bees return to the hive by backward pass method.

Step 4: Evaluate the objective function value partially carried by each bee.

Step 5: For each bee, verify whether to carry on with its own exploration and become a recruiter, or turn into a follower. In BCO, a loyalty decision strategy is introduced at this point (Teodorovic, Davidovic & Selmic, 2011). The probability of bth bee to be loyal is its previously obtained partial solution.

Step 6: This probability can be expressed as shown in equation 29

$$P_b^{u+1} = e^{\frac{o_{max} - o_b}{u}} \qquad b = 1,2,......B \qquad (29)$$

where Ob refers to the normalized value of the objective function carried by the bth bee, Ob signify the maximum over all normalized values of partial solution to be calculated, and the ordinary number of the forward pass is indicated by u.

Step 7: For each of the follower bees, select a new solution from the recruiters using the roulette wheel method. Perform the recruiting mechanism. The probability of the b's partial solution to be selected by an unallocated bee is defined by equation 30.

$$P_b = \frac{O_b}{\sum_{k=1}^{R} o_k} \qquad ,b = 1,2....,R \qquad (30)$$

where, Ok is the normalized value of the objective function of the kth partial solution, and the number of recruiters is represented by R.

Step 8: If the termination criteria are not reached, go to Step 2. Else select the best available solution.

The experimental result shows that BCO is very promising. Other than this, several enhanced versions of BCO can also be found in the literature (Zeng et al., 2010; Low, Chandramohan & Choo, 2009).

Bees Algorithm

Bees Algorithm (BeA) is a population based search technique that mimics food foraging behavior of the bee colonies (Pham et al., 2006). The algorithm performs neighborhood search shared with the global search. This algorithm can be used for both continuous and combinatorial optimization. The only clause in the application of the Be is that the calculation of topological distance between the solutions should be well defined.

The basic Bees algorithm (BeA) working procedures of BeA are listed as explained as follows (Pham & Ghanbarzadeh, 2007; Pham & Koc, 2010; Pham et al, 2006; Pham, Afify & Koc, 2007a):

Step 1: Initialize the population with random solutions. Set parameters: number of scout bees (n), a number of the sites chosen (m), a number of the best selected sites (e), the number of bees employed for the best e sites (nep), the number of bees employed for the other (m-e) selected sites (nsp), and initial size of the patch (ngh) which includes the site and its neighborhood.

Step 2: Assess the fitness of the population.

Step 3: Create the new population.

Step 4: Choose the sites for neighborhood search. The bees with the better fitness values are chosen.

Step 5: Recruit the bees for selected sites (more bees for best s sites), and estimate the fitness function.

Step 6: Choose the fittest bee from each patch. The bees with good fitness value are selected to from the next bee population (Pham, Afify & Koc, 2007a).

Step 7: Assign the remaining bees for random searches, and evaluating their fitness.

Step 8: Terminate the loop once stopping criterion is met.

Wasp Swarm Optimization

Wasp swarm optimization (WSO) mimics the attribute of the wasp colony in which they assign resources to different wasps in the nest (Theraulaz, Godd, Gervet & Deneubourg, 1991). In WSO, resources will be allocated to the individual candidate solution and such allocation will be completed in a random ways based on the strength of its members (Pino, Runkler & Sousa, 2006; Runkler, 2008). The wasp colony consists of fertile queens, workers, i.e. sterile female, and males respectively (Lucchetta et al, 2008; Satchidananda, Cho & Ghosh, 2008). In late summer the queens mate the male members. The male and workers die and the fertilized queen generates next generation during winters in a protected site. During the springs, queen collects material from plants such as fiber and other cellulose, mixes it with saliva and then constructs a typical paper type nest. Wasps are very defensive about their nests. They will make use of the nest for one season only. The nest can contain as many as 10,000 to 30, 000 individual wasps. They are considered to be beneficial for the reason that they feed on a variety of other insects. Over and above the assignment of foraging and brooding, wasp colonies systematize themselves in a hierarchy through proper communication between the individuals. The steps of WSO are given bellow-

Step 1: Initialize the wasps.

Step 2: Apply tournament selection process. The fighter wasps can update and replicate themselves while the non fighters who are neighbors of a fighter wasp will also be replicated in the next generation. The winning probability of fighter wasp is given in equation 31.

$$p_{ij} = \frac{s_j^2}{s_i^2 + s_j^2} \qquad i,j = 1,2\ldots\ldots,c \tag{31}$$

Step 3: Fill the position of the dead wasps using crossover operation on the fighter wasps.

Step 4: Calculate the fitness value and update next generation.

Step 5: Repeat till termination criteria are reached.

Ant Colony Optimization

Ant colonies optimization technique is based on the social and organizational behavior of the ants (Dorgio & Stutzle, 2004). The swarm of ants can accomplish complex tasks that in some cases exceed the capabilities of a single ant. The field of "ant algorithms" study models derived from the study of real ants' behavior, for the design of novel algorithms for the solution of optimization and distributed control problems.

Ant colony optimization (ACO) is one of the most unbeaten examples of ant algorithms inspired by the foraging behavior of ant colonies (Dorgo & Stutzle, 2004; Dorgio, Maniezzo & Colorni, 1996). Cooperation of the members is the key design component of ACO algorithms. The choice is to allocate the computational resources to a set of relatively simple agents (artificial ants) that communicate indirectly using stigmergy, that is, by indirect communication mediated by the environment. Good solutions are an emergent property of the agents' cooperative interaction. The steps of the algorithm for ACO are given below:

Step 1: Initialize m ants for n cities, pheromone constant $\tau_{ij}(t) = c$ for time t.

Step 2: Initialize tabu list.

Step 3: Ants Action:

Each ant builds its route iteratively. Calculate the length of the route Lk for all ants.

Update the shortest route.

Calculate $\Delta\tau_{ij}(t)$ and update $\tau_{ij}(t+1)$.

Step 4: Increment the time.

Step 5: Check if termination criteria are reached. If not, then go to step 3.

Observation on Hymenoptera Family

- The Hymenoptera family gives a wide range of bees, wasps and ants inspired computational intelligence techniques that solve many combinatorial and linear optimization problems.

- Here ABC and ACO were found to be the most popular amongst the rest. These techniques because of simplicity and flexibility are not only popular in the group of insects, but are amongst the world wide popular techniques. The ACO and ABC can also be termed as stepping stones for insect based computational intelligence algorithm.
- This group of insects had caught the maximum attention of the researchers with their ability of self organization, food foraging, division of labor, selecting partners for mating and many others. Out of which food foraging and mating behavior had conquered the field. Most of the techniques are based on these two attribute of the insects.
- Several enhanced versions of these algorithms [72-76] are also available.
- These algorithms are successfully applied in many problems. Some of them are mentioned in section 9 of this chapter.

Arachnida Family

Arachnids are a class of eight legged invertebrate animals (arthropods) (Beccaloni, 2009). The term "Arachnida" is derived from a Greek word which means "spider". Unlike other classes of six legged insects Arachnida have two extra pairs adapted for feeding, defense, and sensory perception. Social Spider Optimization Algorithm is based on this class of insects.

Social Spider Optimization Algorithm

Social-Spider Optimization is inspired by the supportive conducts of social-spiders (Whitehourse & Lubin, 1999). These algorithms take into account both males and females search spiders. Based on its gender, agents are conducted by a set of different operators. The search space is assumed to be a web and a spider's position represents an optimal solution state. The number of male spiders hardly reaches 30% of the total population, while the number of females is about 65% to 90% (Pereira et al., 2014). The steps of the algorithm are given below.

Step 1: Set the total number of the n-dimensional colony and define the number of male Nmale and female Nfemale spiders in the entire colony S based on equation 32.

$$N_{Male} = N - N_{Female}$$

$$N_{Female=} floor[(0.9 - rand.0.25).N]$$

(32)

where rand stands for a random number within the range [0,1] and floor() indicates the mapping between a real and an integer number.

Step 2: Initialize stochastically the male and the female members. Compute the mating radius according to equation number 33 (Cuevas & Perez-Cisneros, 2013b).

$$r = \frac{\sum_{j=1}^{n}(p_j^{high} - p_j^{low})}{2n} \tag{33}$$

Step 3: Calculate the weight of each spider in colony S using the equation 34.

$$w_i = \frac{J(S_i) - worst_s}{best_s - worst_s} \tag{34}$$

where $J(S_i)$ denotes the fitness value acquired through the calculation of the spider position si with regard to the objective function j (.).

Step 4: Move female spiders according to the female cooperative operator model as shown in equation

$$m_i^{k+1} = \begin{cases} m_i^k + \alpha Vibf(sf - m_i^k) + \delta(rand - .5) & \text{if } w_{NFemale+i} > w_{NFemale+i} + m \\ m_i^k + \alpha \left(\dfrac{\sum_{h=1}^{N_{male}} m_h^k WN_{female} + h}{\sum_{h=1}^{N_{Male}} WN_{female} + h} - m_i^k \right) & \text{if } WN_{female} + WN_{female} + m \end{cases} \tag{35}$$

where Sf indicates nearest male spider to the female spider.

Step 5: Perform the mating operation.
Step 6: Terminate if stopping criteria are met. Else return to step 3.

SUMMARY OF INSECTS INSPIRED COMPUTATIONAL INTELLIGENCE

The Table 2 shown bellow reviews all the algorithms discussed above. This table highlights the inspirations and mark out some important observation given as remarks. It also gives a summary of implementation of the techniques.

CONCLUSION

Here in this chapter we have discussed computational intelligence algorithms inspired by the insect family. The algorithms were discussed and grouped as per their origin and family. A comparative study was carried out and merits, demerits and application areas are highlighted in section 9. The source of

Table 2. A summary of algorithms and their implementations

Algorithm	Inspiration	Implementation	Remark
Artificial Bee Colony (Karaboga & Basturk, 2007; Feng, Lau & Gau, 2009)	Foraging behavior of honey bees	Structural optimization, (Farooq, 2006) Traffic optimization (Niknam, 2011) Continuous Optimization (Stützle, 1997) Network routing (Niknam, 2009) Pathological brain detection (Forghany, Davarynejad & Snaar-Jagalska, 2012)	Swarm is grouped into sets of Employed bees, Unemployed bees (scouts bees, onlooker bees Employ fewer control parameters than DE, GA and PSO. Better convergence speed than GA and DE. ABC emploies a greedy selection process between the parent and the candidate solution. Unlike DE and GA, ABC avoids premature convergence. Solves multimodal and multidimensional optimization problem
BeeHive (Wedde & Farooq, 2006; Wedde, Farooq & Zhang, 2004; Farooq, 2006)	Dance language and foraging behavior of honey bee	Network routing (Wedde & Farooq, 2006; Wedde, Farooq & Zhang, 2004; Farooq, 2006)	Swarm is grouped into a set of Short distance bee agent, long distance bee agents. Implemented for the Japanese internet backbone scenario (Wedde & Farooq, 2006; Wedde, Farooq & Zhang, 2004; Farooq, 2006).
Bees Life Algorithm (Pham & Ghanbarzadeh, 2007; Pham & Koc, 2010; Pham et al., 2006; Pham, Afify & Koc, 2007a)	Reproduction and foraging behavior of bees	Vehicular ad hoc network (VANET) problem (Pham & Ghanbarzadeh, 2007; Pham & Koc, 2010; Pham et al., 2006; Pham, Afify & Koc, 2007a)	Swarm is grouped into sets of Queen bees, drone bees and newly born bumblebees Found to be more efficient than GA and HBMO Uses a low number of nodes. Efficient, less complex
Cockroach Swarm Optimization (Chen & Tang, 2011, 2013)	Chase swarming, dispersing and ruthless behavior of cockroach	Vehicle routing problem (Chen & Tang, 2011, 2013)	Higher optimal rate and shorter time than PSO.
Firefly Algorithm (Yang, 2008)	Social conduct of firefly and the trend of bioluminescent communication.	Digital Image Compression and Image Processing (Horng & Jiang, 2010; Horng, 2011; Horng & Liou, 2011) Antenna Design (Badu & Mahanti, 2011; Chatterjee, Mahante & Chatterjee, 2012; Chaterjee, Mahanti & Gourab, 2014) Scheduling and TSP (Khadwilard et al., 2011)	Decreasing random step size. Outperform Particle Swarm Optimization in 11 bench mark problem (Yang, 2008)
Fruit Fly Optimization Algorithm (Pan, 2012)	Oshresis and sensitive vision of fruit flies for food foraging	Traffic flow control (Zhu, Li, Shi, & Chen, 2013) Multidimensional knapsack problem (Wang, Zheng, Wang, 2013) Control Optimization (Liu, Wang & Li, 2012)	Ranking of solution is needed. Solves combinatorial optimization problems. A cmputational process is simple and easy implementation. Tested for maximum and minimum value problem in (Pan, 2012)
Glowworm Swarm Optimization (Krishnanand et al, 2006; Krishnanand & Ghose, 2005)	Luciferin-update phase and the movement of glowworm	Deployment of wireless sensor nodes (Pradhan & Panda, 2012), Sensor Deployment (Liao, Kao & Li, 2011)	A set of standard functions is tested in Huang, Zhou, and Wang (2011). Compared to PSO, PSO with chaos (CPSO), artificial fish swarm algorithm (AFSA), and AFSA with chaos (CAFSA), the experimental results showed that MNGSO is an effective global algorithm for finding optimal results.
Honeybee Social Foraging (Quijano & Passino, 2010)	Foraging behavior of bees	VANET (Bitam & Mellouk, 2013)	Grouped as Queen, drone, workers, brood. Ranking of solution. It outperforms GA and HBMO (Bitam & Mellouk, 2013)
Honeybees Mating Optimization (Abbass, 2001a, 2001b)	Probabilistic mating of drones with queen bee	Vehicle routing problem (Marinakis, Marinaki & Dounias, 2008)	Grouped as Queen bee, male honey bees (drones), neuters/underdeveloped honey bees. Queen represents the best solution. Weaker solutions are replaced using fitness function. In comparison to several nature inspired metaheuristic method, it is one of the best method (Xing & Gau, 2014)
Mosquito Host-Seeking Algorithm (Feng, Lau, & Gau, 2009)	Host seeking behavior of artificial mosquitoes by smelling odor like CO_2	Travelling sales person problem (Feng, Lau, & Gau, 2009)	Performs well, but gets into local minima, Easy to adapt into a wide range of problems like TSP.

Continued on next page

Table 2. Continued

Algorithm	Inspiration	Implementation	Remark
Termite-hill Algorithm (Cranshaw, 2013; Keller & Gordon, 2009)	The behavior of termite to allow simulation in a restricted environment.	Wireless sensor network routing problem. (Cranshaw, 2013; Keller & Gordon, 2009)	Proposed for wireless sensor network routing problem. Competent routing algorithm in terms of energy consumption, throughput, and network
Bees Algorithm[68]	Food foraging behavior of bees.	Clustering systems (Pham et al, 2007; Pham & Darwish, 2010) Manufacturing (Pham, Castellani & Ghanbarzadeh, 2008; Pham, Koc, Lee & Phrueksanant, 2007; Baykasoglu, Ozbakir & Tapkan, 2009; Ozbakir & Tapkan, 2011; Xu et al., 2012) Multi-objective optimization (Lee & Darwish, 2008; Sayadi et al, 2009; Mansouri & Shisheh, 2012) Bioengineering (Bahamish, Abdullah & Salam, 2008; Ruz & Goles, 2013)	Performs neighbor search as well as global search. Used for both combinatorial and continuous optimization problem.
Wasp Swarm Optimization (Theraulaz, Goss, Gervet & Deneubourg, 1991; Lucchetta et al., 2008; Satchidananda, Cho & Ghosh, 2008)	Importance of individual wasp in the colony and resource allocation for them.	Vehicle routing problem (Song, Hu, Tian & Xu, 2005) Scheduling optimization (Wang, Zhang, Wan & Zhu, 2006) Image processing (Fan & Zhong, 2012)	Tournament selection process for resource allocation amongst the wasp. Perform well for problems with more dynamic properties.
Ant Colony Optimization (Dorigo & Stutzle, 2004; Dorigo, Maniezzo & Colorni, 1996)	Organizational and food foraging behavior of ants	Travelling sales person. (Sahana & Jain, 2011) Vehicle routing problem (Baskan et al, 2009; Srivastava et al, 2015; Nanry & Barnes, 2000; Bent & Hentenryck, 2003; Rusell & Chiang, 2006; Donati, et al, 2008) Railway scheduling (Sahana, Jain & Mahanti, 2014) Quadratic assignment problem (Stutzle, 1997) Scheduling Problems (Adhikari & Sahana, 2013; Pfahring, 1996; Blem, 2003; Stutzle, 1994; Baucer et al, 2000; dan Besten, 2000; dan Besten, Stutzle & Dorigo, 2000; Merkle, Middendorf & Schmeck, 2000)	The solution represents a structural graph form. Solves all types of linear and nonlinear problems. High tendency of premature convergence. One of the most popular algorithms with simple implementation.

inspiration in not limited to these only. There are several other notable techniques as mentioned in this chapter. As per the temperament of the problem most appropriate algorithm can be selected. One of the interesting observations is that till the year 2007-08 most of the scientists studied bees and wasps' behavior but gradually different species like cockroaches, termites, firefly, fruit-fly and spiders also came into picture with their unique attributes. These are the budding techniques and till date limited number of work is cited in the literature. The major fascinations of these techniques are flexibility and simplicity in the application part. The algorithms can be merged with other techniques and modified as desired by the researcher so that better results can be obtained.

REFERENCES

Abbass, H. A. (2001a). MBO: Marriage in honey bees optimization. A haplometrosis polygynous swarming approach. *IEEE Proceedings of the Congress on Evolutionary Computation*, 207–214.

Abbass, H. A. (2001b). A monogenous MBO approach to satisfiability. *Proceeding of the International Conference on Computational Intelligence for Modelling, Control and Automation (CIMCA)*.

Abbass, H. A. (2001a). MBO: Marriage in honey bees optimization. A haplometrosis polygynous swarming approach. *IEEE Proceedings of the Congress on Evolutionary Computation*, 207–214.

Adhikari, A., & Sahana, S. K. (2013). Job Shop Scheduling Based on Ant Colony Optimization. *Proceedings of 2nd International Conference ICACM-2013*, 13-19.

Bahamish, H. A. A., Abdullah, R., & Salam, R. A. (2008). Protein Conformational Search Using Bees Algorithm. *Second Asia International Conference on Modeling & Simulation (AICMS 08)*, 911-916.

Baskan, O., Haldenbilen, S., & Ceylan, H. (2009). A new solution algorithm for improving performance of ant colony optimization. *Applied Mathematics and Computation, 211*(1), 75-84.

Basu, B., & Mahanti, G. K. (2011). Firefly and artificial bees colony algorithm for synthesis of scanned and broadside linear array antenna. *Progress in Electromagnetic Research B., 32*, 169–190. doi:10.2528/PIERB11053108

Baucer, A., Bullnheimer, B., Hartl, R. F., & Strauss, C. (2000). Minimizing total tardiness on a single machine using ant colony optimization. *Central European Journal for Operations Research and Economics, 8*(2), 125–141.

Baykasoğlu, A., Ozbakır, L., & Tapkan, P. (2009). The bees algorithm for workload balancing in examination job assignment. *European Journal of Industrial Engineering, 3*(4), 424–435. doi:10.1504/EJIE.2009.027035

Beccaloni, J. (2009). *Arachnids. University of California Press*.

Bent, R., & Hentenryck, P. V. (2003). A two-stage hybrid algorithm for pickup and delivery vehicle routing problems with time windows. *Computers & Operations Research, 33*(4), 875–893. doi:10.1016/j.cor.2004.08.001

Bezdek, J. C. (1994). What is computational intelligence? In *Computational Intelligence Imitating Life* (pp. 1–12). New York: IEEE Press.

Bitam, S., & Mellouk, A. (2013). Bee life-based multi constraints multicast routing optimization for vehicular ad hoc networks. *Journal of Network and Computer Applications, 36*(3), 981–991. doi:10.1016/j.jnca.2012.01.023

Bitam, S., & Mellouk, A. (2013). Bee life-based multi constraints multicast routing optimization for vehicular ad hoc networks. *Journal of Network and Computer Applications, 36*(3), 981–991. doi:10.1016/j.jnca.2012.01.023

Blem, C. (2003). *Beam-ACO, Hybridizing ant colony optimization with beam search. An application to open shop scheduling*. Technical report TR/IRIDIA/2003-17.

Bouchard, P. (2014). *The Book of Beetles: A Life-Size Guide to Six Hundred of Nature's Gems. University Of Chicago Press*. doi:10.7208/chicago/9780226082899.001.0001

Chapman, A. D. (2006). Numbers of living species in Australia and the World. Canberra: Australian Biological Resources Study.

Chapman, R. F. (2013). *The insects: structure and function* (S. J. Simpson & A. E. Douglas, Eds.). New York: Cambridge University Press.

Chatterjee, A., Mahanti, G. K., & Chatterjee, A. (2012). Design of a fully digital controlled reconfigurable switched beam conconcentric ring array antenna using firefly and particle swarm optimization algorithm. *Progress in Elelectromagnetic Research B, 36*, 113–131. doi:10.2528/PIERB11083005

Chatterjee, A., Mahanti, K., & Ghatak, G. (2014). Synthesis of satellite footprint patterns from rectangular planar array antenna by using swarm-based optimization algorithms. *Int. J. Satell. Commun. Network, 32*(1), 25–47. doi:10.1002/sat.1055

Chaves-González, J. M., Vega-Rodríguez, M. A., & Granado-Criado, J. M. (2013). A multiobjective swarm intelligence approach based on artificial bee colony for reliable DNA sequence design. *Engineering Applications of Artificial Intelligence, 26*(9), 2045–2057. doi:10.1016/j.engappai.2013.04.011

Chen, Z., & Tang, H. (2010). Cockroach swarm optimization. *IEEE 2nd International Conference on Computer Engineering and Technology (ICCET)*, 652–655.

Chen, Z., & Tang, H. (2011). Cockroach swarm optimization for vehicle routing problems. *Energy Procedia, 13*, 30–35. doi:10.1016/j.proenv.2012.01.003

Cranshaw, W. (2013). *Bugs Rule!: An Introduction to the World of Insects*. Princeton, NJ: Princeton University Press.

Cuevas, E., Zaldívar, D., & Pérez-Cisneros, M. (2013b). A swarm optimization algorithm for multimodal functions and its application in multicircle detection. *Mathematical Problems in Engineering, 2013*, 1–22.

Cummins, B., Cortez, R., Foppa, I. M., Walbeck, J., & Hyman, J. M. (2012). A spatial model of mosquito host-seeking behavior. *PLoS Computational Biology, 8*(5), 1–13. doi:10.1371/journal.pcbi.1002500 PMID:22615546

Danillo, R., Pereira, M. A., Pazoti, L. A. M., & Pereira, J. P. P. (2014). A social-spider optimization approach for support vector machines parameters tuning. *Swarm Intelligence (SIS), IEEE Symposium*.

Dehuri, S., Cho, S.-B., & Ghosh, A. (2008). Wasp: A Multi-agent System for Multiple Recommendations Problem. *4th International Conference on Next Generation Web Services Practices*.

den Besten, M. (2000). *Ants for the single machine total weighted tardiness problem* (Master's thesis). University of Amsterdam.

den Bseten, M., Stützle, T., & Dorigo, M. (2000). Ant colony optimization for the total weighted tardiness problem. *Proceedings of PPSN-VI, Sixth International Conference on Parallel Problem Solving from Nature, 1917*, 611-620. doi:10.1007/3-540-45356-3_60

Donati, A. V., Montemanni, R., Casagrande, N., Rizzoli, A. E., & Gambardella, L. M. (2008). Time Dependent Vehicle Routing Problem with a Multi Ant Colony System. *European Journal of Operational Research, 185*(3), 1174–1191. doi:10.1016/j.ejor.2006.06.047

Dorigo, M., Maniezzo, V., & Colorni, A. (1996). The ant system: optimization by a colony of cooperating agents. IEEE Transaction on Systems, Man, and Cybernetics- Part B, 26(1).

Dorigo, M., & Stutzle, T. (2004). *Ant Colony Optimization-A Bradford Book*. The MIT Press.

Fan, H., & Zhong, Y. (2012). A rough set approach to feature selection based on wasp swarm optimization. *Journal of Computer Information Systems*, 8, 1037–1045.

Farooq, M. (2006). *From the wisdom of the hive to intelligent routing in telecommunication networks: A step towards intelligent network management through natural engineering* (Unpublished doctoral thesis). Universität Dortmund.

Feng, X., Lau, F. C. M., & Gao, D. (2009). A new bio-inspired approach to the traveling salesman problem. In J. Zhou (Ed.), *Complex Part II, LNICST* (Vol. 5, pp. 1310–1321). Institute for Computer Sciences, Social Informatics and Telecommunications Engineering. doi:10.1007/978-3-642-02469-6_12

Feng, X., Lau, F. C. M., & Gao, D. (2009). A new bio-inspired approach to the traveling salesman problem. In J. Zhou (Ed.), *Complex 2009, Part II, LNICST* (Vol. 5, pp. 1310–1321). Institute for Computer Sciences, Social Informatics and Telecommunications Engineering. doi:10.1007/978-3-642-02469-6_12

Forghany, Z., Davarynejad, M., & Snaar-Jagalska, B. E. (2012). Gene regulatory network model identification using artificial bee colony and swarm intelligence. In *IEEE World Congress on Computational Intelligence (WCCI)* (pp. 1–6). Brisbane, Australia: IEEE. doi:10.1109/CEC.2012.6256461

Hölldobler & Wilson. (2009). *The Superorganism - The Beauty Elegance and Strangeness of Insect Societies*. W. W. Norton & Company.

Horng, M.-H. (2011). vector quantization using the firefly algorithm for image compression. *Expert Systems with Applications*, 38.

Horng, M.-H., & Jiang, T. W. (2010). The codebook design of image vector quantization based on the firefly algorithm. Computational Collective Intelligence. *Technologies and Applications, LNCS, 6423*, 438–447.

Horng, M.-H., & Liou, R.-J. (2011). Multilevel minimum cross entropy threshold selection based on the firefly algorithm. *Expert Systems with Applications, 38*(12), 14805–14811. doi:10.1016/j.eswa.2011.05.069

Hsieh, T.-J., & Yeh, W.-C. (2012). Penalty guided bees search for redundancy allocation problems with a mix of components in series–parallel systems. *Computers & Operations Research, 39*(11), 2688–2704. doi:10.1016/j.cor.2012.02.002

Huang, K., Zhou, Y., & Wang, Y. (2011). Niching glowworm swarm optimization algorithm with mating behavior. *Journal of Information and Computational Science*, 8, 4175–4184.

Karaboga, D. (2005). *An idea based on honey bee swarm for numerical optimization*. Technical Report TR06, Computer Engineering Department, Engineering Faculty, Erciyes University.

Karaboga, D., & Akay, B. (2009). A comparative study of Artificial Bee Colony Algorithm. *Applied Mathematics and Computation*, 214.

Karaboga, D., & Basturk, B. (2007). On the performance of artificial bee colony (ABC) algorithm'. *Applied Soft Computing*, 687–697.

Karaboga, D., & Basturk, B. (2007). A powerful and efficient algorithm for numerical function optimization: Artificial bee colony (ABC) algorithm. *Journal of Global Optimization*, *39*(3), 459–471. doi:10.1007/s10898-007-9149-x

Keller, L., & Gordon, É. (2009). *The lives of ants* (J. Grieve, Trans.). Oxford, UK: Oxford University Press Inc.

Khadwilard, A., Chansombat, S., Thepphakorn, T., Thapatsuwan, P., Chainat, W., & Pongcharoen, P. (2011). *Application of firefly algorithm and its parameter setting for job shop scheduling*. First Symposius on Hands-On Research and Development.

Krishnanand, K. N., Amruth, P., Guruprasad, M. H., Bidargaddi, S. V., & Ghose, D. (2006). Glowworm-inspired robot swarm for simultaneous taxis towards multiple radiation sources. In *IEEE International Conference on Robotics and Automation (ICRA)*, (pp. 958–963). IEEE. doi:10.1109/ROBOT.2006.1641833

Krishnanand, K. N., & Ghose, D. (2005). Detection of multiple source locations using glowworm metaphor with applications to collective robotics. In *IEEE Swarm Intelligence Symposium (SIS)* (pp. 84–91). IEEE. doi:10.1109/SIS.2005.1501606

Lee, J. Y., & Darwish, A. H. (2008). Multi-objective Environmental/Economic Dispatch Using the Bees Algorithm with Weighted Sum. *Proceedings of the EU-Korea Conference on Science and Technology (EKC2008)*, 267-274. doi:10.1007/978-3-540-85190-5_28

Liao, W.-H., Kao, Y., & Li, Y.-S. (2011). A sensor deployment approach using glowworm swarm optimization algorithm in wireless sensor networks. *Expert Systems with Applications*, *38*(10), 12180–12188. doi:10.1016/j.eswa.2011.03.053

Liu, Y., Wang, X., & Li, Y. (2012). A modified fruit-fly optimization algorithm aided PID controller designing. In *IEEE 10th World Congress on Intelligent Control and Automation* (pp. 233–238). Beijing, China: IEEE. doi:10.1109/WCICA.2012.6357874

Low, M. Y. H., Chandramohan, M., & Choo, C. S. (2009). Application of multi-objective bee colony optimization algorithm to automated red teaming. Proceedings of IEEE 2009 Winter Simulation Conference, 1798–1808. doi:10.1109/WSC.2009.5429184

Lucchetta, P., Bernstein, C., Théry, M., Lazzari, C., & Desouhant, E. (2008). Foraging and associative learning of visual signals in a parasitic wasp. *Animal Cognition*, *11*(3), 525–533. doi:10.1007/s10071-008-0144-5 PMID:18274795

Mansouri Poor, M., & Shisheh Saz, M. (2012). Multi-Objective Optimization of Laminates with Straight Free Edges and Curved Free Edges by Using Bees Algorithm. *American Journal of Advanced Scientific Research*, *1*(4), 130–136.

Marinakis, Y., Marinaki, M., & Dounias, G. (2008). Honey bees mating optimization algorithm for the vehicle routing problem. *Studies in Computational Intelligence*, *129*, 139–148.

Marshall, S. (2012). *Flies: The Natural History and Diversity of Diptera. Firefly Books*.

Merkle, D., Middendorf, M., & Schmeck, H. (2000). Ant colony optimization for resource-constrained project scheduling. *Proceedings of the Genetic and Evolutionary Computation Conference (GECCO 2000)*, 893-900.

Mezura-Montes, E., & Velez-Koeppel, R. E. (2012). Elitist artificial bee colony for constrained real-parameter optimization. In *IEEE World Congress on Computational Intelligence (WCCI)* (pp. 2068–2075). Barcelona, Spain: CCIB. doi:10.1109/CEC.2010.5586280

Nanry, W. P., & Barnes, J. W. (2000). Solving the pickup and delivery problem with time windows using reactive tabu search. *Transportation Research Part B: Methodological*, *34*(2), 107–121. doi:10.1016/S0191-2615(99)00016-8

Niknam, T. (2009). An efficient hybrid evolutionary algorithm based on PSO and HBMO algorithms for multi-objective distribution feeder reconfiguration. *Energy Conversion and Management*, *50*(8), 2074–2082. doi:10.1016/j.enconman.2009.03.029

Niknam, T. (2009). An efficient hybrid evolutionary algorithm based on PSO and HBMO algorithms for multi-objective distribution feeder reconfiguration. *Energy Conversion and Management*, *50*(8), 2074–2082. doi:10.1016/j.enconman.2009.03.029

Niknam, T. (2011). An efficient multi-objective HBMO algorithm for distribution feeder reconfiguration. *Expert Systems with Applications*, *38*(3), 2878–2887. doi:10.1016/j.eswa.2010.08.081

Özbakır, L., & Tapkan, P. (2011). Bee colony intelligence in zone constrained two-sided assembly line balancing problem. *Expert Systems with Applications*, *38*(9), 11947–11957. doi:10.1016/j.eswa.2011.03.089

Pan, W. T. (2012). A new fruit fly optimization algorithm: Taking the financial distress model as an example. *Knowledge-Based Systems*, *26*, 69–74. doi:10.1016/j.knosys.2011.07.001

Pfahring, B. (1996). *Multi-agent search for open scheduling: adapting the Ant-Q formalism*. Technical report TR-96-09.

Pham, D. T., Afify, A. A., & Koç, E. (2007a). Manufacturing cell formation using the bees algorithm. In *Third International Virtual Conference on Intelligent Production Machines and Systems (IPROMS)* (pp. 1–6). Dunbeath, UK: Whittles.

Pham, D. T., & Castellani, M. (2009). The bees algorithm: Modelling foraging behaviour to solve continuous optimization problems. *Proceedings of the Institution of Mechanical Engineers. Part C, Journal of Mechanical Engineering Science*, *223*(12), 2919–2938. doi:10.1243/09544062JMES1494

Pham, D. T., Castellani, M., & Ghanbarzadeh, A. (2007) Preliminary design using the Bees Algorithm. *Proceedings Eighth LAMDAMAP International Conference on Laser Metrology, CMM and Machine Tool Performance*, 420-429.

Pham, D. T., & Darwish, A. H. (2010). Using the bees' algorithm with Kalman filtering to train an artificial neural network for pattern classification. *Journal of Systems and Control Engineering*, *224*(7), 885–892.

Pham, D. T., & Ghanbarzadeh, A. (2007). Multi-objective optimisation using the bees algorithm. In *Third International Virtual Conference on Intelligent Production Machines and Systems (IPROMS)* (pp. 1–5). Dunbeath, UK: Whittles.

Pham, D. T., Ghanbarzadeh, A., Koç, E., Otri, S., Rahim, S., & Zaidi, M. (2006). The bees algorithm—a novel tool for complex optimisation problems. In *Proceedings of Second International Virtual Conference on Intelligent production machines and systems (IPROMS)* (pp. 454–459). Oxford, UK: Elsevier. doi:10.1016/B978-008045157-2/50081-X

Pham, D. T., Ghanbarzadeh, A., Koç, E., Otri, S., Rahim, S., & Zaidi, M. (2007b). Using the bees algorithm to schedule jobs for a machine. In *Proceedings of Eighth International Conference on Laser metrology, CMM and machine tool performance (LAMDAMAP)* (pp. 430–439). Euspen.

Pham, D. T., Ghanbarzadeh, A., Otri, S., & Koç, E. (2009). Optimal design of mechanical components using the bees algorithm. *Proceedings of the Institution of Mechanical Engineers. Part C, Journal of Mechanical Engineering Science*, 223(5), 1051–1056. doi:10.1243/09544062JMES838

Pham, D. T., & Koç, E. (2010). Design of a two-dimensional recursive filter using the bees algorithm. *International Journal of Automation and Computing*, 7(3), 399–402. doi:10.1007/s11633-010-0520-x

Pham, D. T., Koç, E., Lee, J. Y., & Phrueksanant, J. (2007). Using the Bees Algorithm to Schedule Jobs for a Machine. *Proceedings 8th international Conference on Laser Metrology, CMM and Machine Tool Performance (LAMDAMAP)*, 430-439.

Pham, D. T., Zaidi, M., Mahmuddin, M., Ghanbarzadeh, A., Koç, E., & Otri, S. (2007). Using the bees' algorithm to optimize a support vector machine for wood defect classification, IPROMS. *Innovative Production Machines and Systems Virtual Conference.*

Pinto, P. C., Runkler, T. A., & Sousa, J. M. C. (2006). Agent based optimization of the MAX-SAT problem using wasp swarms. In *7th Portuguese Conference on Automatic Control (CONTROLO)* (pp. 1–6). Lisboa, Portugal: Instituto Superior Técnico.

Pradhan, P. M., & Panda, G. (2012). Connectivity constrained wireless sensor deployment using multi objective evolutionary algorithms and fuzzy decision making. *Ad Hoc Networks*, 10(6), 1134–1145. doi:10.1016/j.adhoc.2012.03.001

Quijano, N., & Passino, K. M. (2010). Honey bee social foraging algorithms for resource allocation: Theory and application. *Engineering Applications of Artificial Intelligence*, 23(6), 845–861. doi:10.1016/j.engappai.2010.05.004

Runkler, T. A. (2008). Wasp swarm optimization of the c-means clustering model. *International Journal of Intelligent Systems*, 23(3), 269–285. doi:10.1002/int.20266

Rusell, R. A., & Chiang, W. C. (2006). Scatter search for the vehicle routing problem with time windows. *European Journal of Operational Research*, 169(2), 606–622. doi:10.1016/j.ejor.2004.08.018

Ruz, G. A., & Goles, E. (2013). Learning gene regulatory networks using the bees algorithm. *Neural Computing & Applications*, 22(1), 63–70. doi:10.1007/s00521-011-0750-z

Sahana, S. K., & Jain, A. (2011). An Improved Modular Hybrid Ant Colony Approach for Solving Traveling Salesman Problem. *International Journal on Computing, 1*(2), 123-127.

Sahana, S.K., Jain, A., & Mahanti, P.K. (2014). Ant Colony Optimization for Train Scheduling: An Analysis. *I.J. Intelligent Systems and Applications, 6*(2), 29-36. doi:,10.5815/ijisa.2014.02.04

Sayadi, F., Ismail, M., Misran, N., & Jumari, K. (2009). Multi-Objective Optimization Using the Bees Algorithm in Time-Varying Channel for MIMO MC-CDMA Systems. *European Journal of Scientific Research, 33*(3), 411–428.

Song, J., Hu, J., Tian, Y., & Xu, Y. (2005). Re-optimization in dynamic vehicle routing problem based on wasp-like agent strategy. *Proceedings of 8th International Conference on Intelligent Transportation Systems*, 688–693.

Srivastava, Sahana, Pant, & Mahanti.(2015). Hybrid Synchronous Discrete Distance Time Model for Traffic Signal Optimization. *Journal of Next Generation Information Technology, 6.*

Stützle, T. (1997). *MAX-MIN Ant System for the quadratic assignment problem.* Technical Report AIDA-97-4, FB Informatik, TU Darmstadt, Germany.

Stützle, T. (1997). *An ant approach to the flow shop problem.* Technical report AIDA-97-07.

Tasgetiren, M. F., Pan, Q.-K., Suganthan, P. N., & Chen, A. H.-L. (2011). A discrete artificial bee colony algorithm for the total flowtime minimization in permutation flow shops. *Information Sciences, 181*(16), 3459–3475. doi:10.1016/j.ins.2011.04.018

Tasgetiren, M. F., Pan, Q.-K., Suganthan, P. N., & Chen, A. H.-L. (2010). A discrete artificial bee colony algorithm for the permutation flow shop scheduling problem with total flowtime criterion. In *IEEE World Congress on Computational Intelligence* (pp. 137–144). Barcelona, Spain: CCIB. doi:10.1109/CEC.2010.5586300

Tasgetiren, M. F., Pan, Q.-K., Suganthan, P. N., & Oner, A. (2013). A discrete artificial bee colony algorithm for the no-idle permutation flowshop scheduling problem with the total tardiness criterion. *Applied Mathematical Modelling, 37*(10-11), 6758–6779. doi:10.1016/j.apm.2013.02.011

Teodorovic´, D. (2008). Swarm intelligence systems for transportation engineering: Principles and applications. *Transportation Research Part C, Emerging Technologies, 16*(6), 651–667. doi:10.1016/j.trc.2008.03.002

Teodorovic´, D. (2009a). Bee colony optimization (BCO). In C. P. Lim, L. C. Jain, & S. Dehuri (Eds.), Innovations in swarm intelligence (Vol. 248, pp. 39–60). Springer.

Teodorovic´, D. (2009b). Bee colony optimization (BCO). In C. P. Lim, L. C. Jain, & S. Dehuri (Eds.), *Innovations in swarm intelligence.* Berlin: Springer. doi:10.1007/978-3-642-04225-6_3

Teodorovic´, D., & Dell'Orco, M. (2005). Bee colony optimization: A cooperative learning approach to complex transportation problems. *16th Mini-EURO Conference on Advanced OR and AI Methods in Transportation*, 51–60.

Teodorovic, D. U. Š. A. N., Davidovic, T., & Selmic, M. (2011). Bee colony optimization: The applications survey. *ACM Transactions on Computational Logic, 1529*, 3785.

Theraulaz, G., Goss, S., Gervet, J., & Deneubourg, J. L. (1991). Task differentiation in polistes wasps colonies: A model for self-organizing groups of robots. In *First International Conference on Simulation of Adaptive Behavior* (pp. 346–355). Cambridge, MA: MIT Press.

Wang, D.-Z., Zhang, J.-S., Wan, F., & Zhu, L. (2006). A dynamic task scheduling algorithm in grid environment. *5th WSEAS International Conference on Telecommunications and Informatics*, 273–275.

Wang, L., Zheng, X.-L., & Wang, S.-Y. (2013). A novel binary fruit fly optimization algorithm for solving the multidimensional knapsack problem. *Knowledge-Based Systems*, *48*, 17–23. doi:10.1016/j.knosys.2013.04.003

Wedde, H. F., & Farooq, M. (2006). A comprehensive review of nature inspired routing algorithms for fixed telecommunication networks. *Journal of Systems Architecture*, *52*(8-9), 461–484. doi:10.1016/j.sysarc.2006.02.005

Wedde, H. F., & Farooq, M. (2006). A comprehensive review of nature inspired routing algorithms for fixed telecommunication networks. *Journal of Systems Architecture*, *52*(8-9), 461–484. doi:10.1016/j.sysarc.2006.02.005

Wedde, H. F., Farooq, M., & Zhang, Y. (2004). Beehive: An efficient fault-tolerant routing algorithm inspired by honey bee behavior. In M. Dorigo (Ed.), ANTS 2004 (Vol. 3172, pp. 83–94). Springer.

Whitehouse, M. E. A., & Lubin, Y. (1999). Competitive foraging in the social spider Stegodyphus dumicola. *Animal Behaviour*, *58*(3), 677–688. doi:10.1006/anbe.1999.1168 PMID:10479384

Xing & Gao. (2014). *Innovative Computational Intelligence: A Rough Guide to 134 Clever Algorithms*. Springer International Publishing. DOI 10.1007/978-3-319-03404-1(2014)

Xu, W., Zhou, Z., Pham, D. T., Liu, Q., Ji, C., & Meng, W. (2012). Quality of service in manufacturing networks: A service framework and its implementation. *International Journal of Advanced Manufacturing Technology*, *63*(9-12), 1227–1237. doi:10.1007/s00170-012-3965-y

Yang, X.-S. (2008). Nature-inspired metaheuristic algorithms. Luniver Press.

Yang, X.-S. (2010a). Firefly algorithm, Lévy flights and global optimization. In M. Bramer (Ed.), Research and development in intelligent systems (vol. 26, pp. 209–218). London, UK: Springer-Verlag.

Yang, X.-S. (2010b). Firefly algorithm, stochastic test functions and design optimisation. *International Journal of Bio-inspired Computation*, *2*(2), 78–84. doi:10.1504/IJBIC.2010.032124

Yang, X.-S. (2013). Multiobjective firefly algorithm for continuous optimization. *Engineering with Computers*, *29*(2), 175–184. doi:10.1007/s00366-012-0254-1

Zeng, F., Decraene, J., Low, M. Y. H., Hingston, P., Cai, W., Zhou, S., & Chandramohan, M. (2010). Autonomous bee colony optimization for multi-objective function. In *IEEE World Congress on Computational Intelligence (WCCI)* (pp. 1279–1286). Barcelona, Spain: CCIB. doi:10.1109/CEC.2010.5586057

Zhu, W., Li, N., Shi, C., & Chen, B. (2013). SVR based on FOA and its application in traffic flow prediction. *Open Journal of Transportation Technologies*, *2*(01), 6–9. doi:10.12677/OJTT.2013.21002

Zungeru, A. M., Ang, L.-M., & Seng, K. P. (2012). Termite-hill: Performance optimized swarm intelligence based routing algorithm for wireless sensor networks. *Journal of Network and Computer Applications*, *35*(6), 1901–1917. doi:10.1016/j.jnca.2012.07.014

Zungeru, A. M., Ang, L.-M., & Seng, K. P. (2012). Termite-hill: Performance optimized swarm intelligence based routing algorithm for wireless sensor networks. *Journal of Network and Computer Applications*, *35*(6), 1901–1917. doi:10.1016/j.jnca.2012.07.014

Chapter 14
Bio–Inspired Computational Intelligence and Its Application to Software Testing

Abhishek Pandey
UPES Dehradun, India

Soumya Banerjee
BIT Mesra, India

ABSTRACT

Bio inspired algorithms are computational procedure inspired by the evolutionary process of nature and swarm intelligence to solve complex engineering problems. In the recent times it has gained much popularity in terms of applications to diverse engineering disciplines. Now a days bio inspired algorithms are also applied to optimize the software testing process. In this chapter authors will discuss some of the popular bio inspired algorithms and also gives the framework of application of these algorithms for software testing problems such as test case generation, test case selection, test case prioritization, test case minimization. Bio inspired computational algorithms includes genetic algorithm (GA), genetic programming (GP), evolutionary strategies (ES), evolutionary programming (EP) and differential evolution(DE) in the evolutionary algorithms category and Ant colony optimization(ACO), Particle swarm optimization(PSO), Artificial Bee Colony(ABC), Firefly algorithm(FA), Cuckoo search(CS), Bat algorithm(BA) etc. in the Swarm Intelligence category(SI).

1. INTRODUCTION

During the last few decades many new algorithms has been developed in order to solve complex mathematical problems. The development of such algorithms was mandatory due to the fact that many of the computational problems form the set of complex problems that are known to be NP complete problem (M.R Garey, & D.S Johnson, 1979). Bio inspired computational intelligence algorithms are gaining its popularity by the fact that these algorithms performed well on various parameters and give the converged optimized solution. Here it will be worth noting that many conventional methods such as newton's method

DOI: 10.4018/978-1-5225-2128-0.ch014

or gradient descent method, simplex method requires lot of assumption in order to model the problem and thus unable to model the real world problem correctly and precisely. Linear programming methods are also unable to model the real world problem because many of the real world problems had been proved as a nonlinear problem. These algorithms fail to find the feasible solution in large and highly nonlinear environment. Many of the software testing problems such as test data generation problem, test suite selection and minimization problems has been modeled as a search based problems in order to find the optimized solutions. These problems too fall in the category of nonlinear optimization problem. In the next section authors will review the various bio inspired computational intelligence algorithms and then discuss its application to various software testing problems. A brief but complete description of popular Genetic Algorithm and some other evolutionary algorithms will be discussed with proposing algorithms to solve test data generation problem.

2. BACKGROUNDS

2.1. Computational Methods Inspired by Biological Processes of Nature

Inspiration from nature and biological processes have motivated to the development of various computational algorithms in order to solve complex problems. These algorithms are classified as evolutionary and swarm intelligence based algorithms. Evolutionary algorithms are based on the principle of survival of the fittest or natural selection (J.H Holland, 1975). Swarm intelligence is based on the cooperative group intelligence of swarms or collective behavior of insect colonies and other animal colonies (E.Bonabeau, M. Dorigo, & G.Theraulaz, 1999).

2.2. Evolutionary Algorithms

Evolutionary algorithms are inspired by the evolutionary process of nature. According to natural selection theory of evolution, competition among individual to survive in the nature results in the survival of the fittest individual over weaker one. This results in the success of achieving variety of life and its suitability for the nature. Evolutionary algorithms are generic Meta heuristic based optimization algorithms. An EA uses the mechanism inspired by biological process such as reproduction, mutation, recombination and selection (J.H Holland, 1975). An objective function is defined based on the problem and initial population is randomly generated; randomization helps in elimination of local minima problem, now the operators such as selection, recombination and mutation are applied iteratively to find the best individuals survived in the environment of objective function. The progress in search is achieved by evaluating the fitness of individuals and selecting the individual with highest fitness. In general any abstract task to be accomplished can be thought of as solving a problem. This can also be assumed to have a search through a space of the potential solution. Here comes the existence of optimization because search is for the best solution. The method of evolutionary computation is among this category, they are stochastic methods whose search spaces models some of the natural phenomena, survival of the fittest (L. Davis, & (ed.), 1991) . Evolutionary algorithms are widely used to solve complex engineering and science problems. Here it is very important to realize to find the problems that are most suited for the application of evolutionary algorithms. The major goal of research in evolutionary algorithm is to find out the class of problems that are most suited for the application of evolutionary algorithms. The most popular algorithms that constitute the evolutionary computation are Genetic algorithm, evolutionary programming, evolutionary strategies, genetic programming and differential evolution.

2.2.1. Genetic Algorithm

The most popular EAs are Genetic Algorithm. Initially developed by Holland. The standard GA as developed by Holland step by step procedure consists of following steps.

1. A population of n random individuals is initialized.
2. Fitness scores are assigned to each individual.
3. Using roulette wheel parent selection n/2 pairs of parents are chosen from the current population to form a new population.
4. With probability P_c, children are formed by performing crossover on the n/2 pairs of parents. The children replace the parents in the new population.
5. With probability P_n, mutation is performed on the new population.
6. The new population becomes the current population.
7. If the termination conditions are satisfied exit, otherwise go to step3.

GAs was engineered to model adaptation processes, mainly operated on binary strings and mainly used a recombination operator and mutation operator as a background operators (L. Davis, & (ed.), 1991). Mutations flip the bit in the chromosomes and cross over exchanges the genetic between two parents. The combined effect of selection, cross over and mutation gives the reproductive schema growth equation (I. M. Oliver, D. J. Smith, and J. R. C. Holland,1987). Many successful versions of GA also evolved over time (Z. Michalewicz,1992; D.E Goldberg,1989). GA has the property of implicit parallelism. GAs has been successfully applied to wide area of areas (Michalewicz, Z. & D.B Fogel, 2004; J.Brownlee, 2011)

2.2.2. Evolutionary Programming

Evolutionary Programming (EP) technique was developed by Lawrence Fogel (Fogel, L.J., Owens, A.J., & Walsh, M.J, 1966). The main motive behind development of EP was to introduce machine intelligence to predict the change in the environment. The environment was described as the sequence of symbols and the algorithm supposed to predict the output as a new symbol. The output symbol should maximize the fitness function. Evolutionary programming maintains the population of finite state machine with each representing the potential solution of the problem. The fitness function takes an account of overall performance of prediction. Evolutionary programming first generates the offspring and then select population for next generation. Offspring are created by random mutation of parent population. Evolutionary programming (D.B Fogel, 1992, 1993, L.J Fogel, & J.W Atmar, 1998) techniques were generalized to handle various numerical optimization problems.

2.2.3. Evolutionary Strategies

Evolutionary Strategies was developed by Rechenberg and Schwefel (H.P Schwefel, 1994). Evolution Strategies (ESs) are bio-inspired direct search and optimization methods belonging to the family of Evolutionary Algorithm (EAs) which uses mutation, recombination, and selection operators that are applied to the population of candidate solution. It was developed back to mid-1960s when P. Bienert, I. Rechenberg, and H.P. Schwefel at the Technical University of Berlin, Germany, developed the first bionics-inspired schemes for evolving optimal shapes of minimal drag bodies in a wind tunnel using Darwin's evolution principle (J. Zurada, R. Marks, & C. Robinson, (Editors),1994).

2.2.4. Genetic Programming

The objective of computers to automatically solve problems is also the goal of machine intelligence (Alan M. Turing, 1949). The main goal of artificial intelligence and machine intelligence is to develop intelligent algorithm to get machines acts like human and involve use of intelligence (J.R Koza, 1992). Genetic programming is based on the evolution of programs. Instead of solving the problem using genetic algorithm search of possible program for the best one is done (J.R. Koza, 1990, 1992). There are five main steps involved in use of Genetic Programming.

- Selection of terminals.
- Selection of function.
- Identification of evaluation function.
- Selection of parameters of the system.
- Selection of the terminal condition.

It is important to note that the structure that undergoes evolution is hierarchical structure of computer programs. These structures form the initial population. This population is initialised such that some of the structure generates the correct result. The main operator involved is the crossover operator. Other operator such as mutation, permutation, editing, define building block operators. In addition to above mentioned steps Koza added another feature known as set of procedures. These set of procedures are called automatically defined function (ADF).

2.2.5. Differential Evolution

Differential evolution is a nature inspired intelligent algorithm for optimization over continuous domain (R. Storn & K. Price, 1997; Shi Y & R.C Eberhart, 1998). It is a real parameter based optimization algorithm. Differential evolution is a parallel direct search method that utilizes K, N dimensional parameter vectors as a population for each generation. K does not change with population. Initial vector population is chosen randomly to avoid local minima. Uniform probability distribution is used for all random decisions. DE uses mutation as a main operator which is applied using weighted difference of two parameters vectors with the third one. Mutated real parameters are then applied to the crossover; this is known as parameter mixing. Selection is done by comparing the trial vector to the target vector in a greedy approach.

2.2.6. Comparison of Evolutionary Algorithms

See Table 1.

Table 1. Characteristic of various Evolutionary Algorithms

Characteristic of Algorithm	Genetic Algorithm	Evolutionary programming	Evolutionary strategies	Genetic programming	Differential evolution
Algorithm Types	Genotypic/ Phenotypic	Phenotypic	Phenotypic	Phenotypic	Phenotypic
Developed by	Holland	Fogel	Rechenberg Schwefel	Koza	Storn and Price
Basic principle	Natural selection or survival of the fittest	Survival of the fittest	Survival of the fittest	Survival of the fittest	Survival of the fittest
Solution representation	Binary/real valued	Finite state machines	Float valued vectors	Expression trees	Real valued
Fitness	Scaled objective value	Payoff function value	Objective function value	Scaled objective value	Objective function value
Selection	Probabilistic preservative	Probabilistic extinctive	Probabilistic extinctive	Probabilistic extinctive	Deterministic extinctive
Evolutionary operators	Mainly cross over other mutation	Mutation recombination	Mutation cross over	Cross over and mutation	Mainly mutation other cross over

3. SWARM INTELLIGENCE

The swarming behaviour of social insects provides the inspiration for exploration of many important facts of artificial life (T.Seeley, 1985; M.M Millonas, 1994). Basic principles of swarm intelligence include the following points.

1. Proximity principle.
2. Quality principle.
3. Principle of diverse response.
4. Principle of stability.
5. Principle of adaptability.

Swarm intelligence is based on the collective behaviour of social insect and is based on the above-mentioned rules. Proximity principle is easily correlated with the space and time computation (M. Dorigo, V. Maniezzo, & A. Colorni, 1991). The group should be able to response not only in space and time considerations but it must also consider the safety of food locations etc. for betterment. There should also be diversity in response of the insects.

3.1. Ant Colony Optimization

The ACO is inspired by the foraging search behaviour of real ants and their ability in finding the shortest paths. It is a population-based general search technique for the solution of difficult combinatorial optimization problems. The first ant system algorithm was proposed based on the foraging behaviour exhibited by real ant colonies in their search for food. The details can be found in (Thomas Stutzle; Marco Dorigo, 2003).

4. APPLICATIONS OF EVOLUTIONARY ALGORITHMS IN SOFTWARE TEST OPTIMIZATION

Software testing is most time consuming as well as laborious task (Alan M. Turing, 1949; G. Myers, 1979). The first idea of testing is due to Turing. Lot of research is carried out in order to automate the process of software testing. Search based software engineering is the name given to the area of research into which search based optimization techniques are applied to the field of software engineering (M. Harman, B.F. Jones, 2001). Search based software engineering emerged back for fifteen years (Mark Harman, 2010). SBSE formulates the software engineering problems as a search problem.

4.1. Test Data Generation Problem

Test data generation refers to generate valid input data to test the program for the intention of finding out the program behaviour. Test data generation requires lot of efforts in terms of time and cost. Test data generation is automated with the help of intelligent Computer Algorithms that automatically generate the test data for a particular program. Search based software testing refers to field of study in which software testing problem is modelled as a search problem.

Evolutionary testing refers to the application of evolutionary Algorithm to various Problems of software testing such as test data generation, test data validation, test case minimization problem etc. (N. Tracey, J. Clark, K. Mander, and J. McDermid, 1998). Different techniques exist to Generate test data using evolutionary Algorithms is based on the choices for fitness functions. Coverage-Oriented Approaches use the fitness function on the basis of covered program structures (S. Xanthakis, C. Ellis, C. Skourlas, A. Le Gall, S. Katsikas, and K. Karapoulios, 1992). Fitness values are based on the basis of the covered program structures by the test cases. The objective function penalizes individuals that follow already covered paths, by assigning a value that is the inverse of the number of times the path has already been executed during the search (M. Roper1997; Watkins, 1995).

4.2. A Framework for Application of Genetic Algorithm for Test Data Generation Problem

Though various methodology of application of evolutionary Algorithms to test data generation problem exists (B.Jones, H.Sthamer, & D.Eyres,1996; G.McGraw, C.Michael, & M.Schatz,2001). In this paper a modified test data generation using GA is proposed. It is based on the modified fitness function and uses uniform cross over and bit flip mutation. In this framework program to be tested is taken as input. Programs consist of various statements that reflect instructions. For the purpose of program testing Cyclomatic Complexity (cc) is the most important metric (M. Harman, A. Mansouri, & Y. Zhang,2009). It is a measure of different independent path to be tested. Suppose the cyclomatic complexity of a particular program is 3 than there exist 3 independent paths that has to tested.

4.2.2. Control Flow Graph (B. Korel, 1990)

Test adequacy criteria such as branch coverage are calculated using control flow graph. The input for proposed model will be the test program which will generate a control flow graph. The objective function will also be derived from the CFG data. Control flow graph represent the flow of control for a particular test input data. Initial population of test cases are generated using boundary conditions and some test cases will be randomly generated. In the case of regression testing previously available test suite are used. In the case of program modification new test cases are seeded.

4.2.3. Branch Distance (B. Korel, 1990)

See Table 2 and Figure 1.

4.2.4. Proposed Method to Select the Fitness Function

In this proposed work Fitness function is selected based on the normalized branch distance (B. Korel, 1990) with inclusion of weights of the particular path.

Fitness function = α (normalized branch distance) + β (weight of the particular path selected)

where α and β are parameters that is selected by the user to improve the fitness of the particular test cases. In this method weights are assigned as an integer value of the branches which constitute the branch predicate and assigned higher value in following decreasing order.

1. If else condition.
2. Relational operators
3. Assignment operator
4. Loops

4.2.5. Proposed Algorithm

Input: Software under Test (SUT), max.gen
Output: Optimized Test Suite
Begin;
Initialization;
Generate an initial population of test cases id T_i (i= 1,2,3.....k)based on some boundary conditions and solving the branch predicate);
Repeat until max.gen reached do;

Table 2. Objective function for branch predicates

Branch Predicates	Branch Function F(Branch Distance)	rel
E1 > E2	E2- E1	<
E1>= E2	E2- E1	<=
E1< E2	E1- E2	<
E1 <= E2	E1- E2	<=
E1= E2	Abs (E1-E2)	=
E1 ≠ E2	Abs (E1-E2)	≠

Figure 1. Flowchart of Application of GA to test data generation problem

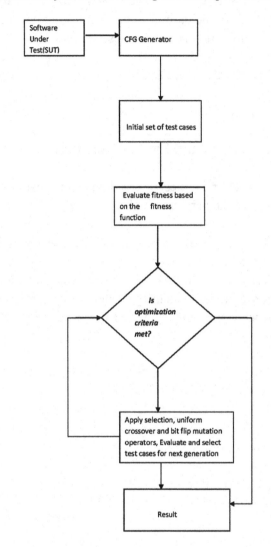

for(1 to k test cases) do
{
Evaluate Fitness according to branch functions;
Apply uniform cross over and bit flip mutation operators;
}
End

4.2.6. Experimental Analysis

We have performed our experiments using (MATLAB® & Simulink® Release,2008a) on the following set of programs

Table 3. Set of programs on which experiments are performed

Serial No.	Program Name	No. of Variables	Cyclomatic Complexity
1.	Triangle classification problem	3	8
2.	Even Odd	1	3
3.	Quadratic equation	3	4
4.	Largest of three numbers	3	3

Figure 2. Graph showing the cyclomatic complexity and no. of variables

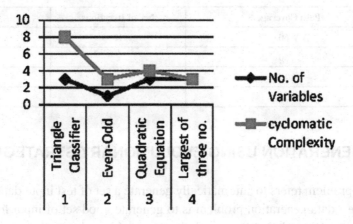

4.2.7. Results and Analysis

We have applied Genetic algorithm to successfully generating the test data for the selected test cases. Parameters we have used in applying GA is uniform cross over, binary encoding and bit flip wise mutation operator. It has been observed that GA is efficient tool for generation the test data for selected paths of the control flow graph. In our example we have taken the program code as our input data. It has been showed that the various test data could be automatically generated from the branch distance knowledge of the test data itself. In the comparison section the performance of GA in test data generation problem is compared with the random method of generating test data. The GA has clearly outperformed Random generation.

Comparison is performed on the basis of three parameters that are Path coverage percentage, no. of iterations, Time taken. GA has outperformed the random generation on all these parameters.

4.2.8. Comparison

In this section comparison of results on application of proposed algorithm to test data generation problem with random generation is given in tabular form.

Table 4. Random Generation of test cases

Serial No.	Path Coverage %	No. of Iterations	Time Taken(s)
1.	40	14	7
2.	34	15	7
3.	27	19	5
4.	57	17	7

Table 5. Result of applying the proposed Algorithm based on Genetic Algorithm

Serial No.	Path Coverage %	No. of Iterations	Time Taken(s)
1.	60	10	3
2.	50	2	1
3.	30.57	2	3
4.	75	3	2

5. TEST DATA GENERATION USING EVOLUTIONARY STRATEGIES

Test data generation problem refers to automatically generate a set of test input data for a program to be tested. The goal of test data generation problem is to generate good set of input for the program to be tested. This problem can be modelled as an optimization problem that optimizes the set of input data. Recently this approach is known as a search based software testing. Test data is generated according to the test adequacy criteria (P.R. Srivastava, K. Baby, & G. Raghurama,2009; Doungsa-ard, K. Dahal, A. Hossain, & T. Suwannasart, 2008). Test adequacy criteria consist of the any of the criteria such as branch coverage, condition coverage, statement coverage. Applications of Meta heuristics to test data generation problem is considered as an important goal of search based software engineering community.

In this section application of evolutionary strategy to test data generation problem is described. Initially a population of μ individuals are randomly generated that fulfils some of the test adequacy criteria in this case branch decision coverage. In every generation λ individuals are selected based on the variation operator, Mutation operator in case of effect to only one individual or recombination operator to effect two individuals from the population. In evolutionary strategy each individual is consists of the vector of real value, a vector of standard deviation and optionally a vector of angles.

The input data values for a test program are either real or integer. Each of these values is the problem variable in the ES applications. This is in contrast to the Genetic algorithm which uses the binary representations. Fitness functions is taken same as the objective functions given in (N. Tracey, J. Clark, K. Mander, & J. McDermid, 1998). In the next section experimental evaluations is carried out.

We take the same set of C programs as taken in the previous approach of GA.

In addition we are taking GCD C program also with others.

Table 6. List of Programs on which experiments are performed

Serial No.	Program Name	No. of Variables	Cyclomatic Complexity
1.	Triangle classification problem	3	8
2.	Even Odd	1	3
3.	Quadratic equation	3	4
4.	Largest of three numbers	3	3

5.1. Results and Discussion

In this work initial population of size $\mu = 30$ individuals are taken. 10% of these individuals are seeded that is 3 individuals. The number of off springs $\lambda = 1$. We have performed 100 evaluations and the test data generator has 30 runs using MATLAB^R. The results are tabulated below. For some program 100% coverage is never achieved because of programming constructs such as infinite loop present.

6. APPLICATION OF ACO, ABC TO THE SOFTWARE TEST DATA GENERATION PROBLEM

Ant colony optimization and ABC has been applied to the test case generation problem in various studies (P.R. Srivastava; K. Baby, & G. Raghurama, 2009; W Pedrycz, J.F Peters, 1998). In this research study an innovative approach of ant colony optimization is proposed.

begin
1. Initially N no. of ants are initialized.
2. Each ant corresponds to a test case so N no. of test cases are initialized using random selection.
3. Fitness of the test cases are evaluated on the basis of branch distance with pheromone index i.(fitness= branch distance × pheromone index)
4. Repeat following steps
5. Each generation update pheromone index.
6. Generate new test cases based on the value of pheromone index and fitness value.
End

Table 7. Results

Program	Path Coverage%	No. of Iterations	Time (s)
Triangle problem	98.54	1965	12.8
Even-odd	100	15	0.0
Quadratic	96.65	1129	24.8
GCD	100	15	0.0
Largest of three numbers	100	15	0.0

6.1. Experimental Setup

Set of bench marked programs has been chosen for the experiments. Application of GA, ACO, ABC has been done to generate the optimized set of test cases and a comparison is shown in tabular form. Experiments are performed using MATLAB[R].

6.2. Results and Discussions

Following Tables and Graphs shows the results. Based on the results, it is obvious that ABC algorithm gives better performance in terms of both execution time as well as Path coverage while the random algorithms are worst performance in terms of execution time as well as path coverage.

7. CONCLUSION

Many of the real world mathematical problems are nonlinear optimization problem. Software testing problem is also modelled as an optimization problem. In fact search based software engineering is a

Table 8. Set of program on which experiments performed

Serial No.	Program Name	No. of Variables	Cyclomatic Complexity
1.	Triangle classification problem	3	8
2.	Even Odd	1	3
3.	Quadratic equation	3	4
4.	Largest of three numbers	3	3

Table 9. Results: Application of ABC Algorithm

Serial No.	Path Coverage %	No. of Iterations	Time Taken(s)
1.	94	44	0.04
2.	100	20	0.005
3.	100	4	0.016
4.	100	2	0.003

Table 10. Results: Application of ACO Algorithm

Serial No.	Path Coverage %	No. of Iterations	Time Taken(s)
1.	75	19	1.05
2.	90	10	1.50
3.	50	40	1.52
4.	100	10	1.53

Figure 3. Comparison bar chart based on path coverage

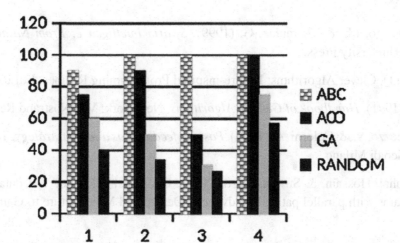

Figure 4. Comparison bar chart based on time taken

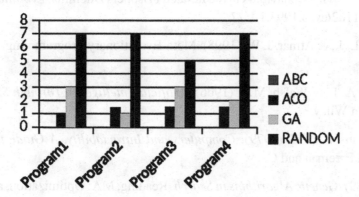

research area that is focussed on optimization of software engineering task. Many problems such as software test data generation, regression test suite minimization, non-functional testing of software are solved using search based techniques. In this paper, brief but complete background of popular bio inspired Algorithms with their possible applications in software testing domain is discussed. An algorithm to solve test data generation problem with the applications of Genetic Algorithm, Evolutionary strategies and ant colony optimization Algorithm are proposed. Results of application of evolutionary Algorithms have been compared. Some of the key issues discussed are test data generation problem and applications of Genetic Algorithm, Evolutionary Strategies, Ant Colony Optimization and Artificial Bee Colony Optimization Algorithm to test data generation problem. Results are compared on the basis of path coverage as well as execution time. Key findings are Genetic Algorithm performed well on the selected problem when compared to Random search. ABC algorithm performed well when compared to others such as ACO and GA on path coverage as well as on execution time.

REFERENCES

Bonabeau, E., Dorigo, M., & Theraulaz, G. (1999). *Swarm Intelligence: From Natural to Artificial Systems*. Oxford University Press.

Brownlee, J. (2011). Clever Algorithms: Nature-inspired Programming Recipes. LuLu.com.

Davis, L. (Ed.). (1991). *Handbook of Genetic Algorithms*. New York: Van Nostrand Reinhold.

Dorigo, M., Maniezzo, V., & Colorni, A. (1991). *Positive feedback as a search strategy*. Technical Report 91-016, Politecnico di Milano.

Doungsa-ard, Dahal, Hossain, & Suwannasart. (2008). GA-based automatic test data generation for UML state diagrams with parallel paths. In Advanced Design and Manufacture to Gain a Competitive Edge. Springer.

Fogel, D. B. (1992). *Evolving Artificial Intelligence* (Ph.D. Thesis). University of California, San Diego, CA.

Fogel, D. B. (1993). Evolving Behaviours in the Iterated Prisoners Dilemma. *Evolutionary Computation*, *1*(1), 77–97. doi:10.1162/evco.1993.1.1.77

Fogel, D. B., Fogel, L. J., & Atmar, J. W. (1998). Meta-Evolutionary Programming. *Informatica*, *18*(4), 387–398.

Fogel, L. J., Owens, A. J., & Walsh, M. J. (1966). *Artificial Intelligence Through Simulated Evolution*. Chichester, UK: John Wiley.

Garey, M. R., & Johnson, D. S. (1979). *Computers and Intractability. A Guide to the theory of NP Completeness*. W.H. Freeman and Co.

Goldberg, D. E. (1989). *Genetic Algorithms in Search*. Reading, MA: Optimization, and Machine Learning, Addison Wiley.

Harman, M. (2010). Why source code analysis and manipulation will always be important (keynote). *10th IEEE International Working Conference on Source Code Analysis and Manipulation*.

Harman, M., & Jones, B. F. (2001). Search based software engineering. *Information and Software Technology*, *43*(14), 833–839. doi:10.1016/S0950-5849(01)00189-6

Harman, Mansouri, & Zhang. (2009). *Search based software engineering: A comprehensive analysis and review of trends techniques and applications*. Technical Report TR-09-03, Department of Computer Science, King's College London.

Holland, J. H. (1975). *Adaptation in Natural and Artificial Systems*. The MIT Press.

Jones, B., Sthamer, H., & Eyres, D. (1996). Automatic structural testing using genetic algorithms. *Software Engineering Journal*, *11*(5), 299–306. doi:10.1049/sej.1996.0040

Korel, B. (1990). Automated Software Test Data Generation. *Transactions on Software Engineering*, *SE-16*(8), 870–879. doi:10.1109/32.57624

Koza, J. R. (1990). *Genetic Programming: A Paradigm for Genetically Breeding Populations of Computer Programs to Solve Problems*. Report No. STAN-CS-90-1314, Stanford University.

Koza, J. R. (1992). *Genetic Programming: On the Programming of Computers by Means of Natural Selection*. Cambridge, MA: MIT Press.

McGraw, G., Michael, C., & Schatz, M. (2001). Generating software test data by evolution. *IEEE Transactions on Software Engineering*, 27(12), 1085–1110. doi:10.1109/32.988709

Michalewicz, Z. (1992). *Genetic Algorithms C+ Data Structures = Evolution Programs*. Berlin: Springer. doi:10.1007/978-3-662-02830-8

Michalewicz, Z., & Fogel, D. B. (2004). How to Solve It: Modern Heuristics. Springer. doi:10.1007/978-3-662-07807-5

Millonas, M. M. (1994). Swarms, phase transitions, and collective intelligence. In *Artificial Life III* (pp. 417–445). Reading, MA: Addison-Wesley.

Myers, G. (1979). *The Art of Software Testing*. New York: Wiley.

Pedrycz, W., & Peters, J. F. (1998). *Computational Intelligence in Software Engineering*. World Scientific Publishers Singapore. doi:10.1142/3821

Roper. (1997). *Computer aided software testing using genetic algorithms*. In 10th International Software Quality Week, San Francisco, CA.

Schwefel, H. P. (1994). On the Evolution of Evolutionary Computation. In Computational Intelligence: Imitating Life, (pp. 116-124). Academic Press.

Seeley, T. (1985). *Honeybee Ecology, A Study of Adaptation in Social Life*. Princeton, NJ: Princeton University Press. doi:10.1515/9781400857876

Shi, Y., & Eberhart, R. C. (1998). Parameter Selection in Particle Swarm Optimization, Evolutionary Programming VII, Springer. *Lecture Notes in Computer Science*, 1447, 591–600. doi:10.1007/BFb0040810

Srivastava, P. R. (2013). Swarm and Evolutionary Computation. Elsevier.

Srivastava, P. R., Baby, K., & Raghurama, G. (2009). An approach of optimal path generation using ant colony optimization. *Proceedings of the TENCON 2009 - 2009 IEEE Region 10 Conference*, 1–6. doi:10.1109/TENCON.2009.5396088

Storn, R., & Price, K. (1997). Differential Evolution – A Simple and Efficient Heuristic for Global Optimization Over Continuous Spaces. *Journal of Global Optimization*, 11(4), 341–359. doi:10.1023/A:1008202821328

Stutzle & Dorigo. (2003). *The ant colony optimization metaheuristic: algorithms, applications, and advances*. New York: Springer.

Tracey, N., Clark, J., Mander, K., & McDermid, J. (1998). An automated framework for structural test data generation. *Proceedings of the International Conference on Automated Software Engineering*, 285-288. doi:10.1109/ASE.1998.732680

Turing, A. M. (1949). Checking a large routine. In *Report of a Conference on High Speed Automatic Calculating Machines*, (pp. 67–69). Cambridge, UK: University Mathematical Laboratory.

Watkins, A. E. L. (1995) A Tool for the Automatic Generation of Test Data using Genetic Algorithms. *Proc. Software Quality Conf.*

Xanthakis, S., Ellis, C., Skourlas, C., Le Gall, A., Katsikas, S., & Karapoulios, K. (1992). Application of genetic algorithms to software testing. *5th International Conference on Software Engineering and its Applications*, 625-636.

Zurada, J., Marks, R., & Robinson, C. (Eds.). (1994). *Computational Intelligence: Imitating Life*. IEEE Press.

Chapter 15

Quantum–Inspired Computational Intelligence for Economic Emission Dispatch Problem

Fahad Parvez Mahdi
Universiti Teknologi Petronas, Malaysia

Vish Kallimani
Universiti Teknologi Petronas, Malaysia

Pandian Vasant
Universiti Teknologi Petronas, Malaysia

M. Abdullah-Al-Wadud
King Saud University, Saudi Arabia

Junzo Watada
Universiti Teknologi Petronas, Malaysia

ABSTRACT

Economic emission dispatch (EED) problems are one of the most crucial problems in power systems. Growing energy demand, limited reserves of fossil fuel and global warming make this topic into the center of discussion and research. In this chapter, we will discuss the use and scope of different quantum inspired computational intelligence (QCI) methods for solving EED problems. We will evaluate each previously used QCI methods for EED problem and discuss their superiority and credibility against other methods. We will also discuss the potentiality of using other quantum inspired CI methods like quantum bat algorithm (QBA), quantum cuckoo search (QCS), and quantum teaching and learning based optimization (QTLBO) technique for further development in this area.

INTRODUCTION

Electrical power system of almost all countries in the world mainly consists of thermal plants which use fossil fuel such as coal, oil and gas to produce electricity. The use of fossil fuels increases tremendously due to the rapid economic growth in the developing countries especially in China and India. At the same time, the capacity to deliver fossil fuels as per their growing demand are limited due to limited production capacity and lack of infrastructure such as pipelines, refineries and terminal capacities. In order to

DOI: 10.4018/978-1-5225-2128-0.ch015

build such infrastructure to support such increasing demand of fossil fuels could cost trillions of dollars (Birol, 2004). Moreover fossil fuels are always not easily accessible to all as fossil fuel reserves are concentrated in a small number of countries. Almost 85% of the world's total coal reserves are located in just eight countries (Dudely, 2015). Again, more than 65% world's total gas stock has been found in only four countries (Agency, 2015) and eight countries (six of them are OPEC members) have almost 80% of the world's total proved oil reserves (Dudely, 2015). Some of these countries may exercise their power to restrict supply or influence the supply of fossil fuels. On the other hand, with the increase of economic growth fossil fuels reserves are declining. According to a research conducted by S. Shafiee and E. Topal, coal will be the only fossil fuel remains after 2042 (Shafiee & Topal, 2009). Several other studies indicate that projected crude oil reserves will run out between 2050 and 2075 (Ivanhoe, 1995; Walsh, 2000). From these studies, it is very clear that fossil fuels will become distinct and too expensive in the near future, which will lead the electricity production to be much more expensive.

In addition, thermal plant is one of the main sources that releases polluted particulates and gases into the air such as sulfur dioxide (SO_2), carbon dioxide (CO_2), nitrogen dioxide (NO_2), ozone (O_3) etc. Burning coal can even cause to emit radioactive materials (McBride, Moore, Witherspoon, & Blanco, 1978) and toxic heavy materials like arsenic, mercury etc. Sulfur and nitrogen dioxide contribute to smog and acid rain, whereas large emission of carbon dioxide is contributing to the greenhouse effect which ultimately leads us to global warming. Global warming has far-reaching, long-lasting and, in many cases, devastating consequences on environment. As the temperature is rising due to global warming, lower areas of the world will soon be flooded by sea water.

Therefore, it is important to employ a model that optimizes both the generation/fuel cost as well as the cost associated with the control of emissions from thermal unit operation and other constraints. Both the objectives cannot be optimized simultaneously and hence there exist a conflict between them. This conflicting behavior gives rise to a type of optimization called multi-objective optimization. The economic emission dispatching (EED) option is an attractive option (Kumar, Bavisetti, & Kiran, 2012), where the objective is to minimize fuel cost and polluted emission while satisfying all constraints including transmission loss, load balance, upper and lower generation of thermal unit, ramp rate limit, prohibited zone of thermal unit etc. Multiobjective optimization with two or more objective functions that are usually noncommensurable and conflicting in nature often gives rise to a set of optimal solutions rather than a single optimal solution. It is because that none of the solution can be considered to be better than any other solutions with respect to the objective functions. All these optimal solutions are known as Pareto-optimal solutions. Fuzzy set theory (Vasant, 2006) often utilized to get the best compromised solution from obtained Pareto-optimal set of nondominated solutions (Abido, 2003).

Computational Intelligence (CI)

Being a relatively new field for the researchers, Computational Intelligence (CI) has no such fixed accepted definition (Xing & Gao, 2014). However, researchers have tried to define CI through their own understanding about it. Roughly, CI can be said to be a heterogeneous field of computer science that can be defined as any biologically, naturally, linguistically or any other sciences like Physics, chemistry, mathematics etc. motivated computational paradigms that include, but not limited to, artificial neural network (NN), connectionist machine, fuzzy system (FS), evolutionary computation (EC), autonomous mental development, and hybrid Intelligent System (IS) in which these paradigms are contained (Duch, 2007; Manju & Nigam, 2014; Xing & Gao, 2014). Genetic algorithm, particle swarm optimization, ant colony, harmony search, gravitational search, cuckoo search, artificial bee colony etc. and their hybridization versions are some of the examples of CI methods.

Advantages and Applications of CI

CI methods are gradually replacing classical Artificial Intelligence (AI) approaches for their broad applicability, robustness to dynamic environments and self-optimization capability which established its role as an optimization and design tool in various fields such as in emerging energy technologies (Senvar, Turanoglu, & Kahraman, 2013), prognostic and health management (Bonissone, Hu, & Subbu, 2009), automated insurance underwriting (Bonisone, Subbu, & Aggour, 2002), interpretation of medical images (Tadeusiewicz, 2008), medical diagnosis (Steimann & Adlassnig, 1998), plug-in hybrid electrical vehicle (PHEV) charging stations (Rahman, Vasant, Singh, & Abdullah-Al-Wadud, 2015), supply chain management (Che, 2010) etc. On the other hand, AI based approaches face severe challenges when dealing with multi-object nature of design problems as these are purely rule based approach and when taking an action which involves a number of parameters to decide upon in combination (Manju & Nigam, 2014). Use of synergistic combinations of CI methods are proved efficient in multi-object multi parameter nature of design problems as it allows combining the strength of several CI methods by letting each method to take care of a certain issue constituting the complexity of the problem (Bittermann, 2010).

Quantum Computational Intelligence (QCI)

QCI is the extension of CI into the domain of quantum computing (QC). Quantum computation is a computation based upon the time evolution of a physical system, characterized by certain principles of Quantum Mechanics (QM) and very much probabilistic in nature. Two important and powerful ideas of quantum computation are quantum parallelism and entanglement (Ventura & Martinez, 1998). Quantum parallelism is referred to the fact that a quantum system exists as a superposition of many states at once, and therefore computation involving the system is simultaneously applied to all states represented in the quantum system. Entanglement is the non-classical correlations that can exist between different quantum systems through which the systems may be said to communicate (Ventura, 1999). Quantum genetic algorithm, quantum particle swarm optimization, quantum evolutionary algorithm etc. are some of the known QCI methods.

Advantages of QCI Over Other Methods

Quantum computation is very counterintuitive and even unsettling from a physical standpoint but from a computational standpoint it can predict results with high level of accuracy and has provided us with perhaps the most accurate physical theory ever. The advantage of quantum inspired algorithm is that it can exploit massive quantum parallelism which can be expressed as the principle of superposition. This phenomenon is combined with existing methods of CI, thus instead of a single state, a superposition of states will be used, resulting all these states compute in parallel. As a result it will increase the speed of computation by many orders of magnitude (K.-H. Han & Kim, 2002; Hogg & Portnov, 2000). For this reason Quantum Inspired CI has been shown used in solving a wide range of problems and many efficient strategies have been proposed as improvement (Manju & Nigam, 2014).

Some QCI Methods and Their Applications

Kak first proposed the concept of quantum neural computing (QNC) in 1995 (Kak, 1995). Later T. Menneer and A. Narayanan developed quantum inspired neural network (QNN) where they introduced some basic concepts inspired by quantum theory for use in neural network training (Narayanan & Menneer, 2000). Finally, Gupta et al. presented QNN as a potential way to build scalable parallel computers with the help of quantum computing under very tight constraints (Gupta & Zia, 2001). QNN successfully used in medical application (Gandhi, Prasad, Coyle, Behera, & McGinnity, 2014; Karayiannis et al., 2006), image compression (Kouda, Matsui, & Nishimura, 2002), fault diagnosis in integrated circuits (Zhu, Chen, & Yang, 2005) etc. Researchers begin to introduce quantum computing phenomenon of performing efficient parallel computations into the classical evolutionary methods to overcome their shortcomings thus introducing quantum inspired evolutionary methods (K.-H. Han & Kim, 2002). This technique has proved very resource consuming even a classical computer. Quantum inspired evolutionary algorithms have been used in solving unit commitment problem (Lau, Chung, Wong, Chung, & Ho, 2009), knapsack problem (Zhang, Gheorghe, & Wu, 2008), economic dispatch (Neto, Bernert, & Coelho, 2011), for determining the optimal operating strategy, cost optimization and reducing emissions of a micro-grid etc.(Hosseini, 2014).Other QCI methods like quantum inspired genetic algorithm and quantum inspired particle swarm optimization will be discussed later into this chapter.

BACKGROUND

In electrical power generation system, the goal of economic dispatch (Wood & Wollenberg, 2012) is to find an optimal combination of power generation in order to minimize the total production cost satisfying all other constraints like transmission loss, load demand, generation limit in each generating unit, generator ramp rate limit etc. On the other hand, emission dispatch deals with the minimization of total emission of hazardous gas and particulates in the generation plant. Thus economic emission dispatch (EED) problems of an electrical power generation system can be formulated as an optimization problem in which two conflicting parameters i.e. fuel cost and emission of hazardous gases and particulates are minimized simultaneously to ensure optimal output of generated power whilst satisfying all other equal and unequal constraint.

Problem Formulation

The general simplified fuel cost function or the object function can be mathematically formulated as (Kothari, 2012),

$$F(P) = \sum_{i=1}^{n} a_i P_i^2 + b_i P_i + c_i \tag{1}$$

where,

$F\left(P_{gi}\right) =$ Total fuel cost, (in \$/hr)

$P_{gi} =$ Real Power Output of the ith generating unit

$a_i, b_i, c_i =$ Cost coefficients of the ith generating unit

The emission function which can also be defined by a quadratic function (Kothari, 2012) can be formulated as,

$$E(P) = \sum_{i=1}^{n} d_i P_i^2 + e_i P_i + f_i \tag{2}$$

where,

$E\left(P_{gi}\right) =$ Emission Function (in Kg/hr)

$d_i, \ e_i, \ f_i =$ Emission coefficients of ith generating unit

Researchers have also used cubic function to define and formulate economic and emission dispatch problem (Krishnamurthy & Tzoneva, 2012). Polynomial function effectively reduces the nonlinearity and thus gives actual response of power generating unit. However, to limit the scope of this book chapter the authors only focus on quadratic function which is the most used fitness function to solve EED problems.

Fuel cost and emission of hazardous gases and particulates are two conflicting objectives to be achieved. When fuel cost decreases, emission increases and decrease of emission will increase the fuel cost. Thus sometimes both objectives are converted into a single objective function (Krishnamurthy & Tzoneva, 2012) with the help of a penalty factor. The combined economic emission dispatch problem can then be formulated as,

$$OF = F_T = \sum_{i=1}^{n} F(P_{gi}) + \sum_{i=1}^{n} h_{i,\max/\max} E(P_{gi}) \tag{3}$$

where,

Penalty factor, $h_i = \sum_{i=1}^{n} \dfrac{F(P_{i,\max})}{E(P_{i,\max})}$

$$\sum_{i=1}^{n} F(P_{i,\max}) = \sum_{i=1}^{n} a_i P_{i,\max}^2 + b_i P_{i,\max} + c_i \tag{4}$$

$$\sum_{i=1}^{n} E(P_{gi,\max}) = \sum_{i=1}^{n} d_i P_{gi,\max}^2 + e_i P_{gi,\max} + f_i \tag{5}$$

Economic emission dispatch problems are often subjected to constraints. Some of the most common constraints in electrical power generation systems are given as follows,

1. **Equality/Power Balance Constraint:** Total generated power must be able to meet total system demand considering total system loss. It can be formulated as,

$$\sum_{i=0}^{N} P_{gi} = P_{SD} + P_L \tag{6}$$

where,

N = Total number of generation unit.
P_{SD} = Total system load demand.
P_L = Total transmission loss.

2. **Inequality/Generation Limit Constraint:** There will be some upper as well as lower limit for each generation unit. Thus, the power generation of each generation unit must be within these limits. It can be formulated as,

$$(P_{gi})_{\min} < P_{gi} < (P_{gi})_{\max} \tag{7}$$

where,

$(P_{gi})_{max}$ = Maximum power output by i^{th} generating unit.
$(P_{gi})_{min}$ = Minimum power output by i^{th} generating unit.

3. **Generator Ramp Rate Limit:** Generating units are restricted to operate in certain operating zone due to their ramp rate limits and thus operate in two adjacent specific operation zones. To formulate EED accurately, generator ramp rate limit must be taken into account. The power output of each generating unit then can be formulated as,

$$Max(P_i^{\min}, P_i^{t-1} - DR_i) \le P_i^t \le Min(P_i^{\max}, P_i^{t-1} + UR_i) \tag{8}$$

where P_{gi}^{t-1} is active power generation of the ith unit at the $(t\text{-}1)^{th}$ hour, P_{gi}^{t} is real power output of the ith generating unit at the tth hour, DR_i and UR_i are down rate and up rate limits of the ith unit respectively.

Related Works on Economic Dispatch

Classical mathematical programming based methods like lambda iterative method (Zhan, Wu, Guo, & Zhou, 2014), Lagrange multiplier (Thang & Asme, 2012), Lagrangian relaxation (Hindi & Ab Ghani, 1991), interior point methods (Balbo, Souza, Baptista, & Nepomuceno, 2012), Bender's decomposition algorithm (Abdolmohammadi & Kazemi, 2013), gradient method (C.-L. Chen & Wang, 1993), linear programming (Farag, Al-Baiyat, & Cheng, 1995; Somuah & Khunaizi, 1990), nonlinear programming (X. Han, Gooi, & Kirschen, 2001), dynamic programming (Liang & Glover, 1992) etc. had been used to solve economic dispatch problem for their certain advantages like availability to large-scale problems, mathematically proven optimality, fast computational speed (in some algorithms), no problem specific parameters to define etc. (Bansal, 2005). However, some of these conventional methods require the unit input-output curves of generators. But, these curves do not increase monotonically due to operating zones of the approaches. Thus, the conventional dispatch algorithms cannot be directly used to optimize such nonlinear cost function. To overcome these limitations, conventional algorithms often hybridized with other (especially intelligent) algorithms like Hopfield neural network (Dieu & Ongsakul, 2011), differential evolution (Duvvuru & Swarup, 2011) etc. and let these handle the part that cannot be handled efficiently by them (conventional algorithms). In the conventional economic dispatch problem, the cost function for each generator approximately represented by a single quadratic function (Ling, Lam, Leung, & Lee, 2003). But, the characteristics of generating units are highly nonlinear inherently, because of different constraints in the power system. Again, polynomial function can handle nonlinearities in the system (as discussed earlier) for that reason some researchers also used cubic function to solve economic dispatch problem (Adhinarayanan & Sydulu, 2006; Truong, Vasant, Balbir Singh, & Vo, 2015). However, most of the researchers ignored higher order polynomial to avoid excessive complexities and higher computational time. Intelligent and stochastic algorithms like artificial neural networks (ANN) (Yalcinoz & Short, 1998), evolutionary programming (EP) (Sinha, Chakrabarti, & Chattopadhyay, 2003), biogeography based optimization (BBO) (P. Roy, Ghoshal, & Thakur, 2009), nature-inspired meta-heuristic algorithms like genetic algorithm (GA) (Ling et al., 2003), tabu search (TS) (Naama, Bouzeboudja, & Allali, 2013), ant colony optimization (ACO) (Pothiya, Ngamroo, & Kongprawechnon, 2010), particle swarm optimization (PSO) and it's variants (Chaturvedi, Pandit, & Srivastava, 2008; J.-B. Park, Jeong, Shin, & Lee, 2010; J. B. Park, Lee, Shin, & Lee, 2005; Selvakumar & Thanushkodi, 2007), cuckoo search (M. Basu & Chowdhury, 2013), bat algorithm (BA) (Gherbi, Bouzeboudja, & Lakdja, 2014), etc. successfully used for solving economic dispatch problems. ANNs have self-adapting capabilities that make them suitable against nonlinearities, uncertainties and parameter varieties which are common in economic emission dispatch problems. One of the advantages of stochastic optimization methods is that it can solve economic dispatch problem without any or fewer restrictions on the shape of the cost function curves for their ability to seek the global optimal solution. In the meantime, intelligent techniques suffer from the drawbacks of long computation time (in some algorithms) and large number of arbitrary or problem-specific parameters (Xia & Elaiw, 2010).

Related Works on Economic Emission Dispatch Problem

Like economic dispatch problem, scholars previously focused on classical conventional methods like Lagrangian relaxation (Shalini & Lakshmi, 2014), Newton Raphson method (S.-D. Chen & Chen, 2003), Quadratic programming (Ji-Yuan & Lan, 1998), linear programming (El-Keib & Ding, 1994) etc. to solve economic emission dispatch problem. Conventional techniques have certain advantages over other methods like they don't have any problem specific parameters, their optimality are mathematically proven and some of them are computationally fast etc. (Papageorgiou & Fraga, 2007). These methods as usual suffer from non-satisfactory results and take large computational time for nonlinear and nonconvex complex problems. Furthermore, in conventional techniques, the economic emission dispatch problem was tackled considering only one loading condition for a given system (Krishnan & Krishnan, 2011). The impact of different loading conditions on the shape of Pareto optimal set was not addressed in the most of the traditional methods.

In second stage, researchers focused on stand-alone intelligent methods to solve the EED problems and finally most of the researchers are now focusing on hybrid intelligent techniques to tackle economic emission dispatch problems. In the early stages of using intelligent techniques to tackle EED problems, fuzzy logic controlled genetic algorithm has been exploited by Song et al. to solve EED problem and compared with conventional GA and Newton-Raphson method to validate its performance (Song, Wang, Wang, & Johns, 1997). Basu came up with particle swarm optimization based goal-attainment method to solve EED problem considering the ramp rate limit of the generating units (M Basu, 2006) where he used goal-attainment method to convert this multiobjective problem into a single objective problem then solved the problem with the help of PSO. But, PSO technique sometimes prematurely converges to local optima. To counter this problem, different improved and modified versions of PSO later used in solving EED problems (Bahmani-Firouzi, Farjah, & Azizipanah-Abarghooee, 2013; Jadoun, Gupta, Niazi, & Swamkar, 2015; Mandal, Mandal, Bhattacharya, & Chakraborty, 2015). New nature inspired metaheuristic Cuckoo Search (CS) algorithm had been used recently to solve EED in 3-unit and 6-unit thermal system (Thao & Thang, 2014). Obtained result showed that CS gives better result than TS and non-dominated sorting genetic algorithm (NSGA-II) and similar performance as BBO in the first system, whereas it's emission cost is higher than TS and same as in BBO and NSGA-II. However, in both systems CS takes less time to reach the convergence point. Almost in the same time, fuzzy set theory integrated CS algorithm was exploited to solve EED problems (Chandrasekaran, Simon, & Padhy, 2014). This method had been tested in 6-unit test system, IEEE standard 24 and 118 bus system which validated its effectiveness on this complex problem. Apart from these methods, some new intelligent methods like bacterial foraging (Hota, Barisal, & Chakrabarti, 2010), differential evolution (Abou El Ela, Abido, & Spea, 2010), firefly algorithm (Apostolopoulos & Vlachos, 2011), teaching and learning based optimization (Niknam, Golestaneh, & Sadeghi, 2012), bat algorithm (BA) (Ramesh, Chandra Jagan Mohan, & Veera Reddy, 2013) etc. have been exploited to reduce fuel and emission cost in electrical power generation systems.

From the recent literature on solving EED problems, the authors can assume that researchers are now more interested to use hybrid algorithms instead of stand-alone algorithms. An improved version of PSO that can represent the control variables in natural way was introduced with GA to improve the overall performance against EED problems (Roselyn, Devaraj, & Dash, 2011). Combinational approach of biogeography based optimization and powerful differential evolution algorithm presented in (Bhattacharya & Chattopadhyay, 2011). This hybrid algorithm searches for global optimum in two different steps, migration and mutation. Several tests with different number of units confirmed that this proposed method performed better than other methods like NSGA-II, fuzzy logic controlled GA (FCGA), PSO, BBO and Newton-Raphson. regarding solution quality and computational efficiency A novel hybrid PSO with gravitational search algorithm was proposed to solve EED problem considering various practical constraints by Jiang et al. where the authors incorporated the social element of PSO with the motion element of GSA (Jiang, Ji, & Shen, 2014). The result of proposed hybrid method was compared with PSO and GSA separately which showed its superior performance over these methods when used separately. Dieu and Ongsakul proposed a combination of Lagrangian function and continuous Hopfield neural network which gave better global solution and less convergence time (Dieu & Ongsakul, 2010). This method can be considered as a good example of a conventional and intelligent technique hybridization. Hybrid optimization techniques provide better solution for EED problems especially in the cases where the processes are too complex to be analyzed by conventional or stand-alone techniques (Krishnan & Krishnan, 2011).

LITERATURE REVIEW

Quantum Genetic Algorithm (QGA)

Genetic algorithm (GA) is a classical nature inspired algorithm that has been used to solve the combinational or nonlinear optimization problem with non-differential or complicated constraint condition. Figure 1 shows the complete process of GA. Although, GA has been used to solve EED problem for its parallel computing character and the ability of adaptive search (Koridak & Rahli, 2010), its more iterative approach with slow convergence speed easily makes it fall into local optimum. A. Narayanan and M. Moore proposed QGA which introduced the quantum theory into GA (Narayanan & Moore, 1996). Due to its stronger search capability and more efficient and simple characteristics, QGA has been proven to be a favorable technique to tackle economic emission dispatch problems of power generation systems (G.-C. Liao, 2012).

Gwo-Ching Liao, in his developed algorithm (G. C. Liao, 2010), exploited the global optimization ability of genetic algorithms with local searching capability based quantum probability model, the sensitive dependence of chaotic algorithms to initial value and the traverse of the search space to establish a new improved quantum evolution algorithm known as Chaotic QGA (CQGA). More about chaotic systems and their recent implication can be found in (Köse & Arslan, 2013). In CQGA method, quantum bit was adopted for problem coding. One of the features of this algorithm was the quantum choromosome was generated using quantum encoding and it carries information about multiple states which ultimately helped to produce a richer population than the simplistic genetic method. The population possessed inherent diversity with this method, thus it wasn't prone to fall into the local optimal trap during the optimization process. Simulated results showed that CQGA outperformed other well-known methods like QGA, evolutionary programming (EP), GA and dynamic programming (DP) in terms of average convergence of power generation cost.

Wenxia Liu, Yuying Zhang, Bo Zeng, Shuya Niu, Jianhua Zhang, and Yong Xiao (Liu et al., 2014) proposed a hybrid heuristic algorithm for a large-scale nonlinear and non-convex electrical power system. This algorithm utilizes the complementary of multiple techniques including the variable step size opti-

Figure 1. Flow chart of a genetic algorithm (Laboudi & Chikhi, 2012)

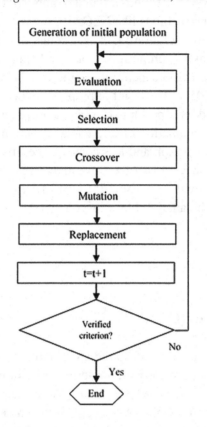

mization, the rotation mutational angle fuzzy control, and the quantum genetic algorithm. This algorithm follows five steps before it gives final optimal output. Steps of this proposed algorithm is given as follows:

Step 1: Population initialization with variable step size chaos algorithm.
Step 2: Encoding and individual measurements to the generator power output where chaotic QGA and EA are probability algorithms.
Step 3: Evaluation of individual targets separately in the obtained solution set.
Step 4: Update the solution set by using suitable quantum rotating gate.
Step 5: Perturbation in the population to escape it from local optima.

Figure 2 shows the steps of VSS_QGA in a flowchart. It shows better performance with superior accuracy and efficiency when comparing with GA, EP approach, QGA and chaotic quantum genetic algorithm (CQGA). One of the reasons of its faster convergence is unlike the searching strategies of GA, EP, and QGA this algorithm obtain the optimal solutions by improving chaos motion ergodicity and local search strategy, which is more suitable and efficient for solving the scheduling optimization problem.

A. A. Mousa and E. E. Elattar (Mousa & Elattar, 2014) presented a hybrid multi-objective quantum genetic algorithm (HM QGA) for solving EED optimization problem where EED problems were formulated as a nonlinear constrained multi-objective optimization problem with both equality and inequality constraints. This technique has been applied successfully to solve EED problems considering two

Figure 2. Flow chart of the variable step-size chaotic fuzzy QGA (VSS_QGA) (Liu et al., 2014)

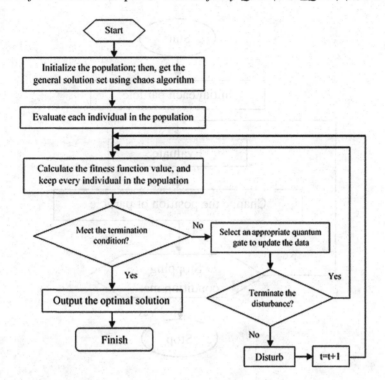

objectives simultaneously where there is no limitation in handling more than two objectives. Instead of a single solution it gives multiple Pareto-optimal solutions in a single simulation run which is useful in giving a reasonable freedom in choosing operating point from the available finite alternative. Overall it provides a sound optimal power flow by simultaneously considering conflicting multi-objective functions.

Quantum Particle Swarm Optimization (QPSO)

Particle swarm optimization (PSO) was first introduced by Kennedy in 1995 (Kennedy & Eberhart, 1995) and later explained more deeply in 1999 (Shi & Eberhart, 1999) by Y. Shi and Eberhart. PSO is inspired by the social behavior of animals such as bird flocking and fish schooling. It gained a lot of attention in various optimal control system applications for its faster convergence, reduced memory requirement, lower computational complexity and easier implementation as compared to other evolutionary algorithms. Many improvements have been achieved in PSO since its introduction in 1995 (Li, Ngambusabongsopa, Mohammed, & Eustache, 2011; Shi & Eberhart, 1998). Inspired by quantum mechanics, Sun et al. proposed QPSO which is a novel variant of the PSO and outperforms the PSO in global search ability (Cai et al., 2008; Sun, Feng, & Xu, 2004). QPSO algorithm has been applied to the power system optimization such as economic load dispatch with valve-point effects (Nie, Xu, & Yue, 2010), engineering design problem (Coelho, 2010) etc.

Songfeng Lu, Chengfu Sun, Zhengding Lu (Lu, Sun, & Lu, 2010) developed an algorithm for hydrothermal power system, where hydrothermal scheduling was formulated as a bi-objective problem. This method combines QPSO algorithm with differential mutation operation to enhance the global search

Figure 3. Flow chart of PSO (S. Yang, Wang, & Jiao, 2004)

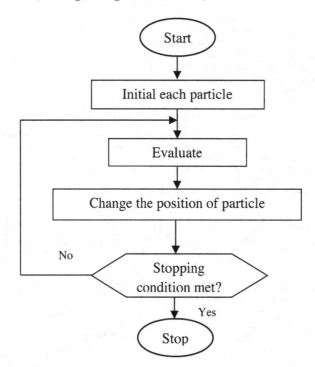

ability. Heuristic strategies were exploited to handle the equality constraints and at the same time a feasibility-based selection technique was also employed to meet the reservoir storage volumes constraints. The simulation results of the case studies revealed that this method had superior features, such as high quality solutions and good convergence properties than the other tested optimization methods like Differential Evolution (DE) or PSO.

PROPOSED METHODS

The use of quantum computational intelligence (QCI) for solving economic emission dispatch (EED) problems is still in its primary stage. The QCI methods so far used to handle EED problems proved successful compared to other methods. In future, different QCI methods like quantum cuckoo search (QCS), quantum bat algorithm (QBA) and quantum teaching and learning based optimization (QTLBO) algorithm etc. should be explored to solve EED problems in power system.

Quantum Cuckoo Search Algorithm (QCSA)

The cuckoo search (CS) method is one of the most recent developed meta-heuristic algorithms (X.-S. Yang & Deb, 2014; X. S. Yang & Suash, 2009) that utilizes the breeding behavior of cuckoos, where each individual searches the most suitable nest to lay an egg (compromise solution) in order to maximize the egg's survival rate and achieve the best habitat society (Chandrasekaran et al., 2014). It gives better solution quality, computational efficiency and robustness than many other classical or nature inspired algorithm like genetic algorithm, PSO etc. (X.-S. Yang & Deb, 2014). QCS algorithm exploits the quantum computing principles like qubit representation, quantum mutation and measure operation in the core of the CS algorithm as explained in Figure 4 (Djelloul, Layeb, & Chikhi, 2015). QCS contains three essential modules to operate. Quantum representation of cuckoo bird is contained in the first module. Quantum representation of cuckoo bird allows QCS to represent the superposition of all potential solutions for a given problem. Fitness function and selection operator are contained in the next module. The function of selection operator is quite similar to the elitism strategy of GA where some portion of the fittest chromosome are kept unchanged into the next generation to ensure the algorithm does not waste time on rediscovering previously discarded past solutions. The last module contains the most important part of the algorithm and it is the main quantum cuckoo dynamics (QCD). Four main operations, inspired by cuckoo search and quantum computing, are done in quantum cuckoo dynamics. They are measurement, mutation, interference and Lévy flight operations. QCS algorithm exploits these operations to evolve the entire swarm through generations (Djelloul et al., 2015). The authors expect that this powerful mechanism of proposed QCS will be very efficient to solve EED problems.

Figure 4. Proposed flowchart of quantum cuckoo search algorithm for economic emission dispatch problems (Layeb, 2011)

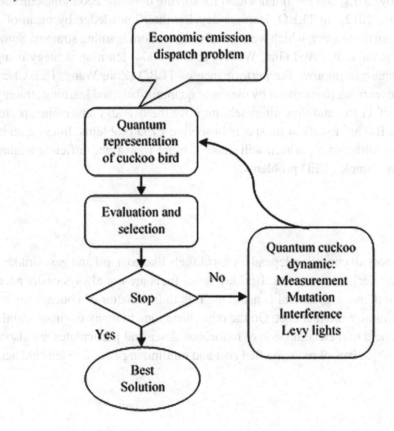

Quantum Bat Algorithm (QBA)

Bat algorithm (BA) was developed by Xin-She Yang that mimics some of the characteristics of micro bats (X.-S. Yang, 2010). It is proved to be easy to implement and has superior features like quality of solution, stable convergence characteristics and superior computational efficiency which is suitable for multiobjective problem (X.-S. Yang, 2011). Bat algorithm has already been successfully implemented to solve EED problems. Comparison with different versions of GAs and artificial bee colony (ABC) reflects its superiority over these methods (Ramesh et al., 2013). The authors believe that integration of the efficient mechanism of quantum computing will boost its search ability and convergence which will be very suitable for complex multiobjective problems like EED problem.

Quantum Teaching and Learning Based Optimization (QTLBO)

Teaching and learning based optimization (TLBO) is an efficient algorithm proposed by Rao et al. (Rao, Savsani, & Vakharia, 2011) and based on teaching-learning phenomena. This algorithm has been proved effective in terms of the quality, speed, and stability of the final solutions when comparing with other state of the arts algorithms (Satapathy, Naik, & Parvathi, 2013). Recently, TLBO algorithm has been successfully applied in different areas of power system such as Hydro-thermal Scheduling (HTS) (P. K. Roy, 2013), optimal capacitor placement (Sultana & Roy, 2014), load frequency control (LFC) (A. Roy, Dutta, & Roy, 2015), transient stability constrained optimal power flow (TSC-OPF) (Mukherjee, Paul, & Roy, 2015), finding optimal location in thyristor controlled series compensator (TCSC) (Mukhopadhyay, Dutta, & Roy, 2015) and last but not least for solving dynamic economic emission dispatch problems (Niknam et al., 2012). In TLBO, learners develop their knowledge by mean of interaction between learners and from the teacher, which we can define as random learning strategy. Some researchers propose to exploit quantum behaved (Jun, Wenbo, & Bin, 2004) learning strategy using a certain probability in learner phase to improve the performance of TLBO (Zou, Wang, Hei, Chen, & Yang, 2014). The probabilistic learning phenomena by means of quantum-behaved learning strategy enhances the exploitative nature of TLBO and thus ultimately improve the overall convergence performance of the algorithm. Thus, TLBO has excellent prospects in solving EED problems. Integration of quantum computing phenomenon with this algorithm will make it more robust and efficient against different nonlinear multiobjective complex EED problems.

DISCUSSION

Power generation of almost all countries depend on fossil fuels like coal, oil and gas. Unlike coal, fossil fuels like oil and gas has declining reserves. Besides, fossil fuels are not always easily accessible due to different infrastructural and geopolitical constraints. It is thus a matter of concern for every power generation system to minimize the fuel cost. On the other hand, due to many environmental issues like global warming, smog, acid rain etc. emission of hazardous gases and particulates are also a matter of concern. But these two objectives of reducing fuel cost and minimizing emission are conflicting to each other. Reduction of fuel cost may cause the emission problem and vice versa. Thus, there rises the need of multi-objective optimization. Many classical, intelligent and hybrid methods have been proposed to achieve both objectives simultaneously. Traditional methods have suffered against the growing nonlinearities of economic emission dispatch (EED) problems; where different intelligent methods suffer from long computational time degrade performance. Quantum based advanced computational intelligence methods show better optimization result than their predecessor. The parallel computing phenomenon of quantum computing reduces computational time to reach optimization point and makes it computationally efficient. In the later part of this chapter, we have proposed quantum inspired cuckoo search (CS), bat algorithm (BA) and teaching and learning based optimization (TLBO) methods for solving EED problems. Previously CS, BA and TLBO methods have successfully been implemented for solving EED problems and thus these methods are very prospectus with the integration of quantum computing phenomenon.

CONCLUSION

In this chapter, authors have shown why it is necessary to be concerned about the fuel cost by describing fossil fuels complex accessibility and declining reserves problem. Authors have also discussed briefly about the necessity of controlling emission of polluted particulates and gases and thus undermining the need of combined economic and emission dispatching. Later, some short discussions are added on computational intelligence (CI), quantum computational intelligence and some of their advantages, and applications. After discussing and comparing a number of heuristic and meta-heuristic methods and optimization algorithms, it can be said that, in handling multiobjective nonlinear and non-convex complex problems like economic emission dispatch problems, where objectives are conflicting with many other equal and inequality constraints, quantum inspired computational intelligence methods are so far very successful. Its quantum computing phenomenon makes it computationally very efficient and robust than the other conventional algorithms. Improved metaheuristic algorithms like artificial bee colony, firefly, cuckoo search, biogeography based optimization etc. also showed good performance in solving economic and emission problem. For further development of electrical power generation system, advanced methods like quantum cuckoo search, quantum bat and quantum teaching and learning based optimization algorithms have been proposed and discussed in this chapter.

ACKNOWLEDGMENT

The authors would like to thank Universiti Teknologi PETRONAS (www.utp.edu.my) for supporting the research under Graduate Assistance Scheme. This research project is financially sponsored by Fundamental Research Grant Scheme (FRGS) of Ministry of Education (MOE) Malaysia (Grant: 0153AB-K45) and the Centre of Graduate study with the support of the Department of Fundamental & Applied Sciences, Universiti Teknologi PETRONAS.

REFERENCES

Abdolmohammadi, H. R., & Kazemi, A. (2013). A benders decomposition approach for a combined heat and power economic dispatch. *Energy Conversion and Management, 71*, 21–31. doi:10.1016/j.enconman.2013.03.013

Abido, M. (2003). Environmental/economic power dispatch using multiobjective evolutionary algorithms. *IEEE Transactions on Power Systems, 18*(4), 1529–1537. doi:10.1109/TPWRS.2003.818693

Abou El Ela, A. A., Abido, M. A., & Spea, S. R. (2010). Differential evolution algorithm for emission constrained economic power dispatch problem. *Electric Power Systems Research, 80*(10), 1286–1292. doi:10.1016/j.epsr.2010.04.011

Adhinarayanan, T., & Sydulu, M. (2006). *Particle swarm optimisation for economic dispatch with cubic fuel cost function*. Paper presented at the TENCON 2006. 2006 IEEE Region 10 Conference. doi:10.1109/TENCON.2006.344059

Agency, C. I. (2015). Comparison: Natural Gas - Proved Reserves. *The World Factbook*. Retrieved from https://www.cia.gov/library/publications/the-world-factbook/rankorder/2253rank.html

Apostolopoulos, T., & Vlachos, A. (2011). Application of the firefly algorithm for solving the economic emissions load dispatch problem. *International Journal of Combinatorics, 23*.

Bahmani-Firouzi, B., Farjah, E., & Azizipanah-Abarghooee, R. (2013). An efficient scenario-based and fuzzy self-adaptive learning particle swarm optimization approach for dynamic economic emission dispatch considering load and wind power uncertainties. *Energy, 50*, 232–244. doi:10.1016/j.energy.2012.11.017

Balbo, A. R., Souza, M. A. D., Baptista, E. C., & Nepomuceno, L. (2012). Predictor-Corrector Primal-Dual Interior Point Method for Solving Economic Dispatch Problems: A Postoptimization Analysis. *Mathematical Problems in Engineering, 26*. doi:10.1155/2012/376546

Bansal, R. (2005). Optimization methods for electric power systems: An overview. *International Journal of Emerging Electric Power Systems, 2*(1). doi:10.2202/1553-779X.1021

Basu, M. (2006). Particle swarm optimization based goal-attainment method for dynamic economic emission dispatch. *Electric Power Components and Systems, 34*(9), 1015–1025. doi:10.1080/15325000600596759

Basu, M., & Chowdhury, A. (2013). Cuckoo search algorithm for economic dispatch. *Energy, 60*, 99–108. doi:10.1016/j.energy.2013.07.011

Bhattacharya, A., & Chattopadhyay, P. K. (2011). Solving economic emission load dispatch problems using hybrid differential evolution. *Applied Soft Computing, 11*(2), 2526–2537. doi:10.1016/j.asoc.2010.09.008

Birol, F. (2004). *World Energy Outlook* (S. Sullivan, Ed.). International Energy Agency.

Bittermann, M. (2010). Artificial Intelligence (AI) versus Computational Intelligence (CI) for treatment of complexity in design. *Design Computing and Cognition (DCC10)*.

Bonisone, P., Subbu, R., & Aggour, K. S. (2002). Evolutionary optimization of fuzzy decision systems for automated insurance underwriting. *Paper presented at the Fuzzy Systems, 2002. FUZZ-IEEE'02. Proceedings of the 2002 IEEE International Conference on.* doi:10.1109/FUZZ.2002.1006641

Bonissone, P., Hu, X., & Subbu, R. (2009). A systematic PHM approach for anomaly resolution: A hybrid neural fuzzy system for model construction. *Proc. PHM 2009.*

Cai, Y., Sun, J., Wang, J., Ding, Y., Tian, N., Liao, X., & Xu, W. (2008). Optimizing the codon usage of synthetic gene with QPSO algorithm. *Journal of Theoretical Biology, 254*(1), 123–127. doi:10.1016/j.jtbi.2008.05.010 PMID:18579159

Chandrasekaran, K., Simon, S. P., & Padhy, N. P. (2014). Cuckoo Search Algorithm for Emission Reliable Economic Multi-objective Dispatch Problem. *Journal of the Institution of Electronics and Telecommunication Engineers, 60*(2), 128–138. doi:10.1080/03772063.2014.901592

Chaturvedi, K. T., Pandit, M., & Srivastava, L. (2008). Self-organizing hierarchical particle swarm optimization for nonconvex economic dispatch. *IEEE Transactions on Power Systems, 23*(3), 1079–1087. doi:10.1109/TPWRS.2008.926455

Che, Z.-H. (2010). Using fuzzy analytic hierarchy process and particle swarm optimisation for balanced and defective supply chain problems considering WEEE/RoHS directives. *International Journal of Production Research, 48*(11), 3355–3381. doi:10.1080/00207540802702080

Chen, C.-L., & Wang, S.-C. (1993). Branch-and-bound scheduling for thermal generating units. *Energy Conversion. IEEE Transactions on, 8*(2), 184–189.

Chen, S.-D., & Chen, J.-F. (2003). A direct Newton–Raphson economic emission dispatch. *International Journal of Electrical Power & Energy Systems, 25*(5), 411–417. doi:10.1016/S0142-0615(02)00075-3

Coelho, L. D. (2010). Gaussian quantum-behaved particle swarm optimization approaches for constrained engineering design problems. *Expert Systems with Applications, 37*(2), 1676–1683. doi:10.1016/j.eswa.2009.06.044

Dieu, V. N., & Ongsakul, W. (2010). Economic dispatch with emission and transmission constraints by augmented Lagrange Hopfield network. *Transaction in Power System Optimization, 1.*

Dieu, V. N., & Ongsakul, W. (2011). Hopfield Lagrange Network for Economic Load Dispatch. *Innovation in Power, Control, and Optimization: Emerging Energy Technologies: Emerging Energy Technologies, 57.*

Djelloul, H., Layeb, A., & Chikhi, S. (2015). Quantum inspired cuckoo search algorithm for graph colouring problem. *International Journal of Bio-inspired Computation, 7*(3), 183–194. doi:10.1504/IJBIC.2015.069554

Duch, W. (2007). *What is Computational Intelligence and where is it going? In Challenges for computational intelligence* (pp. 1–13). Springer.

Dudely, B. (2015). BP Statistical Review of World Energy (64th ed.). BP.

Duvvuru, N., & Swarup, K. S. (2011). A Hybrid Interior Point Assisted Differential Evolution Algorithm for Economic Dispatch. *IEEE Transactions on Power Systems*, *26*(2), 541–549. doi:10.1109/TPWRS.2010.2053224

El-Keib, A., & Ding, H. (1994). Environmentally constrained economic dispatch using linear programming. *Electric Power Systems Research*, *29*(3), 155–159. doi:10.1016/0378-7796(94)90010-8

Farag, A., Al-Baiyat, S., & Cheng, T. (1995). Economic load dispatch multiobjective optimization procedures using linear programming techniques. *IEEE Transactions on Power Systems*, *10*(2), 731–738. doi:10.1109/59.387910

Gandhi, V., Prasad, G., Coyle, D., Behera, L., & McGinnity, T. M. (2014). Quantum Neural Network-Based EEG Filtering for a Brain-Computer Interface. *Ieee Transactions on Neural Networks and Learning Systems*, *25*(2), 278–288. doi:10.1109/TNNLS.2013.2274436 PMID:24807028

Gherbi, Y. A., Bouzeboudja, H., & Lakdja, F. (2014). Economic dispatch problem using bat algorithm. *Leonardo Journal of Sciences, *(24), 75-84.

Gupta, S., & Zia, R. (2001). Quantum neural networks. *Journal of Computer and System Sciences*, *63*(3), 355–383. doi:10.1006/jcss.2001.1769

Han, K.-H., & Kim, J.-H. (2002). Quantum-inspired evolutionary algorithm for a class of combinatorial optimization. *IEEE Transactions on Evolutionary Computation*, *6*(6), 580–593. doi:10.1109/TEVC.2002.804320

Han, X., Gooi, H., & Kirschen, D. S. (2001). Dynamic economic dispatch: Feasible and optimal solutions. *IEEE Transactions on Power Systems*, *16*(1), 22–28. doi:10.1109/59.910777

Hindi, K. S., & Ab Ghani, M. (1991). Dynamic economic dispatch for large scale power systems: A Lagrangian relaxation approach. *International Journal of Electrical Power & Energy Systems*, *13*(1), 51–56. doi:10.1016/0142-0615(91)90018-Q

Hogg, T., & Portnov, D. (2000). Quantum optimization. *Information Sciences*, *128*(3), 181–197. doi:10.1016/S0020-0255(00)00052-9

Hosseini, S. M. (2014). Optimization of Microgrid Using Quantum Inspired Evolutionary Algorithm. *International Journal of Intelligent Systems and Applications*, *6*(9), 47–53. doi:10.5815/ijisa.2014.09.06

Hota, P., Barisal, A., & Chakrabarti, R. (2010). Economic emission load dispatch through fuzzy based bacterial foraging algorithm. *International Journal of Electrical Power & Energy Systems*, *32*(7), 794–803. doi:10.1016/j.ijepes.2010.01.016

Ivanhoe, L. (1995). Future world oil supplies: There is a finite limit. *World Oil*, *216*, 77–77.

Jadoun, V. K., Gupta, N., Niazi, K. R., & Swamkar, A. (2015). Modulated particle swarm optimization for economic emission dispatch. *International Journal of Electrical Power & Energy Systems*, *73*, 80–88. doi:10.1016/j.ijepes.2015.04.004

Ji-Yuan, F., & Lan, Z. (1998). Real-time economic dispatch with line flow and emission constraints using quadratic programming. *IEEE Transactions on Power Systems*, *13*(2), 320–325. doi:10.1109/59.667345

Jiang, S., Ji, Z., & Shen, Y. (2014). A novel hybrid particle swarm optimization and gravitational search algorithm for solving economic emission load dispatch problems with various practical constraints. *International Journal of Electrical Power & Energy Systems, 55*, 628–644. doi:10.1016/j.ijepes.2013.10.006

Jun, S., Wenbo, X., & Bin, F. (2004). *A global search strategy of quantum-behaved particle swarm optimization.* Paper presented at the Cybernetics and Intelligent Systems, 2004 IEEE Conference on.

Kak, S. C. (1995). Quantum neural computing. *Advances in Imaging and Electron Physics, 94*, 259–313. doi:10.1016/S1076-5670(08)70147-2

Karayiannis, N. B., Mukherjee, A., Glover, J. R., Frost, J. D., Hrachovy, R. A., & Mizrahi, E. M. (2006). An evaluation of quantum neural networks in the detection of epileptic seizures in the neonatal electro-encephalogram. *Soft Computing, 10*(4), 382–396. doi:10.1007/s00500-005-0498-4

Kennedy, J., & Eberhart, R. (1995). *Particle swarm optimization.* Paper presented at the Neural Networks, IEEE International Conference on.

Koridak, L. A., & Rahli, M. (2010). Optimization of the emission and economic dispatch by the genetic algorithm. *Przeglad Elektrotechniczny, 86*(11A), 363–366.

Köse, U., & Arslan, A. (2013). Chaotic Systems and Their Recent Implementations on Improving Intelligent Systems. Handbook of Research on Novel Soft Computing Intelligent Algorithms: Theory and Practical Applications, 69.

Kothari, D. P. (2012). *Power system optimization.* Paper presented at the Computational Intelligence and Signal Processing (CISP), 2012 2nd National Conference on. doi:10.1109/NCCISP.2012.6189669

Kouda, N., Matsui, N., & Nishimura, H. (2002). Image compression by layered quantum neural networks. *Neural Processing Letters, 16*(1), 67–80. doi:10.1023/A:1019708909383

Krishnamurthy, S., & Tzoneva, R. (2012). *Impact of Price Penalty Factors on the Solution of the Combined Economic Emission Dispatch Problem using Cubic Criterion Functions.* New York: IEEE. doi:10.1109/PESGM.2012.6345312

Krishnan, G., & Krishnan, A. (2011). Study on techniques for combined economic and emission dispatch. *Global Journal of Researches in Engineering, Electrical and Electronical Engineering, 11*(5).

Kumar, R. M., Bavisetti, T., & Kiran, K. (2012). Optimization of combined economic and emission dispatch problem: a comparative study for 30 bus systems. *J Electr Electron Eng, 2*, 37-43.

Laboudi, Z., & Chikhi, S. (2012). Comparison of genetic algorithm and quantum genetic algorithm. *Int. Arab J. Inf. Technol., 9*(3), 243–249.

Lau, T. W., Chung, C. Y., Wong, K. P., Chung, T. S., & Ho, S. L. (2009). Quantum-Inspired Evolutionary Algorithm Approach for Unit Commitment. *IEEE Transactions on Power Systems, 24*(3), 1503–1512. doi:10.1109/TPWRS.2009.2021220

Layeb, A. (2011). A novel quantum inspired cuckoo search for knapsack problems. *International Journal of Bio-inspired Computation, 3*(5), 297–305. doi:10.1504/IJBIC.2011.042260

Li, Z., Ngambusabongsopa, R., Mohammed, E., & Eustache, N. (2011). A novel diversity guided particle swarm multi-objective optimization algorithm. *Optimization, 8*(10), 12.

Liang, Z.-X., & Glover, J. D. (1992). A zoom feature for a dynamic programming solution to economic dispatch including transmission losses. *IEEE Transactions on Power Systems, 7*(2), 544–550. doi:10.1109/59.141757

Liao, G. C. (2010). *Using chaotic quantum genetic algorithm solving environmental economic dispatch of smart microgrid containing distributed generation system problems.* Paper presented at the 2010 International Conference on Power System Technology: Technological Innovations Making Power Grid Smarter, POWERCON2010. doi:10.1109/POWERCON.2010.5666468

Liao, G.-C. (2012). Solve environmental economic dispatch of Smart MicroGrid containing distributed generation system - Using chaotic quantum genetic algorithm. *International Journal of Electrical Power & Energy Systems, 43*(1), 779–787. doi:10.1016/j.ijepes.2012.06.040

Ling, S., Lam, H., Leung, F. H., & Lee, Y. (2003). *Improved genetic algorithm for economic load dispatch with valve-point loadings.* Paper presented at the Industrial Electronics Society, 2003. IECON'03. The 29th Annual Conference of the IEEE. doi:10.1109/IECON.2003.1280021

Liu, W., Zhang, Y., Zeng, B., Niu, S., Zhang, J., & Xiao, Y. (2014). An Environmental-Economic Dispatch Method for Smart Microgrids Using VSS_QGA. *Journal of Applied Mathematics, 2014*, 1–11. doi:10.1155/2014/623216

Lu, S., Sun, C., & Lu, Z. (2010). An improved quantum-behaved particle swarm optimization method for short-term combined economic emission hydrothermal scheduling. *Energy Conversion and Management, 51*(3), 561–571. doi:10.1016/j.enconman.2009.10.024

Mandal, K. K., Mandal, S., Bhattacharya, B., & Chakraborty, N. (2015). Non-convex emission constrained economic dispatch using a new self-adaptive particle swarm optimization technique. *Applied Soft Computing, 28*, 188–195. doi:10.1016/j.asoc.2014.11.033

Manju, A., & Nigam, M. J. (2014). Applications of quantum inspired computational intelligence: A survey. *Artificial Intelligence Review, 42*(1), 79–156. doi:10.1007/s10462-012-9330-6

McBride, J., Moore, R., Witherspoon, J., & Blanco, R. (1978). Radiological impact of airborne effluents of coal and nuclear plants. *Science, 202*(4372), 1045–1050. doi:10.1126/science.202.4372.1045 PMID:17777943

Mousa, A. A., & Elattar, E. E. (2014). Best compromise alternative to EELD problem using hybrid multiobjective quantum genetic algorithm. *Applied Mathematics and Information Sciences, 8*(6), 2889–2902. doi:10.12785/amis/080626

Mukherjee, A., Paul, S., & Roy, P. K. (2015). Transient Stability Constrained Optimal Power Flow Using Teaching Learning Based Optimization. *International Journal of Energy Optimization and Engineering, 4*(1), 18–35. doi:10.4018/ijeoe.2015010102

Mukhopadhyay, P., Dutta, S., & Roy, P. K. (2015). Optimal Location of TCSC Using Opposition Teaching Learning Based Optimization. *International Journal of Energy Optimization and Engineering, 4*(1), 85–101. doi:10.4018/ijeoe.2015010106

Naama, B., Bouzeboudja, H., & Allali, A. (2013). *Solving the economic dispatch problem by using Tabu Search algorithm*. Paper presented at the Energy Procedia. doi:10.1016/j.egypro.2013.07.080

Narayanan, A., & Menneer, T. (2000). Quantum artificial neural network architectures and components. *Information Sciences, 128*(3–4), 231–255. doi:10.1016/S0020-0255(00)00055-4

Narayanan, A., & Moore, M. (1996). Quantum-inspired genetic algorithms. *Evolutionary Computation, 1996., Proceedings of IEEE International Conference on.*

Neto, J. X. V., Bernert, D. L. D., & Coelho, L. D. S. (2011). Improved quantum-inspired evolutionary algorithm with diversity information applied to economic dispatch problem with prohibited operating zones. *Energy Conversion and Management, 52*(1), 8–14. doi:10.1016/j.enconman.2010.05.023

Nie, R., Xu, X., & Yue, J. (2010). *A novel quantum-inspired particle swarm algorithm and its application*. Paper presented at the Natural Computation (ICNC), 2010 Sixth International Conference on. doi:10.1109/ICNC.2010.5583225

Niknam, T., Golestaneh, F., & Sadeghi, M. S. (2012). theta-Multiobjective Teaching-Learning-Based Optimization for Dynamic Economic Emission Dispatch. *IEEE Systems Journal, 6*(2), 341–352. doi:10.1109/JSYST.2012.2183276

Papageorgiou, L. G., & Fraga, E. S. (2007). A mixed integer quadratic programming formulation for the economic dispatch of generators with prohibited operating zones. *Electric Power Systems Research, 77*(10), 1292–1296. doi:10.1016/j.epsr.2006.09.020

Park, J.-B., Jeong, Y.-W., Shin, J.-R., & Lee, K. Y. (2010). An improved particle swarm optimization for nonconvex economic dispatch problems. *Power Systems. IEEE Transactions on, 25*(1), 156–166.

Park, J. B., Lee, K. S., Shin, J. R., & Lee, K. Y. (2005). A particle swarm optimization for economic dispatch with nonsmooth cost functions. *IEEE Transactions on Power Systems, 20*(1), 34–42. doi:10.1109/TPWRS.2004.831275

Pothiya, S., Ngamroo, I., & Kongprawechnon, W. (2010). Ant colony optimisation for economic dispatch problem with non-smooth cost functions. *International Journal of Electrical Power & Energy Systems, 32*(5), 478–487. doi:10.1016/j.ijepes.2009.09.016

Rahman, I., Vasant, P., Singh, B. S. M., & Abdullah-Al-Wadud, M. (2015). Swarm intelligence-based optimization for PHEV charging stations. Handbook of Research on Swarm Intelligence in Engineering, 374.

Ramesh, B., Chandra Jagan Mohan, V., & Veera Reddy, V. C. (2013). Application of BAT algorithm for combimned economic load and emission dispatch. *Journal of Electrical Engineering, 13*(2), 214–219.

Rao, R. V., Savsani, V. J., & Vakharia, D. (2011). Teaching–learning-based optimization: A novel method for constrained mechanical design optimization problems. *Computer Aided Design*, *43*(3), 303–315. doi:10.1016/j.cad.2010.12.015

Roselyn, J. P., Devaraj, D., & Dash, S. S. (2011). Economic Emission OPF Using Hybrid GA-Particle Swarm Optimization. In B. K. Panigrahi, P. N. Suganthan, S. Das, & S. C. Satapathy (Eds.), *Swarm, Evolutionary, and Memetic Computing, Pt I* (Vol. 7076, pp. 167–175). doi:10.1007/978-3-642-27172-4_21

Roy, A., Dutta, S., & Roy, P. K. (2015). Load Frequency Control of Interconnected Power System Using Teaching Learning Based Optimization. *International Journal of Energy Optimization and Engineering*, *4*(1), 102–117. doi:10.4018/ijeoe.2015010107

Roy, P., Ghoshal, S., & Thakur, S. (2009). Biogeography-based optimization for economic load dispatch problems. *Electric Power Components and Systems*, *38*(2), 166–181. doi:10.1080/15325000903273379

Roy, P. K. (2013). Teaching learning based optimization for short-term hydrothermal scheduling problem considering valve point effect and prohibited discharge constraint. *International Journal of Electrical Power & Energy Systems*, *53*, 10–19. doi:10.1016/j.ijepes.2013.03.024

Satapathy, S. C., Naik, A., & Parvathi, K. (2013). A teaching learning based optimization based on orthogonal design for solving global optimization problems. *SpringerPlus*, *2*(1), 130. doi:10.1186/2193-1801-2-130 PMID:23875125

Selvakumar, A. I., & Thanushkodi, K. (2007). A new particle swarm optimization solution to nonconvex economic dispatch problems. *IEEE Transactions on Power Systems*, *22*(1), 42–51. doi:10.1109/TPWRS.2006.889132

Senvar, O., Turanoglu, E., & Kahraman, C. (2013). Usage of metaheuristics in engineering: a literature review. *Meta-Heuristics Optimization Algorithms in Engineering, Business, Economics, and Finance*, 484-528.

Shafiee, S., & Topal, E. (2009). When will fossil fuel reserves be diminished? *Energy Policy*, *37*(1), 181–189. doi:10.1016/j.enpol.2008.08.016

Shalini, S. P., & Lakshmi, K. (2014). Solution to economic emission dispatch problem using Lagrangian relaxation method. *2014 International Conference on Green Computing Communication and Electrical Engineering (ICGCCEE)*. doi:10.1109/ICGCCEE.2014.6922314

Shi, Y., & Eberhart, R. (1998). *A modified particle swarm optimizer.* Paper presented at the Evolutionary Computation IEEE World Congress on Computational Intelligence., The 1998 IEEE International Conference on. doi:10.1109/ICEC.1998.699146

Shi, Y., & Eberhart, R. C. (1999). Empirical study of particle swarm optimization. *Evolutionary Computation, 1999. CEC 99. Proceedings of the 1999 Congress on*.

Sinha, N., Chakrabarti, R., & Chattopadhyay, P. (2003). Evolutionary programming techniques for economic load dispatch. *Evolutionary Computation. IEEE Transactions on*, *7*(1), 83–94.

Somuah, C., & Khunaizi, N. (1990). Application of linear programming redispatch technique to dynamic generation allocation. *IEEE Transactions on Power Systems*, *5*(1), 20–26. doi:10.1109/59.49081

Song, Y., Wang, G., Wang, P., & Johns, A. (1997). Environmental/economic dispatch using fuzzy logic controlled genetic algorithms. *IEE Proceedings. Generation, Transmission and Distribution*, *144*(4), 377–382. doi:10.1049/ip-gtd:19971100

Steimann, F., & Adlassnig, K. P. (1998). Fuzzy medical diagnosis. Handbook of Fuzzy Computation, G13.

Sultana, S., & Roy, P. K. (2014). Optimal capacitor placement in radial distribution systems using teaching learning based optimization. *International Journal of Electrical Power & Energy Systems*, *54*, 387–398. doi:10.1016/j.ijepes.2013.07.011

Sun, J., Feng, B., & Xu, W. (2004). *Particle swarm optimization with particles having quantum behavior*. Paper presented at the Congress on Evolutionary Computation. doi:10.1109/CEC.2004.1330875

Tadeusiewicz, R. (2008). *Modern computational intelligence methods for the interpretation of medical images* (Vol. 84). Springer.

Thang, N. T., & ASME. (2012). *Solving economic dispatch problem with piecewise quadratic cost functions using lagrange multiplier theory*. New York: Amer Soc. *Mechanical Engineering*.

Thao, N. T. P., & Thang, N. T. (2014). Environmental economic load dispatch with quadratic fuel cost function using cuckoo search algorithm. *International Journal of u-and e-Service, Science and Technology*, *7*(2), 199–210.

Truong, K. H., Vasant, P., Balbir Singh, M. S., & Vo, D. N. (2015). Swarm Based Mean-Variance Mapping Optimization for Solving Economic Dispatch with Cubic Fuel Cost Function. In T. N. Nguyen, B. Trawiński & R. Kosala (Eds.), *Intelligent Information and Database Systems: 7th Asian Conference, ACIIDS 2015* (pp. 3-12). Cham: Springer International Publishing. doi:10.1007/978-3-319-15705-4_1

Vasant, P. M. (2006). Fuzzy Production Planning and its Application to Decision Making. *Journal of Intelligent Manufacturing*, *17*(1), 5–12. doi:10.1007/s10845-005-5509-x

Ventura, D. (1999). Quantum computational intelligence: Answers and questions. *IEEE Intelligent Systems*, *14*(4), 14–16.

Ventura, D., & Martinez, T. (1998). *Quantum associative memory with exponential capacity*. Paper presented at the Neural Networks Proceedings, 1998. IEEE World Congress on Computational Intelligence. The 1998 IEEE International Joint Conference on. doi:10.1109/IJCNN.1998.682319

Walsh, J. (2000). *Projection of cumulative world conventional oil production, Remaining resources and Reserves to 2050: March*. Academic Press.

Wood, A. J., & Wollenberg, B. F. (2012). *Power generation, operation, and control*. John Wiley & Sons.

Xia, X., & Elaiw, A. (2010). Optimal dynamic economic dispatch of generation: A review. *Electric Power Systems Research*, *80*(8), 975–986. doi:10.1016/j.epsr.2009.12.012

Xing, B., & Gao, W.-J. (2014). *Innovative computational intelligence: a rough guide to 134 clever algorithms* (Vol. 62). Springer. doi:10.1007/978-3-319-03404-1

Yalcinoz, T., & Short, M. J. (1998). Neural networks approach for solving economic dispatch problem with transmission capacity constraints. *IEEE Transactions on Power Systems*, *13*(2), 307–313. doi:10.1109/59.667341

Yang, S., Wang, M., & Jiao, L. (2004). *A quantum particle swarm optimization.* Paper presented at the Evolutionary Computation, 2004. CEC2004. Congress on.

Yang, X.-S. (2010). *A new metaheuristic bat-inspired algorithm. In Nature inspired cooperative strategies for optimization (NICSO 2010)* (pp. 65–74). Springer. doi:10.1007/978-3-642-12538-6_6

Yang, X.-S. (2011). Bat algorithm for multi-objective optimisation. *International Journal of Bio-inspired Computation*, *3*(5), 267–274. doi:10.1504/IJBIC.2011.042259

Yang, X.-S., & Deb, S. (2014). Cuckoo search: Recent advances and applications. *Neural Computing & Applications*, *24*(1), 169–174. doi:10.1007/s00521-013-1367-1

Yang, X. S., & Suash, D. (2009). *Cuckoo Search via Levy flights.* Paper presented at the Nature & Biologically Inspired Computing, 2009. NaBIC 2009. World Congress on.

Zhan, J. P., Wu, Q. H., Guo, C. X., & Zhou, X. X. (2014). Fast lambda-Iteration Method for Economic Dispatch. *IEEE Transactions on Power Systems*, *29*(2), 990–991. doi:10.1109/TPWRS.2013.2287995

Zhang, G. X., Gheorghe, M., & Wu, C. Z. (2008). A Quantum-Inspired Evolutionary Algorithm Based on P systems for Knapsack Problem. *Fundamenta Informaticae*, *87*(1), 93–116.

Zhu, D. Q., Chen, E. K., & Yang, Y. Q. (2005). A quantum neural networks data fusion algorithm and its application for fault diagnosis. In D. S. Huang, X. P. Zhang, & G. B. Huang (Eds.), *Advances in Intelligent Computing, Pt 1, Proceedings* (Vol. 3644, pp. 581–590). Berlin: Springer-Verlag Berlin. doi:10.1007/11538059_61

Zou, F., Wang, L., Hei, X., Chen, D., & Yang, D. (2014). Teaching–learning-based optimization with dynamic group strategy for global optimization. *Information Sciences*, *273*, 112–131. doi:10.1016/j.ins.2014.03.038

Chapter 16
Intelligent Expert System to Optimize the Quartz Crystal Microbalance (QCM) Characterization Test:
Intelligent System to Optimize the QCM Characterization Test

Jose Luis Calvo-Rolle
University of A Coruña, Spain

María del Carmen Meizoso-López
University of A Coruña, Spain

José Luis Casteleiro-Roca
University of A Coruña, Spain

Andrés José Piñón-Pazos
University of A Coruña, Spain

Juan Albino Mendez-Perez
Universidad de La Laguna, Spain

ABSTRACT

This chapter describes an approach to reduce significantly the time in the frequency sweep test of a Quartz Crystal Microbalance (QCM) characterization method based on the resonance principle of passive components. On this test, the spent time was large, because it was necessary carry out a big frequency sweep due to the fact that the resonance frequency was unknown. Moreover, this frequency sweep has great steps and consequently low accuracy. Then, it was necessary to reduce the sweeps and its steps gradually with the aim to increase the accuracy and thereby being able to find the exact frequency. An intelligent expert system was created as a solution to the disadvantage described of the method. This model provides a much smaller frequency range than the initially employed with the original proposal. This frequency range depends of the circuit components of the method. Then, thanks to the new approach of the QCM characterization is achieved better accuracy and the test time is reduced significantly.

DOI: 10.4018/978-1-5225-2128-0.ch016

INTRODUCTION

The Quartz Crystal Microbalances are used as sensors to determine mass variations due to its oscillation frequency changes. Some of their advantages include: their possible use either in gas or liquid medium, high sensitivity, detection capability for density-viscosity or viscoelastic changes in a solution in the bound interfacial material; the possibility of their coating surface with a selective layer to be able to detect a specific substance, etc. (Cooper & Singleton, 2007; Kimmel, LeBlanc, Meschievitz, & Cliffel, 2012; Lucklum & Hauptmann, 2006; Marx, 2003). So, the range of applications includes: detecting vapors, chemical analysis, environmental pollutants, biomolecules, cells, etc. (Hunter, 2009; Lec, 2001; Speight & Cooper, 2012).

In order to achieve an adequate interpretation of the results given by the sensor, a correct measurement of the resonator electrical parameters is needed. This fact includes the development of electronic instrumentation systems and the appropriate model of the pair resonator-load choosing according to a specific application (Torres-Villa, 2013). For most applications, there are two essential parameters which measure offers the information that the sensor gives about the load properties. These two parameters are the frequency shift and the change on the series resistance in the well-established Butterworth–Van Dyke model (BVD) (Schröder, Borngräber, Eichelbaum, & Hauptmann, 2002). But, for a more detailed QCM characterization, it is also necessary to know other crystal parameters such as the parallel capacitance (García-Martinez et al., 2011; Martin, Granstaff, & Frye, 1991).

The QCM electronic interface development has been gradually improved in order to obtain continuous monitoring systems. Then, it can be integrated easily into smaller electronic boards, optimized for fast data measuring and also provides, at least, the two mentioned parameters (frequency shift and series resistance). A comprehensive review of them can be found in (Arnau, 2008a). Systems that offer a complete sensor characterization, like impedance analysis based methods, require costly instrumentation and elaborate fitting procedures to extract the crystal parameters of interest (Calvo, Etchenique, Bartlett, Singhal, & Santamaria, 1997; Martin et al., 1991). Usually, oscillators have been used due to their low-cost circuitry, as well as, the integration capability and continuous monitoring (Arnau, 2008a). Its main drawback is the poor stability of high resonant frequency under high loading conditions (Montagut et al., 2011). New techniques, such as phase locked loop circuits, are being implemented to combine the accuracy of expensive instrumentation and the simplicity of oscillator (Arnau, 2008a; Ferrari, Ferrari, & Kanazawa, 2008).

Creating models based on Intelligent Systems is frequently nowadays, with the aim to settle problems that are difficult to solve in a traditional way. In this sense, it is possible to cite several previous works where different models were created to achieve new goals, or to improve many things. The next works are examples of this fact: (Simic & Dimitrijevic, 2013) proposes the tactical ASR recycling planning model which can be used to assist Japanese vehicle recyclers, improving their profitability and ASR recycling efficiency; in (Kułakowski, Matyasik, & Ernst, 2014) is described foundations for design of a robot to conduct regular and automated audits of lighting quality in office buildings, with emphasis on the modeling its behavior; (Calvo-Rolle, Casteleiro-Roca, Quintián, & Meizoso-López, 2013) shows a hybrid system, where it is modeled the existing knowledge of the PID controller tuning in open loop and, with Artificial Neural Network, it is completed the rule based model that allow to choose the optimal parameters for the controller; (Ferreiro Garcia, Calovo-Rolle, Pérez Castelo, & Romero Gómez, 2014) describes the implementation of a supervision strategy implemented with Artificial Neural Networks associated to recursive rule based techniques.

There are several previous research where intelligent techniques improve tasks based on biosensors. In (Reznik, Galinskaya, Dekhtyarenko, & Nowicki, 2005) the ANNs are used to classify odor data given from a QCM matrix sensor. A time series kernel for two pattern recognition problems is used for machine olfaction in (Vembu, Vergara, Muezzinoglu, & Huerta, 2012). In (Gulbag & Temurtas, 2006) the FeedForward Neural Networks were applied, and an Adaptive Neuro-Fuzzy Inference System was proposed, for quantitative identification of individual gas concentrations (trichloroethylene and acetone) in their gas mixtures, where a QCM type sensors were used as gas sensors. Some intelligent classification algorithms are tested on (del Cueto Belchi et al., 2013) to develop a multisensor olfactory system where 32 metal oxide semiconductor sensors, of 7 different types, and operating at different temperatures, have been used. In (Batzias & Siontorou, 2012) is developed a methodological framework for creating specific domain ontologies by means of a cybernetic infrastructure, where the domain is the biosensors. In (Zilinskas & Baronas, 2011) the problem of evaluation of concentrations of several substrates is tackled by minimizing the discrepancy between the observed and modeled transition processes of the amperometric signal.

The present research shows a method, based on intelligent techniques, that allows to reduce significantly the test time for the QCM characterization method described on (Casteleiro-Roca, Calvo-Rolle, Meizoso-López, Piñón-Pazos, & Rodríguez-Gómez, 2014). If the inductor value used on the proposal is known, then, it is possible to predict the necessary frequency range to make the optimal sweep, and find the resonance frequency to obtain the model values in a shorter time.

This paper is organized as follows: It starts with a description of the case of study, where the equivalent circuit used for the QCM, and the way to characterize the sensor through the previous proposal, is explained. The model approach section is then presented, it introduces the dataset obtaining and the used algorithms to obtain the best model for a good accuracy. Next section gives the results achieved, and at the last section, conclusions reached and future works are shown.

CASE OF STUDY

In this section the approach for the QCM characterization that motivates this research is explained. For this purpose, the section is divided on four subsections. The Quartz Crystal Microbalance is defined and its model is described briefly on the first one. Then, the characterization method is exposed followed by its practical implementation. Finally, the disadvantage, to be corrected, of the test time is commented.

The Quartz Crystal Microbalance: QCM

The QCM is an application of the typical quartz crystal, usually employed in electronic circuits to obtain an exact clock signal based on its oscillation frequency. The use of the quartz crystal as a microbalance starts in 1959, when Saurbrey proves that there is a linear relation between the mass over the QCM surface and its resonance frequency (Cooper & Singleton, 2007). As can be see on Figure 1, the QCM is made by a thin AT-cut quartz crystal disk between two metallic circular electrodes, one of them over each side of the crystal.

The proposal is based on the commonly used Butterworth-Van Dyke equivalent circuit (Ferreira, da Silva, & Tome, 2009; Martin et al., 1991). In its simple topology, the model has the appearance shown in Figure 2. As it can be seen, the scheme has two parallel branches. The first one has the C0 capacitor

Figure 1. Front and back of the QCM with gold electrodes
Source: Wikipedia, 2014

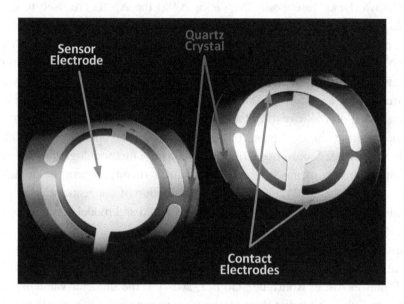

Figure 2. Butterworth-Van Dyke (BVD) equivalent circuit

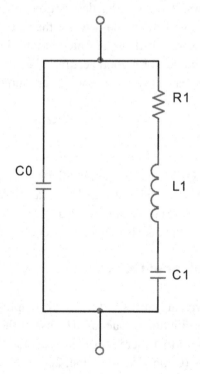

and the other one has a series RLC impedance with R1 resistor, L1 inductor and C1 capacitor. Several alternatives to the simple topology of BVD used in this research, like (Jin, Dong, Luo, & Milne, 2011; Rodahl, Höök, & Kasemo, 1996), have been developed with the aim to allow a better approach, above all, to make approximations to specific cases of QCM uses. But, due to the good results achieved with the simple form, this option has been chosen.

The C0 capacitor is due to the static capacitance and depends on the QCM geometry (Arnau, 2008c). The series RLC branch does not have a specific electric meaning; it models the mechanical phenomena that describe its performance (Arnau, 2008c). The changes on QCM component can be added as additional passive components in the RLC branch to the model shown in Figure 2.

The Characterization Method

The characterization method is explained in detail in (Casteleiro-Roca et al., 2014). The QCM characterization is based on obtaining the BVD electrical equivalent model. The main advantages of the novel method are: it is based on classical theory, it is very intuitive and easy to understand, it is based on BVD model, and finally, it is possible to carry out the method with basic laboratory equipment. In the following subsections the method is summarized because it is necessary to understand the proposal described on the present research.

Background of the Method

The characterization method is based on the theory exposed on (Martin et al., 1991). In it, the expressions are deducted to obtain the parameters of the electric model of the QCM. Different cases are contemplated on the model described: unperturbed QCM, liquid loading and mass loading. The Figure 2 only shows the unperturbed QCM, and the expressions for it are Equations 1 to 4.

$$C0 = \frac{\varepsilon_{22} A}{h} \tag{1}$$

$$C1 = \frac{8K_0^2 C0}{\left(N\pi\right)^2} \tag{2}$$

$$L1 = \frac{1}{\omega_s^2 C1} \tag{3}$$

$$R1 = \frac{\eta_q}{c_{66} C1}\left(\frac{\omega}{\omega_s}\right)^2 \tag{4}$$

where:

- ε_{22} is the quartz permittivity.
- A is the electrode surface area.
- h is quartz thickness.
- K_0 is the electromechanical coupling constant for quartz.
- N overtone or harmonic number = 1, 3, 5…
- ω_s angular series resonant frequency for the unperturbed QCM = $2\,\pi\,f_s$.
- η_q effective quartz viscosity.
- c_{66} quartz elastic constant.
- ω angular excitation frequency = $2\,\pi\,f$.

The four expressions are function of the physical characteristics, material properties and dimensions of the QCM; also, expressions from 3 and 4 are functions of C0, obtained with expression 1, and C1, obtained with expression 2 (and the previous calculated value of C0). Therefore, with the physical features of the QCM, first it is necessary to obtain C0 parameter. When QCM is used, it is usually based on AT-cut quartz. Taking this fact into account, the parameters corresponding of material properties of the expressions (1 to 4) can be considered as constants (Martin et al., 1991). As it can be seen in equations, with C0 it is possible to obtain C1, and then, L1 and R1 values are obtained. As a resume, to get the model, it would only be necessary to obtain the QCM dimension parameters.

Obtaining Parallel Capacitance (C0)

As seen in the previous subsection, the characterization starts by obtaining C0 parameter, and then, with its value, it is possible to obtain the series RLC branch. C0 is the only parameter that depends on the dimensions of the QCM. The problem is that obtaining the dimensions of the QCM could be a difficult task due to different reasons (Arnau, 2008b). That is the reason why, in (Casteleiro-Roca et al., 2014), a novel approach was described to get C0 parameter without the need of obtaining dimensions of the QCM. The new method is based on the circuit shown in Figure 3, where an inductor is added in series with the QCM.

The proposal is based on the operation principle when the series resonance phenomenon occurs between the C0, capacitance of the BVD model of the QCM, and the added inductor at their resonant frequency (ω_r in radians). Then, it is necessary to feed the circuit shown in Figure 3 with an AC source and perform a frequency sweep. When the source frequency is the same as the resonant frequency (ω_r), then the impedance (C0 in series with L) is zero. If the added inductor is known, then it is possible to obtain the C0 capacitance as described in Equation 5.

$$\left.\begin{array}{l} X_L = j\omega L \\ X_{C0} = \dfrac{1}{j\omega C0} \end{array}\right\} \rightarrow j\omega_r L + \dfrac{1}{j\omega_r C0} = 0 \rightarrow C0 = \dfrac{1}{\omega_r^2 L} \tag{5}$$

Figure 3. Circuit approach

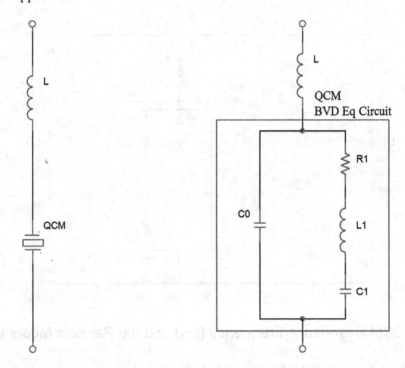

Commonly, the frequency of the laboratory equipment is presented in hertzs (f_r), and then it is only necessary to convert the frequency ω_r with the expression 6.

$$\omega_r = 2\pi f_r \tag{6}$$

If the frequency is obtained in hertzs, the capacitance C0 is obtained through the equation 7, as a result of replacing the equation 6 in 5.

$$C0 = \frac{1}{L\left(2\pi f_r\right)^2} \tag{7}$$

In a practical view, it is necessary to implement the circuit shown in Figure 4, where a resistor has been added. The reason is that when resonance occurs, the impedance (C0 in series with L) is zero, then the source would be in short-circuit, and it is not usually a desired state.

With the aim to obtain a very satisfactory result of the C0 capacitance value, it is necessary to make the tests far from the resonant frequency of the QCM. In (Arnau, 2008b) it is recommended to choose at least the double of the QCM resonant frequency value. Other consideration is to use elements with a good precision and accuracy, above all, the inductor L. The Rcal resistor is not as important, because its main aim is to protect the source from a short-circuit. But, the chosen resistor must have a very precise value too (small tolerance), to solve the following subsections satisfactorily.

Figure 4. Practical circuit

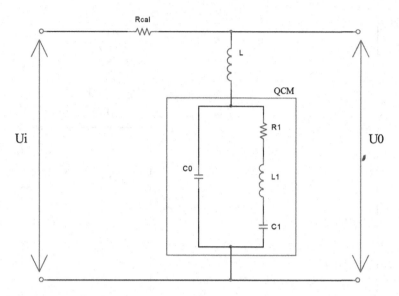

Obtaining the QCM Resonance Frequency (ωs) and the Resistor Model Value (R1)

In several works like (Jin et al., 2011; Martin et al., 1991), it is shown, as a possible method, to obtain the R1 value of the BVD model (Figure 2) through Equation 4. Nonetheless, other studies like (Arnau, 2008b; García-Martinez et al., 2011) prove that the result achieved in this way is wrong, even (Martin et al., 1991) obtains R1 value with other method despite showing the above equation too. For this reason, with the goal to obtain the real value of the resistor, a similar way like in the above subsections is proposed. It is only necessary to remove the L inductor of the circuit shown in Figure 4. For a good understanding of the proposal, Figure 5 is shown.

Like in the above case, it is necessary to apply a frequency sweep to the source and pay special attention when the series resonance phenomenon occurs on the QCM. This value is the QCM resonance frequency (ω_r). Just at series resonant frequency, the impedance of the series RLC branch of the BVD model is equal to the R1 resistance, because L1 and C1 impedances are canceled. In this condition, the circuit is a voltage divider. Since Rcal and the applied voltage to the circuit are known, it is possible to obtain the R1 value by measuring the voltage drop on the QCM as shown in equation 8.

$$V_{QCM} = \frac{R1}{R1 + Rcal} V_{in} \rightarrow R1 = \frac{Rcal \cdot V_{QCM}}{V_{in} - V_{QCM}} \tag{8}$$

Characterization METHOD IMPLEMENTATION

The general scheme to test the novel approach is illustrated in Figure 6.

As it can be seen in the figure, basic equipment present in any electronic laboratory is used to make the characterization of the QCM:

Figure 5. Circuit to obtain R1 value of BVD model

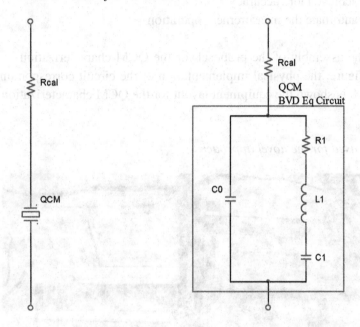

Figure 6. General Scheme to test the novel approach

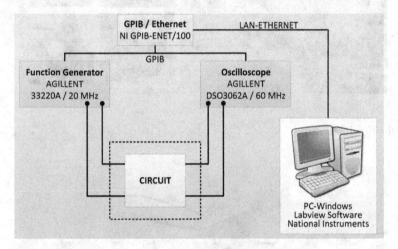

- Function / Arbitrary Waveform Generator, Agilent 33220A, 20 MHz
- Oscilloscope, Agilent DSO3062A, 60 MHz
- GPIB/Ethernet converter, NI GPIB-ENET/100
- PC-Windows with LabView® software

The first two items are essentials, however the last two are optional. The main advantages of the configuration with all the equipment are:

- It is possible to achieve more accuracy
- It is possible to automate the measurement operation

Figure 7 shows the assembly of the proposal for the QCM characterization in air media. On the bottom-right of the figure, the physical implementation of the circuit corresponding with Figure 4 is shown too. In Figure 8 is shown the equipment layout for the QCM characterization in liquid media.

Figure 7. Equipment used for the novel approach

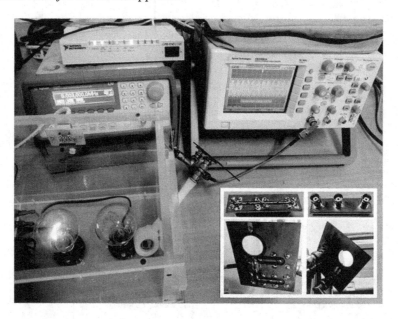

Figure 8. Layout for liquid media

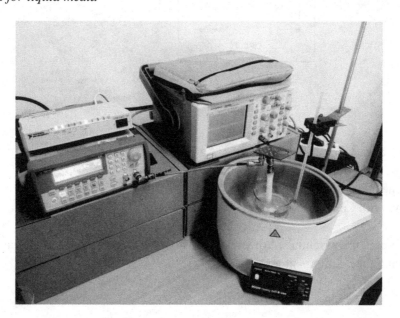

The QCM is allowed in a crystal holder ready to introduce the sensor in a liquid media. The QCM used is the standard sensor of the QCM200 system (N/d, 2009). It consists of a thin disk (1 inch in diameter) of 5 MHz, *AT-cut*, *α-quartz* with circular gold electrodes patterned on both sides. The elements used to connect the circuit with the equipment have a very low attenuation and a very good performance for this purpose. The circuit used in the proposal has been designed to minimize disturbance.

In addition, to create good test conditions, the own holder has been introduced into a methacrylate box. Into it, with the help of an incandescent lamp and a temperature controller, temperature is fixed to *25° C* during the experiments. Even, to depressurize inside the box there is a fan on the top of the box. With this fact, a low level of humidity (between *20%* and *30%*) is achieved.

The frequency sweep could be made manual, but in this case, with the help of the GPIB to Ethernet converter is automated with a program made under LabView® software. Then it is possible to achieve more accuracy and the operation is automated (up to 10^{-1} Hz). The appearance of the developed application is shown in Figure 9.

The Disadvantage of the Test Time

The main disadvantage of the characterization method is the test time, specially when the passive components are not calibrated adequately. For instance, the test showed on Figure 9 has a very wide range of *5 MHz*, and, if the sweep is carry out with increments of *1 kHz*, the test has a duration of more than

Figure 9. Application developed under LabView® software

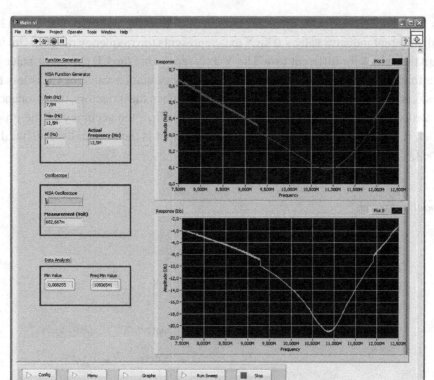

one hour. With the aim to improve the accuracy and to reduce the test time, the frequency ranges must be reduced as possible. The next intelligent model has been created with this goal.

MODEL APPROACH

The model approach proposed on the present research is summarized on the scheme shows in Figure 10. The figure shows that the input of the model is the inductor value used for the test. This inductor is the one shows in Figure 4 as "*L*", and the model was developed to accept a null value that indicates that the test is the corresponding with the Figure 5.

The outputs of the model are the start and stop values of the frequency for the test that is carried out. With this model, the time spent in the test is reduced significantly, because it is not necessary to use a wide frequency range. The basic method proposed in (Casteleiro-Roca et al., 2014), includes a previous scan to detect the range where the resonance frequency appears. Then, the range of the test was reduced, and another test was made until the desired accuracy was achieved.

With the proposal explained in this research, these recurrent steps were avoid. As the model output is the final frequency range for the test.

The second part of the model is used to find the range for specific tests. When there is not previous data for the test, or the change possibility of the resonance frequency, the final solution is to increase the test range to ensure that the new resonance frequency will be measured.

Obtaining the Dataset

Different tests were carried out, with different inductors to develop the model. Figure 11 shows tests carried out with different inductor values. The X axis represents the frequency ranges, which are normalized to compare the values for different test. The Y axis represents the C0 capacitor value obtained for each resonance frequency. As can be seen on this figure, the deviation value of C0 is less than 0.98%.

The values stored to create the dataset was the nominal value of the inductors, the resonance frequency, and the calculated value of C0. The last one is stored to confirm the accuracy of the proposal, not to create the model. It is necessary to clarify that, the model input is the nominal value, but the method to characterize the QCM needs the real inductor value.

Figure 10. Model approach

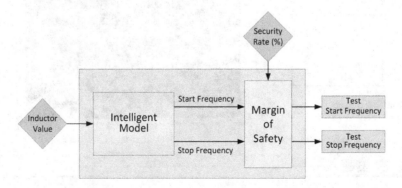

Figure 11. C0 value depending of the frequency range

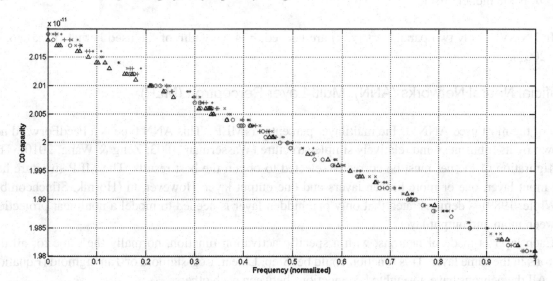

Used Algorithm in the Approach

Support Vector Regression (SVR), Least Square Support Vector Regression (LS-SVR)

The Support Vector Machines (SVM) is and algorithm used for classification. The modification of this algorithm for regression purposes is called Support Vector Regression (SVR). In SVR, a linear regression is made in a space F where the data is mapped by a high-dimensional feature (Cristianini & Shawe-Taylor, 2000; Steinwart & Christmann, 2008).

The LS-SVM is a Least Square formulation for the SVM. The approximation of the solution is obtained by solving a system of linear equations, and it is comparable to SVM in terms of generalization performance (Suykens & Vandewalle, 1999; R. Wang, Wang, & Song, 2012). The application of LS-SVM to regression is known as LS-SVR (Least Square Support Vector Regression) (Guo, Li, Bai, & Ma, 2012; L. Wang & Wu, 2012). In LS-SVR, the insensitive loss function is replaced by a classical squared loss function, which constructs the Lagragian by solving a linear KarushKuhn-Tucker *KKT* (Equation 9).

$$\begin{bmatrix} 0 & I_n^T \\ I_n & K + \gamma_{-1}I \end{bmatrix}\begin{bmatrix} b_0 \\ b \end{bmatrix} = \begin{bmatrix} 0 \\ y \end{bmatrix}$$

(9)

where:

- I_n is a vector of n ones.
- T means transpose of a matrix or vector.
- γ a weight vector.
- b is the regression vector.

481

- b_0 is the model offset.

In LS-SVR, only two parameters (γ, σ) are needed, σ is the width of the used kernel (Li, Shao, & Cai, 2007).

Artificial Neural Networks (ANN). Multi-Layer Perceptron (MLP)

One of the most used ANNs is the multilayer perceptron (MLP). This ANN type is a FeedForward net known by its robustness and relatively simple structure (Wasserman, 1993; Zeng & Wang, 2010). The configuration of the net must be correctly selected to obtain the best results. The MLP structure has one input layer, one or more hidden layers and one output layer. However, in (Hornik, Stinchcombe, & White, 1989) is demonstrated that only one hidden layer is needed to model a nonlinear projection between input and output layer.

Each layer is made of neurons, with a specific activation function, normally the same for all the neurons in the same layer. This function could be: Step, Linear, Log-sigmoid or Tan-sigmoid (Equation 10). All the neurons have a weighted connections between each others.

$$F(t) = \frac{e^t - e^{-t}}{e^t + e^{-t}} \tag{10}$$

It is possible to define the output of a MLP as shown in equation 11 (Rynkiewicz, 2012).

$$f_\theta(x) = \beta + \sum_{i=1}^{k} a_i \phi\left(w_i^T x + b_i\right) \tag{11}$$

where:

- $x = (x(1), \ldots, x(d))^T \in \mathfrak{R}^d$ is the vector of inputs
- k is the number of hidden layers
- ϕ is a bounded transfer function
- $\theta = (\beta, a_1, \ldots, a_k, b_1, \ldots, b_k, w_{11}, \ldots, w_{kd})$ is the parameter vector of the model
- $w_i = (w_{i1}, \ldots, w_{id})^T \in \mathfrak{R}^d$ is the parameter vector for the hidden unit i

Polynomial Regression

A polynomial regression model may be defined as a linear summation of basis functions (Heiberger & Neuwirth, 2009; Wu, 2007; Zhang & Chan, 2011). Basically, the number of basis functions depends on the number of the model inputs, but also depends of the polynomial degree. Equation 12 shows a polynomial regression with two inputs and degree *1*. The model becomes more complex as the degree increases, equation 13 shows a model with the same number of inputs, but with degree *2*.

$$F(x) = a_0 + a_1 x_1 + a_2 x_2 \tag{12}$$

$$F\left(x\right) = a_0 + a_1 x_1 + a_2 x_2 + a_3 x_1 x_2 + a_4 x_1^2 + a_5 x_2^2 \tag{13}$$

Ensemble Regression

The ensembles are a classification learning method (Uysal & Gövenir, 1999) that could be used for regression purposes when the dataset is large (Mozaffari & Azad, 2013). With the aim to increase the predictive performance, a regularization process is made for choosing fewer weak learners of an ensemble. The method tries to minimize the expression 14, finding a set of weights α_t.

$$\sum_{n=1}^{N} w_n g\left(\left(\sum_{t=1}^{T} \alpha_t h_t\left(x_n\right)\right), y_n\right) + \lambda \sum_{t=1}^{T} |\alpha_t| \tag{14}$$

where:

- $\lambda \geq 0$ is the regularization parameter.
- h_t is a weak learner in the ensemble trained on N observations with predictors x_n, responses y_n, and weights w_n.
- $g(f,y) = (f-y)^2$ is the square error.

RESULTS

The dataset was divided into two different sets of data, one for the algorithms training (2/3 of the data), and the other one for testing the performance of each model (1/3 of the samples). The algorithms' performance was measured attending to the MSE (Mean Square Error) achieved with the test data. Given that the test data is not used to train the models, the overfit of them was avoided. The training data was normalized to ensure the best results.

- Least Square Support Vector Regression (LS-SVR):
  ○ The LS-SVR tuning is automatic, and then, configuration parameters are not needed. The optimal parameters obtained for this method are: $\gamma = 2.1474\ e^4$, $\sigma^2 = 0.0095$.
- Artificial Neural Network. Multi-Layer Perceptron (MLP):
  ○ Only one hidden layer was configured, its activation function is Tan-sigmoid. The output layer has a linear activation function. The number of neurons in the hidden layer was from 2 to 15. The best results with this method was obtained with 5 neurons in the hidden layer.
- Polynomial Regression:
  ○ The polynomial regression models were trained for different degrees, from 3 to 9. The best approximation with this algorithm was obtained using a 4 degree polynomial.
- Ensemble Regression:
  ○ The ensemble learning method used was "*LSBoost*", it was 5000 trained cycles and a regression tree algorithm was training.

The best results for the tested algorithms are shown in Table 1.

Table 1. Best MSE for each regression algorithm

Method	Parameters	MSE
LS-SVR	$\gamma = 2.1474\ e^4$, $\sigma^2 = 0.0095$	3.4048E-5
ANN-MLP	1 hidden layer, 5 neurons, Tan-Sigmoid	3.2903E-5
Polynomial	Degree = 4	5.2635E-4
Ensemble	"LSBoost" learning method, 5000 training cycles	3.4296E-5

The created model has been tested several times with different inductor values to the input. The resonance frequency is achieved in all cases with the frequency sweep predicted by the model, when the Security Rate increases the range 5%.

CONCLUSION

The present research shows a solution that brings a large decrease in the frequency sweep test time of the above described QCM characterization method. The achieved model is based on intelligent techniques. As can be seen, this model provides the minimum values of the Start and the Stop sweep frequency. Also, it is possible to add a Security Rate with the aim to ensure the resonance frequency location for the parameters calculation.

Very good results have been obtained in general terms with the novel approach proposed in this research. During the model creation, the best algorithm to implement the model was the ANN-MLP with 5 neurons in the hidden layer, that achieves a MSE of *3.2903E-5*. When the Start and Stop frequencies provides by the model are tested over the characterization method, the resonance frequency is achieved in all cases with the frequency sweep predicted by the model, when the Security Rate increases the range 5%.

The reduction over the test time for the characterization of the QCM was, at least, *75%*. As was explained, the previous method required a recursive testing to improve the accuracy, and, with the novel model, the number of necessary tests were reduced to only one.

The method could be applied to obtain the model of typical Quartz Crystal employed on electronics. With the present contribution described on this work, the task could be accomplished more quickly than with the original method due to the sweep range reduction.

REFERENCES

Arnau, A. (2008a). A Review of Interface Electronic Systems for AT-cut Quartz Crystal Microbalance Applications in Liquids. *Sensors (Basel, Switzerland)*, 8(1), 370–411. doi:10.3390/s8010370 PMID:27879713

Arnau, A. (2008b). A review of interface electronic systems for AT-cut Quartz Crystal Microbalance applications in liquids. *Sensors (Basel, Switzerland)*, 8(1), 370–411. doi:10.3390/s8010370 PMID:27879713

Arnau, A. (2008c). *Piezoelectric transducer and applications* (2nd ed.). Springer.

Batzias, F. A., & Siontorou, C. G. (2012). Creating a specific domain ontology for supporting R&D in the science-based sector – The case of biosensors. *Expert Systems with Applications*, *39*(11), 9994–10015. doi:10.1016/j.eswa.2012.01.216

Calvo, E. J., Etchenique, R., Bartlett, P. N., Singhal, K., & Santamaria, C. (1997). Quartz crystal impedance studies at 10 MHz of viscoelastic liquids and films. *Faraday Discussions*, *107*, 141–247. doi:10.1039/a703551i

Calvo-Rolle, J. L., Casteleiro-Roca, J. L., Quintián, H., & Meizoso-López, M. C. (2013). A hybrid intelligent system for PID controller using in a steel rolling process. *Expert Systems with Applications*, *40*(13), 5188–5196. doi:10.1016/j.eswa.2013.03.013

Casteleiro-Roca, J. L., Calvo-Rolle, J. L., Meizoso-López, M. C., Piñón-Pazos, A. P., & Rodríguez-Gómez, B. A. (2014). New approach for the QCM sensors characterization. *Sensors and Actuators. A, Physical*, *207*(0), 1–9. doi:10.1016/j.sna.2013.12.002

Cooper, M. A., & Singleton, V. T. (2007). Review A survey of the 2001 to 2005 quartz crystal microbalance biosensor literature: Applications of acoustic physics to the analysis of biomolecular interactions. *Journal of Molecular Recognition*, *20*(3), 154–184. doi:10.1002/jmr.826 PMID:17582799

Cristianini, N., & Shawe-Taylor, J. (2000). *An introduction to Support Vector Machines and other kernel-based learning methods*. New York, NY: Cambridge University Press. doi:10.1017/CBO9780511801389

del Cueto Belchi, A., Rothpfeffer, N., Pelegrí-Sebastia, J., Chilo, J., Rodriguez, D. G., & Sogorb, T. (2013). Sensor characterization for multisensor odor-discrimination system. *Sensors and Actuators. A, Physical*, *191*(0), 68–72. doi:10.1016/j.sna.2012.11.039

Ferrari, M., Ferrari, V., & Kanazawa, K. K. (2008). Dual-harmonic oscillator with frequency and resistance outputs for quartz resonator sensors. *Sensors, IEEE*, *1261–1264*. doi:10.1109/ICSENS.2008.4716673

Ferreira, G. N. M., da Silva, A. C., & Tome, B. (2009). Acoustic wave biosensors : Physical models and biological applications of quartz crystal microbalance. *Trends in Biotechnology*, *27*(October), 689–697. doi:10.1016/j.tibtech.2009.09.003 PMID:19853941

Ferreiro Garcia, R., Calovo-Rolle, J. L., Pérez Castelo, J., & Romero Gómez, M. (2014). On the monitoring task of solar thermal fluid transfer systems using NN based models and rule based techniques. *Engineering Applications of Artificial Intelligence*, *27*(0), 129–136. doi:10.1016/j.engappai.2013.06.011

García-Martinez, G., Bustabad, E. A., Perrot, H., Gabrielli, C., Bucur, B., Lazerges, M., & Vives, A. A. et al. (2011). Development of a Mass Sensitive Quartz Crystal Microbalance (QCM)-Based DNA Biosensor Using a 50 MHz Electronic Oscillator Circuit. *Sensors (Basel, Switzerland)*, *11*(8), 7656–7664. doi:10.3390/s110807656 PMID:22164037

Gulbag, A., & Temurtas, F. (2006). A study on quantitative classification of binary gas mixture using neural networks and adaptive neuro-fuzzy inference systems. *Sensors and Actuators. B, Chemical*, *115*(1), 252–262. doi:10.1016/j.snb.2005.09.009

Guo, Y., Li, X., Bai, G., & Ma, J. (2012). Time Series Prediction Method Based on LS-SVR with Modified Gaussian RBF. In T. Huang, Z. Zeng, C. Li, & C. Leung (Eds.), *Neural Information Processing* (Vol. 7664, pp. 9–17). Springer Berlin Heidelberg; doi:10.1007/978-3-642-34481-7_2

Heiberger, R. M., & Neuwirth, E. (2009). Polynomial regression. In *R Through Excel* (pp. 269–284). Springer New York; doi:10.1007/978-1-4419-0052-4_11

Hornik, K., Stinchcombe, M., & White, H. (1989). Multilayer feedforward networks are universal approximators. *Neural Networks*, *2*(5), 359–366. doi:10.1016/0893-6080(89)90020-8

Hunter, A. C. (2009). Application of the quartz crystal microbalance to nanomedicine. *J. Biomed. Nanotechnol.*, *5*(6), 669–675. doi:10.1166/jbn.2009.1083 PMID:20201228

Jin, H., Dong, S. R., Luo, J. K., & Milne, W. I. (2011). Generalised Butterworth-Van Dyke equivalent circuit for thin-film bulk acoustic resonator. *Electronics Letters*, *47*(7), 424–426. doi:10.1049/el.2011.0343

Kimmel, D. W., LeBlanc, G., Meschievitz, M. E., & Cliffel, D. E. (2012). Electrochemical Sensors and Biosensors. *Analytical Chemistry*, *84*(2), 685–707. http://doi.org/doi:10.1021/ac202878q doi:10.1021/ac202878q PMID:22044045

Kułakowski, K., Matyasik, P., & Ernst, S. (2014). Modeling indoor lighting inspection robot behavior using Concurrent Communicating Lists. *Expert Systems with Applications*, *41*(4), 984–998. doi:10.1016/j.eswa.2013.06.065

Lec, R. M. (2001). Piezoelectric biosensors: recent advances and applications. *Proceedings of the 2001 IEEE International Frequency Control Symposium and PDA Exhibition*, 419–429. http://doi.org/doi:10.1109/FREQ.2001.956265

Li, Y., Shao, X., & Cai, W. (2007). A consensus least squares support vector regression (LS-SVR) for analysis of near-infrared spectra of plant samples. *Talanta*, *72*(1), 217–222. doi:10.1016/j.talanta.2006.10.022 PMID:19071605

Lucklum, R., & Hauptmann, P. (2006). Acoustic microsensors the challenge behind microgravimetry. *Analytical and Bioanalytical Chemistry*, *384*(3), 667–682. doi:10.1007/s00216-005-0236-x PMID:16544392

Martin, S. J., Granstaff, V. E., & Frye, G. C. (1991). Characterization of a quartz crystal microbalance with simultaneous mass and liquid loading. *Analytical Chemistry*, *63*(20), 2272–2281. doi:10.1021/ac00020a015

Marx, K. (2003). Quartz Crystal Microbalance: A Useful Tool for Studying ThinPolymer Films and Complex Biomolecular Systems at the Solution-Surface Interface. *Biomacromolecules*, *4*(5), 1099–1120. doi:10.1021/bm020116i PMID:12959572

Montagut, Y., García, J. V., Jiménez, Y., March, C., Montoya, A., & Arnau, A. (2011). Validation of a phase-mass characterization concept and interface for acoustic biosensors. *Sensors (Basel, Switzerland)*, *11*(12), 4702–4720. doi:10.3390/s110504702 PMID:22163871

Mozaffari, A., & Azad, N. L. (2013). Optimally pruned extreme learning machine with ensemble of regularization techniques and negative correlation penalty applied to automotive engine coldstart hydrocarbon emission identification. *Neurocomputing*.

Reznik, A. M., Galinskaya, A. A., Dekhtyarenko, O. K., & Nowicki, D. W. (2005). Preprocessing of matrix QCM sensors data for the classification by means of neural network. *Sensors and Actuators. B, Chemical, 106*(1), 158–163. doi:10.1016/j.snb.2004.05.047

Rodahl, M., Höök, F., & Kasemo, B. (1996). QCM Operation in liquids: An explanation of measured variations in frequency and Q factor with liquid conductivity. *Analytical Chemistry, 68*(13), 2219–2227. doi:10.1021/ac951203m PMID:21619308

Rynkiewicz, J. (2012). General bound of overfitting for MLP regression models. *Neurocomputing, 90*(0), 106–110. doi:10.1016/j.neucom.2011.11.028

Schröder, J., Borngräber, R., Eichelbaum, F., & Hauptmann, P. (2002). Advanced interface electronics and methods for QCM. *Sensors and Actuators. A, Physical, 97–98*, 543–547. doi:10.1016/S0924-4247(02)00036-5

Simic, V., & Dimitrijevic, B. (2013). Modelling of automobile shredder residue recycling in the Japanese legislative context. *Expert Systems with Applications, 40*(18), 7159–7167. doi:10.1016/j.eswa.2013.06.075

Speight, R. E., & Cooper, M. A. (2012). A Survey of the 2010 Quartz Crystal Microbalance Literature. *Journal of Molecular Recognition, 25*(May), 451–473. doi:10.1002/jmr.2209 PMID:22899590

Steinwart, I., & Christmann, A. (2008). *Support Vector Machines* (1st ed.). Springer Publishing Company, Incorporated.

Suykens, J. A. K., & Vandewalle, J. (1999). Least squares support vector machine classifiers. *Neural Processing Letters, 9*(3), 293–300. doi:10.1023/A:1018628609742

Torres-Villa, R. A. (2013). *Instrumental techniques for improving the measurements based on quartz crystal microbalances*. Universidad Politécnica de Valencia.

Uysal, I., & Gövenir, H. A. (1999). An overview of regression techniques for knowledge discovery. *The Knowledge Engineering Review, 14*(04), 319–340. doi:10.1017/S026988899900404X

Vembu, S., Vergara, A., Muezzinoglu, M. K., & Huerta, R. (2012). On time series features and kernels for machine olfaction. *Sensors and Actuators. B, Chemical, 174*(0), 535–546. doi:10.1016/j.snb.2012.06.070

Wang, L., & Wu, J. (2012). Neural network ensemble model using PPR and LS-SVR for stock market eorecasting. In D.-S. Huang, Y. Gan, V. Bevilacqua, & J. Figueroa (Eds.), *Advanced Intelligent Computing* (Vol. 6838, pp. 1–8). Springer Berlin Heidelberg. doi:10.1007/978-3-642-24728-6_1

Wang, R., Wang, A., & Song, Q. (2012). Research on the alkalinity of sintering process based on LS-SVM Algorithms. In D. Jin & S. Lin (Eds.), *Advances in Computer Science and Information Engineering* (Vol. 168, pp. 449–454). Springer Berlin Heidelberg; doi:10.1007/978-3-642-30126-1_71

Wasserman, P. D. (1993). *Advanced methods in neural computing* (1st ed.). New York, NY: John Wiley & Sons, Inc.

Wikipedia. (2014). *Quartz crystal microbalance*. Retrieved from http://en.wikipedia.org/wiki/Quartz_crystal_microbalance

Wu, X. (2007). *Optimal designs for segmented polynomial regression models and web-based implementation of optimal design software*. Stony Brook, NY: State University of New York at Stony Brook.

Zeng, Z., & Wang, J. (2010). *Advances in neural network research and applications* (1st ed.). Springer Publishing Company, Incorporated. doi:10.1007/978-3-642-12990-2

Zhang, Z. G., & Chan, S. C. (2011). On kernel selection of multivariate local polynomial modelling and its application to image smoothing and reconstruction. *J. Signal Process. Syst.*, *64*(3), 361–374. doi:10.1007/s11265-010-0495-4

Zilinskas, A., & Baronas, D. (2011). Optimization-Based Evaluation of Concentrations in Modeling the Biosensor-Aided Measurement. *Informatica, 22*(4), 589–600. http://doi.org/http://www.mii.lt/informatica/htm/INFO844.htm

Chapter 17
Optimization Through Nature–Inspired Soft–Computing and Algorithm on ECG Process

Goutam Kumar Bose
Haldia Institute of Technology, India

Pritam Pain
Haldia Institute of Technology, India

ABSTRACT

In the present research work selection of significant machining parameters depending on nature-inspired algorithm is prepared, during machining alumina-aluminum interpenetrating phase composites through electrochemical grinding process. Here during experimentation control parameters like electrolyte concentration (C), voltage (V), depth of cut (D) and electrolyte flow rate (F) are considered. The response data are initially trained and tested applying Artificial Neural Network. The paradoxical responses like higher material removal rate (MRR), lower surface roughness (Ra), lower overcut (OC) and lower cutting force (Fc) are accomplished individually by employing Cuckoo Search Algorithm. A multi response optimization for all the response parameters is compiled primarily by using Genetic algorithm. Finally, in order to achieve a single set of parametric combination for all the outputs simultaneously fuzzy based Grey Relational Analysis technique is adopted. These nature-driven soft computing techniques corroborates well during the parametric optimization of ECG process.

1. INTRODUCTION

Our modern lifestyle is improving day by day because of the swift improvements and developments in modern technology. To overcome our daily life problems, it is important to achieve more efficient solution. Mathematical dynamics of the related solution based on nature has a remarkable impact. Nature servers various possible approach to think about solution and helps to develop efficient scientific methods.

Eventually, the connection between science and nature has made several possibilities for new research work. There is countless nature inspired techniques which can be utilize for the modern intelligent solution

DOI: 10.4018/978-1-5225-2128-0.ch017

approach. As these nature-inspired techniques are very much effective on forming efficient algorithm, they are quite popular amongst modern Artificial Intelligence research. This is also remarkable that these techniques can easily use with other associated intelligent techniques in order to form new hybrid techniques. Mostly, correlative characteristics by the swarm in the nature had given researcher to develop various types of algorithm methods inspired from swarm such as bat, bee, firefly, cuckoo etc. Then again it is similarly possible to generate new nature-inspired techniques based on the theory of evolution. It is also remarkable that efforts are always given for optimizing the pre-deigned techniques to accomplish a more possible ideal solution to the real life problems. Genetic Algorithm is one such nature-inspired technique which is developed based on the theory of survival of the fittest by Darwin.

The ever-increasing precision machining requirements ultimately call for optimized machining process to sustain in the competition in the global market. To sustain in this competitive business industries are introducing several modifications by altering the traditional manufacturing process to non-traditional manufacturing process. Electrochemical Grinding (ECG) is one such non-traditional machining process which is a collective process of electrochemical dissolution and mechanical grinding. This method is generally applied for generating complex shape with high surface finish of high strength electro conductive material, low machinability alloy with high brittleness. In ECG process a small gap between conductive cathode grinding wheel and anode work piece is filled with flowing electrolyte through which dielectric current passes. The main factors affecting ECG process are Electrolyte concentration (C), Machining Voltage (V), Depth of cut (D), Flow rate of electrolyte (F), type of the abrasive wheel, physical properties of the work piece, relative speed in between tool and work piece, particle size on the abrasive wheel etc. As the machining process is mainly governed by the electrochemical dissolution of the work piece material, the generating surface is free from burr and residual stress as a result there is almost no chance of rejecting a material due to the surface cracks. Apparently, ECG process generate finished surface, therefore there is no need of time consuming additional finishing operations.

Some review of the past research works is presented here. Zhang et al. (2015) employed ECG process on Inconel 718. To elongate the wheel life, the brazed diamond wheel is utilised as a tool in place of the electrodeposited diamond wheel. Experiments showed that the tool durability has been improved significantly from 15 hours to 50 hours while a brazed diamond wheel is employed to replace an electrodeposited diamond wheel. Roy et al. (2007) investigated an experimental study, organized by statistical procedure, is made to calculate the effect of the major effecting parameter 'voltage' on the roughness of P-20 grade cemented carbide. The roughness data are investigated for different voltages. Lyubimov et al. (1998) are presented of diamond consumption in electrochemical in comparison with the routine grinding process. Initiation, development and the mutual correlation of various components of the diamond deterioration - adhesion, abrasion, diffusion, chemical wear and cracking at the electrochemical grinding - are discussed. Maksoud and Brooks (1995) investigates the electrochemical grinding process when used to machine metal-bonded diamond composite wheels. These wheels are utilise as form tools to grind ceramics. Operational parameters such as feed rate, electrolyte flow and current density, are investigated. The optimum operating conditions are evaluated. A comparison with conventional grinding methods is made also. Ilhan et al. (1992) has studied to optimize electrochemical grinding (ECG) process responses simultaneously by an off-line multi response optimization methodology. The responses considered as objectives are side and bottom overcuts, total metal removal rate, surface finish, spindle load and cutting wheel wear. It is shown in this paper that the multi-objective optimization technique can be utilise for an ECG operation, and that the optimal operating conditions for any given combination of weights can be achieved depending upon the objectives. Samanta (2009) presented to model roughness of the work surface in end milling by employing adaptive neuro-fuzzy inference system (ANFIS) and genetic algorithms (GAs). The results illustrate the effectiveness of the suggested approach in modelling the surface roughness. This article of Panda and Yadava (2012) reports an intelligent approach for the modelling of DS-ECSM process using finite element method (FEM) and then artificial neural network (ANN) in integrated manner. The ANN model is found to accurately predict Die sinking-electrochemical spark machining process responses for chosen process conditions. The primary objective of Sanjay and Prithvi is the prediction of suitable process control parameters for roughness of the work surface in drilling. Cutting force, cutting speed and machining time are taken as inputs of the adaptive fuzzy neural network and neuro-fuzzy analysis to estimate the values of surface roughness by employing 2, 3, 4, and 5 membership functions. The ideal structures are selected based on minimum of summation of square with the actual values with the predicated values by employing artificial neural-fuzzy inference system (ANFIS) and neuro-fuzzy systems. Zhang el. al (2013) analyzed the work piece surface quality and the material removal rate on process parameters through machining SKD11 by medium speed wire electrical discharge machining (MS-WEDM). The trial data are utilized to model MRR and Ra at optimal parametric combination by a back-propagation neural network combined with genetic algorithm (BPNN-GA) technique. Hossaina et al. (2016) make an effort to build up an intelligent fuzzy expert system (FES) model to calculate the kerf width in CO_2 laser cutting. The employed input parameters are assisting gas pressure, cutting speed, standoff distance and laser power. The fuzzy logic is performed on fuzzy toolbox in MATLAB R2009b by employing Mamdani technique. Ding et al. (2005) presents an optimization approach for process sequencing based on multi-objective fitness: minimum machining cost, lowest possible manufacturing time and best satisfaction of manufacturing sequence rules. A newly developed hybrid approach is planned to incorporate a neural network, genetic algorithm and analytical hierarchical process (AHP) for process sequencing. Zaina et al. (2012) proposed a new approach in estimating a minimum value for machining performance. In this methodology, artificial neural network and genetic algorithm techniques are integrated in order to search for a combination of ideal cutting condition points that achieve the lowest value of machining performance. Yip-Hoi and Dutta (1996) presented various aspects of parallel machining which effect the generation of process plans are discussed. Further a process planner is described with the use of a genetic algorithm for sequencing operations. Implementation results are also included. Shie (2006) focused on finding an ideal cutting parameter setting of high-purity graphite in dry machining conditions by using an artificial neural network and then employing the Sequential Quadratic Programming method. This algorithm yielded better performance than the traditional methods for instance the Taguchi method and the Design of Experiments (DOE) approach. Du et al. (2015) proposed an improved Quantum-inspired cuckoo search algorithm (QCSA) created on the basis of self-adapting adjusting of search range known as IQCSA. The evolution speed factor and aggregation degree factor are primarily initiated into the proposed algorithm. In each iteration process, IQCSA can regulate the search step size dynamically depending on the current evolution speed factor and also aggregation degree factor, what will deliver the search process with more possible dynamic adaptability. Wang et al. (2015) proposed an improved hybrid cooperative algorithm which combines cooperative cuckoo search (CS) algorithm and particle swarm optimization (HC CS-PSO). The cooperative co-evolutionary structure is introduced in cuckoo search algorithm to implement dimensional cooperation. Yang and Deb (2010) presented a wider comparison study by means of some standard test functions and recently designed stochastic test functions. Then the CS algorithm is applied to evaluate engineering design optimization problems, including the design of springs and welded beam structures. The optimized solutions achieved by CS are far better than the best solutions obtained by an efficient particle swarm optimizer. Madi et al. (2012) aimed at investigating the possibilities of using novel meta-heuristic algorithms for example improved harmony search algorithm (IHSA) and cuckoo search (CS) algorithm for training ANNs in laser cutting modelling. The effectiveness of the algorithms is verified by comparing the outcomes with ANN model trained with real coded genetic algorithm (RCGA). Chawla and Duhan (2014) reviewed some of the applications of three newly developed algorithms, such as biogeography-based optimization, cuckoo search and bat algorithm, in various domains of biomedical engineering, i.e. biomedical instrumentation, clinical diagnosis, artificial neural networks, biomedical image processing, biological control system and biomechanics, bioelectronics, and illustrated how these fields have benefitted over the recently introduced MOA based on evolutionary computation. Ma et al. (2012) exhibited on the basis of analyzing the uncommon objectives in hazardous material transportation (HMT), a new multi-objective optimization model for hazardous material transportation (MOMHMT) is verified, which can take into account transportation risk, operation time, risks fairness, the number of sensitive population and multi-batch transportation simultaneously. Afterwards a fuzzy adaptive weighted genetic algorithm (FAWGA) is arranged in order to solve the MOMHMT by designing priority-based encoding method, fuzzy logic control with adaptive weighted assignment mechanism and partial matching crossover. Bose et al. (2011) studied on the identification of process control variables that have significant importance during electrochemical grinding of alumina-aluminium interpenetrating phase composites (Al_2O_3/Al IPC). The two important responses, i.e. better surface finish (Ra) along with possible maximum material removal rate (MRR) are evaluated as objectives that are to be satisfied simultaneously by a set of process control variables like electrolyte concentration, machining voltage, depth of cut and electrolyte flow rate keeping other parameters unaltered.

It is noted that few research study have been done to establish the optimum process variables so as to achieve maximum material removal rate, lowest surface roughness, minimum overcut and least cutting force. However, there is hardly any research study has been done in this field which includes comprehensive use of nature driven metaheuristic technology that can successfully optimize all the output responses simultaneously. Therefore, this is a clear case of multi objective optimization, which stands very challenging to accomplish simultaneously by a distinct set of process variables.

The current research study emphasises on machining of alumina-aluminum (Al_2O_3/Al) interpenetrating phase composite (IPC) material through electrochemical grinding process to reveal the effect of machine control parameters namely electrolyte concentration (C), machining voltage (V), depth of cut (D) and electrolyte flow rate (F), keeping other process control parameters unaltered, on performance responses like material removal rate (MRR), surface roughness (Ra), overcut (OC) and cutting force (Fc). A well-designed experimental combination is employed to reduce the total number of experiments in order to save both time and production cost. The control parameters are varied in three levels for twenty-seven experimental run based on the Taguchi methodology. Primarily the responses data are tested and trained by applying Artificial Neural Network (ANN) for investigating the validity of the experimental runs. This is followed by individual optimization of responses using Cuckoo Search (CS) algorithm. Next Genetic algorithm (GA) is applied to find the ideal or near ideal parametric condition which can simultaneously satisfy the contradictory objectives. Eventually, a well-known Grey relational analysis (GRA) is conducted where the weights of the responses are calculated using fuzzy set theory to full fill the multi criteria decision making (MCDM) process.

2. PLANNING FOR EXPERIMENTATION

Here in this current research study electrochemical grinding (ECG) of Al_2O_3/Al interpenetrating phase composites (IPC) material (Al_2O_3-68.9% and Al-31.1%) synthesized at 1150°C (for 24 hours) has been considered. The mechanical characteristics of the work material are shown in Table 1.

The experimentation is performed in an improved (microprocessor controlled) and modified surface grinder that uses a grinding wheel having 150 mm diameter with 12.27 mm width where the surface consists of metal bonding and diamond abrasive particles. The abrasive grit size is 100 and the width of the layer comprising the diamond is 3 mm thick. The grinding wheel is mounted at the tip of the rotating spindle which is governed by a DC motor rotating at a 3500 rpm.

During machining, the machining current is noted by using an ammeter connected to the circuit. Figure 1 displays the machining setup along with attachment feed drive mechanism.

Present work consists of the experimental study of the characteristic properties of the ECG process depending on various process control parametric combinations like electrolytic concentration, machining voltage, depth of cut and electrolyte flow rate on MRR, Ra, Overcut and force. However, there are other factors such as type of power (continuous), feed rate (0.4 mm/sec) etc. which may affect the performance, are kept constant during the experimentation. Sodium chloride (NaCl) solution is used as flowing electrolyte. The dimension of the flat rectangular work piece is 23 mm x 15 mm x 5 mm. Table 2 displays the various levels of process control parameters during machining operation.

Throughout machining, the feed movement of the worktable is upheld by a microprocessor controller unit. The feed drive system is controlled by a stepper motor (Type: STM - 1100), generating torque of 10 kg-cm having angular resolution of 1.8° / step, voltage phase of 24 VDC and current phase of 0.67 Ampere. The machining time is recorded using stopwatch. Before and after each machining run the work pieces are cleaned properly and the respective weights are measured with the help of an electronic weighing machine (Maker: Mettler Toledo; Model no: AG285) of precision 0.0002 mg. Perthometer-M1, of Mahr Gmbh make is utilized to measure the surface roughness. For every combination three trials were performed and average is taken for analysis. Table 3 displays the different combinations of process control variables and the associated responses.

Table 1. Properties of the work material (Al_2O_3/Al IPC)

Properties	Values (Synthesis condition is 11500/24 hour)
Fracture origin: Principal	Separation at Al_2O_3/Al grain boundary
Grain size (micron)	Al_2O_3 – 4.27, Al - 1.42
Bulk density (gm/cm³)	3.54
Bend Strength (MPa)	458 ± 15
Compressive Strength (MPa)	576
Elastic modulus (GPa)	67
Micro hardness No.(VHN)	364
Conductivity (10^5ohm^{-1}cm^{-1}at RT)	0.4

Figure 1. The machining setup for the Electrochemical grinding

Table 2. Control parameters and their levels

Control Parameters	Sign	Units	Levels		
			L_1	L_2	L_3
Electrolyte Concentration	C	gm/lit	20	25	30
Machining Voltage	V	volts	15	20	25
Depth of Cut	D	mm	0.04	0.08	0.12
Electrolyte Flow Rate	F	lit/sec	0.1	0.2	0.3

3. ARTIFICIAL NEURAL NETWORK

Artificial Neural Network (ANN) is globally accepted for self-adaptive approach of non-linear experimental model. They are very powerful tool for experimental modelling, particularly when the relationship between the data are unknown. ANN can find out the interrelationship and associate pattern in between the data sets and expected target values. After training, ANN helps in predicting the result of new independent data. This algorithm is basically developed on the basis of neural network.

Table 3. Combination of parameters and responses

Exp. No.	Control Parameter				Responses			
	C (gm/lit)	V (volts)	D (mm)	F (lit/sec)	MRR (gm/min)	Ra (μm)	OC (mm)	Fc (kgf)
1	25	15	0.12	0.2	0.242	0.348	0.174	0.168
2	30	25	0.08	0.2	0.402	0.805	0.125	0.608
3	30	20	0.12	0.2	0.322	0.602	0.175	0.445
4	25	25	0.04	0.2	0.335	0.825	0.102	0.688
5	20	20	0.12	0.2	0.118	1.160	0.065	0.588
6	25	20	0.04	0.1	0.213	0.424	0.174	0.537
7	20	25	0.08	0.2	0.130	1.434	0.043	0.944
8	25	25	0.12	0.2	0.197	1.414	0.067	0.864
9	25	20	0.12	0.3	0.287	1.021	0.134	0.394
10	30	20	0.08	0.1	0.262	0.415	0.206	0.489
11	25	20	0.08	0.2	0.303	0.688	0.162	0.489
12	20	20	0.04	0.2	0.162	0.628	0.100	0.501
13	25	15	0.08	0.3	0.486	0.304	0.275	0.330
14	20	20	0.08	0.1	0.104	0.750	0.074	0.686
15	25	20	0.08	0.2	0.303	0.688	0.162	0.489
16	25	20	0.12	0.1	0.152	0.741	0.106	0.638
17	25	25	0.08	0.1	0.171	0.957	0.076	1.101
18	25	20	0.08	0.2	0.303	0.688	0.162	0.489
19	25	25	0.08	0.3	0.361	1.282	0.093	0.451
20	25	15	0.08	0.1	0.195	0.208	0.204	0.074
21	25	20	0.04	0.3	0.561	0.566	0.233	0.387
22	20	20	0.08	0.3	0.176	1.038	0.091	0.402
23	20	15	0.08	0.2	0.149	0.354	0.122	0.144
24	30	15	0.08	0.2	0.532	0.158	0.357	0.260
25	30	20	0.08	0.3	0.672	0.549	0.277	0.379
26	30	20	0.04	0.2	0.612	0.362	0.307	0.423
27	25	15	0.04	0.2	0.439	0.164	0.305	0.236

Each neuron takes a set of inputs (X_i, i=1, 2…., n-1, n) from associated neurons and issue the adjusted output signals (O_i, i= 1to K) to the end nodes. The function of the synapses is to multiply each input data, X_i by the associated weight W_i value and send the modified signal to the next hidden layer. Equation 1 displays the net input to each neuron in the hidden layer.

$$I_i = \sum_{i=1}^{n} W_i X_i \tag{1}$$

In general, there will be no output response if the activation level of the node exceeds a predetermined threshold value. The output signal of a neuron is generally noted by a sigmoid function expressed as in equation 2.

$$O_i = f(I_i) = \frac{1}{1+e^{-I_i}} \tag{2}$$

Figure 2 displays the schematic diagram of an artificial neuron.
The most usually used neural network architectures are

- Self-organizing neural networks.
- Feedback neural networks.
- Feed forward neural networks

Figure 3 illustrates the architecture of a neural network.

Problems having nonlinear or complex data can be very easily handled even if the data are not much related and date set is incomplete. The technique is very much suited for modelling a complex process like ECG.

Result Analysis

The statistical design of the data set is done by using the software Matlab R2015a. The algorithms considered in Matlab during calculating are as follows: the data has been randomly divided using the Divider and function, Levenberg-Marquardt while training, Mean Squared Error (MSE) for performance. The simulink model of ANN for considering four input parameters to optimize the outputs is shown in Figure 4. In this ANN model 27 experimental run are conducted for analysing.

In the present work back-propagation algorithm is employed to develop the gradient and the Jacobian. The backpropagation computation is designed using the chain rule of calculus backward throughout the artificial network. Amongst the network output and target value of ANN's model Mean Squared Error

Figure 2. Schematic diagram of an artificial neural

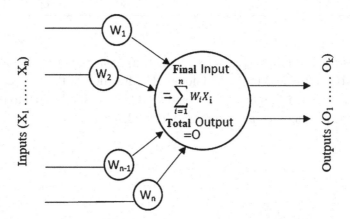

Figure 3. Architecture of a neural network

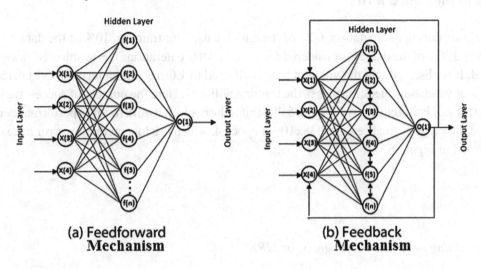

(a) Feedforward
Mechanism

(b) Feedback
Mechanism

Figure 4. Simulink diagram of ANN analyse

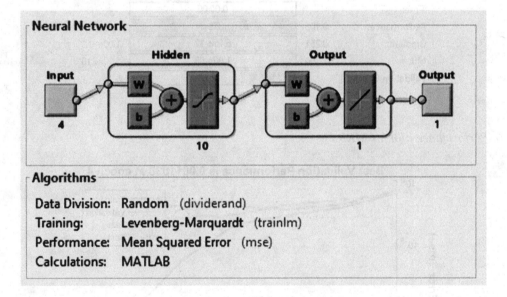

(MSE) is applied. Epoch is the demonstration in the set of training (input and/or target) vectors to a network and use for evaluating the new weights and biases for the data. Primarily the maximum number of 1000 epoch is set to terminate the training for each case. Also, for every investigation, if the magnitude of the gradient falls below 1 x10^{-7}, the training will stop.

A regression plot shows the correlation between the outputs of the network with the targets value. The four plots indicate the training, validation, testing along with overall data. The dotted line in every plot signifies the perfect result – outputs = targets. The continuous line signifies the best fit linear regression line in between outputs with targets. If R = 1, this signifies that there is an exact linear relationship in between outputs and targets. If R is close to zero, then there is a non-linear relationship in between outputs and targets.

Analysis to Maximize MRR

In this analysis, during computation, 60% of the data are used for training, 10% of the data are used for validation and 30% of the data are considered for testing. After 6 iterations it is terminated since the MSE is achieved. It is observed that the gradient here is allowed to $1.0\text{x}10^{-7}$ and it terminates at $6.15\text{x}10^{-12}$. If the number of validation check reaches 6, the training will stop. Here the number of successive iterations performed for validation checks is 2. Figure 5 illustrates the neural network training performance progress.

Best validation performance is $1.1038\text{x}10^{-3}$ at epoch 4, which is a low prediction error measured with MSE revealed in Figure 6.

Figure 5. Training performance progress for MRR

Progress			
Epoch:	0	6 iterations	1000
Time:		0:00:00	
Performance:	0.102	1.85e-21	0.00
Gradient:	0.251	6.15e-12	1.00e-07
Mu:	0.00100	1.00e-08	1.00e+10
Validation Checks:	0	2	6

Figure 6. Performance plot for MRR

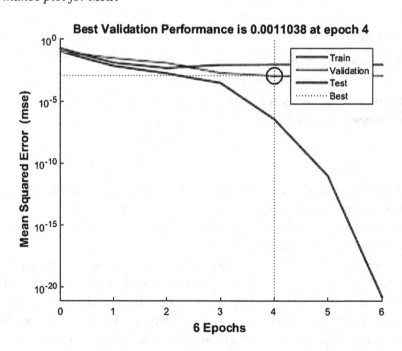

The figure also specifies the iteration where the validation performance reached to its minimum. The training continued up to 6 iterations before the training terminate. As validation and testing curve flows the similar trained, this plot doesn't indicate major problems. The regression is shown in Figure 7.

In Figure 7, regression plot in case of training R=0.99999, in case of validation R=0.99351 and in case of testing R=0.89376. Hence overall R=0.95306. Therefore, the training data directs a good fit as the validation and test results mutually show R values closer to 1.

Analysis to Minimize Ra

In this analyse, during computation 75% of the data are used for training, 15% of the data are used for validation and for testing 10% of the data are considered. After 9 iterations it got terminated since the MSE is achieved. It is observed that the gradient here is allowed to 1.0×10^{-7} and it terminates at 7.29×10^{-8}. If the number of validation check reaches 6, the training will stop. Here the number of successive iterations performed for validation checks is 4. Figure 8 illustrates the neural network training performance progress.

Figure 7. Regression plot of MRR

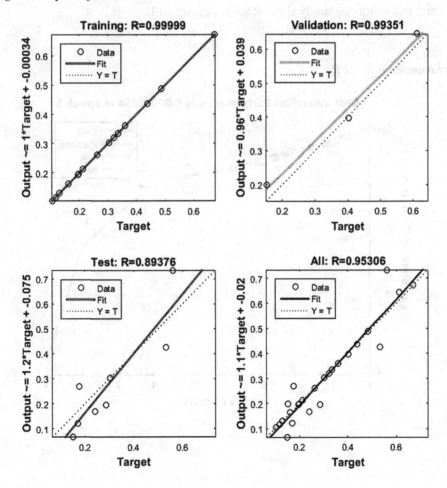

Figure 8. Training performance progress for Ra

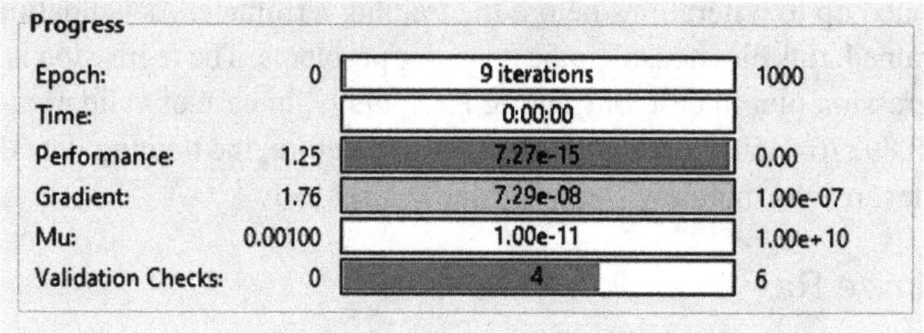

Progress			
Epoch:	0	9 iterations	1000
Time:		0:00:00	
Performance:	1.25	7.27e-15	0.00
Gradient:	1.76	7.29e-08	1.00e-07
Mu:	0.00100	1.00e-11	1.00e+10
Validation Checks:	0	4	6

Best validation performance is 0.32954×10^{-3} at epoch 5, which is a low prediction error measured with MSE revealed in Figure 9.

The figure also specifies the iteration where the validation performance reached to its minimum. The training continued up to 9 iterations before the training terminated. As all the curves follow the similar trend till 5 Epochs therefore this plot doesn't indicate any major problems. The regression is illustrated in Figure 10.

In Figure 10, regression plot in case of training R=0.99566, in case of validation R=0.99911 and in case of testing R=0.99402. Hence overall R=0.9958. Therefore, the training data shows a decent fit as the validation and test results mutually show R values closer to 1.

Figure 9. Performance plot for Ra

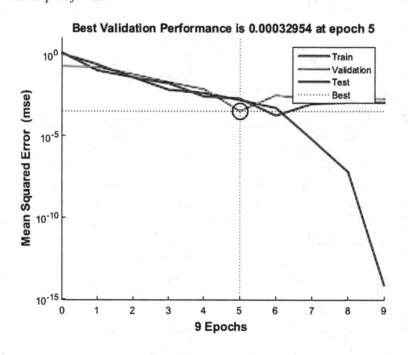

Figure 10. Regression plot of MRR

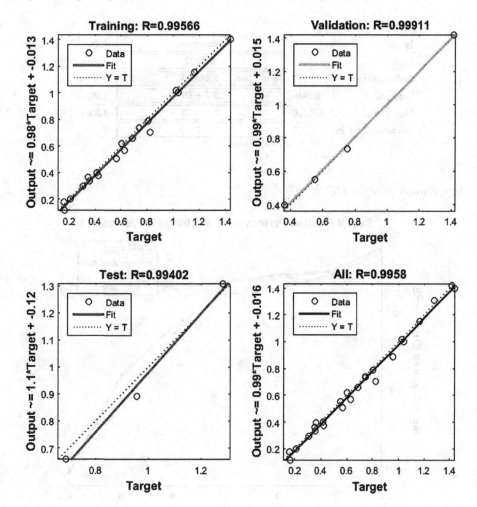

Analysis to Minimize OC

While computing for training 65% of the data are considered, for validation 15% of the data are considered and for testing 20% of the data are considered. After 6 iterations it is terminated as mean square error has been attained. It is noted that the gradient here is 5378×10^{-9}. If the number of validation check reaches 6, the training will stop. Here the number of successive iterations performed for validation checks is 0. Figure 11 represents the neural network training performance progress.

Best validation performance is 0.24101×10^{-3} at epoch 6, which is the lowest possible error measured with MSE exposed in Figure 12.

The figure also specifies the iteration where the validation performance reached to its minimum. The training continued up to 6 iterations before the training terminate. All the curves here follow almost similar trend. The regression plot is shows in Figure 13.

Figure 11. Training performance progress for OC

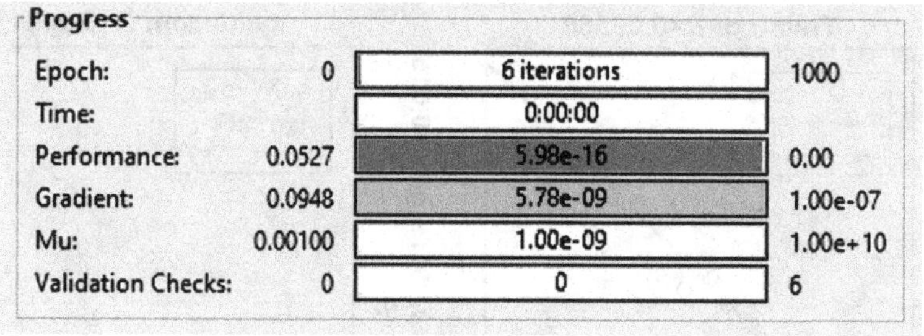

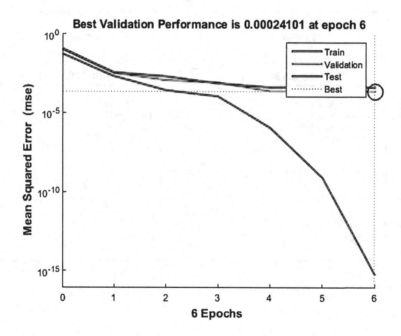

Figure 12. Performance plot for OC

Here in the Figure 13 in case of training R=0.1, in case of validation R=0.99148 and in case of testing R=0.9907. Hence overall R=0.99237. Therefore, the training data shows a decent fit as the validation and test results mutually show R values closer to 1.

Analysis to Minimize Fc

While computing for training 55% of the data are considered, for validation 25% of the data are considered and for testing 20% of the data are considered. After 6 successful iterations it is terminated which point out that the mean square error is arrived. It is also observed that the gradient here is 5.35×10^{-12}. If the number of validation check reaches 6, the training will stop. Here successive iterations performed for validation checks is 3. Figure 14 shows the neural network training performance progress for Fc.

Best validation performance is 22.566×10^{-3} at epoch 3, which is the lowest possible error measured with MSE exposed in Figure 15.

Figure 13. Regression plot of OC

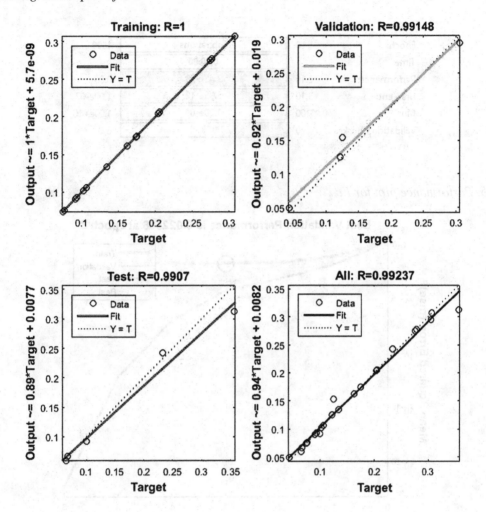

The figure also specifies the iteration where the validation performance reached to its minimum. The training continued up to 6 iterations before the training terminated. As all the curves follow the similar trend till 3 epochs, this plot doesn't indicate major problems. The regression plot is shown in Figure 16.

Here in Figure 16 in case of training R=0.99877, in case of validation R=0.91995 and in case of testing R=0.90642. Hence overall R=0.91007. Therefore, the training data shows a decent fit as the validation and test results mutually show R values closer to 1.

4. CUCKOO SEARCH ALGORITHM FOLLOWING LEVY FLIGHTS

Cuckoo Search (CS) algorithm is a new metaheuristics algorithm which is developed based on mimicking the characteristics of cuckoo. In this algorithm each egg in a nest is represented by a possible solution and each cuckoo egg denotes a new solution. The objective is to apply the new and probably superior solu-

Figure 14. Training performance progress for Fc

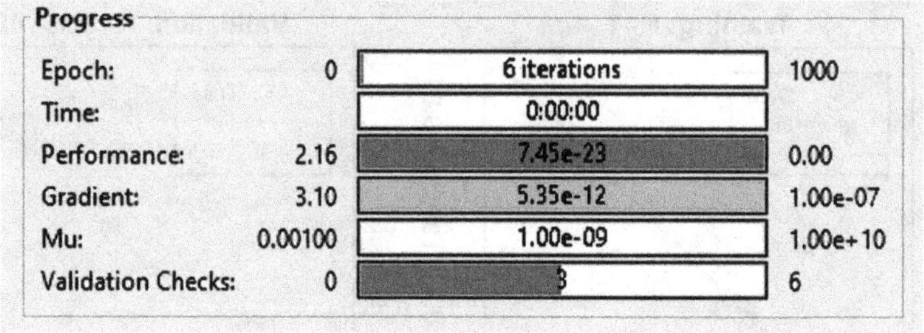

Progress
Epoch: 0 6 iterations 1000
Time: 0:00:00
Performance: 2.16 7.45e-23 0.00
Gradient: 3.10 5.35e-12 1.00e-07
Mu: 0.00100 1.00e-09 1.00e+10
Validation Checks: 0 3 6

Figure 15. Performance plot for Fc

Best Validation Performance is 0.022566 at epoch 3
Mean Squared Error (mse)
10^0
10^-5
10^-10
10^-15
10^-20
0 1 2 3 4 5 6
6 Epochs
Train
Validation
Test
Best

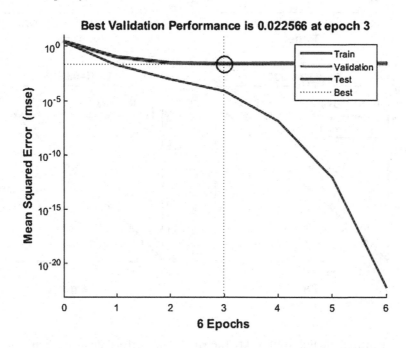

tions to substitute a lower solution in the nests. More complicated cases such as multiple eggs in a nest, implying a set of solution, can be merged in this algorithm. This algorithm follows three steps as follows:

1. First individual cuckoo lays one egg at a randomly chosen host nest.
2. The next generation will inherit best nest with excellent quality of eggs

Finally, the number of available host nest is constant and the possibility of parasitic egg recognition by the host bird is $p_a \in [0,1]$. The host bird can either throw away the sponging egg or ditch that nest for a better new nest. For practicality, in the later hypothesis it can be assumed that fraction p_a of the host nests is substituted by new nests (with new random possible solutions). Generally, the quality or fitness of a solution is suggested to be proportional to the value of the objective function in case of a maximization problem.

Figure 16. Regression plot of Fc

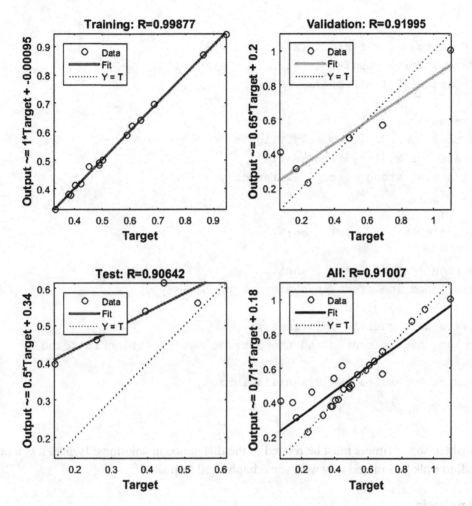

Guided by the above three rules, the CS is abridged by the pseudo code (see Algorithm 1). When making new solutions $x_i(t+1)$ for the ith cuckoo, the following Lévy flight is performed

$$x_i(t+1) = x_i(t) + \alpha \otimes L\acute{e}vy(\lambda) \qquad (3)$$

where a >0 is the size of stage, which should be connected to the scale of the problem of interest. The product $\otimes$ denotes entry-wise multiplications. In this experimentation, a Lévy flight is considered, in which the step-lengths are distributed according to the following possibility spreading

$$L\acute{e}vy \ u = t^{-\lambda}, 1 < \lambda \leq 3 \qquad (4)$$

It has an infinite alteration. Here, the successive steps of a cuckoo essentially outline an arbitrary walk process which obey a power-law step-length distribution to a heavy tail. It is significant that, in the real world, if a cuckoo's egg is very alike to a host's eggs, then this cuckoo's egg is most unlikely to

Algorithm 1. Cuckoo Search via Le'vy Flights

```
begin
    Objective function f(x), x=(x1, x2,........xd)ᵀ
    Generate initial population of
    n host nests xi (i=1, 2, 3......, n)
while
    (t<Maxgeneration) or (stop criterion)
    Get a cuckoo randomly by Levy Flights
    calculate its quality/fitness Fi
    Choose a nest among n (say, j) randomly
if
    (Fi > F j),
    Replace j by the new solution;
end
    A function (pa) of inferior nests
    are discarded and fresh ones are built;
    Keep the best solutions
    (or nests with quality solutions);
    The solutions are ranked and the current best solution is found
end while
    Post process results and visualization
end
```

be distinguished, so the fitness must be related to the difference in solutions. Hence, it is a decent idea to do a random walk in a biased way with some haphazard step sizes.

Result Analysis

In the preliminary study, four parameters are analysed specifically on their implicit effects on material removal rate (MRR), surface roughness (Ra), overcut (OC) and cutting force (Fc). To optimize the experimental test functions, a MATLAB code is generated, by using MATLAB Version R2015a, is established based on the CS. During analysis, the numbers smaller than $4.9407e^{-324}$ are taken as zero. The PC used is an Intel(R) Core i5 3230 M CPU @ 2.60GHz having 4GB of internal memory, with 64 Bit OS.

Optimization problem can be formulated as follows:

Find C, V, D, F
To Maximize: MRR and
To Minimize: Ra, OC, Fc
The cutting parameters are varied as:

$$20 \leq C \leq 30 \tag{5}$$

$$15 \leq V \leq 25 \tag{6}$$

$$0.04 \leq D \leq 0.12 \tag{7}$$

$$0.1 \leq F \leq 0.3 \tag{8}$$

At first each response is individually optimized applying Cuckoo Search algorithm via Levy flights. α is size of the population, i.e. number of the host nest, and Pa is the probability of the discovery rate. In this calculation, α assumed a value of 25 and Pa assumed a value of 0.25. The step size factor is calculated as L/100 and the total number of iteration is allowed up to 50,000 iterations.

Maximum MRR is obtained 0.975 gm/min for parametric combination of C = 30 gm/lit, v = 15 volts, D = 0.04 mm and F = 0.3 lit/sec. Whereas minimum Ra is obtained 0.115 μm with the parametric combination of C = 30 gm/lit, v = 15 volts, D = 0.04 mm and F = 0.3 lit/sec. Lowest OC is obtained at 0.036 mm having parametric combination of C = 20 gm/lit, v = 25 volts, D = 0.04 mm and F = 0.1 lit/sec. Finally, lowest Fc is obtained 0.054 kgf while the parametric combination is C = 20 gm/lit, v = 15 volts, D = 0.04 mm and F = 0.1 lit/sec.

To check the proposed results, developed from the algorithm, verification experiments have been done and the results are illustrated in the Table 4.

From the validation table, it is observed that the forecast values through developed model are virtually similar to the experimental results. Therefore, this model is acceptable for prediction.

5. GENETIC ALGORITHM

Genetic algorithm (GA) is a nature inspired techniques which can find out the global best or near best solution from a set of contradictory objective function when the variables are discrete, non-linear and non-convex. This algorithm is developed on the basis of the theory of survival of the fittest by Darwin.

To find out the finest solution the function need to make two modifications. Using the penalty function, the first alteration changed the original constrained function into a variable function, as:

Table 4. Verification experiments

Responses	Control Parameter				Predicted Result	Validate Result	Error %
	C (gm/lit)	V (volts)	D (mm)	F (lit/sec)			
MRR	30	15	0.04	0.3	0.975	0.861	11.718
Ra	30	15	0.04	0.3	0.115	0.107	6.851
OC	20	25	0.04	0.1	0.036	0.031	13.331
FC	20	15	0.04	0.1	0.054	0.051	5.433

Minimize $f(X) + R\sum_{i=1}^{n}\Phi\big(g_i(X)\big)$ (9)

Subjected to $x_j^{(l)} \leq x_j \leq x_j^{(u)}$, $j = 1,2,....,n$ (10)

Where Φ is a general penalty function define as:

$$\Phi = (Z) = \langle Z \rangle^2$$ (11)

Where

$$\langle Z \rangle = \begin{cases} Z & if \quad Z > 0 \\ 0 & if \quad Z \leq 0 \end{cases}$$ (12)

R is the constant penalty parameter.

Maximizing the fitness objective function, F(X), the second alteration function is minimized as:

$$F(X) = F_{max} - \left(f(X) + R\sum_{i=1}^{n}\Phi\big(g_i(X)\big) \right) = F_{max} - f'(X)$$ (13)

where,

$$F_{max} > f'(X)$$ (14)

F(X) denotes the general fitness function.

It usually works with structures of typically binary numbers (0-1) repressing the problem variables. A binary structure can consider as a biological chromosome.

Analysis of the Result for Multi-Objective Global Optimization

Multi-objective optimization of all the responses is carried out by applying Genetic Algorithm (GA). The objective functions are optimized so that four contradictory objectives i.e. maximum MRR, lower OC, lower Ra and minimum Fc are satisfied simultaneously. The control parameters are varied within a range as shown in equation 5-8.

The following conditions are contemplated during computation:

- *Population*
  - ○ Population size: 50 (As the input variables are less than 5)
  - ○ Population type: Double vector
  - ○ Creation function: Constraint dependent
  - ○ Initial range: [-10;10]
  - ○ Initial population: NULL
  - ○ Initial Scores: NULL
- *Selection*
  - ○ Selection function: Tournament
  - ○ Tournament size: 2
- *Reproduction*
  - ○ Crossover fraction: 0.8
- *Mutation*
  - ○ Mutation function: Constant dependent
- *Crossover*
  - ○ Crossover function: Intermediate
  - ○ Ratio: 1
- *Migration*
  - ○ Direction: Forward
  - ○ Interval: 20
  - ○ Fraction: 0.2
- *Multiobjective problem settings*
  - ○ Distance measure function: @ distancecrowding
  - ○ Pareto front population fraction: 0.35
- *Hybrid function*
  - ○ Hybrid function: None
- *Stopping Criteria*
  - ○ Generations: 100 x number of variables
  - ○ Stall generations: 100
  - ○ Fitness limit: -infinity
  - ○ Time limit: infinity
  - ○ Stall time limit: infinity
  - ○ Function tolerance: 1×10^{-4}
  - ○ Constrain tolerance: 1×10^{-3}
- *Display to command window*
  - ○ Level of display: off
- *User function evaluation*
  - ○ Evaluation fitness function: in serial

Figure 17 illustrate the different plot functions of GA where four opposing objectives are optimized simultaneously.

Here the total number of iteration required for optimization is 102 and it gives 45 combinations for the control parameters which also gives the corresponding responses. Optimization terminated as the average change in the spread of Pareto solutions has been attained to its tolerance value. As the general

Figure 17. Different plot functions for GA

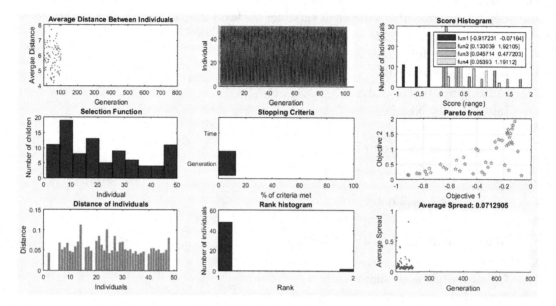

setting of the genetic algorithm is to minimize the objective function, the negative sign is eliminated for maximizing MRR. From Figure 17 it is evident that the responses are varied within a range. For MRR the range is 0.917 gm/min to 0.072 gm/min, for Ra it varies between 1.921 μm to 0.133 μm, for OC it is 0.477 mm to 0.046 mm and for Fc it is between 1.191 kgf to 0.054 kgf. Therefore, in order to accomplish at an optimal or near optimal parametric combination which will all together satisfy opposing nature of the responses, Fuzzy Gray Relational Analysis is conducted. The output combination is illustrated in Table 5.

Table 5. Parametric combination with responses

Exp. No	Control Parameters				Responses			
	C (gm/lit)	V (volts)	D (mm)	F (lit/sec)	MRR (gm/min)	Ra (μm)	Overcut (mm)	Force (kgf)
1	20	15	0.04	0.1	0.072	0.137	0.134	0.054
2	29	16	0.05	0.3	0.849	0.192	0.435	0.444
3	21	25	0.12	0.3	0.121	1.921	0.046	0.637
4	21	25	0.08	0.1	0.138	1.179	0.058	1.191
5	21	25	0.11	0.2	0.144	1.687	0.053	0.848
6	28	15	0.04	0.3	0.776	0.169	0.413	0.425
7	21	25	0.08	0.2	0.147	1.236	0.056	1.039
8	23	25	0.09	0.1	0.168	1.163	0.069	1.066
9	29	17	0.05	0.3	0.785	0.262	0.389	0.425
10	27	20	0.04	0.3	0.673	0.485	0.284	0.396
11	22	25	0.09	0.2	0.176	1.503	0.057	0.757

continued on next page

Table 5. Continued

Exp. No	Control Parameters				Responses			
	C (gm/lit)	V (volts)	D (mm)	F (lit/sec)	MRR (gm/min)	Ra (μm)	Overcut (mm)	Force (kgf)
12	24	16	0.05	0.2	0.363	0.242	0.255	0.248
13	21	25	0.12	0.2	0.134	1.782	0.050	0.817
14	30	15	0.04	0.3	0.917	0.145	0.472	0.478
15	22	25	0.1	0.3	0.170	1.648	0.057	0.624
16	27	17	0.04	0.2	0.527	0.275	0.318	0.340
17	27	18	0.09	0.3	0.489	0.513	0.247	0.369
18	22	25	0.09	0.2	0.160	1.404	0.058	0.969
19	21	25	0.05	0.1	0.099	0.929	0.046	1.154
20	28	16	0.04	0.1	0.428	0.184	0.341	0.206
21	27	23	0.09	0.3	0.406	1.015	0.139	0.457
22	25	15	0.04	0.2	0.344	0.166	0.279	0.175
23	24	19	0.06	0.1	0.194	0.474	0.155	0.443
24	29	17	0.07	0.3	0.627	0.342	0.324	0.382
25	27	25	0.07	0.2	0.395	0.954	0.121	0.567
26	26	17	0.06	0.3	0.557	0.336	0.301	0.365
27	22	17	0.06	0.2	0.319	0.404	0.196	0.309
28	23	23	0.1	0.2	0.216	1.287	0.086	0.623
29	23	25	0.08	0.3	0.239	1.323	0.075	0.658
30	28	18	0.06	0.3	0.649	0.405	0.310	0.398
31	29	16	0.05	0.3	0.828	0.175	0.433	0.441
32	24	18	0.08	0.2	0.335	0.565	0.189	0.358
33	28	22	0.05	0.2	0.551	0.629	0.207	0.449
34	25	22	0.11	0.3	0.268	1.240	0.108	0.461
35	22	25	0.09	0.3	0.177	1.553	0.055	0.716
36	21	25	0.1	0.2	0.154	1.525	0.055	0.909
37	28	18	0.04	0.3	0.755	0.359	0.344	0.410
38	24	24	0.08	0.2	0.255	1.033	0.100	0.719
39	28	16	0.06	0.3	0.743	0.213	0.391	0.414
40	23	17	0.05	0.1	0.164	0.307	0.167	0.273
41	26	23	0.04	0.3	0.499	0.722	0.174	0.461
42	25	21	0.04	0.2	0.293	0.542	0.168	0.553
43	21	24	0.08	0.2	0.161	1.216	0.062	0.930
44	22	23	0.08	0.2	0.180	1.110	0.076	0.807
45	30	15	0.04	0.3	0.908	0.133	0.477	0.470

6. MULTI OBJECTIVE MODEL USING GREY RELATION ANALYSIS

Grey Relation Analysis (GRA) can utilize to optimize reliable responses simultaneously which opposes one another in nature. The grey system theory was developed by Deng in 1989's and at the present time it is frequently used for analysing experimental design in which the model is undetermined or the information is not complete indicating a combination of known and unknown information's.

GRA builds the relationship in between desired (best/ ideal) with real experimental data. Grey grade is computed by averaging the grey coefficient of respective response. In this study multiple response optimizations are found out by converting into a single grey relational grade. The calculated grey relational grade range varies in between 0 to 1, where closer to 1 values indicate its closeness towards the global possible idle solution. Finally, among all the combinations of process control variables, one that attains the maximum grey relational grade is taken to be the best parametric combination.

If higher value is for the better performance such as MRR then it is normalized as per equation,

$$X_{ij} = \frac{Y_{ij} - Min[Y_{ij,} i = 1, 2, ...n]}{Max[Y_{ij,} i = 1, 2, ...n] - Min[Y_{ij,} i = 1, 2, ...n]} \tag{15}$$

If lower value for the better performance such as F_c, OC and Ra then it is expressed as,

$$X_{ij} = \frac{Max[Y_{ij,} i = 1, 2, ...n] - Y_{ij}}{Max[Y_{ij,} i = 1, 2, ...n] - Min[Y_{ij,} i = 1, 2, ...n]} \tag{16}$$

The grey relational co-efficient is utilised to articulate the relationship between actual normalized experimental output with reference. This relation co-efficient can be evaluated as;

$$Y(X_{oj}, X_{ij}) = \frac{\nabla_{min} + \varsigma\nabla_{max}}{\nabla_{ij} + \varsigma\nabla_{max}} [i = 1, 2, ...n \ \& \ j = 1, 2, ...m] \tag{17}$$

where,

$$\nabla_{ij} = |X_{oj} - X_{ij}|$$
,

$$\nabla_{min} = Min[\nabla_{ij}, i = 1, 2, ...n \ \& \ j = 1, 2, ...m]$$

and

$$\nabla_{max} = Max[\nabla_{ij}, i = 1, 2, ...n \ \& \ j = 1, 2, ...m]$$

ς = Distinguished co-efficient (varied with in a range 0-1)

Usually, the notable co-efficient can be regulated to fit the partial requirements. MRR and Ra both of them are given equal weights that assume a value of 0.5. The expression is as follows:

$$\Gamma\left(X_0, X_i\right) = \frac{1}{m}\sum_{i=1}^{m} Y\left(X_{0j}, X_{ij}\right) \tag{18}$$

where, m = Number of response parameter.

To optimize both the response at a time by single combination of process variables, GRA is performed. The combination with the rank 1 full fill multiple response parameters optimization.

Fuzzy Set Theory

Fuzzy set theory is the finest controlling tool to solve the uncertainty in decision making problem. Rarely unclear judgments of decision maker(s) makes it difficult to evaluate accurate mathematical assessment. Use of linguistic assessments values of weights of the conditions in the problem is a more valuable approach as compared to numerical values (Keufmann & Gupta, 1991). Decision matrix can be changed into a fuzzy decision matrix and associated with weighted normalized fuzzy decision matrix while considering the decision makers' fuzzy ratings. In a cosmos of discussion X, a fuzzy set $\hat{d}$ is characterized by an associated function $\mu_{\hat{d}}\left(x\right)$ i.e., degree of association of x in $\hat{d}$ which maps each element x in X to a real number in the interval [0-1]. Triangular fuzzy number (TFN), $\hat{d}$ can be defined as a triplet (d_1, d_2, d_3) and the membership function is defined (Dubois & Prade, 1979) as shown by equation 19.

$$\mu_{\hat{d}}(x) = \begin{cases} 0, & x \leq d_1 \\ \dfrac{x - d_1}{d_2 - d_1}, & d_1 \leq x \leq d_2 \\ \dfrac{d_3 - x}{d_3 - d_2}, & d_2 \leq x \leq d_3 \\ 0, & x > d_3 \end{cases} \tag{19}$$

The transformation technique of fuzzy number into non-fuzzy number, that is, crisp value is recognized as defuzzyfication. In this study 'centroid of area' technique for determining Best Non-Fuzzy Performance (BNP) value is applied.

$$BNP = \frac{[(d_3 - d_1) - (d_2 - d_1)]}{3} + d_1 \tag{20}$$

Choosing the linguistic ratings for criteria:

These linguistic variables can be shown in positive triangular fuzzy numbers as Table 6.

Table 6. Linguistic terms for criteria

Linguistic Terms	Fuzzy Number
Very High (VH)	(0.9,1.0,1.0)
High (H)	(0.7,0.9,1.0)
Moderate High (MH)	(0.5,0.7,0.9)
Moderate (M)	(0.3,0.5,0.7)
Moderate Low (ML)	(0.1,0.3,0.5)
Low (L)	(0.0,0.1,0.3)
Very Low (VL)	(0.0,0.0, 0.1)

Multi Criteria Decision Making (MCDM) Analysis

In the present research study, the four contradictory responses i.e. MRR, Ra, OC and Fc have got different level of importance. Here importance is given on Ra rather than on other parameters because ECG is mainly used for finishing purpose.

From fuzzy set theory, the criteria weights are calculated for respective criteria as tabulated in Table 7.

Here 45 experimental data set as obtained through GA are further evaluated. In this MCDM analysis of the MRR is aimed to be maximum i.e. larger is better and other responses are aimed to be minimum, i.e. smaller is better.

Optimization of the Parameters

The calculated weights for MRR, Ra, OC and Fc are 23.94%, 38.03%, 30.99% and 7.04% respectively. Table 8 illustrate the grey relation co-efficient along with grades corresponding to parametric settings and responses for Table 5 material.

The results show that experiment number 1 has the maximum grey relational grade value. As defined above, this testing setup fulfils multiple response parameter optimizations. Hence, the experimental run of 1 which having parametric combination as C 20 gm/lit, V 15 volts, D 0.04 mm and F 0.1 lit/sec is the best among other experimental setup for having high MRR, low Ra, OC and Fc.

The confirmation experiment performed with the above optimal combination results in grey relational grade MRR, Ra, OC and Fc obtained 0.072 gm/min, 0.137 μm, 0.134 mm and 0.054 kgf respectively. It is found that MRR, Ra, OC and Fc increase considerably as appeared from computational results by using ideal machining variables combinations. Table 9 displays the validation results while machining at elevate condition.

Table 7. Weight criteria for deference responses

Criteria	Linguistic Terms	Fuzzy Number	BNP
MRR	MH	0.5,0.7,0.9	0.2394
Ra	VH	0.9,1.0,1.0	0.3803
OC	H	0.7,0.9,1.0	0.3099
Fc	Ml	0.1,0.3,0.5,	0.0704

Table 8. Grey relation co-efficient along with grades and ranks

Exp. No.	Response				Grey Co-efficient				GREY Grade	Rank
	MRR (gm/ min)	Ra (μm)	OC (mm)	Fc (kgf)	MRR (gm/ min)	Ra (μm)	OC (mm)	Fc (kgf)		
1	0.072	0.137	0.134	0.054	0.19	0.99	0.60	1.00	0.70	1
2	0.849	0.192	0.435	0.444	0.75	0.92	0.26	0.17	0.52	4
3	0.121	1.921	0.046	0.637	0.20	0.28	1.00	0.12	0.40	22
4	0.138	1.179	0.058	1.191	0.21	0.39	0.92	0.07	0.40	24
5	0.144	1.687	0.053	0.848	0.21	0.30	0.95	0.09	0.39	35
6	0.776	0.169	0.413	0.425	0.59	0.95	0.27	0.18	0.50	6
7	0.147	1.236	0.056	1.039	0.21	0.38	0.93	0.08	0.40	23
8	0.168	1.163	0.069	1.066	0.21	0.40	0.85	0.07	0.38	38
9	0.785	0.262	0.389	0.425	0.61	0.84	0.28	0.18	0.48	8
10	0.673	0.485	0.284	0.396	0.45	0.66	0.36	0.19	0.42	20
11	0.176	1.503	0.057	0.757	0.21	0.33	0.92	0.10	0.39	27
12	0.363	0.242	0.255	0.248	0.27	0.86	0.39	0.29	0.45	11
13	0.134	1.782	0.050	0.817	0.21	0.29	0.97	0.09	0.39	30
14	0.917	0.145	0.472	0.478	1.00	0.98	0.24	0.16	0.60	2
15	0.170	1.648	0.057	0.624	0.21	0.31	0.92	0.12	0.39	28
16	0.527	0.275	0.318	0.340	0.34	0.83	0.33	0.22	0.43	15
17	0.489	0.513	0.247	0.369	0.32	0.64	0.40	0.20	0.39	29
18	0.160	1.404	0.058	0.969	0.21	0.35	0.92	0.08	0.39	33
19	0.099	0.929	0.046	1.154	0.20	0.46	1.00	0.07	0.43	14
20	0.428	0.184	0.341	0.206	0.29	0.93	0.31	0.34	0.47	10
21	0.406	1.015	0.139	0.457	0.28	0.44	0.59	0.17	0.37	44
22	0.344	0.166	0.279	0.175	0.26	0.95	0.36	0.40	0.49	7
23	0.194	0.474	0.155	0.443	0.22	0.67	0.55	0.17	0.40	21
24	0.627	0.342	0.324	0.382	0.41	0.77	0.32	0.20	0.42	16
25	0.395	0.954	0.121	0.567	0.28	0.45	0.64	0.13	0.38	41
26	0.557	0.336	0.301	0.365	0.36	0.77	0.34	0.20	0.42	17
27	0.319	0.404	0.196	0.309	0.25	0.72	0.47	0.24	0.42	18
28	0.216	1.287	0.086	0.623	0.22	0.37	0.77	0.12	0.37	42
29	0.239	1.323	0.075	0.658	0.23	0.36	0.82	0.12	0.38	39
30	0.649	0.405	0.310	0.398	0.43	0.71	0.34	0.19	0.42	19
31	0.828	0.175	0.433	0.441	0.69	0.94	0.26	0.17	0.52	5
32	0.335	0.565	0.189	0.358	0.26	0.61	0.48	0.21	0.39	31
33	0.551	0.629	0.207	0.449	0.36	0.58	0.45	0.17	0.39	34
34	0.268	1.240	0.108	0.461	0.24	0.38	0.68	0.16	0.37	45
35	0.177	1.553	0.055	0.716	0.21	0.32	0.94	0.11	0.40	25
36	0.154	1.525	0.055	0.909	0.21	0.33	0.94	0.09	0.39	32

continued on next page

Table 8. Continued

Exp. No.	Response				Grey Co-efficient				GREY Grade	Rank
	MRR (gm/min)	Ra (μm)	OC (mm)	Fc (kgf)	MRR (gm/min)	Ra (μm)	OC (mm)	Fc (kgf)		
37	0.755	0.359	0.344	0.410	0.56	0.75	0.31	0.18	0.45	13
38	0.255	1.033	0.100	0.719	0.23	0.43	0.71	0.11	0.37	43
39	0.743	0.213	0.391	0.414	0.54	0.89	0.28	0.18	0.47	9
40	0.164	0.307	0.167	0.273	0.21	0.80	0.52	0.27	0.45	12
41	0.499	0.722	0.174	0.461	0.33	0.54	0.51	0.16	0.38	37
42	0.293	0.542	0.168	0.553	0.24	0.62	0.52	0.14	0.38	40
43	0.161	1.216	0.062	0.930	0.21	0.39	0.89	0.08	0.39	26
44	0.180	1.110	0.076	0.807	0.22	0.41	0.82	0.10	0.38	36
45	0.908	0.133	0.477	0.470	0.96	1.00	0.24	0.16	0.59	3

Table 9. Results of machining performance using optimal machining parameters

Settings Levels	Predicted Result	Experimental Result
MRR	0.072	0.091
Ra	0.137	0.141
OC	0.134	0.157
Fc	0.054	0.083
Grey Grade	0.70	0.62
Improvement of the grey relation grade: **0.08**		

7. CONCLUSION

The present study attempts to validate and optimize the machining parameters while machining of Al_2O_3/ Al IPC material by ECG. Nature Inspired intelligent systems has proven their effectiveness in answering complex optimization problems. Nature driven techniques can definitely optimize a problem whose objectives are opposing in nature along with a wide variety of possible solutions. Artificial Neural Network (ANN) can simply train and validate the trial data and also test in the trained background. While analysing the experimental data using ANN in order to attain maximum MRR, lower Ra, minimum OC and least Fc the training, validation and testing data indicates that the values of R is closer to 1. This signifies that there is a specific relationship between outputs and targets.

Nature inspired techniques like Cuckoo Search (CS) algorithm can note the best parametric combination to satisfy the maximum MRR and lowest Ra, minimum OC and least Fc separately. Then the individual responses are optimized where the following parametric combinations are found: Maximum MRR 0.975 gm/min is obtained at C = 30 gm/lit, V = 15 volts, D = 0.04 mm and F = 0.3 lit/sec. Minimum Ra 0.115 μm is obtained at C = 30 gm/lit, V = 15 volts, D = 0.04 mm and F = 0.3 lit/sec. Lower OC 0.036 mm is obtained at C = 20 gm/lit, V = 25 volts, D = 0.04 mm and F = 0.1 lit/sec. Minimum Fc 0.054 kgf is obtained at C = 20 gm/lit, V = 15 volts, D = 0.04 mm and F = 0.1 lit/sec.

The contradictory objective functions can have achieved simultaneously by using Genetic Algorithm (GA) through a possible range of the control parameters. For MRR the range is 0.917 gm/min to 0.072 gm/min, for Ra it varies between 1.921 μm to 0.133 μm, for OC it is 0.477 mm to 0.046 mm and for Fc it is between 1.191 kgf to 0.054 kgf.

Finally, the results obtained from Genetic Algorithm is hybridized with Fuzzy set theory to obtain an exact parametric combination of the process control variables which satisfies these four conflicting objective function simultaneously. Weights of the outputs are considered as linguistic variables, where importance is given on Ra instead of on other parameters because ECG is mainly a finishing operation. The result of GA is approached for evaluating the best parametric combination during machining is C 20 gm/lit, V 15 volts, D 0.04 mm and F 0.1 lit/sec. Conclusively, the results are validated and the grey relation grade upgrades to 0.17.

Therefore, the experimental study as presented here for determining the optimum ECG parametric combination during machining of Alumina-Aluminium IPC materials can provide a valuable and an effective guideline for manufacturing of products of similar material.

REFERENCES

Bose, G. K., Jana, T. K., & Mitra, S. (2011). Identification of the significant process parameters by Taguchi methodology during electrochemical grinding of Al2O3/Al – interpenetrating phase composite. *International Journal of Computational Materials Science and Surface Engineering*, *4*(3), 232–246. doi:10.1504/IJCMSSE.2011.042821

Chawla, M., & Duhan, M. (2014). Applications of recent metaheuristics optimization algorithms in biomedical engineering: A review. *International Journal of Biomedical Engineering and Technology*, *16*(3), 268–278. doi:10.1504/IJBET.2014.065807

Deng, J. (1989). Introduction to Grey System. *Journal of Grey System*, *1*(1), 1–24.

Ding, L., Yue, Y., Ahmet, K., Jakson, M., & Parkin, R. (2005). Global optimization of a feature-based process sequence using GA and ANN techniques. *International Journal of Production Research*, *43*(15), 3247–3272. doi:10.1080/00207540500137282

Du, C. B., Quan, H. D., & Cui, P. Z. (2015). Improved quantum-inspired cuckoo search algorithm based on self-adapting adjusting of search range. *International Journal of Reasoning-based Intelligent Systems*, *7*(3-4), 152–160. doi:10.1504/IJRIS.2015.072941

Dubois, D., & Prade, H. (1979). Operations in a Fuzzy-Valued Logic. *Information and Control*, *43*(2), 224–240. doi:10.1016/S0019-9958(79)90730-7

Hossaina, A., Hossaina, A., Nukmana, Y., Hassanab, M. A., Harizama, M. Z., Sifullaha, A. M., & Parandousha, P. (2016). A Fuzzy Logic-Based Prediction Model for Kerf Width in Laser Beam Machining. *Materials and Manufacturing Processes*, *31*(5), 679–684. doi:10.1080/10426914.2015.1037901

Ilhan, R. E., Sathyanarayanan, G., Storer, R. H., & Liao, T. W. (1992). Off-line multi response optimization of electrochemical surface grinding by a multi-objective programming method. *International Journal of Machine Tools & Manufacture*, *32*(3), 435–451. doi:10.1016/0890-6955(92)90013-7

Keufmann, A., & Gupta, M. M. (1985). *Introduction to Fuzzy Arithmetic: Theory and Applications.* New York: Van Nostrand Reinhold.

Lyubimov, V. V., Yerokhin, A. L., & Tchmir, M. Y. (1998). Mechanisms of synthetic diamond wear in tools for electrochemical grinding. *Diamond and Related Materials, 7*(9), 1267–1271. doi:10.1016/S0925-9635(98)00179-4

Ma, C., Li, Y., He, R., Duan, G., Sun, L., & Qi, B. (2012). New optimization model and fuzzy adaptive weighted genetic algorithm for hazardous material transportation. *International Journal of Computing Science and Mathematics, 3*(4), 341–352. doi:10.1504/IJCSM.2012.051621

Madi, M., Markovi, D., & Radovanovi, M. (2012). Performance comparision of meta-heuristic algorithms for training artificial neural networks in modelling laser cutting. *International Journal of Advance Intelligence Paradigms, 4*(3-4), 299–312. doi:10.1504/IJAIP.2012.052073

Maksoud, T. M. A., & Brooks, A. J. (1995). Electrochemical grinding of ceramic form tooling. *Journal of Materials Processing Technology, 55*(2), 70–75. doi:10.1016/0924-0136(95)01787-9

Panda, M. C., & Yadava, V. (2012). Intelligent Modelling and Multi-Objective Optimization of Die Sinking Electrochemical Spark Machining Process. *Materials and Manufacturing Processes. Materials and Manufacturing Processes, 27*(1), 10–25. doi:10.1080/10426914.2010.544812

Qu, N. S., Zhang, Q. L., Fang, X. L., Ye, E. K., & Zhu, D. (2015). Experimental Investigation on Electrochemical Grinding of Inconel 718. *Procedia CIRP, 35*, 16–19. doi:10.1016/j.procir.2015.08.055

Roy, S., Bhattacharya, A., & Banerjee, S. (2007). Analysis of effect of voltage on surface texture in electrochemical grinding by autocorrelation function. *Tribology International, 40*(9), 1387–1393. doi:10.1016/j.triboint.2007.03.008

Samanta, B. (2009). Surface roughness prediction in machining using soft computing. *International Journal of Computer Integrated Manufacturing, 22*(3), 257–266. doi:10.1080/09511920802287138

Sanjay, C., & Prithvi, C. (2014). Hybrid intelligence systems and artificial neural network (ANN) approach for modelling of surface roughness in drilling. *Cogent Engineering, 1*(1).

Shie, J. R. (2006). Optimization of Dry Machining Parameters for High-Purity Graphite in End-Milling Process by Artificial Neural Networks: A Case Study. *Materials and Manufacturing Processes, 21*(8), 838–845. doi:10.1080/03602550600728257

Wang, L., Zhong, Y., & Yin, Y. (2015). A hybrid cooperative cuckoo search algorithm with particle swarm optimization. *International Journal of Computing Science and Mathematics, 6*(1), 18–29. doi:10.1504/IJCSM.2015.067537

Yang, X. S., & Deb, S. (2010). Engineering optimization by cuckoo search. *International Journal of Mathematical Modelling and Numerical Optimization, 1*(4), 330–343. doi:10.1504/IJMMNO.2010.035430

Yip-Hoi, D., & Dutta, D. (1996). A genetic algorithm application for sequencing operations in process planning for parallel machining. *IIE Transactions*, *50*(1), 55–68. doi:10.1080/07408179608966252

Zaina, A. M., Harona, H., & Sharif, S. (2012). Integrated ANN–GA for estimating the minimum value for machining performance. *International Journal of Production Research*, *50*(1), 191–213. doi:10.1080/00207543.2011.571454

Zhanga, G., Zhanga, Z., Guoa, J., Minga, W., Lia, M., & Huangab, Y. (2013). Modelling and Optimization of Medium-Speed WEDM Process Parameters for Machining SKD11. *Materials and Manufacturing Processes*, *28*(10), 1124–1132. doi:10.1080/10426914.2013.773024

Chapter 18
An Overview of the Last Advances and Applications of Artificial Bee Colony Algorithm

Airam Expósito Márquez
University of La Laguna, Spain

Christopher Expósito-Izquierdo
University of La Laguna, Spain

ABSTRACT

Swarm Intelligence is defined as collective behavior of decentralized and self-organized systems of a natural or artificial nature. In the last years and today, Swarm Intelligence has proven to be a branch of Artificial Intelligence that is able to solving efficiently complex optimization problems. Some of well-known examples of Swarm Intelligence in natural systems reported in the literature are colony of social insects such as bees and ants, bird flocks, fish schools, etc. In this respect, Artificial Bee Colony Algorithm is a nature inspired metaheuristic, which imitates the honey bee foraging behaviour that produces an intelligent social behaviour. ABC has been used successfully to solve a wide variety of discrete and continuous optimization problems. In order to further enhance the structure of Artificial Bee Colony, there are a variety of works that have modified and hybridized to other techniques the standard version of ABC. This work presents a review paper with a survey of the modifications, variants and applications of the Artificial Bee Colony Algorithm.

INTRODUCTION

Nature is a constant source of inspiration in the development of new approximate algorithms for solving optimization problems. Specifically, nature intelligent entities that are able to work efficiently and autonomously in unknown and changing environments. Nature-inspired algorithms have high relevance when solving hard and complex optimization problems by mimicking the behaviour arisen in nature in various forms and these algorithms are always hot research topics in the area of Artificial Intelligence (AI). Some general categories grouping nature-inspired algorithms are evolutionary algorithms, swarm

DOI: 10.4018/978-1-5225-2128-0.ch018

intelligence algorithms, and natural ecosystems algorithms. This chapter aims to focus on specific case of swarm intelligence algorithm.

Swarm Intelligence (SI) concept was first introduced in the context of cellular robotics systems (Beni & Wang, 1989). This field of study focuses on the collective behaviour those results from the local interactions of the people with each other and with their surrounding conditions. The main aim of SI is to increase the performance and robustness (Fleischer, 2003). Nowadays, SI is also strongly correlated with a new branch of AI that is used as collective behaviour of swarms in nature, such as colonies of ants, flocking of birds, honey bees. In (Bonabeau & Theraulaz, 1999), SI is defined as any attempt to design algorithms or distributed problem-solving devices inspired by the collective behaviour of social insect colonies and other animal societies. Overall, the term swarm is used for a large number of insects or other small organisms, especially when they are in motion. Roughly speaking, SI systems consist of a population of simple agents exchanging information locally with another simple agents and with their environment. The agent capabilities are simple and limited by interacting direct and indirect with other agents, they follow simple rules. An example of direct communication between agents is e.g. birds where they interact with each other through sound. Birds have very high immense vision power they go in search of food source. Some birds smell the best quality of food source and spread the information to all other birds. Hence they have good communication and cooperation between them. Indirect iterations are defined as interaction with the environment, i.e., one agent changes the environment and other agents respond to the change. An example, the pheromone trail lay by the ants during the search of food. Ants are able to search their food in shortest path and they communicate through environment by chemical substances called pheromone. They cannot communicate directly with each other. Generally speaking, the swarm system is characterized in terms of individuals, interactions and environment. There is no centralized control systems, individual agents of these swarms behave without supervision and each of these agents has a stochastic behaviour due to their perception of the neighborhood. The swarm can be seen as a decentralized and self-organized system. Through this simple and local behaviour, an intelligent and global behaviour of the swarm is generated.

Over the last decades, numerous research efforts have been devoted to the development and study of SI meta-heuristics. In the literature there are many of these meta-heuristics. Some relevant examples are Ant Colony Optimization (ACO) (Dorigo, 1992), Artificial Bee Colony (ABC) (Karaboga, 2005), Bat Algorithm (BA) (Yang, 2010), Particle Swarm Optimization (PSO) (Kennedy & Eberhart, 1995), and many others are some of the natural examples of swarm which are a smart and efficient problem solving techniques. The good reception of these meta-heuristics relies on its ability to obtain high-quality solutions in reasonable times in highly complex optimization problems. This is the reason that encompasses a wide range of practical applications covering areas such as computer networks, engineering, bio-medical applications, control systems, parallel processing, data mining, security, robotics, general optimization and many other application areas. SI is becoming increasingly important research area for computer scientists, engineers, economists, bioinformaticians, operational researchers, and many other disciplines. This is because the problems that the natural intelligent swarms can solve (finding food, building nests, dividing labor among nest mates, etc.) have important counterparts in several engineering areas of real world.

ABC is an interesting and practical algorithm to the scientific community used in a wide range of applications. Its advantage of being easily hybridized with other techniques makes it a robust and viable alternative to the search solutions in many years to come. That is the reason behind the interest of this chapter to organize the most important works around of this technique and identify future lines of work that are still to come. In particular, this chapter aims to present an updated overview on the main works related to ABC, practical applications, and future research perspectives. The main intention is to provide a starting point document for researchers with interest in developmental knowledge of ABC, variants and its applications.

The remaining parts of the paper are organized as follows. Section 2 describes the fundamentals of behaviour of honey bee in nature and the basic structure of the ABC algorithm. Section 3 describes the wide range of applications of the ABC in several fields. Finally, Section 4 draws some concluding remarks from the chapter.

ARTIFICIAL BEE COLONY AND VARIANTS

The ABC is a swarm intelligence meta-heuristic introduced by Karaboga in 2005 (Karaboga, 2005). ABC is based on the foraging behaviour of honey bees. Each bee individually can perform different actions, such as communicating information, save the environment to share it, and make decisions based on that information. The swarm evolves according to changes in the environment, based on social learning behaviour of bees, combining global exploration search with local search.

Foraging Behaviour of Honey Bees

ABC is inspired from the foraging behaviour of honey bees. This process has some features like bees can communicate the information, can memorize the environment, can store and share the information and take decisions based on that. The swarm updates itself, through social behaviour generated by bees, and with respect to changes in the environment. Generally speaking, the foraging behaviour of honey bees is based on five essential components food sources, employed bees, unemployed bees, foraging behaviour, and dances.

Regarding the food sources, while searching the food, a particular bee select a flower for herself. Once selected, the bee collect the information about this food source. The information is basically how much nectar contains the food source, how expensive it is to extract nectar from the selected flower, and how far and in which direction it is with respect to the nest. Generally the quality of a food source can be represented as a single quantity for the sake of simplicity. This single quantity determines the profitability of the food source.

The available food sources are exploited by particular kind of bees. Employed foragers are responsible for exploiting a particular food source. Additionally, they keep the profitability of associated food source and report to the nest about this particular food source. The information reported can be the direction and distance from the nest and the efficiency of the source.

The information shared by the employed bees is transmitted to the unemployed bees. Unemployed bees assimilate the information in order to select a food source to exploit. There are two kinds of them, onlooker bees and scouts bees, both of them with different purpose in the foraging process. The scout bees, continually looking around the nest in search of new food sources and the onlookers bees receive the information from the employed bees while waiting in the nest. The onlookers bees analyses this information with the aim of establish a food source for themselves. If any of the food sources is exhausted then these bees start searching around the nest and find new food sources randomly. Generally, in a honey bee swarm there on average 50% of employed bees and 50% of unemployed bees. Referring to the unemployed bees about 10% are scouts.

The ultimate purpose and most important process of the bee swarm is foraging behaviour. In this process, bees leave the nest in search of food. Once they found a food source, bees collect the nectar from food source and save the nectar in their stomachs. Depending on the food source richness and the distance from the nest, bees take about 20 to 120 minutes to extract the nectar from the food sources. With the help of digestive enzymes, honey begins to be created in the bee stomach. Then she stores nectar in empty cells when she reach the nest. Finally, through different types of dances, she shares the information with other bees are in the nest.

Employed bees performs different kinds of dance on different parts of the nest as transmission mechanism of information about profitability, distance, and direction of food source. This information is transmitted to other bees residing in the nest. The idea to inform other bees is that whether they should follow or not follow her food source to extract. Employed bees perform their dance moves in different areas of the nest, thereby increasing the ability to inform more bees about the food source associated with her. When she is dancing, the other bees taste the nectar of her food source touching her with their antenna. Employed bees performs different kinds of dance depends on the profitability of food source. The round dance is a kind of dance that bees do when food source is near to the nest, this dance does not inform about direction of food source. The tremble dance is used when an employed bee takes a long time to store the nectar and she indicates that does not know about profitability of her food source. Finally, the waggle dance is used to inform the other bees about the direction of food source that is far from the nest. The direction of food source is informed with regard to the sunlight. And the speed of waggle dance is proportional to the distance of food source from the nest.

Algorithmic Structures of ABC

As in the foraging process of the real honey bees, the ABC algorithm has three kinds of artificial bees: employed foragers, onlookers and scouts. The onlooker bee makes the decision to choose a food source whereas the employed bee visit the food source to obtain information before to make the decision. The scout bees search randomly for new food sources. The employed bees are linked to particular food sources therefore there are so many employed bees as food sources for the hive. The bees follow three simple rules to do the process of search food sources. The first of them is evaluate the quality of food sources using the employed bees. Next, the election of the food sources after obtaining information from employed bees by onlookers. And last selecting the scout bees and sending them onto possible food sources.

Every food source positions are located by scout bees and the quality of the each food source is measured. Next the employed bees share the information of the food source with the bees are waiting. Once the information has been shared by employed bees, they choose another food source in the neighborhood of the present one. Finally, the onlooker bees uses the information shared by the employed bees to select a food source. The probability of selecting a food source is dependent on the quality of it. The higher the quality of the food source increases the probability of being selected. Hence, the employed bee with information of a food source with the highest quality recruits the onlookers to that food source. Subsequently, it selects another food source in the neighborhood of the present one comparing food source positions through visual information. Afterwards, the food sources are used by employed and continuously exploited to become unusable. Then the employed bee which used food source becomes a scout bee with the aim of seeking food sources once again. A scout bee generates randomly a new food source to replace the one abandoned by the onlooker bees.

The general algorithmic structure of the ABC optimization approach is given in Table 1.

In ABC meta-heuristic, the number of food sources is equal to the number of solutions in the population. The localization of a food source represents the position of a solution to the optimization problem and the quality of the food source is equal to the fitness cost of the related solution. Basically, bees exploit the sources by local searches in the neighborhood of the solutions selected. The selection of the food source is based on deterministic selection by employed bee and probabilistic selection by the onlooker bee.

In the initialization phase, the population of food sources or solutions is initialized by artificial scout bees, the population size is defined, maximum number of generations is set, and a limit used to diversify the search is set, this limit specifies the number of maximum generations for which each non- improved food source is to be abandoned.

In employed bees step, each artificial employed bee search for new food sources within the neighborhood of the food source in their memory. Employed bees find a neighbor food source and evaluate its fitness, subsequently a greedy selection is applied between the new food source and the previous food source. Finally, the information about food source is transmitted by employed bees to onlooker bees that are waiting in the nest for this information.

On the matter of the onlooker bee step, onlooker bees select their food sources with a probability weighted according to the information provided by the employed bees. A neighborhood source is determined and its fitness value is computed by an onlooker, once the food source for an onlooker bee is chosen. Finally a greedy selection is applied between two food sources.

With regard to the scout bee step, the solutions that employed bees cannot improved after a predetermined number of generations, given in initialization phase, are abandoned. And these employed bees become scout bees. Next, the scout bees start to search randomly new solutions. Therefore, the food sources that have initially poor quality or due to be used by employed bee to become unusable are abandoned.

These three steps discussed above are repeat until a stop criterion is met. These stop criteria could be a maximum execution time or a maximum cycle number.

Table 1. The general algorithmic structure of the ABC optimization approach

---

Algorithm 1 ABC Procedure

1: Initialize phase and problem parameters
2: **repeat**
3:     Send the employed bees to the food sources.
4:     Send the onlookers to select a food source.
5:     Send the scouts to search possible new food.
6:     Memorize the best food source.
7: **until** *termination − criteria − are − met*

Variants of Artificial Bee Colony

This section presents different variations of the basic ABC in order to enhance or improve its performance. Multiple effective variants of the ABC have been proposed in the scientific literature so far to adapt the general method to a wide range of optimization problems.

ABC in its conception was created for solving unconstrained optimization problems. First introduction of the constrained handling procedure to the original ABC was proposed by (Karaboga & Basturk, 2007) to approach constrained optimization problems. The modification is introduced in workers, which use Deb's rules of handling constrained in the ABC selection process instead of greedy selection procedure. This new variation of ABC was compared with PSO and DE methods with excellent results. An improved version of ABC for constrained optimization problems was proposed in (Brajevic et al., 2010). This variant has been tested on several engineering benchmarks with discrete and continuous variables. A new algorithm base on the ABC was introduced in (Mezura-Montes & Velez-Koeppel, 2010) in order to solve constrained real parameter optimization problems. A dynamic tolerance control for equality constraints was introduced in this variant in order to guide the search in the solution space. An approach with"smart bee" having a memory to keep the location and quality of food sources for constrained problems was presented in (Stanarevic et al., 2010). In (Karaboga & Akay, 2011a) is presented a modified ABC algorithm for constrained optimization problems. This approach was compared to a set of algorithms for constrained optimization problems. An ABC algorithm for large-scale problems was presented in (Akay & Karaboga, 2012). This approach was tested on well-known large scale unconstrained tests and in constrained engineering problems.

The versatility and performance of the ABC algorithm has helped researches to use the ABC algorithm in other areas. Applied ABC to integer programming problems was introduced in (Akay B, 009b) with some beneficial results. A new version of ABC, termed DisABC, was proposed in (Kashan et al., 2011). This version was designed for binary optimization, in essence, DisABC uses a differential expression that introduces a measure of dissimilarity between binary vectors instead of the vector subtraction operator used in the classic ABC algorithm. With the goal of determine free parameters of support vector machine an ABC was proposed and a binary ABC is used for intrusion detection systems in (Wang et al., 2010).

Parameter tuning and different strategies in ABC have been proposed by several authors in order to improve its performance. Regarding the control parameters in ABC tuning studied was proposed in (Akay & Karaboga, 2009). Several selection mechanisms in ABC have been analyzed in (Bao L, 2009). In this work the authors consider several selection strategies, for example disruptive selection strategy, rank selection strategy and tournament selection strategy. For scheduling manufacture and assemble of complex products in (Pansuwan et al., 2010) is studied setting ABC algorithm parameters. The influence of the population size of ABC algorithm is studied in (Aderhold et al., 2010). A new adaptation of mutation step size of ABC is introduced in (Alam MS, 2010). A new diversity strategy improved is proposed in (Lee & Cai, 2011). Two new variants of ABC with new methods for update the position of the artificial bees is presented in (Diwold et al., 2011). In (Stanarevic, 2011) was studied the comparison of different mutation strategies applied to ABC. An improved version of ABC algorithm with mutation based on Levy probability distributions is presented on (Rajasekhar et al., 2011). A new variant of ABC based on Von Neumann topology structure is proposed in (Zou W, 2011).

In (Mezura-Montes & Cetina-Dominguez, 2012) is proposed a modified ABC algorithm to solve constrained numerical optimization problems. Four modifications related with the selection mechanism, the scout bee operator, and the equality and boundary constraints are made to the algorithm with the aim to modify its behaviour in a constrained search space.

A non-linear factor for convergence control is introduced in the algorithm to enhance the balance of global and local searches. In (Wang et al., 2013) is considered an modified ABC that is able to generate good solutions for a two-stage make-to-order production system characterized by limited production capacity and tight order due dates. In (Luo et al., 2013), a modified algorithm called converge-onlookers ABC (COABC) algorithm is proposed. In order to improve the exploitation of ABC, a new solution search equation in the onlooker stage by applying the best solution of the previous iteration to guide the search of new candidate solutions was presented. In (Beloufa & Chikh, 2013) a novel ABC algorithm is proposed for diagnosis of diabetes disease. A mutation operator is added to an ABC for improving its performance. When the current best solution cannot be updated, a blended crossover operator (BLX) of genetic algorithm is applied, in order to enhance the diversity of ABC, without compromising with the solution quality.

In order to improve the poor exploitation performance of ABC, (Yurtkuran & Emel, 2015) proposes an adaptive ABC, which employs six different search rules that have been successfully used in the literature. In (Secui, 2015) a new modified ABC, termed MABC, is proposed to solve the economic dispatch problem. The MABC algorithm introduces a new relation to update the solutions within the search space, in order to increase the algorithm ability to avoid pre- mature convergence and to find stable and high quality solutions. A modified ABC algorithm is proposed in (Zhou et al., 2015) for parameters estimation in ultrasonic echo problems. The modified ABC is given by adding an adjusting factor to the neighborhood search formula of traditional ABC algorithm in or- der to enhance its performance. In (Zhang et al., 2015), in order to improve the exploitation of the ABC, two modified versions of ABC are proposed. For this purpose the Grenade Explosion Method (GEM) is introduced in ABC. The two modified versions are termed GABC1 and GABC2. GEM is embedded in the employed bee phase of GABC1, whereas it is embedded in the onlooker bee phase of GABC2. In order to solve a proposed constrained objective function of photovoltaic system module power loss and mitigate the shading effect a modified ABC is proposed in (Fathy, 2015). The solution approach is compared with GA, PSO and standard ABC. In (Anuar et al., 2016) a modified ABC, termed ABC-ROC, is proposed in order to study the performance of solution approach for a set of benchmark problems. ABC-ROC models the behaviour of scout bees to improve the performance of the standard ABC in terms of explorations.

Hybridization of Artificial Bee Colony

Other fast-growing variants is the ABC hybridization, where the major aim is enhancing the weaknesses of the algorithm by hybridizing it with other tech- niques. In this regard, there are three main groups of methods with which hybridize ABC: ABC with hybridization of population-based algorithms, with the local search-based algorithms, and with other techniques.

In (Baykasoglu & Tapkan, 2007) was incorporated the ABC with shift neighborhood searches and Greedy Randomized Adaptive Search Procedure (GRASP) heuristic. A combination of Nelder-Mead simplex and ABC is presented in (Kang & Xu, 2009). In (Jatoth & Rajasekhar, 2010) is proposed a hybridized GA and ABCA. Another combination of GA and ABC is presented in (Zhao et al., 2010b). The main idea of the approach is the information sharing between GA population and ABC population. In (Duan et al., 2010) the local search capacity of the ABC is improved hybridization with Quantum

Evolutionary Algorithm (QEA).The QEA can jump out of the local optimum in order to achieve the global optimal value.

A hybridization of ABC and Forward Neural Network (FNN) is presented by (Zhang & Wu, 2011). A proposal of hybridization between Multi-level Maximum Entropy Thresholding (MET) and ABC is presented in (Horng, 2011). A combination of ABC and Differential Evolution (DE) is proposed in (Gao Wei-feng, 2011). A new search strategy is introduced into ABC in order to improve the convergence rate. DE simulates evolution and individuals are taken into account in each generation. The combination of Pareto archive set and ABC is proposed by (Li & Wang, 2011). In this hybridization the scout bees have two purposes. Some of them perform randomly search tin the predefined region and the other ones select one non-dominated solution from the Pareto archive set. In (Tasgetiren et al., 2011) is proposed a hybridized Discrete ABC with a variant of iterated greedy algorithm for the total flow-time minimization in permutation flow shops. In order to solve container loading problems, in (Dereli & Das, 2011) is proposed a hybrid ABC with the heuristic filling procedure.

A combined ABC with Harmony Search (HS) algorithm termed Collaborative Artificial Bee Colony Algorithm (CABC) is presented by (Shanthi & Amalraj, 2012). A proposal of a hybrid ABC algorithm is presented by (Yan et al., 2012) introducing the crossover operator of GA to ABC in information exchange phase between bees for data clustering. Hybridization between ABC and Particle Swarm Optimization (PSO) is proposed by (Lien & Cheng, 2012). In (Wu et al., 2012) is proposed improvement of Global Swarm Optimization (GSO) by hybridizing it with ABC and PSO.

In (Li et al., 2013) a hybrid approach between Differential Evolution (DE) and ABC is proposed in order to solve Optimal Reactive Power Flow (ORPF) problem. This solution approach, termed DE-ABC, combines X goodness to solve ORPF and the good global search ability of the ABC. An integration of ABC algorithm and the Sequential Quadratic Programming is proposed in (Eslami et al., 2013), termed ABC-SQP. In order to solve global optimization problems and damping of low frequency oscillations in power system stability analyses. In (Yildiz, 2013), a novel hybrid optimization method (HRABC) based on ABC and Taguchi method is proposed to solve a multi-tool milling optimization problem. A hybrid ABC with Harmony Search (HS) for solving the Flexible Job-Shop Scheduling Problem (FJSP) with the criteria to minimize the maximum completion time (makespan) is proposed in (Dagli et al., 2013). In order to minimize the makespan in permutation flow-shop scheduling problems, a hybrid discrete ABC (HDABC) algorithm is presented in (Liu & Liu, 2013). The initial population with certain quality and diversity is generated from GRASP based on Nawaz Enscore Ham (NEH) heuristics. A hybrid ABC algorithm is proposed for solving the The Job-Shop Scheduling Problem (JSSP) in (Zhang et al., 2013). A tree search algorithm is used to enhance the exploitation capability of ABC.

In order to solve the Reliable Hierarchical Maximal Covering Location Problem (RHMCLP) and hybrid ABC algorithm is presented in (Farahani et al., 2014). The ABC is hybridized with 2-opt as a local search. A hybrid ABC algorithm is developed to solve the bi-level problem in (Szeto & Jiang, 2014). The ABC is used to design route structures and a descent direction search method is used to determine an optimal frequency setting for a given route structure. In (Zhang et al., 2014) a hybrid ABC is designed to solve the Environmental Vehicle Routing Problem (EVRP). A novel hybrid evolutionary algorithm name Hybrid ABCDE is proposed in (Xiang et al., 2014), which integrates a modified ABC and a modified DE to solve numerical optimization problems.

A hybrid algorithm termed PSABC is proposed in (Li et al., 2015), which combines the local search phase in PSO with two global search phases in ABC in order to solve high-dimensional optimization problems. In (Li & Pan, 2015) is proposed a novel hybrid algorithm, termed TABC, that combines ABC and Tabu Search (TS) to solve the Hybrid Flow Shop (HFS) scheduling problem with limited buffers. A hybrid discrete ABC algorithm is proposed in (Kalayci et al., 2015) to solve a fuzzy extension of the Disassembly Line Balancing Problem (DLBP). A hybrid ABC is proposed in (Awadallah et al., 2015) for The Nurse Rostering Problem (NRP). The process of the employed bee operator is replaced with the Hill Climbing Optimizer (HCO) to empower its exploitation capability. In (Kefayat et al., 2015) a hybrid configuration of ACO with ABC algorithm, termed hybrid ACOABC algorithm, is presented for optimal location and sizing of Distributed Energy Resources (DERs) problem. In (Wu et al., 2016) an adaptive hybrid ABC algorithm with Chaotic Search, termed AHABCC, is proposed.

Applications

The ABC has encompassed a wide range of applications covering different fields because of its robustness and easy to apply. The ABC was firstly applied to numerical optimization problems in (Karaboga & Basturk, 2007) and was applied to train neural networks (Karaboga & Akay, 2007) to medical pattern classification and clustering problems. The control mechanism of local optimal solution is studied in (Xing & Haijun, 2007). The main objective is to improve the global search ability of the ABC to solve TSP problems. An ABC is applied to network reconfiguration problem in a radial distribution system in (Rao & Ramalingaraju, 2008). In order to minimize the real power loss and improve voltage profile. The ABC proved able to obtain high quality and computation efficiency solutions. In (Pawar & Shankar, 2008) an ABC is applied to some problems such as multi-objective optimization of electro-chemical machining process parameters, optimization of process parameters of the abrasive flow machining process and the milling process. The Leaf-Constrained Minimum Spanning Tree (LCMST) problem is solved using an ABC in (Singh & Sundar, 2011). The solution approach is compared to GA, ACO and TS. (Karaboga, 2009) used the ABC in the signal processing area for designing digital IIR filters. An ABC is used in (Hsu et al., 2012) to propose a personalized auxiliary material recommendation system on Facebook to recommend suitable learning materials according to learning interests and difficulty.

ABC has been applied to other fields such as engineering and real-world optimization problems. Electronics engineering is one of the most interesting fields with works relating to image processing, networking and other several applications. An ABC solution approach to solve cluster-based wireless sensor network routings problem is proposed by (Karaboga et al., 2012). An efficient ABC is proposed to deal with sensor deployment in 3-D terrain in (Mini et al., 2010). An efficient load balancing for a resilient packet ring based on ABC is presented in (Bernardino et al., 2010). An ABC is used in order to CMOS inverter design considering propagation delays (Delican et al., 2010). An ABC is proposed with a novel expression in calculating resonant frequency of H shaped compact micro-strip antennas (Akdagli & Toktas, 2010). In (Taherdangkoo et al., 2010) a segmentation of MR brain images using FCM is improved by ABC. A magnetic resonance brain image classification using ABC is proposed by (Zhang & Wu, 2011). A multi-circle detection on images using ABC is designed by (Cuevas et al., 2014). Mapping for application specific network-on- chip design with help of ABC is presented in (Deng et al., 2011). In order to tackling the static RWA problem an ABC is proposed in (Rubio-Largo et al., 2011). Multilevel thresholding selection for image segmentation with help of ABC is presented in (Horng, 2011). An ABC is development for optimal multi- level thresholding based on maximum Tsallis entropy in (Zhang & Wu, 2011). An ABC with simple formulas for calculating resonant frequencies of C and H shaped compact microstrip antennas is proposed in (Toktas et al., 2011). An efficient ABC is proposed in (Kavian et al., 2012) to solve routing and wavelength assignment in optical networks. In (Karaboga

& Latifoglu, 2013) an approach based on digital IIR filters are described for the elimination of noise on transcranial Doppler by using ABC is proposed. (Draa & Bouaziz, 2014) proposes a new ABC algorithm for image contrast enhancement. A grey-level mapping technique and a new image quality measure are used. The algorithm has been tested on some test images, and the comparisons of the obtained results with the genetic algorithm have proven its superiority. In (Draa & Bouaziz, 2014) an ABC algorithm for image contrast enhancement is proposed. Further qualitative and statistical comparisons of the proposed ABC to the Cuckoo Search (CS) algorithm are also presented.

Other related area in which ABC has an extensive range of applications is the electrical engineering. An ABC is used in direction finding of maximum likelihood algorithm in the impulsive noise proposed by (Zhao et al., 2010a). An ABC is proposed in (Sumpavakup et al., 2010) to solve the optimal power flow problem. An economic load dispatch problem with non-smooth cost functions is solved using ABC in (Hemamalini & Simon, 2010). Proportional-integral- derivative controller design by using ABC is proposed by (Karaboga & Akay, 2010). An ABC for transient performance augmentation of grid connected distributed generation is proposed by (Chatterjee et al., 2010). In (Yousefi-Talouki & Valiollahi, 2010) is presented a solution of optimal power flow incorporating unified power flow controller (UPFC), as a powerful and versatile FACTS de- vices, using artificial bee colony (ABC). An ABC is proposed to Synthesis of Thinned Mutually Coupled Linear Array Using Inverse Fast Fourier Transform in (Basu & Mahanti, 2011). Partial transmit sequences based on artificial bee colony algorithm for peak-to-average power ratio reduction in multi-carrier code division multiple access systems proposed by (Karaboga & Akay, 2011b). Dynamic economic dispatch using ABC for units with valve-point effect is proposed in (Hemamalini & Simon, 2011). An application of ABC with least squares sup- port vector machine for real and reactive power tracing in deregulated power system is presented in (Sulaiman et al., 2012). A performance investigation of ABC algorithm for automatic generation control of a three area interconnected power system is proposed by (Gozde et al., 2012). Model order reduction of single input single output systems using ABC is proposed in (Bansal & Arya, 2012). In (Huang & Liu, 2013) an artificial bee colony algorithm to enhance the fault section estimation performance in power systems. The algorithm owns exploitation and exploration procedures to constitute an effective near-optimal search mechanism. (Luo & Duan, 2014) proposes an aircraft Automatic Landing System (ALS) that uses Chaotic Artificial Bee Colony (CABC) optimization. In (ZHANG et al., 2014) an improved ABC, which combines cyclic exchange neighborhood with chaos (CNC-ABC), is proposed for the sake of tuning the parameters of FOPID controller. In (Develi et al., 2015), a channel model which is based on practical channel measurements obtained from electrical networks in Turkey is proposed for power line communication (PLC) systems. Parameters of the derived mathematical model are optimized by using artificial bee colony algorithm. (Sag & Unka, 2015) presents a new color image segmentation method based on a multi-objective optimization algorithm, named improved ABC for multi-objective optimization (IBMO). In (Mishra et al., 2015) a design technique of a robust power system stabilizer using different performance indices obtained from artificial bee colony (ABC) algorithm is proposed. The parameters of a power system stabilizer (PSS) are tuned by using the ABC algorithm to achieve an acceptable overshoot and settling time at all load points within a wide region of operation.

In mechanical engineering, ABC algorithm has many applications. The ABC is used in optimized edge potential function (EPF) approach to target recognition for low-altitude aircraft in (Xu & Duan, 2010). Chaotic ABC approach to Uninhabited Combat Air Vehicle (UCAV) path planning is proposed in (Xu et al., 2010). In (Shi et al., 2010), ABC is applied to solve scheduling related problems like resource-constrained project scheduling. A discrete ABC for lot-streaming flow-shop with total flowtime minimization is proposed by (Pan et al., 2011). A pareto-based discrete ABC for multi-objective flexible job shop scheduling problems is proposed in (Li et al., 2011). Using ABC to solve stochastic resource constrained project scheduling problem is proposed in (Tahooneh & Ziarati, 2011). A discrete ABC for the total flowtime minimization in permutation flow shops is proposed by (Tasgetiren et al., 2011). A parametric optimization of some non-traditional machining processes using ABC is proposed by (Samanta & Chakraborty, 2011). In (Banharnsakun et al., 2012) the job shop scheduling problem is solved using the best-so-far ABC.

ABC has an extensive range of applications in computer engineering optimization problems. An ABC approach for clustering is presented in (Zhang et al., 2010). An improved ABC and its application in data clustering is presented in (Lei & Zhang, 2010). A clustering approach using cooperative ABC is presented in (Zou, 2010). A fuzzy clustering problem with ABC is proposed by (Yunbin et al., 2014). An ABC to solve the 0-1 multidimensional knapsack problem is proposed in (Sundar et al., 2010). Relative to software testing there are paper such as (Mala et al., 2010) and (Dahiya et al., 2010) which use ABC to software test suite optimization. An ABC in order to solve the multiple sequence alignment is presented in (Lei et al., 2010). An ABC on distributed environments is proposed by (Banharnsakun et al., 2010). A real time intrusion detection systems based on ABC-support vector machine algorithm is proposed in (Wang et al., 2010). Automated generation of independent paths and test suite optimization using ABC is proposed in (Sumesh et al., 2012). In (Nseef et al., 2016) an adaptive multi-population ABC algorithm for dynamic optimization problems (DOPs). Experimental results show that the proposed ABC is superior to the ABC on all tested instances. Compared to state of the art methodologies, the proposed ABC algorithm produces high quality results.

In Civil engineering also exists several ABC applications. In (Sonmez, 2011) an ABC is used for optimization of truss structures. An ABC is used for risk analysis of dam with fuzzy c-means clustering in (LiHaojin et al., 2011). Reliability analysis of engineering structures in (Li & Kang, 2011). In (Sonmez, 2011) for discrete optimum design of truss structures an ABC is used. To solve leak detection of pipeline an ABC is proposed in (Mandal et al., 2012). An ABC for large-scale problems and engineering design optimization is proposed by (Akay & Karaboga, 2012). An interesting application area of ABC is data mining. The above fields are just a small sample of the range of ABC application, there are other uses of ABC in fields such as mathematics, decision sciences, biochemistry genetics and molecular biology, physics and astronomy, energy, agricultural and biological sciences, environmental science, materials science, medicine, chemistry, and neuroscience.

CONCLUSION

The optimization problems in the real world increases their complexity. This problems demands robust, accurate and fast optimization approaches. The ABC algorithm was introduced by Karaboga in 2005, relatively recent algorithm. During this time the ABC algorithm has come to be recognized as a powerful and robust global optimization algorithm. Basic ABC has great recognition, but it was clear to the researches from different disciplines have made several improvements to the original structure in order to enhance the performance and efficiency of the ABC.

This paper includes an overview of ABC, its variants, and applications. Firstly the foraging behaviour of honey bees is described, with emphasis of the different elements that composes this process as food sources, employed bees, unemployed bees, foraging behaviour and dances. Also the basic structure of

ABC algorithm is described. In the subsequent section, an extensive review of ABC modifications is provided. Finally the applications of ABC in a wide range of applications that covering different fields is described.

In brief, ABC is a promising and interesting metaheuristic. The number of publications related to ABC in the literature increases exponentially. This shows that ABC would continue to be extensively used by researchers across diverse fields. One of its main and most important qualities is its ability to easily hybridize with other metaheuristics and exact methods. In addition to its enhancement possibilities over the basic structure. These features make ABC, one metaheuristic with clear possibilities to follow being use in several application fields in the coming years.

REFERENCES

Aderhold, A., Diwold, K., Scheidler, A., & Middendorf, M. (2010). *Artificial Bee Colony Optimization: A New Selection Scheme and Its Performance*. Academic Press.

Akay, B. (2009). Solving integer programming problems by using artificial bee colony algorithm. In *Lecture Notes in Artificial Intelligence: Vol. 5883. AI (ASTERISK) IA 2009: Emergent perspectives in artificial intelligence* (pp. 355–364). Berlin: Springer.

Akay, B. & Karaboga, D. (2009). *Parameter Tuning for the Artificial Bee Colony Algorithm*. Academic Press.

Akay, B., & Karaboga, D. (2012). Artificial bee colony algorithm for large-scale problems and engineering design optimization. *Journal of Intelligent Manufacturing*, 23(4), 1001–1014. doi:10.1007/s10845-010-0393-4

Akdagli, A., & Toktas, A. (2010). A novel expression in calculating resonant fre- quency of h shaped compact microstrip antennas obtained by using artificial bee colony algorithm. *Journal of Electromagnetic Waves and Applications*, 24(14-15), 2049–2061.

Alam, M. S., & Ul Kabir, M. W. I. M. (2010). Self-adaptation of mutation step size in artificial bee colony algorithm for continuous function optimization. *13th international conference on computer and information technology (ICCIT)*.

Anuar, S., Selamat, A., & Sallehuddin, R. (2016). A modified scout bee for artificial bee colony algorithm and its performance on optimization problems. *Journal of King Saud University - Computer and Information Sciences*, 28(4), 395 – 406.

Awadallah, M. A., Bolaji, A. L., & Al-Betar, M. A. (2015). A hybrid artificial bee colony for a nurse rostering problem. *Applied Soft Computing*, 35, 726–739. doi:10.1016/j.asoc.2015.07.004

Banharnsakun, A., Achalakul, T., & Sirinaovakul, B. (2010). Artificial bee colony algorithm on distributed environments. In *Nature and Biologically Inspired Computing (NaBIC), 2010 Second World Congress on*, 13–18. doi:10.1109/NABIC.2010.5716309

Banharnsakun, A., Sirinaovakul, B., & Achalakul, T. (2012). Job shop scheduling with the best-so-far ABC. *Engineering Applications of Artificial Intelligence*, 25(3), 583–593. doi:10.1016/j.engappai.2011.08.003

Bansal, J. S.-H., & Arya, K. (2012). Model order reduction of single input single output systems using artificial bee colony optimization algorithm. *Nature Inspired Cooperative Strategies for Optimization (NICSO 2011), 387*, 85–100.

Bao, L. Z. J. (2009). Comparison and analysis of the selection mechanism in the artificial bee colony algorithm. *International Conference Hybrid Intelligence System.* doi:10.1109/HIS.2009.319

Basu, B., & Mahanti, G. K. (2011). Artificial bees colony optimization for synthesis of thinned mutually coupled linear array using inverse fast Fourier transform. *Devices and Communications (ICDeCom), 2011 International Conference on,* 1–5. doi:10.1109/ICDECOM.2011.5738513

Baykasoglu, A. O. L., & Tapkan. (2007). Artificial bee colony algorithm and its application to generalized assignment problem. *Swarm Intelligence: Focus on Ant and Particle Swarm Optimization.*

Beloufa, F., & Chikh, M. (2013). Design of fuzzy classifier for diabetes disease using modified artificial bee colony algorithm. *Computer Methods and Programs in Biomedicine, 112*(1), 92–103. doi:10.1016/j.cmpb.2013.07.009 PMID:23932385

Beni, G., & Wang, J. (1989). Swarm Intelligence in Cellular Robotic Systems. Academic Press.

Bernardino, A. M., Bernardino, E. M., S´anchez-P´erez, J. M., G´omez-Pulido, J. A., & Vega-Rodr´ıguez, M. A. (2010). *Efficient Load Balancing for a Resilient Packet Ring Using Artificial Bee Colony.* Academic Press.

Bonabeau, E. D. M., & Theraulaz, G. (1999). Swarm intelligence: From natural to artificial systems. Oxford University Press.

Brajevic, I., Tuba, M., & Subotic, M. (2010). Improved artificial bee colony al- gorithm for constrained problems. *Proceedings of the 11th WSEAS Interna- tional Conference on Nural Networks and 11th WSEAS International Confer- ence on Evolutionary Computing and 11th WSEAS International Conference on Fuzzy Systems,* 185–190.

Chatterjee, A., Ghoshal, S. P., & Mukherjee, V. (2010). Artificial Bee Colony Algorithm for Transient Performance Augmentation of Grid Connected Distributed Generation. Academic Press.

Cuevas, E., Sencio´n-Echauri, F., Zaldivar, D., & Cisneros, M. A. P. (2014). *Multi circle detection on images using artificial bee colony (ABC) optimization.* CoRR, abs/1406.6560.

Dagli, C. H., Thammano, A., & Phu-ang, A. (2013). Complex adaptive systems a hybrid artificial bee colony algorithm with local search for flexible job-shop scheduling problem. *Procedia Computer Science, 20*, 96–101. doi:10.1016/j.procs.2013.09.245

Dahiya, S. S., Chhabra, J. K., & Kumar, S. (2010). Application of artificial bee colony algorithm to software testing. In *Proceedings of the 2010 21st Australian Software Engineering Conference*, (pp. 149–154). IEEE Computer Society. doi:10.1109/ASWEC.2010.30

Delican, Y., Vural, R. A., & Yildirim, T. (2010). Artificial bee colony optimization based cmos inverter design considering propagation delays. In *Symbolic and Numerical Methods, Modeling and Applications to Circuit Design (SM2ACD), 2010 XIth International Workshop on* (pp. 1–5). doi:10.1109/SM2ACD.2010.5672326

Deng, Z., Gu, H., Feng, H., & Shu, B. (2011). *Artificial Bee Colony Based Mapping for Application Specific Network-on-Chip Design*. Academic Press.

Dereli, T., & Das, G. S. (2011). A hybrid bee(s) algorithm for solving container loading problems. *Applied Soft Computing*, *11*(2), 2854–2862. doi:10.1016/j.asoc.2010.11.017

Develi, I., Kabalci, Y., & Basturk, A. (2015). Artificial bee colony optimization for modelling of indoor PLC channels: A case study from turkey. *Electric Power Systems Research*, *127*, 73–79. doi:10.1016/j.epsr.2015.05.021

Diwold, K., Aderhold, A., Scheidler, A., & Middendorf, M. (2011). Performance evaluation of artificial bee colony optimization and new selection schemes. *Memetic Computing*, *3*(3), 149–162. doi:10.1007/s12293-011-0065-8

Dorigo, M. (1992). *Optimization, learning and natural algorithms* (PhD thesis). Dipartimento di Elettronica, Politecnico di Milano, Italy.

Draa, A., & Bouaziz, A. (2014). An artificial bee colony algorithm for image contrast enhancement. *Swarm and Evolutionary Computation*, *16*, 69–84. doi:10.1016/j.swevo.2014.01.003

Duan, H.-B., Xu, C.-F., & Xing, Z.-H. (2010). A hybrid artificial bee colony optimization and quantum evolutionary algorithm for continuous optimization problems. *International Journal of Neural Systems*, *20*(01), 39–50. doi:10.1142/S012906571000222X PMID:20180252

Eslami, M., Shareef, H., & Khajehzadeh, M. (2013). Optimal design of damping controllers using a new hybrid artificial bee colony algorithm. *International Journal of Electrical Power & Energy Systems*, *52*, 42–54. doi:10.1016/j.ijepes.2013.03.012

Farahani, R. Z., Hassani, A., Mousavi, S. M., & Baygi, M. B. (2014). A hybrid artificial bee colony for disruption in a hierarchical maximal covering location problem. *Computers & Industrial Engineering*, *75*, 129–141. doi:10.1016/j.cie.2014.06.012

Fathy, A. (2015). Reliable and efficient approach for mitigating the shading effect onphotovoltaic module based on modified artificial bee colony algorithm. *Renewable Energy*, *81*, 78–88. doi:10.1016/j.renene.2015.03.017

Fleischer, M. (2003). *Foundations of swarm intelligence: From principles to practice*. Institute for Systems Research University of Maryland College Park.

Gao & Liu. (2011). Hybrid artificial bee colony algorithm. *Systems Engineering and Electronics*, *33*(5), 1167.

Gozde, H., & Taplamacioglu, M. C. (2012). Comparative performance analysis of artificial bee colony algorithm in automatic generation control for interconnected reheat thermal power system. *International Journal of Electrical Power & Energy Systems*, *42*(1), 167–178. doi:10.1016/j.ijepes.2012.03.039

Hemamalini, S., & Simon, S. (2010). Artificial bee colony algorithm for economic load dispatch problem with non-smooth cost functions. *Electric Power Components and Systems*, *38*(7), 786–803. doi:10.1080/15325000903489710

Hemamalini, S. & Simon, S. P. (2011). Dynamic economic dispatch using artificial bee colony algorithm for units with valve-point effect. *European Transactions on Electrical Power, 21*(1), 70–81.

Horng, M.-H. (2011). Multilevel thresholding selection based on the artificial bee colony algorithm for image segmentation. *Expert Systems with Applications, 38*(11), 13785–13791.

Hsu, C.-C., Chen, H.-C., Huang, K.-K., & Huang, Y.-M. (2012). A personalized auxiliary material recommendation system based on learning style on face- book applying an artificial bee colony algorithm. *Computers & Mathematics with Applications (Oxford, England), 64*(5), 1506–1513. doi:10.1016/j.camwa.2012.03.098

Huang, S.-J., & Liu, X.-Z. (2013). Application of artificial bee colony-based optimization for fault section estimation in power systems. *International Journal of Electrical Power & Energy Systems, 44*(1), 210–218. doi:10.1016/j.ijepes.2012.07.012

Jatoth, R. K., & Rajasekhar, A. (2010). Speed control of pmsm by hybrid genetic artificial bee colony algorithm. *Communication Control and Computing Technologies (ICCCCT), 2010 IEEE International Conference on,* 241– 246.

Kalayci, C. B., Hancilar, A., Gungor, A., & Gupta, S. M. (2015). Multi-objective fuzzy disassembly line balancing using a hybrid discrete artificial bee colony algorithm. *Journal of Manufacturing Systems, 37*(Part 3), 672–682. doi:10.1016/j.jmsy.2014.11.015

Kang, F. L. J., & Xu, Q. (2009). Hybrid simplex artificial bee colony algorithm and its application in material dynamic parameter back analysis of concrete dams. *Journal of Hydraulic Engineering*.

Karaboga, D. (2005). *An idea based on honey bee swarm for numerical optimization techn.* Erciyes Univ. Press.

Karaboga, D., & Akay, B. (2007). *Artificial bee colony (abc) algorithm on training artificial neural networks. Signal Processing and Communications Applications, SIU 2007, IEEE 15th* (p. 14). IEEE.

Karaboga, D., & Akay, B. (2010). Proportional integral derivative controller design by using artificial bee colony, harmony search, and the bees algorithms. *Proceedings of the Institution of Mechanical Engineers. Part I, Journal of Systems and Control Engineering, 224*(7), 869–883. doi:10.1243/09596518JSCE954

Karaboga, D., & Akay, B. (2011a). A modified artificial bee colony (abc) algorithm for constrained optimization problems. *Applied Soft Computing, 11*(3), 3021–3031. doi:10.1016/j.asoc.2010.12.001

Karaboga, D., & Akay, B. (2011b). Partial transmit sequences based on artificial bee colony algorithm for peak-to-average power ratio reduction in multicarrier code division multiple access systems. *IET Communications, 5*(8), 1155–1162. doi:10.1049/iet-com.2010.0379

Karaboga, D. & Basturk, B. (2007). *Artificial Bee Colony (ABC) Optimization Algorithm for Solving Constrained Optimization Problems*. Academic Press.

Karaboga, D., Okdem, S., & Ozturk, C. (2012). Cluster based wireless sensor network routing using artificial bee colony algorithm. *Wireless Networks, 18*(7), 847–860. doi:10.1007/s11276-012-0438-z

Karaboga, N. (2009). A new design method based on artificial bee colony algorithm for digital IIR filters. *Journal of the Franklin Institute*, *346*(4), 328–348. doi:10.1016/j.jfranklin.2008.11.003

Karaboga, N., & Latifoglu, F. (2013). Elimination of noise on transcranial doppler signal using iir filters designed with artificial bee colony abc- algorithm. *Digital Signal Processing*, *23*(3), 1051–1058. doi:10.1016/j.dsp.2012.09.015

Kashan, M. H., Nahavandi, N., & Kashan, A. H. (2011). Disabc: A new artificial bee colony algorithm for binary optimization. *Applied Soft Computing*, *12*(1), 342–352. doi:10.1016/j.asoc.2011.08.038

Kavian, Y. S., Rashedi, A., Mahani, A., & Ghassemlooy, Z. (2012). Routing and wavelength assignment in optical networks using artificial bee colony algorithm. *Optik - International Journal for Light and Electron Optics*, *124*(12), 1243 – 1249.

Kefayat, M., Ara, A. L., & Niaki, S. N. (2015). A hybrid of ant colony optimization and artificial bee colony algorithm for probabilistic optimal placement and sizing of distributed energy resources. *Energy Conversion and Management*, *92*, 149–161. doi:10.1016/j.enconman.2014.12.037

Kennedy, J., & Eberhart, R. (1995). Particle swarm optimization. *Neural Networks, 1995. Proceedings. IEEE International Conference on*, *4*, 1942–1948. doi:10.1109/ICNN.1995.488968

Lee, W. P., & Cai, W. T. (2011). A novel artificial bee colony algorithm with diversity strategy. In *Natural Computation (ICNC), 2011 Seventh International Conference on*, *3*, 1441–1444. doi:10.1109/ICNC.2011.6022505

Lei, X., Sun, J., Xu, X., & Guo, L. (2010). Artificial bee colony algorithm for solving multiple sequence alignment. In *Bio-Inspired Computing: Theories and Applications (BIC-TA), 2010 IEEE Fifth International Conference on*, 337–342.

Lei, X. H. X., & Zhang, A. (2010). *Improved artificial bee colony algorithm and its application in data clustering. In Bio-Inspired Computing: Theories and Applications*. BIC-TA.

Li, H., Li, J., & Kang, F. (2011). Risk analysis of dam based on artificial bee colony algorithm with fuzzy c-means clustering. *Canadian Journal of Civil Engineering*, *38*(5), 483–492. doi:10.1139/l11-020

Li, H. L. J., & Kang, F. (2011). Artificial bee colony algorithm for reliability analysis of engineering structures. *Materials Research*, *163-167*, 3103–3109. doi:10.4028/www.scientific.net/AMR.163-167.3103

Li, J., Xie, S., Pan, Q., & Wang, S. (2011). A hybrid artificial bee colony algorithm for flexible job shop scheduling problems. *International Journal of Computers, Communications & Control*, *6*(2), 286–296. doi:10.15837/ijccc.2011.2.2177

Li, J.-Q., & Pan, Q.-K. (2015). Solving the large-scale hybrid flow shop scheduling problem with limited buffers by a hybrid artificial bee colony algorithm. *Information Sciences*, *316*, 487–502. doi:10.1016/j.ins.2014.10.009

Li, J.-Q., Pan, Q.-K., & Gao, K.-Z. (2011). Pareto-based discrete artificial bee colony algorithm for multi-objective flexible job shop scheduling problems. *International Journal of Advanced Manufacturing Technology*, *55*(9), 1159–1169. doi:10.1007/s00170-010-3140-2

Li, Y., Wang, Y., & Li, B. (2013). A hybrid artificial bee colony assisted differential evolution algorithm for optimal reactive power flow. *International Journal of Electrical Power & Energy Systems*, *52*, 25–33. doi:10.1016/j.ijepes.2013.03.016

Li, Z., Wang, W., Yan, Y., & Li, Z. (2015). Psabc: A hybrid algorithm based on particle swarm and artificial bee colony for high-dimensional optimization problems. *Expert Systems with Applications*, *42*(22), 8881–8895. doi:10.1016/j.eswa.2015.07.043

Lien, L.-C., & Cheng, M.-Y. (2012). A hybrid swarm intelligence based particle- bee algorithm for construction site layout optimization. *Expert Systems with Applications*, *39*(10), 9642–9650. doi:10.1016/j.eswa.2012.02.134

Liu, Y.-F., & Liu, S.-Y. (2013). A hybrid discrete artificial bee colony algorithm for permutation flow-shop scheduling problem. *Applied Soft Computing*, *13*(3), 1459–1463. doi:10.1016/j.asoc.2011.10.024

Luo, J., Wang, Q., & Xiao, X. (2013). A modified artificial bee colony algorithm based on converge-onlookers approach for global optimization. *Applied Mathematics and Computation*, *219*(20), 10253–10262. doi:10.1016/j.amc.2013.04.001

Luo, Q., & Duan, H. (2014). Chaotic artificial bee colony optimization approach to aircraft automatic landing system. *IFAC Proceedings*, *47*(3), 876– 881.

Mala, D. J., Mohan, V., & Kamalapriya, M. (2010). Automated software test optimisation framework - an artificial bee colony optimisation-based approach. *IET Software*, *4*(5), 334–348. doi:10.1049/iet-sen.2009.0079

Mandal, S. K., Chan, F. T., & Tiwari, M. (2012). Leak detection of pipeline: An integrated approach of rough set theory and artificial bee colony trained SVM. *Expert Systems with Applications*, *39*(3), 3071–3080. doi:10.1016/j.eswa.2011.08.170

Mezura-Montes, E., & Cetina-Dominguez, O. (2012). Empirical analysis of a modified artificial bee colony for constrained numerical optimization. *Applied Mathematics and Computation*, *218*(22), 10943–10973. doi:10.1016/j.amc.2012.04.057

Mezura-Montes, E., & Velez-Koeppel, R. E. (2010). Elitist artificial bee colony for constrained real-parameter optimization. *IEEE Congress on Evolutionary Computation*, 1–8. doi:10.1109/CEC.2010.5586280

Mini, S., Udgata, S. K., & Sabat, S. L. (2010). Sensor Deployment in 3-D Terrain Using Artificial Bee Colony Algorithm. Academic Press.

Mishra, S. E., Taplamacolu, M., & Lee, K. Y. (2015). 9th IFAC symposium on control of power and energy systems CPES 2015 robust tuning of power system stabilizer by using orthogonal learning artificial bee colony. *IFAC- PapersOnLine*, *48*(30), 149 – 154.

Nseef, S. K., Abdullah, S., Turky, A., & Kendall, G. (2016). An adaptive multi- population artificial bee colony algorithm for dynamic optimization problems. *Knowledge-Based Systems*, *104*, 14–23. doi:10.1016/j.knosys.2016.04.005

Pan, Q.-K., Tasgetiren, M. F., Suganthan, P., & Chua, T. (2011). A discrete artificial bee colony algorithm for the lot-streaming flow shop scheduling problem. *Information Sciences, 181*(12), 2455–2468. doi:10.1016/j.ins.2009.12.025

Pansuwan, P., Rukwong, N., & Pongcharoen, P. (2010). Identifying optimum artificial bee colony (abc) algorithm's parameters for scheduling the manufacture and assembly of complex products. *Computer and Network Technology (ICCNT), 2010 Second International Conference on,* 339–343.

Pawar, P. R.-R., & Shankar, R. (2008). *Multi-objective optimization of electro- chemical machining process parameters using artificial bee colony (abc) algorithm.* Academic Press.

Rajasekhar, A., Abraham, A., & Pant, M. (2011). Levy mutated artificial bee colony algorithm for global optimization. *Systems, Man, and Cybernetics (SMC), 2011 IEEE International Conference on,* 655–662. doi:10.1109/ICSMC.2011.6083786

Rao, R.S., & Ramalingaraju, M. (2008). Optimization of distribution network configuration for loss reduction using artificial bee colony algorithm. *International Journal of Electrical Power and Energy Systems Engineering, 1,* 116–122.

Rubio-Largo, A., Vega-Rodríguez, M. A., Gómez-Pulido, J. A., & Sánchez-Pérez, J.M. (2011). *Tackling the Static RWA Problem by Using a Multi- objective Artificial Bee Colony Algorithm.* Academic Press.

Sag, T., & Çunkaş, M. (2015). Color image segmentation based on multiobjective artificial bee colony optimization. *Applied Soft Computing, 34,* 389–401. doi:10.1016/j.asoc.2015.05.016

Samanta, S., & Chakraborty, S. (2011). Parametric optimization of some non- traditional machining processes using artificial bee colony algorithm. *Engineering Applications of Artificial Intelligence, 24*(6), 946–957. doi:10.1016/j.engappai.2011.03.009

Secui, D. C. (2015). A new modified artificial bee colony algorithm for the economic dispatch problem. *Energy Conversion and Management, 89,* 43–62. doi:10.1016/j.enconman.2014.09.034

Shanthi, D., & Amalraj, R. (2012). Collaborative artificial bee colony optimization clustering using spnn. *Procedia Engineering, 30,* 989–996. doi:10.1016/j.proeng.2012.01.955

Shi, Y.-j., Qu, F.-Z., Chen, W., & Li, B. (2010). *An Artificial Bee Colony with Random Key for Resource-Constrained Project Scheduling.* Academic Press.

Singh, A., & Sundar, S. (2011). An artificial bee colony algorithm for the mini- mum routing cost spanning tree problem. *Soft Computing, 15*(12), 2489–2499. doi:10.1007/s00500-011-0711-6

Sonmez, M. (2011). Artificial bee colony algorithm for optimization of truss structures. *Applied Soft Computing, 11*(2), 2406–2418. doi:10.1016/j.asoc.2010.09.003

Stanarevic, N. (2011). Comparison of different mutation strategies applied to artificial bee colony algorithm. *Proceedings of the 5th European Conference on European Computing Conference,* 257–262.

Stanarevic, N., Tuba, M., & Bacanin, N. (2010). Enhanced artificial bee colony algorithm performance. *Proceedings of the 14th WSEAS International Conference on Computers: Part of the 14th WSEAS CSCC Multiconference, 2,* 440–445.

Sulaiman, M. H., Mustafa, M. W., Shareef, H., & Khalid, S. N. A. (2012). An application of artificial bee colony algorithm with least squares support vector machine for real and reactive power tracing in deregulated power system. *International Journal of Electrical Power & Energy Systems, 37*(1), 67–77. doi:10.1016/j.ijepes.2011.12.007

Sumesh, E. P., Lam, S. S. B., Raju, M. L. H. P. M., U. K., C. S., & Srivastav, P. R. (2012). International conference on communication technology and system design 2011 automated generation of independent paths and test suite optimization using artificial bee colony. *Procedia Engineering, 30*, 191 – 200.

Sumpavakup, C., Srikun, I., & Chusanapiputt, S. (2010). A solution to the optimal power flow using artificial bee colony algorithm. *Power System Technology (POWERCON), 2010 International Conference on,* 1–5. doi:10.1109/POWERCON.2010.5666516

Sundar, S., Singh, A., & Rossi, A. (2010). *An Artificial Bee Colony Algorithm for the 0–1 Multidimensional Knapsack Problem.* Academic Press.

Szeto, W., & Jiang, Y. (2014). Transit route and frequency design: Bi-level modeling and hybrid artificial bee colony algorithm approach. *Transportation Research Part B: Methodological, 67*, 235–263. doi:10.1016/j.trb.2014.05.008

Taherdangkoo, M., Yazdi, M., & Rezvani, M. H. (2010). Segmentation of Mr Brain images using fcm improved by artificial bee colony (abc) algorithm. *Proceedings of the 10th IEEE International Conference on Information Technology and Applications in Biomedicine,* 1–5. doi:10.1109/ITAB.2010.5687803

Tahooneh, A. & Ziarati, K. (2011). *Using Artificial Bee Colony to Solve Stochastic Resource Constrained Project Scheduling Problem.* Academic Press.

Tasgetiren, M. F., Pan, Q.-K., Suganthan, P., & Chen, A. H.-L. (2011). A discrete artificial bee colony algorithm for the total flowtime minimization in permutation flow shops. *Information Sciences, 181*(16), 3459–3475. doi:10.1016/j.ins.2011.04.018

Toktas, A., Bicer, M. B., Akdagli, A., & Kayabasi, A. (2011). Simple formulas for calculating resonant frequencies of c and h shaped compact microstrip antennas obtained by using artificial bee colony algorithm. *Journal of Electromagnetic Waves and Applications, 25*(11-12), 1718–1729. doi:10.1163/156939311797164855

Wang, J., Li, T., & Ren, R. (2010). A real time idss based on artificial bee colony-support vector machine algorithm. *Advanced Computational Intelligence (IWACI), 2010 Third International Workshop on,* 91–96.

Wang, X., Xie, X., & Cheng, T. (2013). A modified artificial bee colony algorithm for order acceptance in two-machine flow shops. *International Journal of Production Economics, 141*(1), 14–23. doi:10.1016/j.ijpe.2012.06.003

Wu, B., Qian, C., Ni, W., & Fan, S. (2012). The improvement of glowworm swarm optimization for continuous optimization problems. *Expert Systems with Applications, 39*(7), 6335–6342. doi:10.1016/j.eswa.2011.12.017

Wu, D., Ren, F., & Zhang, W. (2016). An energy optimal thrust allocation method for the marine dynamic positioning system based on adaptive hybrid artificial bee colony algorithm. *Ocean Engineering, 118*, 216–226. doi:10.1016/j.oceaneng.2016.04.004

Xiang, W., Ma, S., & An, M. (2014). habcde: A hybrid evolutionary algorithm based on artificial bee colony algorithm and differential evolution. *Applied Mathematics and Computation, 238*, 370–386. doi:10.1016/j.amc.2014.03.055

Xing, F. F. L., & Haijun, D. (2007). *The parameter improvement of bee colony algorithm in tsp problem.* Science Paper Online.

Xu, C., & Duan, H. (2010). Artificial bee colony (abc) optimized edge potential function (epf) approach to target recognition for low-altitude aircraft. *Pattern Recognition Letters, 31*(13), 1759–1772. doi:10.1016/j.patrec.2009.11.018

Xu, C., Duan, H., & Liu, F. (2010). Chaotic artificial bee colony approach to uninhabited combat air vehicle (ucav) path planning. *Aerospace Science and Technology, 14*(8), 535–541. doi:10.1016/j.ast.2010.04.008

Yan, X., Zhu, Y., Zou, W., & Wang, L. (2012). A new approach for data clustering using hybrid artificial bee colony algorithm. *Neurocomputing, 97*, 241–250. doi:10.1016/j.neucom.2012.04.025

Yang, X. S. (2010). *Nature Inspired Cooperative Strategies for Optimization.* New Metaheuristic Bat-Inspired Algorithm.

Yildiz, A. R. (2013). A new hybrid artificial bee colony algorithm for robust optimal design and manufacturing. *Applied Soft Computing, 13*(5), 2906–2912. doi:10.1016/j.asoc.2012.04.013

Yousefi-Talouki, A., & Valiollahi, S. (2010). Optimal power flow with unified power flow controller using artificial bee colony algorithm. *International Review of Electrical Engineering, 5*, 2773.

Yunbin, H., Yupeng, X., Jing, W., & Song, L. (2014). The fuzzy clustering combined an improved artificial bee colony algorithm with new rank fitness selection. *Software Intelligence Technologies and Applications International Conference on Frontiers of Internet of Things 2014, International Conference on*, 261–265. doi:10.1049/cp.2014.1572

Yurtkuran, A., & Emel, E. (2015). An adaptive artificial bee colony algorithm for global optimization. *Applied Mathematics and Computation, 271*, 1004–1023. doi:10.1016/j.amc.2015.09.064

Zhang, C., Ouyang, D., & Ning, J. (2010). An artificial bee colony approach for clustering. *Expert Systems with Applications, 37*(7), 4761–4767. doi:10.1016/j.eswa.2009.11.003

Zhang, C., Zheng, J., & Zhou, Y. (2015). Two modified artificial bee colony algorithms inspired by grenade explosion method. *Neurocomputing, 151*(3), 1198–1207. doi:10.1016/j.neucom.2014.04.082

Zhang, D.-L., Tang, Y.-G., & Gguan, X.-P. (2014). Optimum design of fractional order pid controller for an avr system using an improved artificial bee colony algorithm. *Acta Automatica Sinica, 40*(5), 973–979. doi:10.1016/S1874-1029(14)60010-0

Zhang, R., Song, S., & Wu, C. (2013). A hybrid artificial bee colony algorithm for the job shop scheduling problem. *International Journal of Production Economics, 141*(1), 167–178. doi:10.1016/j.ijpe.2012.03.035

Zhang, S., Lee, C., Choy, K., Ho, W., & Ip, W. (2014). Design and development of a hybrid artificial bee colony algorithm for the environmental vehicle routing problem. *Transportation Research Part D, Transport and Environment, 31*, 85–99. doi:10.1016/j.trd.2014.05.015

Zhang, Y., & Wu, L. (2011). Optimal multi-level thresholding based on maxi-mum tsallis entropy via an artificial bee colony approach. *Entropy, 4*(12), 841–859. doi:10.3390/e13040841

Zhao, D., Gao, H., Diao, M., & An, C. (2010a). Direction finding of maximum likelihood algorithm using artificial bee colony in the impulsive noise. *Artificial Intelligence and Computational Intelligence (AICI), 2010 International Conference on, 2*, 102–105. doi:10.1109/AICI.2010.144

Zhao, H., Pei, Z., Jiang, J., Guan, R., Wang, C., & Shi, X. (2010b). *A Hybrid Swarm Intelligent Method Based on Genetic Algorithm and Artificial Bee Colony*. Academic Press.

Zhou, J., Zhang, X., Zhang, G., & Chen, D. (2015). Optimization and parameters estimation in ultrasonic echo problems using modified artificial bee colony algorithm. *Journal of Bionics Engineering, 12*(1), 160–169. doi:10.1016/S1672-6529(14)60110-4

Zou, W. Z. Y. C.-H. S. X. (2010). A clustering approach using cooperative artificial bee colony algorithm. Discrete Dynamics in Nature and Society.

Zou, W., & Zhu, Y. (2011). Clustering approach based on von neumann topology artificial bee colony algorithm. *International conference on data mining (DMIN11)*, 121–126.

Chapter 19
A Survey of the Cuckoo Search and Its Applications in Real-World Optimization Problems

Christopher Expósito-Izquierdo
University of La Laguna, Spain

Airam Expósito-Márquez
University of La Laguna, Spain

ABSTRACT

The chapter at hand seeks to provide a general survey of the Cuckoo Search Algorithm and its most highlighted variants. The Cuckoo Search Algorithm is a relatively recent nature-inspired population-based meta-heuristic algorithm that is based upon the lifestyle, egg laying, and breeding strategy of some species of cuckoos. In this case, the Lévy flight is used to move the cuckoos within the search space of the optimization problem to solve and obtain a suitable balance between diversification and intensification. As discussed in this chapter, the Cuckoo Search Algorithm has been successfully applied to a wide range of heterogeneous optimization problems found in practical applications over the last few years. Some of the reasons of its relevance are the reduced number of parameters to configure and its ease of implementation.

1. INTRODUCTION

Optimization is a term which has arisen in a natural way from behind multitude of aspects of our daily lives, both at familiar, professional, and scientific levels (Koziel & Yang, 2011). Its practical applications cover a wide range of fields, such as economics, engineering, medicine, agriculture, sports, image processing, data mining, software design, and operations research, among others. For example, determining the shortest path to get to work, selecting the most suitable place to set up a new logistic infrastructure, choosing the best portfolio in such a way that the expected value is as high as possible, or even calculating the optimal timing of organ transplants. In all of these cases and from a mathematical perspective,

DOI: 10.4018/978-1-5225-2128-0.ch019

the goal is to select the best element from a given set of available alternatives according to one or several criteria. This means selecting that element which maximizes or minimizes a given mathematical function.

Nature has become an excellent source of inspiration for the conceptual development of efficient solving methods to tackle optimization problems. In this regard, nature-inspired algorithms are a revolutionary class of approximate solving techniques based on the principles found behind some nature processes. Over the last years, multitude of meta-heuristic algorithms underpinned by diverse

nature-inspired paradigms have been already proposed in the scientific literature with the aim of solving a wide range of real-world optimization problems. Due to their numerous and successful application contexts, some of the most outstanding nature-inspired meta-heuristic algorithms are Genetic Algorithms (Holland, 1975), Ant Colony Optimization Algorithms (Dorigo et al., 1996), Particle Swarm Optimization Algorithms (Kennedy and Eberhart, 1995), and Artificial Bee Colony Algorithms (Karaboga, 2005), among others. These optimization techniques mimic the evolutionary ideas of natural selection and genetics, the behavior of ants when seeking a path between their home colony and a source of food, the behavior of particles in nature, and the behavior of a honey bee swarm, respectively.

Broadly speaking, the popularity of nature-inspired algorithms lies in the fact that current practical optimization problems are nowadays becoming increasingly more complex in terms of dimensions, constraints, dynamism, uncertainty, etc. In this regard, nature-inspired algorithms are usually able to identify promising regions within the search space of a given optimization problem and extract high-quality solutions by means of a reasonable amount of computational time. However, it is worth mentioning that these optimization techniques have certain limitations that must be appropriately analyzed before their effective application in practice. In general terms, they present an asymptotic convergence, and therefore they no guarantee to identify the optima solutions of all the optimization problems in finite computational time. Also, the performance of these techniques is highly dependent on the values of its internal running parameters. In addition, the number of parameters to configure is high in some techniques. Lastly, some of these techniques are computationally very expensive, and consequently they cannot be easily adapted to address real-time or dynamic optimization problems.

The present chapter is aimed at providing to the reader an overview of a recent nature-inspired meta-heuristic termed Cuckoo Search and the main variants of it published in the scientific literature so far. In this regard, its key components are analyzed, whereas, due to its high efficiency in computational terms, some of its most successful application contexts in the real world are also

discussed. As pointed out in this chapter, this optimization technique presents some of the most outstanding advantages associated with nature-inspired methods while the aforementioned limitations are somewhat mitigated.

The remainder of the chapter at hand is organized as follows. Firstly, Section 2 describes the Cuckoo Search from a general point of view. Afterwards, some of the most relevant variants of the Cuckoo Search are discussed in Section 3. Later, a brief overview of successful applications of this optimization technique in a wide range of fields is presented in Section 4. Finally, Section 5 draws some concluding remarks from the chapter.

2. CUCKOO SEARCH

2.1. Introduction

In order to find the origin of the optimization technique termed Cuckoo Search, in short CS, we must look back to the life of Edward Jenner (1749-1823), towering figure in the field of medicine, in particular due to his contribution to immunization and eradication of smallpox. Notwithstanding that, Edward Jenner is nowadays a Fellow of the Royal Society thanks to his discoveries in zoology.

In 1788, Edward Jenner published a paper describing his study about the behavior of the nested cuckoo. In particular, he described how the newly hatched cuckoo pushes the eggs of its host and the existing fledgling chicks out of the nest in which it was born.

2.2. General Description

The CS is a relatively recent nature-inspired population-based meta-heuristic algorithm proposed by Xin-She Yang and Suash Deb (Yang and Deb, 2009). This optimization technique is based upon the lifestyle, egg laying, and breeding strategy of some species of cuckoos. Specifically, these birds lay their own fertilized eggs in nests belonging to other host birds with the goal of being hatched by the surrogate parents. In some cases, cuckoos even take some of the eggs of the host bird away from their nests to increase the hatching probability of their eggs. Regrettably, these intruding eggs can be suddenly discovered by the host birds and consequently these can be thrown out from the incumbent nest or the host birds can renounce the nest definitively and build a new one in another location. Under this scenario, the CS mimics such breeding behavior in order to solve any given optimization problem.

The CS makes multiple analogies between the field of optimization and the aforementioned behaviour of cuckoos in nature. That is, a cuckoo egg in the CS represents a new solution of the optimization problem under study. This means that the larger the number of eggs during the execution of the CS, the larger the probability of covering the whole search space. Furthermore, an egg in a nest represents a feasible solution of the optimization problem to solve. In this environment, the main purpose of the CS is to introduce the best possible cuckoo eggs in a pre-defined set of nests. In fact, those eggs placed inside the nests are replaced over the generations considered in the execution of the optimization technique with the aim of obtaining the subsequent populations. This has several advantages in terms of effectiveness of the search. It allows to reach new promising regions of the search space while avoiding stagnation of the exploration process. In most of cases, only those solutions with the worst objective function value are discarded, *i.e.*, elitism criterion. In the simplest variant of the CS, the number of nests is pre-specified by the user and, in addition, each nest can have only one egg. However, the simplest approach of the technique can be easily extended to consider an adaptive number of nests and multiple eggs per nest.

Broadly speaking, the general behavior of the CS seeks to evolve a population of n host nests over generations with the aim of identifying the optima solutions of the search space. For this purpose, the CS is based upon the following principles:

- One egg is laid by each cuckoo in the CS at a time in a nest which is selected at random.
- Only those nests having the best eggs in terms of objective function value will be included into the next generation.
- The eggs can be discovered by the host birds with a certain probability. In practice, this means that new feasible solutions generated at random are introduced while some of the solutions included into the last population are discarded. The probability of discarding an egg at each generation is denoted as $p\_a \in [0, 1]$. It is easy to check that this parameter controls the diversity of the population used by the optimization technique, in such a way that the higher the value of p a the higher the diversity and the lower the convergence speed. In the same vein, low values of p a give rise to a poor diversity and a high probability of being trapped into local optima solutions within the search space.

Furthermore, one of the most highlighted advantages derived from the use of CS is related to the tuning of its parameters. In fact, the user only has to set up the values of the population size, n, and the probability associated with abandoning the worse nests and being replaced by new ones, p_a, to solve real-world optimization problems in an efficient way.

2.3. Pseudo-Code

In order to facilitate an appropriate understanding of the behavior of the general CS, in the following a pseudo-code of its general structure is summarized in Algorithm 1.

Algorithm 1. General pseudo-code of the Cuckoo Search
Require: P, optimization problem to solve
Require: f ($\cdot$), objective function of P
Require: n, size of the population
Require: p_a, probability of discarding eggs at each generation for P
1. Generate an initial population of n host nests
2. while (stop criterion) do
3. i $\leftarrow$ Get a cuckoo at random (or according to some criterion)
4. Replacing the solution of i by performing Lévy flight
5. Evaluate the objective function value of i, f (i)
6. j $\leftarrow$ Select a nest at random (or according to some criterion)
7. if (f (i) > f (j)) then
8. Replace solution j by i
9. end if
10. Discard a fraction p_a of the worse nests
11. Generate new solutions until fill the population
12. Rank the solutions into the population according to their objective function values
13. end while
14. return Best solution from the population

Without loss of generality, it is assumed in this case that an objective function, f ($\cdot$), of a known maximization optimization problem, P, is provided. It should be noted at this point that the described pseudo-code can be easily modified to also address minimization optimization problems. The first step of the algorithm is aimed at filling an initial population of n host nests (line 1). In most of cases, these solutions are generated at random. However, alternative greedy procedures or another optimization techniques can be also used with this goal in mind. At each generation, one solution is modified according to the Lévy flight (lines 3-4). This process is described in Section 2.4. The new solution replaces an old one selected at random from the population whenever the former has a better objective function value (lines 7-9). Afterwards, some of the worst solutions included into the population are discarded to avoid stagnation and increase the diversification capabilities of the search. In particular, a fraction of p_a solutions are discarded (line 10) and replaced by new solutions (line 11). It should be noted that the population must be sorted according to the objective function values of the solutions included into it to discard, compare, and select the solutions during the execution of the CS. Thus, the last step to carry out at each generation is to rank the solutions of the population (line 12). Lastly, the best solution, in terms of objective function value, is reported by the optimization technique (line 14).

It is worth mentioning that (Yang and Deb, 2010) provide an efficient implementation of the CS by exploiting the vector capabilities of Matlab with the goal of reducing the computational times of the optimization technique. In addition, object-oriented and parallel implementations in CUDA architectures are provided by (Bacanin, 2012) and (Jovanovic et al., 2013), respectively.

2.4. Lévy Flight

The authors of (Yang and Deb, 2009) indicate that the Lévy flight performed by some animals and insects has already demonstrated promising capabilities when adapted to the movement of individuals in population-based optimization techniques. This way, the cuckoos in the CS move according to random walks in which the step-lengths are made in isotropic random directions and are distributed by following a heavy-tailed probability distribution. In particular, the random walks used in the CS are Markov chains in which the next location to explore only depends on the current location and a transition probability given by a Lévy distribution, which has infinite mean and variance.

Given a p-dimensional space for an optimization problem and a vector of variables which represents a solution of it during generation t with the form $x^t = (x^t_1, x^t_2, \ldots, x^t_p)$, a new solution is obtained from it in the next generation by applying a mapping function, $\Delta(\cdot)$. This is:

$$x^{t+1} = \Delta(x^t)$$

In the case of the CS, the random walk is performed by means of a Lévy flight, which determines the values taken by the solution variables according to their own values in the previous generation. Specifically, given the i-th variable of a solution x at generation t, x^t_i, its value in the next generation is calculated as follows (Yang and Deb, 2014):

$$x^{t+1} = x^t_i + \alpha \cdot L(s, \lambda)$$

where α is a problem-dependent scaling factor, s is a step size, $1 < \lambda \leq 3$ (Yang and Deb, 2009), and $L(s, \lambda)$ is expressed as follows:

$$L(s, \lambda) = (\lambda \cdot \Gamma(\lambda) \cdot \sin(\pi\lambda/2))/\pi \cdot (1/s^{1+\lambda})$$

3. VARIANTS OF THE CUCKOO SEARCH

The seminal definition of the Cuckoo Search, in short CS, introduced in the previous section of the chapter at hand has been broadly tested on different optimization problem so far. In fact, it is worth mentioning that the CS has been used to solve optimization problems belonging to different fields of research. In this regard, high-efficient CS-based approaches are available to solve practical optimization problems of scheduling, flood forecasting, supplier selection, speaker recognition, web service composition, logistics and transportation, business, and engineering, among others. This fact is broadly discussed in Section 4. However, up to now addressing these optimization problems has encouraged the development of some effective variants of the CS in the scientific literature thatworth to analyse. Some of the most highlighted variants are the Discrete Binary CS, Neural-based CS, Quantum-inspired CS, Emotional Chaotic CS, and Modified CS, among others. In addition, the CS has been successfully combined with different machine learning approaches, heuristics, meta-heuristics, exact methods, among others, to exploit the beneficial capabilities of the techniques to combine.

A binary version of the generic CS introduced in the previous section is provided by (Pereira et al., 2014) for tackling feature selection processes. The goal in this case is to determine a suitable subset of representative features in such a way that it can represent a whole dataset. As the authors discuss, the main idea behind this variant of the CS is to model the search space as a l-dimensional Boolean

lattice in such a way that the solutions of the optimization problem under study are updated across the corner of a hypercube. This way, a binary vector is used to represent the potential solutions of the optimization problem, where a given position takes value 1 if and only if the corresponding feature is selected to compose the new dataset. Otherwise, it takes value 0. The values of the lattice

are denoted as $x_{\{ji\}}(t)$, which represents the j-th egg at nest i during generation t, where i = 1, 2, ..., m and j = 1, 2, ..., h, and m and h are the dimensions of the dataset. These values are updated as indicated in the following:

$$S(x^j_i(t)) = 1/(1+e^{\{-x^j_i(t)\}})$$
$$x^j_i(t) =$$
1, if $S(x_{ji}(t)) > \sigma$,
0, otherwise

where $\sigma \sim U(0, 1)$. The binary proposal is compared against three nature-inspired optimization methods and the computational experiments indicate that it is high effective in all the cases.

In the same vein as the previous paper, (Gherboudj et al., 2012) present a discrete binary variant of the CS aimed at tacking binary combinatorial optimization problems. In this case and in a similar way as that used by the binary Particle Swarm Optimization, a sigmoid function is used to compute the flipping chances of the set of cuckoos. The effectiveness of the discrete binary CS is assessed by using one-dimensional and multidimensional knapsack problems.

A new variant of the CS is proposed by (Li and Yin, 2015). In particular, the authors present an algorithm in which a self-adaptive parameter setting and two new search strategies are proposed with the aim of solving global optimization problem with variables in the continuous domain. The proposed parameter setting is based upon a statistical learning strategy that indicates the evolution of each individual included into the population. This is carried out on the basis of the relative success ratio associated with selecting one out of two new parameters in previous generations of the search process. However, it is not easy to deduce how the values of these new parameters have been chosen and how they impact on the overall performance of the optimization technique. Also, the proposed CS considers a repair rule that allows to maintain, after reparation, those individuals whose solution values have moved out of the bounds of the involved search space. Furthermore, a linear decreasing probability rule is used to combine two new search rules based on the particular individuals of the population at each generation to obtain a suitable balance between intensification and diversification. This proposal is compared against some representative evolutionary algorithms from the scientific literature on 16 well-known benchmark functions. In this regard, the computational experiments indicate that the proposed optimization technique is at least as competitive or even better than the reference methods.

In contrast to many proposals found in the scientific literature in which the Lévy flight step size is constant and usually takes value one (Yang and Deb, 2009), the paper by (Walton et al., 2011) proposes a Modified CS to decrease the value of this step size as the generations going on. This is performed with the same reasoning as the reduction in the inertia constant in the Particle Swarm Optimization (Kennedy and Eberhart, 1995). This way, the localized searching level of the eggs within the search space is increased as the generations pass. At the same time, the authors of the paper also consider the information exchange between a subset of eggs as a mean to overcome one of the intrinsic characteristics of the seminal definition of the CS: the lack of communication between individuals. For this purpose, a new egg is generated from the characteristics of two of the best eggs in terms of objective function value that are currently included into the population. The position of this new egg within the search space of the optimization problem to solve is based on the line connecting both reference eggs. The relative position on this line is proportional to the objective function values of the eggs at the ends. In spite of the fact that this information exchange strategy is able to provide a higher diversification level, it introduces a new parameter to configure: the percentage of eggs used to exchange information.

The paper by (Layeb, 2011) presents a novel variant of the CS termed Quantum Inspired Cuckoo Search Algorithm. In this case, some of the principles associated with the quantum computing are integrated into the general description of the CS. Some of these are the qubit representation, quantum mutation, measure operation, and superposition of states. The main goal of this approach is to improve the diversification level by generating high-quality random solutions of the optimization problem to solve. Also, it is worth mentioning that one of the strengths of this optimization technique is the ability to reduce the population size and the number of generations to perform. This is carried out by means of the use of quantum representation, which allows to code the feasible solutions with a certain probability. The effectiveness of the algorithmic proposal is assessed on knapsack problems. Despite the encouraging results obtained, the authors suggest to embed local-search-based methods into the definition of the optimization technique to improve the solutions reported. This technique has been also checked when solving one-dimensional bin packing problem by (Layeb and Boussalia, 2012).

Moreover, multi-objective optimization problems are without doubts present in practically any real-world environment. (Yang and Deb, 2013) propose a multi-objective CS, which is a natural extension of the original CS to deal with multi-objective optimization problems. In this case, the nests can maintain k eggs simultaneously, where k is the number of objectives of the optimization problem to solve. This way, the egg i represents the solution of the i-th objective, where i = 1, 2, . . ., k. As in the original CS, a portion of all the nests are discarded at each generation. This means that k eggs are replaced by new ones when a nest is ruled out. The performance of the multi-objective proposal is analyzed by using a wide range of well-known multi-objective test functions and design problems found in the field of engineering and industry. Despite the good results reported by the optimization technique, the authors indicate that incorporating strategies to obtain diverse Pareto fronts may even improve the performance. Lastly, another multi-objective variant of the CS is proposed by (Zhou et al., 2016). In this paper, the accuracy of the community detection in dynamic networks is improved by means of a multi-objective discrete CS.

The use of the Lévy flight to move the cuckoos within the search space of the optimization problem to solve can give rise to a poor convergence rate of the CS. The reason is found in the heavy tail of the Lévy distribution used in the random walk process performed by the cuckoos. In order to overcome this shortcoming of the original CS, (Zheng and Zhou, 2012) propose to use a diminishing Gaussian distribution. Unfortunately, the computational experiments are not sufficiently reliable to be able to establish conclusions about its impact on the overall performance of the optimization technique.

Finally, it should be said that the interested reader can find an analysis of additional variants of the general CS introduced in Section 2 by (Fister et al., 2014).

4. APPLICATIONS OF CUCKOO SEARCH

It has been proven that the Cuckoo Search, CS, and its multiple variants is a high competitive meta-heuristic to solve optimization problems belonging to a wide range of practical application areas. In most of cases, these optimization problems are highly non-linear and involve complex constraints to satisfy. A literature review and a discussion of the applications of the CS are provided in the remainder of this section. In addition, the interested reader is referred to (Fister et al., 2014) in order to get a brief summary of applications in which the CS has been successfully applied.

Firstly, (Yang and Deb, 2010) provide an overview of the CS and validate its competitiveness using some standard test functions and newly designed stochastic test functions against a Genetic Algorithm and a Particle Swarm Optimization. One of the conclusions extracted from the study carried out in the paper is that, unlike other meta-heuristics, the convergence rate of the technique is insensitive to the algorithm-dependent parameters. The authors also apply the CS to solve engineering design optimisation problems. Some of these problems are the design of springs and welded beam structures. In addition, the performance of the CS has been also assessed when solving well-known benchmark functions from the literature by (Nawi et al., 2014). In this case, the Ackley, Griewank, Beale, Rosenbrock, and Booth functions are considered in the study. In all the cases, the computational results reveal the efficiency of the technique when tackling multi-modal optimization problems.

The Modified Cuckoo Search (MCS) proposed by (Walton et al., 2011) and described in the previous section is compared against Differential Evolution, Particle Swarm Optimization, and the original CS on a series of seven benchmark tests. The authors claim that the proposed MCS would be a suitable optimization technique to solve problems for which the objective function evaluations are computationally expensive and also this technique is the best amongst those involved in the experimental analysis when the number of objective function evaluations is not bounded.

Furthermore, (Vazquez, 2011) put forwards the use of the CS in the field of artificial neural networks. In this case, a methodology in which the CS is applied to adjust the synaptic weights of spiking neural models is discussed. The methodology introduced by the authors reports acceptable results when solving linear and non-linear pattern recognition problems. Additionally, the results obtained after the training process carried out by means of the CS improve those reported by a Differential Evolution Algorithm.

The paper by (Chifu et al., 2012) addresses the Web Service Composition Problem, whose objective is to select the optimal combination of semantic services based on criteria such as the quality of service and semantic quality of the services in the composition. The authors present a cuckoo-inspired approach aimed at identifying the optimal or a near-optimal composition encoded in an enhanced planning graph. With the aim of improving the performance of the optimization technique, an 1-opt heuristic is defined to expand the search space and avoid stagnation in local optima solutions.

The paper by (Kaveh and Bakhshpoori, 2013) focuses on the structure design. In particular, the authors propose a CS aimed at determining the optimum design of two-dimensional steel frames for discrete variables and by minimizing the structural weight. The optimization problem considers the material densities and the length and cross-sectional areas while strength constraints are imposed. The numerical experiments reveal the competitiveness of the CS in comparison with other algorithms due to the fact that it reports the best designs.

The CS has been successfully applied to solve a wide range of structural engineering optimization problems over the last few years. Some examples are described by (Gandomi et al., 2013). The paper addresses multiple standard structural engineering test problems by applying this meta-heuristic. Particularly, these optimization problems are briefly introduced in the following:

- Designing a pin-jointed plane frame with a fixed base for minimum weight.
- Minimizing the vertical deflection of a beam with an I-shaped cross-section by satisfying the cross-sectional area and stress constraints under given loads.
- Determining the components of a piston by minimizing the oil volume when its lever is lifted up from 0 o to 45 o when the payload, lever, maximum bending moment of the lever, and oil pressure are given.
- Determining the minimum weights in the design of the corrugated bulk heads for a tanker when the width, depth, length, and plate thickness are known.
- Computing the best weights for a cantilever beam with square cross section. In this case, the design variables are the heights of the beam elements and the thickness.
- Designing a uniform column of tubular section to carry a given compressive load at minimum cost. The yield stress, modulus of elasticity, and density are here given in advance.
- Evaluating the optimal cross sectional areas by minimizing the volume of a statically loaded 3-bar truss subject to stress constraints on each of the truss members.
- Minimizing the cost of the gear ratio of a gear train by considering the number of teeth of each gearwheel.
- Minimizing the total weight of a speed reducer where the bending stress of the gear teeth, surface stress, transverse deflections of shafts due to transmitted force, and stresses in shafts are imposed.
- Determining the total cost of a reinforced concrete beam in such a way that the area of reinforcement, the width of the beam, and the depth of the beam have to be calculated.
- Computing the optimal solution for an estimation of structural parameter subject to measured strains and analytical strains.
- Minimizing the total cost of a compressed air tank by considering thickness, thickness of the head, the inner radius, and the length of the cylindrical section of the vessel.
- Designing a car side impact by minimizing the weight using nine parameters: thicknesses of B-Pillar inner, B-Pillar reinforcement, floor side inner, cross members, door beam, door beltline reinforcement and roof rail, materials of B-Pillar inner and floor side inner and barrier height, and hitting position.

(Yildiz, 2013) develops a CS to optimize cutting parameters in milling operations. The objective is to maximize the total profit rate according to the unit production time and the unit production cost. The latter is given by the sum of the material cost, setup cost, machining cost, and tool changing cost. However, the optimization problem is subject to maximum machine power, surface finish requirement, and maximum cutting force permitted by the rigidity of the tool. The computational experiments indicate that the performance of the proposal overcomes those of alternative optimization techniques from the scientific literature. At the same time, the high robustness of the proposal is demonstrated.

A Multi-population CS is proposed by (Hlunga-Mbuyamba et al., 2016) as an alternative approach to the traditional Active Contour Model to solve the contour energy minimization problem for image segmentation. The proposed technique seeks to identify targeted object edges by means of a two non-sequential stages algorithm. In this case, the control points belonging to a given contour are handled by local search spaces in the first stage. Afterwards, the control points are randomly placed inside each search window with the aim of obtaining new ones. The Rectangular Shaped Search Windows and Pizza-slice Shaped Search Windows are considered as search window geometries. The optimization technique is validated on real medical and synthetic images and by using different performance metrics. In particular, the optimization technique has been successfully used to analyze several human brain tumour tomographies. As the authors indicate, the proposed approach is computationally more expensive than the traditional technique but it requires a fewer number of iterations.

The CS has been successfully applied in the field of high-power electronics. For instance, a CS is presented by (Abd-Elazim and Ali, 2016) to find the optimal design of static synchronous compensator in a multi-machine environment. Despite the authors consider a standard CS, this optimization technique overcomes several drawbacks associated with previous proposals found in the scientific literature. As discussed in the paper, these are the long computational times required when tackling realistic systems, stagnation of the search, slow convergence, high randomness, or a poor balance between exploration and intensification, among others. The simulation experiments carried out in the paper indicate that the proposed optimization technique manifests a robust performance when reducing oscillations and improving voltage profiles. Some interesting applications can be found in the context of hybrid energy system design problems. This is the case of (Sanajaoba and Fernandez, 2016), where a CS is aimed at determining the optimal sizing of three different system schemes. The optimization objective of the problem to solve is to minimize the total system cost while considering seasonal variation of the load. The system reliability is checked by using the loss of load expected and the expected energy not supplied. The performance of the optimization technique proposed in the paper is tested in a real hybrid energy system design problem. In this regard, the computational results indicate that its overcomes alternative techniques in terms of quality of the solutions reported and fast convergence.

The production of electricity by means of thermal units and heat supplying to a load demand at minimum cost is studied by (Nguyen et al., 2016). In this case, the optimization problem seeks to identify heat and power generation for a given set of power, heat, and cogeneration units. The optimization objective is to minimize the total fuel cost for heat and power generations while considering heat and power demands and capacity associated with each available unit. The CS proposed in the paper uses a slack technique for handling equality constraints. The performance of the CS is tested on five systems with quadratic fuel cost function and non-convex fuel cost function. The computational results reveal the CS obtains solutions with higher quality than other reference techniques by using shorter computational times.

The makespan of a multi-stage hybrid flow shop scheduling problem is minimized by (Marichelvam et al., 2014). The authors propose an Improved CS to solve this optimization problem. In this case, the

CS is combined with a constructive heuristic algorithm which reports high-quality solutions very fast. These solutions are used as initial solutions for the CS. With the aimed of assessing the computational performance of the proposed CS, a real-world application of the optimization problem in the context of a furniture manufacturing company is used. Also, a wide range of benchmark instances is used to compare the CS against other optimization techniques. The results indicate in this case that the CS outperforms several of these approaches.

In the same vein as the previous paper, (Hanoun et al., 2014) present an efficient hybridization of a CS and a Variable Neighbourhood Descent Algorithm to solve two discrete sequencing and scheduling problems. The former seeks to minimize the weighted total tardiness time of jobs to be processed on a continually available single machine. For its part, the second one is a multi-objective optimization problem where the minimization of the tardiness and completion time of jobs in a single machine are considered as objectives. The hybrid proposal requires to modify the Lévy flight by introducing a new discrete operator aimed at handling the discrete nature of the optimization problems to solve. However, in spite of the fact that the technique proposed in the paper is able to report high-quality solutions for both problems, as pointed out by the authors, it requires long computational times. This fact could be a serious limitation for its application in real-time applications.

The Capacitated Vehicle Routing Problem is solved by means of an advanced version of the CS by (Teymourian et al., 2016). This solving approach introduces some interesting features that can be also applied when tackling other optimization problems in further research. For instance, the technique considers the fragmentation of the population of cuckoos. That is, it introduces a percentage of cuckoos with the ability to apply local search to control the balance between intensification and diversification over the exploration. In addition, the proposed technique introduces a dynamic parameter setting that allows to adjust the values of the parameters according to the number of generations of the search. It is worth mentioning that the technique is hybridized with other meta-heuristics to develop sophisticated algorithms that are high competitive in comparison with previous solution methods found in the literature.

A new variant of discrete CS is developed by (Majumder and Laha, 2016) with the goal of determining the sequence of robot moves and the sequence of parts in a two-machine robotic cell scheduling of one-unit cycle with sequence-dependent setup times as well as different loading and unloading times. The optimization objective is to minimize the total cycle time. In this case and unlike the standard CS, the step lengths of the Lévy flights distribution are proportional to the number of random or cyclical shift neighborhood operations. These neighborhood structures are also used to exploit some promising solutions found over the execution. The performance of the optimization technique is tested on large problem instances by considering different operating conditions and against two previous approaches already proposed in the literature. The numerical experiments reveal that the CS reports solutions with higher quality than those obtained by the reference approaches.

The field of data analysis has drawn a lot of attention over the last years. In this regard, an improved CS is proposed by (Jia et al., 2016) to optimize the centroids of the well-known Kernel Fuzzy C-Means model. In this case, the individuals considered in the CS are represented by means of quaternions. Also, the authors introduce a variable step length of Lévy flights and a variable discovery probability based on the evolution ratio of the execution. This way, the step size increases as the solutions generated are far from the minimum found in the search space, whereas this size decreases when the solutions are close to the minimum solution.

The optimal design of shell and tube heat exchange is the application field of (Khosravi et al., 2014). The goal is to obtain a suitable trade-off between thermodynamic and economic criteria. In practice, this gives rise to non-linear, discontinues, multi-modal and non-differentiable objective functions, and therefore evolutionary meta-heuristics are promising techniques to solve it. In order to solve this optimization problem, the authors present a CS whose performance overcomes that reported by a Genetic Algorithm in realistic scenarios, providing high-quality solutions by means of a reduced number of iterations. However, one of the advantages highlighted of the optimization technique is the few number of parameters to configure.

Finally, determining the placement of virtual machines in such a way that the number of physical machines is minimized in the context of data center management. In addition, a multi-objective variant of this problem is considered. Particularly, it seeks to simultaneously optimize the power consumption and resource wastage of a given data center. Several CS are proposed to solve both problems and the computational experiments demonstrate that they outperform previous algorithmic proposals for these problems.

5. CONCLUSION

The Cuckoo Search, CS, is a nature-inspired population-based meta-heuristic that has been recently proposed in the scientific literature by Xin-She Yang and Suash Deb. This optimization technique presents a relationship between the lifestyle, egg laying, and breeding strategy of some species of cuckoos in nature and the field of optimization.

The ongoing popularity of the CS has increased considerably since its introduction due to the fact that it overcomes some of the main shortcomings derived from the use of alternative nature-inspired algorithms. Specifically, considering the Lévy flight allows to achieve a suitable balance between intensification and diversification during the search process. However, in its seminal form, there is no information exchange between the cuckoos within the search space. This could have a negative impact of the overall performance in some cases. Also, the reduced number of internal running parameters encourages to develop effective self-tuning strategies which mitigate the problems derived from the individual sensitiveness of the algorithm-dependent parameters. In addition, this fact allows the CS to be highly versatile to adapt itself to a given optimization problem. Furthermore, as indicated along the present chapter, the complexity derived from implementing the technique is lower than in the case of other solving approaches.

In spite of the fact that it is too early to make a definitive statement on the relative performance of the CS in comparison with other proposals from the scientific literature, there are multiple highlighted studies in which its superiority has been empirically demonstrated in practice. For instance, some analyses have indicated that it outperforms well-known nature-inspired algorithms such as the Particle Swarm Optimization. In this regard, it is able to report a high performance in terms of solution quality and computational time when addressing a wide range of heterogeneous optimization problems associated with diverse knowledge areas. In this regard and as discussed in the chapter at hand, this optimization technique has become an essential reference for the multiple practical contexts and, at the same time, it has opened up a new research direction in which further improvements to the general behavior have appeared.

REFERENCES

Abd-Elazim, S., & Ali, E. (2016). Optimal location of STATCOM in multimachine power system for increasing loadability by cuckoo search algorithm. *International Journal of Electrical Power & Energy Systems*, *80*, 240–251. doi:10.1016/j.ijepes.2016.01.023

Bacanin, N. (2012). Implementation and performance of an object-oriented software system for cuckoo search algorithm. *International Journal of Mathematics and Computers in Simulation*, *6*(1), 185–193.

Chifu, V. R., Pop, C. B., Salomie, I., Suia, D. S., & Niculici, A. N. (2012). Optimizing the Semantic Web Service Composition Process Using Cuckoo Search. Springer Berlin Heidelberg.

Dorigo, M., Maniezzo, V., & Colorni, A. (1996). Ant system: optimization by a colony of cooperating agents. Systems, Man, and Cybernetics, Part B: Cybernetics. *IEEE Transactions on*, *26*(1), 29–41.

Fister, I., Yang, X.-S., & Fister, D. (2014). *Cuckoo Search: A Brief Literature Review*. Cham: Springer International Publishing. doi:10.1007/978-3-319-02141-6_3

Gandomi, A. H., Yang, X.-S., & Alavi, A. H. (2013). Cuckoo search algorithm: A metaheuristic approach to solve structural optimization problems. *Engineering with Computers*, *29*(1), 17–35. doi:10.1007/s00366-011-0241-y

Gherboudj, A., Layeb, A., & Chikhi, S. (2012). Solving 01 knapsack problems by a discrete binary version of cuckoo search algorithm. *International Journal of Bio-inspired Computation*, *4*(4), 229–236. doi:10.1504/IJBIC.2012.048063

Hanoun, S., Creighton, D., & Nahavandi, S. (2014). A hybrid cuckoo search and variable neighborhood descent for single and multi-objective scheduling problems. *International Journal of Advanced Manufacturing Technology*, *75*(9), 1501–1516. doi:10.1007/s00170-014-6262-0

Holland, J. H. (1975). *Adaptation in natural and artificial systems: an introductory analysis with applications to biology, control, and artificial intelligence*. University of Michigan Press.

Ilunga-Mbuyamba, E., Cruz-Duarte, J. M., Avina-Cervantes, J. G., Correa-Cely, C. R., Lindner, D., & Chalopin, C. (2016). Active contours driven by cuckoo search strategy for brain tumour images segmentation. *Expert Systems with Applications*, *56*, 59–68. doi:10.1016/j.eswa.2016.02.048

Jia, B., Yu, B., Wu, Q., Yang, X., Wei, C., Law, R., & Fu, S. (2016). Hybrid local diffusion maps and improved cuckoo search algorithm for multiclass dataset analysis. *Neurocomputing*, *189*, 106–116. doi:10.1016/j.neucom.2015.12.066

Jovanovic, R., Tuba, M., & Brajevic, I. (2013). Parallelization of the cuckoo search using cuda architecture. *Proceedings of the 7th International Conference on Applied Mathematics, Simulation, Modelling*.

Karaboga, D. (2005). *An idea based on honey bee swarm for numerical optimization*. Technical report, Technical report-tr06, Erciyes University, Engineering Faculty, Computer Engineering Department.

Kaveh, A., & Bakhshpoori, T. (2013). Optimum design of steel frames using cuckoo search algorithm with Lévy flights. *Structural Design of Tall and Special Buildings*, *22*(13), 1023–1036. doi:10.1002/tal.754

Kennedy, J., & Eberhart, R. (1995). Particle swarm optimization. *Neural Networks, 1995. Proceedings., IEEE International Conference on, 4*, 1942–1948. doi:10.1109/ICNN.1995.488968

Khosravi, R., Khosravi, A., & Nahavandi, S. (2014). *Application of Cuckoo Search for Design Optimization of Heat Exchangers*. Cham: Springer International Publishing. doi:10.1007/978-3-319-12640-1_22

Koziel, S., & Yang, X.-S. (2011). *Computational optimization, methods and algorithms* (Vol. 356). Springer. doi:10.1007/978-3-642-20859-1

Layeb, A. (2011). A novel quantum inspired cuckoo search for knapsack problems. *International Journal of Bio-inspired Computation, 3*(5), 297–305. doi:10.1504/IJBIC.2011.042260

Layeb, A., & Boussalia, S. R. (2012). A novel quantum inspired cuckoo search algorithm for bin packing problem. *International Journal of Information Technology and Computer Science, 4*(5), 58–67. doi:10.5815/ijitcs.2012.05.08

Li, X., & Yin, M. (2015). Modified cuckoo search algorithm with self adaptive parameter method. *Information Sciences, 298*, 80–97. doi:10.1016/j.ins.2014.11.042

Majumder, A., & Laha, D. (2016). A new cuckoo search algorithm for 2-machine robotic cell scheduling problem with sequence-dependent setup times. *Swarm and Evolutionary Computation, 28*, 131–143. doi:10.1016/j.swevo.2016.02.001

Marichelvam, M., Prabaharan, T., & Yang, X. (2014). Improved cuckoo search algorithm for hybrid flow shop scheduling problems to minimize makespan. *Applied Soft Computing, 19*, 93–101. doi:10.1016/j.asoc.2014.02.005

Nawi, N. M., Khan, A., Rehman, M. Z., Herawan, T., & Deris, M. M. (2014). *Comparing Performances of Cuckoo Search Based Neural Networks*. Cham: Springer International Publishing. doi:10.1007/978-3-319-07692-8_16

Nguyen, T. T., Vo, D. N., & Dinh, B. H. (2016). Cuckoo search algorithm for combined heat and power economic dispatch. *International Journal of Electrical Power & Energy Systems, 81*, 204–214. doi:10.1016/j.ijepes.2016.02.026

Pereira, L., Rodrigues, D., Almeida, T., Ramos, C., Souza, A., Yang, X., & Papa, J. (2014). *A Binary Cuckoo Search and Its Application for Feature Selection*. Cham: Springer International Publishing. doi:10.1007/978-3-319-02141-6_7

Sanajaoba, S. & Fernandez, E. (2016). Maiden application of cuckoo search algorithm for optimal sizing of a remote hybrid renewable energy system. *Renewable Energy, 96*(A), 1 –10.

Teymourian, E., Kayvanfar, V., Komaki, G., & Zandieh, M. (2016). Enhanced intelligent water drops and cuckoo search algorithms for solving the capacitated vehicle routing problem. *Information Sciences, 334–335*, 354–378. doi:10.1016/j.ins.2015.11.036

Vazquez, R. A. (2011). Training spiking neural models using cuckoo search algorithm. *2011 IEEE Congress of Evolutionary Computation (CEC)*, 679–686. doi:10.1109/CEC.2011.5949684

Walton, S., Hassan, O., Morgan, K., & Brown, M. (2011). Modified cuckoo search: A new gradient free optimisation algorithm. *Chaos, Solitons, and Fractals, 44*(9), 710–718. doi:10.1016/j.chaos.2011.06.004

Yang, X.-S., & Deb, S. (2009). Cuckoo search via Lévy flights. In *Nature & Biologically Inspired Computing, 2009. NaBIC 2009. World Congress on*, (pp. 210–214). IEEE.

Yang, X.-S., & Deb, S. (2010). Engineering optimisation by cuckoo search. *International Journal of Mathematical Modelling and Numerical Optimisation, 1*(4), 330–343. doi:10.1504/IJMMNO.2010.035430

Yang, X.-S., & Deb, S. (2013). Multiobjective cuckoo search for design optimization. *Computers & Operations Research, 40*(6), 1616–1624. doi:10.1016/j.cor.2011.09.026

Yang, X.-S., & Deb, S. (2014). Cuckoo search: Recent advances and applications. *Neural Computing & Applications, 24*(1), 169–174. doi:10.1007/s00521-013-1367-1

Yildiz, A. R. (2013). Cuckoo search algorithm for the selection of optimal machining parameters in milling operations. *International Journal of Advanced Manufacturing Technology, 64*(1–4), 55–61. doi:10.1007/s00170-012-4013-7

Zheng, H., & Zhou, Y. (2012). A novel cuckoo search optimization algorithm based on gauss distribution. *Journal of Computer Information Systems, 8*(10), 4193–4200.

Zhou, X., Liu, Y., Li, B., & Li, H. (2016). A multiobjective discrete cuckoo search algorithm for community detection in dynamic networks. *Soft Computing*, 1–12.

Compilation of References

Abd-Elazim, S., & Ali, E. (2016). Optimal location of STATCOM in multimachine power system for increasing loadability by cuckoo search algorithm. *International Journal of Electrical Power & Energy Systems*, *80*, 240–251. doi:10.1016/j.ijepes.2016.01.023

Adly, A., & Abd-El-Hafiz, S. (2006). Using the particle swarm evolutionary approach in shape optimization and field analysis of devices involving nonlinear magnetic media. *IEEE Transactions on Magnetics*, *42*(10), 3150–3152. doi:10.1109/TMAG.2006.880103

Akay, B., & Karaboga, D. (2012). Artificial bee colony algorithm for large-scale problems and engineering design optimization. *Journal of Intelligent Manufacturing*, *23*(4), 1001–1014. doi:10.1007/s10845-010-0393-4

Akdagli, A., & Toktas, A. (2010). A novel expression in calculating resonant fre- quency of h shaped compact microstrip antennas obtained by using artificial bee colony algorithm. *Journal of Electromagnetic Waves and Applications*, *24*(14-15), 2049–2061.

Alpaydin, E. (2004). *Introduction to Machine Learning*. London: MIT Press.

Asgarpoor, S. (1994). Comparison of linear, nonlinear, and network flow programming techniques in fuel scheduling. *Electric Power Systems Research*, *30*(3), 169–174. doi:10.1016/0378-7796(94)00851-5

Awadallah, M. A., Bolaji, A. L., & Al-Betar, M. A. (2015). A hybrid artificial bee colony for a nurse rostering problem. *Applied Soft Computing*, *35*, 726–739. doi:10.1016/j.asoc.2015.07.004

Bacanin, N. (2012). Implementation and performance of an object-oriented software system for cuckoo search algorithm. *International Journal of Mathematics and Computers in Simulation*, *6*(1), 185–193.

Bahl, I., & Bhartia, P. (1980). *Microstrip Antennas*. Dedham, MA: Arthec House.

Balamurugan, R., & Subramanian, S. (2007). An improved differential evolution based dynamic economic dispatch with nonsmooth fuel cost function. *Journal of Electrical Systems*, *3*(3), 151–161.

Banharnsakun, A., Sirinaovakul, B., & Achalakul, T. (2012). Job shop scheduling with the best-so-far ABC. *Engineering Applications of Artificial Intelligence*, *25*(3), 583–593. doi:10.1016/j.engappai.2011.08.003

Bao, L. Z. J. (2009). Comparison and analysis of the selection mechanism in the artificial bee colony algorithm. *International Conference Hybrid Intelligence System*. doi:10.1109/HIS.2009.319

Basu, M. (2002). Fuel constrained economic emission load dispatch using Hopfield neural networks. *Electric Power Systems Research*, *63*(1), 51–57. doi:10.1016/S0378-7796(02)00090-1

Beigi, H. (2011). *Fundamentals of Speaker Recognition*. New York: Springer. doi:10.1007/978-0-387-77592-0

Beigi, H. (2012). Speaker Recognition: Advancement and Challenges. In J. Yang (Ed.), *New Trends and Developments in Biometrics* (pp. 3–29). InTech. doi:10.5772/52023

Beloufa, F., & Chikh, M. (2013). Design of fuzzy classifier for diabetes disease using modified artificial bee colony algorithm. *Computer Methods and Programs in Biomedicine, 112*(1), 92–103. doi:10.1016/j.cmpb.2013.07.009 PMID:23932385

Bharti, R., & Bansal, P. (2015). Real Time Speaker Recognition System using MFCC and Vector Quantization Technique. *International Journal of Computers and Applications, 117*(1), 25–31. doi:10.5120/20520-2361

Boeringer, D., & Werner, D. (2005). *Effciency-constrained particle swarm optimization of a modified bernstein polynomial for conformal array excitation amplitude synthesis* (Vol. 53). IEEE Transactions on Antennas and Propagation.

Bouarara, H. A., Hamou, R. M., & Amine, A. (2015). A Novel Bio-Inspired Approach for Multilingual Spam Filtering. *International Journal of Intelligent Information Technologies, 11*(3), 45–87. doi:10.4018/IJIIT.2015070104

Bouarara, H. A., Hamou, R. M., & Amine, A. (2015). Novel Bio-Inspired Technique of Artificial Social Cockroaches (ASC). *International Journal of Organizational and Collective Intelligence, 5*(2), 47–79. doi:10.4018/IJOCI.2015040103

Bouarara, H. A., Hamou, R. M., Rahmani, A., & Amine, A. (2015). Boosting Algorithm and Meta-Heuristic Based on Genetic Algorithms for Textual Plagiarism Detection. *International Journal of Cognitive Informatics and Natural Intelligence, 9*(4), 65–87. doi:10.4018/IJCINI.2015100105

Brajevic, I., Tuba, M., & Subotic, M. (2010). Improved artificial bee colony al- gorithm for constrained problems. *Proceedings of the 11th WSEAS Interna- tional Conference on Nural Networks and 11th WSEAS International Confer- ence on Evolutionary Computing and 11th WSEAS International Conference on Fuzzy Systems,* 185–190.

Cai, J., Ma, X., Li, Q., Li, L., & Peng, H. (2009). A multi-objective chaotic particle swarm optimization for environmental/economic dispatch. *Energy Conversion and Management, 50*(5), 1318–1325. doi:10.1016/j.enconman.2009.01.013

Cai, J., Ma, X., Li, Q., Li, L., & Peng, H. (2010). A multi-objective chaotic ant swarm optimization for environmental/economic dispatch. *International Journal of Electrical Power & Energy Systems, 32*(5), 337–344. doi:10.1016/j.ijepes.2010.01.006

Caorsi, S., Donelli, M., Lommi, A., & Massa, A. (2004). Location and imaging of two-dimensional scatterers by using a Particle Swarm algorithm. *Journal of Electromagnetic Waves and Applications, 18*(4), 481–494. doi:10.1163/156939304774113089

Chawla, M., & Duhan, M. (2014). Applications of recent metaheuristics optimization algorithms in biomedical engineering: A review. *International Journal of Biomedical Engineering and Technology, 16*(3), 268–278. doi:10.1504/IJBET.2014.065807

Clerc, M., & Kennedy, J. (2002). The particle swarm—explosion, stability, and convergence in a multidimensional complex space. *IEEE Transactions on Evolutionary Computation, 6*(1), 58–73. doi:10.1109/4235.985692

Cortes, C., & Vapnik, V. (1995, September). Support-vector networks. *Machine Learning, 20*(3), 273–297. doi:10.1007/BF00994018

Cramer, N. L. (1985, July). A representation for the adaptive generation of simple sequential programs. *Proceedings of the First International Conference on Genetic Algorithms,* 183-187.

Cui, S., & Weile, D. (2006). Application of a parallel particle swarm optimization scheme to the design of electromagnetic absorbers. *IEEE Transactions on Antennas and Propagation, 54*(3), 1107–1110.

Dahiya, S. S., Chhabra, J. K., & Kumar, S. (2010). Application of artificial bee colony algorithm to software testing. In *Proceedings of the 2010 21st Australian Software Engineering Conference*, (pp. 149–154). IEEE Computer Society. doi:10.1109/ASWEC.2010.30

Darwin, C. (1859). *On the origin ofspecies by means of natural selection, or the preservation of favoured races in the struggle for life*. New York, NY: D. Appleton and Company.

Dehak, N., Dehak, R., Reynolds, D. A., & Torres-Carrasquillo, P. A. (2011). *Language Recognition Via I-Vectors And Dimensionality Reduction*. INTERSPEECH.

Dereli, T., & Das, G. S. (2011). A hybrid bee(s) algorithm for solving container loading problems. *Applied Soft Computing*, *11*(2), 2854–2862. doi:10.1016/j.asoc.2010.11.017

Develi, I., Kabalci, Y., & Basturk, A. (2015). Artificial bee colony optimization for modelling of indoor PLC channels: A case study from turkey. *Electric Power Systems Research*, *127*, 73–79. doi:10.1016/j.epsr.2015.05.021

Dhillon, J., Parti, S. C., & Kothari, D. P. (1993). Stochastic economic emission load dispatch. *Electric Power Systems Research*, *26*(3), 179–186. doi:10.1016/0378-7796(93)90011-3

Diwold, K., Aderhold, A., Scheidler, A., & Middendorf, M. (2011). Performance evaluation of artificial bee colony optimization and new selection schemes. *Memetic Computing*, *3*(3), 149–162. doi:10.1007/s12293-011-0065-8

Donelli, M., Azaro, R., Massa, A., & Raffetto, M. (2006). Unsupervised synthesis of microwave components by means of an evolutionary-based tool exploiting distributed computing resources. *Progress in Electromagnetics Research*, *56*, 93–108. doi:10.2528/PIER05010901

Donelli, M., Caorsi, S., De Natale, F., Franceschini, D., & Massa, A. (2004). A versatile enhanced genetic algorithm for planar array design. *Journal of Electromagnetic Waves and Applications*, *18*(11), 1533–1548. doi:10.1163/1569393042954893

Donelli, M., Craddock, I., Gibbins, D., & Sarafianou, M. (2011). A three-dimensional time domain microwave imaging method for breast cancer detection based on an evolutionary algorithm. *Progress in Electromagnetic Research M*, *18*, 179–195. doi:10.2528/PIERM11040903

Donelli, M., Massa, A., Oliveri, G., Pastorino, M., & Randazzo, A. (2010). A differential evolution based multi-scaling algorithm for microwave imaging of dielectric structures. *Proceedings of IEEE International Conferences on Imaging Systems and Techniques, IST*, *2010*, 90–95.

Donelli, M., & Massa, A. (2005). Computational approach based on a particle swarm optimizer for microwave imaging of two-dimensional dielectric scatterers. *IEEE Transactions on Microwave Theory and Techniques*, *53*(5), 1761–1776. doi:10.1109/TMTT.2005.847068

Donelli, M. (2013, February). Design of broadband metal nanosphere antenna arrays with a hybrid evolutionary algorithm. *Optics Letters*, *38*(4), 401–403. doi:10.1364/OL.38.000401 PMID:23455082

Dorigo, M., & Gambardella, L. M. (1997). Ant colonies for the travelling salesman problem. *Bio Systems*, *43*(2), 73–81. doi:10.1016/S0303-2647(97)01708-5 PMID:9231906

Dorigo, M., Maniezzo, V., & Colorni, A. (1996). Ant system: optimization by a colony of cooperating agents. Systems, Man, and Cybernetics, Part B: Cybernetics. *IEEE Transactions on*, *26*(1), 29–41.

Draa, A., & Bouaziz, A. (2014). An artificial bee colony algorithm for image contrast enhancement. *Swarm and Evolutionary Computation*, *16*, 69–84. doi:10.1016/j.swevo.2014.01.003

Dubois, D., & Prade, H. (1979). Operations in a Fuzzy-Valued Logic. *Information and Control*, *43*(2), 224–240. doi:10.1016/S0019-9958(79)90730-7

El-Keib, A. A., Ma, H., & Hart, J. L. (1994). Economic dispatch in view of the clean air act of 1990. *IEEE Transactions on Power Systems*, *9*(2), 972–978. doi:10.1109/59.317648

Eslami, M., Shareef, H., & Khajehzadeh, M. (2013). Optimal design of damping controllers using a new hybrid artificial bee colony algorithm. *International Journal of Electrical Power & Energy Systems*, *52*, 42–54. doi:10.1016/j.ijepes.2013.03.012

Farahani, R. Z., Hassani, A., Mousavi, S. M., & Baygi, M. B. (2014). A hybrid artificial bee colony for disruption in a hierarchical maximal covering location problem. *Computers & Industrial Engineering*, *75*, 129–141. doi:10.1016/j.cie.2014.06.012

Fathy, A. (2015). Reliable and efficient approach for mitigating the shading effect onphotovoltaic module based on modified artificial bee colony algorithm. *Renewable Energy*, *81*, 78–88. doi:10.1016/j.renene.2015.03.017

Fleischer, M. (2003). *Foundations of swarm intelligence: From principles to practice*. Institute for Systems Research University of Maryland College Park.

Forestiere, C., Donelli, M., Walsh, G., Zeni, E., Miano, G., & Dal Negro, L. (2010). Particle-swarm optimization of broadband nanoplasmonic arrays. *Optics Letters*, *35*(2), 133–135. doi:10.1364/OL.35.000133 PMID:20081945

Gherboudj, A., Layeb, A., & Chikhi, S. (2012). Solving 01 knapsack problems by a discrete binary version of cuckoo search algorithm. *International Journal of Bio-inspired Computation*, *4*(4), 229–236. doi:10.1504/IJBIC.2012.048063

Goldberg, D. E. (1989). *Genetic Algorithms in Search, Optimization, and Machine Learning*. Boston, MA: Addison-Wesley.

Grassé, P. P. (1967). Nouvelles experiences sur le termite de Müller (Macrotermes mülleri) et considerations sur la théorie de la stigmergie. *Insectes Sociaux*, *14*(1), 73–101. doi:10.1007/BF02222755

Gregory, M. D., Petko, J. S., Spence, T. G., & Werner, D. H. (2010). Nature-Inspired Design Techniques for Ultra-Wideband Aperiodic Antenna Arrays. *IEEE Antennas and Propagation Magazine*, *52*(3), 28–45. doi:10.1109/MAP.2010.5586571

Haupt, R. (1995). Comparison between genetic and gradient-based optimization algorithms for solving electromagnetics problems. *IEEE Transactions on Magnetics*, *31*(3), 1932–1935. doi:10.1109/20.376418

He, S., Wu, Q. H., & Saunders, J. R. (2009). Group Search Optimizer: An Optimization Algorithm Inspired by Animal Searching Behavior. *IEEE Transactions on Evolutionary Computation*, *13*(5), 973–990. doi:10.1109/TEVC.2009.2011992

Hemamalini, S., & Simon, S. (2010). Artificial bee colony algorithm for economic load dispatch problem with non-smooth cost functions. *Electric Power Components and Systems*, *38*(7), 786–803. doi:10.1080/15325000903489710

Holland, H. (1975). *Adaptation in Natural and Artificial Systems*. Ann Arbor, MI: University of Michigan Press.

Holland, J. H. (1975). *Adaptation in natural and artificial systems*. Ann Arbor, MI: The University of Michigan Press.

Holland, J. H. (1975). *Adaptation in natural and artificial systems: an introductory analysis with applications to biology, control, and artificial intelligence*. University of Michigan Press.

Horng, M.-H. (2011). Multilevel thresholding selection based on the artificial bee colony algorithm for image segmentation. *Expert Systems with Applications*, *38*(11), 13785–13791.

Hsu, C.-C., Chen, H.-C., Huang, K.-K., & Huang, Y.-M. (2012). A personalized auxiliary material recommendation system based on learning style on face- book applying an artificial bee colony algorithm. *Computers & Mathematics with Applications (Oxford, England), 64*(5), 1506–1513. doi:10.1016/j.camwa.2012.03.098

Huang, S.-J., & Liu, X.-Z. (2013). Application of artificial bee colony-based optimization for fault section estimation in power systems. *International Journal of Electrical Power & Energy Systems, 44*(1), 210–218. doi:10.1016/j.ijepes.2012.07.012

Ibraheem, K., Kumar, P., & Kothari, D. P. (2005, February). Recent Philosophies of Automatic Generation Control Strategies in Power Systems. *IEEE Transactions on Power Systems, 20*(1), 346–357. doi:10.1109/TPWRS.2004.840438

Ilhan, R. E., Sathyanarayanan, G., Storer, R. H., & Liao, T. W. (1992). Off-line multi response optimization of electrochemical surface grinding by a multi-objective programming method. *International Journal of Machine Tools & Manufacture, 32*(3), 435–451. doi:10.1016/0890-6955(92)90013-7

Jabr, R. A., Coonick, A. H., & Cory, B. J. (2000). A homogeneous linear programming algorithm for the security constrained economic dispatch problem. *IEEE Transactions on Power Systems, 15*(3), 930–936. doi:10.1109/59.871715

James, J. R., & Hall, P. S. (1989). *Handbook of Microstrip Antennas* (Vols. 1-2). London, UK: Petergrinus.

Jeng, S., Lee, H., Tsao, Y., & Wang, H. (2014). Clustering-based i-vector formulation for speaker recognition.*Proceedings of INTERSPEECH*, 1101-1105.

Jia, B., Yu, B., Wu, Q., Yang, X., Wei, C., Law, R., & Fu, S. (2016). Hybrid local diffusion maps and improved cuckoo search algorithm for multiclass dataset analysis. *Neurocomputing, 189*, 106–116. doi:10.1016/j.neucom.2015.12.066

Jin, N., & Rahmat-Samii, Y. (2005). Parallel particle swarm optimization and finite-difference time-domain (PSO/FDTD) algorithm for multiband and wide-band patch antenna designs. *IEEE Transactions on Antennas and Propagation, 53*(11), 3459–3468. doi:10.1109/TAP.2005.858842

Johnson, J., & Rahmat-Samii, Y. (1997). Genetic algorithms in engineering electromagnetics. *IEEE Transactions on Antennas and Propagation, 39*(4), 7–21. doi:10.1109/74.632992

Kalayci, C. B., Hancilar, A., Gungor, A., & Gupta, S. M. (2015). Multi-objective fuzzy disassembly line balancing using a hybrid discrete artificial bee colony algorithm. *Journal of Manufacturing Systems, 37*(Part 3), 672–682. doi:10.1016/j.jmsy.2014.11.015

Kanagasundaram, A., Dean, D., Sridharan, S., McLaren, M., & Vogt, R. (2014). I-vector Based Speaker Recognition using Advanced Channel Compensation Techniques. *Speech Communication, 28*(1), 121–140.

Kanagasundaram, A., Vogt, R., Dean, D., Sridharan, S., & Mason, M. (2011). i-vector Based Speaker Recognition on Short Utterances.*Proceedings of the 12th Annual Conference of the International Speech Communication Association (ISCA)*, 2341-2344.

Kang, F. L. J., & Xu, Q. (2009). Hybrid simplex artificial bee colony algorithm and its application in material dynamic parameter back analysis of concrete dams. *Journal of Hydraulic Engineering*.

Karaboga, D., & Akay, B. (2007). *Artificial bee colony (abc) algorithm on training artificial neural networks. Signal Processing and Communications Applications, SIU 2007, IEEE 15th* (p. 14). IEEE.

Karaboga, D., & Akay, B. (2011a). A modified artificial bee colony (abc) algorithm for constrained optimization problems. *Applied Soft Computing, 11*(3), 3021–3031. doi:10.1016/j.asoc.2010.12.001

Karaboga, D., Okdem, S., & Ozturk, C. (2012). Cluster based wireless sensor network routing using artificial bee colony algorithm. *Wireless Networks*, *18*(7), 847–860. doi:10.1007/s11276-012-0438-z

Karaboga, N., & Latifoglu, F. (2013). Elimination of noise on transcranial doppler signal using iir filters designed with artificial bee colony abc- algorithm. *Digital Signal Processing*, *23*(3), 1051–1058. doi:10.1016/j.dsp.2012.09.015

Karaboga, N. (2009). A new design method based on artificial bee colony algorithm for digital IIR filters. *Journal of the Franklin Institute*, *346*(4), 328–348. doi:10.1016/j.jfranklin.2008.11.003

Kaveh, A., & Bakhshpoori, T. (2013). Optimum design of steel frames using cuckoo search algorithm with Lévy flights. *Structural Design of Tall and Special Buildings*, *22*(13), 1023–1036. doi:10.1002/tal.754

Kennedy, J., Eberhart, R. C., & Shi, Y. (2001). *Swarm Intelligence*. San Francisco: Morgan Kaufmann.

Khosravi, R., Khosravi, A., & Nahavandi, S. (2014). *Application of Cuckoo Search for Design Optimization of Heat Exchangers*. Cham: Springer International Publishing. doi:10.1007/978-3-319-12640-1_22

Kinnunen, T., & Li, H. (2010). An Overview of Text-independent Speaker Recognition: From Features to Super-vectors. *Speech Communication*, *52*(1), 12–40. doi:10.1016/j.specom.2009.08.009

Kua, J. M. K., Epps, J., & Ambikairajah, E. (2013). i-vector with Sparse Representation Classification for Speaker Verification. *Speech Communication*, *55*(5), 707–720. doi:10.1016/j.specom.2013.01.005

Kumar, A. B., Vemuri, S., Ebrahimzadeh, P., & Farahbakhshian, N. (1986). Fuel resource scheduling-The long-term problem. *IEEE Transactions on Power Systems*, *1*(4), 145–151. doi:10.1109/TPWRS.1986.4335030

Lansberry, J. E., Wozniak, L., & Goldberg, D. E. (1992). Optimal Hydro-generator Governor Tuning with a Genetic Algorithm. *IEEE Transactions on Energy Conversion*, *7*(4), 623–630. doi:10.1109/60.182643

Lasdon, L., Mitter, S., & Waren, A. (1967). The conjugate gradient method for optimal control problems. *IEEE Transactions on Automatic Control*, *12*(2), 132–138. doi:10.1109/TAC.1967.1098538

Layeb, A., & Boussalia, S. R. (2012). A novel quantum inspired cuckoo search algorithm for bin packing problem. *International Journal of Information Technology and Computer Science*, *4*(5), 58–67. doi:10.5815/ijitcs.2012.05.08

Lei, X. H. X., & Zhang, A. (2010). *Improved artificial bee colony algorithm and its application in data clustering. In Bio-Inspired Computing: Theories and Applications*. BIC-TA.

Li, J., Xie, S., Pan, Q., & Wang, S. (2011). A hybrid artificial bee colony algorithm for flexible job shop scheduling problems. *International Journal of Computers, Communications & Control*, *6*(2), 286–296. doi:10.15837/ijccc.2011.2.2177

Li, J.-Q., & Pan, Q.-K. (2015). Solving the large-scale hybrid flow shop scheduling problem with limited buffers by a hybrid artificial bee colony algorithm. *Information Sciences*, *316*, 487–502. doi:10.1016/j.ins.2014.10.009

Li, X., & Yin, M. (2015). Modified cuckoo search algorithm with self adaptive parameter method. *Information Sciences*, *298*, 80–97. doi:10.1016/j.ins.2014.11.042

Li, Y., Wang, Y., & Li, B. (2013). A hybrid artificial bee colony assisted differential evolution algorithm for optimal reactive power flow. *International Journal of Electrical Power & Energy Systems*, *52*, 25–33. doi:10.1016/j.ijepes.2013.03.016

Li, Z., Wang, W., Yan, Y., & Li, Z. (2015). Psabc: A hybrid algorithm based on particle swarm and artificial bee colony for high-dimensional optimization problems. *Expert Systems with Applications*, *42*(22), 8881–8895. doi:10.1016/j.eswa.2015.07.043

Lien, L.-C., & Cheng, M.-Y. (2012). A hybrid swarm intelligence based particle- bee algorithm for construction site layout optimization. *Expert Systems with Applications*, *39*(10), 9642–9650. doi:10.1016/j.eswa.2012.02.134

Lin, C. E., & Viviani, G. L. (1984). Hierarchical economic dispatch for piecewise quadratic cost functions. *IEEE Transactions on Power Apparatus and Systems*, *PAS-103*(6), 1170–1175. doi:10.1109/TPAS.1984.318445

Liu, S. M., & Chen, J.-H. (2015). A multi-label classification based approach for sentiment classification. *Expert Systems with Applications*, *42*(3), 1083–1093. doi:10.1016/j.eswa.2014.08.036

Liu, Y.-F., & Liu, S.-Y. (2013). A hybrid discrete artificial bee colony algorithm for permutation flowshop scheduling problem. *Applied Soft Computing*, *13*(3), 1459–1463. doi:10.1016/j.asoc.2011.10.024

Lu, Y., Zhou, J., Qin, H., Wang, Y., & Zhang, Y. (2011). Chaotic differential evolution methods for dynamic economic dispatch with valve-point effects. *Engineering Applications of Artificial Intelligence*, *24*(2), 378–387. doi:10.1016/j.engappai.2010.10.014

Luo, J., Wang, Q., & Xiao, X. (2013). A modified artificial bee colony algorithm based on converge-onlookers approach for global optimization. *Applied Mathematics and Computation*, *219*(20), 10253–10262. doi:10.1016/j.amc.2013.04.001

Lyubimov, V. V., Yerokhin, A. L., & Tchmir, M. Y. (1998). Mechanisms of synthetic diamond wear in tools for electro-chemical grinding. *Diamond and Related Materials*, *7*(9), 1267–1271. doi:10.1016/S0925-9635(98)00179-4

Ma, C., Li, Y., He, R., Duan, G., Sun, L., & Qi, B. (2012). New optimization model and fuzzy adaptive weighted genetic algorithm for hazardous material transportation. *International Journal of Computing Science and Mathematics*, *3*(4), 341–352. doi:10.1504/IJCSM.2012.051621

Majumder, A., & Laha, D. (2016). A new cuckoo search algorithm for 2-machine robotic cell scheduling problem with sequence-dependent setup times. *Swarm and Evolutionary Computation*, *28*, 131–143. doi:10.1016/j.swevo.2016.02.001

Maksoud, T. M. A., & Brooks, A. J. (1995). Electrochemical grinding of ceramic form tooling. *Journal of Materials Processing Technology*, *55*(2), 70–75. doi:10.1016/0924-0136(95)01787-9

Mandal, S. K., Chan, F. T., & Tiwari, M. (2012). Leak detection of pipeline: An integrated approach of rough set theory and artificial bee colony trained SVM. *Expert Systems with Applications*, *39*(3), 3071–3080. doi:10.1016/j.eswa.2011.08.170

Marichelvam, M., Prabaharan, T., & Yang, X. (2014). Improved cuckoo search algorithm for hybrid flow shop scheduling problems to minimize makespan. *Applied Soft Computing*, *19*, 93–101. doi:10.1016/j.asoc.2014.02.005

Massa, A., Donelli, M., De Natale, F., Caorsi, S., & Lommi, A. (2004, November). Planar antenna array control with genetic algorithms and adaptive array theory. *IEEE Transactions on Antennas and Propagation*, *52*(11), 2919–2924. doi:10.1109/TAP.2004.837523

Massa, A., Pastorino, M., & Randazzo, A. (2006). Optimization of the Directivity of a Monopulse Antenna With a Subarray Weighting by a Hybrid Differential Evolution Method. *IEEE Antennas and Wireless Propagation Letters*, *5*(1), 155–158. doi:10.1109/LAWP.2006.872435

McLaren, M., & Leeuwen, D. V. (2011). Source Normalized and Weighted LDA for Robust Speaker Recognition using i-vector. In *Proceedings of IEEE International Conference on Acoustics, Speech and Signal Processing (ICASSP)* (pp.5456-5459). Prague: IEEE.

Mehrabian, A. R., & Lucas, C. (2006). A novel numerical optimization algorithm inspired from weed colonization. *Ecological Informatics*, *1*(4), 355–366. doi:10.1016/j.ecoinf.2006.07.003

Mezura-Montes, E., & Cetina-Dominguez, O. (2012). Empirical analysis of a modified artificial bee colony for constrained numerical optimization. *Applied Mathematics and Computation, 218*(22), 10943–10973. doi:10.1016/j.amc.2012.04.057

Mikki, S., & Kishk, A. (2006). Quantum particle swarm optimization for electromagnetics. *IEEE Transactions on Antennas and Propagation, 54*(10), 2764–2775. doi:10.1109/TAP.2006.882165

Milani, A. E., & Mozafari, B. (2011, June). Genetic Algorithm based Optimal Load Frequency Control in Two-area Interconnected Power Systems. *Transactions on Power System Optimization, 2*, 6–10.

Mitchell, M. (1998). *An introduction to genetic algorithms.* MIT Press.

Mitchell, T. (1997). *Machine Learning.* Maidenhead, UK: McGraw Hill.

Mitter, S., Lasdon, L. S., & Waren, A. D. (1966). The method of conjugate gradients for optimal control problems. *Proceedings of the IEEE, 54*(6), 904–905. doi:10.1109/PROC.1966.4922

Mohammad, S. M., Zhu, X., Kiritchenko, S., & Martin, J. (2015). Sentiment, emotion, purpose, and style in electoral tweets. *Information Processing & Management, 51*(4), 480–499. doi:10.1016/j.ipm.2014.09.003

Muralidharan, S., Srikrishna, K., & Subramanian, S. (2006). Emission constrained economic dispatch—A new recursive approach. *Electric Power Components and Systems, 34*(3), 343–353. doi:10.1080/15325000500241225

Nawi, N. M., Khan, A., Rehman, M. Z., Herawan, T., & Deris, M. M. (2014). *Comparing Performances of Cuckoo Search Based Neural Networks.* Cham: Springer International Publishing. doi:10.1007/978-3-319-07692-8_16

Nguyen, T. T., Vo, D. N., & Dinh, B. H. (2016). Cuckoo search algorithm for combined heat and power economic dispatch. *International Journal of Electrical Power & Energy Systems, 81*, 204–214. doi:10.1016/j.ijepes.2016.02.026

Niimura, T., & Nakashima, T. (2003). Multiobjective tradeoff analysis of deregulated electricity transactions. *International Journal of Electrical Power & Energy Systems, 25*(3), 179–185. doi:10.1016/S0142-0615(02)00076-5

Nijhawan, G., & Soni, M. K. (2014). Speaker Recognition using MFCC and Vector Quantization. *International Journal on Recent Trends in Engineering and Technology, 11*(1), 211–218.

Nseef, S. K., Abdullah, S., Turky, A., & Kendall, G. (2016). An adaptive multi- population artificial bee colony algorithm for dynamic optimization problems. *Knowledge-Based Systems, 104*, 14–23. doi:10.1016/j.knosys.2016.04.005

Palanichamy, C., & Babu, N. S. (2008). Analytical solution for combined economic and emissions dispatch. *Electric Power Systems Research, 78*(7), 1129–1137. doi:10.1016/j.epsr.2007.09.005

Parikh, J., & Chattopadhyay, D. (1996). A multi-area linear programming approach for analysis of economic operation of the Indian power system. *IEEE Transactions on Power Systems, 11*(1), 52–58. doi:10.1109/59.485985

Park, J. H., Kim, Y. S., Eom, I. K., & Lee, K. Y. (1993). Economic load dispatch for piecewise quadratic cost function using Hopfield neural network. *IEEE Transactions on Power Systems, 8*(3), 1030–1038. doi:10.1109/59.260897

Pereira, L., Rodrigues, D., Almeida, T., Ramos, C., Souza, A., Yang, X., & Papa, J. (2014). *A Binary Cuckoo Search and Its Application for Feature Selection.* Cham: Springer International Publishing. doi:10.1007/978-3-319-02141-6_7

Poli, L., Rocca, P., Manica, L., & Massa, A. (2010, April). Handling sideband radiations in time-modulated arrays through particle swarm optimization. *IEEE Transactions on Antennas and Propagation, 58*(4), 1408–1411. doi:10.1109/TAP.2010.2041165

Pozar, D. M. (2012). *Microwave Engineering.* Wiley & Sons.

Pshenichny, B. N., & Danilin, Y. M. (1978). *Numerical Methods in extrema problems.* Moscow: MIR Publisher.

Qu, B. Y., Suganthan, P. N., Pandi, V. R., & Panigrahi, B. K. (2010, December). Multi objective evolutionary programming to solve environmental economic dispatch problem. In *11th International Conference on Control, Automation, Robotics and Vision, ICARCV 2010, Proceedings*. IEEE. doi:10.1109/ICARCV.2010.5707926

Rajan, P., Kinnunen, T., & Hautamaki, V. (2013). *Effect of Multicondition Training on i-vector PLDA Configurations for Speaker Recognition*. INTERSPEECH.

Rajsekhar, A. G. (2008). *Real Time Speaker Recognition using MFCC and VQ*. Rourkela, India: National Institute of Technology.

Rau, N. S., & Adelman, S. T. (1995). Operating strategies under emission constraints. *IEEE Transactions on Power Systems*, *10*(3), 1585–1591. doi:10.1109/59.466484

Rechenberg, I. (1989). *Evolution strategy: Nature's way of optimization. In Optimization: Methods and applications, possibilities and limitations* (pp. 106–126). Springer Berlin Heidelberg. doi:10.1007/978-3-642-83814-9_6

Reeves, C. (2003). *Genetic algorithms*. Springer, US. doi:10.1007/0-306-48056-5_3

Revathi, A., Ganapathy, R., & Venkataramani, Y. (2009). Text Independent Speaker Recognition and Speaker Independent Speech Recognition using Iterative Clustering Approach. *International Journal of Computer Science and Information Technology*, *1*(2), 31–42.

Reynolds, C. W. (1987, August). Flocks, herds and schools: A distributed behavioral model. *Computer Graphics*, *21*(4), 25–34. doi:10.1145/37402.37406

Reynolds, D. A., Quatieri, T. F., & Dunn, R. B. (2000). Speaker Verification Using Adapted Gaussian Mixture Models. *Digital Signal Processing*, *10*(1-3), 19–41. doi:10.1006/dspr.1999.0361

Reynolds, D. A., & Rose, R. C. (1995). Robust Text-Independent Speaker Identification using Gaussian Mixture Speaker Models. *IEEE Transactions on Speech and Audio Processing*, *3*(1), 72–83. doi:10.1109/89.365379

Reynolds, D. A. (1995). Speaker Identification and Verification using Gaussian Mixture Speaker Models. *Speech Communication*, *17*(1-2), 91–108. doi:10.1016/0167-6393(95)00009-D

Ringlee, R. (1965). Bounds for convex variational programming problems arising in power system scheduling and control. *IEEE Transactions on Automatic Control*, *10*(1), 28–35. doi:10.1109/TAC.1965.1098077

Rocca, P., Manica, L., & Massa, A. (2010, January). Ant colony based hybrid approach for optimal compromise sum difference patterns synthesis. *Microwave and Optical Technology Letters*, *52*(1), 128–132. doi:10.1002/mop.24882

Rocca, P., Oliveri, G., & Massa, A. (2011, February). Differential Evolution as applied to electromagnetics. *IEEE Antennas Propag. Mag.*, *53*(1), 38–49. doi:10.1109/MAP.2011.5773566

Roy, S. S., Mittal, D., Basu, A., & Abraham, A. (2015). Stock market forecasting using LASSO linear regression model. In *Afro-European Conference for Industrial Advancement* (pp. 371–381). Springer International Publishing. doi:10.1007/978-3-319-13572-4_31

Runkler, T. A. (2008). Wasp swarm optimization of the c-means clustering model. *International Journal of Intelligent Systems*, *23*(3), 269–285. doi:10.1002/int.20266

Sacchi, C., De Natale, F., Donelli, M., Lommi, A., & Massa, A. (2004, July). Adaptive antenna array control in presence of interfering signals with stochastic arrivals: Assessment of a GA-based procedure. *IEEE Transactions on Wireless Communications*, *3*(4), 1031–1036. doi:10.1109/TWC.2004.830845

Sadjadi, S. O., Slaney, M., & Heck, L. (2013). *MSR Identity Toolbox v1. 0: a MATLAB Toolbox for Speaker-Recognition Research*. Speech and Language Processing Technical Committee Newsletter.

Sakawa, M., Yano, H., & Yumine, T. (1987). An interactive fuzzy satisficing method for multiobjective linear-programming problems and its application. *IEEE Transactions on Systems, Man, and Cybernetics*, *17*(4), 654–661. doi:10.1109/TSMC.1987.289356

Samanta, B. (2009). Surface roughness prediction in machining using soft computing. *International Journal of Computer Integrated Manufacturing*, *22*(3), 257–266. doi:10.1080/09511920802287138

Samanta, S., & Chakraborty, S. (2011). Parametric optimization of some non- traditional machining processes using artificial bee colony algorithm. *Engineering Applications of Artificial Intelligence*, *24*(6), 946–957. doi:10.1016/j.engappai.2011.03.009

Sashirekha, A., Pasupuleti, J., Moin, N. H., & Tan, C. S. (2013). Combined heat and power (CHP) economic dispatch solved using Lagrangian relaxation with surrogate subgradient multiplier updates. *International Journal of Electrical Power & Energy Systems*, *44*(1), 421–430. doi:10.1016/j.ijepes.2012.07.038

Secui, D. C. (2015). A new modified artificial bee colony algorithm for the economic dispatch problem. *Energy Conversion and Management*, *89*, 43–62. doi:10.1016/j.enconman.2014.09.034

Senoussaoui, M., Kenny, P., Dehak, N., & Dumouchel, P. (2010). *An i-vector Extractor suitable for Speaker Recognition with both Microphone and Telephone Speech*. Odessey.

Shanthi, D., & Amalraj, R. (2012). Collaborative artificial bee colony optimization clustering using spnn. *Procedia Engineering*, *30*, 989–996. doi:10.1016/j.proeng.2012.01.955

Sharma, M., Sarma, M., & Sarma, K. K. (2013). Recurrent Neural Network Based Approach to Recognize Assamese Vowels using Experimentally Derived Acoustic Phonetic Features. In *Proceedings of IEEE 1st International Conference on Emerging Trends and Applications in Computer Science (ICETACS)* (pp.140-143). Shillong, India: IEEE. doi:10.1109/ICETACS.2013.6691411

Shie, J. R. (2006). Optimization of Dry Machining Parameters for High-Purity Graphite in End-Milling Process by Artificial Neural Networks: A Case Study. *Materials and Manufacturing Processes*, *21*(8), 838–845. doi:10.1080/03602550600728257

Singh, A., & Sundar, S. (2011). An artificial bee colony algorithm for the mini- mum routing cost spanning tree problem. *Soft Computing*, *15*(12), 2489–2499. doi:10.1007/s00500-011-0711-6

Sonmez, M. K., Heck, L., Weintraub, M., & Shriberg, E. (1997). A Lognormal Tied Mixture Model of Pitch for Prosody-Based Speaker Recognition. *Proceedings of Eurospeech*, *3*, 1391–1394.

Sonmez, M. (2011). Artificial bee colony algorithm for optimization of truss structures. *Applied Soft Computing*, *11*(2), 2406–2418. doi:10.1016/j.asoc.2010.09.003

Stanarevic, N. (2011). Comparison of different mutation strategies applied to artificial bee colony algorithm. *Proceedings of the 5th European Conference on European Computing Conference*, 257–262.

Storn, R., & Price, K. (1997). Differential Evolution – a simple and efficient heuristic for global optimization over continuous spaces. *Journal of Global Optimization*, *11*(4), 341–359. doi:10.1023/A:1008202821328

Szeto, W., & Jiang, Y. (2014). Transit route and frequency design: Bi-level modeling and hybrid artificial bee colony algorithm approach. *Transportation Research Part B: Methodological*, *67*, 235–263. doi:10.1016/j.trb.2014.05.008

Taherdangkoo, M., Yazdi, M., & Rezvani, M. H. (2010). Segmentation of Mr Brain images using fcm improved by artificial bee colony (abc) algorithm.*Proceedings of the 10th IEEE International Conference on Information Technology and Applications in Biomedicine*, 1–5. doi:10.1109/ITAB.2010.5687803

Teymourian, E., Kayvanfar, V., Komaki, G., & Zandieh, M. (2016). Enhanced intelligent water drops and cuckoo search algorithms for solving the capacitated vehicle routing problem. *Information Sciences*, *334–335*, 354–378. doi:10.1016/j.ins.2015.11.036

Tiwari, V. (2010). MFCC and its applications in Speaker Recognition. *International Journal of Emerging Technologies*, *1*(1), 19–22.

Toktas, A., Bicer, M. B., Akdagli, A., & Kayabasi, A. (2011). Simple formulas for calculating resonant frequencies of c and h shaped compact microstrip antennas obtained by using artificial bee colony algorithm. *Journal of Electromagnetic Waves and Applications*, *25*(11-12), 1718–1729. doi:10.1163/156939311797164855

Vazquez, R. A. (2011). Training spiking neural models using cuckoo search algorithm.*2011 IEEE Congress of Evolutionary Computation (CEC)*, 679–686. doi:10.1109/CEC.2011.5949684

Wallace, A. R. (1870). *Contributions to the theory of natural selection: A series of essays.* Macmillan and Company.

Wang, L., Zhong, Y., & Yin, Y. (2015). A hybrid cooperative cuckoo search algorithm with particle swarm optimization. *International Journal of Computing Science and Mathematics*, *6*(1), 18–29. doi:10.1504/IJCSM.2015.067537

Wang, X., Xie, X., & Cheng, T. (2013). A modified artificial bee colony algorithm for order acceptance in two-machine flow shops. *International Journal of Production Economics*, *141*(1), 14–23. doi:10.1016/j.ijpe.2012.06.003

Weile, D. S., & Michielssen, E. (1997, March). Genetic algorithm optimization applied to electromagnetics: A review. *IEEE Transactions on Antennas and Propagation*, *45*(3), 343–353. doi:10.1109/8.558650

Wood, A. J., & Wollenberg, B. F. (2012). *Power generation, operation, and control.* John Wiley & Sons.

Wu, B., Qian, C., Ni, W., & Fan, S. (2012). The improvement of glowworm swarm optimization for continuous optimization problems. *Expert Systems with Applications*, *39*(7), 6335–6342. doi:10.1016/j.eswa.2011.12.017

Wu, D., Ren, F., & Zhang, W. (2016). An energy optimal thrust allocation method for the marine dynamic positioning system based on adaptive hybrid artificial bee colony algorithm. *Ocean Engineering*, *118*, 216–226. doi:10.1016/j.oceaneng.2016.04.004

Wu, Z. (2001). Tomographic imaging of isolated ground surfaces using radio ground waves and conjugate gradient methods. *IEE Proceedings. Radar, Sonar and Navigation*, *148*(1), 27–34. doi:10.1049/ip-rsn:20010111

Xiang, W., Ma, S., & An, M. (2014). habcde: A hybrid evolutionary algorithm based on artificial bee colony algorithm and differential evolution. *Applied Mathematics and Computation*, *238*, 370–386. doi:10.1016/j.amc.2014.03.055

Xing, F. F. L., & Haijun, D. (2007). *The parameter improvement of bee colony algorithm in tsp problem.* Science Paper Online.

Xu, C., Duan, H., & Liu, F. (2010). Chaotic artificial bee colony approach to uninhabited combat air vehicle (ucav) path planning. *Aerospace Science and Technology*, *14*(8), 535–541. doi:10.1016/j.ast.2010.04.008

Xu, C., & Duan, H. (2010). Artificial bee colony (abc) optimized edge potential function (epf) approach to target recognition for low-altitude aircraft. *Pattern Recognition Letters*, *31*(13), 1759–1772. doi:10.1016/j.patrec.2009.11.018

Yan, X., Zhu, Y., Zou, W., & Wang, L. (2012). A new approach for data clustering using hybrid artificial bee colony algorithm. *Neurocomputing*, *97*, 241–250. doi:10.1016/j.neucom.2012.04.025

Yang, X. S., & Deb, S. (2010). Engineering optimization by cuckoo search. *International Journal of Mathematical Modelling and Numerical Optimization, 1*(4), 330–343. doi:10.1504/IJMMNO.2010.035430

Yang, X. S. (2010). *Nature Inspired Cooperative Strategies for Optimization.* New Metaheuristic Bat-Inspired Algorithm.

Yang, X.-S., & Deb, S. (2013). Multiobjective cuckoo search for design optimization. *Computers & Operations Research, 40*(6), 1616–1624. doi:10.1016/j.cor.2011.09.026

Yi, J., Di Huang, S. F., He, H., & Li, T. (2016). Multi-Objective Bacterial Foraging Optimization Algorithm Based on Parallel Cell Entropy for Aluminum Electrolysis Production Process. *IEEE Transactions on Industrial Electronics, 63*(4).

Yildiz, A. R. (2013). A new hybrid artificial bee colony algorithm for robust optimal design and manufacturing. *Applied Soft Computing, 13*(5), 2906–2912. doi:10.1016/j.asoc.2012.04.013

Yurtkuran, A., & Emel, E. (2015). An adaptive artificial bee colony algorithm for global optimization. *Applied Mathematics and Computation, 271*, 1004–1023. doi:10.1016/j.amc.2015.09.064

Zhang, C., Ouyang, D., & Ning, J. (2010). An artificial bee colony approach for clustering. *Expert Systems with Applications, 37*(7), 4761–4767. doi:10.1016/j.eswa.2009.11.003

Zhang, C., Zheng, J., & Zhou, Y. (2015). Two modified artificial bee colony algorithms inspired by grenade explosion method. *Neurocomputing, 151*(3), 1198–1207. doi:10.1016/j.neucom.2014.04.082

Zhang, R., Song, S., & Wu, C. (2013). A hybrid artificial bee colony algorithm for the job shop scheduling problem. *International Journal of Production Economics, 141*(1), 167–178. doi:10.1016/j.ijpe.2012.03.035

Zhang, S., Lee, C., Choy, K., Ho, W., & Ip, W. (2014). Design and development of a hybrid artificial bee colony algorithm for the environmental vehicle routing problem. *Transportation Research Part D, Transport and Environment, 31*, 85–99. doi:10.1016/j.trd.2014.05.015

Zhang, X., Zhang, X., Yuen, S. Y., Ho, S. L., & Fu, W. N. (2013). An Improved Artificial Bee Colony Algorithm for Optimal Design of Electromagnetic Devices. *IEEE Transactions on Magnetics, 49*(8), 4811–4816. doi:10.1109/TMAG.2013.2241447

Zheng, H., & Zhou, Y. (2012). A novel cuckoo search optimization algorithm based on gauss distribution. *Journal of Computer Information Systems, 8*(10), 4193–4200.

Zhou, J., Zhang, X., Zhang, G., & Chen, D. (2015). Optimization and parameters estimation in ultrasonic echo problems using modified artificial bee colony algorithm. *Journal of Bionics Engineering, 12*(1), 160–169. doi:10.1016/S1672-6529(14)60110-4

Zhou, X., Liu, Y., Li, B., & Li, H. (2016). A multiobjective discrete cuckoo search algorithm for community detection in dynamic networks. *Soft Computing*, 1–12.

Zhu, J., & Momoh, J. A. (2001). Multi-area power systems economic dispatch using nonlinear convex network flow programming. *Electric Power Systems Research, 59*(1), 13–20. doi:10.1016/S0378-7796(01)00131-6

Agarwal, A., Biadsy, F., & Mckeown, K. R. (2009). Contextual phrase-level polarity analysis using lexical affect scoring and syntactic n-grams. In *Proceedings of the 12th Conference of the European Chapter of the Association for Computational Linguistics*, (pp. 24-32). Association for Computational Linguistics. doi:10.3115/1609067.1609069

Al-Muraeb, A., & Abdel-Aty-Zohdy, H. (2015). Optimal Design of Short Fiber Bragg Grating Using Bat Algorithm With Adaptive Position Update. *IEEE Photonics Journal, 8*(1).

Amir, M., Bedra, S., Benkouda, S., & Fortaki, T. (2014). Bacterial foraging optimisation and method of moments for modelling and optimisation of microstrip antennas. *IET Microwaves, Antennas & Propagation, 8*(4), 295–300.

Azaro, R., De Natale, F., Donelli, M., & Massa, A. (2006). PSO-based optimization of matching loads for lossy transmission lines. *Microwave and Optical Technology Letters, 48*(8), 1485–1487. doi:10.1002/mop.21738

Bell, W. J., Roth, L. M., & Nalepa, C. A. (2007). *Cockroaches: ecology, behavior, and natural history*. JHU Press.

Benahmed, K., Merabti, M., & Haffaf, H. (2012). Inspired social spider behavior for secure wireless sensor networks. *International Journal of Mobile Computing and Multimedia Communications, 4*(4), 1–10. doi:10.4018/jmcmc.2012100101

Bevrani, H., & Hiyama, T. (2011). *Intelligent Automatic Generation Control*. CRC Press.

Bhattacharya, R., Bhattacharyya, T. K., & Saha, S. (2011). Sidelobe level reduction of aperiodic planar array using an improved invasive weed optimization algorithm. *Applied Electromagnetics Conference (AEMC)*. IEEE. doi:10.1109/AEMC.2011.6256797

Bose, G. K., Jana, T. K., & Mitra, S. (2011). Identification of the significant process parameters by Taguchi methodology during electrochemical grinding of Al2O3/Al – interpenetrating phase composite. *International Journal of Computational Materials Science and Surface Engineering, 4*(3), 232–246. doi:10.1504/IJCMSSE.2011.042821

Boser, B. E., Guyon, I. M., & Vapnik, V. N. (1992). A training algorithm for optimal margin classifiers. In *Proceedings of the fifth annual workshop on Computational learning theory*, (pp. 144-152). ACM. doi:10.1145/130385.130401

Bouarara, H. A., Hamou, R. M., & Amine, A. (2014). Text Clustering using Distances Combination by Social Bees: Towards 3D Visualisation Aspect. *International Journal of Information Retrieval Research, 4*(3), 34–53.

Bourjot, C., Chevrier, V., & Thomas, V. (2003). A new swarm mechanism based on social spiders colonies: From web weaving to region detection. *Web Intelligence and Agent Systems: An International Journal, 1*(1), 47–64.

Bremermann, H. (1974). Chemotaxis and optimization. *Journal of the Franklin Institute, 297*(5), 397–404. doi:10.1016/0016-0032(74)90041-6

Caorsi, S., Donelli, M., Massa, A., Pastorino, M., & Randazzo, A. (2004). Detection of Buried Objects by an Electromagnetic Method Based on a Differential Evolution Approach. *Proceedings IEEE Instrumentation and Measurement Technology Conference, 2*, 1107-1111. doi:10.1109/IMTC.2004.1351257

Chen, X., ONeill, K., Barrowes, B. E., Grzegorczyk, T. M., & Kong, J. A. (2004). Application of a Spheroidal-Mode Approach and a Differential Evolution Algorithm for Inversion of Magneto-Quasistatic Data in UXO Discrimination. *Inverse Problems, 20*(6), 27–40. doi:10.1088/0266-5611/20/6/S03

Colorni, A., Dorigo, M., Maniezzo, V., & Trubian, M. (1994). Ant System for Job-shop Scheduling. Belgian Journal of Operations Research. *Statistics and Computer Science, 34*(1), 39–53.

Darwin, C. (1991). *On the origin of species by means of natural selection*. London: Murray.

Dave, K., Lawrence, S., & Pennock, D. M. (2003). Mining the peanut gallery: Opinion extraction and semantic classification of product reviews. In *Proceedings of the 12th international conference on World Wide Web*, (pp. 519-528). ACM. doi:10.1145/775152.775226

Deb, K. (2001). *Multi-objective optimization using evolutionary algorithms* (Vol. 16). John Wiley & Sons.

Deb, K. (2005). *Multi-Objective Optimization using Evolutionary Algorithms*. Willey Eastern Limited.

Dehak, N., Kenny, P. J., Dehak, R., Dumouchel, P., & Ouellet, P. (2011). Front End Factor Analysis for Speaker Verification. *IEEE Transactions on Audio. Speech and Language Processing, 19*(4), 788–798. doi:10.1109/TASL.2010.2064307

Deng, J. (1989). Introduction to Grey System. *Journal of Grey System, 1*(1), 1–24.

Dhar, R. N. (1982). *Computer Aided Power System Operation and Analysis.* Tata McGraw-Hill Publishing Company Ltd.

Ding, L., Yue, Y., Ahmet, K., Jakson, M., & Parkin, R. (2005). Global optimization of a feature-based process sequence using GA and ANN techniques. *International Journal of Production Research, 43*(15), 3247–3272. doi:10.1080/00207540500137282

Donelli, M., Azaro, R., De Natale, F., & Massa, A. (2006, March). An innovative computational approach based on a particle swarm strategy for adaptive phased-arrays control. *IEEE Transactions on Antennas and Propagation, 54*(3), 888–898. doi:10.1109/TAP.2006.869912

Du, C. B., Quan, H. D., & Cui, P. Z. (2015). Improved quantum-inspired cuckoo search algorithm based on self-adapting adjusting of search range. *International Journal of Reasoning-based Intelligent Systems, 7*(3-4), 152–160. doi:10.1504/IJRIS.2015.072941

Duan, H.-B., Xu, C.-F., & Xing, Z.-H. (2010). A hybrid artificial bee colony optimization and quantum evolutionary algorithm for continuous optimization problems. *International Journal of Neural Systems, 20*(01), 39–50. doi:10.1142/S012906571000222X PMID:20180252

Elgerd, O. I. (2001). *Electric Energy Systems Theory* (2nd ed.). Tata: McGraw-Hill.

Engelbrecht, A. P. (2007). *Computational intelligence: an introduction.* John Wiley & Sons. doi:10.1002/9780470512517

Feng, X., Lau, F. C., & Gao, D. (2009). A new bio-inspired approach to the traveling salesman problem. In *Complex Sciences* (pp. 1310–1321). Springer Berlin Heidelberg. doi:10.1007/978-3-642-02469-6_12

Fernandes, C. M., Mora, A. M., Merelo, J. J., & Rosa, A. C. (2014). KANTS: A Stigmergic Ant Algorithm for Cluster Analysis and Swarm Art. *IEEE Transactions on Cybernetics, 44*(6), 843–856. doi:10.1109/TCYB.2013.2273495 PMID:23912505

Fuller, T. K., Mech, L. D., & Cockrane, J. F. (2003). Wolf population dynamics. In L. D. Mech & L. Boitani (Eds.), *Wolves: Behavior, Ecology and Conservation* (pp. 161–191). Chicago: University of Chicago Press.

Furui, S. (1997). Recent Advances in Speaker Recognition. In *Proceedings of first International Conference on Audio and Video based Biometric Person Authentication, 1206,* 235-252. doi:10.1007/BFb0016001

Gandomi, A. H., Yang, X. S., & Alavi, A. H. (2013). Cuckoo search algorithm: A metaheuristic approach to solve structural optimization problems. *Engineering with Computers, 29*(1), 17–35. doi:10.1007/s00366-011-0241-y

Genovesi, S., Monorchio, A., Mittra, R., & Manara, G. (2007). A subboundary approach for enhanced particle swarm optimization and its application to the design of artificial magnetic conductors. *IEEE Transactions on Antennas and Propagation, 55*(3), 766–770. doi:10.1109/TAP.2007.891559

Goldberg, D. E. (1989). *Genetic Algorithms in Search, Optimization and Machine Learning.* Addison-Wesley Publishing Company Inc.

Goudos, S. K., Siakavara, K., & Sahalos, J. N. (2014). Novel Spiral Antenna Design Using Artificial Bee Colony Optimization for UHF RFID Applications. *IEEE Antennas and Wireless Propagation Letters, 13,* 528–531. doi:10.1109/LAWP.2014.2311653

Hanoun, S., Creighton, D., & Nahavandi, S. (2014). A hybrid cuckoo search and variable neighborhood descent for single and multi-objective scheduling problems. *International Journal of Advanced Manufacturing Technology, 75*(9), 1501–1516. doi:10.1007/s00170-014-6262-0

Ho, S., Yang, S., Ni, G., & Wong, H. (2006). A particle swarm optimization method with enhanced global search ability for design optimizations of electromagnetic devices. *IEEE Transactions on Magnetics, 42*(4), 1107–1110. doi:10.1109/TMAG.2006.871426

Hofstadter, D. (2013). *Alan Turing: Life and legacy of a great thinker* (C. Teuscher, Ed.). Springer Science & Business Media.

Hossaina, A., Hossaina, A., Nukmana, Y., Hassanab, M. A., Harizama, M. Z., Sifullaha, A. M., & Parandousha, P. (2016). A Fuzzy Logic-Based Prediction Model for Kerf Width in Laser Beam Machining. *Materials and Manufacturing Processes, 31*(5), 679–684. doi:10.1080/10426914.2015.1037901

Ilunga-Mbuyamba, E., Cruz-Duarte, J. M., Avina-Cervantes, J. G., Correa-Cely, C. R., Lindner, D., & Chalopin, C. (2016). Active contours driven by cuckoo search strategy for brain tumour images segmentation. *Expert Systems with Applications, 56*, 59–68. doi:10.1016/j.eswa.2016.02.048

Jain, A. K., Srivastava, S. C., Singh, S. N., & Srivastava, L. (2015). Bacteria Foraging Optimization Based Bidding Strategy Under Transmission Congestion. *IEEE Systems Journal, 9*(1), 141–151. doi:10.1109/JSYST.2013.2258229

Kanagasundaram, A., Dean, D., Sridharan, S., Gonzalez-Dominguez, J., Gonzalez-Rodriguez, J., & Ramos, D. (2014). Improving Short Utterance i-vector Speaker Verification using Utterance Variance Modeling and Compensation Techniques. *Speech Communication, 59*, 69–82. doi:10.1016/j.specom.2014.01.004

Kavousi-Fard, A., Niknam, T., & Fotuhi-Firuzabad, M. (2016). A Novel Stochastic Framework Based on Cloud Theory and \theta -Modified Bat Algorithm to Solve the Distribution Feeder Reconfiguration. *IEEE Transactions on Smart Grid, 7*(2), 740–750.

Keufmann, A., & Gupta, M. M. (1985). *Introduction to Fuzzy Arithmetic: Theory and Applications.* New York: Van Nostrand Reinhold.

Koziel, S., & Yang, X.-S. (2011). *Computational optimization, methods and algorithms* (Vol. 356). Springer. doi:10.1007/978-3-642-20859-1

Kulkarni, S., Kothari, AG, & Kothari, DP, P. (. (. (2000). Combined economic and emission dispatch using improved backpropagation neural network. *Electric Machines &Power Systems, 28*(1), 31–44. doi:10.1080/073135600268496

Kumar, A. B., Vemuri, S., & Imah, A. H. (1985). Fuel Resource Scheduling The Daily Scheduling Problem. *IEEE Transactions on Power Apparatus and Systems, PAS-104*(2), 313–320. doi:10.1109/TPAS.1985.319045

Li, H., Li, J., & Kang, F. (2011). Risk analysis of dam based on artificial bee colony algorithm with fuzzy c-means clustering. *Canadian Journal of Civil Engineering, 38*(5), 483–492. doi:10.1139/l11-020

Li, W.-W., Wang, H., & Zou, Z. J. (2005). Function optimization method based on bacterial colony chemotaxis. *Journal of Circuits and Systems, 10*, 58–63.

Liu, C., Yan, X., Liu, C., & Wu, H. (2011). The wolf colony algorithm and its application. *Chinese Journal of Electronics, 20*, 212–216.

Liu, J., Zheng, S., & Tan, Y. (2013). The improvement on controlling exploration and exploitation of firework algorithm. In *Advances in swarm intelligence* (pp. 11–23). Springer Berlin Heidelberg; doi:10.1007/978-3-642-38703-6_2

Macdonald, D. W., Creel, S., & Mills, M. G. L. (2004). Society: Canid society. In D. W. Macdonald & C. Sillero-Zubiri (Eds.), *Biology and Conservation of Wild Carnivores* (pp. 85–106). Oxford, UK: Oxford University Press. doi:10.1093/acprof:oso/9780198515562.003.0004

Marichelvam, M. K., Prabaharan, T., & Yang, X. S. (2014). A Discrete Firefly Algorithm for the Multi-Objective Hybrid Flowshop Scheduling Problems. *IEEE Transactions on Evolutionary Computation*, *18*(2), 301–305. doi:10.1109/TEVC.2013.2240304

Meyer, D., Leisch, F., & Hornik, K. (2003, September). The support vector machine under test. *Neurocomputing*, *55*(1), 169–186. doi:10.1016/S0925-2312(03)00431-4

Mittal, D., Gaurav, D., & Roy, S. S. (2015, July). An effective hybridized classifier for breast cancer diagnosis. In *2015 IEEE International Conference on Advanced Intelligent Mechatronics (AIM)* (pp. 1026-1031). IEEE. doi:10.1109/AIM.2015.7222674

Mohammad, S. M., Kiritchenko, S., & Zhu, X. (2013). NRC-Canada: Building the state-of-the-art in sentiment analysis of tweets.*Proceedings of the Second Joint Conference on Lexical and Computational Semantics (SEMSTAR'13)*.

Nanda, J., Kothari, M. L., & Satsangi, P. S. (1983, January). Automatic Generation Control of an Interconnected Hydrothermal System in Continuous and Discrete Modes Considering Generation Rate Constraints. *IEE Proceedings. Control Theory and Applications*, *130*(1), 17–27. doi:10.1049/ip-d.1983.0004

Nautsch, A. (2014). *Speaker Verification using i-vector*. Hochschule Darmstadt, Germany: University of Applied Science.

Niknam, T., Azizipanah-Abarghooee, R., Zare, M., & Bahmani-Firouzi, B. (2013). Reserve Constrained Dynamic Environmental/Economic Dispatch: A New Multiobjective Self-Adaptive Learning Bat Algorithm. *IEEE Systems Journal*, *7*(4), 763–776. doi:10.1109/JSYST.2012.2225732

Niu, B., & Wang, H. (2012). Bacterial colony optimization. *Discrete Dynamics in Nature and Society*, *2012*, 1–28.

Panda, M. C., & Yadava, V. (2012). Intelligent Modelling and Multi-Objective Optimization of Die Sinking Electrochemical Spark Machining Process. *Materials and Manufacturing Processes. Materials and Manufacturing Processes*, *27*(1), 10–25. doi:10.1080/10426914.2010.544812

Pang, B., Lee, L., & Vaithyanathan, S. (2002). Thumbs up? Sentiment classification using machine learning techniques. In *Proceedings of the ACL-02 conference on Empirical methods in natural language processing (vol. 10*, pp. 79-86). Association for Computational Linguistics. doi:10.3115/1118693.1118704

Qu, N. S., Zhang, Q. L., Fang, X. L., Ye, E. K., & Zhu, D. (2015). Experimental Investigation on Electrochemical Grinding of Inconel 718. *Procedia CIRP*, *35*, 16–19. doi:10.1016/j.procir.2015.08.055

Rao, R.S., & Ramalingaraju, M. (2008). Optimization of distribution network configuration for loss reduction using artificial bee colony algorithm. *International Journal of Electrical Power and Energy Systems Engineering*, *1*, 116–122.

Rashidi, F., Abiri, E., Niknam, T., & Salehi, M. R. (2014). On-line parameter identification of power plant characteristics based on phasor measurement unit recorded data using differential evolution and bat inspired algorithm IET Science. *Measurement Techniques*, *9*(3), 376–392.

Reynolds, D. A. (2002). An Overview of Automatic Speaker Recognition Technology. In *Proceedings of IEEE International Conference on Acoustics, Speech and Signal Processing (ICASSP)* (pp.4072-4075). Orlando, FL: IEEE. doi:10.1109/ICASSP.2002.5745552

Robinson, J., Sinton, S., & Rahmat-Samii, Y. (2001). Particle swarm, genetic algorithm, and their hybrids: Optimization of a profiled corrugated horn antenna. *IEEE Antennas Propagat. Soc. Int. Symp. Dig.*, 1, 314–317. doi:10.1109/APS.2002.1016311

Roy, G. G., Das, S., Chakraborty, P., & Suganthan, P. N. (2011). Design of Non-Uniform Circular Antenna Arrays Using a Modified Invasive Weed Optimization Algorithm. *IEEE Transactions on Antennas and Propagation*, 59(1), 110–118. doi:10.1109/TAP.2010.2090477

Roy, S., Bhattacharya, A., & Banerjee, S. (2007). Analysis of effect of voltage on surface texture in electrochemical grinding by autocorrelation function. *Tribology International*, 40(9), 1387–1393. doi:10.1016/j.triboint.2007.03.008

Schölkopf, B., Simard, P., Vapnik, V., & Smola, A. J. (1997). Improving the accuracy and speed of support vector machines. *Advances in Neural Information Processing Systems*, 9, 375–381.

Singh, U., & Rattan, M. (2014). Design of thinned concentric circular antenna arrays using firefly algorithm. *IET Microwaves, Antennas & Propagation*, 8(12), 894–900. doi:10.1049/iet-map.2013.0695

Stolcke, A., Ferrer, L., Kajarekar, S., Shriberg, E., & Venkataraman, A. (2005). MLLR Transforms as Features in Speaker Recognition. In *Proceedings of the 9th European Conference on Speech Communication and Technology*, 4, 2424-2427.

Su, H., Yong, B., & Du, Q. (2016). Perspectral Band Selection Using Improved Firefly Algorithm. *IEEE Geoscience and Remote Sensing Letters*, 13(1), 68–72. doi:10.1109/LGRS.2015.2497085

Tang, D. (2015). Sentiment-Specific Representation Learning for Document-Level Sentiment Analysis. In *Proceedings of the Eighth ACM International Conference on Web Search and Data Mining*, (pp. 447-452). ACM. doi:10.1145/2684822.2697035

Tapia, C. G., & Murtagh, B. A. (1991). Interactive fuzzy programming with preference criteria in multiobjective decision-making. *Computers & Operations Research*, 18(3), 307–316. doi:10.1016/0305-0548(91)90032-M

Todorovic, N., & Petrovic, S. (2013). Bee Colony Optimization Algorithm for Nurse Rostering. *IEEE Transactions on Systems, Man, and Cybernetics Systems*, 43(2), 467–473.

Turney, P. D. (2002). Thumbs up or thumbs down?: semantic orientation applied to unsupervised classification of reviews. In *Proceedings of the 40th annual meeting on association for computational linguistics*, (pp. 417-424). Association for Computational Linguistics. doi:10.3115/1073083.1073153

Yang, C., Tu, X., & Chen, J. (2007). Algorithm of marriage in honey bees optimization based on the wolf pack search. In *IEEE International Conference on Intelligent Pervasive Computing (IPC)* (pp. 462–467). doi:10.1109/IPC.2007.104

Yang, L., Sun, X., Peng, L., Yao, X., & Chi, T. (2015). An Agent-Based Artificial Bee Colony (ABC) Algorithm for Hyperspectral Image Endmember Extraction in Parallel. *IEEE Journal of Selected Topics in Applied Earth Observations and Remote Sensing*, 8(10), 4657–4664. doi:10.1109/JSTARS.2015.2454518

Yang, S., Gan, Y. B., & Qing, A. (2002). Sideband Suppression in Time-Modulated Linear Arrays by Differential Evolution Algorithm. *IEEE Antennas and Wireless Propagation Letters*, 1(1), 173–175. doi:10.1109/LAWP.2002.807789

Yip-Hoi, D., & Dutta, D. (1996). A genetic algorithm application for sequencing operations in process planning for parallel machining. *IIE Transactions*, 50(1), 55–68. doi:10.1080/07408179608966252

Yonezawa, Y., & Kikuchi, T. (1996). Micro Machine and Human Science. *Proceedings of the Seventh International Symposium Ecological algorithm for optimal ordering used by collective honey bee behaviour*, 249-256.

Yoshida, H., Kawata, K., Fukuyama, Y., Takayama, S., & Nakanishi, Y. (2000). A particle swarm optimization for reactive power and voltage control considering voltage security assessment. *IEEE Transactions on Power Systems*, *15*(4), 1232–1239. doi:10.1109/59.898095

Yousefi-Talouki, A., & Valiollahi, S. (2010). Optimal power flow with unified power flow controller using artificial bee colony algorithm. *International Review of Electrical Engineering*, *5*, 2773.

Zaina, A. M., Harona, H., & Sharif, S. (2012). Integrated ANN–GA for estimating the minimum value for machining performance. *International Journal of Production Research*, *50*(1), 191–213. doi:10.1080/00207543.2011.571454

Zhang, F., Zhang, F.-S., Lin, C., Zhao, G., & Jiao, Y.-C. (2009). Pattern Synthesis for Planar Array Based on Element Rotation. *Progress In Electromagnetics Research Letters*, *11*, 55–64. doi:10.2528/PIERL09070705

Zhang, J., Chung, H. S.-H., Lo, A. W.-L., & Huang, T. (2009). Extended Ant Colony Optimization Algorithm for Power Electronic Circuit Design. *IEEE Transactions on Power Electronics*, *24*(1), 147–162. doi:10.1109/TPEL.2008.2006175

Zou, W., & Zhu, Y. (2011). Clustering approach based on von neumann topology artificial bee colony algorithm.*International conference on data mining (DMIN11)*, 121–126.

Gao & Liu. (2011). Hybrid artificial bee colony algorithm. *Systems Engineering and Electronics*, *33*(5), 1167.

Anandaraman, C., Sankar, A. V. M., & Natarajan, R. (2012). A new evolutionary algorithm based on bacterial evolution and its applications for scheduling a flexible manufacturing system. *Jurnal Teknik Industri*, *14*(1), 1–12. doi:10.9744/jti.14.1.1-12

Balamurugan, R., & Subramanian, S. (2007). A simplified recursive approach to combined economic emission dispatch. *Electric Power Components and Systems*, *36*(1), 17–27. doi:10.1080/15325000701473742

Bouarara, H. A., & Bouarara, Y. (2016). Swarm Intelligence Methods for Unsupervised Images Classification: Applications and Comparative Study. *International Journal of Organizational and Collective Intelligence*, *6*(2), 50–74. doi:10.4018/IJOCI.2016040104

Bouarara, H. A., Hamou, R. M., & Amine, A. (2015). New Swarm Intelligence Technique of Artificial Social Cockroaches for Suspicious Person Detection Using N-Gram Pixel with Visual Result Mining. *International Journal of Strategic Decision Sciences*, *6*(3), 65–91. doi:10.4018/IJSDS.2015070105

Dagli, C. H., Thammano, A., & Phu-ang, A. (2013). Complex adaptive systems a hybrid artificial bee colony algorithm with local search for flexible job-shop scheduling problem. *Procedia Computer Science*, *20*, 96–101. doi:10.1016/j.procs.2013.09.245

Dorigo, M., & Gambardella, L. M. (1997). Ant colony system: A cooperative learning approach to the traveling salesman problem. Evolutionary Computation. *IEEE Transactions on*, *1*(1), 53–66.

Eberhart, R. C., & Shi, Y. (2001). Tracking and optimizing dynamic systems with particle swarms. *Proc. Congress on Evolutionary Computation 2001*. doi:10.1109/CEC.2001.934376

Fard, A. K., & Niknam, T. (2014). Optimal stochastic capacitor placement problem from the reliability and cost views using firefly algorithm. *IET Science, Measurement & Technology*, *8*(5), 260–269. doi:10.1049/iet-smt.2013.0231

Haupt, R. (1995). An introduction to genetic algorithms for electromagnetics. *IEEE Antennas Propag. Mag.*, *37*(2), 7–15. doi:10.1109/74.382334

Holland, J. H. (1982). *Adaption in Natural and Artificial Systems: An Introductory Analysis with Applications to Biology, Control, and Artificial Intelligence*. MIT Press.

Huang, S.-J., Liu, X.-Z., Su, W.-F., & Ou, T.-C. (2013). Application of Enhanced Honey-Bee Mating Optimization Algorithm to Fault Section Estimation in Power Systems. *IEEE Transactions on Power Delivery*, 28(3), 1944–1951. doi:10.1109/TPWRD.2013.2264142

James, M. (2008). The Self-Organization of Interaction Networks for Nature-Inspired Optimization. *IEEE Transactions on Evolutionary Computation*, 12(2), 220–230. doi:10.1109/TEVC.2007.900327

Karaboga, D., & Akay, B. (2010). Proportional integral derivative controller design by using artificial bee colony, harmony search, and the bees algorithms. *Proceedings of the Institution of Mechanical Engineers. Part I, Journal of Systems and Control Engineering*, 224(7), 869–883. doi:10.1243/09596518JSCE954

Karaboga, D., & Akay, B. (2011b). Partial transmit sequences based on artificial bee colony algorithm for peak-to-average power ratio reduction in multicarrier code division multiple access systems. *IET Communications*, 5(8), 1155–1162. doi:10.1049/iet-com.2010.0379

Kashan, M. H., Nahavandi, N., & Kashan, A. H. (2011). Disabc: A new artificial bee colony algorithm for binary optimization. *Applied Soft Computing*, 12(1), 342–352. doi:10.1016/j.asoc.2011.08.038

Kefayat, M., Ara, A. L., & Niaki, S. N. (2015). A hybrid of ant colony optimization and artificial bee colony algorithm for probabilistic optimal placement and sizing of distributed energy resources. *Energy Conversion and Management*, 92, 149–161. doi:10.1016/j.enconman.2014.12.037

Kirkpatrick, S., Gelatt, C. D., & Vecchi, M. P. (1983). Optimization by Simulated Annealing. *Science New Series*, 220, 671–680. PMID:17813860

Koza, J. R. (1992). *Genetic programming: on the programming of computers by means of natural selection* (Vol. 1). MIT Press.

Li, J.-Q., Pan, Q.-K., & Gao, K.-Z. (2011). Pareto-based discrete artificial bee colony algorithm for multi-objective flexible job shop scheduling problems. *International Journal of Advanced Manufacturing Technology*, 55(9), 1159–1169. doi:10.1007/s00170-010-3140-2

Li, T.-H. S., Kao, M.-C., & Kuo, P.-H. (2015). Recognition System for Home-Service-Related Sign Language Using Entropy-Based K-Means Algorithm and ABC-Based HMM. *IEEE Transactions on Systems, Man, and Cybernetics Systems*, 46(1), 150–162. doi:10.1109/TSMC.2015.2435702

Madi, M., Markovi, D., & Radovanovi, M. (2012). Performance comparision of meta-heuristic algorithms for training artificial neural networks in modelling laser cutting. *International Journal of Advance Intelligence Paradigms*, 4(3-4), 299–312. doi:10.1504/IJAIP.2012.052073

Mala, D. J., Mohan, V., & Kamalapriya, M. (2010). Automated software test optimisation framework - an artificial bee colony optimisation-based approach. *IET Software*, 4(5), 334–348. doi:10.1049/iet-sen.2009.0079

Mohammed, H. J., Abdullah, A. S., Ali, R. S., Abd-Alhameed, R. A., Abdulraheem, Y. I., & Noras, J. M. (2016). Design of a uniplanar printed triple band-rejected ultra-wideband antenna using particle swarm optimisation and the firefly algorithm. *IET Microwaves, Antennas & Propagation*, 10(1), 31–37. doi:10.1049/iet-map.2014.0736

Niknam, T., Bavafa, F., & Azizipanah-Abarghooee, R. (2014). New self-adaptive bat-inspired algorithm for unit commitment problem. *IET Science, Measurement & Technology*, 8(6), 505–517. doi:10.1049/iet-smt.2013.0252

Robinson, J., & Rahmat-Samii, Y. (2004, February). Particle swarm optimization in electromagnetics. *IEEE Transactions on Antennas and Propagation*, 52(2), 397–407. doi:10.1109/TAP.2004.823969

Sharma, M., & Sarma, K. K. (2015). Dialectal Assamese Vowel Speech Detection using acoustic Phonetic Features, KNN and RNN. In *Proceedings of 2nd International Conference on Signal Processing and Integrated Networks (SPIN)* (pp.674-678). New Delhi, India: SPIN. doi:10.1109/SPIN.2015.7095270

Silva, L. I., Belati, E. A., & Ivo, C. S. J. (2016). Heuristic Algorithm for Electrical Distribution Systems Reconfiguration Based on Firefly Movement Equation. *IEEE Latin America Transactions, 14*(2), 752–758. doi:10.1109/TLA.2016.7437219

Sulaiman, M. H., Mustafa, M. W., Shareef, H., & Khalid, S. N. A. (2012). An application of artificial bee colony algorithm with least squares support vector machine for real and reactive power tracing in deregulated power system. *International Journal of Electrical Power & Energy Systems, 37*(1), 67–77. doi:10.1016/j.ijepes.2011.12.007

Sundareswaran, K., Peddapati, S., & Palani, S. (2014). MPPT of PV Systems Under Partial Shaded Conditions Through a Colony of Flashing Fireflies. *IEEE Transactions on Energy Conversion, 29*(2), 463–472. doi:10.1109/TEC.2014.2298237

Teodoro, C. (2012). Bat-Inspired Optimization Approach for the Brushless DC Wheel Motor Problem. *IEEE Transactions on Magnetics, 48*(2), 947–950. doi:10.1109/TMAG.2011.2176108

Xu, Z. (2015). Three-Dimensional Cole-Cole Model Inversion of Induced Polarization Data Based on Regularized Conjugate Gradient Method. *IEEE Geoscience and Remote Sensing Letters, 12*(6), 1180–1184. doi:10.1109/LGRS.2014.2387197

Yang, N.-C., & Le, M.-D. (2015). Multi-objective bat algorithm with time-varying inertia weights for optimal design of passive power filters set. *IET Generation, Transmission & Distribution, 9*(7), 644–654. doi:10.1049/iet-gtd.2014.0965

Yunbin, H., Yupeng, X., Jing, W., & Song, L. (2014). The fuzzy clustering combined an improved artificial bee colony algorithm with new rank fitness selection.*Software Intelligence Technologies and Applications International Conference on Frontiers of Internet of Things 2014, International Conference on*, 261–265. doi:10.1049/cp.2014.1572

Zhang, Y., & Wu, L. (2011). Optimal multi-level thresholding based on maxi-mum tsallis entropy via an artificial bee colony approach. *Entropy, 4*(12), 841–859. doi:10.3390/e13040841

Zhanga, G., Zhanga, Z., Guoa, J., Minga, W., Lia, M., & Huangab, Y. (2013). Modelling and Optimization of Medium-Speed WEDM Process Parameters for Machining SKD11. *Materials and Manufacturing Processes, 28*(10), 1124–1132. doi:10.1080/10426914.2013.773024

Gozde, H., & Taplamacioglu, M. C. (2012). Comparative performance analysis of artificial bee colony algorithm in automatic generation control for interconnected reheat thermal power system. *International Journal of Electrical Power & Energy Systems, 42*(1), 167–178. doi:10.1016/j.ijepes.2012.03.039

Sag, T., & Çunkaş, M. (2015). Color image segmentation based on multiobjective artificial bee colony optimization. *Applied Soft Computing, 34*, 389–401. doi:10.1016/j.asoc.2015.05.016

Yip, P. P. C., & Pao, Y. H. (1995, March). Combinational Optimization with Use of Guided Evolutionary Simulated Annealing. *IEEE Transactions on Neural Networks, 6*(2), 290–295. doi:10.1109/72.363466 PMID:18263313

Zhang, D.-L., Tang, Y.-G., & Gguan, X.-P. (2014). Optimum design of fractional order pid controller for an avr system using an improved artificial bee colony algorithm. *Acta Automatica Sinica, 40*(5), 973–979. doi:10.1016/S1874-1029(14)60010-0

Ibraheem, K. P., & Khatoon, S. (2005). Effect of Parameter Uncertainties on Dynamic Performance of an Interconnected Power System with AC/DC Links. *International Journal of Power and Energy Systems, 25*(3).

Liu, F., Lin, L., Jiao, L., Li, L., Yang, S., Hou, B., & Xu, J. et al. (2015). Nonconvex Compressed Sensing by Nature-Inspired Optimization Algorithms. *IEEE Transactions on Cybernetics, 45*(5), 1042–1053. doi:10.1109/TCYB.2014.2343618 PMID:25148677

Li, H. L. J., & Kang, F. (2011). Artificial bee colony algorithm for reliability analysis of engineering structures. *Materials Research, 163-167*, 3103–3109. doi:10.4028/www.scientific.net/AMR.163-167.3103

Akay, B. (2009). Solving integer programming problems by using artificial bee colony algorithm. In *Lecture Notes in Artificial Intelligence: Vol. 5883. AI (ASTERISK) IA 2009: Emergent perspectives in artificial intelligence* (pp. 355–364). Berlin: Springer.

Aksoy & Afacan. (2009). Planar Antenna Pattern Nulling Using Differential Evolution Algorithm. *International Journal on Electronics and Communications, 63*(2), 116-122.

Alam, M. S., & Ul Kabir, M. W. I. M. (2010). Self-adaptation of mutation step size in artificial bee colony algorithm for continuous function optimization. *13th international conference on computer and information technology (ICCIT)*.

Bansal, J. S.-H., & Arya, K. (2012). Model order reduction of single input single output systems using artificial bee colony optimization algorithm. *Nature Inspired Cooperative Strategies for Optimization (NICSO 2011), 387*, 85–100.

Baykasoglu, A. O. L., & Tapkan. (2007). Artificial bee colony algorithm and its application to generalized assignment problem. *Swarm Intelligence: Focus on Ant and Particle Swarm Optimization*.

Blackwell, T., & Bentley, P. J. (2002). Improvised music with swarms. *Proceedings of the 2002 Congress on Evolutionary Computation CEC 2002*, 1462–1467.

Breard, Perrusson, & Lesselier. (2008). Hybrid Differential Evolution and Retrieval of Buried Spheres in Subsoil. *IEEE Geoscience and Remote Sensing Letters, 5*(4), 788-792.

Choy, Cheong, Laik, & Shung. (2011). *A sentiment analysis of Singapore Presidential Election 2011 using Twitter data with census correction.* arXiv preprint arXiv:1108.5520

Darwin, C. (2009). *The origin of species by means of natural selection: or, the preservation of favored races in the struggle for life.* Academic Press.

Dorigo, M. (1992). *Optimization, learning and natural algorithms* (Ph.D. Thesis). Dipartimento diElettronica, Politecnico di Milano, Italy. (in Italian)

Dorigo, M., Maniezzo, V., & Colorni, A. (1991). *Positive feedback as a search strategy.* Tech. Report 91-016, Dipartimento di Elettronica, Politecnico di Milano, Italy.

Dorigo, M., Maniezzo, V., & Colorni, A. (1996). Ant system: optimization by a colony of cooperating agents. IEEE Trans. Syst. Man Cybern. B, 26(1), 29-41.

Go, A., Bhayani, R., & Huang, L. (2009). *Twitter sentiment classification using distant supervision.* CS224N Project Report, Stanford. Retrieved from https://github.com/maxluk/tweet-sentiment/blob/master/tweet-sentiment/StormTopology/data/dictionary.tsv

Greenberg, C. S., et al. (2014). The NIST 2014 Speaker Recognition i-vector Machine Learning Challenge. *Odyssey- The Speaker and Language Recognition Workshop*, 224-230.

Grimaccia, F., Mussetta, M., & Zich, R. E. (2007). Genetical swarm optimization: self-adaptive hybrid evolutionary algorithm for electromagnetics. IEEE Transactions on Antennas and Propagation, 55(3), 781–785.

Huang, T., & Mohan, A. S. (2007). A microparticle swarm optimizer for the reconstruction of microwave images. IEEE Transactions on Antennas and Propagation, 55(3), 568–576.

Ibraheem & Ahmad. (2004). Dynamic Performance Enhancement of Hydro-power Systems with Asynchronous Tie-lines. *Journal Institution of Engineers, 85*.

Janecek, A., & Tan, Y. (2011, July). Iterative improvement of the multiplicative update nmf algorithm using nature-inspired optimization. In *Natural Computation (ICNC), 2011 Seventh International Conference on* (Vol. 3, pp. 1668-1672). IEEE. doi:10.1109/ICNC.2011.6022356

Jin & Ran. (2015). A Fair-Rank Ant Colony Algorithm in Distributed Mass Storage System. *IEEE Journals & Magazines Canadian Journal of Electrical and Computer Engineering, 38*(4).

Jin, N., & Rahmat-Samii, Y. (2007). Advances in particle swarm optimization for antenna designs: real-number, binary, single-objective and multi-objective implementations. IEEE Transactions on Antennas and Propagation, 55(3), 556–567.

Kenane, E.-H., Djahli, F., & Dumond, C. (2015). A novel Modified Invasive Weeds Optimization for linear array antennas nulls control. *2015 4th International Conference on Electrical Engineering (ICEE),* 1-4. doi:10.1109/INTEE.2015.7416784

King. (2006). Biomimetics: Biologically Inspired Technologies. Bar-Cohen.

Li, J., Zheng, S., & Tan, Y. (2014, July). Adaptive Fireworks Algorithm. In *Evolutionary Computation (CEC), 2014 IEEE Congress on* (pp. 3214-3221). IEEE. doi:10.1109/CEC.2014.6900418

Mishra, S. E., Taplamacolu, M., & Lee, K. Y. (2015). 9th IFAC symposium on control of power and energy systems CPES 2015 robust tuning of power system stabilizer by using orthogonal learning artificial bee colony. *IFAC- PapersOnLine, 48*(30), 149 – 154.

Pang & Lee. (2008). Opinion mining and sentiment analysis. *Foundations and Trends in Information Retrieval, 2*(1-2), 1-135.

Passino, K. M. (2012). Bacterial foraging optimization. *Innovations and Developments of Swarm Intelligence Applications, 219.*

Pawar, P. R.-R., & Shankar, R. (2008). *Multi-objective optimization of electro- chemical machining process parameters using artificial bee colony (abc) algorithm.* Academic Press.

Pei, Y., Zheng, S., Tan, Y., & Takagi, H. (2012, October). An empirical study on influence of approximation approaches on enhancing fireworks algorithm. In *Systems, Man, and Cybernetics (SMC), 2012 IEEE International Conference on* (pp. 1322-1327). IEEE. doi:10.1109/ICSMC.2012.6377916

Poli, R., Langdon, W. B., McPhee, N. F., & Koza, J. R. (2008). *A field guide to genetic programming.* Lulu.com.

Premaratne, U., Samarabandu, J., & Sidhu, T. (2009, December). A new biologically inspired optimization algorithm. In *Industrial and Information Systems (ICIIS), 2009 International Conference on* (pp. 279-284). IEEE. doi:10.1109/ICIINFS.2009.5429852

Rahimi, A., Ahangaran, M., Ramezani, P., & Kashkooli, T. (2011). An Improved Artificial Weed Colony for Continuous Optimization. *Computer Modeling and Simulation (EMS),2011 Fifth UKSim European Symposium on,* 1-5. doi:10.1109/EMS.2011.30

Riham, M., Abdel Hady, M. F., Hosam, E., Amr, H., & Ashour, A. (2015). Feature Selection for Twitter Sentiment Analysis: An Experimental Study. In Computational Linguistics and Intelligent Text Processing, (pp. 92-103). Springer International Publishing.

Roy & Viswanatham. (2016). Classifying Spam Emails Using Artificial Intelligent Techniques. *International Journal of Engineering Research in Africa, 22.*

Sanjay, C., & Prithvi, C. (2014). Hybrid intelligence systems and artificial neural network (ANN) approach for modelling of surface roughness in drilling. *Cogent Engineering, 1*(1).

Sarlan, A., Nadam, C., & Basri, S. (2014). Twitter sentiment analysis. In *Information Technology and Multimedia (ICIMU),2014International Conference on*, (pp. 212-216). IEEE. doi:10.1109/ICIMU.2014.7066632

Semnani, Kamyab, & Rekanos. (2009). Reconstruction of One-Dimensional Dielectric Scatterers Using Differential Evolution and Particle Swarm Optimization. *IEEE Geoscience and Remote Sensing Letters, 6*(4), 671-675.

Shrawankar, U., & Thakare, V. (2013). *Techniques for Feature Extraction in Speech Recognition System: A Comparative Study.* CoRR, abs/1305.1145.

Stumberger, Dolinar, Palmer, & Hameyer. (2000). Optimization of Radial Active Magnetic Bearings Using the Finite Element Technique and Differential Evolution Algorithm. *IEEE Transactions on Magnetics, 36*(4), 1009-1013.

Stützle, T., & Hoos, H. (1997, April). MAX-MIN ant system and local search for the traveling salesman problem. In *Evolutionary Computation, 1997., IEEE International Conference on* (pp. 309-314). IEEE. doi:10.1109/ICEC.1997.592327

van den Berg, J., & Bioch, J. C. (1993). *Constrained optimization with a continuous Hopfield-Lagrange model.* Technical report EUR-CS-93-10, Erasmus University Rotterdam.

Zaman, T. R., Herbrich, R., Van Gael, J., & Stern, D. (2010). Predicting information spreading in twitter. *Workshop on computational social science and the wisdom of crowds, nips*, 104(45), 17599-601.

Zheng, S., Janecek, A., & Tan, Y. (2013, June). Enhanced fireworks algorithm. In *Evolutionary Computation (CEC), 2013 IEEE Congress on* (pp. 2069-2077). IEEE. doi:10.1109/CEC.2013.6557813

Zheng, S., Janecek, A., Li, J., & Tan, Y. (2014, July). Dynamic search in fireworks algorithm. In *Evolutionary Computation (CEC), 2014 IEEE Congress on* (pp. 3222-3229). IEEE. doi:10.1109/CEC.2014.6900485

Aderhold, A., Diwold, K., Scheidler, A., & Middendorf, M. (2010). *Artificial Bee Colony Optimization: A New Selection Scheme and Its Performance.* Academic Press.

Akay, B. & Karaboga, D. (2009). *Parameter Tuning for the Artificial Bee Colony Algorithm.* Academic Press.

Anuar, S., Selamat, A., & Sallchuddin, R. (2016). A modified scout bee for artificial bee colony algorithm and its performance on optimization problems. *Journal of King Saud University - Computer and Information Sciences, 28*(4), 395–406.

Banharnsakun, A., Achalakul, T., & Sirinaovakul, B. (2010). Artificial bee colony algorithm on distributed environments. In *Nature and Biologically Inspired Computing (NaBIC), 2010 Second World Congress on*, 13–18. doi:10.1109/NABIC.2010.5716309

Basu, A., Roy, S. S., & Abraham, A. (2015). A Novel Diagnostic Approach Based on Support Vector Machine with Linear Kernel for Classifying the Erythemato-Squamous Disease. In *Computing Communication Control and Automation (ICCUBEA),2015International Conference on*, (pp. 343-347). IEEE. doi:10.1109/ICCUBEA.2015.72

Basu, B., & Mahanti, G. K. (2011). Artificial bees colony optimization for synthesis of thinned mutually coupled linear array using inverse fast Fourier transform. *Devices and Communications (ICDeCom), 2011 International Conference on*, 1–5. doi:10.1109/ICDECOM.2011.5738513

Beni, G., & Wang, J. (1989). Swarm Intelligence in Cellular Robotic Systems. Academic Press.

Bernardino, A. M., Bernardino, E. M., S´anchez-P´erez, J. M., G´omez-Pulido, J. A., & Vega-Rodr´ıguez, M. A. (2010). *Efficient Load Balancing for a Resilient Packet Ring Using Artificial Bee Colony.* Academic Press.

Bonabeau, E. D. M., & Theraulaz, G. (1999). Swarm intelligence: From natural to artificial systems. Oxford University Press.

Chatterjee, A., Ghoshal, S. P., & Mukherjee, V. (2010). Artificial Bee Colony Algorithm for Transient Performance Augmentation of Grid Connected Distributed Generation. Academic Press.

Chifu, V. R., Pop, C. B., Salomie, I., Suia, D. S., & Niculici, A. N. (2012). Optimizing the Semantic Web Service Composition Process Using Cuckoo Search. Springer Berlin Heidelberg.

Cuevas, E., Sencio´n-Echauri, F., Zaldivar, D., & Cisneros, M. A. P. (2014). *Multi circle detection on images using artificial bee colony (ABC) optimization.* CoRR, abs/1406.6560.

Das, T. K., Acharjya, D. P., & Patra, M. R. 2014, January. Opinion mining about a product by analyzing public tweets in Twitter. In *Computer Communication and Informatics (ICCCI), 2014 International Conference on* (pp. 1-4). IEEE. doi:10.1109/ICCCI.2014.6921727

Delican, Y., Vural, R. A., & Yildirim, T. (2010). Artificial bee colony optimization based cmos inverter design considering propagation delays. In *Symbolic and Numerical Methods, Modeling and Applications to Circuit Design (SM2ACD), 2010 XIth International Workshop on* (pp. 1–5). doi:10.1109/SM2ACD.2010.5672326

Deng, Z., Gu, H., Feng, H., & Shu, B. (2011). *Artificial Bee Colony Based Mapping for Application Specific Network-on-Chip Design.* Academic Press.

Dorigo, M. (1992). *Optimization, learning and natural algorithms* (PhD thesis). Dipartimento di Elettronica, Politecnico di Milano, Italy.

Fujita, G., Shirai, G., & Yokoyama, R. (2002). Automatic Generation Control for DC Link Power System. *IEE Proceedings on Transmission and Distribution Conference and Exhibition: Asia Pacific, 3,* 1584-1588.

Hemamalini, S. & Simon, S. P. (2011). Dynamic economic dispatch using artificial bee colony algorithm for units with valve-point effect. *European Transactions on Electrical Power, 21*(1), 70–81.

Hicklin, J. F. (1986). *Application of the genetic algorithm to automatic program generation.* Academic Press.

Ibraheem & Singh. (2010). Hybrid GA-SA based Optimal AGC of a Multi-area Interconnected Power System with Asynchronous Tie-lines. *International Journal of Electrical and Power Engineering, 4*(2), 78-84.

Jatoth, R. K., & Rajasekhar, A. (2010). Speed control of pmsm by hybrid genetic artificial bee colony algorithm. *Communication Control and Computing Technologies (ICCCCT), 2010 IEEE International Conference on,* 241– 246.

Jovanovic, R., Tuba, M., & Brajevic, I. (2013). Parallelization of the cuckoo search using cuda architecture. *Proceedings of the 7th International Conference on Applied Mathematics, Simulation, Modelling.*

Kanagasundaram, A., Vogt, R., Dean, D., & Sridharan, S. (2012). PLDA Based Speaker Recognition on Short Utterances. Odyssey: The Speaker and Language Recognition Workshop.

Karaboga, D. & Basturk, B. (2007). *Artificial Bee Colony (ABC) Optimization Algorithm for Solving Constrained Optimization Problems.* Academic Press.

Karaboga, D. (2005). *An idea based on honey bee swarm for numerical optimization techn.* Erciyes Univ. Press.

Karaboga, D. (2005). *An idea based on honey bee swarm for numerical optimization.* Technical report, Technical report-tr06, Erciyes University, Engineering Faculty, Computer Engineering Department.

Kavian, Y. S., Rashedi, A., Mahani, A., & Ghassemlooy, Z. (2012). Routing and wavelength assignment in optical networks using artificial bee colony algorithm. *Optik - International Journal for Light and Electron Optics, 124*(12), 1243 – 1249.

579

Koza, J. R. (1994). Genetic programming II: Automatic discovery of reusable subprograms. Cambridge, MA: Academic Press.

Kumar, A. B., Vemuri, S., Gibbs, L. A., Hackett, D. F., & Eisenhauer, J. T. (1984). Fuel Resource Scheduling, Part III: The Short-Term Problem. Power Engineering Review, IEEE, (7), 25-26.

Lee, W. P., & Cai, W. T. (2011). A novel artificial bee colony algorithm with diversity strategy. In *Natural Computation (ICNC), 2011 Seventh International Conference on, 3,* 1441–1444. doi:10.1109/ICNC.2011.6022505

Lei, X., Sun, J., Xu, X., & Guo, L. (2010). Artificial bee colony algorithm for solving multiple sequence alignment. In *Bio-Inspired Computing: Theories and Applications (BIC-TA), 2010 IEEE Fifth International Conference on,* 337–342.

Luo, Q., & Duan, H. (2014). Chaotic artificial bee colony optimization approach to aircraft automatic landing system. *IFAC Proceedings, 47*(3), 876– 881.

Mini, S., Udgata, S. K., & Sabat, S. L. (2010). Sensor Deployment in 3-D Terrain Using Artificial Bee Colony Algorithm. Academic Press.

Pansuwan, P., Rukwong, N., & Pongcharoen, P. (2010). Identifying optimum artificial bee colony (abc) algorithm's parameters for scheduling the manufacture and assembly of complex products. *Computer and Network Technology (ICCNT), 2010 Second International Conference on,* 339–343.

Pohlheim, H. (2005). Evolutionary algorithms: overview, methods and operators. *GEATbx: Gentic & Evolutionary AlgorithmToolbox for Matlab.*

Qing, A. (2007). A Parametric Study on Differential Evolution Based on Benchmark Electromagnetic Inverse Scattering Problem. *Proceedings2007IEEE Congress on Evolutionary Computation (CEC 2007),* 1904-1909. doi:10.1109/CEC.2007.4424706

Rajasekhar, A., Abraham, A., & Pant, M. (2011). Levy mutated artificial bee colony algorithm for global optimization. *Systems, Man, and Cybernetics (SMC), 2011 IEEE International Conference on,* 655–662. doi:10.1109/ICSMC.2011.6083786

Rubio-Largo, A., Vega-Rodríguez, M. A., Gómez-Pulido, J. A., & Sánchez-Pérez, J.M. (2011). *Tackling the Static RWA Problem by Using a Multi- objective Artificial Bee Colony Algorithm.* Academic Press.

Sanajaoba, S. & Fernandez, E. (2016). Maiden application of cuckoo search algorithm for optimal sizing of a remote hybrid renewable energy system. *Renewable Energy, 96*(A), 1 –10.

Saravanan, B., & Vasudevan, E. R. (2014). Emission constrained unit commitment problem solution using invasive weed optimization Algorithm. *Advances in Electrical Engineering (ICAEE),2014International Conference on,* 1-6. doi:10.1109/ICAEE.2014.6838532

Saravanan, B., Vasudevan, E. R., & Kothari, D. P. (2013). A solution to unit commitment problem using Invasive Weed Optimization algorithm. *Power, Energy and Control (ICPEC),2013International Conference on,* 386-393. doi:10.1109/ICPEC.2013.6527687

Sharma, M., & Sarma, K. K. (2015). Soft-Computational Techniques and Spectro-Temporal Features for Telephonic Speech Recognition: an overview and review of current state of the art. In S. Bhattacharyya, P. Banerjee, D. Majumdar, & P. Dutta (Eds.), Handbook of Research on Advanced Hybrid Intelligent Techniques and Applications (pp. 161–189). Academic Press.

Shi, Y.-j., Qu, F.-Z., Chen, W., & Li, B. (2010). *An Artificial Bee Colony with Random Key for Resource-Constrained Project Scheduling.* Academic Press.

Song, Y. H., Wang, G. S., Wang, P. Y., & Johns, A. T. (1997, July). Environmental/economic dispatch using fuzzy logic controlled genetic algorithms. In *Generation, Transmission and Distribution, IEE Proceedings* (Vol. 144, No. 4, pp. 377-382). IET.

Stanarevic, N., Tuba, M., & Bacanin, N. (2010). Enhanced artificial bee colony algorithm performance. *Proceedings of the 14th WSEAS International Conference on Computers: Part of the 14th WSEAS CSCC Multiconference, 2*, 440–445.

Sukor, A. S. (2012). Speaker Identification System using MFCC procedure and Noise Reduction method. University Tun Hussein Onn, Malaysia.

Sumesh, E. P., Lam, S. S. B., Raju, M. L. H. P. M., U. K., C. S., & Srivastav, P. R. (2012). International conference on communication technology and system design 2011 automated generation of independent paths and test suite optimization using artificial bee colony. *Procedia Engineering, 30*, 191 – 200.

Sumpavakup, C., Srikun, I., & Chusanapiputt, S. (2010). A solution to the optimal power flow using artificial bee colony algorithm. *Power System Technology (POWERCON), 2010 International Conference on*, 1–5. doi:10.1109/POWERCON.2010.5666516

Sundar, S., Singh, A., & Rossi, A. (2010). *An Artificial Bee Colony Algorithm for the 0–1 Multidimensional Knapsack Problem*. Academic Press.

Svozil, D., Kvasnicka, V., & Pospichal, J. (1997). Introduction to Multi Layer Feed Forward Neural Network. *Chemo-Metrics and Intelligent Laboratory Systems, 39*(1), 43-62.

Tahooneh, A. & Ziarati, K. (2011). *Using Artificial Bee Colony to Solve Stochastic Resource Constrained Project Scheduling Problem*. Academic Press.

Tokheim, A. E. H. (2012). i-vector Based Language Recognition. Norwegian University of Science and Technology.

Veenhuis, C. (2010). Binary Invasive Weed Optimization. *Nature and Biologically Inspired Computing (NaBIC), 2010 Second World Congress on*, 449-454. doi:10.1109/NABIC.2010.5716311

Wang, J., Li, T., & Ren, R. (2010). A real time idss based on artificial bee colony-support vector machine algorithm. *Advanced Computational Intelligence (IWACI), 2010 Third International Workshop on*, 91–96.

Yang, X.-S., & Deb, S. (2009). Cuckoo search via Lévy flights. In *Nature & Biologically Inspired Computing, 2009. NaBIC 2009. World Congress on*, (pp. 210–214). IEEE.

Zhao, D., Gao, H., Diao, M., & An, C. (2010a). Direction finding of maximum likelihood algorithm using artificial bee colony in the impulsive noise. *Artificial Intelligence and Computational Intelligence (AICI), 2010 International Conference on, 2*, 102–105. doi:10.1109/AICI.2010.144

Zhao, H., Pei, Z., Jiang, J., Guan, R., Wang, C., & Shi, X. (2010b). *A Hybrid Swarm Intelligent Method Based on Genetic Algorithm and Artificial Bee Colony*. Academic Press.

Zou, W. Z. Y. C.-H. S. X. (2010). A clustering approach using cooperative artificial bee colony algorithm. Discrete Dynamics in Nature and Society.

Abbass, H. A. (2001a). MBO: Marriage in honey bees optimization. A haplometrosis polygynous swarming approach. *IEEE Proceedings of the Congress on Evolutionary Computation*, 207–214.

Abbass, H. A. (2001b). A monogenous MBO approach to satisfiability. *Proceeding of the International Conference on Computational Intelligence for Modelling, Control and Automation (CIMCA)*.

Abdolmohammadi, H. R., & Kazemi, A. (2013). A benders decomposition approach for a combined heat and power economic dispatch. *Energy Conversion and Management, 71*, 21–31. doi:10.1016/j.enconman.2013.03.013

Abido, M. (2003). Environmental/economic power dispatch using multiobjective evolutionary algorithms. *IEEE Transactions on Power Systems, 18*(4), 1529–1537. doi:10.1109/TPWRS.2003.818693

Abou El Ela, A. A., Abido, M. A., & Spea, S. R. (2010). Differential evolution algorithm for emission constrained economic power dispatch problem. *Electric Power Systems Research, 80*(10), 1286–1292. doi:10.1016/j.epsr.2010.04.011

Adhikari, A., & Sahana, S. K. (2013). Job Shop Scheduling Based on Ant Colony Optimization. *Proceedings of 2nd International Conference ICACM-2013,* 13-19.

Adhinarayanan, T., & Sydulu, M. (2006). *Particle swarm optimisation for economic dispatch with cubic fuel cost function.* Paper presented at the TENCON 2006. 2006 IEEE Region 10 Conference. doi:10.1109/TENCON.2006.344059

Adriansyah, A., & Amin, S. (2006). Analytical and empirical study of particle swarm optimization with a sigmoid decreasing inertia weight. *Regional Conference on Engineering and Science*, Johor.

Agency, C. I. (2015). Comparison: Natural Gas - Proved Reserves. *The World Factbook*. Retrieved from https://www.cia.gov/library/publications/the-world-factbook/rankorder/2253rank.html

Akay, B., & Karaboga, D. (2015). A survey on the applications of artificial bee colony in signal, image, and video processing. *Signal. Image and Video Processing, 9*(4), 967–990. doi:10.1007/s11760-015-0758-4

Alias, A., Abdullah, B., & Abbas, N. M. (2012). Influence of machined feed rate in WEDM of titanium Ti-6Al-4V with constant current (6A) using brass wire. *Procedia Engineering, 41*, 1806–1811. doi:10.1016/j.proeng.2012.07.387

Altiparmak, F., Gen, M., Lin, L., & Paksoy, T. (2006). A genetic algorithm approach for multi-objective optimization of supply chain networks. *Computers & Industrial Engineering, 51*(1), 196–215. doi:10.1016/j.cie.2006.07.011

Angeline, P. (1995). Adaptive and self-adaptive evolutionary computations. Computational Intelligence: A Dynamic Systems Perspective. IEEE Press.

Angus, D., & Woodward, C. (2009). Multiple objective ant colony optimisation. *Swarm Intelligence, 3*(1), 69–85. doi:10.1007/s11721-008-0022-4

Antony, J. (2000). Multi-response optimization in industrial experiments using Taguchis quality loss function and principal component analysis. *Quality and Reliability Engineering International, 16*(1), 3–8. doi:10.1002/(SICI)1099-1638(200001/02)16:1<3::AID-QRE276>3.0.CO;2-W

Apostolopoulos, T., & Vlachos, A. (2011). Application of the firefly algorithm for solving the economic emissions load dispatch problem. *International Journal of Combinatorics, 23*.

Ardizzon, G., Cavazzini, G., & Pavesi, G. (2015). Adaptive acceleration coefficients for a new search diversification strategy in particle swarm optimization algorithms*Information Sciences, 299*, 337–378..

Arnau, A. (2008a). A Review of Interface Electronic Systems for AT-cut Quartz Crystal Microbalance Applications in Liquids. *Sensors (Basel, Switzerland), 8*(1), 370–411. doi:10.3390/s8010370 PMID:27879713

Arnau, A. (2008c). *Piezoelectric transducer and applications* (2nd ed.). Springer.

Arumugam, M., Chandramohan, A., & Rao, M. (2005). Competitive Approaches to PSO Algorithms via New Acceleration Co-efficient Variant with Mutation Operators. *Sixth International Conference on Computational Intelligence and Multimedia Applications*, 225-230. doi:10.1109/ICCIMA.2005.18

Aslam, M. W., Zhu, Z., & Nandi, A. K. (2013). Feature generation using genetic programming with comparative partner selection for diabetes classification. *Expert Systems with Applications, Elsevier, 40*(13), 5402–5412. doi:10.1016/j.eswa.2013.04.003

Atanassov, K. T. (1986). Intuitionistic fuzzy sets. *Fuzzy Sets and Systems, 20*(1), 87–96. doi:10.1016/S0165-0114(86)80034-3

Bahamish, H. A. A., Abdullah, R., & Salam, R. A. (2008). Protein Conformational Search Using Bees Algorithm. *Second Asia International Conference on Modeling & Simulation (AICMS 08)*, 911-916.

Bahmani-Firouzi, B., Farjah, E., & Azizipanah-Abarghooee, R. (2013). An efficient scenario-based and fuzzy self-adaptive learning particle swarm optimization approach for dynamic economic emission dispatch considering load and wind power uncertainties. *Energy, 50*, 232–244. doi:10.1016/j.energy.2012.11.017

Balaprakash, P., Birattari, M., & Stutzle, T. (2007). Improvement strategies for the F-race algorithm: Sampling design and iterative refinement. In *Lecture Notes in Computer Science: vol. 4771. Hybrid Metaheuristics, 4th International Workshop, Proceedings* (pp. 108-122). Berlin: Springer.

Balbo, A. R., Souza, M. A. D., Baptista, E. C., & Nepomuceno, L. (2012). Predictor-Corrector Primal-Dual Interior Point Method for Solving Economic Dispatch Problems: A Postoptimization Analysis. *Mathematical Problems in Engineering, 26*. doi:10.1155/2012/376546

Banks, A., Vincent, J., & Anyakoha, C. (2007). A review of particle swarm optimization. Part I: Background and development. *Natural Computing, 6*(4), 467–484. doi:10.1007/s11047-007-9049-5

Bansal, J. C., Sharma, H., & Jadon, S. S. (2013). Artificial bee colony algorithm: A survey. *International Journal of Advanced Intelligence Paradigms, 5*(1-2), 123–159. doi:10.1504/IJAIP.2013.054681

Bansal, R. (2005). Optimization methods for electric power systems: An overview. *International Journal of Emerging Electric Power Systems, 2*(1). doi:10.2202/1553-779X.1021

Barakat, N. (2007). *Rule extraction from support vector machines: Medical diagnosis prediction and explanation* (Ph.D. thesis). School Inf. Technol. Electr. Eng. (ITEE), Univ. Queensland, Brisbane, Australia.

Barakat, N. H., & Bradley, A. P. (2007). Rule Extraction from Support Vector Machines: A Sequential Covering Approach. *IEEE Transactions on Knowledge and Data Engineering, 19*(6), 2007. doi:10.1109/TKDE.2007.190610

Barakat, N. H., Bradley, A. P., & Barakat, M. N. H. (2010). Intelligible Support Vector Machines for Diagnosis of Diabetes Mellitus. *IEEE Transactions on Information Technology in Biomedicine, 14*(4), 1114–1120. doi:10.1109/TITB.2009.2039485 PMID:20071261

Bartz-Beielstein, T., Lasarczyk, C., & Preuss, M. (2005). Sequential parameter optimization. *IEEE Congress on Evolutionary Computation*, 773-780.

Baskan, O., Haldenbilen, S., & Ceylan, H. (2009). A new solution algorithm for improving performance of ant colony optimization. *Applied Mathematics and Computation, 211*(1), 75-84.

Bass, I. (2007). *Six Sigma Statistics with Excel and Minitab*. McGraw Hill.

Basu, B., & Mahanti, G. K. (2011). Firefly and artificial bees colony algorithm for synthesis of scanned and broadside linear array antenna. *Progress in Electromagnetic Research B., 32*, 169–190. doi:10.2528/PIERB11053108

Basu, M. (2006). Particle swarm optimization based goal-attainment method for dynamic economic emission dispatch. *Electric Power Components and Systems, 34*(9), 1015–1025. doi:10.1080/15325000600596759

Basu, M., & Chowdhury, A. (2013). Cuckoo search algorithm for economic dispatch. *Energy*, *60*, 99–108. doi:10.1016/j.energy.2013.07.011

Batzias, F. A., & Siontorou, C. G. (2012). Creating a specific domain ontology for supporting R&D in the science-based sector – The case of biosensors. *Expert Systems with Applications*, *39*(11), 9994–10015. doi:10.1016/j.eswa.2012.01.216

Baucer, A., Bullnheimer, B., Hartl, R. F., & Strauss, C. (2000). Minimizing total tardiness on a single machine using ant colony optimization. *Central European Journal for Operations Research and Economics*, *8*(2), 125–141.

Baykasoğlu, A., Ozbakır, L., & Tapkan, P. (2009). The bees algorithm for workload balancing in examination job assignment. *European Journal of Industrial Engineering*, *3*(4), 424–435. doi:10.1504/EJIE.2009.027035

Beccaloni, J. (2009). *Arachnids. University of California Press*.

Beheshti, Z., Mariyam, S., & Shamsuddin, H. (2014). CAPSO: Centripetal accelerated particle swarm optimization. *Information Sciences*, *258*, 54–79. doi:10.1016/j.ins.2013.08.015

Beheshti, Z., Shamsuddin, S., & Sulaiman, S. (2013). Fusion global-local-topology particle swarm optimization for global optimization problems. *Mathematical Problems in Engineering*.

Beni, G., & Wang, J. (1993). Swarm Intelligence in Cellular Robotic Systems. In P. Dario, G. Sandini, & P. Aebischer (Eds.), *Robots and Biological Systems: Towards a New Bionics?* (pp. 703–712). Berlin: Springer Berlin Heidelberg. doi:10.1007/978-3-642-58069-7_38

Bent, R., & Hentenryck, P. V. (2003). A two-stage hybrid algorithm for pickup and delivery vehicle routing problems with time windows. *Computers & Operations Research*, *33*(4), 875–893. doi:10.1016/j.cor.2004.08.001

Bergh, F. (2002). An Analysis of Particle Swarm Optimizers, PhD thesis. Pretoria, South Africa: Department of Computer Science, University of Pretoria. Retrieved from repository.up.ac.za/bitstream/handle/2263/24297/00thesis.pdf

Bergh, F., & Engelbrecht, A. (2004). A cooperative approach to particle swarm optimization. *IEEE Transactions on Evolutionary Computation*, *8*(3), 225–239. doi:10.1109/TEVC.2004.826069

Bertini, I., Ceravolo, F., Citterio, M., De Felice, M., Di Pietra, B., Margiotta, F., & Puglisi, G. et al. (2010). Ambient temperature modelling with soft computing techniques. *Solar Energy*, *84*(7), 1264–1272. doi:10.1016/j.solener.2010.04.003

Bezdek, J. C. (1994). What is computational intelligence? In *Computational Intelligence Imitating Life* (pp. 1–12). New York: IEEE Press.

Bhattacharya, A., & Chattopadhyay, P. K. (2011). Solving economic emission load dispatch problems using hybrid differential evolution. *Applied Soft Computing*, *11*(2), 2526–2537. doi:10.1016/j.asoc.2010.09.008

Bia, P., Caratelli, D., Mescia, L., Cicchetti, R., Maione, G., & Prudenzano, F. (2015). A novel FDTD formulation based on fractional derivatives for dispersive Havriliak–Negami media. *Signal Processing, 107*, 312-318.

Bia, P., Caratelli, D., Mescia, L., & Gielis, J. (2013). Electromagnetic Characterization of Supershaped Lens Antennas for High-Frequency Applications. *Proceedings of the 10th European Radar Conference (EuRAD)*, 1679-1682.

Bia, P., Caratelli, D., Mescia, L., & Gielis, J. (2015). Analysis and Synthesis of Supershaped Dielectric Lens Antennas. IET Microwaves. *Antennas & Propagation*, *9*, 1497–1504.

Birattari, M., Stutzle, T., Paquete, L., & Varrentrapp, K. (2002). A racing algorithm for configuring metaheuristics. In *GECCO 2002: Proceedings of the Genetic and Evolutionary Computation Conference*. Morgan Kaufmann Publishers.

Birol, F. (2004). *World Energy Outlook* (S. Sullivan, Ed.). International Energy Agency.

Bitam, S., & Mellouk, A. (2013). Bee life-based multi constraints multicast routing optimization for vehicular ad hoc networks. *Journal of Network and Computer Applications*, *36*(3), 981–991. doi:10.1016/j.jnca.2012.01.023

Bittermann, M. (2010). Artificial Intelligence (AI) versus Computational Intelligence (CI) for treatment of complexity in design. *Design Computing and Cognition (DCC10)*.

Blem, C. (2003). *Beam-ACO, Hybridizing ant colony optimization with beam search. An application to open shop scheduling*. Technical report TR/IRIDIA/2003-17.

Blum, C. (2005). Ant colony optimization: Introduction and recent trends. *Physics of Life Reviews*, *2*(4), 353–373. doi:10.1016/j.plrev.2005.10.001

Bonabeau, E., Dorigo, M., & Theraulaz, G. (1999). *Swarm Intelligence: From Natural to Artificial Systems*. Oxford University Press.

Bonisone, P., Subbu, R., & Aggour, K. S. (2002). Evolutionary optimization of fuzzy decision systems for automated insurance underwriting. *Paper presented at the Fuzzy Systems, 2002. FUZZ-IEEE'02. Proceedings of the 2002 IEEE International Conference on*. doi:10.1109/FUZZ.2002.1006641

Bonissone, P. P. (1997). Soft computing: The convergence of emerging reasoning technologies. *Soft Computing*, *1*(1), 6–18. doi:10.1007/s005000050002

Bonissone, P., Hu, X., & Subbu, R. (2009). A systematic PHM approach for anomaly resolution: A hybrid neural fuzzy system for model construction. *Proc. PHM 2009*.

Bonyadi, M. R., & Michalewicz, Z. (2014). A locally convergent rotationally invariant particle swarm optimization algorithm. *Swarm Intelligence*, *8*(3), 159–198. doi:10.1007/s11721-014-0095-1

Bonyadi, M. R., Michalewicz, Z., & Li, X. (2014). An analysis of the velocity updating rule of the particle swarm optimization algorithm. *Journal of Heuristics*, *20*(4), 417–452. doi:10.1007/s10732-014-9245-2

Bouchard, P. (2014). *The Book of Beetles: A Life-Size Guide to Six Hundred of Nature's Gems*. University Of Chicago Press. doi:10.7208/chicago/9780226082899.001.0001

Bratton, D., & Kennedy, J. (2007). Defining a Standard for Particle Swarm Optimization. *Proceedings of the IEEE Swarm Intelligence Symposium*, 120–127. doi:10.1109/SIS.2007.368035

Brownlee, J. (2011). Clever Algorithms: Nature-inspired Programming Recipes. LuLu.com.

Cai, X., Cui, Y., & Tan, Y. (2009). Predicted modified PSO with time-varying accelerator coefficients. *International Journal of Bio-inspired Computation*, *1*(1-2), 50–60. doi:10.1504/IJBIC.2009.022773

Cai, Y., Sun, J., Wang, J., Ding, Y., Tian, N., Liao, X., & Xu, W. (2008). Optimizing the codon usage of synthetic gene with QPSO algorithm. *Journal of Theoretical Biology*, *254*(1), 123–127. doi:10.1016/j.jtbi.2008.05.010 PMID:18579159

Calvo, E. J., Etchenique, R., Bartlett, P. N., Singhal, K., & Santamaria, C. (1997). Quartz crystal impedance studies at 10 MHz of viscoelastic liquids and films. *Faraday Discussions*, *107*, 141–247. doi:10.1039/a703551i

Calvo-Rolle, J. L., Casteleiro-Roca, J. L., Quintián, H., & Meizoso-López, M. C. (2013). A hybrid intelligent system for PID controller using in a steel rolling process. *Expert Systems with Applications*, *40*(13), 5188–5196. doi:10.1016/j.eswa.2013.03.013

Campos, M., Krohling, M., & Enriquez, I. (2014). Bare Bones Particle Swarm Optimization With Scale Matrix Adaptation. *IEEE Transactions on Cybernetics*, *44*(9), 1567–1578. doi:10.1109/TCYB.2013.2290223 PMID:25137686

Caratelli, D., Mescia, L., Bia, P., & Stukach, O. V. (2016). Fractional-Calculus-Based FDTD Algorithm for Ultrawide-band Electromagnetic Characterization of Arbitrary Dispersive Dielectric Materials. *IEEE Transactions on Antennas and Propagation, 64*(8), 3533–3544. doi:10.1109/TAP.2016.2578322

Carlisle, A., & Dozier, G. (2001) An off-the-shelf PSO. *Workshop on Particle Swarm Optimization.*

Casteleiro-Roca, J. L., Calvo-Rolle, J. L., Meizoso-López, M. C., Piñón-Pazos, A. P., & Rodríguez-Gómez, B. A. (2014). New approach for the QCM sensors characterization. *Sensors and Actuators. A, Physical, 207*(0), 1–9. doi:10.1016/j.sna.2013.12.002

Chandrasekaran, K., Simon, S. P., & Padhy, N. P. (2014). Cuckoo Search Algorithm for Emission Reliable Economic Multi-objective Dispatch Problem. *Journal of the Institution of Electronics and Telecommunication Engineers, 60*(2), 128–138. doi:10.1080/03772063.2014.901592

Chandrasekaran, M., Muralidhar, M., Krishna, C. M., & Dixit, U. S. (2010). Application of soft computing techniques in machining performance prediction and optimization: A literature review. *International Journal of Advanced Manufacturing Technology, 46*(5-8), 445–464. doi:10.1007/s00170-009-2104-x

Chantraine-Bars, B., Sauleau, R., & Coq, L. L. (2005). A new accurate design method for millimeter-wave homogeneous dielectric substrate lens antennas. *IEEE Transactions on Antennas and Propagation, 53*(3), 1069–1082. doi:10.1109/TAP.2004.842644

Chapman, A. D. (2006). Numbers of living species in Australia and the World. Canberra: Australian Biological Resources Study.

Chapman, R. F. (2013). *The insects: structure and function* (S. J. Simpson & A. E. Douglas, Eds.). New York: Cambridge University Press.

Chatterjee, A., Mahanti, G. K., & Chatterjee, A. (2012). Design of a fully digital controlled reconfigurable switched beam conconcentric ring array antenna using firefly and particle swarm optimization algorithm. *Progress in Elelectromagnetic Research B, 36*, 113–131. doi:10.2528/PIERB11083005

Chatterjee, A., Mahanti, K., & Ghatak, G. (2014). Synthesis of satellite footprint patterns from rectangular planar array antenna by using swarm-based optimization algorithms. *Int. J. Satell. Commun. Network, 32*(1), 25–47. doi:10.1002/sat.1055

Chaturvedi, D. K. (2008). *Soft computing: techniques and its applications in electrical engineering.* Berlin: Springer. doi:10.1007/978-3-540-77481-5

Chaturvedi, K. T., Pandit, M., & Srivastava, L. (2008). Self-organizing hierarchical particle swarm optimization for non-convex economic dispatch. *IEEE Transactions on Power Systems, 23*(3), 1079–1087. doi:10.1109/TPWRS.2008.926455

Chaves-González, J. M., Vega-Rodríguez, M. A., & Granado-Criado, J. M. (2013). A multiobjective swarm intelligence approach based on artificial bee colony for reliable DNA sequence design. *Engineering Applications of Artificial Intelligence, 26*(9), 2045–2057. doi:10.1016/j.engappai.2013.04.011

Chawla, M., & Duhan, M. (2015). Bat algorithm: A survey of the state-of-the-art. *Applied Artificial Intelligence, 29*(6), 617–634. doi:10.1080/08839514.2015.1038434

Chen, C.-L., & Wang, S.-C. (1993). Branch-and-bound scheduling for thermal generating units. *Energy Conversion. IEEE Transactions on, 8*(2), 184–189.

Chen, G. (2006). Natural exponential Inertia Weight strategy in particle swarm optimization. *Intelligent Control and Automation, WCICA, 1*, 3672–3675. doi:10.1109/WCICA.2006.1713055

Cheng, R., & Jin, Y. (2015, February). A Competitive Swarm Optimizer for Large Scale Optimization. *IEEE Transactions On Cybernetics*, *45*(2), 191–204. doi:10.1109/TCYB.2014.2322602 PMID:24860047

Cheng, S., Shi, Y., Qin, Q., & Ting, T. (2012). Population Diversity Based Inertia Weight Adaptation in Particle Swarm Optimization. *IEEE International Conference on Advanced Computational Intelligence*, 395-403. doi:10.1109/ICACI.2012.6463194

Chen, S.-D., & Chen, J.-F. (2003). A direct Newton–Raphson economic emission dispatch. *International Journal of Electrical Power & Energy Systems*, *25*(5), 411–417. doi:10.1016/S0142-0615(02)00075-3

Chen, Z., Li, J., & Wei, L. (2007). A multiple kernel support vector machine scheme for feature selection and rule extraction from gene expression data of cancer tissue. *Artificial Intelligence in Medicine*, *41*(2), 161–175. doi:10.1016/j.artmed.2007.07.008 PMID:17851055

Chen, Z., & Tang, H. (2010). Cockroach swarm optimization. *IEEE 2nd International Conference on Computer Engineering and Technology (ICCET)*, 652–655.

Chen, Z., & Tang, H. (2011). Cockroach swarm optimization for vehicle routing problems. *Energy Procedia*, *13*, 30–35. doi:10.1016/j.proenv.2012.01.003

Che, Z.-H. (2010). Using fuzzy analytic hierarchy process and particle swarm optimisation for balanced and defective supply chain problems considering WEEE/RoHS directives. *International Journal of Production Research*, *48*(11), 3355–3381. doi:10.1080/00207540802702080

Chiang, K. T., & Chang, F. P. (2006). Optimization of the WEDM process of particle-reinforced material with multiple performance characteristics using grey relational analysis. *Journal of Materials Processing Technology*, *180*(1-3), 96–101. doi:10.1016/j.jmatprotec.2006.05.008

Choubey & Sanchita. (2016). GA_MLP NN: A Hybrid Intelligent System for Diabetes Disease Diagnosis. *International Journal of Intelligent Systems and Applications, 8*(1), 49-59.

Choubey, D. K., & Paul, S. (2016). Classification Techniques for Diagnosis of Diabetes Disease: A Review. *International Journal of Biomedical Engineering and Technology, 21*(1), 15-39.

Choubey, D. K., & Paul, S. (2017). GA_RBF NN: A Classification System for Diabetes. *International Journal of Biomedical Engineering and Technology, 23*(1), 71-93.

Choubey, D. K., & Sanchita. (2015). GA_J48graft DT: A Hybrid Intelligent System for Diabetes Disease Diagnosis. *International Journal of Bio-Science and Bio-Technology, 7*(5), 135–150.

Choubey, D. K., Paul, S., & Bhattacharjee, J. (2014). Soft Computing Approaches for Diabetes Disease Diagnosis: A Survey. *International Journal of Applied Engineering Research, 9*, 11715-11726.

Choubey, D. K., Paul, S., Kuamr, S., & Kumar, S. (2017). Classification of Pima Indian Diabetes Dataset using Naive Bayes with Genetic Algorithm as an Attribute Selection. In *Communication and Computing Systems: Proceedings of the International Conference on Communication and Computing System (ICCCS 2016)*, pp. 451-455. CRC Press Taylor Francis.

Ciuprina, G., Ioan, D., & Munteanu, I. (2002). Use of Intelligent-Particle Swarm Optimization in Electromagnetics. *IEEE Transactions on Magnetics*, *38*(2), 1037–1040. doi:10.1109/20.996266

Clerc, M. (1999). The swarm and the queen: towards a deterministic and adaptive particle swarm optimization. *Proc. 1999 ICEC*, 1951 – 1957. doi:10.1109/CEC.1999.785513

Clerc, M. (2010). *Particle Swarm Optimization*. Academic Press.

Clerc, M. (2012). *Standard Particle Swarm Optimisation, Particle Swarm Central*. Technical Report. Retrieved from http://clerc.maurice.free.fr/pso/SPSOdescriptionspdf

Clerc, M. (2006). *Particle Swarm Optimization*. International Scientific and Technical Encyclopedia. doi:10.1002/9780470612163

Clerc, M. (2010). From Theory to Practice in Particle Swarm Optimization. In *Handbook of Swarm Intelligence: Adaptation, Learning, and Optimization*. Springer.

Coelho, L. D. (2010). Gaussian quantum-behaved particle swarm optimization approaches for constrained engineering design problems. *Expert Systems with Applications*, *37*(2), 1676–1683. doi:10.1016/j.eswa.2009.06.044

Coello, C. A. C. (2002). Theoretical and numerical constraint-handling techniques used with evolutionary algorithms: A survey of the state of the art. *Computer Methods in Applied Mechanics and Engineering*, *191*(11–12), 1245–1287. doi:10.1016/S0045-7825(01)00323-1

Coello, C., Pulido, G. T., & Lechuga, M. S. (2004). Handling multiple objectives with particle swarm optimization. *IEEE Transactions on Evolutionary Computation*, *8*(3), 256–279. doi:10.1109/TEVC.2004.826067

Cooper, M. A., & Singleton, V. T. (2007). Review A survey of the 2001 to 2005 quartz crystal microbalance biosensor literature: Applications of acoustic physics to the analysis of biomolecular interactions. *Journal of Molecular Recognition*, *20*(3), 154–184. doi:10.1002/jmr.826 PMID:17582799

Cranshaw, W. (2013). *Bugs Rule!: An Introduction to the World of Insects*. Princeton, NJ: Princeton University Press.

Cristianini, N., & Shawe-Taylor, J. (2000). *An introduction to Support Vector Machines and other kernel-based learning methods*. New York, NY: Cambridge University Press. doi:10.1017/CBO9780511801389

Cuevas, E., Zaldívar, D., & Pérez-Cisneros, M. (2013b). A swarm optimization algorithm for multimodal functions and its application in multicircle detection. *Mathematical Problems in Engineering*, *2013*, 1–22.

Cui, Z., Zeng, J., & Yin, Y. (2008). An improved PSO with time-varying accelerator coefficients. *Eighth International conference on intelligent systems design and applications*, 638–643. doi:10.1109/ISDA.2008.86

Cummins, B., Cortez, R., Foppa, I. M., Walbeck, J., & Hyman, J. M. (2012). A spatial model of mosquito host-seeking behavior. *PLoS Computational Biology*, *8*(5), 1–13. doi:10.1371/journal.pcbi.1002500 PMID:22615546

Daho, M. E. H., Settouti, N., Lazouni, M. E. A., & Chikh, M. A. (2013). Recognition Of Diabetes Disease Using A New Hybrid Learning Algorithm For Nefclass. *8th International Workshop on Systems, Signal Processing and their Applications (WoSSPA)*.

Danillo, R., Pereira, M. A., Pazoti, L. A. M., & Pereira, J. P. P. (2014). A social-spider optimization approach for support vector machines parameters tuning. *Swarm Intelligence (SIS), IEEE Symposium*.

Darwin, C. (1859). *On the origins of species by means of natural selection*. London: Murray.

Datta, S., & Mahapatra, S. S. (2010). Modeling, simulation and parametric optimization of wire EDM process using response surface methodology coupled with grey-Taguchi technique. *International Journal of Engineering Science and Technology*, *2*(5), 162–183. doi:10.4314/ijest.v2i5.60144

Datta, S., Nandi, G., Bandyopadhyay, A., & Pal, P. K. (2009). Application of PCA based hybrid Taguchi method for multi-criteria optimization of submerged arc weld: A case study. *International Journal of Advanced Manufacturing Technology*, *45*(3-4), 276–286. doi:10.1007/s00170-009-1976-0

Davis, L. (Ed.). (1991). *Handbook of Genetic Algorithms*. New York: Van Nostrand Reinhold.

Deb, K., Pratap, A., Agarwal, S., & Meyarivan, T. (2002). A fast and elitist multiobjective genetic algorithm: NSGA-II. *IEEE Transactions on Evolutionary Computation, 6*(2), 182–197. doi:10.1109/4235.996017

Dehuri, S., Cho, S.-B., & Ghosh, A. (2008). Wasp: A Multi-agent System for Multiple Recommendations Problem. *4th International Conference on Next Generation Web Services Practices*.

del Cueto Belchi, A., Rothpfeffer, N., Pelegrí-Sebastia, J., Chilo, J., Rodriguez, D. G., & Sogorb, T. (2013). Sensor characterization for multisensor odor-discrimination system. *Sensors and Actuators. A, Physical, 191*(0), 68–72. doi:10.1016/j.sna.2012.11.039

del Valle, Y., Venayagamoorthy, G. K., Mohagheghi, S., Hernandez, J.-C., & Harley, R. G.del. (2008). Particle swarm optimization: Basic concepts, variants and applications in power systems. *IEEE Transactions on Evolutionary Computation, 12*(2), 171–195. doi:10.1109/TEVC.2007.896686

den Besten, M. (2000). *Ants for the single machine total weighted tardiness problem* (Master's thesis). University of Amsterdam.

den Bseten, M., Stützle, T., & Dorigo, M. (2000). Ant colony optimization for the total weighted tardiness problem. *Proceedings of PPSN-VI, Sixth International Conference on Parallel Problem Solving from Nature*, 1917, 611-620. doi:10.1007/3-540-45356-3_60

Deng, J. (1989). Introduction to Grey System. *Journal of Grey System, 1*, 1–24.

Dey, S., & Tripathi, B. (2013). Analyzing the effects of process variables (cutting rate surface roughness and gap current) of the wire electric discharge machining (WEDM)-a study. *International Journal of Engineering and Science Research, 3*, 168–172.

Dieu, V. N., & Ongsakul, W. (2010). Economic dispatch with emission and transmission constraints by augmented Lagrange Hopfield network. *Transaction in Power System Optimization, 1*.

Dieu, V. N., & Ongsakul, W. (2011). Hopfield Lagrange Network for Economic Load Dispatch. *Innovation in Power, Control, and Optimization: Emerging Energy Technologies: Emerging Energy Technologies*, 57.

Djelloul, H., Layeb, A., & Chikhi, S. (2015). Quantum inspired cuckoo search algorithm for graph colouring problem. *International Journal of Bio-inspired Computation, 7*(3), 183–194. doi:10.1504/IJBIC.2015.069554

Dogantekin, E., Dogantekin, A., Avci, D., & Avci, L. (2010). An Intelligent Diagnosis System For Diabetes On Linear Discriminant Analysis and Adaptive Network Based Fuzzy Inference System: LDA–ANFIS. *Digital Signal Processing, Elsevier, 20*(4), 1248–1255. doi:10.1016/j.dsp.2009.10.021

Donati, A. V., Montemanni, R., Casagrande, N., Rizzoli, A. E., & Gambardella, L. M. (2008). Time Dependent Vehicle Routing Problem with a Multi Ant Colony System. *European Journal of Operational Research, 185*(3), 1174–1191. doi:10.1016/j.ejor.2006.06.047

Dorigo, M., Maniezzo, V., & Colorni, A. (1991). *Positive feedback as a search strategy*. Technical Report 91-016, Politecnico di Milano.

Dorigo, M., Maniezzo, V., & Colorni, A. (1996). The ant system: optimization by a colony of cooperating agents. IEEE Transaction on Systems, Man, and Cybernetics- Part B, 26(1).

Dorigo, M. (1992). *Optimization, Learning and Natural Algorithm*. Milan, Italy: Dipartimento di Elettronica, Politecnico di Milano.

Dorigo, M., & Caro, G. D. (1999). Ant colony optimization: a new meta-heuristic. In *Proceedings of the 1999 Congress on Evolutionary Computation, 1999. CEC 99* (Vol. 2, p. 1477). http://doi.org/ doi:10.1109/CEC.1999.782657

Dorigo, M., Di, C., & Gambardella, L. M. (1999). Ant algorithms for discrete optimization. *Artificial Life*, *5*(2), 137–172. doi:10.1162/106454699568728 PMID:10633574

Dorigo, M., Maniezzo, V., & Colorni, A. (1996). Ant system: Optimization by a colony of cooperating agents. *IEEE Transactions on Systems, Man, and Cybernetics. Part B, Cybernetics*, *26*(1), 29–41. doi:10.1109/3477.484436 PMID:18263004

Dorigo, M., & Stutzle, T. (2004). *Ant Colony Optimization-A Bradford Book*. The MIT Press.

dos Santos Coelho, L. (2008). A quantum particle swarm optimizer with chaotic mutation operator. *Chaos, Solitons, and Fractals*, *37*(5), 1409–1418. doi:10.1016/j.chaos.2006.10.028

Doungsa-ard, Dahal, Hossain, & Suwannasart. (2008). GA-based automatic test data generation for UML state diagrams with parallel paths. In Advanced Design and Manufacture to Gain a Competitive Edge. Springer.

Duan, H., Yu, Y., Zou, J., & Feng, X. (2012). Ant colony optimization-based bio-inspired hardware: Survey and prospect. *Transactions of the Institute of Measurement and Control*, *34*(2-3), 318–333. doi:10.1177/0142331210366689

Duch, W. (2007). *What is Computational Intelligence and where is it going? In Challenges for computational intelligence* (pp. 1–13). Springer.

Dudely, B. (2015). BP Statistical Review of World Energy (64th ed.). BP.

Durairaj, M., Sudharsun, D., & Swamynathan, N. (2013). Analysis of Process Parameters in Wire EDM with Stainless Steel Using Single Objective Taguchi Method and Multi Objective Grey Relational Grade. *Procedia Engineering*, *64*, 868–877. doi:10.1016/j.proeng.2013.09.163

Durgun, I., & Yildiz, A. R. (2012). Structural design optimization of vehicle components using Cuckoo search Algorithm. *Materialpruefung/Materials Testing*, *54*(3), 185–188.

Duvvuru, N., & Swarup, K. S. (2011). A Hybrid Interior Point Assisted Differential Evolution Algorithm for Economic Dispatch. *IEEE Transactions on Power Systems*, *26*(2), 541–549. doi:10.1109/TPWRS.2010.2053224

Eberhart, R., & Shi, Y. (2001). Particle swarm optimization: developments, applications and resources. *Proc. IEEE Int. Conf. on Evolutionary Computation*, 81-86. doi:10.1109/CEC.2001.934374

Eberhart, R. C., & Shi, Y. 2000. Comparing inertia weights and constriction factors in particle swarm optimization. *Proc. of Congress on Evolutionary Computing*, 84–89. doi:10.1109/CEC.2000.870279

Eberhart, R., & Kennedy, J. (1995). A new optimizer using particle swarm theory. *Proceedings of the Sixth International Symposium on Micro Machine and Human Science*, 39 – 43. doi:10.1109/MHS.1995.494215

Eiben, A. E., Hinterding, R., & Michalewicz, Z. (1999). Parameter Control in Evolutionary Algorithms. *IEEE Transactions on Evolutionary Computation*, *3*(2), 124–141. doi:10.1109/4235.771166

El-Keib, A., & Ding, H. (1994). Environmentally constrained economic dispatch using linear programming. *Electric Power Systems Research*, *29*(3), 155–159. doi:10.1016/0378-7796(94)90010-8

Engelbrecht, A. P. (2013a). Particle swarm optimization: Global best or local best? *2013 BRICS Congress on Computational Intelligence and 11th Brazilian Congress on Computational Intelligence*, 124-135.

Engelbrecht, A. P. (2013b). Particle Swarm Optimization: Iteration Strategies Revisited. *BRICS Congress on Computational Intelligence & 11th Brazilian Congress on Computational Intelligence*.

Engelbrecht, P. (2005). *Fundamentals of Computational Swarm Intelligence.* John Wiley & Sons Ltd.

Ephzibah, E. P. (2011). Cost Effective Approach on Feature Selection using Genetic Algorithms and Fuzzy Logic for Diabetes Diagnosis. International Journal on Soft Computing, 2(1).

Esme, U., Sagbas, A., & Kahraman, F. (2009). Prediction of surface roughness in wire electrical discharge machining using design of experiments and neural networks, *Iranian Journal of Science and Technology, Transaction B, Engineering, 33,* 231-240.

Espejo, P. G., Ventura, S., & Herrera, F. (2010). A survey on the application of genetic programming to classification. *IEEE Transactions on Systems, Man and Cybernetics. Part C, Applications and Reviews, 40*(2), 121–144. doi:10.1109/TSMCC.2009.2033566

Evers, G. I., & Ben Ghalia, M. (2009). Regrouping Particle Swarm Optimization: A New Global Optimization Algorithm with Improved Performance Consistency Across Benchmarks. *IEEE International Conference on Systems, Man and Cybernetics, 3901-3908.* doi:10.1109/ICSMC.2009.5346625

Fang, Q., Meaney, P. M., & Paulsen, K. D. (2004). Microwave image reconstruction of tissue property dispersion characteristics utilizing multiple-frequency information. *IEEE Transactions on Microwave Theory and Techniques, 52*(8), 1866–1875. doi:10.1109/TMTT.2004.832014

Fan, H., & Zhong, Y. (2012). A rough set approach to feature selection based on wasp swarm optimization. *Journal of Computer Information Systems, 8,* 1037–1045.

Farag, A., Al-Baiyat, S., & Cheng, T. (1995). Economic load dispatch multiobjective optimization procedures using linear programming techniques. *IEEE Transactions on Power Systems, 10*(2), 731–738. doi:10.1109/59.387910

Farooq, M. (2006). *From the wisdom of the hive to intelligent routing in telecommunication networks: A step towards intelligent network management through natural engineering* (Unpublished doctoral thesis). Universität Dortmund.

Feng, Y., Teng, G., Wang, A., & Yao, Y. (2007). Chaotic Inertia Weight in Particle Swarm Optimization. *Innovative Computing, Information and Control, ICICIC'07. Second International Conference on,* 475.

Ferrari, M., Ferrari, V., & Kanazawa, K. K. (2008). Dual-harmonic oscillator with frequency and resistance outputs for quartz resonator sensors. *Sensors, IEEE, 1261–1264.* doi:10.1109/ICSENS.2008.4716673

Ferreira, G. N. M., da Silva, A. C., & Tome, B. (2009). Acoustic wave biosensors : Physical models and biological applications of quartz crystal microbalance. *Trends in Biotechnology, 27*(October), 689–697. doi:10.1016/j.tibtech.2009.09.003 PMID:19853941

Ferreiro Garcia, R., Calovo-Rolle, J. L., Pérez Castelo, J., & Romero Gómez, M. (2014). On the monitoring task of solar thermal fluid transfer systems using NN based models and rule based techniques. *Engineering Applications of Artificial Intelligence, 27*(0), 129–136. doi:10.1016/j.engappai.2013.06.011

Fhager, A., Gustafsson, M., & Nordebo, S. (2012). Image reconstruction in microwave tomography using a dielectric Debye model. *IEEE Transactions on Microwave Theory and Techniques, 59,* 156–166. PMID:21937340

Filipovic, D. F., & Rebeiz, G. M. (1993). Double-slot antennas on extended hemispherical and elliptical quartz dielectric lenses. *International Journal of Infrared and Millimeter Waves, 14*(10), 1905–1924. doi:10.1007/BF02096363

Fisher, R. A. (1951). *Design of experiments, Edinburgh.* Oliver and Boyd.

Fister, J., Fister, D., & Yang, X.-S. (2013). A hybrid bat algorithm. *Elektrotehniski Vestnik/Electrotechnical Review, 80*(1-2), 1–7.

Fister, I. Jr, Perc, M., Kamal, S. M., & Fister, I. (2015). A review of chaos-based firefly algorithms: Perspectives and research challenges. *Applied Mathematics and Computation, 252*, 155–165. doi:10.1016/j.amc.2014.12.006

Fister, I., Yang, X.-S., & Fister, D. (2014). Firefly algorithm: A brief review of the expanding literature. *Studies in Computational Intelligence, 516*, 347–360. doi:10.1007/978-3-319-02141-6_17

Fister, I., Yang, X.-S., Fister, D., & Fister, I. (2014). Cuckoo Search: A Brief Literature Review. In X.-S. Yang (Ed.), *Cuckoo Search and Firefly Algorithm* (Vol. 516, pp. 49–62). Cham: Springer International Publishing. doi:10.1007/978-3-319-02141-6_3

Fister, J., Fister, D., & Fistar, I. (2013). A comprehensive review of Cuckoo search: Variants and hybrids. *International Journal of Mathematical Modelling and Numerical Optimisation, 4*(4), 387–409. doi:10.1504/IJMMNO.2013.059205

Fleming, P. J., & Pashkevich, A. P. (1985). Computer aided control system design using a multiobjective optimization approach. *Proceedings of the IEE Control 85 Conference*, 174–179.

Fogel, D. B. (1992). *Evolving Artificial Intelligence* (Ph.D. Thesis). University of California, San Diego, CA.

Fogel, D. B. (1993). Evolving Behaviours in the Iterated Prisoners Dilemma. *Evolutionary Computation, 1*(1), 77–97. doi:10.1162/evco.1993.1.1.77

Fogel, D. B., Fogel, L. J., & Atmar, J. W. (1998). Meta-Evolutionary Programming. *Informatica, 18*(4), 387–398.

Fogel, L. J., Owens, A. J., & Walsh, M. J. (1966). *Artificial Intelligence Through Simulated Evolution*. Chichester, UK: John Wiley.

Fonseca, C. M., & Fleming, P. J. (1995). Multiobjective genetic algorithms made easy: Selection, sharing, and mating restriction. In A. M. S. Zalzala (Ed.), *Proceedings of the First International Conference on Genetic Algorithms in Engineering Systems: Innovations and Applications (GALESIA 95)*. Institution of Electrical Engineers.

Fonseca, C. M., & Fleming, P. J. (1993). Genetic algorithms for multiobjective optimization: Formulation, discussion and generalization. In S. Forrest (Ed.), *Proceedings of the Fifth International Conference on Genetic Algorithms*. Morgan Kauffman Publishers.

Forghany, Z., Davarynejad, M., & Snaar-Jagalska, B. E. (2012). Gene regulatory network model identification using artificial bee colony and swarm intelligence. In *IEEE World Congress on Computational Intelligence (WCCI)* (pp. 1–6). Brisbane, Australia: IEEE. doi:10.1109/CEC.2012.6256461

Fornarelli, G., Giaquinto, A., & Mescia, M. (2013). *Optimum design and characterization of rare earth-doped fibre amplifiers by means of particle swarm optimization approach*. Hershey, PA: IGI Global.

Fornarelli, G., & Mescia, M. (2013). *Swarm Intelligence for Electric and Electronic Engineering*. Hershey, PA: IGI Global. doi:10.4018/978-1-4666-2666-9

Fourman, M. P. (1985). Compaction of symbolic layout using genetic algorithms. In J. Grefenstette (Ed.), *Proceedings of the First International Conference on Genetic Algorithms*. Lawrence Erlbaum Associates.

Fu, X., Liu, W., Zhang, B., & Deng, H. (2013). Quantum Behaved Particle Swarm Optimization with Neighborhood Search for Numerical Optimization. *Mathematical Problems in Engineering, 2013*, 469723. doi:10.1155/2013/469723

Gambardella, L. M., Taillard, É. D., & Dorigo, M. (1999). Ant colonies for the quadratic assignment problem. *The Journal of the Operational Research Society, 50*(2), 167–176. doi:10.1057/palgrave.jors.2600676

Gandhi, V., Prasad, G., Coyle, D., Behera, L., & McGinnity, T. M. (2014). Quantum Neural Network-Based EEG Filtering for a Brain-Computer Interface. *Ieee Transactions on Neural Networks and Learning Systems*, *25*(2), 278–288. doi:10.1109/TNNLS.2013.2274436 PMID:24807028

Gandomi, A. H., & Yang, X.-S. (2014). Chaotic bat algorithm. *Journal of Computational Science*, *5*(2), 224–232. doi:10.1016/j.jocs.2013.10.002

Gandomi, A. H., Yang, X.-S., & Alavi, A. H. (2011). Mixed variable structural optimization using Firefly Algorithm. *Computers & Structures*, *89*(23-24), 2325–2336. doi:10.1016/j.compstruc.2011.08.002

Gandomi, A. H., Yang, X.-S., Alavi, A. H., & Talatahari, S. (2013). Bat algorithm for constrained optimization tasks. *Neural Computing & Applications*, *22*(6), 1239–1255. doi:10.1007/s00521-012-1028-9

Gandomi, A. H., Yang, X.-S., Talatahari, S., & Alavi, A. H. (2013). Firefly algorithm with chaos. *Communications in Nonlinear Science and Numerical Simulation*, *18*(1), 89–98. doi:10.1016/j.cnsns.2012.06.009

Ganji, M. F., Abadeh, M. S. (2010). Using fuzzy Ant Colony Optimization for Diagnosis of Diabetes Disease. *Proceedings of ICEE.*

Gao, Y., An, X., & Liu, J. (2008). A Particle Swarm Optimization Algorithm with Logarithm Decreasing Inertia Weight and Chaos Mutation. *Computational Intelligence and Security, International Conference on*, *1*, 61-65.

Gao, C., Zhan, Z., Wang, S., He, N., & Li, L. (2013). Research on WEDM Process Optimization for PCD Micro Milling Tool. *Procedia CIRP*, *6*, 209–214. doi:10.1016/j.procir.2013.03.035

Gao, W.-F., & Liu, S.-Y. (2012). A modified artificial bee colony algorithm. *Computers & Operations Research*, *39*(3), 687–697. doi:10.1016/j.cor.2011.06.007 PMID:23086528

Gao, Y., & Duan, Y. (2007). A New Particle Swarm Optimization Algorithm with Random Inertia Weight and Evolution Strategy. *International Conference on Computational Intelligence and Security Workshops*, 199-203.

García-Martinez, G., Bustabad, E. A., Perrot, H., Gabrielli, C., Bucur, B., Lazerges, M., & Vives, A. A. et al. (2011). Development of a Mass Sensitive Quartz Crystal Microbalance (QCM)-Based DNA Biosensor Using a 50 MHz Electronic Oscillator Circuit. *Sensors (Basel, Switzerland)*, *11*(8), 7656–7664. doi:10.3390/s110807656 PMID:22164037

Garey, M. R., & Johnson, D. S. (1979). *Computers and Intractability. A Guide to the theory of NP Completeness*. W.H. Freeman and Co.

Garg, M. P., Jain, A., & Bhushan, G. (2012). Modelling and multi-objective optimization of process parameters of wire electrical discharge machining using non-dominated sorting genetic algorithm-II. *Proceedings of the IMechE, Part B: Journal of Engineering Manufacture.*, *226*(12), 1986–2001. doi:10.1177/0954405412462778

Gauri, S. K., & Chakraborty, S. (2009). Multi-response optimisation of WEDM process using principal component analysis. *International Journal of Advanced Manufacturing Technology*, *41*(7-8), 741–748. doi:10.1007/s00170-008-1529-y

Gherbi, Y. A., Bouzeboudja, H., & Lakdja, F. (2014). Economic dispatch problem using bat algorithm. *Leonardo Journal of Sciences,* (24), 75-84.

Ghodsiyeh, D., Lahiji, M. A., Ghanbari, M., Golshan, A., & Shirdar, M. R. (2012). Optimizing rough cut in WEDMing titanium alloy (Ti6Al4V) by brass wire using the Taguchi method. *Journal of Basic and Applied Scientific Research*, *2*, 7488–7496.

Goldberg, D. E. (1989). Genetic algorithms in search, optimization, and machine learning. *NN Schraudolph and J.*, *3*, 1.

Goldberg, D. E. (1989). *Genetic Algorithms in Search*. Reading, MA: Optimization, and Machine Learning, Addison Wiley.

Goldberg, D. E., & Richardson, J. (1987). Genetic algorithms with sharing for multimodal function optimization. In J. Grefenstette (Ed.), *Proceedings of the Second International Conference on Genetic Algorithms*. Lawrence Erlbaum Associates.

Goncalves, L. B., Bernardes, M. M., & Vellasco, R. (2006). Inverted Hierarchical Neuro–Fuzzy BSP System: A Novel Neuro-Fuzzy Model for Pattern Classification and Rule Extraction in Databases. IEEE Transactions on Systems, Man, and Cybernetics—Part C: Applications and Reviews, 36(2).

Grattan-Guinness, I. (1976). Fuzzy Membership Mapped onto Intervals and Many-Valued Quantities. *Mathematical Logic Quarterly*, 22(1), 149–160. doi:10.1002/malq.19760220120

Gulbag, A., & Temurtas, F. (2006). A study on quantitative classification of binary gas mixture using neural networks and adaptive neuro-fuzzy inference systems. *Sensors and Actuators. B, Chemical*, 115(1), 252–262. doi:10.1016/j.snb.2005.09.009

Guo, Y., Li, X., Bai, G., & Ma, J. (2012). Time Series Prediction Method Based on LS-SVR with Modified Gaussian RBF. In T. Huang, Z. Zeng, C. Li, & C. Leung (Eds.), *Neural Information Processing* (Vol. 7664, pp. 9–17). Springer Berlin Heidelberg; doi:10.1007/978-3-642-34481-7_2

Gupta, S., & Zia, R. (2001). Quantum neural networks. *Journal of Computer and System Sciences*, 63(3), 355–383. doi:10.1006/jcss.2001.1769

Haleja, P., & Lin, C.-Y. (1992). Genetic search strategies in multicriterion optimal design. *Structural Optimization*, 4(2), 99–107. doi:10.1007/BF01759923

Han, F., Jiang, J., & Yu, D. (2007). Influence of machining parameters on surface roughness in finish cut of WEDM. *International Journal of Advanced Manufacturing Technology*, 34(5-6), 538–546. doi:10.1007/s00170-006-0629-9

Han, K.-H., & Kim, J.-H. (2002). Quantum-inspired evolutionary algorithm for a class of combinatorial optimization. *IEEE Transactions on Evolutionary Computation*, 6(6), 580–593. doi:10.1109/TEVC.2002.804320

Han, X., Gooi, H., & Kirschen, D. S. (2001). Dynamic economic dispatch: Feasible and optimal solutions. *IEEE Transactions on Power Systems*, 16(1), 22–28. doi:10.1109/59.910777

Harman, Mansouri, & Zhang. (2009). *Search based software engineering: A comprehensive analysis and review of trends techniques and applications*. Technical Report TR-09-03, Department of Computer Science, King's College London.

Harman, M. (2010). Why source code analysis and manipulation will always be important (keynote). *10th IEEE International Working Conference on Source Code Analysis and Manipulation*.

Harman, M., & Jones, B. F. (2001). Search based software engineering. *Information and Software Technology*, 43(14), 833–839. doi:10.1016/S0950-5849(01)00189-6

Hassanien, A. E., & Emary, E. (2015). *Swarm Intelligence: Principles, Advances, and Applications*. CRC Press. doi:10.1201/b19133

Heiberger, R. M., & Neuwirth, E. (2009). Polynomial regression. In *R Through Excel* (pp. 269–284). Springer New York; doi:10.1007/978-1-4419-0052-4_11

Helwig, S., Branke, J., & Mostaghim, S. M. (2013). Experimental Analysis of Bound Handling Techniques in Particle Swarm Optimization. *Evolutionary Computation. IEEE Transactions*, 17(2), 259–271.

Hemant & Pushpavathi. (2007). *A novel approach to predict diabetes by Cascading Clustering and Classification*. Academic Press.

Hewidy, M. S., El-Taweel, T. A., & El-Safty, M. F. (2005). Modelling the machining parameters of wire electrical discharge machining of Inconel 601 using RSM. *Journal of Materials Processing Technology, 169*(2), 328–336. doi:10.1016/j.jmatprotec.2005.04.078

Hidalgo, D., Melin, P., & Castillo, O. (2012). An optimization method for designing type-2 fuzzy inference systems based on the footprint of uncertainty using genetic algorithms. *Expert Systems with Applications, 39*(4), 4590–4598. doi:10.1016/j.eswa.2011.10.003

Hindi, K. S., & Ab Ghani, M. (1991). Dynamic economic dispatch for large scale power systems: A Lagrangian relaxation approach. *International Journal of Electrical Power & Energy Systems, 13*(1), 51–56. doi:10.1016/0142-0615(91)90018-Q

Hinterding, R., Michalewicz, Z., & Peachey, T. (1996). Self-adaptive genetic algorithm for numeric functions. *Lecture Notes in Computer Science, 1141*, 420–429. doi:10.1007/3-540-61723-X_1006

Hogg, T., & Portnov, D. (2000). Quantum optimization. *Information Sciences, 128*(3), 181–197. doi:10.1016/S0020-0255(00)00052-9

Hölldobler & Wilson. (2009). *The Superorganism - The Beauty Elegance and Strangeness of Insect Societies*. W. W. Norton & Company.

Horng, M.-H. (2011). vector quantization using the firefly algorithm for image compression. *Expert Systems with Applications, 38*.

Horng, M.-H., & Jiang, T. W. (2010). The codebook design of image vector quantization based on the firefly algorithm. Computational Collective Intelligence. *Technologies and Applications, LNCS, 6423*, 438–447.

Horng, M.-H., & Liou, R.-J. (2011). Multilevel minimum cross entropy threshold selection based on the firefly algorithm. *Expert Systems with Applications, 38*(12), 14805–14811. doi:10.1016/j.eswa.2011.05.069

Hornik, K., Stinchcombe, M., & White, H. (1989). Multilayer feedforward networks are universal approximators. *Neural Networks, 2*(5), 359–366. doi:10.1016/0893-6080(89)90020-8

Horn, J., & Nafpliotis, N. (1993). Multiobjective optimization using the niched Pareto genetic algorithm. In *IlliGAL Report 93005*. Urbana, IL: University of Illinois at Urbana-Champaign.

Hosseini, S. M. (2014). Optimization of Microgrid Using Quantum Inspired Evolutionary Algorithm. *International Journal of Intelligent Systems and Applications, 6*(9), 47–53. doi:10.5815/ijisa.2014.09.06

Hota, P., Barisal, A., & Chakrabarti, R. (2010). Economic emission load dispatch through fuzzy based bacterial foraging algorithm. *International Journal of Electrical Power & Energy Systems, 32*(7), 794–803. doi:10.1016/j.ijepes.2010.01.016

Hsieh, T.-J., & Yeh, W.-C. (2012). Penalty guided bees search for redundancy allocation problems with a mix of components in series–parallel systems. *Computers & Operations Research, 39*(11), 2688–2704. doi:10.1016/j.cor.2012.02.002

Hu, X., & Eberhart, R. (2002). Adaptive Particle Swarm Optimization: Detection And Response to Dynamic Systems. *Proceedings of the IEEE Congress on Evolutionary Computation, CEC2002*, 1666-1670.

Huang, J. T., & Liao, Y. S. (2003). Application of grey relational analysis to machining parameter determination of wire electrical discharge machining. *International Journal of Production Research, 41*, 1244–1256. doi:10.1080/1352816031000074973

Huang, J. T., Liao, Y. S., & Hsue, W. J. (1999). Determination of finish-cutting operation number and machining-parameters setting in wire electrical discharge machining. *Journal of Materials Processing Technology, 87*(1-3), 69–81. doi:10.1016/S0924-0136(98)00334-3

Huang, K., Zhou, Y., & Wang, Y. (2011). Niching glowworm swarm optimization algorithm with mating behavior. *Journal of Information and Computational Science, 8,* 4175–4184.

Huang, M. S., & Lin, T. Y. (2008). Simulation of a regression-model and PCA based searching method developed for setting the robust injection molding parameters of multi-quality characteristics. *International Journal of Heat and Mass Transfer, 51*(25-26), 5828–5837. doi:10.1016/j.ijheatmasstransfer.2008.05.016

Huang, T., & Mohan, A. S. (2004). A hybrid boundary condition for robust particle swarm optimization. *IEEE Antennas and Wireless Propagation Letters, 4*(1), 112–117. doi:10.1109/LAWP.2005.846166

Hu, M., Wu, T., & Weir, J. (2013). An Adaptive Particle Swarm Optimization With Multiple Adaptive Methods. *IEEE Transactions On Evolutionary Computation, VOL., 17*(5), 705–720. doi:10.1109/TEVC.2012.2232931

Hunter, A. C. (2009). Application of the quartz crystal microbalance to nanomedicine. *J. Biomed. Nanotechnol., 5*(6), 669–675. doi:10.1166/jbn.2009.1083 PMID:20201228

Immanuel Selvakumar, A., & Thanushkodi, K. (2007, February). A New Particle Swarm Optimization Solution to Nonconvex Economic Dispatch Problems. *IEEE Transactions on Power Systems, 22*(1), 42–51. doi:10.1109/TPWRS.2006.889132

Ivanhoe, L. (1995). Future world oil supplies: There is a finite limit. *World Oil, 216,* 77–77.

Iwasaki, N., Yasuda, K., & Ueno, G. (2006). Dynamic Parameter Tuning of Particle Swarm Optimization. *IEEJ Trans, 1,* 353–363.

Jaco, F., Schutte, F., & Groenwold, A. A. (2005). A study of global optimization using particle swarms. *Journal of Global Optimization, 31*(1), 93–108. doi:10.1007/s10898-003-6454-x

Jadoun, V. K., Gupta, N., Niazi, K. R., & Swamkar, A. (2015). Modulated particle swarm optimization for economic emission dispatch. *International Journal of Electrical Power & Energy Systems, 73,* 80–88. doi:10.1016/j.ijepes.2015.04.004

Jahn, K.-U. (1975). Intervall-wertige Mengen. *Mathematische Nachrichten, 68*(1), 115–132. doi:10.1002/mana.19750680109

Jangra, K., Grover, S., & Aggarwal, A. (2011). Simultaneous optimization of material removal rate and surface roughness for WEDM of WCCo composite using grey relational analysis along with Taguchi method. *International Journal of Industrial Engineering Computations, 2*(3), 479–490. doi:10.5267/j.ijiec.2011.04.005

Janson, S., & Middendorf, M. (2005). A hierarchical particle swarm optimizer and its adaptive variant. *IEEE Transactions on Systems, Man, and Cybernetics. Part B, Cybernetics, 35*(6), 1272–1282. doi:10.1109/TSMCB.2005.850530 PMID:16366251

Jayalakshmi, T., & Santhakumaran, A. (2010). A Novel Classification Method for Diagnosis of Diabetes Mellitus Using Artificial Neural Networks. *International Conference on Data Storage and Data Engineering,* 159-163. doi:10.1109/DSDE.2010.58

Jiang, S., Ji, Z., & Shen, Y. (2014). A novel hybrid particle swarm optimization and gravitational search algorithm for solving economic emission load dispatch problems with various practical constraints. *International Journal of Electrical Power & Energy Systems, 55,* 628–644. doi:10.1016/j.ijepes.2013.10.006

Jin, Y., Okabe, T., & Sendhoff, B. (2001). Adapting weighted aggregation for multiobjective evolutionary optimization. *Proceedings of the Genetic and Evolutionary Computation Conference (GECCO 2001),* 1042–1049.

Jin, H., Dong, S. R., Luo, J. K., & Milne, W. I. (2011). Generalised Butterworth-Van Dyke equivalent circuit for thin-film bulk acoustic resonator. *Electronics Letters, 47*(7), 424–426. doi:10.1049/el.2011.0343

Jin, J., & Rahmat-Samii, Y. (2007). Advances in Particle Swarm Optimization for Antenna Designs: Real-Number, Binary, Single-Objective and Multiobjective Implementations. *IEEE Transactions on Antennas and Propagation, 55*(3), 556–567. doi:10.1109/TAP.2007.891552

Jin, X., Liang, Y., Tian, D., & Zhuang, F. (2013). Particle swarm optimization using dimension selection methods. *Applied Mathematics and Computation, 219*(10), 5185–5197. doi:10.1016/j.amc.2012.11.020

Jin, Y., Okabe, T., & Sendhoff, B. (2001). Dynamic weighted aggregation for evolutionary multi-objective optimization: Why does it work and how?. In *Proceedings of the 2001enetic and Evolutionary Computation Conference (GECCO 2001)*. Morgan Kaufmann Publishers.

Ji-Yuan, F., & Lan, Z. (1998). Real-time economic dispatch with line flow and emission constraints using quadratic programming. *IEEE Transactions on Power Systems, 13*(2), 320–325. doi:10.1109/59.667345

Johnson, D. E. (1998). *Applied multivariate methods for data analysis*. Pacific Grove, CA: Duxbury.

Jones, B., Sthamer, H., & Eyres, D. (1996). Automatic structural testing using genetic algorithms. *Software Engineering Journal, 11*(5), 299–306. doi:10.1049/sej.1996.0040

Jordehi, A. (2015). Enhanced leader PSO (ELPSO): A new PSO variant for solving global optimisation problems. *Applied Soft Computing, 26*, 401–417. doi:10.1016/j.asoc.2014.10.026

Ju, L., Du, Q., & Gunzburger, M. (2001). *Probabilistic methods for centroidal Voronoi tessellations and their parallel implementations*. Penn State Department of Mathematics Report No. AM250

Jun, S., Wenbo, X., & Bin, F. (2004). *A global search strategy of quantum-behaved particle swarm optimization*. Paper presented at the Cybernetics and Intelligent Systems, 2004 IEEE Conference on.

Kacprzyk, J. (2015). Computational Intelligence and Soft Computing: Closely Related but Not the Same. In L. Argüelles Méndez & R. Seising (Eds.), *Accuracy and Fuzziness. A Life in Science and Politics* (Vol. 323, pp. 267–280). Cham: Springer International Publishing. doi:10.1007/978-3-319-18606-1_26

Kahraman, C., Öztayşi, B., & Çevik Onar, S. (2016). A Comprehensive Literature Review of 50 Years of Fuzzy Set Theory. *International Journal of Computational Intelligence Systems, 9*(sup1), 3–24. http://doi.org/10.1080/18756891.2016.1180817

Kahramanli, H., & Allahverdi, N. (2008). Design of a hybrid system for the diabetes and heart diseases. *Expert Systems with Applications, Elsevier, 35*(1-2), 82–89. doi:10.1016/j.eswa.2007.06.004

Kak, S. C. (1995). Quantum neural computing. *Advances in Imaging and Electron Physics, 94*, 259–313. doi:10.1016/S1076-5670(08)70147-2

Kalaiselvi & Nasira. (2014). A New Approach for Diagnosis of Diabetes and Prediction of Cancer using ANFIS. *World Congress on Computing and Communication Technologies*. IEEE. doi:10.1109/WCCCT.2014.66

Kamalapur, S., & Patil, V. (2012). Analysis of particle trajectories and monitoring velocity behaviour in particle swarm optimization. *International Conference on Hybrid Intelligent Systems*, 4-7.

Kamalapur, S., & Patil, V. (2014). Adaptive Random Link PSO with Link Change Variations and Confinement Handling. *International Journal of Intelligent Systems and Applications, 7*(1), 62–72. doi:10.5815/ijisa.2015.01.06

Kanlayasiri, K., & Boonmung, S. (2007). Effects of wire-EDM machining variables on surface roughness of newly developed DC 53 die steel: Design of experiments and regression model. *Journal of Materials Processing Technology, 192-193*, 59–464. doi:10.1016/j.jmatprotec.2007.04.085

Kapoor, J., Singh, S., & Khamba, J. S. (2012). Effect of cryogenic treated brass wire electrode on material removal rate in wire electrical discharge machining, *Proc. Inst. Mech. Eng. Part C. Journal of Mechanical Engineering Science*, *226*(11), 2750–2758. doi:10.1177/0954406212438804

Karaboga, D. (2005). *An idea based on honey bee swarm for numerical optimization*. Technical Report TR06, Computer Engineering Department, Engineering Faculty, Erciyes University.

Karaboga, D. (2005). *An idea based on honey bee swarm for numerical optimization*. Technical report-tr06, Erciyes University, Engineering Faculty, Computer Engineering Department.

Karaboga, D., & Akay, B. (2009). A comparative study of Artificial Bee Colony algorithm. *Applied Mathematics and Computation*, *214*(1), 108–132. doi:10.1016/j.amc.2009.03.090

Karaboga, D., & Akay, B. (2009). A comparative study of Artificial Bee Colony Algorithm. *Applied Mathematics and Computation*, 214.

Karaboga, D., & Basturk, B. (2007). A powerful and efficient algorithm for numerical function optimization: Artificial bee colony (ABC) algorithm. *Journal of Global Optimization*, *39*(3), 459–471. doi:10.1007/s10898-007-9149-x

Karaboga, D., & Basturk, B. (2007). On the performance of artificial bee colony (ABC) algorithm'. *Applied Soft Computing*, 687–697.

Karaboga, D., & Ozturk, C. (2011). A novel clustering approach: Artificial Bee Colony (ABC) algorithm. *Applied Soft Computing*, *11*(1), 652–657. doi:10.1016/j.asoc.2009.12.025

Karatsiolis, S., & Schizas, C. N. (2012). Region based Support vector machine algorithm for Medical Diagnosis on PIMA Indian Diabetes Dataset. *Proceedings of the IEEE 12th International Conference on Bioinformatics & Bioengineering (BIBE)*, 11-13.

Karayiannis, N. B., Mukherjee, A., Glover, J. R., Frost, J. D., Hrachovy, R. A., & Mizrahi, E. M. (2006). An evaluation of quantum neural networks in the detection of epileptic seizures in the neonatal electroencephalogram. *Soft Computing*, *10*(4), 382–396. doi:10.1007/s00500-005-0498-4

Karegowda, A. G., Manjunath, A.S., & Jayaram, M.A. (2011). Application Of Genetic Algorithm Optimized Neural Network Connection Weights For Medical Diagnosis Of Pima Indians Diabetes. International Journal On Soft Computing, 2(2).

Kayaer, K., & Yildirim, T. (2003). Medical Diagnosis on Pima Indian Diabetes Using General Regression Neural Networks. IEEE.

Keller, L., & Gordon, É. (2009). *The lives of ants* (J. Grieve, Trans.). Oxford, UK: Oxford University Press Inc.

Kennedy, J. (2003). Bare bones particle swarms. *Swarm Intelligence Symposium, SIS '03. Proceedings of the 2003 IEEE*, 80-87.

Kennedy, J., & Eberhart, R. (1995). *Particle swarm optimization*. Paper presented at the Neural Networks, IEEE International Conference on.

Kennedy, J., & Eberhart, R. C. (1997). Discrete binary version of the particle swarm algorithm. *Proceedings of the IEEE International Conference on Systems, Man and Cybernetics*, *5*, 4104-4108. doi:10.1109/ICSMC.1997.637339

Kennedy, J. (1997). The particle swarm social adaptation of knowledge. *Proc. IEEE Int. Conf. Evolutionary Computation*, 303–308. doi:10.1109/ICEC.1997.592326

Kennedy, J. (1999). Small Worlds and Mega-Minds: Effects of Neighborhood Topology on Particle Swarm Performance. *Proceedings of the IEEE Congress on Evolutionary Computation*, 1931–1938. doi:10.1109/CEC.1999.785509

Kennedy, J. (2000). Stereotyping: Improving Particle Swarm Performance with Cluster Analysis. *Proceedings of the IEEE Congress on Evolutionary Computation*, 2, 1507–1512. doi:10.1109/CEC.2000.870832

Kennedy, J., & Eberhart, R. (1995). Particle swarm optimization. *IEEE International Conference on Neural Networks, 1995. Proceedings* (Vol. 4, pp. 1942–1948). http://doi.org/ doi:10.1109/ICNN.1995.488968

Kennedy, J., & Mendes, R. (2002). Population structure and particle swarm performance. *Proc. 2002 Cong. Evol. Comput.*, 1671-1675.

Kennedy, J., & Mendes, R. (2006). Neighborhood topologies in fully informed and best-of-neighborhood particle swarms. *IEEE Transactions on Systems, Man and Cybernetics. Part C, Applications and Reviews*, 36(4), 515–519. doi:10.1109/TSMCC.2006.875410

Kentzoglanakis, K., & Poole, M. (2009). Particle swarm optimization with an oscillating Inertia Weight. *Proceedings of the 11th Annual conference on Genetic and evolutionary computation*, 1749-1750. doi:10.1145/1569901.1570140

Khadwilard, A., Chansombat, S., Thepphakorn, T., Thapatsuwan, P., Chainat, W., & Pongcharoen, P. (2011). *Application of firefly algorithm and its parameter setting for job shop scheduling*. First Symposius on Hands-On Research and Development.

Khan, N. Z., Khan, Z. A., Siddiquee, A. N., & Chanda, A. K. (2014). Investigation on the effect of wire EDM process parameters on surface integrity of HSLA: A multi-performance characteristics optimization. *Prod. Manuf. Res*, 2(1), 501–518.

Khanna, R., & Singh, H. (2013). Performance analysis for D-3 material using response surface methodology on WEDM. *Int. J. Machining and Machinability of Materials*, 14(1), 45–65. doi:10.1504/IJMMM.2013.055120

Kimmel, D. W., LeBlanc, G., Meschievitz, M. E., & Cliffel, D. E. (2012). Electrochemical Sensors and Biosensors. *Analytical Chemistry*, 84(2), 685–707. http://doi.org/doi:10.1021/ac202878q doi:10.1021/ac202878q PMID:22044045

Kiranyaz, S., Ince, T., Yildirim, A., & Gabbouj, M. (2010, April). AlperYildirim, and Moncef Gabbouj, "Fractional Particle Swarm Optimization in Multidimensional Search Space. *IEEE Transactions on Systems, Man, and Cybernetics. Part B, Cybernetics*, 40(2), 298–319. doi:10.1109/TSMCB.2009.2015054

Komaki, G. M., & Kayvanfar, V. (2015). Grey Wolf Optimizer algorithm for the two-stage assembly flow shop scheduling problem with release time. *Journal of Computational Science*, 8, 109–120. doi:10.1016/j.jocs.2015.03.011

Konak, A., Coit, D. W., & Smith, A. E. (2006). Multi-objective optimization using genetic algorithms: A tutorial. *Reliability Engineering & System Safety*, 91(9), 992–1007. doi:10.1016/j.ress.2005.11.018

Konar, A. (2000). *Artificial intelligence and soft computing: behavioral and cognitive modeling of the human brain*. Boca Raton, FL: CRC Press.

Korel, B. (1990). Automated Software Test Data Generation. *Transactions on Software Engineering, SE-16*(8), 870–879. doi:10.1109/32.57624

Koridak, L. A., & Rahli, M. (2010). Optimization of the emission and economic dispatch by the genetic algorithm. *Przeglad Elektrotechniczny*, 86(11A), 363–366.

Köse, U., & Arslan, A. (2013). Chaotic Systems and Their Recent Implementations on Improving Intelligent Systems. Handbook of Research on Novel Soft Computing Intelligent Algorithms: Theory and Practical Applications, 69.

Kothari, D. P. (2012). *Power system optimization*. Paper presented at the Computational Intelligence and Signal Processing (CISP), 2012 2nd National Conference on. doi:10.1109/NCCISP.2012.6189669

Kouda, N., Matsui, N., & Nishimura, H. (2002). Image compression by layered quantum neural networks. *Neural Processing Letters, 16*(1), 67–80. doi:10.1023/A:1019708909383

Koza, J. R. (1990). *Genetic Programming: A Paradigm for Genetically Breeding Populations of Computer Programs to Solve Problems*. Report No. STAN-CS-90-1314, Stanford University.

Koza, J. R. (1992). *Genetic Programming: On the Programming of Computers by Means of Natural Selection*. Cambridge, MA: MIT Press.

Kozak, J., Rajurkar, K. P., & Wang, S. Z. (1994). Material removal in WEDM of PCD Blanks. *Journal of Manufacturing Science and Engineering, 116*, 363–369.

Krishnamurthy, S., & Tzoneva, R. (2012). *Impact of Price Penalty Factors on the Solution of the Combined Economic Emission Dispatch Problem using Cubic Criterion Functions*. New York: IEEE. doi:10.1109/PESGM.2012.6345312

Krishnan, G., & Krishnan, A. (2011). Study on techniques for combined economic and emission dispatch. *Global Journal of Researches in Engineering, Electrical and Electronical Engineering, 11*(5).

Krishnanand, K. N., Amruth, P., Guruprasad, M. H., Bidargaddi, S. V., & Ghose, D. (2006). Glowworm-inspired robot swarm for simultaneous taxis towards multiple radiation sources. In *IEEE International Conference on Robotics and Automation (ICRA)*, (pp. 958–963). IEEE. doi:10.1109/ROBOT.2006.1641833

Krishnanand, K. N., & Ghose, D. (2005). Detection of multiple source locations using glowworm metaphor with applications to collective robotics. In *IEEE Swarm Intelligence Symposium (SIS)* (pp. 84–91). IEEE. doi:10.1109/SIS.2005.1501606

Krohling, R., & Mendel, E. (2009). Bare bones particle swarm optimization with Gaussian or Cauchy jumps. *Proceeding of IEEE Congress of Evolutionary Computation*, 3285–3291. doi:10.1109/CEC.2009.4983361

Kułakowski, K., Matyasik, P., & Ernst, S. (2014). Modeling indoor lighting inspection robot behavior using Concurrent Communicating Lists. *Expert Systems with Applications, 41*(4), 984–998. doi:10.1016/j.eswa.2013.06.065

Kumar, R. M., Bavisetti, T., & Kiran, K. (2012). Optimization of combined economic and emission dispatch problem: a comparative study for 30 bus systems. *J Electr Electron Eng, 2*, 37-43.

Kumar, A., Kumar, V., & Kumar, J. (2012). Prediction of surface roughness in wire electrical discharge machining (WEDM) process based on response surface methodology. *IACSIT International Journal of Engineering and Technology, 2*, 708–719.

Kumar, A., Kumar, V., & Kumar, J. (2013). Multi-response optimization of process parameters based on response surface methodology for pure titanium using WEDM process. *International Journal of Advanced Manufacturing Technology, 68*(9-12), 2645–2688. doi:10.1007/s00170-013-4861-9

Kumar, M., & Mishra, S. K. (2015). Particle swarm optimization-based functional link artificial neural network for medical image denoising. In *Computational Vision and Robotics* (pp. 105–111). Springer India. doi:10.1007/978-81-322-2196-8_13

Kumar, M., Mishra, S. K., & Sahu, S. S. (2016). *Cat Swarm Optimization Based Functional Link Artificial Neural Network Filter for Gaussian Noise Removal from Computed Tomography Images*. Applied Computational Intelligence and Soft Computing, Hindawi.

Kuriakose, S., & Shunmugam, M. S. (2004). Characteristics of wire-electro discharge machined Ti6Al4V surface. *Materials Letters, 58*(17-18), 2231–2237. doi:10.1016/j.matlet.2004.01.037

Kuriakose, S., & Shunmugam, M. S. (2005). Multi-objective optimization of wire-electro discharge machining process by non-dominated sorting genetic algorithm. *Journal of Materials Processing Technology, 170*(1-2), 133–141. doi:10.1016/j.jmatprotec.2005.04.105

Kursawe, F. (1990). A variant of evolution strategies for vector optimization. In Parallel Problem Solving from Nature. Berlin, Germany: Springer-Verlag. doi:10.1007/BFb0029752

Laboudi, Z., & Chikhi, S. (2012). Comparison of genetic algorithm and quantum genetic algorithm. *Int. Arab J. Inf. Technol., 9*(3), 243–249.

Lau, T. W., Chung, C. Y., Wong, K. P., Chung, T. S., & Ho, S. L. (2009). Quantum-Inspired Evolutionary Algorithm Approach for Unit Commitment. *IEEE Transactions on Power Systems, 24*(3), 1503–1512. doi:10.1109/TPWRS.2009.2021220

Layeb, A. (2011). A novel quantum inspired cuckoo search for knapsack problems. *International Journal of Bio-inspired Computation, 3*(5), 297–305. doi:10.1504/IJBIC.2011.042260

Lec, R. M. (2001). Piezoelectric biosensors: recent advances and applications. *Proceedings of the 2001 IEEE International Frequency Control Symposium and PDA Exhibition*, 419–429. http://doi.org/ doi:10.1109/FREQ.2001.956265

Lee, C.-S. (2011). A Fuzzy Expert System for Diabetes Decision Support Application. Transactions on Systems, Man, and Cybernetics—Part B: Cybernetics, IEEE, 41(1).

Lee, J. Y., & Darwish, A. H. (2008). Multi-objective Environmental/Economic Dispatch Using the Bees Algorithm with Weighted Sum. *Proceedings of the EU-Korea Conference on Science and Technology (EKC2008)*, 267-274. doi:10.1007/978-3-540-85190-5_28

Lee, J., Yoo, M., & Lim, S. (2015). A Study of Ultra-Thin Single Layer Frequency Selective Surface Microwave Absorbers With Three Different Bandwidths Using Double Resonance. *IEEE Transactions on Antennas and Propagation, 63*(1), 221–230. doi:10.1109/TAP.2014.2365826

Li & Deb. (2010). Comparing lbest PSO Niching algorithms Using Different Position Update Rules. *WCCI 2010 IEEE World Congress on Computational Intelligence*, 1564-1571.

Li, C., & Yang, S. (2009). An Adaptive Learning Particle Swarm Optimizer for Function Optimization. *Proceeding of IEEE Congress on Evolutionary Computation*, 381-388. DOI doi:10.1109/CEC.2009.4982972

Li, H., & Gao, Y. (2009a). Particle Swarm Optimization Algorithm with Adaptive Threshold Mutation. *Proceeding of International Conference on Computational Intelligence and Security*, 129-132.

Li, J. W., Cheng, Y. M., & Chen, K. Z. (2014). Chaotic particle swarm optimization algorithm based on adaptive inertia weight. *The 26th Chinese Control and Decision Conference*, 1310-1315. doi:10.1109/CCDC.2014.6852369

Li, X., Fu, H., & Zhang, C. (2008). A self-adaptive particle swarm optimization algorithm. *Proceeding of International Conference on Computer Science and Software Engineering*, 186-189. DOI doi:10.1109/CSSE.2008.142

Li, Z., Ngambusabongsopa, R., Mohammed, E., & Eustache, N. (2011). A novel diversity guided particle swarm multi-objective optimization algorithm. *Optimization, 8*(10), 12.

Liang, Z.-X., & Glover, J. D. (1992). A zoom feature for a dynamic programming solution to economic dispatch including transmission losses. *IEEE Transactions on Power Systems, 7*(2), 544–550. doi:10.1109/59.141757

Liao, & Wang, J. (2011). Nonlinear, Inertia Weight Variation for Dynamic Adaptation in Particle Swarm Optimization ICSI, Part I. *LNCS, 6728*, 80-85.

Liao, G. C. (2010). *Using chaotic quantum genetic algorithm solving environmental economic dispatch of smart microgrid containing distributed generation system problems.* Paper presented at the 2010 International Conference on Power System Technology: Technological Innovations Making Power Grid Smarter, POWERCON2010. doi:10.1109/POWERCON.2010.5666468

Liao, G.-C. (2012). Solve environmental economic dispatch of Smart MicroGrid containing distributed generation system - Using chaotic quantum genetic algorithm. *International Journal of Electrical Power & Energy Systems, 43*(1), 779–787. doi:10.1016/j.ijepes.2012.06.040

Liao, H. C. (2006). Multi-response optimization using weighted principal component. *International Journal of Advanced Manufacturing Technology, 2006*(7-8), 720–725. doi:10.1007/s00170-004-2248-7

Liao, T., Aydin, D., & Stützle, T. (2013). Artificial bee colonies for continuous optimization: Experimental analysis and improvements. *Swarm Intelligence, 7*(4), 327–356. doi:10.1007/s11721-013-0088-5

Liao, W.-H., Kao, Y., & Li, Y.-S. (2011). A sensor deployment approach using glowworm swarm optimization algorithm in wireless sensor networks. *Expert Systems with Applications, 38*(10), 12180–12188. doi:10.1016/j.eswa.2011.03.053

Liao, Y. S., Huang, J. T., & Chen, Y. H. (2004). A study to achieve a fine surface finish in Wire EDM. *Journal of Materials Processing Technology, 149*(1-3), 165–171. doi:10.1016/j.jmatprotec.2003.10.034

Li, H., & Gao, Y. (2009b). Particle Swarm Optimization Algorithm with Exponent Decreasing Inertia Weight and Stochastic Mutation. *Second International Conference on Information and Computing Science*, 66-69. doi:10.1109/ICIC.2009.24

Lim, W., & Isa, N. (2014a). Particle swarm optimization with increasing topology connectivity. *Engineering Applications of Artificial Intelligence, 27*, 80–102. doi:10.1016/j.engappai.2013.09.011

Lim, W., & Isa, N. (2014b). Particle swarm optimization with adaptive time-varying topology connectivity. *Applied Soft Computing, 24*, 623–642. doi:10.1016/j.asoc.2014.08.013

Ling, S., Lam, H., Leung, F. H., & Lee, Y. (2003). *Improved genetic algorithm for economic load dispatch with valve-point loadings.* Paper presented at the Industrial Electronics Society, 2003. IECON'03. The 29th Annual Conference of the IEEE. doi:10.1109/IECON.2003.1280021

Lin, K. W., & Wang, C. C. (2010). Optimizing multiple quality characteristics of wire electrical discharge machining via Taguchi method-based gray analysis for magnesium alloy. *Journal of C.C.I.T., 39*, 23–34.

Liu, H., Su, R., Gao, Y., & Xu, R. (2009). Improved Particle Swarm Optimization Using Two Novel Parallel Inertia Weights. *Second International Conference on Intelligent Computation Technology and Automation*, 185-188 doi:10.1109/ICICTA.2009.53

Liu, W., Zhang, Y., Zeng, B., Niu, S., Zhang, J., & Xiao, Y. (2014). An Environmental-Economic Dispatch Method for Smart Microgrids Using VSS_QGA. *Journal of Applied Mathematics, 2014*, 1–11. doi:10.1155/2014/623216

Liu, Y., Qin, Z., Shi, Z., & Lu, J. (2007). Center particle swarm optimization. *Neurocomputing, 70*(4-6), 672–679. doi:10.1016/j.neucom.2006.10.002

Liu, Y., Wang, X., & Li, Y. (2012). A modified fruit-fly optimization algorithm aided PID controller designing. In *IEEE 10th World Congress on Intelligent Control and Automation* (pp. 233–238). Beijing, China: IEEE. doi:10.1109/WCICA.2012.6357874

Li, X. (2010). Niching Without Niching Parameters: Particle Swarm Optimization Using a Ring Topology. *IEEE Transactions on Evolutionary Computation, 14*(1), 150–169. doi:10.1109/TEVC.2009.2026270

Li, X., & Yao, X. (2012, April). Cooperatively Coevolving Particle Swarms for Large Scale Optimization. *IEEE Transactions on Evolutionary Computation, 16*(2), 210–224. doi:10.1109/TEVC.2011.2112662

Li, Y., Shao, X., & Cai, W. (2007). A consensus least squares support vector regression (LS-SVR) for analysis of near-infrared spectra of plant samples. *Talanta, 72*(1), 217–222. doi:10.1016/j.talanta.2006.10.022 PMID:19071605

Lok, Y. K., & Lee, T. C. (1997). Processing of advanced ceramics using the wire-cut EDM process. *Journal of Materials Processing Technology, 63*(1-3), 839–843. doi:10.1016/S0924-0136(96)02735-5

Low, M. Y. H., Chandramohan, M., & Choo, C. S. (2009). Application of multi-objective bee colony optimization algorithm to automated red teaming. Proceedings of IEEE 2009 Winter Simulation Conference, 1798–1808. doi:10.1109/WSC.2009.5429184

Lucchetta, P., Bernstein, C., Théry, M., Lazzari, C., & Desouhant, E. (2008). Foraging and associative learning of visual signals in a parasitic wasp. *Animal Cognition, 11*(3), 525–533. doi:10.1007/s10071-008-0144-5 PMID:18274795

Lucklum, R., & Hauptmann, P. (2006). Acoustic microsensors the challenge behind microgravimetry. *Analytical and Bioanalytical Chemistry, 384*(3), 667–682. doi:10.1007/s00216-005-0236-x PMID:16544392

Lu, S., Sun, C., & Lu, Z. (2010). An improved quantum-behaved particle swarm optimization method for short-term combined economic emission hydrothermal scheduling. *Energy Conversion and Management, 51*(3), 561–571. doi:10.1016/j.enconman.2009.10.024

Luukka, P. (2011). Feature selection using fuzzy entropy measures with similarity classifier. *Expert Systems with Applications, Elsevier, 38*(4), 4600–4607. doi:10.1016/j.eswa.2010.09.133

Lynn, N., & Suganthan, P. (2015). Heterogeneous comprehensive learning particle swarm optimization with enhanced exploration and exploitation. *Swarm and Evolutionary Computation, 24*, 11–24. doi:10.1016/j.swevo.2015.05.002

Maca, P., & Pech, P. (2015). The Inertia Weight Updating Strategies in Particle Swarm Optimisation Based on the Beta Distribution. *Mathematical Problems in Engineering, 2015*, 790465. doi:10.1155/2015/790465

Mahanfar, A., Bila, S., Aubourg, M., & Verdeyme, S. (2007). Cooperative particle swarm optimization of passive microwave devices. *Int. J. Numer. Model., 21*(1-2), 151–168. doi:10.1002/jnm.655

Mahapatra, S. S., & Patnaik, A. (2006). Optimization of wire electrical discharge machining (WEDM) process parameters using genetic algorithm. *Indian Journal of Engineering and Materials Science, 13*, 494–502.

Mahapatra, S. S., & Patnaik, A. (2007). Optimization of wire electrical discharge machining (WEDM) process parameters using Taguchi method. *International Journal of Advanced Manufacturing Technology, 34*(9-10), 911–925. doi:10.1007/s00170-006-0672-6

Mandal, K. K., Mandal, S., Bhattacharya, B., & Chakraborty, N. (2015). Non-convex emission constrained economic dispatch using a new self-adaptive particle swarm optimization technique. *Applied Soft Computing, 28*, 188–195. doi:10.1016/j.asoc.2014.11.033

Manju, A., & Nigam, M. J. (2014). Applications of quantum inspired computational intelligence: A survey. *Artificial Intelligence Review, 42*(1), 79–156. doi:10.1007/s10462-012-9330-6

Manna, A., & Bhattacharyya, B. (2006). Taguchi and Gauss elimination method: A dual response approach for parametric optimization of CNC wire cut EDM of PRAlSiCMMC. *International Journal of Advanced Manufacturing Technology, 28*(1-2), 67–75. doi:10.1007/s00170-004-2331-0

Mansouri Poor, M., & Shisheh Saz, M. (2012). Multi-Objective Optimization of Laminates with Straight Free Edges and Curved Free Edges by Using Bees Algorithm. *American Journal of Advanced Scientific Research*, *1*(4), 130–136.

Marinakis, Y., Marinaki, M., & Dounias, G. (2008). Honey bees mating optimization algorithm for the vehicle routing problem. *Studies in Computational Intelligence*, *129*, 139–148.

Marshall, S. (2012). *Flies: The Natural History and Diversity of Diptera. Firefly Books*.

Martin, S. J., Granstaff, V. E., & Frye, G. C. (1991). Characterization of a quartz crystal microbalance with simultaneous mass and liquid loading. *Analytical Chemistry*, *63*(20), 2272–2281. doi:10.1021/ac00020a015

Marx, K. (2003). Quartz Crystal Microbalance: A Useful Tool for Studying Thin Polymer Films and Complex Biomolecular Systems at the Solution-Surface Interface. *Biomacromolecules*, *4*(5), 1099–1120. doi:10.1021/bm020116i PMID:12959572

McBride, J., Moore, R., Witherspoon, J., & Blanco, R. (1978). Radiological impact of airborne effluents of coal and nuclear plants. *Science*, *202*(4372), 1045–1050. doi:10.1126/science.202.4372.1045 PMID:17777943

McCulloch, W. S., & Pitts, W. (1943). A logical calculus of the ideas immanent in nervous activity. *The Bulletin of Mathematical Biophysics*, *5*(4), 115–133. doi:10.1007/BF02478259

McGraw, G., Michael, C., & Schatz, M. (2001). Generating software test data by evolution. *IEEE Transactions on Software Engineering*, *27*(12), 1085–1110. doi:10.1109/32.988709

Mehdad, Y., & Magnini, B. (2009). Optimizing Textual Entailment Recognition Using Particle Swarm Optimization. *Proceedings of the 2009 Workshop on Applied Textual Inference*, 36–43. doi:10.3115/1708141.1708148

Mendes, R., Kennedy, J., & Neves, J. (2003). Watch thy Neighbor or How the Swarm can Learn from its Environment. *Proceedings of the IEEE Swarm Intelligence Symposium*, 88–94. doi:10.1109/SIS.2003.1202252

Mendes, R., Kennedy, J., & Neves, J. (2004). The Fully Informed Particle Swarm: Simpler, Maybe Better. *IEEE Transactions on Evolutionary Computation*, *8*(3), 204–210. doi:10.1109/TEVC.2004.826074

Merkle, D., Middendorf, M., & Schmeck, H. (2000). Ant colony optimization for resource-constrained project scheduling. *Proceedings of the Genetic and Evolutionary Computation Conference (GECCO 2000)*, 893-900.

Mescia, L., Bia, P., & Caratelli, D. (2015). Fractional-calculus-based FDTD method for solving pulse propagation problems. *International Conference on Electromagnetics in Advanced Applications (ICEAA)*, 460-463.

Mescia, L., Bia, P., Caratelli, D., Chiapperino, M. A., Stukach, O., & Gielis, J. (2016). Electromagnetic Mathematical Modeling of 3-D Supershaped Dielectric Lens Antennas. Mathematical Problems in Engineering.

Mescia, L., Bia, P., & Caratelli, D. (2014). Fractional Derivative Based FDTD Modeling of Transient Wave Propagation in Havriliak-Negami Media. *IEEE Transactions on Microwave Theory and Techniques*, *62*(9), 1920–1929. doi:10.1109/TMTT.2014.2327202

Mescia, L., Bia, P., & Caratelli, D. (2015). Authors. *Reply. IEEE Trans. Microw. Theory Techn.*, *63*(12), 4191–4193. doi:10.1109/TMTT.2015.2495263

Mezura-Montes, E., & Velez-Koeppel, R. E. (2012). Elitist artificial bee colony for constrained real-parameter optimization. In *IEEE World Congress on Computational Intelligence (WCCI)* (pp. 2068–2075). Barcelona, Spain: CCIB. doi:10.1109/CEC.2010.5586280

Michalewicz, Z., & Fogel, D. B. (2004). How to Solve It: Modern Heuristics. Springer. doi:10.1007/978-3-662-07807-5

Michalewicz, Z. (1992). *Genetic Algorithms C+ Data Structures = Evolution Programs*. Berlin: Springer. doi:10.1007/978-3-662-02830-8

Michalewicz, Z. (1996). *Genetic algorithms + data structures = evolution programs*. Springer. doi:10.1007/978-3-662-03315-9

Miller, S. F., Shih, A. J., & Qu, J. (2004). Investigation of the spark cycle on material removal rate in wire electrical discharge machining of advanced materials. *International Journal of Machine Tools & Manufacture, 44*(4), 39–400. doi:10.1016/j.ijmachtools.2003.10.005

Millonas, M. M. (1994). Swarms, phase transitions, and collective intelligence. In *Artificial Life III* (pp. 417–445). Reading, MA: Addison-Wesley.

Mirjalili, S. (2015). How effective is the Grey Wolf optimizer in training multi-layer perceptrons. *Applied Intelligence, 43*(1), 150–161. doi:10.1007/s10489-014-0645-7

Mirjalili, S., Lewis, A., & Sadiq, A. S. (2014). Autonomous Particles Groups for Particle Swarm Optimization. *Arab J Sci Eng, 39*(6), 4683–4697. doi:10.1007/s13369-014-1156-x

Mirjalili, S., Mirjalili, S. M., & Lewis, A. (2014). Grey Wolf Optimizer. *Advances in Engineering Software, 69*, 46–61. doi:10.1016/j.advengsoft.2013.12.007

Mohamad, A. B., Zain, A. M., & Bazin, N. E. N. (2014). Cuckoo search algorithm for optimization problems - A literature review and its applications. *Applied Artificial Intelligence, 28*(5), 419–448. doi:10.1080/08839514.2014.904599

Mohri, N., Fukuzawa, Y., Tani, T., & Sata, T. (2002). Some considerations to machining characteristics of insulating ceramics towards practical use in industry. *Ann CIRP, 51*(1), 112–116. doi:10.1016/S0007-8506(07)61490-5

Montagut, Y., García, J. V., Jiménez, Y., March, C., Montoya, A., & Arnau, A. (2011). Validation of a phase-mass characterization concept and interface for acoustic biosensors. *Sensors (Basel, Switzerland), 11*(12), 4702–4720. doi:10.3390/s110504702 PMID:22163871

Montgomery, D. C. (2001). *Design and Analysis of Experiments*. New York: Wiley.

Moravej, Z., & Akhlaghi, A. (2013). A novel approach based on cuckoo search for DG allocation in distribution network. *International Journal of Electrical Power & Energy Systems, 44*(1), 672–679. doi:10.1016/j.ijepes.2012.08.009

Mousa, A. A., & Elattar, E. E. (2014). Best compromise alternative to EELD problem using hybrid multiobjective quantum genetic algorithm. *Applied Mathematics and Information Sciences, 8*(6), 2889–2902. doi:10.12785/amis/080626

Mozaffari, A., & Azad, N. L. (2013). Optimally pruned extreme learning machine with ensemble of regularization techniques and negative correlation penalty applied to automotive engine coldstart hydrocarbon emission identification. *Neurocomputing*.

Mukherjee, A., Paul, S., & Roy, P. K. (2015). Transient Stability Constrained Optimal Power Flow Using Teaching Learning Based Optimization. *International Journal of Energy Optimization and Engineering, 4*(1), 18–35. doi:10.4018/ijeoe.2015010102

Mukherjee, R., Chakraborty, S., & Samanta, S. (2012). Selection of wire electrical discharge machining process parameters using non-traditional optimization algorithms. *Applied Soft Computing, 12*(8), 2506–2516. doi:10.1016/j.asoc.2012.03.053

Mukhopadhyay, P., Dutta, S., & Roy, P. K. (2015). Optimal Location of TCSC Using Opposition Teaching Learning Based Optimization. *International Journal of Energy Optimization and Engineering, 4*(1), 85–101. doi:10.4018/ijeoe.2015010106

Muttamara, A., Fukuzawa, Y., Mohri, N., & Tani, T. (2003). Probability of precision micro-machining of insulating Si3N4 ceramics by EDM. *Journal of Materials Processing Technology, 140*(1-3), 243–247. doi:10.1016/S0924-0136(03)00745-3

Myers, G. (1979). *The Art of Software Testing*. New York: Wiley.

Naama, B., Bouzeboudja, H., & Allali, A. (2013). *Solving the economic dispatch problem by using Tabu Search algorithm*. Paper presented at the Energy Procedia. doi:10.1016/j.egypro.2013.07.080

Nannen, V., & Eiben, A. (2007).Relevance estimation and value calibration of evolutionary algorithm parameters. *Proceedings of the 20th International Joint Conference on Artificial Intelligence*, 975-980. doi:10.1109/CEC.2007.4424460

Nanry, W. P., & Barnes, J. W. (2000). Solving the pickup and delivery problem with time windows using reactive tabu search. *Transportation Research Part B: Methodological, 34*(2), 107–121. doi:10.1016/S0191-2615(99)00016-8

Narayanan, A., & Moore, M. (1996). Quantum-inspired genetic algorithms. *Evolutionary Computation, 1996., Proceedings of IEEE International Conference on*.

Narayanan, A., & Menneer, T. (2000). Quantum artificial neural network architectures and components. *Information Sciences, 128*(3–4), 231–255. doi:10.1016/S0020-0255(00)00055-4

Nasir, M., Das, S., Maity, D., Sengupta, S., Halder, U., & Suganthan, P. (2012). A dynamic neighborhood learning based particle swarm optimizer for global numerical optimization. *Information Sciences, 209*, 16–36. doi:10.1016/j.ins.2012.04.028

Nayak, B.B. and Mahapatra, S.S. (2016). Optimization of WEDM process parameters using deep cryo-treated Inconel 718 as work material. *Engineering Science and Technology, an International Journal, 19*(1), 161–170.

Neto, J. X. V., Bernert, D. L. D., & Coelho, L. D. S. (2011). Improved quantum-inspired evolutionary algorithm with diversity information applied to economic dispatch problem with prohibited operating zones. *Energy Conversion and Management, 52*(1), 8–14. doi:10.1016/j.enconman.2010.05.023

Nie, R., Xu, X., & Yue, J. (2010). *A novel quantum-inspired particle swarm algorithm and its application*. Paper presented at the Natural Computation (ICNC), 2010 Sixth International Conference on. doi:10.1109/ICNC.2010.5583225

Nikabadi, A., Ebadzadeh, M. (2008). Particle swarm optimization algorithms with adaptive InertiaWeight: A survey of the state of the art and a Novel method. *IEEE Journal of Evolutionary Computation*.

Niknam, T. (2009). An efficient hybrid evolutionary algorithm based on PSO and HBMO algorithms for multi-objective distribution feeder reconfiguration. *Energy Conversion and Management, 50*(8), 2074–2082. doi:10.1016/j.enconman.2009.03.029

Niknam, T. (2011). An efficient multi-objective HBMO algorithm for distribution feeder reconfiguration. *Expert Systems with Applications, 38*(3), 2878–2887. doi:10.1016/j.eswa.2010.08.081

Niknam, T., Golestaneh, F., & Sadeghi, M. S. (2012). theta-Multiobjective Teaching-Learning-Based Optimization for Dynamic Economic Emission Dispatch. *IEEE Systems Journal, 6*(2), 341–352. doi:10.1109/JSYST.2012.2183276

Omkar, S. N., Khandelwal, R., Ananth, T. V. S., Narayana Naik, G., & Gopalakrishnan, S. (2009). Quantum behaved Particle Swarm Optimization (QPSO) for multi-objective design optimization of composite structures. *Expert Systems with Applications, 36*(8), 11312–11322. doi:10.1016/j.eswa.2009.03.006

Orkcu, H., & Bal, H. (2011). Comparing performances of backpropagation and genetic algorithms in the data classification. *Expert Systems with Applications, Elsevier, 38*(4), 3703–3709. doi:10.1016/j.eswa.2010.09.028

Özbakır, L., & Tapkan, P. (2011). Bee colony intelligence in zone constrained two-sided assembly line balancing problem. *Expert Systems with Applications, 38*(9), 11947–11957. doi:10.1016/j.eswa.2011.03.089

Ozcan, E., & Mohan, C. K. (1999). Particle swarm optimization: surfing the waves. In *Evolutionary Computation, 1999. CEC 99. Proceedings of the 1999 Congress on (Vol. 3)*. IEEE

Ozcan, E., & Mohan, C. (1998). Analysis of a Simple Particle Swarm Optimization System. *Intelligent Engineering Systems Through Artifocial Neural Networks, 8*, 253–258.

Ozdemir, N., & Ozek, C. (2006). An investigation on machinability of nodular cast iron by WEDM. *International Journal of Advanced Manufacturing Technology, 28*(9-10), 869–872. doi:10.1007/s00170-004-2446-3

Pan, Q.-K., Fatih, T., Suganthan, P. N., & Chua, T. J. (2011). A discrete artificial bee colony algorithm for the lot-streaming flow shop scheduling problem. *Information Sciences, 181*(12), 2455–2468. doi:10.1016/j.ins.2009.12.025

Pant, M., Thangaraj, R., & Abraham, A. (2008). A new quantum behaved particle swarm optimization. *Proceedings of the 10th Annual Conference on Genetic and Evolutionary Computation*, 87–94. doi:10.1145/1389095.1389108

Pant, M., Thangaraj, R., & Singhl, V. P. (2009). Sobal mutated quantum particle swarm optimization. *International Journal of Recent Trends in Engineering, 1*(1), 95–99.

Pant, M., Thangaraj, R., & Singh, V. (2007). A simple diversity guided particle swarm optimization. *Proceedings of IEEE Congress Evolutionary Computation*, 3294–3299. doi:10.1109/CEC.2007.4424896

Pan, W. T. (2012). A new fruit fly optimization algorithm: Taking the financial distress model as an example. *Knowledge-Based Systems, 26*, 69–74. doi:10.1016/j.knosys.2011.07.001

Papageorgiou, L. G., & Fraga, E. S. (2007). A mixed integer quadratic programming formulation for the economic dispatch of generators with prohibited operating zones. *Electric Power Systems Research, 77*(10), 1292–1296. doi:10.1016/j.epsr.2006.09.020

Park, J. B., Lee, K. S., Shin, J. R., & Lee, K. Y. (2005). A particle swarm optimization for economic dispatch with non-smooth cost functions. *IEEE Transactions on Power Systems, 20*(1), 34–42. doi:10.1109/TPWRS.2004.831275

Park, J.-B., Jeong, Y.-W., Shin, J.-R., & Lee, K. Y. (2010). An improved particle swarm optimization for nonconvex economic dispatch problems. *Power Systems. IEEE Transactions on, 25*(1), 156–166.

Parpinelli, R. S., Lopes, H. S., & Freitas, A. A. (2002). Data mining with an ant colony optimization algorithm. *IEEE Transactions on Evolutionary Computation, 6*(4), 321–332. doi:10.1109/TEVC.2002.802452

Parsopoulos, K., & Vrahatis, M. (2004). UPSO: a Unified Particle Swarm Optimization Scheme. *Lecture Series on Computational Sciences*, 868–873.

Parsopoulos, K. E., & Vrahatis, M. N. (2010). *Particle Swarm Optimization and Intelligence: Advances and Applications*. Hershey, PA: IGI Global. doi:10.4018/978-1-61520-666-7

Patil, B. M., Joshi, R. C., & Toshniwal, D. (2010). Association rule for classification of type -2 diabetic patients. *Second International Conference on Machine Learning and Computing*. IEEE. doi:10.1109/ICMLC.2010.67

Pedemonte, M., Nesmachnow, S., & Cancela, H. (2011). A survey on parallel ant colony optimization. *Applied Soft Computing, 11*(8), 5181–5197. doi:10.1016/j.asoc.2011.05.042

Pedrycz, W., & Peters, J. F. (1998). *Computational Intelligence in Software Engineering*. World Scientific Publishers Singapore. doi:10.1142/3821

Peram, T., Veeramachaneni, K., & Mohan, C. (2003). Fitness-distance-ratio based particle swarm optimization. *Proceedings of the IEEE Swarm Intelligence Symposium*, 174–181.

Pfahring, B. (1996). *Multi-agent search for open scheduling: adapting the Ant-Q formalism*. Technical report TR-96-09.

Phadke, M. S. (1989). *Quality engineering using robust design*. Englewood Cliffs, NJ: Prentice Hall.

Pham, D. T., & Ghanbarzadeh, A. (2007). Multi-objective optimisation using the bees algorithm. In *Third International Virtual Conference on Intelligent Production Machines and Systems (IPROMS)* (pp. 1–5). Dunbeath, UK: Whittles.

Pham, D. T., Afify, A. A., & Koç, E. (2007a). Manufacturing cell formation using the bees algorithm. In *Third International Virtual Conference on Intelligent Production Machines and Systems (IPROMS)* (pp. 1–6). Dunbeath, UK: Whittles.

Pham, D. T., Castellani, M., & Ghanbarzadeh, A. (2007) Preliminary design using the Bees Algorithm. *Proceedings Eighth LAMDAMAP International Conference on Laser Metrology, CMM and Machine Tool Performance*, 420-429.

Pham, D. T., Ghanbarzadeh, A., Koç, E., Otri, S., Rahim, S., & Zaidi, M. (2007b). Using the bees algorithm to schedule jobs for a machine. In *Proceedings of Eighth International Conference on Laser metrology, CMM and machine tool performance (LAMDAMAP)* (pp. 430–439). Euspen.

Pham, D. T., Koç, E., Lee, J. Y., & Phrueksanant, J. (2007). Using the Bees Algorithm to Schedule Jobs for a Machine. *Proceedings 8th international Conference on Laser Metrology, CMM and Machine Tool Performance (LAMDAMAP)*, 430-439.

Pham, D. T., & Castellani, M. (2009). The bees algorithm: Modelling foraging behaviour to solve continuous optimization problems. *Proceedings of the Institution of Mechanical Engineers. Part C, Journal of Mechanical Engineering Science*, *223*(12), 2919–2938. doi:10.1243/09544062JMES1494

Pham, D. T., & Darwish, A. H. (2010). Using the bees' algorithm with Kalman filtering to train an artificial neural network for pattern classification. *Journal of Systems and Control Engineering*, *224*(7), 885–892.

Pham, D. T., Ghanbarzadeh, A., Koç, E., Otri, S., Rahim, S., & Zaidi, M. (2006). The bees algorithm—a novel tool for complex optimisation problems. In *Proceedings of Second International Virtual Conference on Intelligent production machines and systems (IPROMS)* (pp. 454–459). Oxford, UK: Elsevier. doi:10.1016/B978-008045157-2/50081-X

Pham, D. T., Ghanbarzadeh, A., Otri, S., & Koç, E. (2009). Optimal design of mechanical components using the bees algorithm. *Proceedings of the Institution of Mechanical Engineers. Part C, Journal of Mechanical Engineering Science*, *223*(5), 1051–1056. doi:10.1243/09544062JMES838

Pham, D. T., & Koç, E. (2010). Design of a two-dimensional recursive filter using the bees algorithm. *International Journal of Automation and Computing*, *7*(3), 399–402. doi:10.1007/s11633-010-0520-x

Pham, D. T., Zaidi, M., Mahmuddin, M., Ghanbarzadeh, A., Koç, E., & Otri, S. (2007). Using the bees' algorithm to optimize a support vector machine for wood defect classification, IPROMS. *Innovative Production Machines and Systems Virtual Conference*.

Pinto, P. C., Runkler, T. A., & Sousa, J. M. C. (2006). Agent based optimization of the MAX-SAT problem using wasp swarms. In *7th Portuguese Conference on Automatic Control (CONTROLO)* (pp. 1–6). Lisboa, Portugal: Instituto Superior Técnico.

Piro, G., Bia, P., Boggia, G., Caratelli, D., Grieco, L. A., & Mescia, L. (2016). Terahertz electromagnetic field propagation in human tissues: a study on communication capabilities. *Nano Communication Networks*.

Polat, K., & Güneş, S. (2007). An expert system approach based on principal component analysis and adaptive neuro-fuzzy inference system to diagnosis of diabetes disease. *Digital Signal Processing, Elsevier, 17*(4), 702–710. doi:10.1016/j.dsp.2006.09.005

Polat, K., Güneş, S., & Arslan, A. (2008). A cascade learning system for classification of diabetes disease: Generalized Discriminant Analysis and Least Square Support Vector Machine. *Expert Systems with Applications, Elsevier, 34*(1), 482–487. doi:10.1016/j.eswa.2006.09.012

Poli, R., Kennedy, J., & Blackwell, T. (2007). Particle swarm optimization. *Swarm Intelligence, 1*(1), 33–57. doi:10.1007/s11721-007-0002-0

Pongchairerks, P. (2009). Particle swarm optimization algorithm applied to scheduling problems. *ScienceAsia, 35*(1), 89–94. doi:10.2306/scienceasia1513-1874.2009.35.089

Pothiya, S., Ngamroo, I., & Kongprawechnon, W. (2010). Ant colony optimisation for economic dispatch problem with non-smooth cost functions. *International Journal of Electrical Power & Energy Systems, 32*(5), 478–487. doi:10.1016/j.ijepes.2009.09.016

Pradhan, P. M., & Panda, G. (2012). Connectivity constrained wireless sensor deployment using multi objective evolutionary algorithms and fuzzy decision making. *Ad Hoc Networks, 10*(6), 1134–1145. doi:10.1016/j.adhoc.2012.03.001

Qasem, S. N., & Shamsuddin, S. M. (2011). Radial basis function network based on time variant multi objective particle swarm optimization for medical diseases diagnosis. *Applied Soft Computing, Elsevier, 11*(1), 1427–1438. doi:10.1016/j.asoc.2010.04.014

Qu, Suganthan, & Das. (2013). A Distance-based Locally Informed Particle Swarm Model for Multi-modal Optimization. *IEEE Transactions on Evolutionary Computation, 17*(3), 387-402.

Quijano, N., & Passino, K. M. (2010). Honey bee social foraging algorithms for resource allocation: Theory and application. *Engineering Applications of Artificial Intelligence, 23*(6), 845–861. doi:10.1016/j.engappai.2010.05.004

Rada-Vilela, J., Zhang, M., & Seah, W. (2011b). A performance study on synchronous and asynchronous updates in particle swarm optimization. Genetic and evolutionary computation conference, 21–28. doi:10.1145/2001576.2001581

Rada-Vilela, J., Zhang, M., & Seah, W. (2012). A performance study on the effects of noise and evaporation in particle swarm optimization. IEEE congress on evolutionary computation, 873–880. doi:10.1109/CEC.2012.6256451

Rada-Vilela, J., Zhang, M., & Seah, W. (2011a). Random asynchronous PSO. *5th international conference on automation, robotics and applications*, 220–225. doi:10.1109/ICARA.2011.6144885

Rada-Vilela, J., Zhang, M., & Seah, W. (2013). performance study on synchronicity and neighborhood size in particle swarm optimization. *Soft Computing, 17*(6), 1019–1030. doi:10.1007/s00500-013-1015-9

Rahman, I., Vasant, P., Singh, B. S. M., & Abdullah-Al-Wadud, M. (2015). Swarm intelligence-based optimization for PHEV charging stations. Handbook of Research on Swarm Intelligence in Engineering, 374.

Raicu, V. (1999). Dielectric dispersion of biological matter: Model combining Debye-type and universal responses. *Physical Review E: Statistical Physics, Plasmas, Fluids, and Related Interdisciplinary Topics, 60*(4), 4677–4680. doi:10.1103/PhysRevE.60.4677 PMID:11970331

Ramakrishnan, R., & Karunamoorthy, L. (2006). Multi response optimization of wire EDM operations using robust design of experiments. *International Journal of Advanced Manufacturing Technology, 29*(1-2), 105–112. doi:10.1007/s00170-004-2496-6

Ramakrishnan, R., & Karunamoorthy, L. (2008). Modeling and multi-response optimization of Inconel 718 on machining of CNC WEDM process. *Journal of Materials Processing Technology, 207*(1-3), 343–349. doi:10.1016/j.jmatprotec.2008.06.040

Raman, S., Barker, N. S., & Rebeiz, G. M. (1998). AW-band dielectric lens-based integrated monopulse radar receiver. *IEEE Transactions on Microwave Theory and Techniques, 46*(12), 2308–2316. doi:10.1109/22.739216

Ramesh, B., Chandra Jagan Mohan, V., & Veera Reddy, V. C. (2013). Application of BAT algorithm for combimned economic load and emission dispatch. *Journal of Electrical Engineering, 13*(2), 214–219.

Rao, C. V. S. P., & Sarcar, M. M. M. (2009). Evolution of optimal parameters for machining brass with wire cut EDM. *Journal of Scientific and Industrial Research, 68*, 32–35.

Rao, R. V., Savsani, V. J., & Vakharia, D. (2011). Teaching–learning-based optimization: A novel method for constrained mechanical design optimization problems. *Computer Aided Design, 43*(3), 303–315. doi:10.1016/j.cad.2010.12.015

Ratnaweera, A., Saman, K., & Watson, H. C. (2004). Self–Organizing Hierarchical Particle Swarm Optimizer with Time–Varying Acceleration Coefficients. *IEEE Transactions on Evolutionary Computation, 8*(3), 240–255. doi:10.1109/TEVC.2004.826071

Ravindranadh B. R., Madhu, V. & Gogia, A.K. (2015). Multi response optimization of wire-EDM process parameters of ballistic grade aluminium alloy. *Engineering Science and Technology, an International Journal, 18*(4), 720–726.

Ravishankar, S., & Dharshak, B. (2014). A rapid direction of arrival estimation procedure for adaptive array antennas covered by a shaped dielectric lens. *Proc. IEEE Radio and Wireless Symposium (RWS '14)*, 124-126.

Reyes-Medina, T., & Ramirez-Tores, J. (2011). A Statistical Study of the Effects of Neighborhood Topologies in Particle Swarm Optimization. *Studies in Computational Intelligence, 343*, 179–192.

Reznik, A. M., Galinskaya, A. A., Dekhtyarenko, O. K., & Nowicki, D. W. (2005). Preprocessing of matrix QCM sensors data for the classification by means of neural network. *Sensors and Actuators. B, Chemical, 106*(1), 158–163. doi:10.1016/j.snb.2004.05.047

Riget, J., & Vesterstrom, J. (2002). *A Diversity Guided Particle Swarm Optimizer- the ARPSO*. EVALife Technical Report no. 2002-02.

Rodahl, M., Höök, F., & Kasemo, B. (1996). QCM Operation in liquids: An explanation of measured variations in frequency and Q factor with liquid conductivity. *Analytical Chemistry, 68*(13), 2219–2227. doi:10.1021/ac951203m PMID:21619308

Rodriguez, R. M., Martinez, L., & Herrera, F. (2012). Hesitant Fuzzy Linguistic Term Sets for Decision Making. *IEEE Transactions on Fuzzy Systems, 20*(1), 109–119. doi:10.1109/TFUZZ.2011.2170076

Roper. (1997). *Computer aided software testing using genetic algorithms*. In 10th International Software Quality Week, San Francisco, CA.

Roselyn, J. P., Devaraj, D., & Dash, S. S. (2011). Economic Emission OPF Using Hybrid GA-Particle Swarm Optimization. In B. K. Panigrahi, P. N. Suganthan, S. Das, & S. C. Satapathy (Eds.), *Swarm, Evolutionary, and Memetic Computing, Pt I* (Vol. 7076, pp. 167–175). doi:10.1007/978-3-642-27172-4_21

Ross, P. J. (1996). Taguchi Techniques for Quality Engineering (2nd ed.). New York: McGraw Hill.

Roy, A., Dutta, S., & Roy, P. K. (2015). Load Frequency Control of Interconnected Power System Using Teaching Learning Based Optimization. *International Journal of Energy Optimization and Engineering, 4*(1), 102–117. doi:10.4018/ijeoe.2015010107

Roy, P. K. (2013). Teaching learning based optimization for short-term hydrothermal scheduling problem considering valve point effect and prohibited discharge constraint. *International Journal of Electrical Power & Energy Systems, 53*, 10–19. doi:10.1016/j.ijepes.2013.03.024

Roy, P., Ghoshal, S., & Thakur, S. (2009). Biogeography-based optimization for economic load dispatch problems. *Electric Power Components and Systems, 38*(2), 166–181. doi:10.1080/15325000903273379

Roy, R. K. (1990). *A primer on the Taguchi method.* Dearborn, MI: Society of Manufacturing Engineers.

Roy, R., Furuhashi, T., & Chawdhry, P. (Eds.). (1999). *Advances in soft computing: engineering design and manufacturing.* London: Springer. doi:10.1007/978-1-4471-0819-1

Roy, S., Roy, S. D., Tewary, J., Mahanti, A., & Mahanti, G. K. (2015). Particle Swarm Optimization for Optimal Design of Broadband Multilayer Microwave Absorber for Wide Angle of Incidence. *Progress in Electromagnetics Research, 62*, 121–135. doi:10.2528/PIERB14122602

Ruan, D. (2010). *Computational Intelligence in Complex Decision Systems* (Vol. 2). Paris: Atlantis Press. doi:10.2991/978-94-91216-29-9

Rusell, R. A., & Chiang, W. C. (2006). Scatter search for the vehicle routing problem with time windows. *European Journal of Operational Research, 169*(2), 606–622. doi:10.1016/j.ejor.2004.08.018

Ruz, G. A., & Goles, E. (2013). Learning gene regulatory networks using the bees algorithm. *Neural Computing & Applications, 22*(1), 63–70. doi:10.1007/s00521-011-0750-z

Rynkiewicz, J. (2012). General bound of overfitting for MLP regression models. *Neurocomputing, 90*(0), 106–110. doi:10.1016/j.neucom.2011.11.028

Sadeghi, M., Razavi, H., Esmaeilzadeh, A., & Kolahan, F. (2011). Optimization of cutting conditions in WEDM process using regression modelling and Tabu-search algorithm. *Proceedings of the Institution of Mechanical Engineers. Part B, Journal of Engineering Manufacture, 225*(10), 1825–1834. doi:10.1177/0954405411406639

Sahana, S. K., & Jain, A. (2011). An Improved Modular Hybrid Ant Colony Approach for Solving Traveling Salesman Problem. *International Journal on Computing, 1*(2), 123-127.

Sahana, S.K., Jain, A., & Mahanti, P.K. (2014). Ant Colony Optimization for Train Scheduling: An Analysis. *I.J. Intelligent Systems and Applications, 6*(2), 29-36. doi:,10.5815/ijisa.2014.02.04

Saha, P., Singha, A., Pal, S. K., & Saha, P. (2008). Soft computing models based prediction of cutting speed and surface roughness in wire electro-discharge machining of tungsten carbide cobalt composite. *International Journal of Advanced Manufacturing Technology, 39*(1-2), 74–78. doi:10.1007/s00170-007-1200-z

Sahoo, P. (2005). *Engineering Tribology.* New Delhi: Prentice Hall of India.

Saremi, S., Mirjalili, S. Z., & Mirjalili, S. M. (2015). Evolutionary population dynamics and grey wolf optimizer. *Neural Computing & Applications, 26*(5), 1257–1263. doi:10.1007/s00521-014-1806-7

Sarkar, S., Mitra, S., & Bhattacharyya, B. (2005). Parametric analysis and optimization of wire electrical discharge machining of γ-titanium aluminide alloy. *Journal of Materials Processing Technology, 159*(3), 286–294. doi:10.1016/j.jmatprotec.2004.10.009

Sastry, K., Goldberg, D., & Kendall, G. (2005). Genetic algorithms. In *Search Methodologies* (pp. 97–125). Introductory Tutorials in Optimization and Decision Support Techniques. doi:10.1007/0-387-28356-0_4

Satapathy, S. C., Naik, A., & Parvathi, K. (2013). A teaching learning based optimization based on orthogonal design for solving global optimization problems. *SpringerPlus*, *2*(1), 130. doi:10.1186/2193-1801-2-130 PMID:23875125

Sayadi, F., Ismail, M., Misran, N., & Jumari, K. (2009). Multi-Objective Optimization Using the Bees Algorithm in Time-Varying Channel for MIMO MC-CDMA Systems. *European Journal of Scientific Research*, *33*(3), 411–428.

Schaffer, J. D. (1985). Multiple objective optimization with vector evaluated genetic algorithms. In J. Grefenstette (Ed.), *Proceedings of the First International Conference on Genetic Algorithms*. Lawrence Erlbaum Associates.

Schröder, J., Borngräber, R., Eichelbaum, F., & Hauptmann, P. (2002). Advanced interface electronics and methods for QCM. *Sensors and Actuators. A, Physical*, *97–98*, 543–547. doi:10.1016/S0924-4247(02)00036-5

Schwefel, H. P. (1994). On the Evolution of Evolutionary Computation. In Computational Intelligence: Imitating Life, (pp. 116-124). Academic Press.

Seeley, T. (1985). *Honeybee Ecology, A Study of Adaptation in Social Life*. Princeton, NJ: Princeton University Press. doi:10.1515/9781400857876

Seera, M., & Lim, C. P. (2014). A hybrid intelligent system for medical data classification. *Expert Systems with Applications, Elsevier*, *41*(5), 2239–2249. doi:10.1016/j.eswa.2013.09.022

Selvakuberan, K., Kayathiri, D., Harini, B., & Devi, M. I. (2011). An efficient feature selection method for classification in Health care Systems using Machine Learning Techniques. IEEE.

Senthilnath, J., Omkar, S. N., & Mani, V. (2011). Clustering using firefly algorithm: Performance study. *Swarm and Evolutionary Computation*, *1*(3), 164–171. doi:10.1016/j.swevo.2011.06.003

Senvar, O., Turanoglu, E., & Kahraman, C. (2013). Usage of metaheuristics in engineering: a literature review. *Meta-Heuristics Optimization Algorithms in Engineering, Business, Economics, and Finance*, 484-528.

Shafiee, S., & Topal, E. (2009). When will fossil fuel reserves be diminished? *Energy Policy*, *37*(1), 181–189. doi:10.1016/j.enpol.2008.08.016

Shalini, S. P., & Lakshmi, K. (2014). Solution to economic emission dispatch problem using Lagrangian relaxation method. *2014 International Conference on Green Computing Communication and Electrical Engineering (ICGCCEE)*. doi:10.1109/ICGCCEE.2014.6922314

Sharma, N., Khanna, R., & Gupta, R. D. (2013). Multi Quality Characteristics Of WEDM Process Parameters With RSM. *Procedia Engineering*, *64*, 710–719. doi:10.1016/j.proeng.2013.09.146

Sharma, N., Khanna, R., Gupta, R. D., & Sharma, R. (2013). Modeling and multiresponse optimization on WEDM for HSLA by RSM. *International Journal of Advanced Manufacturing Technology*, *67*(9-12), 2269–2281. doi:10.1007/s00170-012-4648-4

Sharma, N., Singh, A., Sharma, R., & Deepak, . (2014). Modelling the WEDM Process Parameters for Cryogenic Treated D-2 Tool Steel by Integrated RSM and GA. *Procedia Engineering*, *97*, 1609–1617. doi:10.1016/j.proeng.2014.12.311

Shi, Y., & Eberhart, R. (1998). A modified particle swarm optimizer. *Evolutionary Computation Proceedings, 1998. IEEE World Congress on Computational Intelligence*, 69 – 73.

Shi, Y., & Eberhart, R. (1998). *A modified particle swarm optimizer.* Paper presented at the Evolutionary Computation IEEE World Congress on Computational Intelligence., The 1998 IEEE International Conference on. doi:10.1109/ICEC.1998.699146

Shi, Y., & Eberhart, R. C. (1999). Empirical study of particle swarm optimization. *Evolutionary Computation, 1999. CEC 99. Proceedings of the 1999 Congress on.*

Shi, Y., & Eberhart, R.C. (1999). Empirical Study of Particle Swarm Opimization. *Proc. IEEE Int. Conf. on Evolutionary Computation, 3,* 101–106.

Shi, Y., & Eberhart, R. (1998). A modified particle swarm optimizer. *Proc. IEEE International Conference on Evolutionary Computation (ICEC),* 69-73.

Shi, Y., & Eberhart, R. (1999). Empirical study of particle swarm optimization. *Proceedings of the 1999 Congress on Evolutionary Computation,* 1945-1950. doi:10.1109/CEC.1999.785511

Shi, Y., & Eberhart, R. (2001). Fuzzy adaptive particle swarm optimization, Evolutionary Computation. *Proceedings of the 2001 Congress, 1,* 101-106. doi:10.1109/CEC.2001.934377

Shi, Y., & Eberhart, R. (2008). Population diversity of particle swarms, Evolutionary Computation, 2008. *CEC 2008. IEEE World Congress on Computational Intelligence,* 1063 – 1067.

Shi, Y., & Eberhart, R. C. (1998). Parameter Selection in Particle Swarm Optimization, Evolutionary Programming VII, Springer. *Lecture Notes in Computer Science, 1447,* 591–600. doi:10.1007/BFb0040810

Simeoni, M., Cicchetti, R., Yarovoy, A., & Caratelli, D. (2011). Plastic-based supershaped dielectric resonator antennas for wide-band applications. *IEEE Transactions on Antennas and Propagation, 59*(12), 4820–4825. doi:10.1109/TAP.2011.2165477

Simic, V., & Dimitrijevic, B. (2013). Modelling of automobile shredder residue recycling in the Japanese legislative context. *Expert Systems with Applications, 40*(18), 7159–7167. doi:10.1016/j.eswa.2013.06.075

Singh, H., & Garg, R. (2009). Effects of process parameters on material removal rate in WEDM. *Journal of Achievements in Materials and Manufacturing Engineering, 32,* 70–74.

Sinha, N., Chakrabarti, R., & Chattopadhyay, P. (2003). Evolutionary programming techniques for economic load dispatch. *Evolutionary Computation. IEEE Transactions on, 7*(1), 83–94.

Skaar, J., & Haakestad, M. W. (2012). Inverse scattering of dispersive stratified structures. *Journal of the Optical Society of America. B, Optical Physics, 29*(9), 2438–2445. doi:10.1364/JOSAB.29.002438

Smith, J., & Fogarty, T. (1996). Self adaptation of mutation rates in a steady state genetic algorithm. *International Conference on Evolutionary Computation,* 318-323. doi:10.1109/ICEC.1996.542382

Socha, K., & Dorigo, M. (2008). Ant colony optimization for continuous domains. *European Journal of Operational Research, 185*(3), 1155–1173. doi:10.1016/j.ejor.2006.06.046

Somuah, C., & Khunaizi, N. (1990). Application of linear programming redispatch technique to dynamic generation allocation. *IEEE Transactions on Power Systems, 5*(1), 20–26. doi:10.1109/59.49081

Song, J., Hu, J., Tian, Y., & Xu, Y. (2005). Re-optimization in dynamic vehicle routing problem based on wasp-like agent strategy. *Proceedings of 8th International Conference on Intelligent Transportation Systems,* 688–693.

Song, X., Tang, L., Zhao, S., Zhang, X., Li, L., Huang, J., & Cai, W. (2015). Grey Wolf Optimizer for parameter estimation in surface waves. *Soil Dynamics and Earthquake Engineering, 75,* 147–157. doi:10.1016/j.soildyn.2015.04.004

Song, Y., Wang, G., Wang, P., & Johns, A. (1997). Environmental/economic dispatch using fuzzy logic controlled genetic algorithms. *IEE Proceedings. Generation, Transmission and Distribution, 144*(4), 377–382. doi:10.1049/ip-gtd:19971100

Spedding, T. A., & Wang, Z. Q. (1997a). Parametric optimization and surface characterization of wire electrical discharge machining process. *Precision Engineering, 20*(1), 5–15. doi:10.1016/S0141-6359(97)00003-2

Spedding, T. A., & Wang, Z. Q. (1997b). Study on modeling of wire EDM process. *Journal of Materials Processing Technology, 69*(1-3), 18–28. doi:10.1016/S0924-0136(96)00033-7

Speight, R. E., & Cooper, M. A. (2012). A Survey of the 2010 Quartz Crystal Microbalance Literature. *Journal of Molecular Recognition, 25*(May), 451–473. doi:10.1002/jmr.2209 PMID:22899590

Srinivas, N., & Deb, K. (1994). Multiobjective Optimization Using Nondominated Sorting in Genetic Algorithms". *Evolutionary Computation, 2*(3), 221–248. doi:10.1162/evco.1994.2.3.221

Srivastava, P. R. (2013). Swarm and Evolutionary Computation. Elsevier.

Srivastava, P. R., Baby, K., & Raghurama, G. (2009). An approach of optimal path generation using ant colony optimization. *Proceedings of the TENCON 2009 - 2009 IEEE Region 10 Conference*, 1–6. doi:10.1109/TENCON.2009.5396088

Srivastava, Sahana, Pant, & Mahanti.(2015). Hybrid Synchronous Discrete Distance Time Model for Traffic Signal Optimization. *Journal of Next Generation Information Technology, 6.*

Stach, W., Kurgan, L., Pedrycz, W., & Reformat, M. (2005). Genetic learning of fuzzy cognitive maps. *Fuzzy Sets and Systems, 153*(3), 371–401. doi:10.1016/j.fss.2005.01.009

Steimann, F., & Adlassnig, K. P. (1998). Fuzzy medical diagnosis. Handbook of Fuzzy Computation, G13.

Steinwart, I., & Christmann, A. (2008). *Support Vector Machines* (1st ed.). Springer Publishing Company, Incorporated.

Stutzle & Dorigo. (2003). *The ant colony optimization metaheuristic: algorithms, applications, and advances.* New York: Springer.

Stützle, T. (1997). *An ant approach to the flow shop problem.* Technical report AIDA-97-07.

Stützle, T. (1997). *MAX-MIN Ant System for the quadratic assignment problem.* Technical Report AIDA-97-4, FB Informatik, TU Darmstadt, Germany.

Stützle, T., & Hoos, H. H. (2000). MAX-MIN Ant System. *Future Generation Computer Systems, 16*(8), 889–914. doi:10.1016/S0167-739X(00)00043-1

Su, C. T., & Tong, L. I. (1997). Multi-response robust design by principal component analysis. *Total Quality Management, 8*(6), 409–416. doi:10.1080/0954412979415

Suganthan, P. (1999). Particle swarm optimizer with neighbourhood operator. *IEEE Congress on Evolutionary Computation, 3,* 1958-1962.

Sulaiman, S., Shamsuddin, S. M., Forkan, F., & Abraham, A. (2008). Intelligent Web Caching Using Neurocomputing and Particle Swarm Optimization Algorithm. *AMS, 2008, Asia International Conference on Modelling & Simulation, Asia International Conference on Modelling & Simulation,* 642-647. doi:10.1109/AMS.2008.40

Sulaiman, M. H., Mustaffa, Z., Mohamed, M. R., & Aliman, O. (2015). Using the gray wolf optimizer for solving optimal reactive power dispatch problem. *Applied Soft Computing, 32,* 286–292. doi:10.1016/j.asoc.2015.03.041

Sultana, S., & Roy, P. K. (2014). Optimal capacitor placement in radial distribution systems using teaching learning based optimization. *International Journal of Electrical Power & Energy Systems, 54,* 387–398. doi:10.1016/j.ijepes.2013.07.011

Sun J., Lai, C-H., & Wu, X-J. (2011). *Particle Swarm Optimisation: Classical and Quantum Perspectives*. CRC Press, Inc.

Sun, J., Fang, W., Palade, V., Wua, X., & Xu, W. (2011). Quantum-behaved particle swarm optimization with Gaussian distributed local attractor point. *Applied Mathematics and Computation, 218*, 3763–3775,

Sun, J., Feng, B., & Xu, W. B. (2004). Particle swarm optimization with particles having quantum behavior. *Proc. IEEE Congress on Evolutionary Computation (CEC '04)*, 325–331. doi:10.1109/CEC.2004.1330875

Sun, J., Xu, B., & Fang, W. (2006). A diversity-guided quantum-behaved particle swarm optimization algorithm. *International Conference on Simulated Evolution and Learning*, 497–504. doi:10.1007/11903697_63

Sun, J., Xu, W., & Feng, B. (2005). Adaptive parameter control for quantum-behaved particle swarm optimization on individual level. *Proceedings of IEEE International Conference on Systems, Man, and Cybernetics*, 3049–3054. doi:10.1109/ICSMC.2005.1571614

Suraj, T. P., Ghosh, S., & Sinha, R.K. (2015). Classification of two class motor imagery tasks using hybrid GA-PSO based K-means Clustering. Computational Intelligence and Neuroscience.

Suykens, J. A. K., & Vandewalle, J. (1999). Least squares support vector machine classifiers. *Neural Processing Letters, 9*(3), 293–300. doi:10.1023/A:1018628609742

Syafrullah & Salim. (2010). Improving Term Extraction Using Particle Swarm Optimization Techniques. *Journal of Computing, 2*(2), 116-120.

Tadeusiewicz, R. (2008). *Modern computational intelligence methods for the interpretation of medical images* (Vol. 84). Springer.

Taguchi, G. (1990). *Introduction to Quality Engineering*. Tokyo: Asian Productivity Organization.

Tanweer, M. R., Suresh, S., & Sundararajan, N. (2015). Self regulating particle swarm optimization algorithm. *Information Sciences, 294*, 182–202. doi:10.1016/j.ins.2014.09.053

Tarng, Y. S., Ma, S. C., & Chung, L. K. (1995). Determination of optimal cutting parameters in wire electrical discharge machining. *International Journal of Machine Tools & Manufacture, 35*(12), 1693–1701. doi:10.1016/0890-6955(95)00019-T

Tasgetiren, M. F., Pan, Q.-K., Suganthan, P. N., & Chen, A. H.-L. (2010). A discrete artificial bee colony algorithm for the permutation flow shop scheduling problem with total flowtime criterion. In *IEEE World Congress on Computational Intelligence* (pp. 137–144). Barcelona, Spain: CCIB. doi:10.1109/CEC.2010.5586300

Tasgetiren, M. F., Pan, Q.-K., Suganthan, P. N., & Chen, A. H.-L. (2011). A discrete artificial bee colony algorithm for the total flowtime minimization in permutation flow shops. *Information Sciences, 181*(16), 3459–3475. doi:10.1016/j.ins.2011.04.018

Tasgetiren, M. F., Pan, Q.-K., Suganthan, P. N., & Oner, A. (2013). A discrete artificial bee colony algorithm for the no-idle permutation flowshop scheduling problem with the total tardiness criterion. *Applied Mathematical Modelling, 37*(10-11), 6758–6779. doi:10.1016/j.apm.2013.02.011

Temurtas, H., Yumusak, N., & Temurtas, F. (2009). A Comparative Study On Diabetes Disease Diagnosis Using Neural Networks. *Expert Systems With Applications, Elsevier, 36*(4), 8610–8615. doi:10.1016/j.eswa.2008.10.032

Teodorovic´, D. (2009a). Bee colony optimization (BCO). In C. P. Lim, L. C. Jain, & S. Dehuri (Eds.), Innovations in swarm intelligence (Vol. 248, pp. 39–60). Springer.

Teodorovic´, D. (2008). Swarm intelligence systems for transportation engineering: Principles and applications. *Transportation Research Part C, Emerging Technologies, 16*(6), 651–667. doi:10.1016/j.trc.2008.03.002

Teodorovic´, D. (2009b). Bee colony optimization (BCO). In C. P. Lim, L. C. Jain, & S. Dehuri (Eds.), *Innovations in swarm intelligence*. Berlin: Springer. doi:10.1007/978-3-642-04225-6_3

Teodorovic´, D., & Dell'Orco, M. (2005). Bee colony optimization: A cooperative learning approach to complex transportation problems. *16th Mini-EURO Conference on Advanced OR and AI Methods in Transportation*, 51–60.

Teodorovic, D. U. Š. A. N., Davidovic, T., & Selmic, M. (2011). Bee colony optimization: The applications survey. *ACM Transactions on Computational Logic*, *1529*, 3785.

Thangaraj, R., Pant, M., Abraham, A., & Bouvry, P. (2011). Particle swarm optimization: Hybridization perspectives and experimental illustrations. *Applied Mathematics and Computation*, *217*(12), 5208–5226. doi:10.1016/j.amc.2010.12.053

Thang, N. T., & ASME. (2012). *Solving economic dispatch problem with piecewise quadratic cost functions using lagrange multiplier theory*. New York: Amer Soc. *Mechanical Engineering*.

Thao, N. T. P., & Thang, N. T. (2014). Environmental economic load dispatch with quadratic fuel cost function using cuckoo search algorithm. *International Journal of u-and e-Service, Science and Technology*, *7*(2), 199–210.

Theraulaz, G., Goss, S., Gervet, J., & Deneubourg, J. L. (1991). Task differentiation in polistes wasps colonies: A model for self-organizing groups of robots. In *First International Conference on Simulation of Adaptive Behavior* (pp. 346–355). Cambridge, MA: MIT Press.

Torra, V. (2010). Hesitant fuzzy sets. *International Journal of Intelligent Systems*. http://doi.org/10.1002/int.20418

Torres-Villa, R. A. (2013). *Instrumental techniques for improving the measurements based on quartz crystal microbalances*. Universidad Politécnica de Valencia.

Tosun, N., & Cogun, C. (2003). An investigation on wire wears in WEDM. *Journal of Materials Processing Technology*, *134*(3), 273–278. doi:10.1016/S0924-0136(02)01045-2

Tosun, N., Cogun, C., & Tosun, G. (2004). A study on kerf and material removal rate in wire electrical discharge machining based on Taguchi method. *Journal of Materials Processing Technology*, *152*(3), 316–322. doi:10.1016/j.jmatprotec.2004.04.373

Tracey, N., Clark, J., Mander, K., & McDermid, J. (1998). An automated framework for structural test data generation. *Proceedings of the International Conference on Automated Software Engineering*, 285-288. doi:10.1109/ASE.1998.732680

Trelea, I. C. (2003). The particle swarm optimization algorithm: Convergence analysis and parameter selection. *Information Processing Letters*, *85*(6), 317–325. doi:10.1016/S0020-0190(02)00447-7

Truong, K. H., Vasant, P., Balbir Singh, M. S., & Vo, D. N. (2015). Swarm Based Mean-Variance Mapping Optimization for Solving Economic Dispatch with Cubic Fuel Cost Function. In T. N. Nguyen, B. Trawiński & R. Kosala (Eds.), *Intelligent Information and Database Systems: 7th Asian Conference, ACIIDS 2015* (pp. 3-12). Cham: Springer International Publishing. doi:10.1007/978-3-319-15705-4_1

Turing, A. M. (1949). Checking a large routine. In *Report of a Conference on High Speed Automatic Calculating Machines*, (pp. 67–69). Cambridge, UK: University Mathematical Laboratory.

UCI Repository of Bioinformatics Databases. (n.d.). Available: http://www.ics.uci.edu./~mlearn/ML Repository.html

Ursem, R. (2003). *Models for evolutionary algorithms and their applications in system identification and control optimization* (Ph.D. thesis). Univ. Aarhus, Denmark. Retrieved from www.brics.dk/DS/03/6/BRICS-DS-03-6.pdf

Uysal, I., & Gövenir, H. A. (1999). An overview of regression techniques for knowledge discovery. *The Knowledge Engineering Review*, *14*(04), 319–340. doi:10.1017/S026988899900404X van den Bergh, F. (2002). *An analysis of particle swarm optimizers* (Ph.D. dissertation). Dept. Comput. Sci., Univ. Pretoria, Pretoria, South Africa.

van den Bergh, F., & Engelbrecht, A. P. (2004). A Cooperative Approach to Particle Swarm Optimization. *IEEE Trans. on Evolutionary Computation, 8,* 225-239.

van den Bergh, F., & Engelbrecht, A. P. (2006). A study of particle swarm optimization particle trajectories. *Information Sciences, 176*(8), 937–971. doi:10.1016/j.ins.2005.02.003

Vapnik, V. N. (1995). *The nature of statistical learning theory.* New York, NY: Springer-Verlag New York, Inc. doi:10.1007/978-1-4757-2440-0

Vasant, P. M. (2006). Fuzzy Production Planning and its Application to Decision Making. *Journal of Intelligent Manufacturing, 17*(1), 5–12. doi:10.1007/s10845-005-5509-x

Vembu, S., Vergara, A., Muezzinoglu, M. K., & Huerta, R. (2012). On time series features and kernels for machine olfaction. *Sensors and Actuators. B, Chemical, 174*(0), 535–546. doi:10.1016/j.snb.2012.06.070

Ventura, D., & Martinez, T. (1998). *Quantum associative memory with exponential capacity.* Paper presented at the Neural Networks Proceedings, 1998. IEEE World Congress on Computational Intelligence. The 1998 IEEE International Joint Conference on. doi:10.1109/IJCNN.1998.682319

Ventura, D. (1999). Quantum computational intelligence: Answers and questions. *IEEE Intelligent Systems, 14*(4), 14–16.

Walsh, J. (2000). *Projection of cumulative world conventional oil production, Remaining resources and Reserves to 2050: March.* Academic Press.

Walton, S., Hassan, O., Morgan, K., & Brown, M. R. (2011). Modified cuckoo search: A new gradient free optimisation algorithm. *Chaos, Solitons, and Fractals, 44*(9), 710–718. doi:10.1016/j.chaos.2011.06.004

Wang, M.-H., Lee, C.-S., Li, H.-C., & Ko, W.-M. (2007). Ontology-based Fuzzy Inference Agent for Diabetes Classification. IEEE.

Wang, D.-Z., Zhang, J.-S., Wan, F., & Zhu, L. (2006). A dynamic task scheduling algorithm in grid environment. *5th WSEAS International Conference on Telecommunications and Informatics,* 273–275.

Wang, H. (2007). Opposition-based particle swarm algorithm with Cauchy mutation. *Proceedings of the IEEE Congress on Evolutionary Computation,* 4750-4756.

Wang, H., Moon, I., Yang, S., & Wang, D. (2012). A memetic particle swarm optimization algorithm for multimodal optimization problems. *Information Sciences, 197,* 38–52. doi:10.1016/j.ins.2012.02.016

Wang, L., & Wu, J. (2012). Neural network ensemble model using PPR and LS-SVR for stock market eorecasting. In D.-S. Huang, Y. Gan, V. Bevilacqua, & J. Figueroa (Eds.), *Advanced Intelligent Computing* (Vol. 6838, pp. 1–8). Springer Berlin Heidelberg. doi:10.1007/978-3-642-24728-6_1

Wang, L., Zheng, X.-L., & Wang, S.-Y. (2013). A novel binary fruit fly optimization algorithm for solving the multidimensional knapsack problem. *Knowledge-Based Systems, 48,* 17–23. doi:10.1016/j.knosys.2013.04.003

Wang, R., Wang, A., & Song, Q. (2012). Research on the alkalinity of sintering process based on LS-SVM Algorithms. In D. Jin & S. Lin (Eds.), *Advances in Computer Science and Information Engineering* (Vol. 168, pp. 449–454). Springer Berlin Heidelberg; doi:10.1007/978-3-642-30126-1_71

Wasserman, P. D. (1993). *Advanced methods in neural computing* (1st ed.). New York, NY: John Wiley & Sons, Inc.

Watkins, A. E. L. (1995) A Tool for the Automatic Generation of Test Data using Genetic Algorithms. *Proc. Software Quality Conf.*

Wedde, H. F., Farooq, M., & Zhang, Y. (2004). Beehive: An efficient fault-tolerant routing algorithm inspired by honey bee behavior. In M. Dorigo (Ed.), ANTS 2004 (Vol. 3172, pp. 83–94). Springer.

Wedde, H. F., & Farooq, M. (2006). A comprehensive review of nature inspired routing algorithms for fixed telecommunication networks. *Journal of Systems Architecture*, 52(8-9), 461–484. doi:10.1016/j.sysarc.2006.02.005

Weng, F., & Her, M. (2002). Study of the batch production of micro parts using the EDM process. *International Journal of Advanced Manufacturing Technology*, 19(4), 266–270. doi:10.1007/s001700200033

Whitehouse, M. E. A., & Lubin, Y. (1999). Competitive foraging in the social spider Stegodyphus dumicola. *Animal Behaviour*, 58(3), 677–688. doi:10.1006/anbe.1999.1168 PMID:10479384

Wikipedia. (2014). *Quartz crystal microbalance*. Retrieved from http://en.wikipedia.org/wiki/Quartz_crystal_microbalance

Woolfson, M. M., & Pert, G. J. (1999). *An Introduction to Computer Simulation*. New York, NY: Oxford University Press.

Wu, X. (2007). *Optimal designs for segmented polynomial regression models and web-based implementation of optimal design software*. Stony Brook, NY: State University of New York at Stony Brook.

Xanthakis, S., Ellis, C., Skourlas, C., Le Gall, A., Katsikas, S., & Karapoulios, K. (1992). Application of genetic algorithms to software testing. *5th International Conference on Software Engineering and its Applications*, 625-636.

Xia, X., & Elaiw, A. (2010). Optimal dynamic economic dispatch of generation: A review. *Electric Power Systems Research*, 80(8), 975–986. doi:10.1016/j.epsr.2009.12.012

Xi, M., Sun, J., & Xu, W. (2008). An improved quantum-behaved particle swarm optimization algorithm with weighted mean best position. *Applied Mathematics and Computation*, 205(2), 751–759. doi:10.1016/j.amc.2008.05.135

Xing & Gao. (2014). *Innovative Computational Intelligence: A Rough Guide to 134 Clever Algorithms*. Springer International Publishing. DOI 10.1007/978-3-319-03404-1(2014)

Xing, B., & Gao, W.-J. (2014). *Innovative computational intelligence: a rough guide to 134 clever algorithms* (Vol. 62). Springer. doi:10.1007/978-3-319-03404-1

Xu, W., Zhou, Z., Pham, D. T., Liu, Q., Ji, C., & Meng, W. (2012). Quality of service in manufacturing networks: A service framework and its implementation. *International Journal of Advanced Manufacturing Technology*, 63(9-12), 1227–1237. doi:10.1007/s00170-012-3965-y

Yalcinoz, T., & Short, M. J. (1998). Neural networks approach for solving economic dispatch problem with transmission capacity constraints. *IEEE Transactions on Power Systems*, 13(2), 307–313. doi:10.1109/59.667341

Yang, S., Wang, M., & Jiao, L. (2004). *A quantum particle swarm optimization*. Paper presented at the Evolutionary Computation, 2004. CEC2004. Congress on.

Yang, Wang, & Jiao. (2004). A Quantum Particle Swarm Optimization. *Proceedings of the IEEE Congress on Evolutionary Computation (CEC 2004)*, 320 – 324.

Yang, X. S. (2008). Firefly algorithm. *Nature-Inspired Metaheuristic Algorithms*, 79–90.

Yang, X. S., & Suash, D. (2009). *Cuckoo Search via Levy flights*. Paper presented at the Nature & Biologically Inspired Computing, 2009. NaBIC 2009. World Congress on.

Yang, X.-S. (2008). Nature-inspired metaheuristic algorithms. Luniver Press.

Yang, X.-S. (2010a). Firefly algorithm, Lévy flights and global optimization. In M. Bramer (Ed.), Research and development in intelligent systems (vol. 26, pp. 209–218). London, UK: Springer-Verlag.

Yang, X.-S., Cui, Z., Xiao, R., Gandomi, A. H., & Karamanoglu, M. (2013). *Swarm Intelligence and Bio-Inspired Computation*. Academic Press.

Yang, X. S., & He, X. (2013). Bat algorithm: Literature review and applications. *International Journal of Bio-inspired Computation, 5*(3), 141. doi:10.1504/IJBIC.2013.055093

Yang, X.-S. (2010). A new metaheuristic Bat-inspired Algorithm. *Studies in Computational Intelligence, 284*, 65–74. doi:10.1007/978-3-642-12538-6_6

Yang, X.-S. (2010b). Firefly algorithm, stochastic test functions and design optimisation. *International Journal of Bio-inspired Computation, 2*(2), 78–84. doi:10.1504/IJBIC.2010.032124

Yang, X.-S. (2011). Bat algorithm for multi-objective optimisation. *International Journal of Bio-inspired Computation, 3*(5), 267–274. doi:10.1504/IJBIC.2011.042259

Yang, X.-S. (2013b). Multiobjective firefly algorithm for continuous optimization. *Engineering with Computers, 29*(2), 175–184. doi:10.1007/s00366-012-0254-1

Yang, X.-S. (2014). Cuckoo search and firefly algorithm: Overview and analysis. *Studies in Computational Intelligence, 516*, 1–26. doi:10.1007/978-3-319-02141-6_1

Yang, X.-S., & Deb, S. (2009). Cuckoo Search via Levy Flights. *World Congress on Nature & Biologically Inspired Computing (NaBIC 2009)*, (pp. 210-214). IEEE. doi:10.1109/NABIC.2009.5393690

Yang, X.-S., & Deb, S. (2014). Cuckoo search: Recent advances and applications. *Neural Computing & Applications, 24*(1), 169–174. doi:10.1007/s00521-013-1367-1

Yang, X.-S., & He, X. (2015). Swarm Intelligence and Evolutionary Computation: Overview and Analysis. In X.-S. Yang (Ed.), *Recent Advances in Swarm Intelligence and Evolutionary Computation* (Vol. 585, pp. 1–23). Cham: Springer International Publishing. doi:10.1007/978-3-319-13826-8_1

Yang, Z., Tang, K., & Yao, X. (2008, August). Large scale evolutionary optimization using cooperative coevolution. *Inform. Sci., 178*(15), 2986–2999. doi:10.1016/j.ins.2008.02.017

Yasuda, K., Ide, A., & Iwasaki, N. (2003). Adaptive particle swarm optimization. *Proceedings of the IEEE International Conference on Systems, Man, and Cybernetics*, 1554-1559.

Yasuda, K., Iwasaki, N., Ueno, G., & Aiyoshi, E. (2008). Particle Swarm Optimization: A Numerical Stability Analysis and Parameter Adjustment Based on Swarm Activity. *IEEJ Trans, 3*, 642–659.

Yildiz, A. R. (2013). Cuckoo search algorithm for the selection of optimal machining parameters in milling operations. *International Journal of Advanced Manufacturing Technology, 64*(1-4), 55–61. doi:10.1007/s00170-012-4013-7

Yuan, B., & Gallagher, M. (2004). Statistical racing techniques for improved empirical evaluation of evolutionary algorithms. In Lecture Notes in Computer Science: Vol. 3242. Parallel Problem Solving from Nature - PPSN VIII (pp. 172-181). Springer-Verlag. doi:10.1007/978-3-540-30217-9_18

Yumin, D., & Li, Z. (2014). Quantum Behaved Particle Swarm Optimization Algorithm Based on Artificial Fish Swarm. *Mathematical Problems in Engineering, 2014*, 592682. doi:10.1155/2014/592682

Zadeh, L. A. (1965). Fuzzy sets. *Information and Control, 8*(3), 338–353. doi:10.1016/S0019-9958(65)90241-X

Zadeh, L. A. (1975). The concept of a linguistic variable and its application to approximate reasoning—I. *Information Sciences*, *8*(3), 199–249. doi:10.1016/0020-0255(75)90036-5

Zadeh, L. A. (1978). Fuzzy sets as a basis for a theory of possibility. *Fuzzy Sets and Systems*, *1*(1), 3–28. doi:10.1016/0165-0114(78)90029-5

Zadeh, L. A. (1994). Fuzzy logic, neural networks, and soft computing. *Communications of the ACM*, *37*(3), 77–84. doi:10.1145/175247.175255

Zeng, F., Decraene, J., Low, M. Y. H., Hingston, P., Cai, W., Zhou, S., & Chandramohan, M. (2010). Autonomous bee colony optimization for multi-objective function. In *IEEE World Congress on Computational Intelligence (WCCI)* (pp. 1279–1286). Barcelona, Spain: CCIB. doi:10.1109/CEC.2010.5586057

Zeng, Z., & Wang, J. (2010). *Advances in neural network research and applications* (1st ed.). Springer Publishing Company, Incorporated. doi:10.1007/978-3-642-12990-2

Zhang, G. X., Gheorghe, M., & Wu, C. Z. (2008). A Quantum-Inspired Evolutionary Algorithm Based on P systems for Knapsack Problem. *Fundamenta Informaticae*, *87*(1), 93–116.

Zhang, W., Wei, D., & Liang, H. (2014). A parameter selection strategy for particle swarm optimization based on particle positions. *Expert Systems with Applications*, *41*(7), 3576–3584. doi:10.1016/j.eswa.2013.10.061

Zhang, Z. G., & Chan, S. C. (2011). On kernel selection of multivariate local polynomial modelling and its application to image smoothing and reconstruction. *J. Signal Process. Syst.*, *64*(3), 361–374. doi:10.1007/s11265-010-0495-4

Zhan, J. P., Wu, Q. H., Guo, C. X., & Zhou, X. X. (2014). Fast lambda-Iteration Method for Economic Dispatch. *IEEE Transactions on Power Systems*, *29*(2), 990–991. doi:10.1109/TPWRS.2013.2287995

Zhan, Z., & Zhang, J. (2009). Adaptive Particle Swarm Optimization. *IEEE Transactions on Systems, Man, and Cybernetics. Part B, Cybernetics*, *39*(6), 1362–1381. doi:10.1109/TSMCB.2009.2015956 PMID:19362911

Zheng, Y. (2003). Empirical study of particle swarm optimizer with an increasing inertia weight. *Proceeding of the IEEE Congress on Evolutionary Computation*, 221-226.

Zhu, D. Q., Chen, E. K., & Yang, Y. Q. (2005). A quantum neural networks data fusion algorithm and its application for fault diagnosis. In D. S. Huang, X. P. Zhang, & G. B. Huang (Eds.), *Advances in Intelligent Computing, Pt 1, Proceedings* (Vol. 3644, pp. 581–590). Berlin: Springer-Verlag Berlin. doi:10.1007/11538059_61

Zhu, W., Li, N., Shi, C., & Chen, B. (2013). SVR based on FOA and its application in traffic flow prediction. *Open Journal of Transportation Technologies*, *2*(01), 6–9. doi:10.12677/OJTT.2013.21002

Zilinskas, A., & Baronas, D. (2011). Optimization-Based Evaluation of Concentrations in Modeling the Biosensor-Aided Measurement. *Informatica*, *22*(4), 589–600. http://doi.org/http://www.mii.lt/informatica/htm/INFO844.htm

Zou, F., Wang, L., Hei, X., Chen, D., & Yang, D. (2014). Teaching–learning-based optimization with dynamic group strategy for global optimization. *Information Sciences*, *273*, 112–131. doi:10.1016/j.ins.2014.03.038

Zungeru, A. M., Ang, L.-M., & Seng, K. P. (2012). Termite-hill: Performance optimized swarm intelligence based routing algorithm for wireless sensor networks. *Journal of Network and Computer Applications*, *35*(6), 1901–1917. doi:10.1016/j.jnca.2012.07.014

Zurada, J., Marks, R., & Robinson, C. (Eds.). (1994). *Computational Intelligence: Imitating Life*. IEEE Press.

About the Contributors

Shishir K. Shandilya (Senior Member-IEEE), Dean (Academics) & Head-CSE, Ph.D. (Computer Engineering) and M.Tech (CSE), is an excellent academician and active researcher with proven record of teaching and research. Dr. Shandilya is awarded by the title of "Young Scientist" for consecutive two years (2005 & 2006) by Indian Science Congress & MP Council of Science & Technology for Computer Engineering. He also carries various awards like Computer Wizard-2002 and Excellent Mentor-2008. He has written six books of international-fame and published over 50 quality research papers in international & national journals & conferences. He is actively steering the international conferences as Conference Chair and international journals as Reviewer & Coordinator. He is an active member of over 20 international professional bodies. He has achieved excellent results in all the subjects he taught. He is also an excellent programmer and credited various software projects in his account. He is also giving consultancy in IT as Sr. Consultant. He has recently delivered an expert lecture on 'Opinion Mining' at Oxford-United Kingdom.

Smita Shandilya (Senior Member-IEEE) is an eminent scholar and energetic researcher with excellent teaching and research skills. She achieved excellent result in all the subjects she has taught till date. She has over 20 quality research papers in international & national journals & conferences to her credits. She has delivered several invited talks in national seminars of high repute. Her research interests are Power System Planning and Smart Micro Grids. She is one of the core members of the research and development section of her Institute. She is also involved in various projects like the establishment of Energy Lab in the Institute (first in any Private Institute in M.P.), Establishment of Training cum Incubator centre in Collaboration with iEnergy.

Kusum Deep is a Professor, with the Department of Mathematics, Indian Institute of Technology Roorkee, India. Born on August 15, 1958, she pursued B.Sc Hons and M.Sc Hons. School from Centre for Advanced Studies, Panjab University, Chandigarh. A M.Phil Gold Medalist, she earned her PhD from IIT Roorkee in 1988. She was awarded UGC National Merit Scholarship and UGC National Education Test Scholarship. She carried out research at Loughborough University, UK during 1993-94, under an International Post Doctorate Bursary funded by Commission of European Communities, Brussels. She was awarded the Khosla Research Award in 1991; UGC Career Award in 2002; Starred Performer of IIT – Roorkee Faculty continuously from 2001 to 2005; best technical paper, Railway Bulletin of Indian Railways for 2005; special facilitation in memory of late Prof. M. C. Puri during 40th Convention of Operations Research Society of India held at New Delhi in 2007. She has nearly 60 research publications in refereed International Journals and more than 52 research papers in International / National Conferences. She is on the editorial board of a number of International and National Journals. She is a Senior Member of Operations Research Society of India, IEEE, Computer Society of India, Indian Mathematical Society and Indian Society of Industrial Mathematics. She is on the Expert Panel of the Department of Science and Technology, Govt. of India. Recently she has been nominated as a member of the Seneta of IIT Roorkee. Dr. Deep is having International Collaboration with Liverpool Hope University, Liverpool, UK and Machine Intelligence Research Labs, USA. Her areas of specialization are numerical optimization and their applications to engineering, science and industry. Currently she is working on Evolutionary Computations, particularly, Genetic Algorithms, Memetic Algorithms, Particle Swarm Optimization and their applications to solve real life problems. She has co-authored a book entitled "Optimization Techniques" by New Age Publishers New Delhi in 2009 with an International edition by New Age Science, UK. She successfully organized (as convener) an International Conference on Soft Computing for Problem Solving, held at IIT Roorkee campus during December 20-22, 2011. She is the General Chair of two forthcoming Conferences: Second International Conference on Soft Computing for Problem Solving Dec 28-30, 2012, Jaipur, India and 7th Her research interests include Numerical Optimization, Evolutionary Algorithms, Genetic Algorithms, Particle Swarm Optimization, etc.

Atulya K. Nagar is the Foundation Professor of Computer and Mathematical Sciences at Liverpool Hope University and is Head of Department of Computer Science. A mathematician by training, Prof. Nagar brings multi-disciplinary expertise in computational science, bioinformatics, operations research and systems engineering to the Faculty of Business & Computer Sciences. He received a prestigious Commonwealth Fellowship for pursuing his Doctorate in applied non-linear mathematics, which he received from the University of York in 1996. Prof. Nagar is an internationally recognised scholar working at the cutting edge of theoretical computer science, applied mathematical analysis, operations research, and industrial systems engineering. The centre of his research expertise lies in his IDS group, which pursues strategic and applied research into advancing applications of engineering, computational and biological systems. The research of the group seeks to contribute to the general body of knowledge and to influence IT practice in systems modelling and planning, scheduling, optimisation, and informatics. One such innovative theme is DNA sequence analysis using sophisticated computational techniques. The work of the group is highly theoretical, and primarily benefits the scientific community, with demonstrable potential for practical applications and relevance to society as a whole. Prof. Nagar has published a substantial number of research papers in reputed outlets such as the IEE and IEEE publications. He has co-edited a volume on Intelligent Systems area and serves on editorial boards for a number of prestigious journals including the International Journal of Artificial Intelligence and Soft Computing, and the Journal of Universal Computer Science. Prof. Nagar was a Conference Chair for the European Modelling Symposium (EMS 2008); currently he is a Conference and TPC Chair for the Developments in E-Systems Engineering (DeSE'09) Conference (www.dese.org.uk); and he serves on International Programme Committees (IPC) for several international conferences. He has been an expert reviewer for the Biotechnology and Biological Sciences Research Council (BBSRC) grants peer-review committee for Bioinformatics Panel and has been selected to serve on the prestigious Peer-Review College of the Arts and Humanities Research Council (AHRC) as a Scientific/Technical expert member. He is a member of numerous professional organisations including the IEE; a fellow of the Higher Education Academy (FHEA); he is a member of the Council of Professors and Heads of Computing (CPHC); and has been listed in the invaluable reference Marquis' Who's Who in Science and Engineering. Prof. Nagar supervises PhD research projects in Computer Science and serves on PhD external examiner panels. He holds a Visiting Professorship at the University of Madras; and Adjunct Professorship at the Mathematics department at the Indian Institute of Technology (IIT), Roorkee. He is a member of the Board of Studies at Stella Maris College, India; external examiner for MSc Computer Science programme at Staffordshire University. His teaching expertise is in Applied Analysis, Systems Engineering and Computational Biology. Prof. Nagar earned his PhD in Applied Nonlinear Mathematics from the University of York (UK) in 1996. He holds BSc (Hons.), MSc and MPhil (with distinction) degrees, in Mathematical Sciences, from the MDS University of Ajmer, India. Prior to joining Liverpool Hope University, Prof. Nagar has worked for several years as a Senior Research Scientist, on various EPSRC sponsored research projects, in the department of Mathematical Sciences, and later in the department of Systems Engineering, at Brunel University. In the work at Brunel he has contributed to the development of new techniques based on mathematical control systems theory for modelling and analysis of uncertainty in complex decision making systems.

***

M. Donelli received his M.Sc. in Electronic Engineering and Ph.D. degree in Space Science and Engineering from the University of Genoa, Genoa, Italy, in 1998 and 2003, respectively. He is currently an Associate professor of electromagnetic field with the department of Information and Communication Technology, University of Trento, Trento, Italy, and a member of the ELEDIA Research Center. He is the author/coauthor of over 160 peer-reviewed papers in international journals and conferences. His current research interests include microwave devices and systems design, electromagnetic inverse scattering, adaptive antenna synthesis, optimization techniques for microwave imaging, wave propagation in superconducting materials, and urban environments.

Pandian Vasant is a senior lecturer at Department of Fundamental and Applied Sciences, Faculty of Science and Information Technology, Universiti Teknologi PETRONAS in Malaysia. He holds PhD (UNEM, Costa Rica) in Computational Intelligence, MSc (UMS, Malaysia, Engineering Mathematics) and BSc (Hons, Malayan University (MU), Malaysia) in Mathematics. His research interests include Soft Computing, Hybrid Optimization, Holistic Optimization, Innovative Computing and Applications. He has co-authored research papers and articles in national journals, international journals, conference proceedings, conference paper presentation, and special issues lead guest editor, lead guest editor for book chapters' project, conference abstracts, edited books, keynote lecture and book chapters (162 publications indexed in SCOPUS). In the year 2009, Dr. Pandian Vasant was awarded top reviewer for the journal Applied Soft Computing (Elsevier) and awarded outstanding reviewer in the year 2015 for ASOC (Elsevier) journal. He has 25 years of working experience at the various universities from 1989-2016. Currently he is Editor-in-Chief of IJCO, IJSIEC, IEM, IJEOE, Associate Editor of IJFSA and Editor of GJTO and Cogent Engineering. H-Index SCOPUS Citations = 35, H-Index Google Scholar = 25 and i10-index = 75.

Index

A

B

C

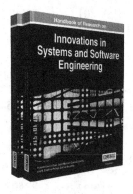

Stay Current on the Latest Emerging Research Developments

Become an IGI Global Reviewer for Authored Book Projects

Premier Reference Source
Solutions for High-Touch Communications in a High-Tech World

Premier Reference Source
Advanced Research on Biologically Inspired Cognitive Architectures

Premier Reference Source
Workforce Development Theory and Practice in the Mental Health Sector

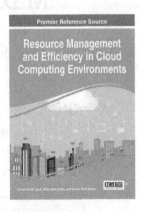
Premier Reference Source
Resource Management and Efficiency in Cloud Computing Environments

The overall success of an authored book project is dependent on quality and timely reviews.

In this competitive age of scholarly publishing, constructive and timely feedback significantly decreases the turnaround time of manuscripts from submission to acceptance, allowing the publication and discovery of progressive research at a much more expeditious rate. Several IGI Global authored book projects are currently seeking highly qualified experts in the field to fill vacancies on their respective editorial review boards:

Applications may be sent to:
development@igi-global.com

Applicants must have a doctorate (or an equivalent degree) as well as publishing and reviewing experience. Reviewers are asked to write reviews in a timely, collegial, and constructive manner. All reviewers will begin their role on an ad-hoc basis for a period of one year, and upon successful completion of this term can be considered for full editorial review board status, with the potential for a subsequent promotion to Associate Editor.

If you have a colleague that may be interested in this opportunity, we encourage you to share this information with them.

Encyclopedia of Information Science and Technology, Third Edition (10 Vols.)

Mehdi Khosrow-Pour, D.B.A. (Information Resources Management Association, USA)
ISBN: 978-1-4666-5888-2; **EISBN:** 978-1-4666-5889-9; © 2015; 10,384 pages.

The **Encyclopedia of Information Science and Technology, Third Edition** is a 10-volume compilation of authoritative, previously unpublished research-based articles contributed by thousands of researchers and experts from all over the world. This discipline-defining encyclopedia will serve research needs in numerous fields that are affected by the rapid pace and substantial impact of technological change. With an emphasis on modern issues and the presentation of potential opportunities, prospective solutions, and future directions in the field, it is a relevant and essential addition to any academic library's reference collection.

Take An Extra
30% Off[1]

[1] 30% discount offer cannot be combined with any other discount and is only valid on purchases made directly through IGI Global's Online Bookstore (www.igi-global.com/books), not intended for use by distributors or wholesalers. Offer expires December 31, 2016.

Free Lifetime E-Access with Print Purchase

Take 30% Off Retail Price:

Hardcover with <u>Free E-Access</u>:[2] **$2,765**
~~List Price: $3,950~~

E-Access with <u>Free Hardcover</u>:[2] **$2,765**
~~List Price: $3,950~~

Recommend this Title to Your Institution's Library: www.igi-global.com/books

[2] IGI Global now offers the exclusive opportunity to receive free lifetime e-access with the purchase of the publication in print, or purchase any e-access publication and receive a free print copy of the publication. You choose the format that best suits your needs. This offer is only valid on purchases made directly through IGI Global's Online Bookstore and not intended for use by book distributors or wholesalers. Shipping fees will be applied for hardcover purchases during checkout if this option is selected.

The lifetime of a publication refers to its status as the current edition. Should a new edition of any given publication become available, access will not be extended on the new edition and will only be available for the purchased publication. If a new edition becomes available, you will not lose access, but you would no longer receive new content for that publication (i.e. updates). Free Lifetime E-Access is only available to single institutions that purchase printed publications through IGI Global. Sharing the Free Lifetime E-Access is prohibited and will result in the termination of e-access.